PS= BASK201

COMPUTERS AND
DATA PROCESSING
concepts and applications

WEST SERIES IN DATA PROCESSING AND INFORMATION SYSTEMS

V. Thomas Dock, Consulting Editor

Clark & Mandell	*A Short Course in PL / I and PL / C*
Dock	*BASIC Programming for Business*
Dock	*Structured COBOL: American National Standard*
Dock	*Structured FORTRAN IV Programming*
Graham	*The Mind Tool: Computers and Their Impact on Society*
Mandell	*Computers and Data Processing: Concepts and Applications*
Mandell	*Principles of Data Processing*
Nolan	*Managing the Data Resource Function*
Wetherbe	*Systems Analysis for Computer-Based Information Systems*
Wetherbe	*Cases in Systems Design*

COMPUTERS AND DATA PROCESSING
concepts and applications

with BASIC

STEVEN L. MANDELL

MIS Institute
Bowling Green State University

WEST PUBLISHING COMPANY

St. Paul   New York   Los Angeles   San Francisco

A study guide has been developed to assist you in mastering concepts presented in this text. The study guide reinforces concepts by presenting them in condensed, concise form. Additional illustrations and examples are also included. The study guide is available from your local bookstore under the title, *Study Guide to Accompany Computers and Data Processing: Concepts and Applications,* prepared by Steven L. Mandell.

LIBRARY OF CONGRESS CATALOGING IN PUBLICATION DATA

Mandell, Steven L.
  Computers and data processing.
  (West series in data processing and information systems).

  Includes Index.
  1. Electronic data processing.   2. Electronic digital computers.   3. BASIC (computer program language).
  I. Title.   II. Series.
QA76.M27472   001.6'4   78–27874
ISBN 0-8299-0247-3   INTERNATIONAL EDITION ISBN 0-8299-0344-5
3rd Reprint 1979

ACKNOWLEDGEMENTS

4 Copyright Art Buchwald. **20** Reprinted by permission of *The Wall Street Journal* © Dow Jones & Company, Inc., 1973. All rights reserved. **44** Reprinted by permission from *Time*, the Weekly Newsmagazine; Copyright Time Inc. 1977. **70** Reprinted from *Popular Science* with permission © 1977 Times Mirror Magazines, Inc. **96** Reprinted by permission of *The Wall Street Journal* © Dow Jones & Company, Inc. 1976. All rights reserved. **120** Copyright 1978 by CW Communications/Inc., Newton, Mass. 02160; Copyright 1977 by Computerworld, Inc., Newton, Mass. 02160. **148** Copyright 1978 by CW Communications/Inc., Newton, Mass. 02160; Copyright 1977 by Computerworld, Inc., Newton, Mass. 02160. **200** Permission from *Science Digest* and from Roger Field, Health & Science Editor, CBS Chicago (WBBM-TV). **218** Reprinted by permission from *Sports Illustrated*, August 22, 1977, Copyright 1977 Time Inc. **248** Reprinted with permission from *High Fidelity/Backbeat*, August, 1977. All rights reserved. **286** Reprinted with permission from the *Toledo Blade*. **308** Copyright 1978 by CW Communications/Inc., Newton, Mass. 02160; Copyright 1977 by Computerworld, Inc., Newton, Mass. 02160. **330** Copyright 1978 by CW Communications/Inc., Newton, Mass. 02160; Copyright 1977 by Computerworld, Inc., Newton, Mass. 02160. **356** Reprinted by permission from *Time*, The Weekly Newsmagazine; Copyright Time Inc., 1978. **374** Reprinted from the *Journal of Systems Management*. **406** Reprinted by permission of *The Wall Street Journal* © Dow Jones & Company, Inc. 1977. All rights reserved. **428** Copyright Art Buchwald.

CREDITS

22, 23, 24, 25, 26 Courtesy of IBM. **27, 28** Courtesy of Sperry Univac, A Division of the Sperry Rand Corporation. **30, 31** Courtesy of IBM. **32** Courtesy of Burroughs Corporation. **33** Courtesy of Digital Equipment Corporation. **37** Courtesy of the Department of the Navy. **58** Courtesy of IBM. **60** Courtesy of Bell Laboratories. **61, 64, 75, 76** Courtesy of IBM.

77 Courtesy of Bowling Green State University. **80, 81** Courtesy of IBM. **83** Courtesy of Bowling Green State University. **84** Courtesy of IBM. **91** Courtesy of United Life Insurance Company. **99** Courtesy of Anderson Jacobson, Inc. **100** Courtesy of Northwestern Bell. **105** Courtesy of Data 100 Corporation. **115, 117** Courtesy of West Publishing Company. **124** Courtesy of IBM. **125** Courtesy of Inforex Inc. **131, 132** Courtesy of IBM. **133** Courtesy of Tektronix, Inc. **134** Courtesy of AT&T. **135** Courtesy of IBM. **136** Courtesy of California Computer Products, Inc. (CalComp). **137** Courtesy of Applicon Incorporated. **143** Courtesy of Federal Reserve System. **148** Courtesy of United States Machines Works, Inc. **150** Courtesy of IBM. **153** Courtesy of Honeywell, Inc. **155** Courtesy of NCR Corporation. **157** Courtesy of IBM. **158** Courtesy of Control Data Corporation. **160** Courtesy of California Computer Products, Inc. (CalComp). **162** Courtesy of IBM. **166** Courtesy of The Procter & Gamble Company. **172, 173** Courtesy of Blaupunkt. **176, 177** Courtesy of Burroughs Corporation. **178** Courtesy of Honeywell, Inc. **179** Courtesy of IBM. **180** Courtesy of Burroughs Corporation. **181** (*right*) Reprinted by permission of Itel Corporation, Copyright 1978; (*left*) Courtesy of Motorola Semiconductor, Inc. **182** Courtesy of Digital Equipment Corporation. **192** Courtesy of Southern Railway Co. **214** Courtesy of NCR Corporation. **243** Courtesy of Eli Lilly and Company. **248** Courtesy of Designer, James M. Troxel. **282** Courtesy of Ohio Citizens Trust Company. **302** Courtesy of Armco, Inc. **321** Courtesy of The Kroger Co. **350** Courtesy of Marathon Oil Company. **368** Courtesy of Dana Corporation. **397** Courtesy of Ford Motor Company. **422** Courtesy of the Civil Service Commission.

To an inspiration,
GRACE MURRAY HOPPER

CONTENTS

Preface   xv

SECTION I   INFORMATION PROCESSING   1

1   INTRODUCTION TO DATA PROCESSING   3

Background   6
Data Processing   8
A Data-Processing Application   10
Stored-Program Concept   11
Computer Impact   13
Summary   14
Review Questions   16
application: Introduction to Applications   17

2   EVOLUTION OF COMPUTERS   19

Early Development   22
First Generation: 1951 through 1958   27
Second Generation: 1959 through 1964   29
Third Generation: 1965 through ?   31
State of the Art: The Present   32
Summary   35
Review Questions   36
application: United States Navy   37

SECTION II   TECHNOLOGY   41

3   HARDWARE   43

Digital and Analog Computers   46
The Central Processing Unit   46
   Basic Functions   46
   Storage Locations and Addresses   49
   Registers   49
Data Representation   50
   Binary Representation   50
   Computer Codes   52
   Hexadecimal Representation   55
Storage   57
   Primary Storage   57
   Read-Only Memory (ROM)   59
Summary   62
Review Questions   63
application: IBM   64

4 CARD INPUT AND PRINTER OUTPUT   69

Punched Cards   71
Data Representation   71
Punched-Card Processing   73
Card Punch   74
Verifying Machines   74
Card Readers   76
Unit-Record Concept   77
Punched-Card Systems—A Perspective   82
Printers   82
Impact Printers   83
Nonimpact Printers   85
Summary   88
Review Questions   90
application: American United Life Insurance Company   91

5 REMOTE-ACCESS/COMMUNICATION SYSTEMS   95

Data Communication   98
Message Transmission   98
Communication Channels   99
Multiplexers and Concentrators   101
Programmable Communications Processors   101
Remote-Access Computing   103
Online Systems   103
Online Real-Time Systems   104
Interactive/Time-Sharing Systems   107
Distributed Systems   110
Summary   113
Review Questions   114
application: WESTLAW   115

6 DATA-ENTRY/INFORMATION-RESPONSE   119

Data Input   122
Magnetic-Ink Character Readers   122
Key-to-Tape and Key-to-Disk Devices   122
Source-Data Automation   125
Optical Recognition   127
Remote Terminals   130
Special-Purpose Output   135
Plotters   135
Computer Output Microfilm (COM)   137
Input/Output Operations   138
Control Units   138
Channels   138
Summary   140
Review Questions   141
application: Federal Reserve Bank of Cincinnati   143

7 STORAGE DEVICES   147

Storage-Media Classifications   149
Sequential-Access Storage   150
    Paper Tape   150
    Magnetic Tape   151
Direct-Access Storage   156
    Magnetic Disk   156
    Advantages and Disadvantages   160
Mass Storage   161
Future Trends in Data Storage   162
Summary   163
Review Questions   165
application: The Procter & Gamble Company   166

8 COMPUTER SYSTEMS   171

Overview of Computer Systems   175
    Large Computer Systems   175
    Medium-Size Computer Systems   177
    Small Computer Systems   178
    Minicomputer Systems   179
    Microcomputer Systems   181
Industry Structure   183
    Main-Frame Sector   183
    Minicomputer Sector   183
    Plug-Compatible Peripheral Equipment Sector   184
    Other Sectors   185
Computer Systems—A Management Perspective   186
    Purchase and Rental Price Considerations   187
    Cost and Availability of Maintenance   187
    Vendor Support and Training   187
    Software Costs and Capabilities   187
    Speed, Storage Capacity, and Peripherals   188
    Computer Staff Requirements   188
    Flexibility and Compatibility Considerations   188
    Discussion   189
Summary   190
Review Questions   191
application: Southern Railway Company   192

SECTION III PROGRAMMING   **197**

9 SYSTEM AND APPLICATIONS SOFTWARE   199

Programs   202
    System Programming   202
    Applications Programming   202
Operating Systems   203
    Operating-System Functions   203

Types of Operating Systems 203
Operating-System Components 204
Levels of Language 207
Machine Language 207
Assembly Language 207
High-Level Programming Languages 209
Language Translation 209
Summary 212
Review Questions 213
application: NCR Corporation 214

10 THE PROGRAMMING PROCESS 217

Program Development 220
Defining the Problem 220
Planning a Problem Solution 221
Writing the Program 221
Program Debugging 222
Testing the Program 222
Basic Logic Patterns 224
Program Flowcharting 224
Modular and Detailed Flowcharting 226
Developing a Flowchart 229
Documentation 235
Programming Case Study 237
Summary 239
Review Questions 242
application: Eli Lilly and Company 243

11 PROGRAMMING LANGUAGES 247

Batch-Oriented Programming Languages 250
Assembly Language 251
COBOL 254
FORTRAN 263
PL/1 269
RPG 271
Interactive Programming Languages 271
BASIC 273
APL 276
Programming Languages—A Comparison 277
Summary 279
Review Questions 281
application: Ohio Citizens Trust Company 282

12 STRUCTURED-DESIGN CONCEPTS 285

Structured-Design Methodology 288
Top-Down Design 288
Documentation and Design Tools 290

Structured Programming 291
Management of System Projects 297
   Chief Programmer Team 298
   Structured Review and Evaluation 299
Summary 300
Review Questions 301
application: Armco Inc. 302

13 ADVANCED SOFTWARE TOPICS 307

Multiprogramming 309
Virtual Storage 311
Multiprocessing 314
Software Packages 317
   System Packages 317
   Applications Packages 318
   Choosing Packages 318
Summary 319
Review Questions 320
application: The Kroger Company 321

SECTION IV SYSTEMS **327**

14 SYSTEM ANALYSIS AND DESIGN 329

System Analysis 331
   Data Gathering 332
   Data Analysis 333
System Design 340
   Review of Goals and Objectives 341
   Development of System Model 342
   Evaluation of Organizational Constraints 342
   Defining I/O Requirements 343
   Developing Alternative Designs 343
   Cost/Benefit Analysis of Alternatives 344
   System Recommendation 344
System Implementation 345
   Personnel Training 345
   Testing the System 346
   System Conversion 346
   System Auditing 347
   System Maintenance and Follow-up 348
Summary 348
Review Questions 349
application: Marathon Oil Company 350

15 PROCESS DESIGN 355

Batch/Sequential Processing 357
   Example of Batch Processing 359
   Interrogating Sequential Files 360

Assessment of Batch/Sequential Processing 361
Inline/Direct-Access Processing 362
  Direct-Access Addressing 362
  Examples of Inline/Direct-Access Processing 362
  Interrogating Direct-Access Files 364
  Assessment of Inline/Direct-Access Processing 364
Indexed-Sequential File Organization 365
Summary 366
Review Questions 367
application: Dana Corporation 368

16 MANAGEMENT INFORMATION SYSTEMS 373

Information Requirements of Managers 376
Effectiveness of MIS 379
Decision-Oriented Reporting of MIS 380
Design Alternatives 381
Data Base Concepts 384
  Data Organization 384
  Data Base Management System (DBMS) 387
  Data Base Administrator 388
Managing Information Systems 389
  Organization of Data Processing 389
  Top-Management and User Involvement 390
  Managing System Development 391
  Managing Computer Operations 392
Security 392
  Major Hazards 393
  Security Measures 394
Summary 395
Review Questions 396
application: Ford Motor Company 397

SECTION V   ISSUES OF INDIVIDUAL CONCERN 403

17 CAREER OPPORTUNITIES 405

People and Their Roles 409
  Information System Manager 409
  System Analyst 409
  Programming Personnel 410
  Data-Processing Operations Personnel 411
  Data Base Administrator 412
University Programs 413
Professional Associations 417
  American Federation of Information Processing
  Societies (AFIPS) 417
  Association for Computing Machinery (ACM) 417
  Data Processing Management Association (DPMA) 418

Association for Systems Management (ASM) 418
Institute for Certification of Computer
Professionals (ICCP) 419
Summary 419
Review Questions 421
application: Civil Service Commission 422

18 COMPUTERS AND SOCIETY 427

The Privacy Issue 430
Automation 432
Artificial Intelligence 434
Personal Computing 436
Societal Impact 438
Perspective 440
Summary 441
Review Questions 442
application: Walt Disney Productions 443

APPENDIX: BASIC PROGRAMMING 447

Glossary/Index 543

PREFACE

The term *data processing* is widely accepted as a reference to the major use of computers in organizations. The objective of this book is to present introductory material that is in keeping with the spirit of this orientation. The book is extremely unique in its approach and contains a variety of teaching vehicles.

The most inspiring lectures on computers that I have had the fortune to attend were presented by Captain Grace Hopper, a legend in her own time. In analyzing her material, which always seemed so interesting, it became apparent to me that no new concept was permitted to remain abstract. Rather, actual examples were described, encouraging the listener to visualize its application. In like manner, each chapter in this book is followed by an application that shows how a corporation or government agency implements the concepts presented.

Several other important features are included within each chapter. An opening article invokes attention and acts as a motivator. A meaningful outline of the subject matter follows. The introductory section serves a dual purpose: transition between chapters and preview of material. A chapter summary and review questions are also provided. At the end of the text is a comprehensive, combined glossary and index.

I have had one paramount objective throughout the development of this book: The material is designed to be student-oriented, and all incorporated approaches are designed to assist students in the learning process. Important concepts are never avoided, regardless of their complexity. Many books on data processing emphasize one of two aspects of data processing—informational relationships or computer capabilities. This text attempts to balance and blend both subjects.

The material is structured according to an approach used successfully by several thousand business and computer science students in a course entitled "Introduction to Computers" at Bowling Green State University. The book is divided into five parts: Information Processing, Technology, Programming, Systems, and Issues of Individual Concern. The Information Processing section presents an introduction to the basic concepts of data processing and a historical perspective. The Technology section concentrates on computer hardware, including internal storage and input/output devices. System and applications software, program development, languages, and structural approaches constitute the Programming section. The System section provides a discussion of the methods and approaches to designing information systems. Finally, the Issues of Individual Concern section includes material for career planning and a look at some aspects of the impact of computers on society.

The study guide for this text includes numerous materials for student reinforcement. The instructor material is designed to reduce administrative efforts. A second version of the text that includes extensive coverage of the BASIC programming language is also available.

PREFACE

Many individuals and companies have been involved in the development of the material for this book. The corporations and government agencies whose applications appear in this book have provided invaluable assistance. Captain Grace Hopper has managed to sustain a watchful eye over this project. Faculty and staff of the Management Information Systems Institute at Bowling Green provided the assistance required for the completion of a text of this magnitude: James Bernot and Devendra Gulati on student material; Michael Heim and Becky Nicholas with corporate research; Norma Morris and Terrye Gregory in manuscript preparation; and Barbara Wensel with typing. Comments by reviewers Peter L. Irwin, Ronald S. Lemos, Peter Simis, and R. Fedrick were greatly appreciated. The rough material was again transformed into a polished book through the efforts of a remarkable editor, Marilyn Bohl. The design of the book is a tribute to the many talents of Janet Bollow. One final acknowledgement goes to the series editor, V. Thomas Dock, and the publisher, Clyde Perlee, for their unfaltering support.

Steven L. Mandell

COMPUTERS AND
DATA PROCESSING
concepts and applications

section 1

INFORMATION PROCESSING

1

INTRODUCTION TO DATA PROCESSING

2

EVOLUTION OF COMPUTERS

INTRODUCTION TO DATA PROCESSING 1

OUTLINE

I. Background
  A. Functions
  B. Speed
  C. Accuracy
  D. Memory
II. Data Processing
  A. Evolution
  B. Data vs. Information
  C. Processing Functions
    1. Classify
    2. Sort
    3. Calculate
    4. Summarize
    5. Store

III. A Data-Processing Application
IV. Stored-Program Concept
  A. Development
  B. Non-Destructive Read, Destructive Write
  C. Next-Sequential-Instruction Feature
  D. Program Execution
V. Computer Impact
  A. Business Applications
  B. Government Use
  C. Education and Health Care Utilization

INTRODUCTION

The computer has become a dominant force in society today. Business corporations, government agencies, and other organizations depend on the computer to process data and make information available for use in decision-making. Computers are responsible, to a large extent, for our present standard of living. As the costs for computer equipment continue to decrease, computers will become an even more integral part of our daily lives. It is therefore essential that people gain a basic understanding of computers—their capabilities, limitations, and applications.

In this chapter, a basic description of the computer and its uses in data processing is given. The distinction between data and information is presented. A computerized example of payroll processing is used to demonstrate how computers can be programmed to provide meaningful information. Finally, some of the major advances and problems resulting from computers are presented as evidence of the growing impact computers have had on all parts of society.

THE GREAT DATA FAMINE

Art Buchwald

Washington Post,
September 28, 1969

One of the major problems we face in the 1970s is that so many computers will be built in the next decade that there will be a shortage of data to feed them.

Prof. Heinrich Applebaum, director of the Computer Proliferation Center at Grogbottom, has voiced concern about the crisis and has urged a crash program to produce enough data to get our computers through the seventies.

"We didn't realize," the professor told me, "that computers would absorb so much information in such a fast period of time. But if our figures are correct, every last bit of data in the world will have been fed into a machine by Jan. 12, 1984, and an information famine will follow, which could spread across the world."

"It sounds serious," I said.

"It is serious," he replied. "Man has created his own monster. He never realized when he invented the computer that there would not be enough statistics to feed it. Even now, there are some computers starving to death because there is no information to put into them. At the same time, the birth rate of computers is increasing by thirty percent a year. Barring some sort of worldwide holocaust, we may soon have to find data for 30,000,000 computers with new ones being born every day."

"You make it sound so frightening."

"It is frightening," Prof. Applebaum said. "The new generation of computers is more sophisticated than the older generation, and the computers will refuse to remain idle just because there is nothing to compute, analyze, or calculate. Left to their own devices, the Lord only knows what they will do."

"Is there any solution, professor?"

"New sources of data must be found. The government must expand, and involved studies must be thought up to make use of the computers' talents. The scientific community, instead of trying to solve problems with computers, must work on finding problems for the computers to solve."

"Even if the scientists really don't want the answer?"

"Naturally. The scientific community invented the computer. Now it must find ways of feeding it. I do not want to be an alarmist, but I can see the day coming when millions of computers will be fighting for the same small piece of data, like savages."

"Is there any hope that the government will wake up to the data famine in time?"

"We have a program ready to go as soon as the bureaucrats in Washington give us the word. We are recommending that no computer can be plugged in more than three hours a day.

"We are also asking the government for $50 billion to set up data manufacturing plants all over the country. This data, mixed with soy beans, could feed hundreds of thousands of computer families for months.

"And finally we are advocating a birth control program for computers. By forcing a computer to swallow a small bit of erroneous information, we could make it sterile forever, and it would be impossible for it to reproduce any more of its kind."

"Would you advocate abortions for computers?" I asked Applebaum.

"Only if the Vatican's computer gives us its blessing."

Buchwald's satirical article is both humorous and instructive. The importance of data and its transformation into information useful for decision-making is the computer's reason for being. The first chapter explains this basic computer process.

BACKGROUND

When many individuals think of the word *computer*, they envision an electronic marvel with mystical powers. In reality, its capabilities are quite limited. Its success can be directly attributed to the imagination of people. A computer possesses no independent intelligence. It cannot perform any tasks that a person has not predetermined. Therefore, the computer's IQ is zero!

Computers can perform only three basic functions:

1. Add, subtract, multiply, and divide

2. Compare (test the relationship of two values to see if they are equal, if the first is greater than the second, or vice versa; values can be either numeric or alphabetic)

3. Store and retrieve information

The number of different instructions required to direct a computer to perform these three functions is quite limited, often fewer than one hundred. These instructions govern fundamental logical and arithmetic procedures such as addition, subtraction, and comparison. Together, they constitute the *instruction set* of the computer. Engineers design the instruction set into the electronic circuitry of the machine. By manipulating this small instruction set, people can create computer programs and thus harness the computer's power to achieve desired results. Most computers can be used for many purposes. They are referred to as general-purpose machines. Special-purpose, or dedicated, machines are similar to general-purpose computers but have been specifically adapted to perform specialized tasks. In all cases, a human determines the combination of instructions that a machine will perform.

Computers derive most of their amazing power from three features: speed, accuracy, and memory. In fact, modern computers are capable of performing millions of calculations in one second. Their speed is fast reaching the physical limitation of the speed of light. Generally, computer speed is expressed as the time required to perform one operation. The following units of time apply.

UNIT	SYMBOL	FRACTION OF A SECOND
Millisecond	ms	one-thousandth (1/1,000)
Microsecond	μs	one-millionth (1/1,000,000)
Nanosecond	ns	one-billionth (1/1,000,000,000)
Picosecond	ps	one-trillionth (1/1,000,000,000,000)

The time required to perform one addition ranges from 4 microseconds to 200 nanoseconds. This means that some machines can do in excess of one million additions in one second. Obviously, such speed of processing far exceeds human capabilities.

Two factors control the speed of a computer:

The switching speed of the electronic circuits that make up the computer

The distances that electric currents have to travel

Electricity travels at a speed of 186,000 miles per second. This is approximately one foot per nanosecond. Recent advances in technology have made it possible to increase the switching speed of electronic circuits. Other advances have made it possible to reduce the lengths of interconnections by packing circuits closer together. To appreciate the ability of modern computers to perform operations in nanoseconds, see Figure 1–1.

The accuracy of computers is due in part to the inherent reliability of the electronic circuits that make up a computer. In our daily lives, we take advantage of this aspect of circuitry every time we switch on an electric device and assume it will come on. Our assumption is based upon our past experience. We expect the same activity to yield the same result. And the device comes on. Similarly, in a computer, passing the same type of current through the same electrical circuits yields the same result. The constancy of computer-generated results is referred to as accuracy.

Error-free computation by computers is further assured by the incorporation of internal, self-checking features in electronic circuits. However, we must realize that the accuracy of a computer relates to its internal operations. To say that a computer is accurate does not imply that what comes out of the computer is correct unless what was put into it was correct. If the *input* that is collected and fed into the computer is incorrect or not relevant to the problem being solved, then it is impossible for the computer to manipulate that input and produce meaningful *output*. Bad programs will also produce bad output, so the correctness of programs used to manipulate the data is also important. The phrase *"garbage in—garbage out"* (*GIGO*) is fundamental to understanding computer "mistakes."

FIGURE 1–1
A Nanosecond

NANOSECOND

If one person is equivalent to a nanosecond, then it would take the total population of the following countries to make up a second:

1.	U.S.	**8.**	U.K.
2.	U.S.S.R.	**9.**	Philippines
3.	Japan	**10.**	France
4.	Brazil	**11.**	Spain
5.	Nigeria	**12.**	Iran
6.	W. Germany	**13.**	Canada
7.	Italy	**14.**	Yugoslavia

7

The part of the computer that is able to store data is the computer's *memory*, or storage. Computers are capable of storing a virtually unlimited amount of data and of retrieving this data at incredible speeds. Though storage of vast quantities of data in manually maintained files of paper is possible, the files tend to become extremely bulky. They require a good deal of storage space. The job of manually extracting data from such a file becomes increasingly tedious and time-consuming as the size of the file increases. Through the memory capabilities of a computer, the same data can be stored in considerably less space and retrieved in a fraction of the time otherwise required.

The amount of storage available in today's computers can be increased or decreased according to user requirements. Continuing advances in technology have led to steady reductions in the cost of memory. Users can purchase the amount of memory needed to satisfy their storage requirements. Once data has been placed in the computer's memory, efficient processing and retrieval operations can be performed. The enormous memory capacities of computers are vital to their successful application.

DATA PROCESSING

In the past, our manual techniques of collecting, manipulating, and disseminating data to achieve certain objectives were known as *data processing*. As technology advanced, electromechanical machines were developed to do these functions. The term *automatic data processing* (*ADP*) was introduced. Today, technology is at the point where the electronic computer can achieve results formerly accomplished by humans and machines. This is known as *electronic data processing* (*EDP*). (The term *data processing* is sometimes used as a shorthand reference to EDP.)

The objective of all data processing, whether manual, electromechanical, or electronic, is to convert raw data into information that can be used in decision-making. Thus, we must distinguish data from information. *Data* refers to raw facts that have been collected from different sources and, as such, cannot be the basis for meaningful conclusions. For example, a daily list of all checks and deposit slips of all branch offices may mean very little to a bank manager. But once the data has been manipulated according to certain predetermined criteria, it may provide useful information. This information may be presented in the form of a summary report giving the number and amount of deposits at each branch, and the number and amount of withdrawals at each branch. Therefore, *information* is data that has been organized and processed. It can be used to increase understanding and to make intelligent decisions.

All data processing follows the same basic flow pattern (see Figure 1–2).

Input involves collecting data, verifying it to insure its correctness, and then converting it to a machine-readable form so that it can be entered into the data-processing system.

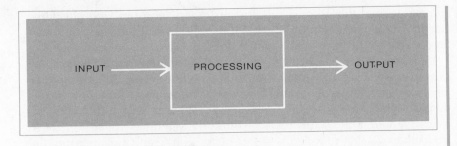

FIGURE 1–2
Data Flow

The terms *classify, sort, calculate, summarize,* and *store* are used to refer to the steps involved in processing data.

● Classify: This step involves categorizing data according to certain characteristics so that it is meaningful to the user. For example, sales data can be grouped according to salesperson, product type, customer, or any other classification useful to management.

● Sort: This step follows the classification step. It involves arranging the data elements into a predetermined sequence to facilitate processing. For example, an employee file may be sorted by social security number or by employee last name. Sorting can be done on numbers, letters, special characters ($+$, $-$, ¢, etc.), or a combination of these. However, a strictly numeric sort is usually faster than other sorts in computer-based data-processing systems.

● Calculate: The arithmetic and/or logical manipulation of data is referred to as calculating. Examples include computation of student grade-point averages, customer bank balances, and employee wages.

● Summarize: Reducing large amounts of data to a concise, usable form is called summarizing. This logical reduction of data is necessary to provide only information that is useful, and eliminate everything else. An example of reduced data is a top-management report which summarizes the profit performance of each division of a company. No further breakdown (say, by departments within divisions) is needed for top-management decision-making purposes.

● Store: Keeping processed data for future reference is storing. The data is placed on a storage medium such as paper, magnetic tape, or microfilm for retrieval when needed. Obviously, only facts that may be needed later should be stored. The cost of storage should not exceed the benefit of having the facts available for future use.

Once data has been processed according to the steps outlined above, the output is ready for dissemination and communication to the user. Often, several users may require the output. This necessitates duplication. Some types of equipment (for example, Xerox duplicators) reproduce human-readable copies; other types of equipment duplicate data in machine-readable form on media such as punched cards and magnetic disks. Examples of output are sales reports for marketing

9

managers, monthly phone bills for customers, and updated checking account balances for customers. Ultimately, all output must be communicated to the user in an intelligible form.

To achieve effective data processing, data is organized in an integrated way to answer all anticipated user information needs. For example, a business firm may want to maintain specific data about all employees— home address, social security number, wage per hour, withholding tax, gross income, and so on. Each of these data items is called a *field*. A collection of fields, or individual data items, that relate to a single unit (in this case a single employee) is a *record*. A grouping of all related records (in this case all employee records) is a *file*. The structuring of data to satisfy a wider variety of information needs than can be supported by a single file is a *data base*. We shall consistently use the terms field, record, file, and data base in this manner.

A DATA-PROCESSING APPLICATION

One common application of data processing is payroll preparation. The inputs to this application are employee time cards and a personnel file. This data is processed to provide paychecks for all employees and a payroll report containing summary information for management (see Figure 1–3).

Payroll preparation is suitable for electronic data processing because it involves a well-defined, repetitive procedure and a large number of

FIGURE 1–3

Payroll Processing

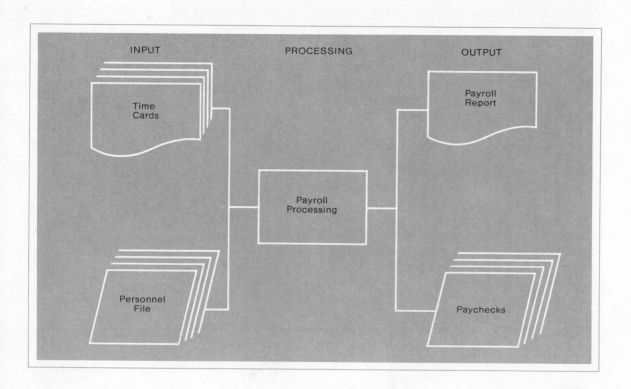

records. The computer must take the following steps in preparing a paycheck:

1. Read total hours worked from time card.

2. Compute gross pay by multiplying total hours worked by employee hourly wage rate.

3. Calculate withholding tax and social security tax.

4. Deduct withholding tax and social security tax from gross pay to get net pay.

5. Write paycheck.

In most payroll applications, the computer must also check for other conditions. Among them are overtime, maximum or minimum allowable work hours, other deductions, and special wage rates for overtime work.

The payroll report includes information such as number of employees paid, total dollar value of payroll for the period, total withholdings, and breakdowns of payments for all departments of the company. This report aids management in its decision-making with respect to labor costs, cash flow planning, and the like.

STORED-PROGRAM CONCEPT

A *program* is a series of instructions to direct the computer in performing a given task. In early computers, the instructions had to be either (a) wired on control panels and plugged into the computer at the beginning of a job, or (b) read into the computer from punched cards in discrete steps as the job progressed. The latter approach limited the speed of processing because the computer had to wait for instructions to be fed in on cards made available to it by a human operator. To overcome this limitation, the memory of the computer was used to store both data and the instructions required to manipulate the data. This development—the stored-program concept—was significant. Since the instructions were stored in the computer's memory in electronic form, no human intervention was required during processing.

Most modern computers are stored-program computers. Once the instructions required for a particular application have been determined, they are placed into the computer memory so that the appropriate operations can be performed. The storage unit operates in a manner similar to that of a tape recorder. Once a copy of the instructions and data have been stored, they remain in storage until new instructions and data are stored over them. Therefore, it is possible to perform the same instructions and process the same data, over and over again, until a change is desired. The same principle then applies to the new instructions and data. This basic characteristic of memory is known as *nondestructive read, destructive write*. Each series of instructions placed into memory is called a *stored program*.

11

The computer performs instructions in a sequential manner unless instructed to do otherwise. This *next-sequential-instruction feature* requires that the instructions that constitute a program be placed in consecutive locations in memory. Since input must be brought into the computer for processing, a separate area must be designated for the input. Output generated by the program will also require an area isolated from the instructions. Figure 1–4 depicts graphically the required memory allocation.

Assume a four-instruction program is placed in computer memory (see Figure 1–5). It directs the computer to calculate and print output paychecks for employees, based upon input time sheets. The computer can process timesheets in the same way a human payroll clerk does. Because of the sequential nature of program execution, the instructions are performed in the following ordered manner:

Instruction 1:   Read a time sheet

Instruction 2:   Calculate net pay

Instruction 3:   Write out a paycheck

Instruction 4:   Repeat Instructions 1, 2, and 3 (Go to Instruction 1)

When the first instruction is executed, time sheet data (name, hours, rate) is brought into the input area. Since the data must be in machine-readable form, a device that can read the time sheet and translate the data into electronic pulses is used in this step. Next, the mathematical operations needed to calculate net pay are performed and the result is placed into the output area. The third instruction causes the printing of that information. If there are more employee time sheets, it is necessary to repeat these three instructions. Therefore, to override the next-sequential-instruction feature of the computer, we command it to go back to Instruction 1.

When the second time sheet is read and the data placed into the input area, the previous employee's time data is replaced by the new data (a result of the destructive-write feature). Prior to calculation of net pay based upon the second time sheet, the input area holds the second time sheet data but the output area still holds the result of the first pay calculation. When Instruction 2 is executed again, the net pay for the

FIGURE 1–4
Stored-Program Concept

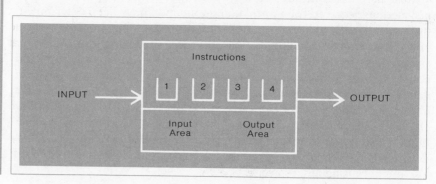

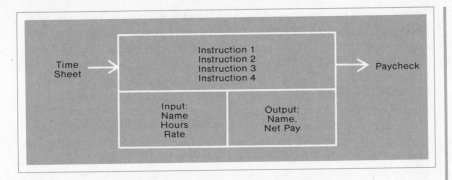

FIGURE 1—5
Program Execution

second employee is moved into the output area. It overlays, or destroys, the net pay of the first employee. Now the second paycheck, containing the appropriate name and net pay, can be printed out. When the computer has processed all input time sheets, it will stop.

At this time, assume the sales office needs the computer's help in preparing invoices. The program to accept sales data as input and prepare invoices as output is placed into computer memory on top of the payroll program. It destroys the stored copy of the payroll program. The computer that generated paychecks is now used to prepare sales invoices. This demonstrates the general-purpose nature of the computer.

COMPUTER IMPACT

We are in the midst of the computer revolution. During the past two decades, the cost of computing has decreased significantly. So has the size of computers. The rapid decline in cost has fostered a pervasive use of computers in today's society. The ability of the computer to store, retrieve, and analyze data at tremendous speeds and at low cost has made possible such advances as space travel, electronic banking, and body scanners. The potential of computers seems unlimited—new applications are appearing every day.

The advantages of a new technology are often obvious, but the problems that may arise are much more difficult to assess. This was so with automobiles. It may very well be the case with computers. We have all been exposed to the impact of computers—from the utility bill on a computer card which says "do not fold, staple, or mutilate," to the 24-hour automated tellers which accept deposits and cash checks at banks. Many people are excited about the uses of computers, but many others are concerned about the problems they may create—problems like worker displacement, invasion of privacy, and depersonalization in business operations. We can take heart from the fact that the computer is a general-purpose machine; it can be used to solve many of the problems it creates.

Perhaps the greatest impact of computers has been on business. Today, most businesses are involved in electronic data processing. The power to process data rapidly and disseminate the results of processing to users is critical to technological progress. Business organizations are concerned with using scarce resources in an optimal manner to achieve their objectives of profit and growth. Managers must make various decisions as they attempt to achieve these goals. The computer, by providing information that is timely, concise, and relevant, has improved the decision-making process.

The computer is much like any other tool used by humans. It has not replaced people, but it has enhanced their problem-solving capabilities and increased their capacity to handle complex relationships. Thus, computers are being used for straightforward clerical tasks (payroll processing, inventory control, and billing) and for complex applications (budgeting, facilities planning, market research, and corporate planning).

Government use of computers parallels business use as far as conventional data processing is concerned. But the government also uses computers extensively in its development of military weapons and defense systems. Examples of the latter include computerized radar systems and automatically guided missiles. The government is also using computers for land resource planning, health service planning, transportation planning, and police telecommunication systems.

In addition to governments and businesses, computers have had a significant impact on education and health care. Education is one of society's largest industries. Like business, it would not function smoothly without computers to store and process large amounts of data. Recently, computers are also being used in teaching. Computer-assisted instruction (CAI) involves direct interaction between a computer and a student. This method of teaching holds promise since the computer can deal with a large number of students on an individual basis.

In the health-care field, computers are being used for medical diagnoses, patient monitoring, and maintaining medical histories. The advantage of computer monitoring of intensive-care patients is that critical factors like pulse rate, breathing, and body temperature can be checked several times a second. This type of monitoring could not be provided by an individual. Moreover, the computer does not suffer fatigue, and it makes no mistakes once it has been correctly set up.

Computers are here to stay. We could not maintain our present life styles if we did away with them. Indeed, it is essential that we be familiar with their capabilities, limitations, and real and potential social impact. This text introduces the basic workings of the computer, discusses recent computer innovations, and points to some of the issues that face the computer generation.

SUMMARY

● A computer is a general-purpose machine. It derives its power from speed, accuracy, and memory. It possesses no intelligence. It can perform only tasks which are predetermined by humans.

● The basic pattern of all data processing is (1) input, (2) processing, and (3) output. All computer processing involves the basic machine functions of simple arithmetic (addition, subtraction, etc.), comparing values (either numeric or alphabetic), and storage and retrieval of information.

● The speed of computer processing is limited by the switching speed of its electronic circuits and the distances that electric currents must travel through these circuits. Advances in technology have resulted in computers that can perform operations in nanoseconds (billionths of a second).

● Computer accuracy is enhanced by the internal, self-checking features of electronic circuits. Although the internal operations of the computer are essentially error-free, there is no guarantee of the validity of the input to the computer. "Garbage in—garbage out" (GIGO) is fundamental to understanding computer "mistakes."

● The collection, manipulation, and dissemination of data is known as data processing. The use of machines to perform these functions is called automatic data processing. When an electronic computer is used, electronic data processing (EDP) is performed.

● Data refers to raw facts that have been collected from different sources and, as such, cannot be the basis for meaningful conclusions. Information is data that has been organized and processed so that it can be used to make intelligent decisions. The conversion of data into information involves classifying, sorting, calculating, summarizing, and storing the data in a meaningful way. The information must then be communicated to the user in an intelligible form.

● In order for data to be processed effectively, it must be organized. A data item is called a field; a collection of fields relating to a single unit is a record. A grouping of related records is called a file. The structuring of data to support the information needs of a wide variety of users is a data base.

● The stored-program concept involves storing both data and instructions in the computer's memory, thus eliminating the need for human intervention during processing.

● The non-destructive read, destructive write characteristic of memory allows a program to be executed repeatedly, yet remain intact in memory until another program is stored over it. The computer performs instructions in a sequential manner (as they have been placed in consecutive locations in memory) unless instructed to do otherwise.

● The capability of the computer to store, retrieve, and analyze data at tremendous speeds has made possible new advances such as space travel and electronic banking. Computers have had a growing impact on society as we have become more dependent on them in our daily lives. Unfortunately, there are no simple answers to problems such as worker displacement and invasion of privacy that may be created by computers.

15

REVIEW QUESTIONS

1. Describe what is meant by the stored-program concept and explain why it is significant to electronic data processing.

2. Although computer processing is essentially error-free, mistakes can and do occur. Explain how computer mistakes occur, and what is meant by the phrase "garbage in—garbage out."

3. Distinguish between data and information. What are some of the functions performed in converting data into information? Give an example of how a computer can be used to perform these functions.

4. List five ways that the computer has had some impact on you.

5. What are some of the problems created by computers? Can these problems be solved? Discuss.

At the conclusion of each subsequent chapter of this book, an application will be discussed. Each discussion will show how a corporation or government agency uses computers. The applications complement the text material. The concepts presented in a chapter become the focus of the associated application.

The organizations represented in these application sections were selected primarily on the basis of two criteria—nature of operations and computer technology. An effort was made to include as wide a variety of operations as possible. A breakdown of the applications by classification of operation is given in Table 1—1. Because the intent is to match the computer use described in an application and the chapter content, some technological efforts of the organizations are not detailed in this book.

To understand an application, you must have mastered the preceding text material. Only with this knowledge is it possible to maximize the benefits that can be derived from this approach. Since the subject matter is cumulative in nature, the applications are similarly structured. Table 1—2 lists the principal concepts associated with the applications.

The ability to transform a concept from an abstraction to a reality is essential. The essence of data processing is the harnessing of computer power by organizations for their benefit. Hopefully, you, the reader, will find the applications challenging but rewarding, and benefit accordingly.

applications

INTRODUCTION TO APPLICATIONS

TYPE OF OPERATION	ORGANIZATION
Government	United States Navy
	Federal Reserve Bank
	Civil Service Commission
Distribution and Retail	Kroger Company
	Marathon Oil
Entertainment	Walt Disney Productions
Computer Manufacturers	IBM
	NCR Corporation
Manufacturing	Dana Corporation (industrial)
	Procter & Gamble Company (consumer)
	Eli Lilly & Company (drug)
	Armco Inc. (steel)
	Ford Motor Company (integrated)
Banking and Insurance	American United Life
	Ohio Citizens Bank
Transportation	Southern Railways
Service	WESTLAW

TABLE 1—1
CORPORATE
CLASSIFICATIONS

TABLE 1—2
NATURE OF APPLICATIONS

ORGANIZATION	CHAPTER	FOCUS
United States Navy	2	Historical involvement
IBM	3	Computer equipment
American United Life	4	Unit-record punched card
WESTLAW	5	Remote computing
Federal Reserve Bank	6	Data-entry
Procter & Gamble Company	7	Storage criteria
Southern Railways	8	Computer systems integration
NCR Corporation	9	Software development
Eli Lilly & Company	10	Programming management
Ohio Citizens Bank	11	Language selection
Armco Inc.	12	Structured approach
Kroger Company	13	Technological advances
Marathon Oil	14	Systems methodology
Dana Corporation	15	Processing alternatives
Ford Motor Company	16	Corporate applications
Civil Service Commission	17	Training program
Walt Disney Productions	18	Automation

EVOLUTION OF COMPUTERS | 2

OUTLINE

I. Early Development
   A. Abacus, Pascal's Adding
      Machine, Babbage's Difference
      Engine, Hollerith's First Census
      Tabulator
   B. Accounting Machines
   C. Mark I, ENIAC, EDSAC
II. First Generation: 1951
    Through 1958
   A. Vacuum-Tube Technology
   B. Machine Language
   C. Symbolic Language

III. Second Generation: 1959
     Through 1964
   A. Transistor Technology
   B. Magnetic Cores
   C. Disk Storage, Modular
      Hardware, Improved I/O
      Devices
   D. High-Level Languages
IV. Third Generation: 1965 Through ??
   A. Technological Advances
   B. Software Improvements
V. State of the Art: The Present
   A. Large-Scale Integrated
      Circuitry

INTRODUCTION

Although the computer is a relatively recent innovation, its development rests on centuries of research, thought, and discoveries. Advances in information-processing technology are a response to the growing need to find better, faster, cheaper, and more reliable methods of handling data. The search for better ways to store and process data is not recent—data-processing equipment has gone through generations of changes and improvements. An understanding of the evolution of data processing is especially helpful in understanding the capabilities and limitations of modern computers.

This chapter presents significant events leading to the development of the computer. A brief history of data processing is given, beginning with the earliest calculating machines and ending with the state of the art today. Since developments in computer programs (*software*) are as important as developments in computer equipment (*hardware*), major advances in both areas are presented.

Jeffrey A. Tannenbaum
Staff Reporter of *The Wall Street Journal*

The Wall Street Journal,
Feb. 13, 1973, p. 1, col. 4

We have some bad news to report.

While some of the nation's drinkers have been quietly downing an occasional drink on the house, and while some of the nation's bartenders have been quietly dipping into the till, some of the nation's bar owners have been quietly buying little computers. And the little computers can do two things: They can mix drinks, and they can count. They can do both tasks very precisely.

And you know what that means.

It means no more drinks on the house. It means no more little extras for bartenders. It means no heavy hand on the gin on those nights when you really need a heavy hand on the gin.

It also means more profits for bar owners, and that, of course, is why bar owners are putting out thousands of dollars for computers.

It is already too late to stop this trend. "The sales outlook is unbelievable," says one man who sells these mechanical bartenders. Another says, "The industry is only in its infancy, but we've started to see extremely rapid growth in the last several months." Some large companies are entering the field, and you know what that means.

National Cash Register Co. of Dayton has sold more than 500 of its Elektra-Bar systems and has orders for over 100 of a newer model; the systems, introduced in late 1970, cost around $10,000 apiece. Other companies, among them Bar Boy, Inc. of San Diego, Electronic Dispensers International of Concord, Calif., and an Illinois-based subsidiary of a German company called Anker-Werke, agree. Their models, which sell for $600 to over $15,000, are selling as fast as you can say "very dry Beefeater martini on the rocks, with a twist."

WHIR, BUZZ, HUM, $1.25

But why? Because computers don't drink. Because computers don't hand out free drinks to other computers who might stop by for a fast one or two. Because computers keep track of the inventory. And because computers don't dip into the till to get a little extra money to make car payments. "The average (human-type) bartender steals enough to make a car payment," contends Homer Lum, food and beverage manager at the Sheraton Inn-Hopkins at Cleveland's Hopkins Airport. "If they're driving a Chevy, they're taking in enough on the side to pay for a Chevy. If they're driving a Cadillac, they're taking in enough to pay for a Cadillac."

The machines also eliminate overpouring by bartenders, the bar owners say with as much enthusiasm as bar owners ever muster. "For consistency of drink, the machine is great," says John J. Urban, food and beverage manager at a Holiday Inn in North Randall, Ohio. His machine is programmed to mete out precisely an ounce and a quarter of liquor for each $1.25 drink. (Actually, that's not too bad a deal. A machine at the Charter One Club in Daytown, Texas, pours exactly three-fourths of an ounce of booze into each $1.10 drink, says assistant manager Bill Mitchell. The machine, he adds, "is very accurate.")

And every time those machines pour, they go whir, buzz, hum and put it on your tab. Bartenders, hoping for big tips, don't always go whir, buzz, hum. The computers are so conscientious that they pay for themselves rapidly, maintains William L. Ohman, director of food service development for Holiday Inns (which is developing its very own machines). "It's an absolute must to have this equipment in a lounge or bar," he asserts.

It's generally agreed that the machines are not good at listening sympathetically to a drinker's troubles. It's generally agreed that the machines are not good at sending you home when you have had enough. But it isn't generally agreed that the machines make especially good drinks—or especially bad ones.

YES AND NO

Chuck Hobbs, a policeman who was in the bar at the Holiday Inn in North Randall the other day, says a machine-made vodka collins "doesn't taste as good as a hand-mixed one; it doesn't have the flavor or the body." But Walter Quinn, another customer, says he "can't tell the difference" between a hand-mixed Scotch-and-soda and one made by a machine.

Drinkers might be mixed in their reactions, but bartenders aren't. So far, computers are just supplementing bartenders, not replacing them, but even so the machine "takes away the art of being a bartender," says a bartender named Antonio who works at North Randall. Other bartenders say many drinkers fear getting short shots from machines they can't see.

But Pete Hamm, a bartender-psychologist (he has a psychology degree) at Sir Henry's in Cleveland, which tried a $13,000 machine but decided against it, points out that while the machines won't cheat the bar owner neither will they cheat the bar goer. And you can't always say that about bartenders, he says. "Most bartenders can pour you a short shot in front of your eyes," he says, "and you'll never know it."

"HEY BARTENDER! POUR ME ANOTHER SCOTCH!" WHIR, BUZZ, POCKETA

This article presents another example of the expanding uses of computers. The evolution of the computer from the abacus to the monstrous electromechanical Mark I to sophisticated minicomputers has culminated in remarkable applications like the one just described.

EARLY DEVELOPMENT

People have always needed to keep track of information. The progress toward the concept of a computer has extended over several centuries, though many of the technological advances are recent. Often an invention in a widely different field has found an application in the growth of the computer concept.

One of the earliest computational devices was the abacus, used by the Chinese since 1000 B.C. It consisted of a number of beads strung on rows of wires set in a rectangular frame (see Figure 2–1).

The climb to the computer concept originated when Blaise Pascal invented a mechanical adding machine in 1642. The machine used gears with teeth to store digits. When a gear rotated past the tooth representing the digit 9, the next gear to the left shifted one tooth, or digit (see Figure 2–2). This concept was expanded by Gottfried Leibnitz, a German mathematician, who constructed a machine to add, subtract, multiply, divide, and calculate square roots. His mechanical calculating machine was first demonstrated in 1694. Mechanical technology continued to advance with the invention of more complex machines.

In 1822, Charles Babbage developed the concept of a machine that could execute complex computations and print results without human intervention. Using this idea, Babbage built a machine called the *difference engine* (see Figure 2–3). This machine was used to compute mathematical tables with results up to five significant digits in length. When Babbage tried to build a larger model, he found that parts could not be produced to meet necessary tolerances for accuracy.

Babbage did not give up, however. In 1833 he developed the idea for an *analytical engine.* This machine was to be capable of addition, subtraction, multiplication, division, and storage of intermediate results in a memory unit. It was to have a "mill," or arithmetic unit, to perform computations, a punched-card input system, and an external storage

FIGURE 2–1
The Abacus

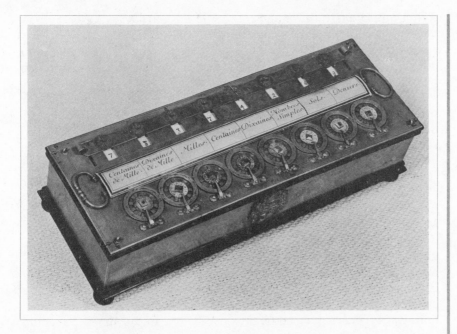

FIGURE 2–2
Pascal's Adding Machine

FIGURE 2–3
Babbage's Difference
Engine

unit. Unfortunately, the analytical engine was too advanced for its time, and parts could not be manufactured for it. Babbage's work was essentially forgotten for nearly a century. It was not rediscovered until after the concepts and ideas that he advocated had been implemented by other men.

In the 1880s, Dr. Herman Hollerith developed a device to code data for the United States Bureau of Census (see Figure 2–4). He showed that by using a punched card with census data on it and a machine that did sorting, 250 cards could be sorted in one minute. This reduced the time needed to process the 1890 census data from $7\frac{1}{2}$ years to $2\frac{1}{2}$ years. In 1896 Hollerith founded the Tabulating Machine Company to commercially manufacture and market punched-card equipment. Fifteen years later this company merged with 12 others to form International Business Machines Corporation (IBM).

Significant advances in punched-card equipment design were made during the late 1920s and early 1930s. Punched cards with increased record lengths of 80 and 90 columns were introduced. Machines that could not only add and subtract, but also multiply were developed. The capability to perform full-scale record-keeping and accounting functions was further enhanced by the introduction of machines that could handle alphabetic data. These machines were referred to as *accounting machines* (tabulators).

FIGURE 2–4
The First Census Tabulator

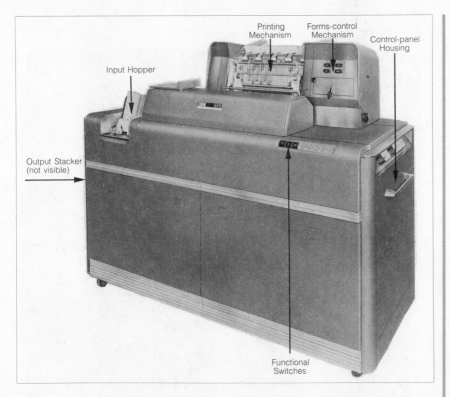

Printing Mechanism
Forms-control Mechanism
Control-panel Housing
Input Hopper
Output Stacker (not visible)
Functional Switches

FIGURE 2–5
Accounting Machine

Accounting machines could read data from punched cards, perform summary calculations such as addition and subtraction, rearrange data to meet user requirements, and print results in a wide variety of formats (see Figure 2–5). These operations were controlled by hand-wired control panels. Different calculations and report formats could be obtained by changing the wiring in the control panel (see Figure 2–6).

Although punched-card devices were increasingly used for business data processing and statistical computations, they had several limitations. First, the mechanical manipulation of cards limited the speed of the equipment. Second, since each device was designed to perform a specific function, the cards had to be transferred from one machine to another to do different functions. This took time and increased the possibility of error.

Inventions and perfections of techniques and technologies brought entirely new processes to light. In the late 1930s and early 1940s, the first automatic calculator, the *Mark I*, was introduced. It was developed by Professor Howard Aiken of Harvard University in conjunction with engineers from IBM. Since it used electromagnetic relays and mechanical counters, it was an electromechanical computer rather than an electronic one. The machine was controlled by punched cards and paper tapes. It could multiply 10-digit numbers in six seconds (see Figure 2–7). **25**

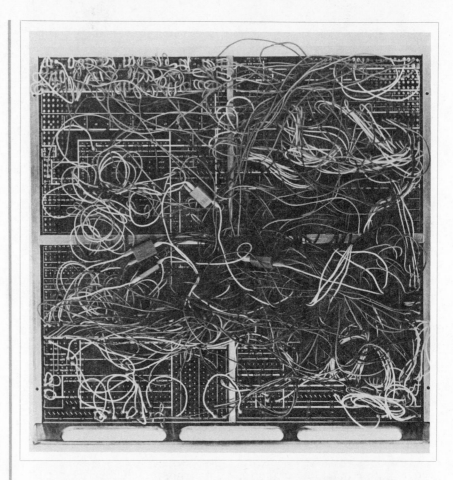

FIGURE 2–6
Control Panel

FIGURE 2–7
The Mark I Computer

In the mid-1940s, the *ENIAC* (*E*lectronic *N*umerical *I*ntegrator *a*nd *C*alculator) was developed at the University of Pennsylvania. It was a 30-ton, 1500-square-foot machine. The ENIAC did not have a memory capable of holding instructions; rather, it was programmed by a combination of switches. Its computational abilities far exceeded those of the Mark I, and it could handle 300 numbers per second. The ENIAC was the first electronic digital computer. Its switching and control functions were performed using vacuum tubes (see Figure 2–8).

The *EDSAC* (*E*lectronic *D*elay-*S*torage *A*utomatic *C*omputer) was completed at Cambridge University in 1949. It was the first stored-program computer. Instead of wired control panels, instructions stored in the computer itself controlled the operation of the machine. Thus, the EDSAC could perform different types of arithmetic and logical manipulations without human intervention, depending solely on the stored-program instructions within it.

FIRST GENERATION: 1951 THROUGH 1958

Computers of various sizes and capabilities were developed in the late 1940s. However, it was not until 1951 that the first commercial electronic computer became available. This was the *UNIVAC I* (*Uni*versal *Auto*matic *C*omputer) built by John W. Mauchly and J. Presper Eckert, who were also responsible for the development of the ENIAC. The UNIVAC I was sold to the Census Bureau of the U.S. Government and marked the

FIGURE 2–8
The ENIAC

beginning of *first-generation computers* (see Figure 2–9). In 1954 another UNIVAC I was installed at General Electric's Appliance Park in Louisville, Kentucky. IBM installed its first commercial computer, an IBM 650, in Boston, Massachusetts.

The characteristic that distinguished first-generation computers from subsequent machines was the use of *vacuum tubes* to control internal operations. The vacuum tubes were fairly large in size, and they generated considerable heat. Consequently, first-generation computers were huge. They required a lot of space and special air-conditioning equipment to dissipate the heat generated by the tubes. Maintenance and reliability were major considerations. Although first-generation computers were much faster than earlier mechanical or electromechanical devices, they were slow in comparison to today's computers. Their internal storage capacity was limited. Many used *magnetic drums* as a storage medium. The magnetic drum was a cylinder, coated with magnetizable material. Data was stored as tiny magnetized spots on tracks on the outer surface of the drum. It could be recorded or read as the drum rotated at high speed. Other types of storage media were also used. Among them were mercury acoustic delay lines and magnetic cores (though cores were not generally available until later; see below). Input and output operations were performed using punched cards. Most first-generation computers were oriented towards scientific applications rather than business data processing.

The computer, a binary machine, can distinguish between only two states—say, "on" or "off," magnetized in one direction or in another. The early first-generation computers were programmed in *machine language*. The machine language consisted of strings of zeroes and ones, specifying the desired electrical states of the computer's two-state internal circuits and memory banks. Obviously, writing a machine-language program was extremely cumbersome and time-consuming.

FIGURE 2–9
The UNIVAC I Computer

To make programming easier, *symbolic languages* were developed. Given such languages, instructions could be written using symbolic codes (called *mnemonics,* or memory aids) rather than strings of ones and zeroes. As a part of symbolic-language development, a method of translating symbolic instructions into corresponding binary codes (machine-language instructions) had to be devised. The first set of programs, or instructions, to tell the computer how to translate mnemonic symbols into machine language was developed by Dr. Grace Hopper in 1952 at the University of Pennsylvania. Subsequent to this breakthrough, most first-generation computers were programmed in symbolic language. Payroll and billing were typical business applications of first-generation computers, since they were easy to program and to cost-justify.

SECOND GENERATION: 1959 THROUGH 1964

In the late 1950s, *transistors* became available for commercial installations. They were used instead of vacuum tubes in computers. The elimination of vacuum tubes greatly reduced the heat generated by an operating machine. It also made possible the development of computers which were significantly smaller and more reliable than their predecessors. They were faster, had increased storage capacity, and required less power to operate. These machines were known as *second-generation computers.*

Magnetic drums were replaced by *magnetic cores* as the primary internal-storage medium of these computers. The cores were very small doughnut-shaped rings of ferromagnetic material strung on thin wires. By passing a current through the wire on which a core was strung, the core could be magnetized (set "on" or "off"), and thus used to store data. Because data stored in magnetic cores can be located and retrieved for processing in a few millionths of a second, core storage is faster than magnetic-drum storage.

In many second-generation computer systems, the *internal,* or *main, storage* capacity of the computer was supplemented by the use of *magnetic tapes* for *external,* or *auxiliary, storage.* Substituting magnetic tapes for punched cards or punched paper tape increased input/output processing speeds by a factor of at least 50 (see Figure 2–10).

Other significant changes occurring during this period were the development of disk storage, modular hardware, and improved input/output devices. *Magnetic disks* can be compared with phonograph records. Data is stored in circular tracks on the outer surfaces of the platter, or disk, which are coated with ferromagnetic material. The main advantage of disk storage is that it is possible to locate a particular record on a set of disks rotating at high speeds in a fraction of a second. The records on the disks do not have to be sorted into a certain sequence before processing. Thus, the disks provide *direct,* or *random, access* to records in a file.

The modular-hardware concept involved using a building-block approach to the design of electronic circuits. With this approach, complete

FIGURE 2—10
A Second-Generation
Computer System

modules could be replaced in case of malfunctions. New modules could be added to the system to increase its capabilities. For example, primary storage modules consisting of 100 or more switching circuits on a single silicon chip could be added to the system to increase the main memory capacity.

The improvement in input/output (I/O) devices related to factors such as faster printing speeds, and automatic detection and correction of input/output errors. These advances allowed the devices to be connected directly to the computer (*online*), without significantly lowering the overall efficiency of the computer system.

Second-generation computers were programmed in *high-level languages*, which had a closer resemblance to English than their predecessors. They were application- and problem-oriented rather than machine-oriented. Eventually, many of the languages were standardized to help insure machine-independence.

The first high-level language to achieve widespread acceptance was called *FORTRAN* (*FOR*mula *TRAN*slator). It was developed during the period from 1954 through 1957 by IBM. The version of the language known as FORTRAN IV was standardized in 1963. It has been extensively used for scientific applications.

Because FORTRAN lacked many features desirable for business data processing, another language, called *COBOL* (*CO*mmon *Business-Oriented Language*), was developed in 1961. Among the significant features of COBOL are its file-processing, editing, and input/output capabilities. Another is its self-documentation.

Second-generation computers, like their predecessors, were designed either for business data processing or for scientific applications. The most popular business-oriented computer was the IBM 1401. Typical applications included payroll processing, invoicing, and maintaining personnel records. All of these applications involved *batch processing*— the collection of data over a certain period of time and the subsequent processing of it in one computer run. Prior to entrance into the computer system, the items in a batch are sorted into a sequential order to match the sequence of the records on the application file. Magnetic tape was the principal storage medium associated with batch processing.

30

THIRD GENERATION: 1965 THROUGH ??

Continued technological advancement in the field of electronics and solid-state physics brought further reductions in computer size, even greater reliability and speed, and lower costs. *Integrated circuits (ICs)* replaced the transistors of second-generation equipment, in machines referred to as *third-generation computers*. Through techniques like etching and printing, hundreds of electronic components were included on circuit chips less than $\frac{1}{8}$-inch square. Such processes made possible still faster processing at a still lower price (see Figure 2–11).

Other important improvements in third-generation equipment included:

● Greater storage capacity

● Versatile programs that automated many tasks previously handled by human operators

● Greater compatibility of components, allowing easier expansion of computer systems

● Use of communication channels to permit remote input and output

● Ability to perform several operations simultaneously

● Capability to handle both business and scientific applications

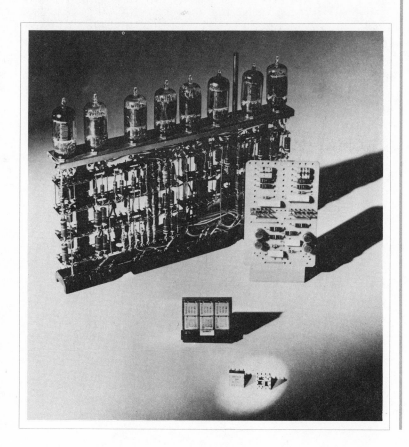

FIGURE 2–11
First-, Second-, and Third-Generation Components

Third-generation computers were programmed almost exclusively in high-level languages such as FORTRAN and COBOL. Progress was also made in the development of *operating-system software,* programs to control the computer's operations and facilitate its use. Computer manufacturers and software firms specializing in this area provided extremely complex operating systems that could handle diverse tasks such as controlling all input/output and scheduling jobs to maximize system efficiency.

Standardized programs for applications like payroll and billing were provided by software firms at low costs. They gained widespread acceptance. Third-generation equipment was not limited to batch-processing applications. Remote terminals at various geographic locations could be used to communicate directly with a central computer. The central computer responded immediately to inquiries from these terminals. Many users were able to interact with the computer at the same time and receive almost instantaneous results in what was called a *time-sharing* environment. Computers were (and are being) used for such diverse applications as inventory control, scheduling labor and materials, and bank credit-card billing.

STATE OF THE ART: THE PRESENT

In 1971 IBM began delivering its System/370 computers (see Figure 2–12). This family of computers, and those developed by other large computer manufacturers in the 1970s, incorporated further refinements; among them were monolithic semi-conductor memories, further miniaturization through *large-scale integrated (LSI) circuits* and widespread use of virtual-storage techniques. LSI is a technological process that allows circuits containing thousands of transistors to be densely packed on a single silicon chip. Figure 2–13 shows a modern *minicomputer* that uses these new technologies.

Computers of this period are sometimes referred to as *third-and-a-half generation computers.* They do not constitute a new (fourth) generation

FIGURE 2–12
A Third-Generation
Computer System

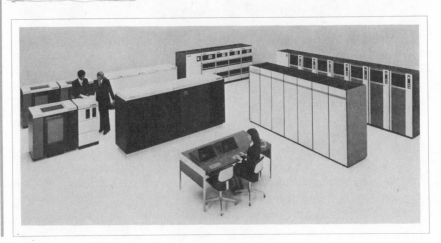

32

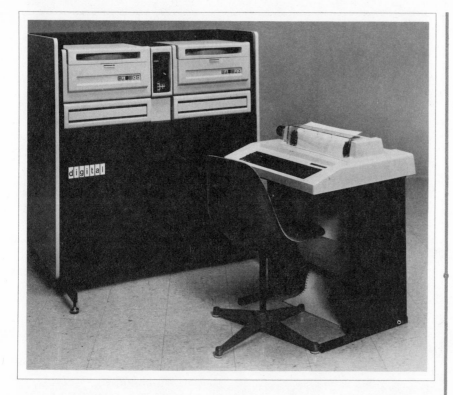

FIGURE 2–13

A Minicomputer That Uses Third-Generation Miniaturization Techniques

because they do not offer the significant price/performance improvements that distinguished the first, second, and third generations. The advent of fourth-generation computer systems will be a gradual, evolving process since systems are now being designed to be compatible with their third-generation counterparts. This *compatibility* is necessary because users are not willing to go through the conversion and incompatibility problems that characterized the change from second-generation to third-generation computer systems.

The present-day computer systems are characterized by large-scale integrated circuitry, increased speeds, greater reliability, and storage capacities approaching billions of characters. The emphasis is on ease of use and application. Most systems have communication capabilities; they permit remote input and output via communication channels such as ordinary telephone lines. The use of TV-like display screens has become increasingly common. Additionally, data-recording equipment to capture data at its point of origin in a form directly suitable for computer processing has been developed. Common examples are magnetic-ink character readers (MICRs) and optical-character recognition (OCR) devices. The former are especially suited for applications like check processing for banks (see Table 2–1). The latter include point-of-sale (POS) terminals that record data about sales transactions as they occur. There is no need for a special data-entry step using other input devices. Thus, accurate and faster entry of data for computer processing is achieved.

33

TABLE 2–1
COMPUTER
ADVANCEMENTS

PERIOD	COMPUTER SYSTEM CHARACTERISTICS
First Generation 1951–1958	Use of vacuum tubes in electronic circuits
	Magnetic drum as primary internal-storage medium
	Limited main-storage capacity
	Slow input/output; punched-card-oriented
	Low-level symbolic-language programming
	Heat and maintenance problems
	Applications: payroll processing and record keeping
	Examples: IBM 650
	UNIVAC I
Second Generation 1959–1964	Use of transistors for internal operations
	Magnetic core as primary internal-storage medium
	Increased main-storage capacity
	Faster input/output; tape orientation
	High-level programming languages (COBOL, FORTRAN)
	Great reduction in size and heat generation
	Increased speed and reliability
	Batch-oriented applications: billing, payroll processing, updating inventory files
	Examples: IBM 1401
	Honeywell 200
	CDC 1604
Third Generation 1965–??	Use of integrated circuits
	Magnetic core and solid-state main storage
	More flexibility with input/output; disk-oriented
	Smaller size and better performance and reliability
	Extensive use of high-level programming languages
	Availability of operating-system programs (software) to control I/O and do many tasks previously handled by human operators
	Applications: airline reservation systems, market forecasting, credit-card billing
	Examples: IBM System/360
	NCR 395
	Burroughs B6500
State of the Art Present	Use of large-scale integrated circuits
	Increased storage capacity and speed
	Remote processing and time-sharing through communication
	Modular design and compatibility between equipment (hardware) provided by different manufacturers (customer no longer tied to one vendor)
	Availability of sophisticated programs for special applications
	Greater versatility of input/output devices
	Increased use of minicomputers
	Applications: mathematical modeling and simulation, electronic funds transfer, and computer-aided instruction
	Examples: IBM 3033
	Burroughs B7700
	HP 3000 (minicomputer)

SUMMARY

● Machines to perform arithmetic calculations were developed as early as the 1600s by Blaise Pascal and Gottfried Leibnitz. The first machine employing concepts similar to those of a computer was the analytical engine designed by Charles Babbage in 1833. This machine was doomed to failure because its production was beyond the technological manufacturing capabilities of its time.

● The use of electromechanical calculating machines was first implemented by Herman Hollerith in the 1890 census. These machines used punched-card input, and performed simple arithmetic calculations and card-sorting operations. Electromechanical punched-card machines such as accounting machines were used extensively in the early and mid-1900s. They were controlled by hand-wired control panels.

● The Mark I was the first automatic calculator. Introduced in the late 1930s, the Mark I used electromagnetic relays and counters for performing calculations. It was an electromechanical computer rather than an electronic one.

● In the mid-1940s, the ENIAC (Electronic Numerical Integrator and Calculator) was developed. The ENIAC was the first electronic digital computer. Its switching and control functions were performed using vacuum tubes. The EDSAC (Electronic Delay-Storage Automatic Computer) was completed in 1949. It was the first stored-program computer.

● The first generation of computers (1951–1958) began with the introduction of the UNIVAC I (Universal Automatic Computer). First-generation computers used vacuum tubes to control internal operations. These machines were very large and generated a lot of heat. They were much faster than earlier machines, but very slow by today's standards.

● Second-generation computers (1959–1964) relied on transistors for controlling internal operation. Transistors were much smaller, faster, and more reliable than vacuum tubes. In addition, significant increases in speed were obtained through the use of magnetic cores for internal storage, or memory. Other important innovations during the second generation were the introduction of high-level programming languages, modular hardware design, and improved input/output devices.

● Third-generation computers (1965–?) used solid-state integrated circuits rather than transistors to obtain reductions in size and cost, together with increased reliability and speed. These machines had a much larger storage capacity than second-generation computers. In addition, third-generation computers were supported by more sophisticated software. Many tasks previously handled by human operators were automated.

● In the future, semiconductor memories and large-scale integrated (LSI) circuitry will lead to further miniaturization and cost reductions in computer equipment. Further improvements can also be expected in

35

data collection and recording equipment. However, the transition to fourth-generation computers will be slow because users want new computers to be compatible with their current equipment.

REVIEW QUESTIONS

1. Calculating machines developed in the 1600s by Pascal and Leibnitz could perform many of the functions of modern computers. Besides the fact that these machines were mechanical, rather than electronic, what was a major difference between these devices and computers?

2. Charles Babbage attempted to build a machine employing the concepts now used in computers. What was this machine called and why was it never built?

3. What was the first automatic calculator? How did this machine differ from first-generation computers?

4. What are the chief characteristics which distinguish first-, second-, and third-generation computers?

5. Why is it important that future computer equipment be compatible with present equipment? When was the compatibility problem first experienced? How will this problem slow the development of fourth-generation computers?

6. Many hardware innovations were accompanied by improvements in software. What were some of the software developments during the second and third generations of computers? Why were improvements in software necessary?

The United States Navy has provided a major impetus to the development of modern computers. Through the Office of Naval Research, much effort and money have been directed toward the development of the basic concepts prevalent in today's computer. The most notable of these are stored programs and magnetic-core memory. Because of the increasing demands for national security, the Navy will no doubt continue to keep at the forefront of technology.

The Office of Naval Research (ONR) was established by Congress in 1946 as a post-war continuation of wartime projects initiated by the National Defense Research Committee (NDRC) and the Office of Scientific Research and Development (OSRD). The purpose of this organization was to encourage scientific research. Such research was believed to be vital to the maintenance of naval power and, in effect, the preservation of national security. For many years following World War II, the ONR was the primary and most reliable source of funds for scientific research in the United States.

The Mathematical Sciences Division in the Natural Sciences group of the ONR heavily supported research in pure mathematics, applied mathematics, and mathematical statistics following World War II. This included the support of increasingly complex methods of numerical analysis. To implement these methods, researchers developed various computing devices and, eventually, large-scale electronic digital computers. A specific application of interest was in the area of hydrodynamics and aerodynamics. The ONR was considering an exciting possibility: replacing tests of actual models of physical systems with studies of mathematical models that simulated the physical systems. Without the aid of the digital computer, such analyses were impossible.

The Navy's first major impact on computer development was their support of the Mark I, developed by Howard Aiken at Harvard and built by IBM. This project was first supported by the Bureau of Ships and then by the Bureau of Ordnance Computation Project. The Mark I was capable of performing the complex

UNITED STATES NAVY

scientific calculations believed to be necessary for national security. In fact, some of the early calculations for the atomic bomb were performed on this machine. The Mark I was electromechanical in nature. It had 72 counters for storing numbers. Each counter was capable of holding 23 digits plus a sign. The machine could perform multiplication in about six seconds but required nearly twice as much time to do division.

Following the successful completion of the Mark I project, the Navy contracted Aiken to construct a machine for the computation of ballistic tables at the Bureau of Ordnance's Naval Proving Ground at Dahlgren, Virginia. This machine, popularly known as the "Ballistic Computer," was a special-purpose, all-relay calculator. It was much faster than the Mark I.

In 1944, J. W. Forrester was contracted by the Navy Office of Research and Invention to build a computer system capable of simulating an airplane's performance. A pilot who provided input was to be part of the system. The system was to respond to the pilot just as the plane actually would. Engineering changes to the plane could be simulated without the expense, time, and possible dangers inherent in building and operating a prototype plane.

In 1946, the ONR began support ot the Whirlwind I project at the Massachusetts Institute of Technology (MIT). This project was also under the direction of Forrester. It was on this project that Forrester developed, and had operable by 1953, a magnetic-core memory that was to become the standard for all digital computers. The MIT Servomechanism Laboratory also did important wartime work on fire control and shipboard radar systems.

Also in 1946, a project under the co-sponsorship of the Army Ordnance Corps and the Office of Naval Research was set up. The project was under the direction of John von Neumann. It was known as the Electronic Computer Project of the Institute for Advanced Study. Four main components—an arithmetic unit, a memory, a control, and an input/output area—were developed for the project machine. These components also exist in today's computers.

In 1952, the Naval Research Laboratory of the ONR developed a scientific calculator known as the Naval Research Laboratory Electronic Digital Computer (NAREC). Its primary function was the reduction of experimental data gathered from missile-control research. The internal storage of this machine consisted of electrostatic tubes. Auxiliary storage was provided by a magnetic drum.

The Naval Ordnance Research Calculator (NORC) was developed in a joint effort by the Naval Bureau of Ordnance and IBM in 1954. At the time of its development, the NORC represented the leading edge of technology. It was a one-of-a-kind device using electrostatic storage tubes and capable of performing multiplication in about 30 microseconds. This rate was much faster than the six seconds needed by the Mark I to perform a similar calculation. The NORC was used to perform general scientific calculations in ordnance research, development, and testing at the Naval Proving Ground.

Beginning in about 1954, commercially available (mass-produced) computers began to replace one-of-a-kind computers. These machines could be adapted to a variety of purposes. The Navy began to utilize them to process their applications. Computers began to appear everywhere in naval operations, from shipboard applications to weaponry and base control. As technology advanced, the Navy's use of computers became increasingly sophisticated.

One such example is a current Navy contract with Control Data Corporation (CDC). CDC is to build standardized airborne computers for use in F18 fighters and 204 LAMPS helicopters. The machines will be used in navigation and weapons firing. They may also be used in other types of aircraft such as the P3 antisubmarine plane. The major production of these computers is not expected to begin until October 1979.

Another current Naval project is a satellite-based system designed to improve the accuracy of global weather forecasts. The system collects data from remote locations on land, aircraft, ships, automatic weather buoys, the Defense Meteorological Satellite, and the Seasat Satellite. A digitized view of the atmosphere, temperature, and humidity, and two profiles of the stratosphere are generated. Important data is collected via the satellites which are able to monitor weather conditions over the oceans. (Few oceanic weather stations have been successful heretofore due to expense and equipment losses.)

Once the data has been collected and transmitted to a computer, it is combined with known hydrodynamic equations and laws to produce a weather forecast. A complete forecast is produced every 12 hours and transmitted over the Naval Environmental Data Network to ships, weather stations, and other government agencies.

The Navy is presently in the process of converting applications processed by large computers on their ships to minicomputers. The size of these minicomputers varies greatly, depending upon the size of the ship. An aircraft carrier, for example, requires a much larger machine than a smaller ship such as a destroyer or frigate needs. The primary functions performed by these shipboard computers are logistics and supply applications.

In summary, the United States Navy has been operating at the forefront of computer technology for over a quarter of a century. All indications are that this trend will continue. The advent of new technology makes possible increased national security, which is the prime concern of naval operations. The Navy will undoubtedly continue to push the development of computer technology into unexplored areas.

DISCUSSION POINTS

1. The Whirlwind I and NORC are members of which generation of computers? What characteristics place them in this generation?

2. What are the characteristics of third-generation computers that allow them to be used in such advanced applications as aircraft and weaponry control?

section **II**

TECHNOLOGY

3

HARDWARE

4

CARD INPUT AND PRINTER OUTPUT

5

REMOTE-ACCESS/COMMUNICATION SYSTEMS

6

DATA-ENTRY/INFORMATION-RESPONSE

7

STORAGE DEVICES

8

COMPUTER SYSTEMS

HARDWARE | 3

OUTLINE

I. Digital and Analog Computers

II. The Central Processing Unit
  A. Basic Functions
    1. Control Unit
    2. Arithmetic/Logic Unit (ALU)
    3. Primary Storage Unit
    4. Instruction and Data Flow
  B. Storage Locations and Addresses
  C. Registers

III. Data Representation
  A. Binary Representation
  B. Computer Codes

    1. BCD, EBCDIC, ASCII Coding Schemes
    2. Code Checking
  C. Hexadecimal Representation

IV. Storage
  A. Primary Storage
    1. Cores
    2. Semiconductor Memory
    3. Bubble Memory
  B. Read-Only Memory (ROM)
    1. Microprogramming
    2. Programmable Read-Only Memory (PROM)

INTRODUCTION

One can acquire a general understanding of electronic data processing without making a detailed study of the computer technology involved. However, we should develop a basic understanding of how the computer operates. With this background, we are better equipped to appreciate computer capabilities and limitations, and to relate this knowledge in a useful manner to data-processing activities.

This chapter focuses on the parts of a computer system. The heart of the computer is the central processing unit, or CPU. The key components of the CPU are identified and their functions explained. The representation of data in ways that are appropriate for computer processing is shown. The chapter concludes with a discussion of primary storage. A brief explanation of read-only memory (ROM) and programmable read-only memory (PROM) is included.

PLUGGING IN EVERYMAN

Time, from the column
entitled "Living,"
Sept. 5, 1977, p. 39.

Michael Mastrangelo, 40, a Manhattan audiovisual consultant, has a servant who keeps the temperature and humidity in his home at just the levels he demands, puts his favorite music on the stereo as he pulls into the driveway, and phones him at the office in case of fire or burglary. If Mastrangelo wanted, his majordomo could also wake him in the morning, make him a cup of tea, brief him on the day's business appointments as he has breakfast, remind him that the car needs an oil change and, after he drives off, water the lawn and roast a turkey dinner for twelve.

Where did Mastrangelo get help like that these days? The answer: from a custom-built household computer and some auxiliary gadgets. The computer cost him $11,000 six years ago, but with advances in technology the same hardware today would be only $4000, and some new models are as compact and inexpensive as a good color TV set. The age of the home computer (or microcomputer, as it is often called) is at hand.

Since Micro Instrumentation & Telemetry Systems Inc. of Albuquerque 2½ years ago introduced its Altair 8800, a 250,000-calculations-per-second computer that retails for $1070, some 30 other manufacturers have begun producing similar equipment. Tandy Corp. next week will begin delivering a $600 microcomputer (only $399 if hooked up to one's own viewing screen) to the firm's 6756 Radio Shack stores. Heath Co., the nation's largest producer of build-it-yourself electronic gadgets, is selling a $1240 Heathkit and will introduce a souped-up $2500 model in November. Such industrial giants as Timex and Texas Instruments are also said to be pondering a move into home computers, and Sears, Montgomery Ward, and a number of other large chains are considering selling them. "Some day soon every home will have a computer," says Byron Kirkwood, a Dallas microcomputer retailer. "It will be as standard as a toilet."

A slight exaggeration, perhaps. But already some 50,000 microcomputers have been sold, largely for home use, and industry analysts predict sales of three times that many in the next year alone. Some 500 retail outlets have opened in the past couple of years to sell and service microcomputers—and serve as hangouts for the growing legions of home-computer nuts, or "hackers," as they call themselves. For further companionship, hackers have formed at least 150 computer clubs across the country and launched a dozen home-computer magazines. Says Theodor Nelson, author of a book called *Computer Lib:* "The lid is off. There's going to be an avalanche as there was with hi-fi, calculators, and CB radio."

Like their big brothers in business and government, microcomputers have a central processing unit to do the thinking, an input/output device (typically an electric typewriter connected to a video-display screen) for giving instructions and receiving answers, and a memory for storing information. A microcomputer can easily perform such sedentary chores as keeping track of an investment portfolio, maintaining an up-to-date Christmas card list, collating menus, or entertaining the kids with a vast Olympiad of electronic games, from TV tennis to Star Trek (destroy the Klingons before they capture the starship *Enterprise*). Other tasks—reporting on water seepage in the basement, watering the lawn when it reaches a given aridity, locking the front door at night—require the addition of various switches, sensors, and motors that can send a house-proud hacker's outlay soaring. Says James Warren, a California microcomputer consultant: "You keep adding components until you exceed your yearly income."

So far the hardware is more easily available than the software, or ready-made programs telling the computer what to do. But addicts nevertheless manage to find plenty of applications for their new toys. Robert Goodyear, 62, a Framingham, Mass., physicist, uses his computer to tap out and edit his personal correspondence. Manhattan physician Joseph J. Sanger cross-indexes his medical journals to provide him with instant, tailor-made refresher courses on any disease he asks for. Ham radio operator Irving Osser of Beverly Hills has programmed his computer to keep a log of the people he talks to on his radio and to translate Morse code into a typewritten message. Boston pediatrician Lawrence Reiner uses his machine to relax by playing TV games with his children. Robert Phillips, president of Gimix Inc., a Chicago firm that computerizes entire households,

has installed terminals in every room of his Chicago apartment. He uses them to dim and brighten his lights, tune his stereo, turn his television on and off, even to open and close his drapes.

For many household operations, however, microcomputers are clearly inferior to simpler and less expensive devices. Like fingers. Michael Mastrangelo finds it easier to make his own tea than program a computer for the task. Says David Korman, who has an IMSAI 8080 in his Belmont, Mass., apartment: "I tried doing my checkbook on it. It's a lot faster by hand." And even though prices have dropped, microcomputers remain complicated devices that require long hours of study to use properly. When Robert Phillips let his sister give a party in his computerized Chicago apartment, he dutifully left a long list of instructions. Not long enough. Someone accidentally hit a button that killed all the power, reducing the puzzled guests to carrying candles. "The hard part," says Phillips, "is making the computer compatible with people."

Basic computer hardware—the CPU, input/output devices, and storage—has finally moved into the personal arena as illustrated in this article. The internal workings of this hardware are explained in this chapter.

DIGITAL AND ANALOG COMPUTERS

In the first section of this book, the term *computer* was used several times. Each use assumed a specific type of computer—the *digital computer*. However, there are also *analog computers.* It is important to distinguish between these two types.

A digital computer is a machine that operates directly on binary digits. These digits represent numbers, letters, or other distinct symbols. A digital computer receives input and produces output in the form of numbers, letters, and special characters represented by holes in punched cards, magnetized areas on tapes or disks, printing on paper, and so on. Digital computers are commonly used in business applications.

Digital computers achieve varying degrees of accuracy, depending on their particular construction and machine characteristics. For example, some digital computers can achieve results accurate to hundreds or even thousands of decimal places. Such computers are often used in scientific applications. For business applications, results accurate to only a few decimal places are sufficient. Therefore, computer manufacturers build various models of digital computers, in order to meet the different needs of the ultimate users of these machines.

In contrast to digital computers, analog computers do not operate directly on digits. Instead, they measure continuous physical or electrical magnitudes such as pressure, temperature, current, voltage, length, or shaft rotations. For example, a gasoline pump contains an analog computer that measures (1) the quantity of gasoline pumped (to the nearest tenth of a gallon) and (2) the price of that gasoline (to the nearest penny). Another example of an analog computer is a car speedometer. Here, driveshaft rotations are measured and converted to a number that indicates the speed of the car.

It is important to note that numerical results can be obtained from analog computers, but they are arrived at indirectly. For this reason, analog computers are less accurate than digital computers. For example, it is not uncommon for a car speedometer to be "off" by one or two miles per hour. The remainder of this book will continue to focus on digital computers.

THE CENTRAL PROCESSING UNIT

Basic Functions

It is not necessary to acquire a working knowledge of the internal electronic circuitry of a computer in order to obtain valid output from it. However, a basic understanding of computer technology is essential. The simple diagram in Figure 3–1 shows the principal components of a computer system.

The input to a computer can take many forms: magnetic tape, the pressing of keys on a terminal keyboard, punched cards, and so on. Representing data on punched cards and entering this data into the

46

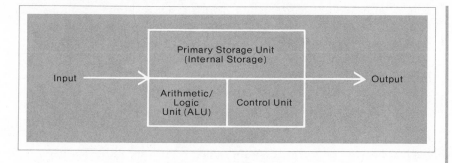

FIGURE 3—1
Computer-System
Components

system through a card reader is a common method. (Input devices will be discussed in greater detail in Chapters 4 and 6.)

The *central processing unit* (*CPU*), also known as the *main frame*, is the heart of the computer system. It is composed of three units: (1) the control unit; (2) the arithmetic/logic unit (ALU); and (3) the primary storage unit. Each unit performs its own, unique functions.

The *control unit*, as its name implies, maintains order and controls activity in the CPU. It does not process or store data. Rather, it directs the sequence of operations. The control unit interprets the instructions of a program in storage and produces signals that act as commands to circuits to execute the instructions. Other functions of the control unit are to communicate with an input device in order to begin the transfer of instructions and data into storage and, similarly, to initiate the transfer of results from storage to an output device.

The *arithmetic/logic unit* (*ALU*) performs arithmetic computations and logical operations. Since the bulk of internal processing involves calculations or comparisons, the capabilities of a computer often depend upon the design and capabilities of the ALU. The ALU does not store data; it merely performs the necessary manipulations.

The *primary storage unit* (*internal storage, memory,* or *main storage*) holds all instructions and data necessary for processing. It also holds intermediate and final results during manipulation. Data is transferred from an input device to the primary storage unit where it is stored until needed for processing. Data that is being processed and intermediate results of ALU calculations are also stored in primary storage. After all computations and manipulations are completed, the final results remain in memory. The control unit directs them to be transferred to an output device.

There are many types of output devices. Among the most widely used are: printers, which provide results on paper; visual-display units, which project results on screens; and tape and disk drives, which produce machine-readable magnetic information. (These will be discussed in Chapters 4 and 7.)

To obtain an overall perspective of the functions of each computer-system component, we need to discuss the instruction and data flow through a computer system. Initially, the control unit directs the input device to transfer instructions and data to primary storage. Then the

47

control unit takes one instruction from storage, examines it, and sends appropriate electronic signals to the ALU and storage, causing the instruction to be carried out. The signals sent to storage may instruct it to transfer data to the ALU, where it is mathematically manipulated. The result is transferred back to primary storage.

After an instruction has been executed, the control unit takes the next instruction from the primary storage unit. Data may be transferred from storage to the ALU and back several times before the execution of an entire series of instructions is complete. When all manipulations have been completed, the control unit directs the storage unit to transfer the processed data (information) to the output device.

These steps can be summarized as listed below. (Steps B through E are also shown in Figure 3–2.) Notice that computers, like humans, can only execute one instruction at a time. However, they work at incredible speeds.

Step A: Instructions and data are stored in primary storage when received from the input device under direction of the control unit.

Step B: The control unit examines one instruction and interprets it.

Step C: The control unit sends appropriate electronic signals to the ALU and primary storage.

Step D: The necessary data items are transferred to the ALU, where calculations and/or comparisons are performed.

Step E: The result is transferred back to the primary storage unit.

Steps B through E: Continued until all instructions have been executed.

Step F: The control unit signals the primary storage unit to transfer the results to the output device.

Computer instructions have two basic parts: the operation code and the operand. The *operation code* (*op code*) tells the control unit what

FIGURE 3–2
CPU Operations

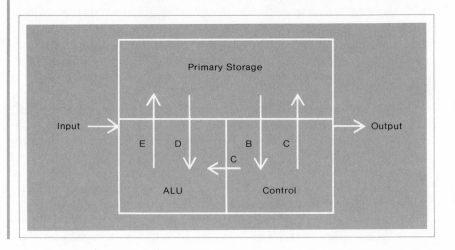

function (i.e., operation) is to be performed (such as ADD, SUBTRACT, MOVE DATA, or COMPARE). The *operand* indicates the location of the data to be operated on. (Op codes and operands will be discussed in more detail in Chapter 11.)

Storage Locations and Addresses

In order to direct processing operations, the control unit of the CPU must be able to locate each instruction and data item in storage. So that it can do this, each location in storage is assigned an *address*. A simple way to understand this concept is to picture computer storage as a large collection of mailboxes. Each mailbox is at a specific location with its own address (see Figure 3–3). Each can hold one item of information. Because each location in storage has a unique address, particular items in storage can be located when they are called for by stored-program instructions.

Suppose the computer is to be directed to subtract TAX from GROSS PAY in order to determine an employee's salary. Suppose further that TAX is stored at location 104 and has a value of 55.60, and that GROSS PAY is stored at location 111 and has a value of 263.00.

To accomplish this task, the programmer instructs the computer to subtract 104 from 111. The computer interprets this to mean that it should subtract the contents of location 104 from the contents of location 111. The programmer must keep track of what is stored at each location. Fortunately, computer manufacturers usually provide pre-written, specialized programs for keeping track of storage locations and addresses. This relieves the programmer of this part of the programming task.

Registers

Registers are devices that facilitate the execution of instructions by acting as temporary holding areas for instructions and data. Registers are located in the CPU, but they are not considered part of primary

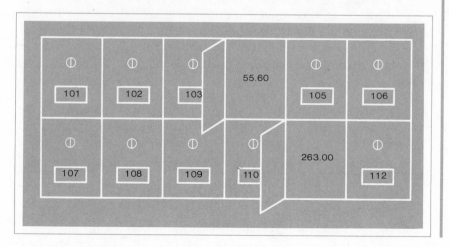

FIGURE 3–3
Each Mailbox Represents a Location in Storage with a Specific Address.

storage. They are capable of receiving information, holding it, and transferring it very quickly as directed by the control unit of the CPU.

A register functions similarly to a standard pocket calculator. A person using the calculator acts as the control unit by transferring numbers from a sheet of paper to the calculator. Here, the paper is analogous to the primary storage unit of the CPU. When the calculation is complete, the calculator displays the result. The person (control unit) then transfers the result displayed on the calculator (register) back to the sheet of paper (primary storage). This process is very similar to the way most modern computers work. Intermediate calculations are performed in registers, and the final results are transferred back to primary storage.

There are different types of registers. Some perform specific functions. They are named according to the functions they perform. For example, an *accumulator* is a register that accumulates results of computations. A *storage register* holds information being sent to or taken from the primary storage unit. During program execution, each instruction is transferred to an *instruction register* where it is decoded by the control unit. The address of a data item called for by an instruction is kept in an *address register.* Some computers do not have registers with specific uses. Instead, they have general-purpose registers, which can be used for both arithmetic and addressing functions.

The number and size of registers in computers vary. Their function, however, remains the same; they are used as temporary storage areas to facilitate the transfer of data and instructions within the CPU.

DATA REPRESENTATION

Throughout history, humans have strived continuously to improve their ability to communicate. Indeed, from the time of the earliest cave dwellers, societal progress has depended heavily on the ability of people to improve their methods of communicating. The computer is one of the tools we have developed to facilitate communication.

Humans communicate by using symbols which have specific meanings. Symbols such as letters or numbers are combined in meaningful ways to represent information. For example, the 26 letters of the English alphabet can be combined to form words, sentences, paragraphs, and so on. By combining the individual letters in different ways, we can construct different messages. This enables us to communicate with one another.

The human mind is much more complex than the computer. A computer is only a machine; it is not capable of understanding the meanings of symbols used by humans to communicate. In order to use a computer, therefore, it is necessary to convert human symbols into a form the computer is capable of "understanding." This is accomplished through binary representation.

Binary Representation

Data is represented in the computer by the presence or absence of electrical signals in the circuitry of the machine. Only two possible states exist: either there is a signal, or there is not one. This two-state system is known as a *binary system*. The use of this system to represent data is known as *binary representation*.

The *binary (base 2) number system* operates in a manner similar to the familiar *decimal number system*. For example, in the decimal number 4672, we have the following:

$$
\begin{array}{l}
4 \quad 6 \quad 7 \quad 2 \\
\;2 \times 10^0 = 2 \quad \text{or} \quad 4 \quad 6 \quad 7 \quad 2 \\
\;7 \times 10^1 = 70 \\
\;6 \times 10^2 = 600 \\
\;4 \times 10^3 = 4000 \quad\quad\quad 10^3 \; 10^2 \; 10^1 \; 10^0 \\
\;\underline{} \\
\;4672
\end{array}
$$

Each position of the number represents a certain power of 10. The progression of powers is from right to left. That is, digits further to the left in a decimal number represent larger powers of 10 than those to the right of them.

10^5	10^4	10^3	10^2	10^1	10^0
100,000	10,000	1,000	100	10	1

FIGURE 3–4
Decimal Place Values

The same principle holds for binary representation. The difference is that in binary representation, each position in the number represents a power of 2. For example, consider the decimal number 14. In binary, the number 14 is written as follows:

$$
\begin{array}{l}
1 \quad 1 \quad 1 \quad 0 \\
\;0 \times 2^0 = 0 \quad\quad 1 \quad 1 \quad 1 \quad 0 \\
\;1 \times 2^1 = 2 \quad \text{or} \\
\;1 \times 2^2 = 4 \\
\;1 \times 2^3 = \underline{8} \quad\quad 2^3 \; 2^2 \; 2^1 \; 2^0 \\
\;14
\end{array}
$$

As a further example, the value represented by the decimal number 300 is represented in binary form as shown below.

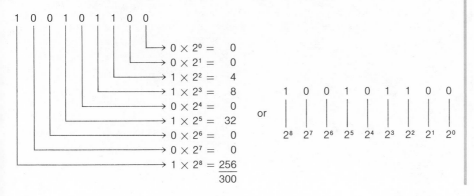

$$
\begin{array}{l}
1 \quad 0 \quad 0 \quad 1 \quad 0 \quad 1 \quad 1 \quad 0 \quad 0 \\
0 \times 2^0 = 0 \\
0 \times 2^1 = 0 \\
1 \times 2^2 = 4 \\
1 \times 2^3 = 8 \\
0 \times 2^4 = 0 \quad\quad\quad\quad 1 \; 0 \; 0 \; 1 \; 0 \; 1 \; 1 \; 0 \; 0 \\
1 \times 2^5 = 32 \quad \text{or} \\
0 \times 2^6 = 0 \\
0 \times 2^7 = 0 \quad\quad 2^8 \; 2^7 \; 2^6 \; 2^5 \; 2^4 \; 2^3 \; 2^2 \; 2^1 \; 2^0 \\
1 \times 2^8 = \underline{256} \\
300
\end{array}
$$

As indicated by the examples above, the binary number system uses 1s and 0s in different combinations to represent numbers. Each digit position in a binary number is called a *bit,* which is simply an abbreviation of *binary digit.* A 1 in a bit position indicates the presence of a specific power of 2, while a 0 indicates the absence of a specific power. A bit is "on" if it contains a 1; it is "off" if it contains a 0. As in the decimal number system, the progression of powers in the binary number system is from right to left.

Notice in Figure 3–5 that any decimal digit (0–9) has a 4-binary-digit equivalent. Each position in the binary number has a specific place value. The rightmost bit position (representing 2^0) has a value of 1; it is called the 1-bit. Similarly, the other three bit positions (from right to left) are called the 2-bit, 4-bit, and 8-bit positions. To find the decimal equivalent value, the place values of the bits that are "on" are added. For example, in the binary number 1001, the 8-bit and the 1-bit are on. Summing 1 and 8, we find that the decimal equivalent is 9.

Computer Codes

The approach just described is used to represent numbers in some computers. The coding scheme is called *4-bit binary coded decimal* (*BCD*). For instance, the decimal number 23 is represented in 4-bit BCD with two sets of four binary digits as shown below.

0 0 1 0	0 0 1 1
2	3

FIGURE 3–5

Binary and Decimal Equivalent Values

2^8	2^7	2^6	2^5	2^4	2^3	2^2	2^1	2^0
256	128	64	32	16	8	4	2	1

DECIMAL EQUIVALENT	PLACE VALUE			
	8	4	2	1
0	0	0	0	0
1	0	0	0	1
2	0	0	1	0
3	0	0	1	1
4	0	1	0	0
5	0	1	0	1
6	0	1	1	0
7	0	1	1	1
8	1	0	0	0
9	1	0	0	1

The representation of a 3-digit decimal number in 4-bit BCD consists of 12 binary digits. For example, the decimal number 637 is coded as follows:

$$
\underbrace{0\ \ 1\ \ 1\ \ 0}_{6}\qquad \underbrace{0\ \ 0\ \ 1\ \ 1}_{3}\qquad \underbrace{0\ \ 1\ \ 1\ \ 1}_{7}
$$

There are 16 (2^4) possible unique bit combinations when using a 4-bit code. We have already seen that 10 of these combinations are used to represent the decimal digits 0–9 in 4-bit BCD. In practice, this code is only used to represent numbers.

To represent letters and special characters as well as numbers, more than four bit positions are needed for each code character. Another coding scheme called *6-bit BCD* allows for 64 (2^6) unique bit combinations. Thus, 6-bit BCD can be used to represent the decimal digits 0–9, the letters A–Z, and 28 special characters such as the period and the comma.

The four rightmost bit positions in 6-bit BCD are called *numeric bits.* The two leftmost bit positions are called *zone bits* (see Figure 3–6). The zone bits are used in different combinations with the numeric bits to represent numbers, letters, and special characters.

ZONE BITS		NUMERIC BITS			
A	B	8	4	2	1

FIGURE 3–6
Bit Positions in 6-Bit BCD Representation

Another common approach used to represent data in some computers is an 8-bit code known as *Extended Binary Coded Decimal Interchange Code (EBCDIC)*. In an 8-bit code, there are 256 (2^8) possible bit combinations. Whereas 6-bit BCD can be used to represent only uppercase letters, 8-bit EBCDIC can be used to represent uppercase and lowercase letters, and additional special characters such as the cent sign and the quotation mark. The EBCDIC bit combinations for uppercase letters and numbers are given in Figure 3–7.

With EBCDIC, the four leftmost bit positions are zone bits. The four rightmost bit positions are numeric bits. As with 6-bit BCD, the zone bits are used in different combinations with the numeric bits to represent numbers, letters, and special characters.

The *American Standard Code for Information Interchange (ASCII)* is a 7-bit code. This code was developed through the cooperation of several computer manufacturers. Their objective was to develop a standard code for all computers. Because certain machines are designed to accept 8-bit characters rather than 7-bit code patterns, an 8-bit version of ASCII, called ASCII-8, was created. ASCII-8 and EBCDIC are similar. The key difference between them is in the bit patterns used for representation of certain characters.

A fixed number of adjacent bits operated on as a unit is called a *byte.* Usually, one alphabetic character or two numeric characters are repre-

Character	EBCDIC Bit Configuration		Character	EBCDIC Bit Configuration	
A	1100	0001	S	1110	0010
B	1100	0010	T	1110	0011
C	1100	0011	U	1110	0100
D	1100	0100	V	1110	0101
E	1100	0101	W	1110	0110
F	1100	0110	X	1110	0111
G	1100	0111	Y	1110	1000
H	1100	1000	Z	1110	1001
I	1100	1001	0	1111	0000
J	1101	0001	1	1111	0001
K	1101	0010	2	1111	0010
L	1101	0011	3	1111	0011
M	1101	0100	4	1111	0100
N	1101	0101	5	1111	0101
O	1101	0110	6	1111	0110
P	1101	0111	7	1111	0111
Q	1101	1000	8	1111	1000
R	1101	1001	9	1111	1001

FIGURE 3–7
EBCDIC Representation:
0–9, A–Z

sented by one byte. This is the case in computers that use 8-bit codes (EBCDIC or ASCII-8) to represent data. Since eight bits are sufficient for any character, 8-bit groupings are the basic units of memory. In these computers, then, a byte is a group of eight adjacent bits. Therefore, one byte of storage is needed for each character. When discussing large amounts of storage, the symbol K is often used. One K equals 1024 (2^{10}) units. Thus, a computer that has 256K bytes of storage can store 256 $\times$ 1024, or 262,144, characters.

Code Checking   Computers do not always function perfectly; errors can and do occur. For example, a bit may be lost while data is being transferred from the ALU to the primary storage unit, or over telephone lines from one location to another. This loss could be caused by dust, moisture, magnetic fields, equipment failure, or other reasons. Thus, it is necessary to have a method for detecting when an error has occurred and isolating the location of the error.

To accomplish this task, most computers have an additional bit in each storage location. This additional bit is called a *parity bit*, or *check bit*. Computers that use parity bits are specifically designed so that there will always be either an even or an odd number of 1 (or "on") bits in each storage location. Regardless of the type of code used, if an odd number of 1 bits is used to represent each character, the characters are said to be

54

written in *odd parity*. Similarly, if an even number of 1 bits is used to represent each character, the characters are written in *even parity*. Internal circuitry in the computer constantly monitors whether a bit has been lost by checking if the required parity exists.

For example, if the 6-bit BCD code is used, a seventh bit is added as a check bit (see Figure 3–8). Suppose the number 6 is to be represented in 6-bit BCD using odd parity (see Figure 3–9). In this case, the check bit must be set to 1, or "on," because the number of 1 bits would be even otherwise. If a parity error is detected, the system informs the computer operator that an error has occurred.

CHECK BIT	ZONE BITS		NUMERIC BITS			
C	B	A	8	4	2	1

FIGURE 3–8
Bit Positions of 6-Bit BCD with Check Bit

	C	B	A	8	4	2	1
Valid $\longrightarrow$	1	0	0	0	1	1	0
Invalid $\longleftarrow$	1	0	0	0	0	1	0

FIGURE 3–9
Detection of Error with Parity Check (Odd Parity).

Notice that the checking circuitry of the computer can only detect the miscoding of characters. It cannot detect the use of incorrect data. In the previous example, for instance, the computer circuitry can determine if a bit has been dropped, making the representation of the number 6 invalid. However, if the number 5 had been mistakenly entered into the computer instead of 6 (say, because of incorrect punching of a card), no error would have been detected.

Hexadecimal Representation

When a program fails to execute correctly, it is sometimes necessary to examine the contents of certain memory locations to discover what went wrong. In such cases, the programmer often finds it useful to have a printout, or *dump*, of the contents of the memory locations. If everything were printed in binary representation, the programmer would be staring at pages upon pages of 1s and 0s. Detection of the error would be difficult.

To alleviate this problem, the contents of 8-bit bytes can be represented by symbols of the *hexadecimal (base 16) number system*. This *hexadecimal representation* is convenient for several reasons: (1) the conversion from binary to hexadecimal is much easier and faster than the conversion from binary to decimal; (2) hexadecimal numbers are much easier to read than binary numbers; and (3) significant savings of both paper and time are possible when the contents of storage are printed in hexadecimal rather than binary notation—the equivalent of a 12-page binary dump is only three pages long in hexadecimal.

	BINARY SYSTEM (PLACE VALUES)			HEXADECIMAL EQUIVALENT	DECIMAL EQUIVALENT
8	4	2	1		
0	0	0	0	0	0
0	0	0	1	1	1
0	0	1	0	2	2
0	0	1	1	3	3
0	1	0	0	4	4
0	1	0	1	5	5
0	1	1	0	6	6
0	1	1	1	7	7
1	0	0	0	8	8
1	0	0	1	9	9
1	0	1	0	A	10
1	0	1	1	B	11
1	1	0	0	C	12
1	1	0	1	D	13
1	1	1	0	E	14
1	1	1	1	F	15

FIGURE 3–10

Binary, Hexadecimal, and Decimal Equivalent Values

In the hexadecimal number system, 16 symbols are used to represent the digits 0 through 15 (see Figure 3–10). Note that the letters A through F designate the numbers 10 to 15, respectively. Each position in a hexadecimal number represents a power of 16. This allows for easy conversion from binary to hexadecimal, since 16 is equal to 2^4. A single hexadecimal digit can be used to represent four binary digits as shown below.

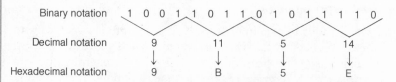

Binary notation	1 0 0 1	1 0 1 1	0 1 0 1	1 1 1 0
Decimal notation	9	11	5	14
Hexadecimal notation	9	B	5	E

Hexadecimal numbers are converted to decimal numbers in the same manner as binary numbers are converted. The decimal equivalent of a hexadecimal number is found by multiplying each symbol by the power of 16 that it represents, and then adding the resulting products. For example, the hexadecimal number A4B2 can be converted to its decimal equivalent, 42162, as shown below.

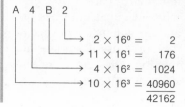

A 4 B 2

$2 \times 16^0 = 2$
$11 \times 16^1 = 176$
$4 \times 16^2 = 1024$
$10 \times 16^3 = \underline{40960}$
42162

STORAGE

All computers must have the capability to hold instructions and data items. This is accomplished by primary storage and other storage devices.

Primary Storage

Primary storage comprises all storage considered part of the CPU. It may, in some cases, be supplemented by *secondary* (also called *auxiliary,* or *external*) *storage,* which is separate from the CPU. Information is transferred between primary and secondary storage via electrical lines. The most common secondary storage devices are magnetic-tape and magnetic-disk units. As discussed earlier, primary storage can be composed of magnetic cores. Each core can store one binary digit, or bit. Core operation is based upon the principle of a magnetic field being created when electricity flows through a wire (Gauss's Law). The direction of the magnetic field, which depends upon the direction of the electric current flow, determines which binary state is represented. Magnetization of a core in a clockwise direction indicates an "on" condition; a counterclockwise direction of magnetization represents an "off" condition (see Figure 3–11).

A large number of cores are strung on a screen, or plane, of wires. If a full current were sent down a wire to set a particular core, all other cores along that wire would also be set. To prevent this, a system of half currents is used. That is, a half current is sent down each of the two wires that intersect at the core. The combination of two half currents at that core results in magnetization of the core, but leaves all other cores along the two wires unaffected. Therefore, setting cores to store bits is a manipulation of the electrical flow of half currents (see Figure 3–12).

The cores in a plane may also be threaded with two other wires (see Figure 3–13). The *sense wire* is used to read a core to determine whether it represents a 0-bit or a 1-bit. The process of sensing (reading) the core sets it to a 0 state. The *inhibit wire* is used to return the core to a 1 state if it was in a 1 state when read. Returning the core to its original state insures that the read operation does not destroy its content. This is the non-destructive read characteristic of memory that we discussed earlier. It is essential if the core is to be read several times during processing.

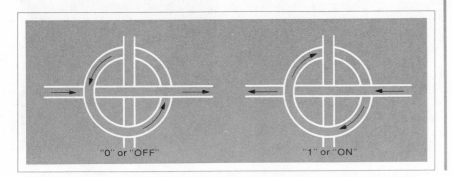

FIGURE 3–11
Magnetizing a Core

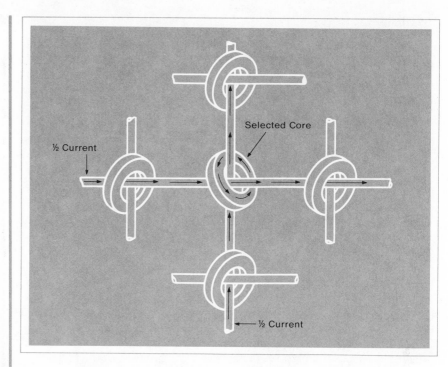

FIGURE 3—12
Selecting a Core

In addition to the 4-wire approach discussed above, there are 2-wire and 3-wire cores. In some systems, the sense and inhibit functions are combined in one wire. In other systems, only the two half-current wires are used, but the same type of bit manipulation takes place.

Technological developments relative to two-state components have led to the use of semiconductors in some primary storage units. *Semiconductor memory* is composed of circuitry on *silicon chips*. One silicon chip, only slightly bigger than one core, may hold the equivalent

FIGURE 3—13
Core Storage

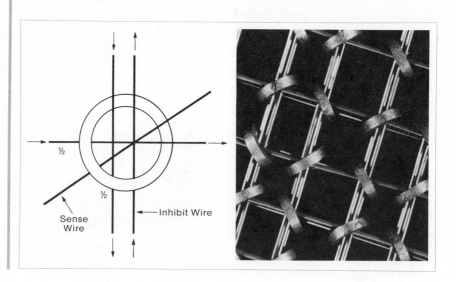

of thousands of cores. The speed of processing with semiconductors is also significantly faster than that with cores.

Semiconductor representation is based on the two-state "on" or "off" principle used with cores. A semiconductor is read by testing to check if it will carry a current. If it will, it is "on"; if it will not, it is "off." One difference between semiconductors and cores is that semiconductors do not need to be restored after they have been read. They automatically have non-destructive read capabilities so there is no need for a restore cycle.

One disadvantage of semiconductor memory is that it requires a constant power source. Since it relies on currents for representation, all stored data is lost if the power source fails unless there is an emergency (*backup*) system. Core memory retains its contents even if the power source fails because it relies on magnetic charges rather than on currents. At present, the cost of semiconductor memory is greater than that of core memory, but improved manufacturing methods have resulted in significant cost reductions. Semiconductors are replacing magnetic cores as the basic internal-storage medium.

Recently, a new memory device called *bubble memory* has been introduced, not only as a replacement medium for primary storage, but also for secondary storage. This memory consists of magnetized spots, or *magnetic domains*, which rest on a thin film of semiconductor material. The magnetic domains (called *bubbles*) are much smaller than magnetic cores so more data can be stored in a smaller area. A bubble memory module only slightly larger than a quarter can store 20,000 characters of data.

The bubbles in a bubble memory have a polarity which is opposite that of the semiconductor material they are on. Data is stored by shifting the positions of the bubbles on the surface of the material (see Figure 3–14). When data is read, the presence of a bubble in a specific location indicates a 1 bit; the absence of a bubble indicates a 0 bit. The bubbles are similar to magnetic cores in that they retain their magnetism indefinitely.

Some manufacturers have introduced bubble memories in their computers. The high cost and difficulty of production has been a major factor limiting wide industry and user acceptance of bubbles as yet.

Read-Only Memory (ROM)

Computers are capable of certain complex functions such as taking square roots and evaluating exponents. These functions can be built into the hardware or software of a computer system. Hardware has the advantages of being very fast and reliable since operations are hand-wired into the computer. Software is more flexible, but it is also slower and more prone to error.

When functions are built into the hardware of a computer, they are placed in *read-only memory* (*ROM*). Read-only memory is a part of the computer hardware in which items are stored in an unalterable form. Unlike other computer memory (such as cores), the read-only memory

59

FIGURE 3—14
Bubble Storage Module

cannot be occupied by common stored-program instructions or data. Furthermore, the items placed in read-only memory are permanent; they cannot be deleted or changed by stored-program instructions. The only method of changing the contents of ROM is by altering the construction of the circuits (see Figure 3–15).

FIGURE 3–15
Read-Only Storage Unit

A direct result of this hardware innovation is called *microprogramming. Microprograms* are sequences of instructions built into read-only memory to carry out functions (e.g., calculating square roots) that otherwise would be directed by stored-program instructions at a much slower speed. Microprograms are usually supplied by computer manufacturers; these programs cannot be altered by users. However, microprogramming allows the basic operations of the computer to be tailored to meet the needs of users. If all instructions that a computer can execute are located in ROM, a complete new set of instructions can be obtained by changing the ROM. When selecting a computer, the user can get the standard features of the machine, plus his choice of the optional features available through microprogramming.

Another type of read-only memory is known as *programmable read-only memory (PROM)*. As mentioned earlier, ROM can only be altered by changing the computer circuitry. PROM is programmed by the manufacturer, but it can be reprogrammed by users to meet unique needs. This feature increases the versatility of the computer system.

A key point worth mentioning is that the concept of read-only memory is entirely different from that of non-destructive read. Under non-destructive read, items in memory can be read repeatedly without loss of information; however, the contents of memory can be altered by reading in new values to replace old ones as directed by stored-program instructions. Read-only memory can be changed solely by rewiring.

61

SUMMARY

● Computers are usually classified as either digital or analog. Digital computers operate on distinct symbols (decimal numbers, letters, etc.) and are commonly used in business applications. Analog computers measure continuous physical or electrical magnitudes such as pressure, temperature, current, or voltage.

● The central processing unit, the heart of the computer, is composed of three units: the primary storage unit, the arithmetic/logic unit (ALU), and the control unit. The control unit maintains order and controls what is happening in the CPU; the ALU performs arithmetic and logical operations; and the primary storage unit holds all data and instructions necessary for processing.

● Each location in storage has a unique address. This allows stored-program instructions and data items to be located by the control unit of the CPU as it directs processing operations.

● Registers are devices that facilitate the execution of instructions. They act as temporary holding areas and are capable of receiving information, holding it, and transferring it very quickly as directed by the control unit of the CPU.

● Data representation in the computer is based on a two-state, or binary, system. A 1 in a position indicates the presence of a power of 2; a 0 indicates its absence. The 4-bit binary coded decimal (BCD) system uses groups of four binary digits to represent the decimal digits 0–9. The 6-bit BCD system allows for 64 unique bit combinations; alphabetic, numeric, and 28 special characters can be represented. Both EBCDIC and ASCII-8 are 8-bit coding systems and are capable of representing up to 256 different characters.

● Hexadecimal notation can be used to represent binary data in a concise form. For this reason, the contents of computer memory are sometimes printed in hexadecimal. Programmers use such printouts to locate errors.

● One method of storing binary digits (bits) in primary storage uses electrical currents to set magnetic cores to "on" or "off" states. Another form of storage is semiconductor memory, which uses circuitry on silicon chips. Semiconductor units are smaller and faster than cores, but they demand a constant power source and cost more than core memory. Bubble memory consists of magnetized spots which rest on a thin film of semiconductor material. These bubbles retain their magnetism indefinitely and have the ability to store much more data in a smaller space than core memory.

● Read-only memory (ROM) is part of the hardware of a computer in which items are stored in an unalterable form. They can be deleted or changed only by rewiring. Microprograms are sequences of instructions built into read-only memory to carry out functions that otherwise would be directed by stored-program instructions at a much slower speed.

● Programmable read-only memory (PROM), although originally programmed by the manufacturer, can be reprogrammed by users to meet unique needs. Thus, it provides greater flexibility and versatility than ROM offers.

REVIEW QUESTIONS

1. Distinguish between analog and digital computers, giving examples of each.

2. What are the three major components of the CPU? Discuss the functions of each.

3. Why are computer coding schemes necessary? What advantages does EBCDIC offer as compared to 6-bit BCD?

4. Why are concepts of the binary number system important for digital computers? What relationship does the hexadecimal number system have to the binary number system?

5. What developments have occurred in primary storage media and what impact have these developments had on modern computers?

6. Explain the concept of read-only memory. How does it relate to microprogramming?

In the 1880s, Herman Hollerith developed a mechanical method of processing census data for the United States Bureau of the Census. His method included two devices: one that coded population data as punched holes in cards, and another that sensed the data. The success of these devices led Hollerith to form his own company in 1896 to manufacture and sell these devices. In 1911 the company became part of the Computing-Tabulating-Recording (C-T-R) Company, which manufactured commercial scales and tabulating and time-recording equipment. In 1924 CTR became the International Business Machines (IBM) Corporation.

Today IBM is the leader of the worldwide data-processing community. It controls over half of the industry's business. IBM's products include data-processing machines and systems, information processors, electric type-writers, copiers, dictation equipment, educational and testing materials, and related supplies and services. Most products can be either leased or purchased through IBM's worldwide marketing organizations.

IBM dominates two industries—electric typewriters and computers. IBM computers range from small, powerful mini-computers to ultra-high-performance computers for high-speed, large-scale scientific and commercial applications. The wide range of computer applications in scientific, industrial, and commercial areas today requires machines of different sizes and capabilities. For example, a computer used to forecast the weather has different capabilities from a computer used mainly for payroll processing. Consequently, computers that are manufactured with similar characteristics are usually grouped together into a family, series, or system of

computers. The family members differ from each other in terms of the range of available memory, the number of input/output channels, the execution speed of the computer, and the types of devices that can be interfaced to it.

As an example, IBM's Series/1 is a family of versatile, small computers. The IBM System/32 combines the advantages of an accounting machine with those of a disk-supported computer to provide flexible computing for small businesses. IBM's System/370 is a family of large, general-purpose computers readily adaptable to a large number of applications. Its predecessor, System/360, is a multipurpose system of computers (and thus named "360," to indicate applicability to the "full circle" of applications). The IBM System/7 is a high-speed computing system designed for applications requiring sensor-based or data-processing input/output operations.

Within each family are many different processor models. The System/370 includes 11 models. Model 115, the smallest of the System/370 models, is a compact, versatile system with 65,000 to 393,000 bytes of main storage. Model 138 can provide over 1,000,000 bytes of main storage while Model 168 provides storage capacities of over 8,000,000 bytes.

A comparison of two of IBM's series, System/7 and System/370, illustrates the differences in the capabilities of the computers and the variety of applications each can perform. The IBM System/7 is designed to support applications such as data acquisition, plant and laboratory automation, and process control. Examples range from hospital patient monitoring and oceanographic research to automated production machines and traffic control.

The processor for the System/7 is the 5010. It is available in three models—A, B, and E. Storage sizes for Models A and B range from 4096 bytes to 32,768 bytes; Model E storage ranges from 32,768 to 131 072 bytes.

The System/7 processors have other characteristics which differentiate them from other processors. They perform high-speed processing with a storage cycle time (the time it takes for information to be transferred to or from main storage) of 400 nanoseconds. Data is transmitted in blocks of 16 data bits with a parity bit for each eight data bits.

System/7 accommodates applications such as production monitoring and control, which permit data to be entered from many different units (see Figure 3–16). It is often necessary for the System/7 processor to stop a current operation in order to receive input from a sensor-based unit whose processing has a higher priority. The processor is designed to recognize the request for attention (*interrupt*) from a sensor-based input or output unit, stop the current operation, service the request, and return to the original operation at the point it was stopped.

System/7 has four levels of interrupt priority. Each level has 16 sublevels. For each interrupt level, the processor contains seven index registers, an instruction address register, six program indicators, and an accumulator. Each register consists of 16 data bits. The 16-bit arrangement allows System/7 to effectively address up to 65,636 bytes of storage.

For sensor-based applications on System/7, the system must also include an analog-to-digital converter (ADC). This electronic device senses an analog signal (for example, a continuous voltage

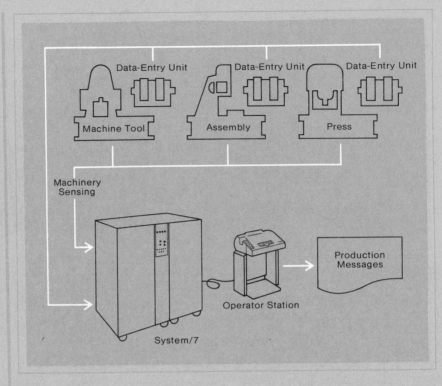

FIGURE 3–16
Plant Automation
(Production Monitoring and
Control)

applied from the machine-tool unit) and converts it to a proportional representation in digital form. The digital form is a 14-bit binary number plus a sign bit.

The IBM System/370 is a general-purpose system readily adaptable to a large number of applications, as opposed to the System/7, which is used for special-purpose applications. As previously indicated, the System/370 has 11 processor models. All have certain characteristics in common. Data can be transferred in blocks ranging in size from 8 to 64 bits (one to eight bytes). Recall that the System/7 transfers data in blocks of 16 bits only. The System/370 addressing arrangement uses a 24-bit binary address, as opposed to the System/7 16-bit arrangement. Thus, System/370 has the capability of addressing as many as 16,777,216 bytes of storage.

System/370 processor models designed with multiple general-purpose

registers are more powerful than System/7 processors in which each register performs a single task. Furthermore, the registers are larger in size and thus offer greater flexibility. System/370 uses control registers to regulate the interrupt system. The system separates interrupts into six general classes, and simultaneous interrupts are serviced in a fixed order of priority.

The System/370 models have main-storage capacities varying from 65,536 bytes to 8,388,608 bytes, depending on the model. Notice that the minimum storage capacity of System/370 is close to the maximum storage capacity of System/7. Model 168, designed for large-scale, high-speed scientific and commercial applications, has the largest main-storage capacity. Its scientific applications range from nuclear physics and theoretical astronomy to weather forecasting. The Model 168 can be used commercially as the control center of complex airline reservations systems, coast-to-coast time-sharing networks, and process-control systems. The power and speed of this advanced system are primarily the result of improved circuit technology. The basic machine cycle time of the central processing unit is 80 nanoseconds, five times faster than that of System/7.

The new IBM 3033 processor is IBM's most powerful one. With faster internal cycle time and up to eight million char-

TABLE 3—1
MAJOR IBM COMPUTERS

SERIES	MODELS	DATE INTRODUCED	COMMENTS
700	701	1953	Vacuum tubes
	702		
	704		Magnetic core
	705		
Type 650		1954	Magnetic-drum machine
1400	1401	1960	
	1410		Oriented to business
7000	7070	1960	Transistors, business-oriented
	7074		Scientific-oriented
1620		1960	Scientific-oriented, decimal minicomputer
1130		1962	Integrated circuits, small, special-purpose
1800		1963	Integrated circuits, small, special-purpose
360	20	1965	
	25		
	30		
	40		
	44		Systems designed for all
	50		purposes—business and
	65		scientific
	67		
	75		
	85		
	90		
	91		
System/7		1968	Replacement for 1800
System/3		1969	Midi/small computer
370	115	1973	
	125		
	135		IBM's most popular
	138		system—extends capabilities of
	145		System/360
	148		
	158		
	168		
	3031	1977	IBM's most powerful processors
	3032		
	3033		
System/32		1974	Small system for business
System/34		1977	Small system for business
Series/1		1977	Versatile small computer for experienced users

acters of high-speed main storage, it is for users needing sizable data storage and having data-communication requirements. Two additional high-performance processors, the IBM 3031 and the IBM 3032, are for intermediate and large system users who need greater speed and capacity but not the power of the IBM 3033. All three processors are compatible members of the System/370 family.

Table 3–1 summarizes the major IBM series and the models within the series. As data-processing requirements have expanded, hardware capabilities have been developed to provide the necessary support.

DISCUSSION POINTS

1. What are some characteristics that a series of computers may have in common? How do family members within a series differ from each other?

2. Name some important hardware characteristics that must be considered when selecting a computer. How do these characteristics relate to processing requirements?

CARD INPUT AND PRINTER OUTPUT | 4

OUTLINE

I. Punched Cards
  A. Data Representation
II. Punched-Card Processing
  A. Card Punch
  B. Verifying Machines
  C. Card Readers
  D. Unit-Record Concept

  1. Reproducer
  2. Interpreter
  3. Collator
  4. Sorter
  E. Punched-Card Systems—
     A Perspective
III. Printers
  A. Impact Printers
  B. Nonimpact Printers

INTRODUCTION

A computer system is much more than a central processing unit. Auxiliary media and devices enter data into and receive output from the CPU. Organizations using computers are more concerned with the overall effectiveness of a system than with the efficiency of the CPU alone. Data input and information output are important activities in any computer-based system because they are the communication links between people and the machine. If these people/machine interfaces are weak, the overall performance of the computer system suffers accordingly.

This chapter describes one of the primary media used for computer input—punched cards. Because punched cards have played such a major role in data processing, the chapter discusses the various types of equipment used for punched-card processing and provides a perspective on punched-card systems. Printers, which are the basic medium for computer output, are also discussed.

COMPUTER APPRAISES YOUR HOME

Popular Science,
May, 1977, p. 168

A typical on-site home appraisal can cost as much as $200. A new service, known as Value Rater, will figure the replacement cost of your home, and send you the computerized evaluation and appraisal certificate by mail within 10 days. The charge: $9.95.

The service, recently announced by GAB Business Services, is available nationwide for residential property valued at less than $125,000. It's made possible by the computerization of locally derived variables such as type of construction, regional variations in labor and materials costs, and building standards.

The one-page form for Value Rater is completed by the homeowner and mailed to GAB's Princeton, N.J., appraisal center. No appraisers visit your home. GAB says that its system takes into account such specific elements as type and extent of foundation, exterior covering, quality of windows and roofing, and wall construction, style of fireplace (if any), floor coverings, air conditioning, and electrical, plumbing, and heating systems.

The system uses real labor and materials costs from 480 selected locations in postal zip-code areas nationwide.

The appraisal certificate, says GAB, can help you determine whether you have sufficient insurance on your home. A $30,000 home in 1965 would cost upwards of $55,000 to replace today; building costs have risen at a rate of 6 to 10 percent per year.

GAB is not an insurance company or agent, but an independent service that's part of the corporate family that owns United Airlines and Western International Hotels. The address: GAB, 1101 State Rd., Princeton, N.J. 08540.

The information that the homeowner supplies to "Value Rater" comprises a unit record. This concept, printers, and punched-card processing are explained in this chapter.

PUNCHED CARDS

Punched cards were used in data processing long before the digital computer was developed. As we saw earlier, they were used by the Census Bureau as early as 1890. It was then that punched cards were first recognized as a medium for data processing. Today, punched cards serve not only as one of the primary media for entering data into computer systems, but also as user-oriented documents—time cards, bills, checks, invoices, and the like.

Punched-card data processing involves (1) the recording of data as holes in cards, and (2) the processing of the data by machines. Punched cards are commonly used to enter data into computer systems. They can also be processed by various electromechanical machines. The electromechanical machines are capable of sorting, calculating, accumulating, and reproducing data that has been stored in a deck of punched cards. Such processing takes place very quickly since the cards are manipulated at machine speeds. The systems are called *punched-card*, or *unit-record, systems*.

Data Representation

The standard punched card has 80 vertical columns and 12 horizontal rows (see Figure 4–1). It is appropriately called an 80-column punched card or Hollerith card. It can hold 80 characters of data in the form of numbers, letters, and special characters. As mentioned earlier, the data is recorded by punching holes in particular locations on the card.

The 80-column punched card is divided horizontally into three sections. The lower ten rows, numbered 0 through 9, are called *digit rows*. They can be used to represent any digit, 0–9. The upper three rows, numbered 12, 11, and 0, are called *zone rows*. (The 0 row is both a digit row and a zone row.) Zone punches can be combined with digit punches in the same column to represent alphabetic and special characters. The third section (at the very top of the card) is used to display what is punched into the card in a form that is easily readable by humans. Named after Herman Hollerith, this method of data representation is known as *Hollerith code.*

For instance, the number 6 is represented in column 21 of the card in Figure 4–1. If that particular column is examined, from the display section to the bottom of the card, it can be seen that a hole has been punched in the digit row 6. The same technique is used to represent any number; that is, a hole is punched in the appropriate digit row. Notice also in Figure 4–1 that one zone punch is used in combination with one or two numeric punches to represent a letter or special character. There can be only one character in a column.

When punched cards are used, data is generally grouped into fields and punched in specific columns on the cards. Each field is a group of related characters treated as a single unit of information. It consists of a group of consecutive columns on the card (see Figure 4–2). A field may be from 1 to 80 characters in length. Related fields are stored on the same card if possible.

71

72

FIGURE 4–1

80-Column Punched Card
and Hollerith Code

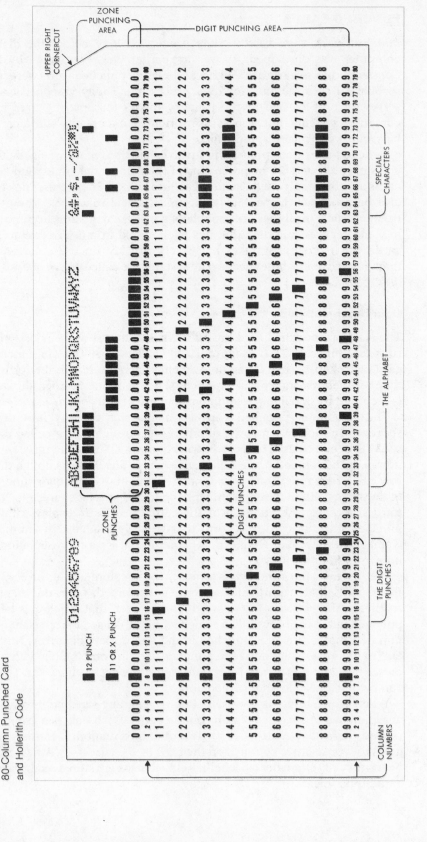

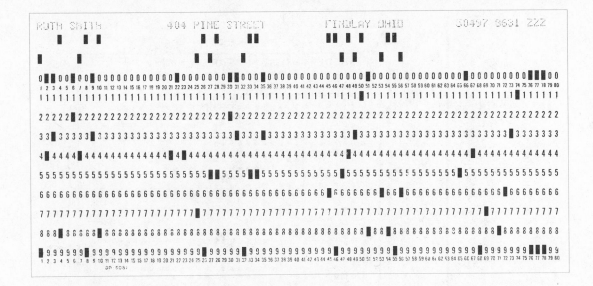

FIGURE 4–2
Data on a Punched Card

The 80-column limitation of the Hollerith card presents major disadvantages. First of all, when records require more than 80 columns, two or more cards must be used. This hinders processing of the cards since punched-card machines are designed to operate on only one card at a time. Second, when less than an entire card is needed for a record, the remaining space is left unused and, thus, wasted.

A second type of punched card is used by IBM in their System/3 series of computers. This card has 96 columns, but it is smaller than the Hollerith card (see Figure 4–3). The 96-column punched card is divided into two areas. The bottom part of the card is the *punch area;* the upper part is the *print area.* The punch area is divided further into three equal, 32-column, horizontal sections called *tiers.* There are six punch positions in each of the 96 columns on the card. Different characters are represented by different combinations of punches in the columns. The coding scheme used is similar to the 6-bit BCD system discussed in the last chapter.

The data represented by punches in columns of the three tiers in the punch area can be printed in three corresponding rows in the print area. Arranging a card in this manner allows more data to be stored in a smaller space than is possible with the standard 80-column punched card.

PUNCHED-CARD PROCESSING

We noted earlier that systems that use a computer for data processing are known as electronic, or computer, data-processing systems. In contrast, systems that use electromechanical punched-card machines for data processing are very mechanically oriented. Although processing takes place at machine speeds, much physical movement is involved

73

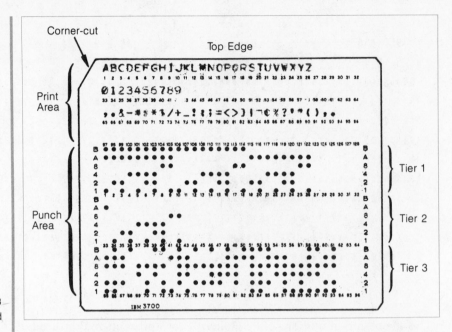

since punched cards must be transferred physically within the systems. These punched-card, or unit-record, systems perform automatic data processing. Although the machines may contain electronic circuits, a punched-card system relies very heavily on electromechanical methods of processing data. A digital computer is not used.

Card Punch

Data is most commonly recorded on punched cards through the use of a *card punch,* or *keypunch* (see Figure 4–4). An operator reads a source document and transcribes the data from the document into cards by pressing keys on a keyboard. This operation is similar to using a typewriter. The machine automatically feeds, positions, and stacks the cards, thus allowing the operator to concentrate on the keying operation.

Keyboards differ on card-punch machines, depending on the uses for which the machines are designed. For example, some keypunches have only alphabetic keyboards; some have only numeric keyboards; and others have combination alphabetic-numeric keyboards. Also, different sets of special characters are available on various machines. Automatic skipping and duplicating are other options available.

Regardless of the number of functions performed automatically, keypunching is probably the slowest and most costly operation in either computer or punched-card systems. One person is needed to operate each machine, and much time is spent keying data.

Verifying Machines

Keypunching is a human process, and even the best keypunch operators make errors. Normally, checking the validity of data on punched cards before processing is much less costly than detecting errors after

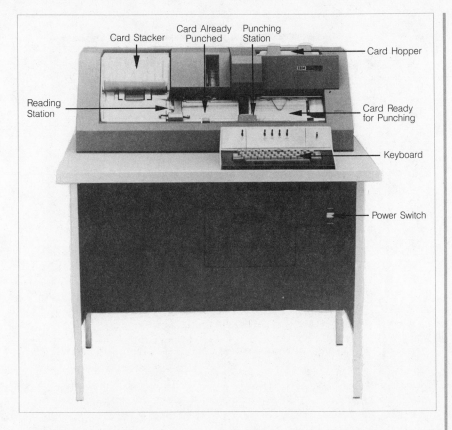

Card Stacker

Card Already
Punched

Punching
Station

Card Hopper

Reading
Station

Card Ready
for Punching

Keyboard

Power Switch

FIGURE 4—4
80-Column Card Punch

processing has been completed and reports printed. There are several approaches to verifying that the data has been punched correctly.

One approach to verification involves a machine called the *verifier* (see Figure 4–5). The verifier is similar to a card punch, except that it does not punch holes in cards. After the cards have been punched, they are loaded into the verifier. The same data is re-keyed by the operator, but the verifier merely senses the data already punched on the cards and compares it with the data re-keyed by the operator. If a mismatch is detected, the card stops and a light comes on. A second attempt can be made to verify the column. If it is unsuccessful, the verifier punches a notch in the card over the incorrect column. The cards with error notches can be spotted easily. Correct cards can be inserted in their places in the card deck.

Another approach to verification involves a machine called the *verifying punch*. This machine is also similar to the card punch, and a keyboard is used to enter data. However, when data is first keyed on this device, it is stored in a memory device within the machine. After all the data is in storage, the operator re-keys identical data. If the data entered the second time matches the original, a card is punched. If an error is detected, the operator simply backspaces and enters the correct data. Efficiency is increased since the error is detected before the card is punched. Also, while one card is being punched, the operator can begin keying data for the next card.

75

FIGURE 4—5
Verifier

A similar approach to verification is used when processing 96-column punched cards. Here, the cards are processed on a machine called a *data recorder*. Data is first entered into storage by a keying operation. A card is punched after the data has been verified by re-keying.

Card Readers

Card readers are devices that read data recorded on punched cards and convert the data into a form that can be processed by a computer. Most card readers have an input hopper where cards are loaded, and one or more output stackers where cards are stacked in their original order after they have been read. Some card readers also contain a built-in punch unit for producing punched-card output. These combination card read/punch machines have a punch input hopper, a read input hopper, and several output stackers (see Figure 4–6).

During the reading process, cards are fed individually to a read station. The presence or absence of holes in the card is translated into electrical pulses. These electrical pulses representing the data on the cards are then sent to the CPU. After each card is read, it is automatically transferred to an output stacker and another card is fed to the read station. The reading of cards continues without human intervention until all cards in the input hopper have been read.

There are two principal methods of translating punched holes into electrical pulses. The first method uses a photoelectric circuit to convert holes into electrical pulses. In this method, a light source is used. As the card moves through the read station, light passes through the holes and strikes photoelectric cells behind the card (see Figure 4–7). The photoelectric cells emit electricity when struck by light. In this manner, electrical pulses are created and transmitted to the CPU. A common reading speed for photoelectric readers is 1000 cards per minute.

A second method of reading punched cards uses metal brushes to determine the positions of holes in a card column. The sensing brushes make electronic contact with a roller below the card, through the holes punched in the column, and generate electrical pulses.

Unit-Record Concept

Unit-record data-processing systems are so named because of their extensive use of punched cards. The unit-record concept implies that each punched card is a complete record; it contains all the necessary data about a transaction. For example, the card in Figure 4–8 can contain all necessary data pertaining to the sale of an item.

The unit-record principle allows a punched card to be processed with other punched cards on a single-record basis, using special punched-card machines. Unit records can be added, sorted, or deleted by

FIGURE 4–6
Card Read/Punch

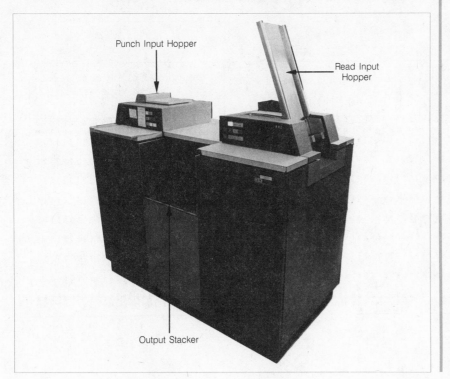

Punch Input Hopper

Read Input
Hopper

Output Stacker

Light
Source
Input
Hopper
Photoelectric
Cells
Card
Stacker
To CPU

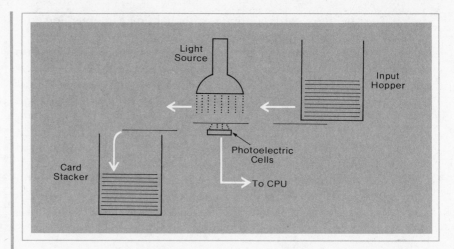

FIGURE 4–7
Photoelectric Card Reading

removing cards or adding cards to a group, or deck. Punched cards can also be arranged in a variety of ways for preparing reports. For example, punched cards containing sales data can be grouped by item number and then processed in groups to produce an inventory status report. They can be arranged by customer number or date to provide other reports. Generally, several machines are involved in this process, and the cards must be carried manually to the different machines. The machines usually involved in a punched-card system are explained briefly below.

FIGURE 4–8
Unit Record

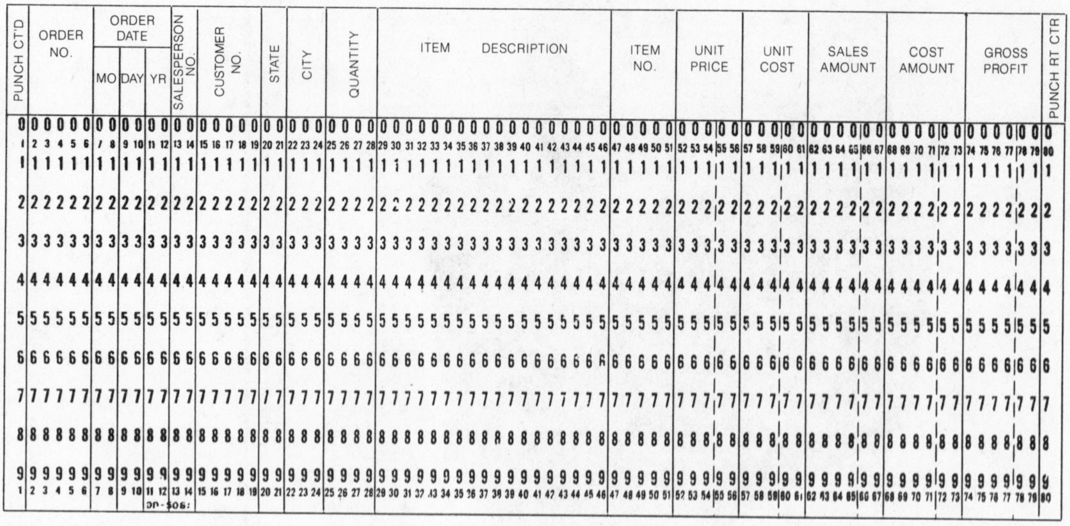

PUNCH CT'D
ORDER NO.
ORDER DATE
MO
DAY
YR
SALESPERSON NO.
CUSTOMER NO.
STATE
CITY
QUANTITY
ITEM DESCRIPTION
ITEM NO.
UNIT PRICE
UNIT COST
SALES AMOUNT
COST AMOUNT
GROSS PROFIT
PUNCH RT CTR

Reproducer   A *reproducer* can perform two functions—reproducing and gangpunching (see Figure 4–9). *Reproducing* is the process of transferring data from one card to another. The data may be punched in the same fields as in the original card or in different fields. *Gangpunching* involves the punching of a single item of data from one master card into several detail cards.

Interpreter   The *interpreter* prints, at the top of a card, all or part of the data represented by the holes in the card (see Figure 4–10). Showing the data in human-readable form greatly facilitates the handling of punched cards by humans.

Collator   The *collator* arranges cards in a predetermined manner (see Figure 4–11). The specific functions performed by the collator are:

● *Sequence-checking*   Determining if cards are in correct sequence.

● *Merging*   Combining two separate files into one. In payroll, for example, new employees' records are punched on cards to form a transaction file. This file is then merged with the old master payroll file to form a new master payroll file.

● *Matching*   Comparing master records with transaction records to see if certain fields are identical, and extracting unmatched records (cards). In the payroll example, an employee's time card indicates how many hours he or she worked (the transaction file). If an employee was newly hired, there may not be a record for him or her in the master file. If the time card cannot be matched, the collator separates it to indicate that no match was found.

● *Selecting*   Extracting particular cards from a file without disturbing the organization of the other cards. For example, if an employee has a change of address, his or her card can be isolated and removed for updating.

● *Match-merging*   Merging only cards which are matched. The unmatched cards from both the master file and the transaction file are separated.

Sorter   Before data on punched cards is processed, the cards usually must be sequenced. The *sorter* is used to arrange punched cards in a predetermined order (see Figure 4–12). Usually, sorting is done before other processing so that the cards can be input sequentially, one right after the other.

   Grouping is another function performed by the sorter. Cards that contain identical data in a particular field are grouped together. For example, suppose that a system uses punched cards to record the purchases of goods. If a customer pays cash, column 5 is punched with a C; if the goods are bought on credit, column 5 is punched with an R. If cards of both types are mixed, they must be grouped before processing.

79

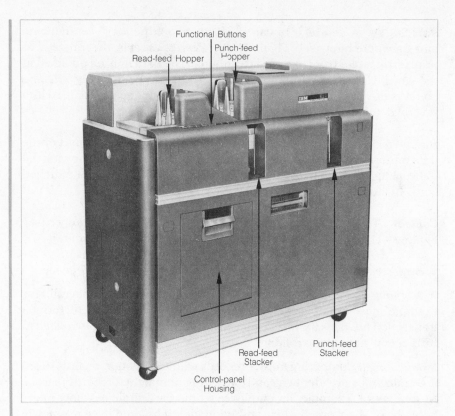

FIGURE 4–9
Reproducer

Read-feed Hopper

Functional Buttons

Punch-feed Hopper

Control-panel Housing

Read-feed Stacker

Punch-feed Stacker

FIGURE 4–10
Interpreter

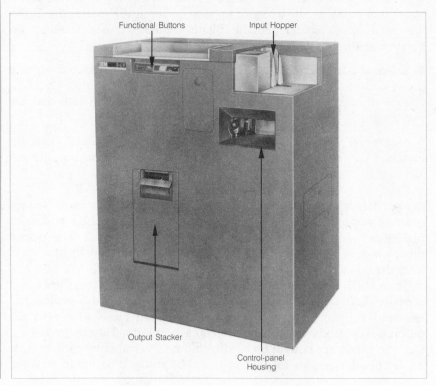

Functional Buttons

Input Hopper

Output Stacker

Control-panel Housing

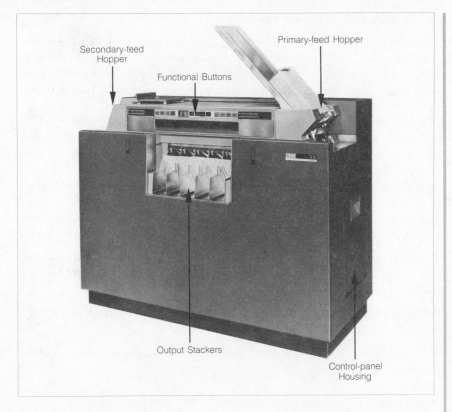

Secondary-feed
Hopper

Functional Buttons

Primary-feed Hopper

Output Stackers

Control-panel
Housing

FIGURE 4—11
Collator

FIGURE 4—12
Sorter

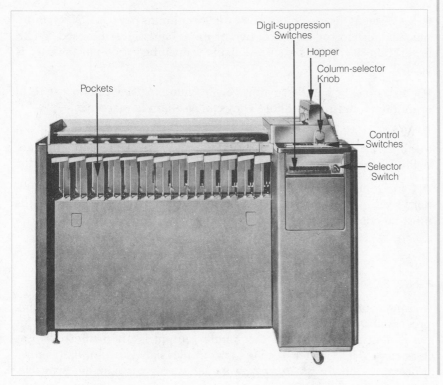

Digit-suppression
Switches

Hopper

Column-selector
Knob

Pockets

Control
Switches

Selector
Switch

Punched-Card Systems—A Perspective

Although punched-card systems are quickly being replaced by computer systems, they are still used successfully in many applications. Punched-card systems sometimes offer a satisfactory alternative when the volume of processing does not justify using a computer. However, as the costs of computer systems continue to decrease, the use of punched-card systems will continue to decline. As Chapter 8 will point out, minicomputers and microcomputers are now performing the tasks that punched-card systems have performed since the turn of the century.

In summary, punched-card systems offer the following advantages:

● Punched cards are standardized, allowing transfer of data between various machines.

● Each card is a unit record. A file can be updated easily by inserting, removing, or changing individual cards, without disturbing the rest of the file.

● Cards are easily handled. They can be written or typed on and easily mailed.

● They provide a fast, efficient means of processing small to moderate amounts of data.

The major disadvantages of punched-card systems are:

● Record lengths are limited to 80 (or 96) columns per card. When more space is needed for a record, two or more cards must be used. When fewer than 80 columns are needed, the remaining portion of the card is wasted.

● Cards must be handled extensively by humans. They can be lost, torn, or mutilated during handling. They can also jam in machines.

● When large volumes of data must be stored on cards, both human and machine processing speeds are limitations. Also, large card files are bulky. They require substantial storage space and are difficult to handle.

● Cards must be processed sequentially. Additional time for preliminary sorting is often required. When records are updated, new cards must be punched, verified, and positioned correctly.

PRINTERS

Computer *printers* serve a straightforward basic function—printing processed data in a form readable by humans (see Figure 4–13). This permanent readable copy of computer output is often referred to as *hard-copy*. The printer receives electronic signals from the central processing unit. In an *impact printer*, these signals activate print ele-

FIGURE 4–13
Printer

ments, which are pressed against paper. A newer development is the *nonimpact printer*. Printers belonging to this group use methods such as heat, laser technology, and photographic techniques to print output.

Impact Printers

Impact printers are designed to print either one character at a time or one line at a time. Printer-keyboards and wire-matrix printers are the two principal character-at-a-time devices. The *printer-keyboard* is similar

83

to an office typewriter except that a program, rather than a person, controls the printing (see Figure 4–14). All instructions, including spacing, carriage returns, and printing of characters, are sent from the CPU to the printer. A printing element with characters on its surface is generally used for printing. The keyboard allows an operator to communicate with the system, for example, to enter data or instructions. The usual print speed of a printer-keyboard is about 900 characters per minute.

Wire-matrix (also called *dot-matrix*) *printers* are based on a design principle similar to that of a football or basketball scoreboard. The matrix is a rectangle composed of pins; usually, it is seven pins high and five pins wide. Certain combinations of pins are activated to represent characters. For example, the number 4 is formed as shown in Figure 4–15. When this combination of pins is pressed against paper, the number 4 results. Wire-matrix printers can typically print up to 900 characters per minute.

The most popular line-at-a-time printers are print-wheel printers, chain printers, and drum printers. A *print-wheel printer* typically contains 120 print wheels, one for each of 120 print positions on a line (see Figure 4–16). Each print wheel contains 48 characters, including alphabetic, numeric, and special characters. Each print wheel rotates until a desired character moves into the corresponding print position on the current print line. When all characters are in their correct positions, a hammer drives the paper against the wheels and an entire line of output is printed. These printers can print about 150 lines per minute.

A *chain printer* has a character set engraved in type and assembled in a chain that revolves horizontally past all print positions (see Figure

FIGURE 4–14
Printer-Keyboard

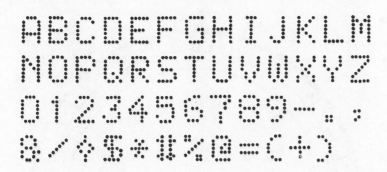

FIGURE 4—15
Wire-Matrix Printer
Character Set

4–17). There is one print hammer for each column on the paper. Characters are printed when the hammer presses the paper against an inked ribbon, which in turn presses against appropriate characters on the print chain. Type fonts can be changed easily on chain printers, allowing a variety of type faces to be used such as italics or boldface. These printers can produce 2000 lines of print per minute.

A *drum printer* has a metal cylinder which contains rows of characters engraved across its surface (see Figure 4–18). Each column on the drum contains the complete character set and corresponds to one print position on the line. As the drum rotates, the appropriate characters reach the print positions. A hammer presses the paper against an ink ribbon and the drum. One line is printed for each revolution of the drum since all characters eventually reach the print positions during one revolution. Drum printers can produce 1600 lines of print per minute.

Nonimpact Printers

As mentioned earlier, nonimpact printers do not print characters by means of a mechanical printing element that strikes paper. Instead, a variety of other methods are used to print output.

An *electrostatic printer* forms an image of a character on paper by means of charged wires, or pins, which supply a charge in the desired pattern (using a dot matrix) on special paper. The paper is moved through a solution containing ink particles that have an opposite charge. The ink particles adhere to each charged pattern on the paper. A visible image of each character is formed.

Electrothermal printers generate characters using heat and heat-sensitive paper. Letter forms are generated by heating selected rods in a matrix. When the ends of the selected rods touch the heat-sensitive paper, the image is transferred.

Both electrothermal and electrostatic printers are silent in operation. They are often used in applications where noise may be a problem. Some of these printers are capable of producing 5000 lines of print per minute.

85

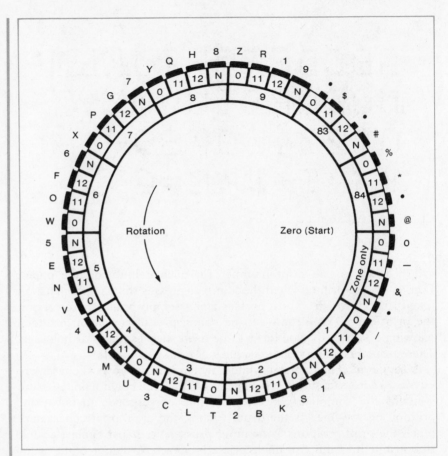

FIGURE 4—16
Print Wheel

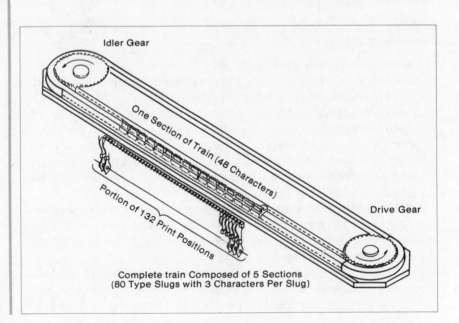

FIGURE 4—17
Chain Printer

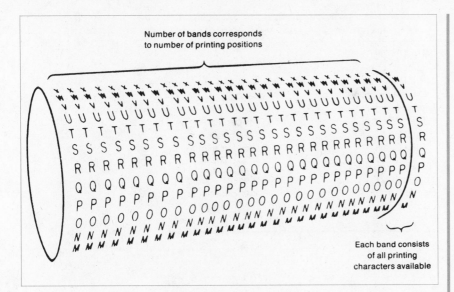

Number of bands corresponds
to number of printing positions

Each band consists
of all printing
characters available

FIGURE 4–18
Print Drum

In an *ink-jet printer*, a nozzle is used to shoot a stream of charged ink towards paper. Before the ink reaches the paper, it passes through an electronic field and is deflected to produce a dot-matrix character.

Other examples of nonimpact printers are *laser printers* and *xerographic printers*. Laser printers combine laser beams and electrophotographic technology to create output images. A beam of light is focused through a rotating disk containing a full font of characters. The character image is projected onto a piece of film or photographic paper. The print or negative is developed and fixed, in a manner similar to that used for ordinary photographs. The output consists of high-quality, letter-perfect images. It is often used in book-making. Laser printers are high-speed printers. Some can print up to 21,000 lines per minute.

Xerographic printers use printing methods much like those used in common xerographic copying machines. The pioneer of this type of printing is Xerox. One of their models, unlike most high-speed printers, prints on single $8\frac{1}{2} \times 11''$ plain paper sheets. Xerographic printers operate at 4000 lines per minute.

Table 4–1 indicates the differences in print speeds of impact and nonimpact printers.

Since nonimpact printers involve much less physical movement than impact printers, they are generally much faster. They offer a wider choice of type faces and better speed/price ratios than impact printers. Their technology implies a higher reliability. The primary disadvantage of nonimpact printers is often declared to be their inability to make carbon copies. But multiple printings of a page can be made in less time than it takes an impact printer to print the page.

New printing systems now being introduced incorporate many features of the printing process in one machine. On one machine, for example, collating, routing, hole-punching, blanking out of proprietary

87

TABLE 4–1

PRINTER TYPES
AND SPEEDS

PRINTER TYPE	PRINTING CAPABILITY
IMPACT PRINTERS	
Character-at-a-Time:	
Printer-Keyboards	900 characters per minute
Wire-Matrix (Dot-Matrix)	900 characters per minute
Line-at-a-Time:	
Print Wheel	150 lines per minute
Print Drum	1600 lines per minute
Print Chain	2000 lines per minute
NONIMPACT PRINTERS	
Xerographic	4000 lines per minute
Electrothermal	5000 lines per minute
Electrostatic	5000 lines per minute
Laser	21,000 lines per minute

information, and perforating are performed automatically. Another printer produces both text and forms designs on plain paper; this reduces the need for preprinted forms.

As the refinement of nonimpact printing technology continues, nonimpact printers will become the predominant means of producing hard-copy output.

SUMMARY

● Punched cards are one of the primary media for entering data into computer systems. Card readers and card punches are the input/output devices used to process punched cards in computer systems. Systems in which cards are processed by electromechanical machines are called unit-record systems.

● There are two types of punched cards. The Hollerith card has 80 vertical columns and 12 horizontal rows. The second type has 96 columns and allows more data to be stored in a smaller space.

● Data is recorded on punched cards by means of a card-punch/keypunch machine. The data is typed from source documents by an operator. Options like automatic skipping and duplicating are available on most keypunches.

● The verifier is used to check the data punched onto cards. The punched cards are loaded into the verifier, and the same data is re-keyed by the operator. If an error is found, the verifier punches a notch in the card over the incorrect column. The verifying punch is also used to check data. It has a memory and is more efficient since errors can be detected before cards are punched.

● The data recorder is used to process 96-column punched cards. Data is first entered into storage by a keying operation. A card is punched after the data has been verified by re-keying.

● Card readers convert data recorded on punched cards into a form that can be processed by a computer. The mechanism for translating punched holes into electrical pulses involves either metal brushes or photoelectric cells.

● The reproducer punches data onto cards. It can transfer data from one card to another (reproducing), and it can punch a single item from one master card into several detail cards (gangpunching).

● The interpreter prints, at the top of a card, the data that has been punched on the card. The fields to be interpreted and the positions where they are to be printed are controlled by the wiring of a control panel.

● The collator arranges cards in a predetermined manner. Its major functions are sequence-checking, merging, matching, selecting, and match-merging.

● The sorter arranges cards in a desired sequence. It can also group cards containing identical data in a particular field.

● The advantages of punched-card systems include standardization, which allows processing of data by different machines; easy updating; and easy handling. The major disadvantages are record-length limitations, mutilation during handling, slow processing speeds, and preliminary sorting requirements. Also, large card files take up space and increase handling costs.

● Printers provide human-readable output in a permanent (hard-copy) form. Impact printers are most commonly used with computers. They can be classified as either character-at-a-time such as printer-keyboards and wire-matrix printers, or line-at-a-time such as print-wheel printers, drum printers, and chain printers.

● Nonimpact printers are a more recent development. They use photographic, thermal, and laser techniques to print output. They are faster than impact printers, offer a wider choice of type faces and better speed/price ratios, and are very reliable.

REVIEW QUESTIONS

1. How does automatic data processing differ from computer data processing?

2. Explain the concept of unit-record systems.

3. Briefly explain keypunch machines. How is card punching verified?

4. Explain the two mechanisms used by card readers to convert data recorded as punched holes into electrical pulses for computer input.

5. Define the following functions: (a) reproducing, (b) gangpunching, (c) interpreting, and (d) sorting.

6. Discuss the two types of printing devices. Which type is more common and why?

7. Distinguish between character-at-a-time printers and line-at-a-time printers, giving examples of each.

American United Life Insurance Company is ranked 47th, based on assets, among the nation's 50 largest life insurance companies in a survey conducted by *Fortune* magazine. With an increase of 11.1 percent, or $864,566,268, in life insurance in force during 1977, American United Life continues the strong growth trend that has characterized the firm since its inception.

The company now offers all forms of individual and group life and health insurance policies, tax-deferred annuities, retirement accounts, and pensions. American United Life also sells mutual funds, has a line of mass-marketed insurance products, and is a leader in the specialized field of re-insurance.

The data-processing area at American United Life is basically a service department. It supports all the firm's product lines as well as the accounting department. Approximately 50 people, including operators, programmers, analysts, and keypunch operators, are employed in this area by American United Life. The move toward computerization began in 1960 with the purchase of an NCR 304 computer. The growing size and complexity of operations necessitated a change to a larger

IBM computer in 1968. The company has continually updated this equipment as needed. Today it has an IBM System/370 Model 148, with a main storage capacity of one million bytes. Peripheral equipment includes eight tape drives, ten disk drives, and two impact printers. Keypunches are used to enter data onto standard 80-column punched cards.

A major application that makes extensive use of punched cards is the group insurance application. Group insurance policies provide coverage for four major types of customers: Employee/Employer groups, which include sole proprietorships, partnerships, and corporations; Associations; Multiple Employer Trust; and Unions. A master policy is prepared for each insured group. This is a contract between the policyholder and the insurer. The master policy tells who is eligible for insurance and the types and amounts of the various benefits. Each master policy applies to all people in a group, so only one master policy is created for each group. Each employee covered by the policy receives a certificate of proof of insurance that provides all the information that the employee may need.

To facilitate the monthly billing of all policyholders, a master file is main-

application

AMERICAN UNITED LIFE INSURANCE COMPANY

American United Life · Indianapolis

We have been guaranteeing futures
for more than 100 years.

91

tained. This master file is kept in policy number order. Within each policy number, the file contains three different card formats (see Figure 4–19). Each of the cards makes extensive use of the unit-record concept.

The first card in each set is the policy-holder name and address card. Since only one master policy is created for each group, this card contains data pertaining to the party to be billed, which in most cases is a business firm. The card is green in color, allowing it to be recognized conveniently from other cards in the file. The letter G punched in column 1 indicates that the billing pertains to a group policy. Columns 2 through 7 contain the policy number. The next 20 columns contain the name of the organization that is to be billed, followed by columns allocated for street address, city, state, and zip code. The remaining columns are used for additional data required in the billing process.

The second card in the set is yellow. It is the group contract rate card. The most important fields on this card are policy number, policyholder name, policy effective date, premium due day, premium mode (indicates whether the billing is to be annually, semi-annually, quarterly, or monthly), regional group office code, and rate of billing for each $1000 of insurance coverage. This data is used to generate the billing statement.

The third card in the set is the enrollee status card. Although there is usually only one policyholder name and address card and one group contract rate card for each group insured, there are anywhere from less than 20 to over 1000 enrollee status cards for each group. These cards are organized alphabetically by enrollee last name within each group. Any card can be

retrieved easily. American United Life has from 2600 to 2700 billing units; this means there are about 2700 policyholder name and address cards and 2700 group contract rate cards. The total number of individuals insured by these policies is nearly 80,000. Thus, the bulk of the file consists of enrollee status cards. The most important items on this card are policy number, enrollee name, birth date, sex, marital status, and effective date of insurance. Also included are the individual premiums applicable to each type of coverage. For example, an insured employee, R.O. Nicholas, is covered under group number 6106482, which is recorded on all three cards. The employee was born in January, 1955, is female, and is single. Columns 28 through 33 indicate that her insurance policy became effective on June 5, 1978. The remaining columns on the card contain data indicating the amount of her coverage and the monthly premiums charged for this coverage.

The major advantage of this card-file organization is the relative ease of updating the master file. When a new employee becomes eligible for a group's insurance plan, the company or group mails to American United Life an enrollment card containing all pertinent data about the enrollee. An enrollee status card can then be keypunched and inserted into the file. Termination can be reflected with the same ease by removing an enrollee status card from the file.

When it is time for a billing, the card file is placed into a card reader. A punched card containing the due date for billing is inserted in front of the file to establish the billing date. The data on the cards is read into the computer and written out on magnetic tape. The cards are returned to the storage area because they

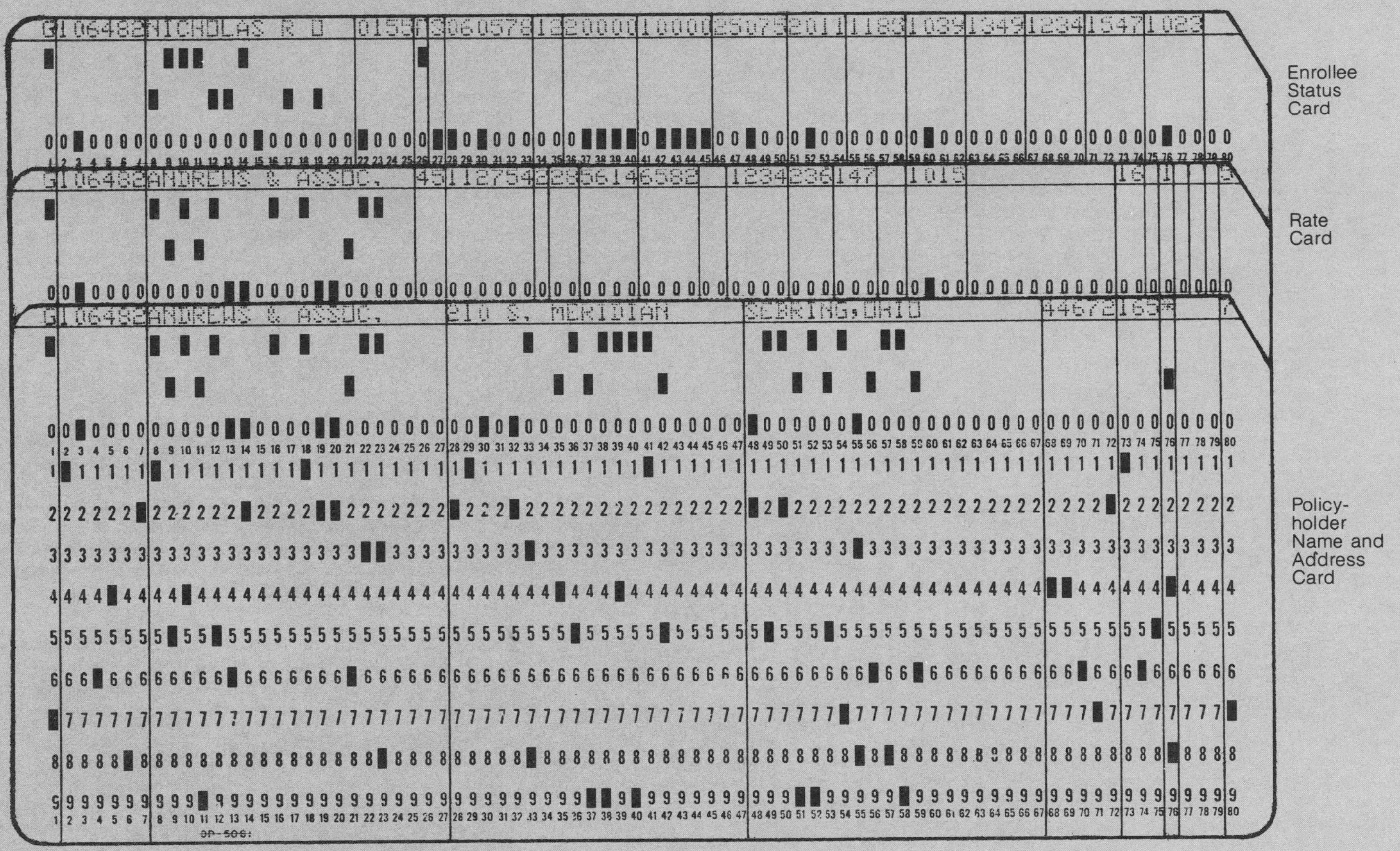

FIGURE 4–19

Master Billing File Consisting
of Three Sets of Punched
Cards

are no longer needed for the billing process.

The magnetic tape is mounted onto a tape drive. The data on the tape is used by the computer to generate a three-part billing statement. With an IBM 3211 printer capable of printing 2000 lines per minute, about 30 billing statements can be generated in one minute. Since the file for a group contains nearly 2700 billing units, all necessary statements can be produced in less than 1½ hours.

The billing statements are then sent to the accounting department. One copy of each is retained, pending payment. The other two copies are forwarded to the billing address. The policyholder keeps one of the copies for his/her files, and returns the other copy with the premium remittance. The returned copy may show changes that have to be made to the master file. When this occurs, a new card is punched for each changed unit record and inserted into the file. Unnecessary cards are removed from the file.

A company insured by American United Life may request information not included on their billing statement. One such instance is a request for an alphabetical listing of all employees insured under a certain policy number. Although the enrollee status card file is maintained in alphabetical order for each group, cards occasionally are misfiled. Rather than use costly CPU time to arrange the file in alphabetical order, American United Life elects to perform the task *offline* (using a device not directly connected to the computer). An IBM Model 84 sorter with a read/sort speed of about 1000 cards per minute is used. Once this sorting is completed, the company's request for a listing can be satisfied.

The punched-card system has served American United well in the group application. A punched-card file works well when only limited data is required and the file is used for a few specific purposes. Changes to a punched-card file can efficiently be made by simply adding cards, changing cards, or pulling cards to keep the file up to date. The manual operations necessary to remove old cards and insert new ones, however, cannot be executed as rapidly as electronic processing of changes through a computer. Life, health, and pension applications have already been converted to magnetic-disk and magnetic-tape files; this group insurance application will probably undergo a similar transformation.

DISCUSSION POINTS

1. What type of verification procedures might American United Life use for their group insurance application?

2. How has the unit-record concept aided in processing this application? What problems has it created?

REMOTE-ACCESS/ COMMUNICATION SYSTEMS | 5

OUTLINE

I. Data Communication
   A. Message Transmission
      1. Modulation and Demodulation
      2. Analog and Digital Transmission
   B. Communication Channels
      1. Channel Transmission Modes
      2. Narrow-Band and Broad-Band Channels
   C. Multiplexers and Concentrators
   D. Programmable Communications Processors

II. Remote-Access Computing
   A. Online Systems
      1. Direct-Access Processing
      2. Remote Job-Entry
   B. Online Real-Time Systems
   C. Interactive/Time-Sharing Systems
   D. Distributed Systems
      1. Spider Configuration
      2. Ring Configuration
      3. Hierarchical Network

INTRODUCTION

Managing today's diverse businesses is a complex task. Management information needs extend beyond periodic summary reports provided on a routine basis. A manager must have current knowledge of company operations to control business activities and to insure that effective customer service is provided. Decisions must be made on short notice, on the basis of data gathered and analyzed from geographically remote locations. An efficient, fast way to capture, process, and distribute large amounts of data is needed. Data communication systems have been developed to meet this need. They help to reduce delays in collection and dissemination of data.

This chapter explains how communication systems allow users at remote locations to gain fast, easy access to computer resources. The concepts and techniques involved in message transmission are discussed. The types of equipment that make data communication possible are introduced. Alternative methods of using communications technology to implement management information systems are presented. Examples of applications that demonstrate the capabilities of these systems are described.

PHYSICIANS CAN GET "ODDS" ON A PATIENT'S RISK OF HEART ATTACK

Wall Street Journal
Staff Reporter

Wall Street Journal,
Feb. 9, 1976, p. 26

SUMMIT, N.J.—Doctors now can get the "track odds" on a patient's chances of having a stroke or a heart attack almost as easily as the patient can get the odds on the daily line at a horse-racing track.

The handicapper is a computer here that any doctor in the country can reach by dialing a toll-free number. The doctor quickly ticks off the patient's age, smoking habits, blood pressure, blood cholesterol level, heart size, and results of a blood sugar test.

Within seconds, a computer operator responds with the patient's risk of having a stroke or heart attack.

For example, if the doctor describes a 49-year-old male who smokes and has blood pressure and cholesterol levels slightly above average but is otherwise normal, the computer would, as it did recently, give a risk analysis something like this: The patient has 2.3 times the average risk of his sex and age group of having a stroke or heart attack. His chances of having a heart attack or stroke in the next eight years are 17 out of 100, compared with 8 out of 100 for a 49-year-old male who doesn't smoke and has normal blood pressure and cholesterol levels.

HOW ODDS WOULD CHANGE

If asked, the computer also can calculate how the odds would change if the man quit smoking, or lowered his blood pressure or his cholesterol level, or did all three.

The service, called Cardio-Dial, is being offered free to doctors throughout the country by Ciba Pharmaceutical Co., a subsidiary of the Swiss-owned Ciba-Geigy Corp. The company makes, among other pharmaceuticals, drugs to control high blood pressure, although it refrains from making any sales pitch with the service. Ciba representatives, during their regular visits to doctors, are providing each physician with a special phone number and authorization number.

The company said it is offering the service nationwide after having tested it with 5000 physicians in several Southeastern states. During the test period the doctors asked for risk analyses on more than 2500 patients, a spokesman said.

REALLY AT A HIGH RISK

"Many of the doctors said they used it to convince patients that they really are at a high risk of a stroke or heart attack," the Ciba spokesman explained. "The doctor thinks that 'maybe this guy will believe me if I can show him exactly what his risks are,'" the spokesman said. It requires only about a minute and a half to get a risk analysis. Thus, one can be obtained while the patient is in the doctor's office. The service doesn't involve the use of any patient identification.

Some doctors have tested the service by asking for risk analyses of patients who have died of heart attacks. In one recent instance, an analysis disclosed that a 40-year-old man who smoked and had a high cholesterol level along with a slight elevation of blood pressure was running a risk of heart attack or stroke 20 times greater than average.

The risk calculations are based on findings of a federal study in Framingham, Mass., where public health experts for the past 25 years have been closely following the incidence of heart attacks and strokes among 5000 people and correlating it with blood pressure, smoking, cholesterol levels, and other suspected heart-disease risk factors.

This type of communication with a computer that is 50 or 2500 miles away is an example of remote-access interactive computing. The combination of data communication and interactive computing as discussed in the article has greatly broadened the computer's impact. Additional information about these topics follows.

DATA COMMUNICATION

Data communication is the electronic transmission of data from one location to another, usually over communication channels such as telephone/telegraph lines or microwaves. In a data communication system, data is transmitted between terminals and a central computer. People and equipment are geographically dispersed. The computer and its input and output devices, or *terminals*, are hooked into a communication network. The combined use of communication facilities, such as a telephone system, and data-processing equipment is called *teleprocessing*.

Message Transmission

Computers store data in *pulse form*. A pulse of current represents a 1 bit; a "no" pulse represents a 0 bit (see Figure 5–1). It is extremely difficult to transmit data in pulse form over long distances. It is much easier to transmit electrical signals which are in *wave form*. Consequently, when data from computers is transmitted over long distances via communication channels, it is first converted from pulse form to wave form. This process is referred to as *modulation*.

An opposite type of conversion, from wave form to pulse form, is required when data that has been transmitted from remote locations is to be entered into a computer. This conversion is called *demodulation*. Both modulation and demodulation are done by devices called *modems*, or *data sets* (see Figure 5–2).

A wave is characterized by three elements: (a) the *amplitude*, or strength, of the signal; (b) the *frequency*, or number of times the wave form is repeated during a specified time interval; and (c) the *phase*, or duration in time, of the wave form. These elements are illustrated in Figure 5–3.

Transmission of data in a continuous wave form is referred to as *analog transmission*. In the past, analog transmission was the only means of relaying data over long distances. But *digital transmission*, which involves transmitting data as distinct "on"/"off" pulses, is now possible. When this mode of transmission is used, the special steps of conversion from pulse form to wave form before transmission, and subsequent reconversion from wave form to pulse form at the destination, are unnecessary. With further developments in communication technology, digital transmission will become more popular.

FIGURE 5–1
Pulse Form

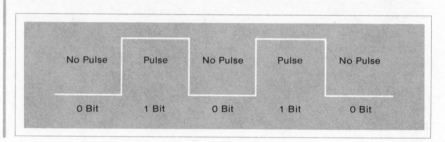

No Pulse	Pulse	No Pulse	Pulse	No Pulse
0 Bit	1 Bit	0 Bit	1 Bit	0 Bit

FIGURE 5—2
Modem

Communication Channels

The purpose of a *communication channel* is to carry data from one location to another. It is the link permitting transmission of electrical signals between distributed locations. The types of communication channels used for data transfer are telegraph lines, telephone lines, coaxial cables, microwave links, communication satellites, high-speed helical waveguides, and laser beams.

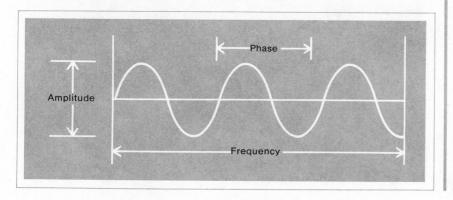

FIGURE 5—3
Amplitude, Frequency, and Phase

frequency

The *grade*, or *bandwidth*, of a channel must be considered for each application because the width of the frequency band is approximately proportional to the quantity of data that can be transmitted via the channel. Telegraph lines are *narrow-bandwidth channels*. They can transmit data at rates of from 45 to 90 bits per second. Telephone lines are voice-grade channels; they offer a broader bandwidth. The transmission rates in this category vary from 300 to 9600 bits per second. Voice-grade channels are used by the Data-Phone (see Figure 5–4) and the Dataspeed equipment of the Bell Telephone System, the Wide Area Telephone Service (WATS), and many others.

For applications that require high-speed transmission of large volumes of data, *broad-band channels* are most suitable. Coaxial cables and microwaves belong in this grade. Leased broad-band services are offered by both Western Union and the Bell System. An example of a leased broad-band service is American Telephone and Telegraph's Telpak system. Such a service is capable of transmitting data at rates of up to 120,000 bits per second.

Another way of classifying communication channels is by the type of transmission. Depending on the application and the terminal equipment used, channels operate in one of three basic transmission modes (see also Figure 5–5):

● *Simplex.*   The simplex channel provides for unidirectional, or one-way, transmission of data.

● *Half-duplex.*   In this mode of transmission, communication can occur in only one direction at a time, but that direction can change.

● *Full-duplex.*   This is the most versatile mode of transmission. A full-duplex channel can transmit data in both directions simultaneously.

FIGURE 5–4
Data-Phone

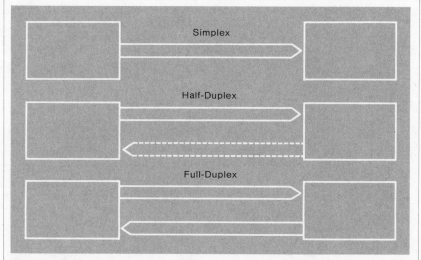

FIGURE 5–5
Channel Transmission
Modes

Multiplexers and Concentrators

The purpose of *multiplexers* and *concentrators* is to increase the number of input and output terminals that can use a communication channel. In many cases, the terminals operate at much slower speeds than the communication channel being used. This is uneconomical, since the channel cannot be used to or near its full capacity. To overcome this difficulty, multiplexers were developed. A multiplexer receives input from several terminals, combines the input into a stream of data, and then transmits the stream over one communication channel. One channel can now handle the data transmission that previously had to be handled by more than one channel.

A concentrator differs from a multiplexer in that data from only one terminal at a time is transmitted over the communication channel. A typical example is a situation where six terminals are linked with only three channels. The concentrator controls access to these channels by polling the terminals when a channel becomes available. The first channel that is ready to send or receive data when polled is given control of the channel until its transmission is completed. If all three channels are being used and a fourth terminal is activated, the user at that terminal must wait until a channel becomes available before transmitting data. The use of concentrators is based on the probability that not all terminals will need to send or receive data simultaneously. Figure 5–6 shows communication systems with and without multiplexers and concentrators.

Programmable Communications Processors

A *programmable communications processor* is a device that relieves the CPU of many of the tasks typically required in a communication system.

101

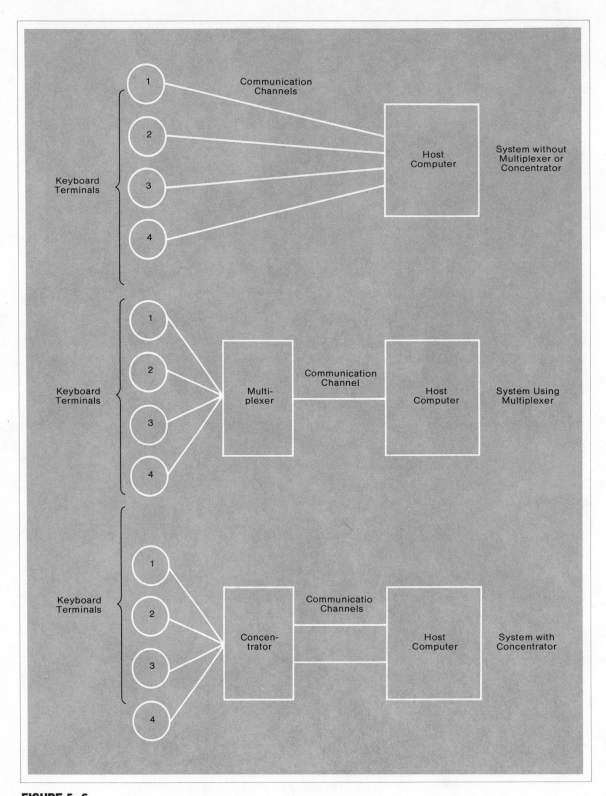

FIGURE 5—6
Communication Systems with Multiplexers and Concentrators

When the volume of data transmission surpasses a certain level, a programmable communications processor can handle these tasks more economically than the CPU. Examples of such tasks include the handling of messages and of priorities, disconnecting after messages have been received, requesting re-transmission of incomplete messages, and verification of successfully transmitted messages.

The two most frequent uses of communications processors are for message-switching and front-end processing. When used for message-switching, the principal task of the processor is to receive messages and route them to appropriate destinations. A *front-end processor* performs message-switching as well as more sophisticated operations such as validation of transmitted data and pre-processing of data prior to transmission to the central computer.

REMOTE-ACCESS COMPUTING

Dramatic advancements in computer technology have been made in the past two decades. The speeds of central processors and of I/O devices have increased tremendously. A wide variety of *peripherals* (I/O devices, secondary storage devices, and other auxiliary computer equipment) offering far greater capabilities has been developed. However, providing high-quality information for effective management of resources involves more than just processing data. An information system may be capable of extremely fast data processing, but it may not provide timely information if there are delays in collection and distribution. *Remote-access computing systems* have been designed to solve this problem. They use data-communication techniques to reduce delays in data collection and dissemination.

Four types of remote-access computing systems are discussed in this section. They are: online systems, online real-time systems, interactive/time-sharing systems, and distributed systems.

Online Systems

Online systems are frequently dependent on *direct-access processing* capabilities. When direct-access processing is used, data is submitted to the computer as it occurs. Online terminals, which are in direct communication with the computer, permit immediate data-entry and retrieval. Thus, data can be sent to, or received from, local I/O devices or remote terminals. Records are updated immediately using direct-access processing capabilities provided by disk storage units or similar *direct-access storage devices* (*DASDs*). A particular record in a master file or disk can be accessed directly and updated, without reading all preceding records on the file. Figure 5–7 shows an online direct-access system for inventory and accounts-receivable (A/R) operations.

Online systems do not always use direct-access processing. Figure 5–9 illustrates an online system operating in a batch-processing mode with *remote job-entry* (*RJE*) capabilities. A remote job-entry terminal is connected to a central computer by a communication channel. It can tell

103

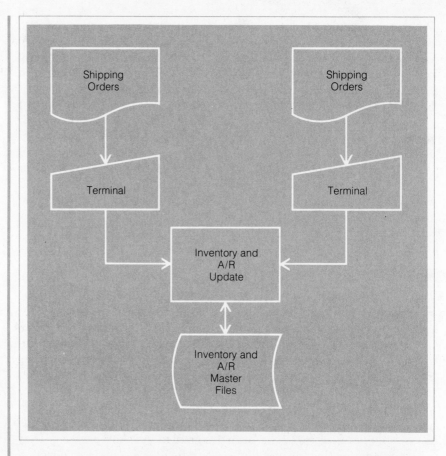

FIGURE 5—7
Online Direct-Access
Inventory and
Accounts-Receivable
System

the central computer to execute an application program (job), submit data to the program, and print the output after program execution. Any I/O device can be converted into an RJE terminal by adding a communication data control unit and linking it to a computer via a communication channel. Thus, an RJE terminal, or station, typically consists of an input device, an output device, and a console to communicate with the central computer (see also Figure 5–8).

The system in Figure 5–9 has three RJE stations connected to a central computer. All three stations have card readers and printers. Jobs are batched at each station before they are transmitted through the card reader to the central computer. The results of the processing are printed by the RJE printer. Such a system can be used to advantage in applications where a fast response is not crucial and can be sacrificed for the lower costs of batch processing.

Online Real-Time Systems

A *real-time system* can receive data, process it, and provide output fast enough to control the activity being performed. Thus, *response time*, defined as the time between completion of data input and start of output,

Printer Card reader Card punch

FIGURE 5—8
Remote Job-Entry Station

FIGURE 5—9
Remote Job-Entry System

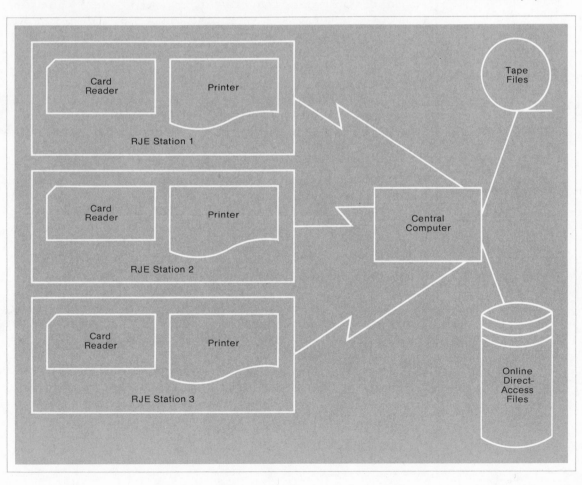

Card Reader

Printer

RJE Station 1

Card Reader

Printer

RJE Station 2

Card Reader

Printer

RJE Station 3

Central Computer

Tape Files

Online Direct– Access Files

is critical in all real-time applications. However, the response time required of a real-time system cannot be fixed in absolute time units. Rather, it depends on the particular application. For example, the registrar's office at a university may be willing to wait up to 30 seconds for responses concerning the records of students. A monitoring system for intensive care patients must have a response time of fractions of a second.

A system that operates in real-time generally must be an online system. However, not all online systems are real-time systems. Generally, then, online real-time systems allow direct access to computer files (stored on direct-access storage devices) and immediate update of the files as transactions occur. Additionally, inquiries can be made via online terminals, and responses received in a few seconds. In cases where the central computer is far from the user terminals, communication channels are used to link the terminals with it. Simply having a remote terminal online does not insure a real-time response; required data files also must be online and on direct-access storage so that the system can respond quickly.

Figure 5–10 shows the major components of an online real-time system for tracking and controlling the inmates of a large correction facility. The terminal-based system helps the prison staff to improve security, reduce tensions, improve efficiency of operations, and thus provide a better environment for the inmates.

The system has multiple online terminals and a data file (containing data about all inmates) that is also online and on direct-access storage. When a prisoner first arrives at the prison, he is assigned an identification number. His answers to personal and medical questions, any other aliases that he may have, and the charges that have been brought against him are entered into the file. Sentence information is also included on his record. Terminal 1 is used for this purpose.

Next, the inmate is sent to the official responsible for cell assignments. The officer assigns a cell based on information retrieved from the system and displayed on the TV-like screen of the officer's terminal (Terminal 2). Other pertinent data such as date of arrival and dates on which the inmate must appear in court are entered via Terminal 3, before the prisoner goes to his cell.

As conditions, for example, court dates or clinic appointments, change, the display terminal at the records office (Terminal 4) is used to enter the new data. Thus, the data file is updated immediately. The system has *security* features built into it so that only certain information can be accessed from each terminal. Special codes are required to access protected data fields, records, or files.

This system operates in real-time. Prison officials can obtain information needed to control ongoing activities. Within a few seconds, the system can provide a population breakdown according to any of several classifications for research purposes. It can track an inmate for a lawyer seeking him as his client for consultation. It can answer queries pertaining to any prisoner at the facility.

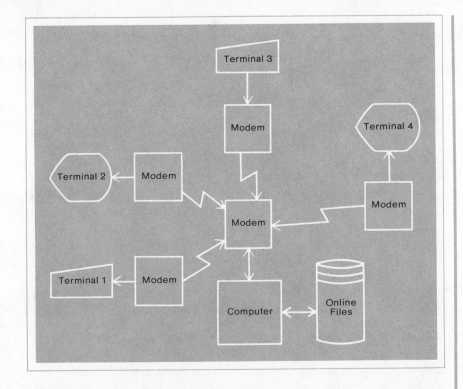

FIGURE 5–10
Online Real-Time System

Interactive/Time-Sharing Systems

Many businesses could benefit from the installation of a computer facility but are prohibited from doing so by its cost. Computer systems are expensive; some cost millions of dollars. Some organizations need the power of a large computer system on an infrequent basis. To meet both of these requirements, *time-sharing systems* have been developed. Under time-sharing, two or more users can access the same central computer resources and receive what seem to be simultaneous results. Each user believes that he or she has total control of the computer. In reality, the computer is dividing its time among them. Each user is charged only for the computer resources he or she actually uses. The users need not be requesting solutions to similar problems; completely unrelated tasks can be carried out. Remote users may access the system via terminals and telephone lines. Nearby users may have I/O devices that are directly connected to it.

A distinguishing feature of a time-sharing system is its ability to provide *interactive computing.* Interaction, or conversation, between users at online terminals and the central computer occurs. Through commands entered at the terminal, the user can write a program, correct errors identified with the help of diagnostic (error) messages provided by the computer, and then run the program. The user can also ask the computer to list files, explain error messages, acknowledge a change that

107

may have been made to the program, and so on. Such interaction is a great advantage to users who are just becoming familiar with computers.

A system that supports interactive computing must have some method of allocating computing time to users. Imagine your frustration if you were forced to wait 30 minutes while another user executed a program that monopolized the CPU's processing facilities. The purpose of the system would be defeated. All users would be reluctant to waste time, waiting for the CPU to become available. To minimize this problem, each user of a time-sharing system is allocated a small portion of processing time through a technique called *time-slicing*. If the user's program is completely executed during this time, or if it reaches a point where input or output activity occurs, the CPU begins (or resumes) execution of another program. If the program is not completely executed, control of the CPU is given to another program, but the first program is placed at the end of a waiting line. This switching between programs occurs at such a rapid rate that the user is usually unaware that execution of the program has stopped.

Several programming languages have been designed primarily for interactive computing. The most popular of these is *BASIC* (*B*eginners *A*ll-purpose *S*ymbolic *I*nstruction *C*ode). It is easy to learn, and it can be used to solve a variety of problems. Although the language does not have to be used exclusively in time-sharing systems, it can be used most effectively in systems that provide interactive-computing facilities.

Figure 5–11 shows a simple interactive payroll program written in BASIC. Notice that the computer is instructed to ask the user to enter the data that is to be processed: name, hours worked, and pay rate per hour. The employee's gross pay is then calculated and printed. Then the computer asks if data for any more employees is to be processed. The user can then enter additional data or stop execution of the program.

There are two methods of establishing time-sharing capability. One is to install a system *in-house;* that is, an organization may set up its own time-sharing system to obtain quick answers to such problems as production and cost analysis, forecasting, and accounts receivable. The other method is to purchase time-sharing capability from a service company equipped to sell the capability. This approach is often taken by small organizations that cannot afford to have their own computers. Due to the high competition in this area, many service companies have expanded to provide not only time-sharing capability but also specialized programs and technical assistance.

The major advantages of time-sharing systems are listed below.

● Quick-response capabilities are provided through online terminals. This allows managers to get answers to problems that need immediate attention, say, those dealing with product marketing, hospital monitoring of patients, accounts receivable, and engineering calculations.

● During the time interval needed for one job to be completed in a batch-processing system, several jobs (or the same job) can be run several times in a time-sharing system.

```
PAYROLL      21:32    AUGUST 3RD, 1978

100  REM THIS PROGRAM CALCULATES A WEEKLY
110  REM PAYROLL FOR ALL EMPLOYEES
120  PRINT "ENTER NAME, HOURS WORKED, PAY RATE"
130  PRINT
140  INPUT N$,H,W
150  PRINT
160  LET P = H*W
170  PRINT "EMPLOYEE NAME," "NET PAY"
180  PRINT
190  PRINT N$,P
200  PRINT
210  PRINT "ANY MORE EMPLOYEES?"
220  INPUT D$
230  IF D$ = "YES" THEN 120
240  END


RUN PAYROLL

PAYROLL      21:33    AUGUST 3RD, 1978

ENTER NAME, HOURS WORKED, PAY RATE

?ROBERTA SCHILLER, 35, 8.00

EMPLOYEE NAME      NET PAY

ROBERTA SCHILLER     280

ANY MORE EMPLOYEES?
?YES
ENTER NAME, HOURS WORKED, PAY RATE

?RICHARD NICKLES, 41, 8.34

EMPLOYEE NAME      NET PAY

RICHARD NICKLES     341.94

ANY MORE EMPLOYEES?
?NO

TIME 0 SECS.
```

FIGURE 5—11
BASIC Payroll Program

● By using portable terminals, users can move from one location to another, and still be able to link to the central computer through telephone lines.

● Utilization of the central computer is greater in a time-sharing system than in a batch-processing system. The central processor is not idle during I/O operations; it proceeds to a different user program.

● Time-sharing may be the only economical alternative for small users who cannot get access to large-scale or complex computing power because of the costs involved. In a time-sharing environment, they need to pay only a flat monthly charge and an additional fee for the computer time they use.

● In time-sharing, each user seems to possess a private computer, but the resource pooling that takes place means lower costs per unit than could be obtained if a private computer were actually owned and operated.

Although time-sharing has many advantages, there are some inherent problems. Some of these are identified below.

● A breakdown in telephone lines or an increase in communication costs may greatly affect users who are connected via the lines. Furthermore, telephone lines are designed primarily for voice communication; they are not the best medium for transmission of data. Thus, applications involving extensive I/O operations may not be suited to time-sharing.

● Because data can be accessed quickly and easily in a time-sharing system, there is an increased concern regarding security. All programs and data must be safeguarded from unauthorized persons or use.

● When speed of response is not a necessity, a time-sharing capability may be needlessly expensive.

● System reliability may be lower than it is in other, non-time-sharing systems. The additional equipment and communication channels create more areas for both mechanical and system-related problems.

A typical in-house time-sharing application—the preparation of sales invoices—is shown in Figure 5–12. The operator at Sales Office A uses a typewriter-like terminal to enter a customer number. The central processor locates that number on the customer master file (on a DASD). It instructs the terminal user at Sales Office A to enter the customer name and address. The operator also enters the product code and quantity of the items ordered by the customer. The computer checks the inventory master file and returns the item description, unit price, and total charge for each item. If an item is not in inventory, an appropriate message is returned to the user. After all items have been processed, the computer figures the total order cost and computes any special discounts that are applicable.

While the terminal at Sales Office A is printing the sales invoice, the central computer may receive input from Warehouse D. It updates the inventory master file to reflect the changes entered by the warehouse operator. Thus, multiple users can independently communicate with the central computer and get quick responses.

Distributed Systems

Distributed systems are characterized by geographically dispersed computers linked together in a communication network. Instead of using

110

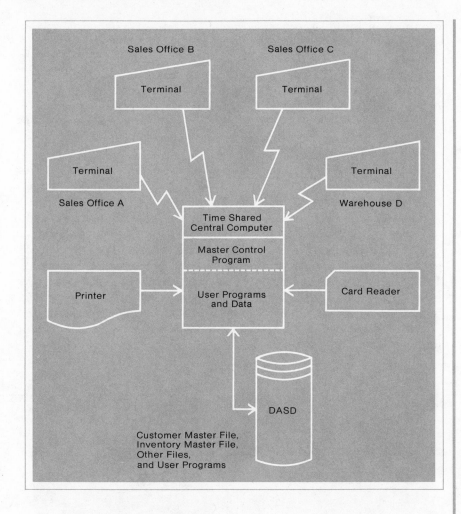

FIGURE 5–12
Time-Sharing Application

one centralized computer for all data input, processing, and output, the distributed approach uses computers at the locations where data is collected and information is required. Such an approach is a natural extension of time-sharing. In both cases, a communication network is employed to collect and disseminate data. However, a significant difference is that a time-sharing system uses one central processor, whereas a distributed system uses multiple processors to provide local processing capabilities. The advantages of distributed data processing include reduced organizational impact, greater flexibility and responsiveness, and increased fault tolerance.

Different types of structures can be used to implement the distributed systems concept. A *spider configuration* uses a central controller. All communication must be routed to a central computer before it can be routed to the appropriate network computer. The effect is to create a central decision point. This facilitates workload distribution and resource sharing, but it exposes the system to single-point vulnerability. An alternative approach uses a number of computers connected to a single

111

transmission line in a *ring configuration.* This type of system can bypass a malfunctioning unit without disrupting operations throughout the network.

An interesting and more sophisticated approach is a *hierarchical network.* Under this approach, an organization's needs are divided into multiple levels. The levels receive different levels of computer support. The lowest level is the user level. At this level, only computing power is supplied. But this level is connected to the next higher level and its associated information system. At each higher level, the machine size increases while the need for distribution decreases. Thus, such a system basically consists of a network of small computers tied into a large central computing complex.

Figure 5–13 shows a distributed system consisting of three dispersed minicomputers connected to a large central computer via communication linkages. The three minicomputers are located in three functional departments of the organization—finance, marketing, and production. Thus, the functional departments can meet their processing requirements locally. Some of the information generated by the minicomputers is communicated to the central computer to be used in corporate-wide planning and control. Such a network provides fast response and great flexibility to local system users. Furthermore, the central facility is

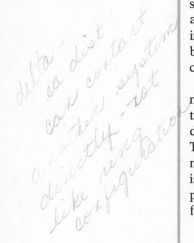

FIGURE 5–13
Distributed System

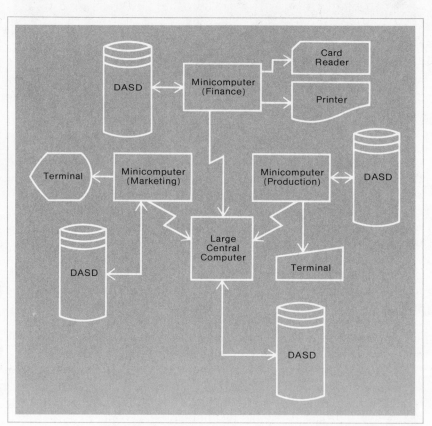

available to them for jobs that require computing power beyond the capabilities of the minicomputers.

SUMMARY

● Data communication is the electronic transmission of data from one location to another, usually over communication channels such as telephone/telegraph lines or microwaves. The combined uses of data-processing equipment and communication facilities, such as a telephone system, is called teleprocessing.

● Modulation is the process of converting data from the pulse form used by the computer to a wave form used for message transmission over communication lines. Demodulation is the process of converting the received message from wave form back into pulse form. The modulation/demodulation functions are performed by devices called modems, or data sets.

● Digital transmission involves transmitting data as distinct "on"/"off" pulses rather than waves. This mode of transmission eliminates the specialized steps of conversion from pulse to wave form and subsequent reconversion from wave to pulse form at the destination.

● A communication channel is the link permitting transmission of electrical signals from one location to another. Types of communication channels include telegraph lines, telephone lines, coaxial cables, micro-wave links, and communication satellites. Communication channels may be classified by (1) the amount of data they can transmit, or bandwidth, or (2) the type of transmission mode they use, such as simplex, half-duplex, or full-duplex.

● Multiplexers, concentrators, and programmable communications processors are devices that have been developed to reduce the costs associated with data transmission in a communication system.

● Remote-access computing systems are designed to reduce delays in data collection and dissemination. Data-communication techniques are used to transfer data from remote locations to a central computer. Remote-access computing can be accomplished through online systems, online real-time systems, interactive/time-sharing systems, and distributed systems.

● Online systems are frequently dependent on direct-access processing capabilities. Online direct-access systems consist of terminals in direct communication with the computer to permit immediate data-entry and retrieval. Remote job-entry (RJE) terminals can also be linked to a computer via communication channels to initiate computer processing from remote locations.

● Online real-time systems can receive data, process it, and provide results fast enough to control activities being performed. Direct-access processing of data files is used to achieve quick responses.

113

● A time-sharing system allows several users to access the same computer resources at the same time. Online terminals can be used for interactive computing. A time-sharing system may be installed in-house, or time-sharing capability may be purchased from a service company.

● Distributed systems are characterized by several geographically dispersed computers linked together in a communication network. This approach uses computers at the locations where data is collected and information is required. Types of distributed systems include spider configurations, ring configurations, and hierarchical networks.

REVIEW QUESTIONS

1. What are modems? What purpose do they serve in data communication systems?

2. Distinguish between simplex, half-duplex, and full-duplex transmission modes. Why are the transmission mode and bandwidth of communication channels of concern to an analyst designing a data communication system?

3. Do all online systems function in real-time? Why or why not? Must a real-time system be online? Give examples to support your answers.

4. What alternative is available to a firm that does not process a sufficient volume of data to justify the installation of a computer? What problems may arise?

5. What is the major difference between a time-sharing system and a distributed system? What advantages are offered by a distributed system over a system using a single, centrally located computer?

Years ago, computer-assisted legal research seemed an unlikely notion: law was an art rather than a science; as such, it could not be reduced to numbers and programs. And even if it could be, the results would be poor and prohibitively expensive.

Today, computer-assisted legal research systems do exist and are successful. One such system, WESTLAW, was created by West Publishing Company. West applied its 100 years of service to the legal profession to create a system tailored to the needs of lawyers and judges.

The primary advantage of a computer-assisted legal research system is speed. Lawyers and judges are able to search thousands of documents and retrieve relevant case law in just a matter of seconds. This is a much-needed service. In the last five years alone, more than 200,000 court decisions were reported.

The WESTLAW system is an online real-time system involving geographically dispersed terminals linked to a central computer. The system features interactive computing.

The central computer in the WESTLAW system is a powerful IBM System/370 Model 158 located at West headquarters in St. Paul, Minnesota. Law firms, courts, and government agencies using the system have terminals that are directly tied to the central computer via dedicated lines. Through these communication lines, the WESTLAW data base can be directly accessed and information retrieved in a matter of seconds. Data is transmitted over the lines at a rate of 4800 bits per second.

A video-display terminal with a typewriter-like keyboard, perhaps located in a lawyer's office or courtroom, is used for inquiries. The inquiries and immediate answers are flashed on a *cathode-ray tube* (*CRT*) screen. The CRT is an

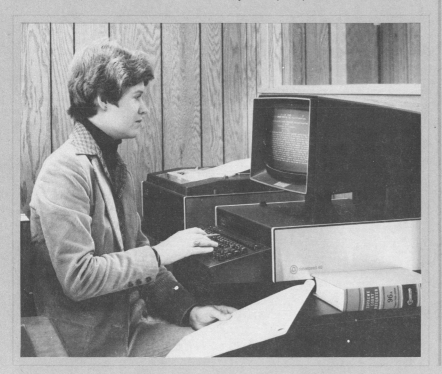

electronic vacuum tube containing a screen, similar to that of a television set, on which information can be displayed.

A printer is also located in the lawyer's office, usually adjacent to the terminal. It allows the lawyer to request copies of any document displayed on the screen by pressing a key on the terminal keyboard.

A great deal of analysis preceded the design of the WESTLAW data base. Currently the data base provides access to the full text and headnotes of all opinions of the United States Supreme Court from 1932 to date; the opinions of the United States Courts of Appeals from 1961 to date and the United States District Courts from 1961 to date. (A headnote is a brief explanatory note prefacing a legal case.) The full text and headnotes of all reported opinions of the state courts are available from January 1, 1978, to date and for some states complete coverage is afforded for earlier years. Both state and federal data is constantly added as new decisions are reported.

Some computer systems can respond only to key words with special connecting symbols. Using this facility, a WESTLAW researcher selects certain words pertinent to the legal problem he or she is handling. The researcher uses the typewriter-like keyboard to type the words with ampersands between them. For example:

ATTORNEY & CLIENT &
PRIVILEGE & INCRIMINATION

The words are communicated to the central computer. It searches the data base for cases in which all of these words are present. The cases are retrieved and flashed onto the CRT screen. This type of query works satisfactorily for situations where getting only documents containing every one of the selected words is sufficient.

West's experience with legal writing indicated that using a key-word system exclusively was not feasible in a computerized legal research system. The English language is imprecise, and synonym—antonym problems are not dealt with. Consequently, WESTLAW also permits a researcher to frame a search query in natural language, just as he or she might otherwise write or state the problem. For example:

MAY AN ATTORNEY IN POSSESSION OF RECORDS BELONGING TO A CLIENT ASSERT THE CLIENT'S PRIVILEGE AGAINST SELF-INCRIMINATION?

The retrieved documents are ranked by the computer on the basis of the frequency of occurrence of the search terms in the documents. The retrieved documents are displayed in the sequence of apparent relevance. The relevant documents are usually among the first 15 to 20 documents displayed.

The query process is illustrated in Figure 5–14. As the researcher types the query on the keyboard, it is displayed on the screen. Then the researcher presses the ENTER key. In only a few seconds, the computer searches all 327,091 documents in the federal data base, ranks the retrieved documents according to the frequency of occurrence of the search terms, and displays the most relevant document first.

The search terms used in the query are highlighted in the displayed document. The display also shows the case name and a citation to the full case, the court, and the year.

The WESTLAW system can perform a variety of other types of searches. For

FIGURE 5–14
The Query Process

Inquiry is
typed and
displayed.

MAY AN ATTORNEY IN POSSESSION OF RECORDS
BELONGING TO A CLIENT ASSERT THE CLIENT'S
PRIVILEGE AGAINST SELF-INCRIMINATION?_

Within seconds
the first
document
is displayed.

410K217
410 WITNESSES
K217. PERSONS ENTITLED TO ASSERT
PRIVILEGE.
C.A.N.Y. 1962
    ATTORNEY, BY MAKING PROPER SHOWING,
MAY RAISE CLIENTS' PRIVILEGE AGAINST
SELF-INCRIMINATION AS A BASIS FOR
REFUSING TO PRODUCE INDEPENDENTLY PRE-
EXISTING RECORDS OR OTHER DOCUMENTS
TURNED OVER TO HIM BY CLIENTS IF CLIENTS
COULD HAVE REFUSED TO PRODUCE THEM UNDER
THAT PRIVILEGE.
COLTON V. U.S.,
306 F.2D 633, CERTIORARI DENIED 83 S.
CT.505, 371 U.S. 951, 9 L.ED.2D 499.
END OF DOCUMENT

instance, when a fact word search is used, the system searches the data base for all documents containing one or more of the words entered. The system also permits phrase-searching. Here, the researcher enters a phrase enclosed in quotes, e.g., ''unsafe food additive.'' Cases can be retrieved by requiring that certain words occur in a document within the same sentence or paragraph. The researcher can retrieve a particular law by entering a statutory citation. He or she can retrieve a case summary by entering a case citation. He or she can limit a search to a particular year, court, judge, or state.

WESTLAW's speed has dramatically changed some aspects of legal research. Its online real-time capabilities allow one lawyer to do the amount of research formerly done by three or four lawyers, in the same amount of time. The approximate yearly cost is equivalent to that of one lawyer, not three or four.

DISCUSSION POINTS

1. What advantages does the real-time capability of the WESTLAW system provide to the legal researcher?

2. The WESTLAW system terminals are linked to the central computer via dedicated communication lines. Yet the system offers to the user the flexibility of accessing other systems' data bases via standard dial-up telephones. Why is this important?

DATA-ENTRY/INFORMATION-RESPONSE | 6

OUTLINE

I. Data Input
   A. Magnetic-Ink Character Readers
   B. Key-to-Tape and Key-to-Disk Devices
II. Source-Data Automation
   A. Optical Recognition
      1. Optical-Mark Recognition
      2. Bar-Code Recognition
      3. Optical-Character Recognition

   B. Remote Terminals
      1. POS Terminals
      2. Visual-Display Terminals
      3. Touch-Tone Devices
      4. Intelligent Terminals
III. Special-Purpose Output
   A. Plotters
   B. Computer Output Microfilm (COM)
IV. Input/Output Operations
   A. Control Units
   B. Channels

INTRODUCTION

In Chapter 4, we discussed card input and printer output. These I/O media have certain limitations that prohibit their use in some computer applications. Punched cards are limited by their bulkiness, high cost, fixed size, and preliminary sorting requirements. Printers are limited by their relatively slow speed and the fixed size of printer output. The I/O devices discussed in this chapter are designed to overcome these limitations and to meet the unique needs of various data-processing applications.

This chapter describes magnetic-ink character readers and key-to-tape and key-to-disk devices. The importance of source-data automation in the capture and preparation of data is stressed, and various input devices that meet this requirement are discussed. Special-purpose output provided by plotters and computer output microfilm are introduced. In addition, the primary functions of both control units and channels in I/O operations are explained. The concept of buffering is introduced in this context.

PERTEC LABORING FOR LOST LOVES

Ann Dooley, CW Staff

Computerworld,
May 22, 1978, p. 1

CHATSWORTH, CALIF. Romeo and Juliet might have lived to tell about it, Penelope might never have taken up knitting while awaiting Odysseus' return, and Prince Charming wouldn't have had to play footsy with anyone but Cinderella if someone had only programmed a computer system to find lost lovers.

Pertec Computer Corp. (PCC) has done just that for present-day lovers who have lost touch and want to find each other again. The vendor is playing Cupid as a promotion for Columbia Pictures' new film, "If Ever I See You Again," the story of a composer reunited with his former sweetheart after 12 years.

PCC went into the lost-love business to "help change the image of computers to a more humane and personal one," according to a spokeswoman. "It's a positive and fun way to introduce computers to people who ordinarily don't have anything to do with them and have misconceptions about them," she said.

Nearly 18 other computer companies turned hard hearts on the project before PCC agreed to the idea. Several were afraid of possible legal implications; others claimed they did not want to be held responsible for breaking up marriages.

The love matching began May 1. Since then nearly 5000 calls have come into PCC facilities. The calls are expected to increase very soon, when the film is released, and continue at a high rate until the project ends July 1.

THREE MATCHES

Out of thousands of calls that have come in, only three verifiable matches have been made, according to the spokeswoman.

Anyone wishing to find a former love can call PCC headquarters on a toll-free line—(800) 423-5250 or, in California, (800) 382-3666—and give his name and phone number, the name of the person to be located, and the city where their romance bloomed.

An operator enters the information into a PCC XL40 data-entry system via one of six 480-character CRTs. If the person being sought has already called PCC, a flashing heart with a moving arrow will appear on the CRT screen to indicate a match. The system also displays the time of the matching call and the phone number where the second caller can be reached.

If a match is not made, the information is entered into the file-inquiry system and stored in case the partner calls.

The system works only if both former lovers are looking for each other and each calls in requesting the other. A caller's privacy is protected since an individual can be reached only by the person he is trying to locate.

The data is coded so a match will be made only if each individual comes up with both the other person's name and the state they were living in when they knew each other. PCC officials further verify matches by calling back both parties.

The system is an XL40 distributed processing, state-of-the-heart microprocessor-based system with 128K memory, three 8.8M-byte disks, and a 300-line/min printer. Its information retrieval package allows an operator to enter, validate, retrieve, and update a file directly at the source.

Innovations in data-entry have greatly extended computer applications. CRTs (visual-display terminals) such as the one described above have helped the computer to be more responsive to human needs.

DATA INPUT

Magnetic-Ink Character Readers

Magnetic ink was introduced in the late 1950s to facilitate check processing by the banking industry. Because magnetic-ink characters are readable by both humans and machines (see Figure 6–1), no special data conversion step is needed. The magnetic-ink characters are already in a form acceptable to the computer.

Magnetic-ink characters are formed using magnetized particles of iron oxide. Each character is composed of certain sections of a 70-section matrix (see Figure 6–2). The characters can be read and converted into machine code by a *magnetic-ink character reader* (*MICR*).

The MICR examines each character area passed to it, to determine the shape of the character represented. The presence of a magnetic field in a section of the area represents a 1 bit; the absence of a magnetic field represents a 0 bit. Each magnetic-ink character is composed of a unique combination of 0 bits and 1 bits. When all sections in a character area are combined and translated into binary notation in this manner, the particular character represented can be determined. The MICR automatically checks each character read to insure accuracy.

The processing of bank checks is a major application of magnetic-ink character recognition. The magnetic-ink characters are printed along the bottom of the check (see Figure 6–3). The *transit field* is preprinted on the check. It includes the bank number, an aid in routing the check through the Federal Reserve System. The customer's checking-account number appears in the *"on-us" field* on the check. A clerk manually inserts the amount of the check in the amount field after the check has been used and received at a bank.

All magnetic-ink characters on checks are formed using the standard 14-character set shown in Figure 6–1. (Other character sets may be used in different applications.) An MICR can read and sort the checks as they are fed into it. The checks are sorted by bank number at the Federal Reserve Bank, and by account number at the issuing bank. In this manner, checks are routed back to each issuing bank and then back to its customers. Between 750 and 1500 checks per minute can be read and sorted by an MICR.

Key-to-Tape and Key-to-Disk Devices

Key-to-tape and *key-to-disk* machines were developed to overcome the disadvantages of punched cards. Magnetic tapes and magnetic disks are the storage media used with these devices.

FIGURE 6–1
Magnetic-Ink Character Set

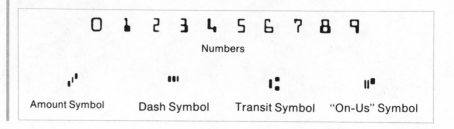

Numbers

Amount Symbol   Dash Symbol   Transit Symbol   "On-Us" Symbol

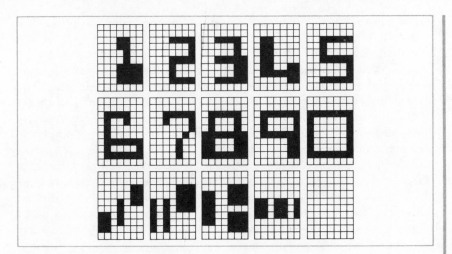

FIGURE 6—2
Matrix Patterns for
Magnetic-Ink Characters

Data is stored as magnetized spots on the surface of a tape or disk. The data can be stored indefinitely because the spots retain their magnetism. It can be replaced with new data when desired. The reusable nature of tapes and disks overcomes a major disadvantage of punched cards, which are not reusable in this manner. Much more data can be stored in a smaller space, when using tapes or disks. For example, as many as 1600 characters are commonly stored on one inch of magnetic tape. Finally, data stored on tape or disk can be read into the CPU at speeds more than 25 times faster than data on cards can be read. Thus, use of magnetic tape or disk can significantly increase the efficiency of data-processing operations.

FIGURE 6—3
Sample Check

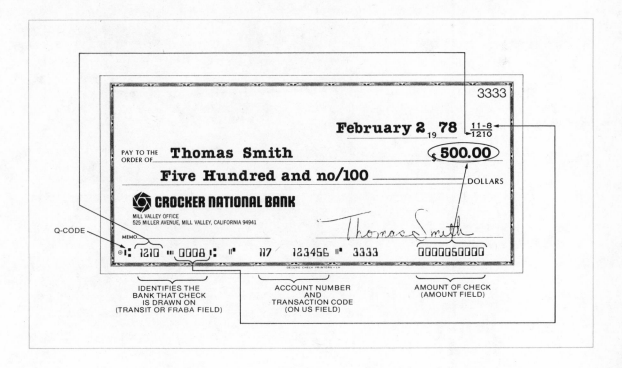

In a key-to-tape or key-to-disk system, data is recorded on tape or disk using a machine similar in appearance to a keypunch (see Figures 6–4 and 6–5). Rather than punch holes in cards, however, the machine records data in the form of magnetized spots. In a key-to-tape system, data is recorded on magnetic-tape reels, cartridges, or cassettes. The data being keyed is usually displayed on a CRT screen to allow easy verification and correction by the operator. An error can be corrected by backspacing and re-keying the correct character(s). As a second check, the tape is rewound and the data is re-keyed a second time.

When key-to-tape devices are used, the data is stored on tape at 20 characters per inch. Another device called a *tape pooler* is used to rewrite the data on the original tape onto another tape in a highly condensed form. For instance, the tape pooler can convert data stored at 20 characters per inch to a condensed form of from 800 to 1600 characters per inch for input to a computer.

When key-to-disk units are used, data is keyed onto magnetic disks (see Figure 6–5). Before data is written onto a disk, however, it is usually stored and edited by a minicomputer. This editing is directed by stored-program instructions in the minicomputer. If an error is detected, the system interrupts the operator and "stands by" until a correction has been entered.

Normally, data is only temporarily stored on disk after editing. The system automatically writes the edited data onto magnetic tape for input to the computer. This process eliminates the need to pool data from one

FIGURE 6—4
Key-to-Tape System

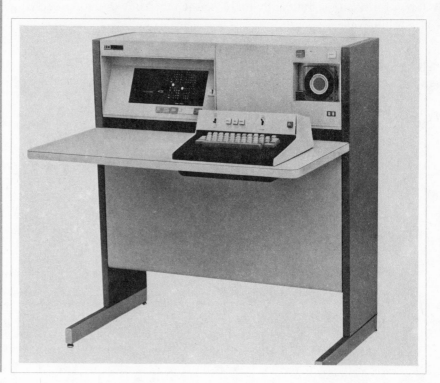

124

FIGURE 6—5
Key-to-Disk System

or several tapes as is done in a key-to-tape system. The characters are automatically condensed when written onto tape from disk storage.

Key-to-tape and key-to-disk data-entry systems offer several advantages over traditional punched-card input:

1. Errors can be corrected by backspacing and re-keying correct data over the incorrect data. Magnetic tapes and magnetic disks are reusable.

2. Since these key-entry devices work electronically rather than mechanically, they are much quieter than card-punch machines. In addition, operators can transcribe data faster from source documents.

3. Record lengths are not limited to 80 characters as with punched cards. Most key-to-disk systems can rearrange data into an 80-column format to facilitate processing by programs originally written to accept punched-card records, if desired.

4. Storage on tape or disk is much more compact than card storage. This reduces data handling and saves storage space.

While key-to-disk and key-to-tape systems offer many advantages over punched-card input, they are also more costly. Generally, these systems are cost-effective where large amounts of data are prepared for processing on medium or large computers.

SOURCE-DATA AUTOMATION

Data-entry has traditionally been the weakest link in the chain of data-processing operations. Although data can be processed electronically at extremely high speeds, significantly more time is required to prepare the data and input it into the computer system.

125

Consider a computer system that uses punched cards for data input. The data is first written on some type of coding form or source document. Then it is keypunched onto cards by an operator. The keypunching operation is relatively slow since each character is recorded at the speed of the operator. Next, the data is verified by duplicating the entire keypunching operation. Incorrect cards must be keypunched and verified a second time.

After all data has been recorded correctly on cards, operations such as sorting and merging must be performed before the cards can be read into the computer. Generally, card files are copied onto magnetic tape for input to the computer at a later time, because magnetic-tape files can be read into the computer much faster than card files can. This type of system is shown graphically in Figure 6–6.

This method of entering data into the computer is very time-consuming and expensive. Some organizations have turned to key-to-tape and key-to-disk systems to simplify keypunching operations. Another approach to data collection and preparation is also gaining in popularity. It is called *source-data automation*. The purpose of source-data automation is to collect data about an event in computer-readable form, when and where the event takes place. By eliminating the intermediate steps used in preparing card input, source-data automation improves the speed, accuracy, and efficiency of data-processing operations (see Figure 6–7).

FIGURE 6–6
Traditional Keypunch
Data-Preparation

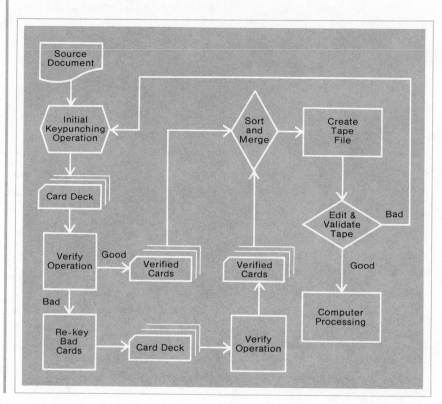

126

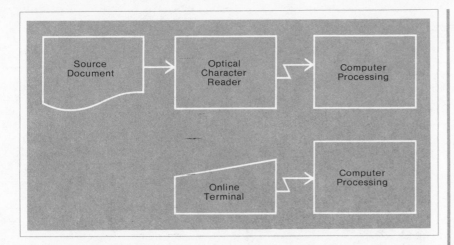

FIGURE 6–7

Typical Methods of Source-Data Automation

Source-data automation is implemented using a variety of methods. Each requires special machines for reading data and converting it into machine language. The most common approaches to source-data automation are discussed below.

Optical Recognition

Optical recognition devices can read marks or symbols coded on paper documents and convert them into electrical pulses. The pulses can then be transmitted directly to the CPU, or stored on magnetic tape or punched cards for input at a later time.

The simplest approach to optical recognition is known as *optical-mark recognition* (*OMR*), or *mark-sensing*. This approach is often used for machine scoring of multiple-choice examinations (see Figure 6–8). A person taking the examination makes a mark with a heavy lead pencil in the location corresponding to each desired answer.

The marks on an OMR document are sensed by an *optical-mark page reader* as the document passes under a light source. The presence of marks in specific locations is indicated by light reflected at those locations. As the document is read, the optical-mark data is automatically translated into machine language. When the optical-mark page reader is directly connected to the computer, up to 2000 forms can be read and processed in an hour.

Optical-mark recognition is also used in order writing, inventory control, surveys and questionnaires, and payroll applications. Since optical-mark data is intially recorded by people, simple, easy-to-complete forms must be devised. Instructions, with examples, are generally provided to aid those who must use the forms. Good forms design helps to prevent errors and lessens the amount of time required to complete the forms.

Another type of optical reader is known as a *bar-code reader*. It can read special line, or bar, codes. The bar codes are actually patterns of

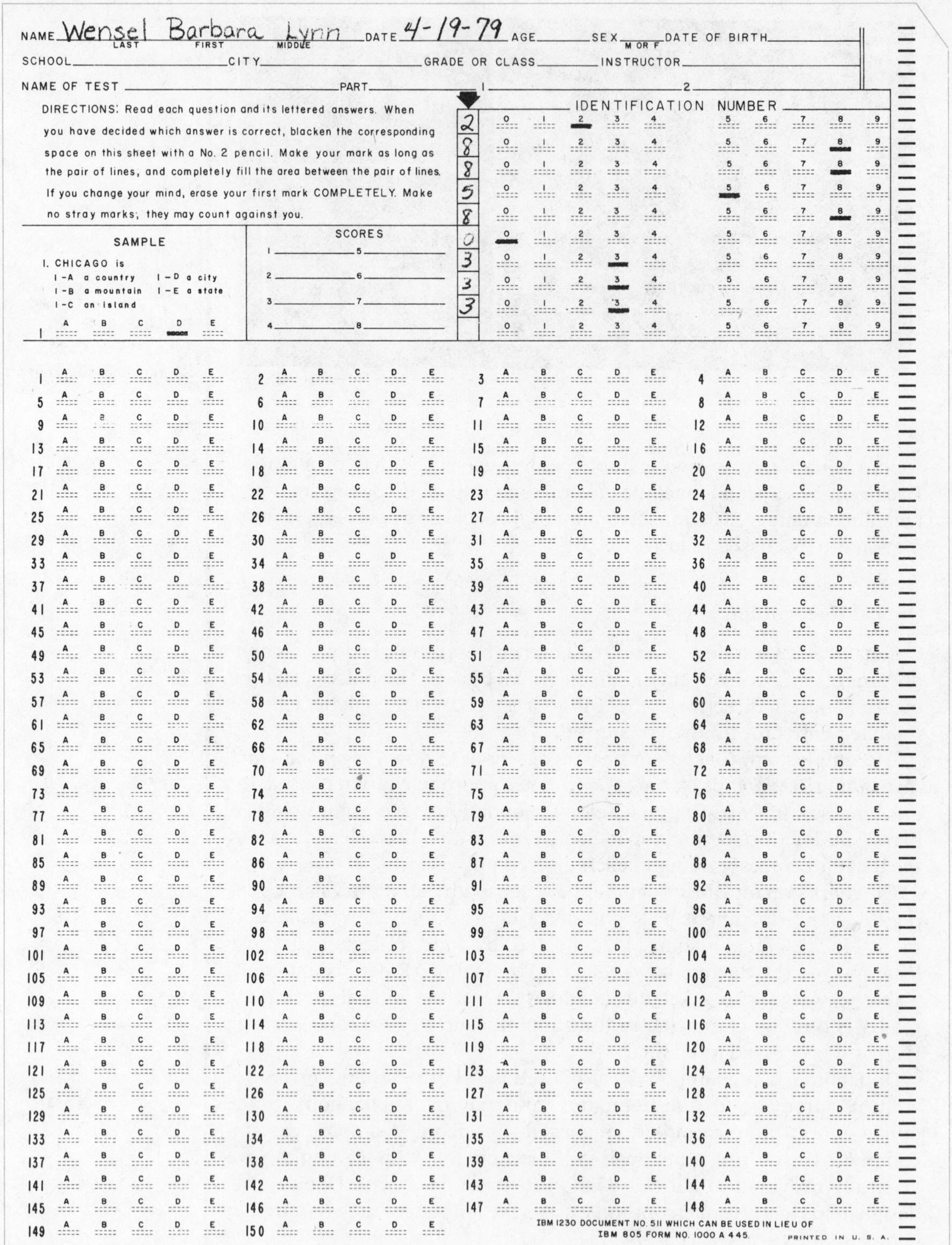
NAME Wensel Barbara Lynn DATE 4-19-79 AGE ____ SEX ____ DATE OF BIRTH ____
LAST FIRST MIDDLE M OR F
SCHOOL ____ CITY ____ GRADE OR CLASS ____ INSTRUCTOR ____
NAME OF TEST ____ PART ____ 1 ____ 2 ____

DIRECTIONS: Read each question and its lettered answers. When you have decided which answer is correct, blacken the corresponding space on this sheet with a No. 2 pencil. Make your mark as long as the pair of lines, and completely fill the area between the pair of lines. If you change your mind, erase your first mark COMPLETELY. Make no stray marks; they may count against you.

IDENTIFICATION NUMBER

2	0	1	2	3	4	5	6	7	8	9
8	0	1	2	3	4	5	6	7	8	9
8	0	1	2	3	4	5	6	7	8	9
5	0	1	2	3	4	5	6	7	8	9
8	0	1	2	3	4	5	6	7	8	9
0	0	1	2	3	4	5	6	7	8	9
3	0	1	2	3	4	5	6	7	8	9
3	0	1	2	3	4	5	6	7	8	9
3	0	1	2	3	4	5	6	7	8	9
	0	1	2	3	4	5	6	7	8	9

SAMPLE

I. CHICAGO is
I-A a country I-D a city
I-B a mountain I-E a state
I-C an island

I A B C D E

SCORES
1 ____ 5 ____
2 ____ 6 ____
3 ____ 7 ____
4 ____ 8 ____

1	A B C D E	2	A B C D E	3	A B C D E	4	A B C D E
5	A B C D E	6	A B C D E	7	A B C D E	8	A B C D E
9	A B C D E	10	A B C D E	11	A B C D E	12	A B C D E
13	A B C D E	14	A B C D E	15	A B C D E	16	A B C D E
17	A B C D E	18	A B C D E	19	A B C D E	20	A B C D E
21	A B C D E	22	A B C D E	23	A B C D E	24	A B C D E
25	A B C D E	26	A B C D E	27	A B C D E	28	A B C D E
29	A B C D E	30	A B C D E	31	A B C D E	32	A B C D E
33	A B C D E	34	A B C D E	35	A B C D E	36	A B C D E
37	A B C D E	38	A B C D E	39	A B C D E	40	A B C D E
41	A B C D E	42	A B C D E	43	A B C D E	44	A B C D E
45	A B C D E	46	A B C D E	47	A B C D E	48	A B C D E
49	A B C D E	50	A B C D E	51	A B C D E	52	A B C D E
53	A B C D E	54	A B C D E	55	A B C D E	56	A B C D E
57	A B C D E	58	A B C D E	59	A B C D E	60	A B C D E
61	A B C D E	62	A B C D E	63	A B C D E	64	A B C D E
65	A B C D E	66	A B C D E	67	A B C D E	68	A B C D E
69	A B C D E	70	A B C D E	71	A B C D E	72	A B C D E
73	A B C D E	74	A B C D E	75	A B C D E	76	A B C D E
77	A B C D E	78	A B C D E	79	A B C D E	80	A B C D E
81	A B C D E	82	A B C D E	83	A B C D E	84	A B C D E
85	A B C D E	86	A B C D E	87	A B C D E	88	A B C D E
89	A B C D E	90	A B C D E	91	A B C D E	92	A B C D E
93	A B C D E	94	A B C D E	95	A B C D E	96	A B C D E
97	A B C D E	98	A B C D E	99	A B C D E	100	A B C D E
101	A B C D E	102	A B C D E	103	A B C D E	104	A B C D E
105	A B C D E	106	A B C D E	107	A B C D E	108	A B C D E
109	A B C D E	110	A B C D E	111	A B C D E	112	A B C D E
113	A B C D E	114	A B C D E	115	A B C D E	116	A B C D E
117	A B C D E	118	A B C D E	119	A B C D E	120	A B C D E
121	A B C D E	122	A B C D E	123	A B C D E	124	A B C D E
125	A B C D E	126	A B C D E	127	A B C D E	128	A B C D E
129	A B C D E	130	A B C D E	131	A B C D E	132	A B C D E
133	A B C D E	134	A B C D E	135	A B C D E	136	A B C D E
137	A B C D E	138	A B C D E	139	A B C D E	140	A B C D E
141	A B C D E	142	A B C D E	143	A B C D E	144	A B C D E
145	A B C D E	146	A B C D E	147	A B C D E	148	A B C D E
149	A B C D E	150	A B C D E				

IBM 1230 DOCUMENT NO. 511 WHICH CAN BE USED IN LIEU OF IBM 805 FORM NO. 1000 A 445.

PRINTED IN U. S. A.

FIGURE 6–8
Optical-Mark Recognition

optical marks. Some of the bar codes in use today are shown in Figure 6–9. They are suitable for many applications, including point-of-sale (POS) systems, credit-card verification, and freight identification to facilitate warehouse operations.

Data representation in a bar code is achieved by the widths of the bars and the distances between them. Probably the most familiar bar code is the *Universal Product Code* (*UPC*) found on most grocery items. This code consists of 10 pairs of vertical bars which represent both the manufacturer's identity and the identity of the item. The code for each product is a unique combination of these vertical bars. The UPC symbol is read by a hand-held *wand reader* or by a fixed scanner linked to a cash-register-like device. The computer system identifies the product, its brand name, and other pertinent information. The price of the item is also available to the computer. It prints out both the name of the item and the price. The computer also keeps track of each item sold and thus aids the store manager in maintaining current inventory status.

Optical-character readers can read special types of characters known as *optical characters*. Some *optical character recognition (OCR)* devices

FIGURE 6–9
Types of Bar Codes

can read characters of several type fonts, including both uppercase and lowercase letters. The most common font is shown in Figure 6–10.

Acceptable OCR input can be produced by computer printers, adding machines, cash registers, accounting machines, and typewriters. Data can be fed into the reader via a *continuous form* such as a cash-register tape, or on *cut forms* such as phone or utility bills. When individual, cut forms are used, the reader can usually sort the forms as well.

A major difference between optical-character recognition and optical-mark recognition is that data is represented by the shapes of characters rather than the positions of marks. However, both OCR and OMR devices rely on reflected light to translate written data into machine-readable form. The most advanced optical-character readers can read handwritten characters also. The handwritten characters must be neat and clear; otherwise, they may not be read correctly (see Figure 6–11). Any characters that cannot be interpreted are rejected by the optical-character readers.

Machine-produced optical-character recognition has been used in credit-card billing, utility billing, and inventory-control applications. Handwritten optical-character recognition has been used widely in sorting mail. The reliability of optical-character recognition systems is generally very good. It is improving as optical-scanning techniques continue to improve.

Remote Terminals

Remote terminals are used to collect data at its source and transmit it to a central computer for processing. Generally, the data is transmitted using telecommunication equipment. Many types of terminals are available. Their use can increase the versatility and expand the applications of the computer.

POS Terminals. Remote terminals that perform the functions of a cash register and also capture sales data are referred to as *point-of-sale (POS) terminals.* Such a terminal has a keyboard for data entry, a panel to display the price, a cash drawer, and a printer that provides a cash receipt. A POS terminal typical of those found in many supermarkets is shown in Figure 6–12.

FIGURE 6–10
OCR Characters

Rule	Correct	Incorrect
1. Write big	0 2 8 3 4	o 2 8 3 4
2. Close loops	0 6 8 8 9	0 6 8 8 9
3. Use simple shapes	0 2 3 7 5	0 2 3 7 5
4. Do not link characters	0 0 8 8 1	0 0 8 8 1
5. Connect lines	4 5 T	4 5 T
6. Block print	C S T X Z	C S T X Z

FIGURE 6–11
Handwritten Optically
Readable Characters

As suggested earlier, some POS terminals have a wand reader that can read the Universal Product Code (UPC) stamped on an item. The sale is registered automatically as the checkout person passes the wand reader over the code. There is no need to enter the item price via a keyboard. Thus, POS terminals enable sales data to be collected at its source. If the terminals are directly connected to a large central computer, useful inventory and sales information can be provided almost instantaneously to the retailer.

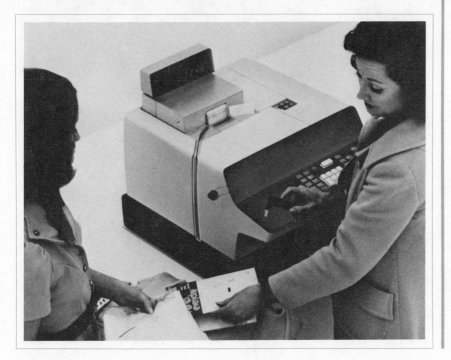

FIGURE 6–12
Point-of-Sale Terminal

Visual-Display Terminals Visual-display terminals display data on a *cathode-ray tube (CRT)* screen similar to that of a television set (see Figure 6–13). A typical screen can hold 24 lines, each containing 80 characters. These terminals supply what is known as *soft-copy* output; that is, they do not provide a permanent record of what is shown on the screen. The terminals are well-suited for applications involving inquiry and response, where no permanent (printed, or hard-copy) records are required. They are also used for entering data to be transmitted from remote offices to a central computer. The data is input via a keyboard on the terminal. It is displayed on the screen as it is keyed, for verification.

Visual-display terminals have some advantages over printer output. First, they can display output much faster than printers. Some CRT terminals can display up to 10,000 characters in a second. Also, they are much quieter in operation than printers. It is usually possible to connect a printer or a copier to a CRT terminal. With this capability, hard-copy output of the screen contents can be provided.

Another type of CRT, known as a *graphic-display device,* is used for displaying drawings as well as characters on a screen (see Figure 6–14). Graphic display devices are generally used to display graphs and charts, but they can also display complex curves and shapes. Data or pictures

FIGURE 6–13
Visual-Display Device

FIGURE 6—14
Graphic-Display Device

displayed on the screen can be altered by using a *light pen*. The light pen is a pen-shaped object with a light-sensitive cell at its end. Lines can be drawn on the screen by specifying the ends of the lines with the light pen. Graphs and line drawings can be altered quickly by applying the light pen at the appropriate locations on the screen.

Touch-Tone Devices Touch-tone devices are used together with ordinary telephone lines to transfer data from remote locations to a central computer. The data is entered via a special keyboard on the terminal. Generally, slight modifications must have been made to the telephone connection to allow data to be transferred over the line.

There are several types of touch-tone devices. One type, shown in Figure 6–15, can read holes punched in cards. This type of terminal is often used to verify credit-card transactions. Another type of touch-tone device can store large amounts of data on a magnetic belt before transmitting it. The magnetic belt is similar to a magnetic tape. This type of terminal is best suited for large-volume processing.

A third type of touch-tone terminal is used in systems offering *audio input/output* capabilities. In these systems, sounds are translated into electrical pulses for transmission over telephone lines. Audio output is achieved through techniques whereby the computer has a vocabulary made up of half-second records of voice sounds. By arranging the records in a particular order, the computer can "speak" to the user. The approach is being used in the banking industry to report customer account balances. It is well-suited for low-volume, highly formal messages.

These types of touch-tone terminals generally have keyboards as an **133**

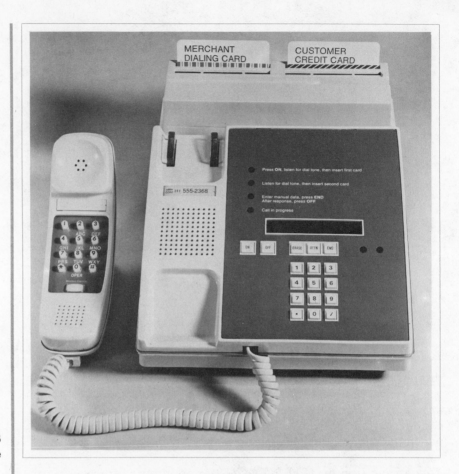

FIGURE 6–15
Touch-Tone Device

alternative form of input. An entire unit may weigh less than 10 pounds. Some are built into briefcases for easy portability (see Figure 6–16).

Intelligent Terminals *Intelligent terminals* can be programmed using stored-program instructions. This capability distinguishes them from other (dumb) terminals (discussed earlier in this chapter), which cannot be programmed. Intelligent terminals have the same kinds of components as a full-sized computer, but they are limited in their storage capability and in the set of instructions they can perform. They are useful for editing data, prior to transferring the data to a central computer. The editing or other manipulating functions are directed by programs stored in the primary storage unit of the terminal.

Most intelligent terminals have a CRT and/or a printer built into them. The CRT is useful when editing data and for displaying responses to inquiries. Its programmable nature extends its applications into other areas. For example, an intelligent terminal can be connected to other I/O devices and used as a stand-alone computer system for low-volume or special-purpose processing. Alternatively, an intelligent terminal can be used to coordinate data entry from non-programmable terminals at other locations. In this case, the data is transmitted to the intelligent terminal for editing and validation. It is transmitted later as a part of batched input from the intelligent terminal to a large central computer.

The use of intelligent terminals will continue to grow as their cost continues to decrease and new applications in which to use them are discovered. They can help in many ways to make data entry and retrieval easier for the user.

SPECIAL-PURPOSE OUTPUT

Plotters

A *plotter* is an output device that converts data emitted from the CPU into graphic form. It can produce lines, curves, and complex shapes. The key difference between a plotter and a graphic-display device is that the plotter produces hard-copy output (paper) whereas the graphic-display device produces soft-copy output (CRT screen image).

A plotter has a pen, movable carriage, drum, and chart-paper holder (see Figure 6–17). Shapes are produced as the pen moves back and forth

FIGURE 6—16
Touch-Tone Audio Terminal

135

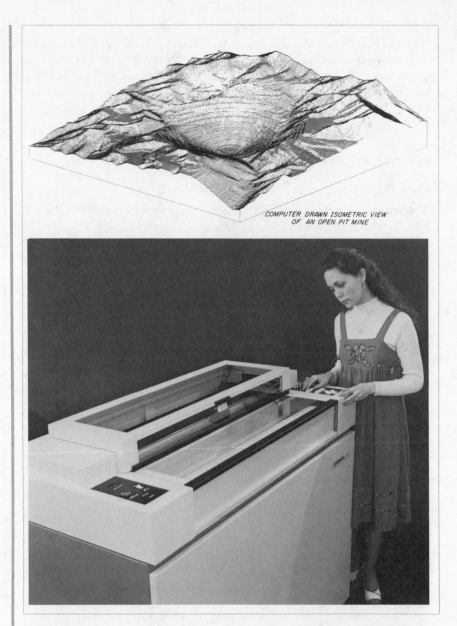

COMPUTER DRAWN ISOMETRIC VIEW
OF AN OPEN PIT MINE

FIGURE 6—17
Plotter

across the paper along a y-axis while the drum moves the paper up and down along the x-axis. Both the paper movement and the pen movement are bi-directional. The pen can be raised and lowered from the paper surface automatically.

The plotter can be used to produce line and bar charts, graphs, organizational charts, engineering drawings, maps, trend lines, supply and demand curves, and so on. The figures are drawn precisely because the pen can be positioned at up to 45,000 points in each square inch of paper. Some new plotters can produce drawings in several colors. The usefulness of the plotter lies in its ability to communicate information in easy-to-understand picture form.

Computer Output Microfilm (COM)

In situations where large volumes of information must be printed and stored for future reference, conventional paper output is not appropriate. It uses much storage space, and particular portions of it are often difficult to access. A possible alternative is *computer output microfilm (COM),* which consists of photographed images produced in miniature using the computer. In some cases, the output is first recorded on magnetic tape. Special photocopying equipment is then used to reproduce the information on the tape in microfilm. In an online operation, the COM equipment is used to display output on a CRT screen. The screen is exposed to microfilm. The microfilm copy can be produced as a roll of film or a 4 × 6″ microfiche card. In such a system, the speed of recording can be 25 to 50 times faster than printing (see Figure 6–18).

The main advantage of COM is that much data can be stored compactly. This reduces both space requirements and storage costs. Character and graphic output can be recorded. Use of a forms-overlay permits headings to be printed and lines superimposed so that output is highly readable. The cost of producing additional microfilm copies is very low. However, high initial investment costs, and the inability to retrieve microfilmed data directly by the computer, have been offsetting disadvantages.

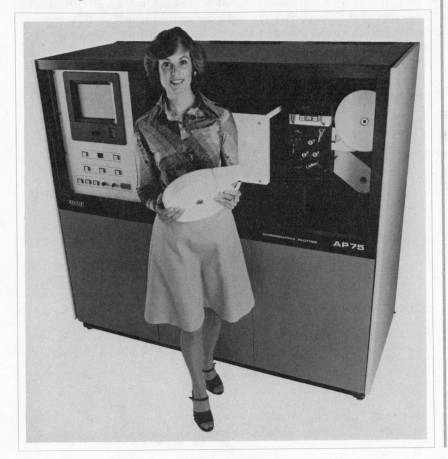

FIGURE 6–18
Producing Computer Output Microfilm

INPUT/OUTPUT OPERATIONS

Control Units

One of the key functions of the I/O subsystem of a computer system is the conversion of data into machine-readable code. For instance, data on punched cards must be converted from Hollerith code into a machine code such as ASCII or BCD. Code conversion must also be performed when data is entered from devices such as remote terminals and magnetic-ink character readers. The code conversion is performed by a device known as an I/O *control unit*. This control unit is different from the control unit of the CPU. It is located between one or more I/O devices and the CPU, and is used only to facilitate I/O operations.

Besides code conversion, I/O control units perform another important function known as *data buffering*. A *buffer* is a separate storage unit (normally contained in the I/O control unit) for a particular input or output device. It is used as a temporary holding area for data being transferred to or from the CPU.

When data is read by an input unit, it is converted to machine code and stored in a buffer. Once a certain amount of data has been collected in the buffer, it is transferred to the CPU as directed. The buffer allows a large quantity of data to be transferred much faster than all the data items could be transferred, individually. For example, a buffer is used to temporarily hold data being entered from a remote terminal. This allows an entire record to be keyed on the terminal, held, and transferred all at once to the CPU. While the record is being keyed, the CPU processes other data (see Figure 6–19). The buffer serves a similar purpose when information is transferred from the computer to a printer or terminal as output.

Channels

Although the CPU is very fast and accurate, it can execute only one instruction at a time. If it is executing an instruction that indicates an input or output operation, it must wait until that operation is completed before it can continue. Compared with CPU internal processing speeds, I/O speeds are extremely slow. Even high-speed I/O devices often work only 1/10 as fast as the CPU. When the CPU is slowed down because of I/O operations, the system is said to be *input/output-bound*.

	TIME 1	TIME 2	TIME 3
INPUT	Item 1		
PROCESS		Item 1	
OUTPUT			Item 1

The CPU is input/output-bound. It can operate on only one item at a time.

The flow of data above indicates that in this system the CPU does the PROCESS step when it can, but it sits idle most of the time, waiting for

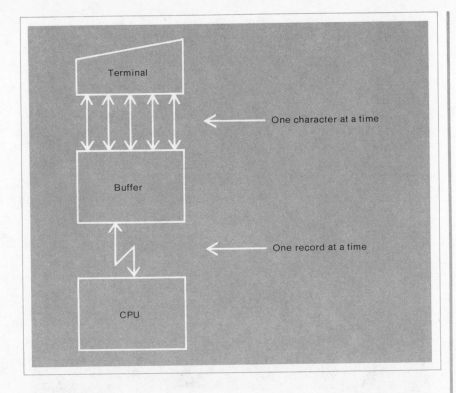

FIGURE 6—19
Data Buffering

INPUT and OUTPUT to occur. To alleviate such situations, *channels* have been developed. Channels take over the tasks of input and output from the CPU. Each channel is a small, limited-capacity computer. It serves as a data roadway upon command from the CPU. It may be within the CPU or a separate piece of equipment connected to the CPU. Because the channel handles I/O operations, the CPU is relieved of its responsibility for data transfer (and, therefore, its need to wait).

	TIME 1	TIME 2	TIME 3
INPUT	Item 1	Item 2	Item 3
PROCESS		Item 1	Item 2
OUTPUT			Item 1

With the aid of channels, the CPU is active a greater percentage of the time.

There are two types of channels: selector and multiplexor. A *selector channel* can accept input from only one device at a time. It is used with a high-speed I/O device such as a magnetic-tape or magnetic-disk unit. A *multiplexor channel* can handle more than one I/O device at a time. It is normally associated with slow-speed devices such as printers, card readers, or terminals (see Figure 6–20).

139

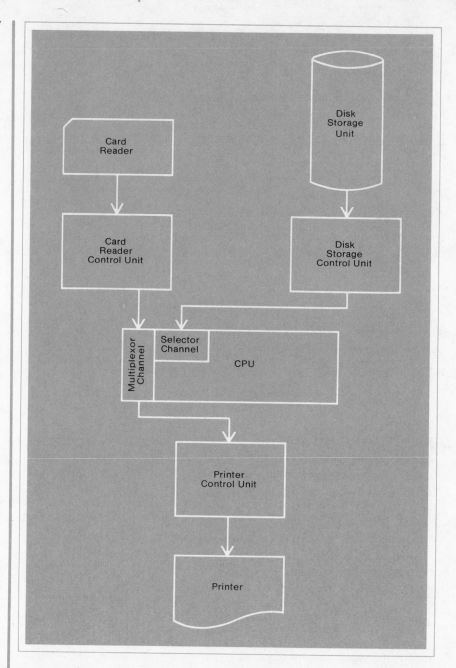

FIGURE 6—20
Channels, Control Units, and
I/O Devices

SUMMARY

● Magnetic-ink characters can be read by humans, and also by machines since they are magnetically inscribed. Magnetic-ink character readers (MICRs) can convert the magnetic characters into machine code for computer processing. MICRs are used extensively for processing checks by the banking industry.

• Key-to-tape and key-to-disk devices are being used increasingly because they overcome the disadvantages of punched cards. Tapes and disks are reusable; they can store more data in less space; and data transfer rates are at least 25 times faster than those possible with cards. These devices also allow verification, formatting, and editing of data as it is recorded.

• Source-data automation refers to collecting data at the points where transactions occur. Common approaches to source-data automation employ optical-recognition devices and other types of remote terminals.

• Optical-mark recognition devices can sense marks made with a heavy lead pencil and convert them into machine code. Other optical-character recognition devices are capable of reading bar codes, documents printed with different type fonts, and even handwritten characters. The main advantage of optical-character recognition is that it eliminates the intermediate process of transcribing data from source documents to an input medium.

• Remote terminals can collect data at its source and transmit it over communication lines for processing by a central computer. Included in this category are point-of-sale (POS) terminals, visual-display devices, touch-tone devices, and intelligent terminals. Each device satisfies distinct needs for input and output. Which device is most appropriate for a certain application depends on the particular I/O requirements of the application.

• Special-purpose output devices include plotters and computer output microfilm (COM) equipment. A plotter can represent computer output in hard-copy graphic form. COM consists of miniature photographed images of computer output. It is suitable for applications involving large volumes of information because it uses less space, thereby reducing storage costs. Disadvantages are high initial investment costs and the computer's inability to directly retrieve microfilmed data.

• I/O control units and channels are used in an I/O subsystem to increase the efficiency of the CPU. Buffers are temporary holding areas which allow faster transfer of data. A control unit converts input data into machine code, and vice versa. It is used in data buffering.

• Channels control I/O operations and free the CPU to do other processing. This allows input, output, and processing to overlap. Selector channels can accommodate only one I/O device at a time. They are used with high-speed devices like magnetic-tape and magnetic-disk units. Multiplexor channels can accommodate multiple I/O devices. They are often used with slow-speed devices such as printers, card readers, or terminals.

REVIEW QUESTIONS

1. Which I/O device is used extensively by the banking industry? Explain how this device works.

2. What advantages are offered by key-to-tape and key-to-disk devices over traditional keypunching? What are some disadvantages of key-to-tape data entry?

3. Explain source-data automation.

4. Discuss three types of optical-recognition devices. Identify applications where each type can be used to advantage.

5. What advantages do visual-display terminals offer over conventional printers?

6. What is an intelligent terminal? Give some examples.

7. What functions does an I/O control unit perform?

8. What are channels used for? Distinguish between selector channels and multiplexor channels.

The Federal Reserve Act of 1913 provided the guidelines for establishing the Federal Reserve System. The primary function of the Federal Reserve System is to regulate monetary and credit conditions. This function involves the creation and destruction of money internally, and the regulation of the creation and destruction of money by commercial banks. Other important functions include check clearing and collection, acting as the fiscal agent for the government, and engaging in operations in the foreign-exchange market.

The internal demands of user departments within the Federal Reserve Bank of Cincinnati, and the external demands of commercial banks, are met by two large computers. A Burroughs B3500 is used to satisfy the processing require-ments of the bank itself. The primary applications run on this computer are general-ledger/accounting functions, fiscal-agency operations, and payroll functions.

The largest department involved in data processing is the check area, which employs 110 people. The CPU that processes checks is a Burroughs B4732 with 150,000 bytes of primary memory and 100,000,000 bytes of disk storage. This computer is extremely important to the bank because check clearing and collection is the most demanding service provided to commercial banks by the Federal Reserve System.

The complexity of check clearing and collection activities is overwhelming. All

FEDERAL RESERVE BANK OF CINCINNATI

143

checks must be sorted and sent in batches to appropriate endpoints. A cash letter indicating the number and dollar value of the enclosed checks accompanies each batch. The initial sorting of these checks takes place on a high-speed reader/sorter manufactured by Burroughs Corporation. The machine handles the majority of checks processed daily (an average of 1.1 million checks per day were handled by the bank in April 1978). Approximately 1.4 percent of the checks contain magnetic-ink characters that cannot be read by the machine. These rejects, added to the reject items deposited by area banks, total nearly 40,000 items per day.

Checks that are rejected by the Burroughs high-speed reader/sorter present serious complications for the bank. The checks have to be read manually, then sorted using a very slow IBM machine. The machine can sort a maximum of 32 locations in one pass of the checks through it. Three or four passes have to be made before the checks are finally ready for shipment. Thus, this processing is extremely tedious and time-consuming.

To alleviate the difficulties encountered in processing checks with unreadable magnetic-ink characters, the Federal Reserve Bank of Cincinnati is evaluating the feasibility of implementing the 7750 Distributed Document Processing System manufactured by NCR Corporation. The system is designed to process documents bearing universal MICR and OCR fonts. Figure 6–21 is a schematic of the system.

Checks can be entered into the 7750 system through an automatic feed hopper or by hand dropping. Fully encoded checks, processed by the bank, are entered through the automatic feed

hopper since it is more convenient and much faster. Each check passes a reader that reads the MICR encoding on the check. The operator station is linked to a general-purpose, programmable minicomputer that supplies the intelligence necessary to interpret the MICR data. The CPU is programmed to validate the transit number, transaction code (deposit or withdrawal), customer account number, and dollar amount of the check.

If the amount field is not encoded on the check, the operator keys in the handwritten amount and places the check in the transport. The entire MICR line is read, validated, and compared with applicable tables within the program in the minicomputer. If a required field is missing, unreadable, or invalid, the program can cause the document to stop at the document view station. A light display indicates the field. The operator must then enter the correct data.

Once validated and accepted, the keyboard-entered and MICR-read data is captured on a magnetic medium. The check proceeds down the transport, where any programmed field encoding is accomplished, any programmed endorsing is done, and a bank stamp is applied. A microfilmer records both sides of the check on tape, and the check proceeds to a programmed pocket destination.

One application at the Federal Reserve Bank of Cincinnati deals exclusively with items rejected by the reader/sorter. If we assume the 7750 system is implemented, that application is processed as follows. Since the reject items are fully encoded, they are entered from the automatic feed hopper. Operator action is required only for fields deemed invalid or unreadable by

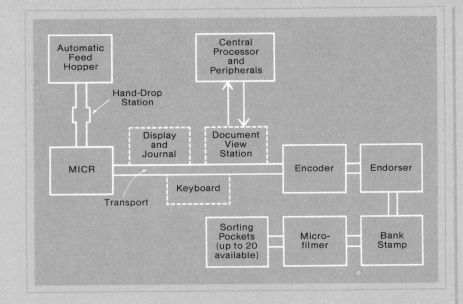

FIGURE 6–21
Check-Processing
Sequence

the reader logic and the program. No encoding is required. An audit-trail number is placed on the back of each document in place of the normal endorsement. The MICR data is captured on magnetic tape, and a variety of totals is maintained. A balancing item is entered at the end of the reject run, to indicate that the entire batch has been processed.

Although more than one pass is still required to sort the checks, the remaining passes can be accomplished with little operator intervention. The magnetic tape can be mounted on a large Burroughs computer at the end of the day, and the cash letters that must accompany the checks can be computer-generated. (The preparation of these cash letters formerly had to be done manually by totaling at the end of the day the dollar values of all batches of reject checks that were to be delivered to the commercial banks involved.)

If the 7750 Distributed Document Processing System is implemented, the Federal Reserve Bank will be able to reduce its number of employees. It will be able to speed up its check clearing and collection activities. Increased capabilities are provided by this equipment. For example, the MICR will permit computer verification of data elements that now have to be verified manually. The collection of source data on magnetic tape will eliminate the manual preparation of cash letters. The capabilities provided by this equipment will permit efficiencies that were once impossible.

DISCUSSION POINTS

1. How does the Federal Reserve Bank of Cincinnati use source-data automation to speed check processing?

2. Would it be possible to process checks using optical characters rather than magnetic-ink characters? Support your answer.

145

STORAGE DEVICES | 7

OUTLINE

I. Storage-Media Classifications
  A. Main Storage
  B. Auxiliary Storage
  C. Sequential-Access vs.
     Direct-Access
II. Sequential-Access Storage
  A. Paper Tape
    1. Data Representation
    2. Utilization
    3. Advantages and
      Disadvantages
  B. Magnetic Tape
    1. Data Representation
    2. Characteristics
    3. Advantages and
      Disadvantages

III. Direct-Access Storage
  A. Magnetic Disk
    1. Characteristics
    2. Disk Packs
    3. Data Access
    4. Flexible Disk
  B. Advantages and Disadvantages
IV. Mass Storage
  A. Advantages and Disadvantages
  B. Characteristics
V. Future Trends in Data Storage
  A. Charge-Coupled Devices
  B. Laser Technology

INTRODUCTION

Organizations store large volumes of data for a variety of purposes. When an organization uses electronic methods of processing data, most of the data must be stored in computer-accessible form. Some media have dual functions. For example, magnetic tapes and disks, which were mentioned in the previous chapter, are used for input and output, and also for data storage. It is important to know how data is stored in a computer system.

This chapter distinguishes between main storage and auxiliary storage. Auxiliary storage devices are further classified according to whether they provide sequential access or direct access to stored data. The most common sequential-access and direct-access storage media are magnetic tapes and magnetic disks. Both are explained in considerable detail here. The chapter also describes paper tape. The major advantages and disadvantages of mass storage systems are discussed.

**MICRO-BASED
BALL SERVER
AIMED AT TENNIS
BUFFS**

Computerworld,
March 27, 1978, p. 17

LANSDALE, PA. The DPer who enjoys hitting a few tennis balls after work now can test his ground strokes against a microprocessor-controlled tennis ball thrower from the United States Machine Works, Inc.

Dubbed "The System," the MOS Technology, Inc., 6504-based unit allows tennis players to program any sequence of up to 99 shots to different court locations, at different speeds, and with different delays between shots.

The $4000 ball launcher even comes with a removable control panel that allows players the joy of bringing it home to pre-program for the next day's practice session. In addition, there is a six-function remote control unit that permits players to control the unit from anywhere on the court.

As an additional feature for the player too harried to pre-program a session, The System will program itself for both singles and doubles.

And for the player who demands the privacy of his own home, United States Machine Works will design full- or half-length practice alleys to meet the player's individual requirements.

Information on installation and prices can be obtained from the firm at 21 Williams Place, Lansdale, Pa. 19446.

This tennis ball thrower uses a tape cassette to store instructions for up to 99 shots. The reason why this type of storage is best for this application is explained in the following chapter. Other types of auxiliary storage are also discussed.

148

STORAGE-MEDIA CLASSIFICATIONS

A computer system contains two types of storage: main storage and auxiliary storage. *Main storage,* which was discussed in Chapter 3, is considered part of the CPU. It is used to store both data and instructions. The most common main-storage media are magnetic cores and semiconductor circuits. Other media such as magnetic bubbles (bubble memory) are also used.

Auxiliary, or *secondary, storage* is not part of the CPU. The most common auxiliary-storage media are magnetic tapes and magnetic disks. Other media such as paper tape, punched cards, and magnetic drums are also used. Auxiliary storage is used to store large amounts of data at a lower cost than would be possible if the data were kept in main storage. Since auxiliary storage devices are connected to the CPU, the data can be read into main storage for processing, and the results can be written back to auxiliary storage (see Figure 7–1). By augmenting main storage in this manner, auxiliary storage greatly enhances the capabilities of a computer system.

Data in auxiliary storage can be accessed either directly or sequentially. A medium such as magnetic tape or paper tape must be read sequentially until the needed data is located. These media provide

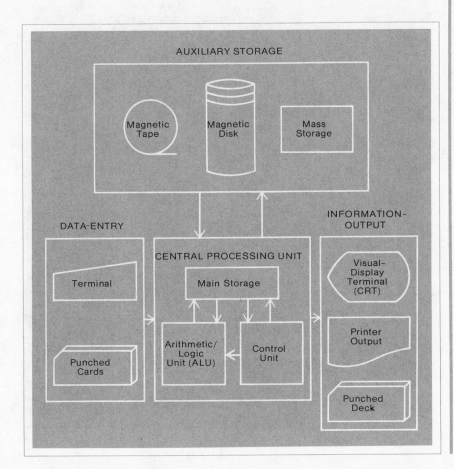

FIGURE 7–1
Computer-System Schematic

149

sequential-access storage. In contrast, a medium such as magnetic disk or magnetic drum does not have to be read sequentially. These media provide *direct-access storage.* Data on direct-access storage can be located much faster than data on sequential-access storage. Many computer systems have both sequential-access and direct-access storage devices.

SEQUENTIAL-ACCESS STORAGE

Paper Tape

Paper tape is a storage medium that resembles cash register or adding machine tape. The tape is a continuous strip, wound on a reel. Data is recorded as vertical combinations of circular holes in the tape. A paper-tape punch is used to record the data (see Figure 7–2). The punching operation is a relatively slow mechanical process similar to that used in punching cards.

Paper tape is sometimes punched in an auxiliary operation performed at the same time that documents are printed or cards punched. For instance, a paper-tape punch can be connected to a typewriter-like

FIGURE 7–2
Paper-Tape Punch

device, and the tape can be punched at the same time that invoices or other messages are typed by the operator.

The data stored on paper tape is read by a paper-tape reader, which translates the punched holes in the tape into electrical pulses. The paper-tape reader can read data stored on tape at speeds ranging from 350 to 2000 characters per second.

One method of representing data on paper tape is via an eight-channel code (see Figure 7–3). The length of the tape is divided into eight horizontal rows, or *channels*. Data is represented vertically, one character per column. The four lower channels (1,2,4,8) are used for numeric data. The digits 0 through 9 are represented by one or more punches in the appropriate channels. As with binary coded decimal, the sum of the position values tells the value that is represented. The X and 0 channels are known as zone punches. They are used in combination with the four lower channels to represent alphabetic and special characters. The check row aids in checking the validity of characters. An eighth channel is provided as an end-of-line channel. A punch in this channel indicates to the tape reader that the end of a record has been reached. Besides eight-channel code, data can be represented on paper tape in five-, six-, and seven-channel codes.

Paper tape can be used as both an input and an output medium in a computer system. It is more often used as an I/O medium with telecommunication equipment transmitting messages to remote places.

Paper tape has several advantages over punched cards as an I/O medium. More data can be stored in a smaller space, and record lengths are not limited by card boundaries. Paper tape is inexpensive, costing even less than cards, and can be read faster than punched cards.

The major disadvantage of paper tape is difficulty in adding or deleting data. Because paper tape is a continuous medium and cannot be erased, changes can only be made either by cutting out unwanted parts of the tape and splicing the ends together or by repunching the entire tape. Normally, paper tape is used for computer input only when relatively small amounts of data are processed.

Magnetic Tape

Like paper tape, *magnetic tape* is a narrow strip capable of holding data. The width of magnetic tape is usually ½ inch, but tape widths of ¾ inch, 1 inch, and 3 inches are also used. The tape is usually stored on a reel that is 10½ inches in diameter. The amount of tape that can fit on one reel ranges from 50 to 3600 feet.

In contrast to paper tape, data is stored on magnetic tape by

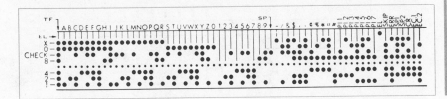

FIGURE 7–3

Paper Tape with Eight-Channel Code

151

magnetizing small areas on the magnetic coating of iron oxide on the surface of the tape. The magnetized areas on the surface of the tape are too small to be seen by the human eye. Because of their small size, a large quantity of data can be stored on a short length of tape. A typical tape reel can hold 2400 feet of tape and can store as much data as 400,000 punched cards.

Magnetic tape is similar to home tape-recorder tape; data can be recorded or stored, played back at a later date, or erased and replaced with new data. A common method of representing data on tape uses a nine-track coding scheme (see Figure 7–4). The tape is divided horizontally into nine channels, or *tracks*. As with paper tape, data is represented vertically. Each character is made up of a combination of magnetized areas (bits) in one vertical column. This method of coding data is identical to the Extended Binary Coded Decimal Interchange Code (EBCDIC) used to represent data in internal storage.

A magnetic tape must be mounted on a *tape drive* (see Figure 7–5) when it is to be used as input to a computer system. The tape drive has a *read/write head* that is actually an electromagnet (see Figure 7–6). The read/write head detects the magnetized areas of the tape as it moves past the head. They are converted into electrical pulses which are sent to the CPU. When data is written on the tape, the head magnetizes the appropriate areas on the tape and erases any data stored previously.

The number of characters that can be stored on one inch of tape is called the *density* of the tape. The storage capacity of the tape depends in part on its density. Current densities range from 100 to more than 6000 bytes per inch. The most common densities are 800 and 1600. The density of the tape and the speed that it travels past the read/write head determine how fast data can be transferred from the tape to the CPU. For example, if a tape has a density of 800 characters per inch, and the tape moves at a speed of 112.5 inches per second, then the data is transferred at a speed of 90,000 characters per second (CPS). Typical tape speeds range from 18.7 to 200 inches per second.

Individual records on magnetic tape are separated by *interrecord gaps* (*IRGs*) as shown in Figure 7–7. These gaps are spaces where no data is stored. When data is read from tape, the tape stops whenever an IRG is detected. After processing of the record has occurred, the remainder of

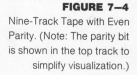

FIGURE 7–4
Nine-Track Tape with Even Parity. (Note: The parity bit is shown in the top track to simplify visualization.)

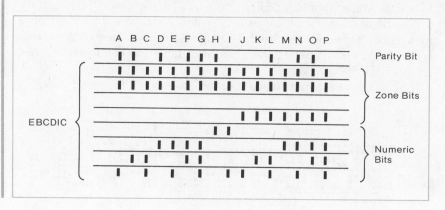

152

FIGURE 7—5
Magnetic-Tape Drive

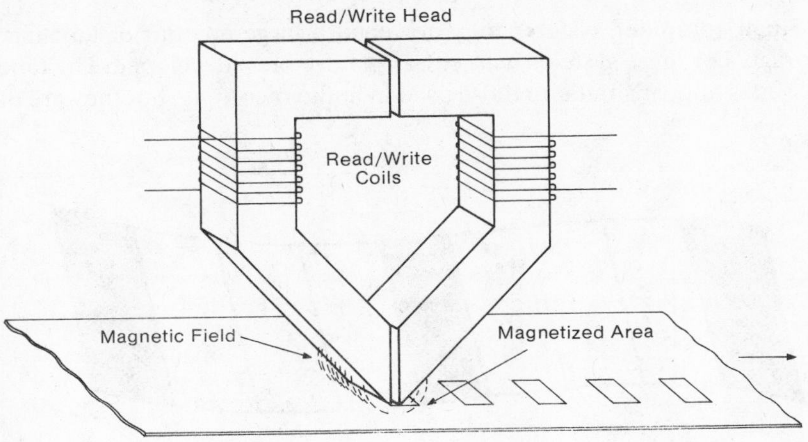

FIGURE 7—6
Recording on Magnetic
Tape

Read/Write Head

Read/Write
Coils

Magnetic Field

Magnetized Area

153

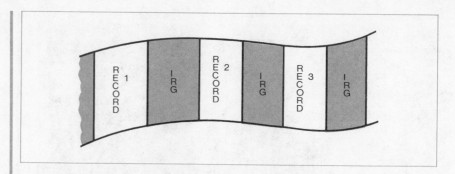

FIGURE 7–7
Magnetic-Tape Records

the gap allows the tape drive to regain speed. During reading or writing, the magnetic tape must move at a certain constant speed past the read/write head. The drive must always have time to reach that speed before the read/write process begins. Thus, the interrecord gap length is dependent upon the acceleration speed of the tape drive. Longer gaps are needed for a higher read/write speed so as to permit the tape drive to reach that speed.

Record lengths are not limited by the physical characteristics of magnetic tape. Therefore, tape is more versatile with respect to record length than punched cards. If records are very short and divided by equally long IRGs, the tape may be more than 50 percent blank. The tape drive must be constantly stopping and accelerating. To avoid this possibility, records may be grouped, or blocked. The *blocked records*, or *blocks*, are separated by *interblock gaps* (*IBGs*) (see Figure 7–8). Now, instead of reading a short record and stopping, reading a short record and stopping, and so on, the read/write head reads a group of short records at once and then stops, reads another group and stops, and so on. This method reduces the overall processing time because the tape drive does not spend so much time starting and stopping. An entire block of records is read into a buffer, and individual records are transferred from the buffer to primary storage for processing. Blocking also limits wasted space on the tape. This permits more records to be stored on one reel.

Small computer systems may not need a large amount of auxiliary storage. For these systems, *tape cassettes* have been developed. The tape cassettes appear similar to those used in audio recording, but they are of

FIGURE 7–8
Blocked Records

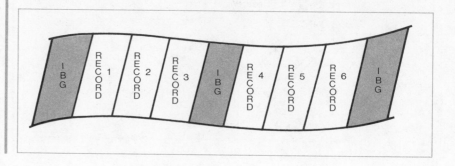

higher quality, suitable for high-density digital recording (see Figure 7–9). The densities range from 125 to 200 characters per inch, and the common tape length is between 150 and 200 feet. Because of the low cost and convenience of tape cassettes, their use for input, output, and storage has increased greatly in small computer systems.

Magnetic tape has many advantages over a storage medium such as punched cards or paper tape:

● Data can be transferred to and from magnetic tape, to and from the CPU, at high speeds.

● Magnetic-tape records can have any number of characters, whereas card records are usually limited to 80 characters.

● Magnetic tapes, because of their high density, require less storage space than cards.

● The erasable nature of magnetic tape allows it to be reused for different data.

● Magnetic tape can provide large-capacity storage and backup storage at a relatively low cost. A 2400-foot magnetic tape costs about $15.

● Magnetic tape is perfectly suited for sequential or batch processing. It is the most common medium in these types of systems.

The disadvantages of magnetic tape follow:

● Since tape is a sequential medium, the entire tape must be read when updating. The amount of time required for updating and accessing records precludes it from being used where instantaneous retrieval of data is required.

FIGURE 7–9
Tape Cassette

● All tapes and reel containers must be labeled for identification purposes.

● The data on magnetic tape is not readable by humans. When the validity of magnetic-tape data is questioned, the contents of the tape must be printed.

● The environment can distort data stored on magnetic tape. Dust, moisture, high or low temperatures, and static electricity can cause improper processing. Therefore, the environment must be carefully controlled.

DIRECT-ACCESS STORAGE

Magnetic Disk

A *magnetic disk* is a metal platter similar to a phonograph record. It is coated on both sides with a magnetic recording material. The physical similarity ends here, though. Records have grooves that spiral into the center, but a disk has no grooves; it has concentric circles called *tracks*. The tracks are enclosed within each other without touching each other (see Figure 7–10). Usually, several disks are assembled to form a *disk*

FIGURE 7–10
Top View of Disk Surface
Showing Concentric Tracks

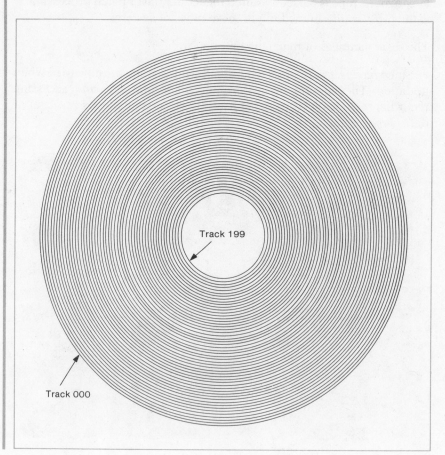

pack (see Figure 7–11). They are connected by a center shaft that spins all disks in the pack at the same time. All the number-1 tracks on the disk surfaces form a *cylinder;* the number-2 tracks on all surfaces form another cylinder enclosed within the first; and so on. There are usually 200 separate tracks on each disk, and, therefore, 200 cylinders in each pack. Data is stored by magnetizing spots on the disk's tracks.

The data is read or written by read/write heads between the disks. Most disk units have one read/write head for each disk recording surface. All read/write heads are permanently connected to an *access mechanism.* When reading or writing occurs, the heads are positioned over the appropriate track by in-and-out movement of the access mechanism. As the access mechanism moves, all read/write heads move in unison (see Figure 7–12). Some disk units have as many as one read/write head for each track. The access time is much faster with this type of disk unit, since the access mechanism does not need to move from track to track. But these disk units are rarely used because of their high cost.

The top surface of the top disk in a pack and the bottom surface of the bottom disk are not used for storing data because they are likely to be scratched or nicked. Thus, if a disk pack contains 11 disks, there are 20 recording surfaces and 20 read/write heads. A disk pack may contain from 5 to 100 disks. The disks may range from 15 inches to 3 feet in diameter.

A disk pack must be positioned in a disk storage unit when the data on the pack is to be processed. The *disk drive* rotates all disks in unison at a speed ranging from 40 to 1000 revolutions per second. In some models,

FIGURE 7–11
Disk Pack

157

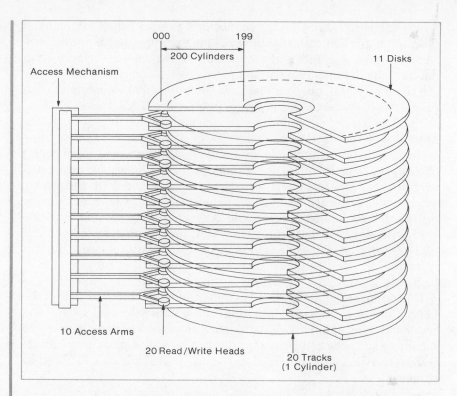

FIGURE 7–12

Access Mechanism of
Disk Unit

the disk packs are removable; in others, the disks are permanently mounted on the disk drive. Removable disk packs allow disk files to be removed when the data they contain is not needed. Systems with removable disk packs typically have many more disk packs than disk drives (see Figure 7–13).

Data stored on a magnetic disk is accessed by disk surface number, track number, and record number. This access information constitutes a

FIGURE 7–13

Disk Storage Units with
Removable Disk Packs

disk address. The disk address of a record immediately precedes the record (see Figure 7–14). Note that disk records are separated by gaps similar to the interrecord gaps on magnetic tape. Thus, more data can be stored on a track by blocking several records together and reducing the number of gaps.

Just as a stereo record needle can be placed anywhere on a phonograph record, the read/write heads of an access mechanism can be positioned directly over any track without reading other tracks to get to it. The appropriate read/write head is then activated, and the track is searched for the desired record. Depending upon the particular disk drive, read speeds of up to 850,000 characters per second are possible. Due to this direct-access capability, disks are used for online file updating. They are also used when frequent inquiries of data files are required.

A more recent innovation that allows for even easier handling is the *flexible disk*, also called a *floppy disk* or *diskette* (see Figure 7–15). Introduced in 1973 to replace punched cards as a medium for data entry, these disks are used to store programs and data files. The disks are made of plastic and sell for considerably less than traditional disks—often as little as $4. One disk has a storage capacity equivalent to that of 3000 punched cards. It is reusable and easy to store, and can be mailed. As with other magnetic disks, data can be read as often as necessary from a

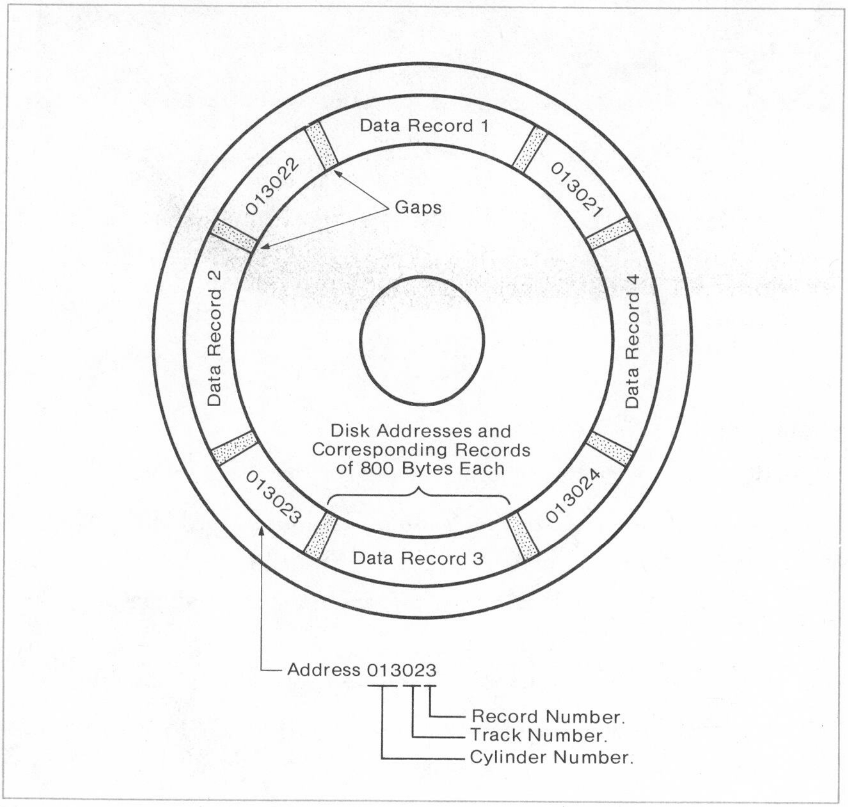

FIGURE 7–14
Disk Address

159

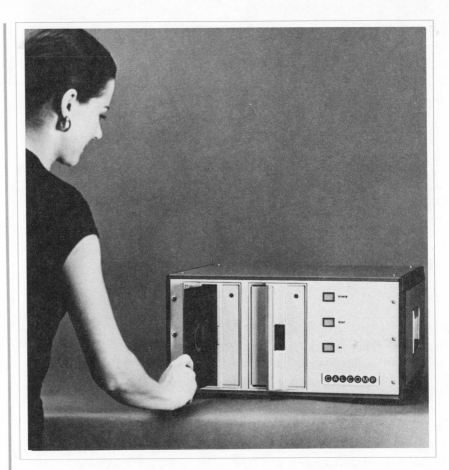

FIGURE 7—15
Flexible Disk

track location; and, similar to other disks, all previous data on an area of disk is lost when new data is written on the area. Although floppy disks are most frequently found on point-of-sale terminals and minicomputers, some large computers use floppy disks to store important control programs.

Advantages and Disadvantages

Magnetic-disk storage has several advantages over magnetic tape:

● Disk files can be organized sequentially and processed like magnetic tape, or they can be organized for direct-access processing.

● The fast access time offered by magnetic-disk storage allows data files to be updated immediately.

● Quick response can be made to inquiries (normally, in seconds).

● Files stored on disks can be linked by software (stored-program instructions) to allow a single transaction to update all files simultaneously.

The major disadvantages of magnetic-disk storage follow:

● Magnetic disk is a relatively expensive storage medium; it may cost 10 times as much as magnetic tape in terms of cost per character stored. However, reductions in disk costs and the introduction of flexible disks are making these storage devices more attractive from a cost standpoint.

● When disk files are updated, the original data is erased and the new data is put in its place. Therefore, there is no backup file in the event of an error. If there are no other provisions for error checking and backup files, errors can go undetected.

● Disk storage requires more sophisticated programming for accessing records and updating files. The hardware itself is also highly sophisticated, and skilled technicians are required for maintenance.

● Security may be a problem, due to the ease of accessing disk files.

MASS STORAGE

Primary storage is very fast because data can be accessed directly without any physical movement. The speed of electricity is, in effect, the limiting factor. However, primary storage is also very expensive. Disk storage is less expensive, and it is fast enough to be used for direct access. But disk storage tends to be an inappropriate alternative from a cost standpoint when very large amounts of data must be stored for direct-access processing.

To meet this need, *mass storage devices* have been developed. They allow rapid access to data, although access times are much slower than those of primary storage or magnetic disk. Large files, backup files, and infrequently used files can be placed in mass storage at a relatively low cost.

One approach to mass storage uses a cartridge tape as the storage medium. The cartridges are similar to cassette tapes; however, since high-density tape is used, there is a 90 percent reduction in storage space needed compared to that of a common magnetic tape. A cartridge-oriented system generally contains a control unit, a reel-selector mechanism, a reel-mounting mechanism, and a tape-drive unit. When a particular set of data is needed, a command is sent from the computer to the control unit of the mass storage device. The control unit then signals the reel-selector mechanism to select the needed cartridge. The reel-mounting mechanism mounts the cartridge on a tape-drive unit. The data is read or written by read/write heads. The same mechanical process is used to remount the cartridge in its original location. A mass storage system such as this can hold the equivalent of up to 8000 tape reels.

Another cartridge-oriented mass storage system uses a slightly different approach. Instead of a cassette-tape cartridge, small sections (about 100 to 200 inches) of magnetic tape are kept in spools and stored in a cartridge. These cartridges are stored in a group of cells which resembles a honeycomb. When a particular data set is needed, the tape cartridge containing it is removed from a storage cell and moved to a read/write station. Here, the tape is removed from the cartridge and wrapped around a drum positioned near the read/write heads. After the data has been read or written, the tape is rewound, placed in the cartridge, and returned to its original location (see Figure 7–16).

Mass storage is not limited to high-density magnetic tape. Recently, a mass storage system for minicomputers using small floppy disks as the storage medium was introduced. However, most mass storage devices require extensive physical movement because the needed files must be found and mounted mechanically before data can be read or written. Although direct access is possible, the retrieval time is relatively slow (normally measured in seconds).

FUTURE TRENDS IN DATA STORAGE

As technology continues to advance, smaller, faster, and less expensive storage devices will become commonplace. Advances are rapidly being made in semiconductor and laser technology. A recent innovation in semiconductor technology is the development of *charge-coupled devices* (*CCDs*) for use in data storage. CCDs are made of silicon, similar to semiconductor memory. They are nearly 100 times faster than magnetic

FIGURE 7–16
Mass Storage

bubbles, but somewhat slower than semiconductor, random-access memories. As in semiconductor memories, data in CCDs may be lost if a power failure occurs.

Laser technology provides an opportunity to store massive quantities of data at greatly reduced costs. A *laser storage system* can store nearly 128 billion characters of data at about one-tenth of the cost of standard magnetic media. In a laser system, data is recorded by the formation of patterns by a laser beam on the surface of a polyester sheet coated with a thin layer of rhodium metal. To read data from this sheet, the laser reflects light off the surface, reconstructing the data into a digital bit stream. Laser data is resistant to alteration, and any attempt at alteration can be detected readily. Unlike magnetic media, laser storage does not deteriorate over time and is immune to electromagnetic radiation. Another advantage is that there is no danger of lost data due to power failure.

A very recent development is a laser system to be used as a mass storage device for minicomputers. This system uses a helium-neon laser, delivering about 10 milliwatts of optical power to a disk coated with a film of non metallic substance (tellurium). Data is recorded when the laser creates a hole approximately one micrometer in diameter in the film. The disk used in this system is 30 centimeters in diameter and can store 10 billion bits on its 40,000 tracks. The data cannot be erased once it is written, so this system is best suited for archival storage or where a great volume of data must be maintained online.

Technology advances occur so rapidly that accurate prediction of future storage media is nearly impossible. The objectives of making storage less expensive, faster, and smaller will continue to be pursued. The current state of the art will remain current for only a relatively short time.

SUMMARY

● Auxiliary storage is not part of the CPU. Large amounts of data and instructions are stored at a lower cost than is possible with main storage. The most common auxiliary-storage media are magnetic tapes and magnetic disks.

● Data in auxiliary storage can be accessed either sequentially or directly. Paper tape and magnetic tape provide sequential-access storage whereas magnetic disks and magnetic drums provide direct-access storage.

● Data is recorded on paper tape by punching circular holes in the tape using a paper-tape punch. Data can be represented on tape in five-, six-, seven-, or eight-channel code. Paper tape is a very inexpensive I/O medium and is especially suitable for use with telecommunication equipment transmitting data over communication lines.

● Magnetic tape consists of a plastic base, coated with iron oxide. Data is stored on magnetic tape by magnetizing small areas on the surface of the tape.

163

● Usually, data is represented on tape using a nine-track coding scheme, such as 8-bit EBCDIC and a ninth bit for parity.

● Tape density refers to the number of characters that can be stored on one inch of tape. The transfer rate of data from tape to CPU depends on the density of the tape and the speed at which it travels past the read/write head.

● Data is recorded on magnetic tape as groups of records called blocks. Blocks are separated from each other by interblock gaps (IBGs). Blocking reduces overall processing time.

● Tape cassettes are similar to audio cassettes. They can store up to 200 characters per inch and are used when small amounts of storage are required.

● The major advantages of magnetic tape are high speed of data transfer, no limit on record length, reusability, and low cost. Disadvantages include requirement for sequential organization, lack of human readability, and susceptibility to environmental factors, which can distort data on tape.

● A disk pack consists of from 5 to 100 metal platters, or disks. In some packs, each platter has 200 tracks on which data is recorded in magnetic form. Data is read or written by read/write heads connected to an access mechanism.

● A disk pack is positioned on a disk drive, which rotates all disks in the pack in unison. Some disk packs are removable, whereas others are permanently mounted on the disk drive.

● Magnetic disks provide direct access. Any record can be accessed by giving the appropriate disk surface number, track number, and record number. The read/write head can be positioned directly over the desired track.

● Flexible, or floppy, disks provide low-cost, direct-access storage. Their storage capacity may be equivalent to that of 3000 punched cards. Floppy disks are reusable and easy to store, and can be mailed. They are frequently used with minicomputers.

● Advantages of disk storage include fast access times and provision for both sequential and direct-access file organization. Major disadvantages are high cost, no backup when updating records, greater programming complexity, and the need for greater security measures.

● Mass storage devices are appropriate when large amounts of data must be stored at a low cost. They provide direct access, although access time is much slower than that of disk. Commonly used mass storage devices are cassette-type cartridge tape, magnetic spools stored in honeycomb-like cells, and small floppy-disk systems.

● Technological advances will continue to make storage devices less expensive, faster, and smaller. Recent innovations include charge-coupled devices and laser storage systems.

REVIEW QUESTIONS

1. Distinguish between main storage and auxiliary storage. Name some common auxiliary storage devices.

2. Which storage media provide direct access and which provide sequential access? Explain how direct-access capabilities are achieved.

3. Compare paper tape, magnetic tape, and magnetic disk as auxiliary storage media. Identify applications for which each is suitable.

4. Explain blocking of records. What is the purpose of blocking? Why are interblock gaps necessary?

5. Describe two types of mass storage devices. What are the advantages and disadvantages of such devices?

THE PROCTER & GAMBLE COMPANY

The Procter & Gamble Company is one of the largest manufacturers and distributors of household products in the United States. If you bathe, wash your clothes, brush your teeth, drink coffee, clean your house, or watch television, you have probably been exposed to a Procter & Gamble product. Although household products accounted for about 88 percent of the company's total 1977 sales of $7,284,000,000, the company was also active in the production of related products for institutional and industrial use. Procter & Gamble has over 40 manufacturing installations in the United States. An additional 23 manufacturing installations are widely dispersed in countries such as Austria, Morocco, Japan, Sweden, and Venezuela.

The Procter & Gamble Company has been engaged in data processing for over 20 years. The original data-processing applications of the company consisted primarily of large, daily batch transaction systems. Computer operations today have been expanded to include not only batch-processed cash and product flow systems, but also analytical/operations, research/statistical models, interactive online systems, and a wide range of information retrieval systems. Over 200 departments routinely budget for data-processing activities, supporting such vital business functions as research and development, engineering, manufacturing, marketing and sales, and finance.

The Corporate Data Center uses two IBM System/370 Model 168 central processing units, multiple 3330/3350 disk drives, more than 20 tape drives, and printing, microfiche, and plotting equipment. This equipment configuration currently supports over 125 remote job-entry stations connected to the system via telecommunication facilities, approximately 600 time-sharing terminals, and local data-entry devices. Nearly 3500 batch jobs and 1000 interactive sessions are processed during an average day's activity to support 5000 direct users. The operations department of the Management Systems

Division employs 180 people in the support, development, and maintenance of these activities.

Both disk and tape storage are needed to support the variety of applications processed at Procter & Gamble. The magnetic tapes are nine-channel, wound on 2400-foot reels, with data recorded at a density of 6250 bytes per inch. The interblock gaps on these tapes measure three-tenths of an inch. The magnetic disks are IBM 3330-11 units. They provide a total storage capacity of 201.7 megabytes (one megabyte equals one million bytes). Each disk pack contains 808 cylinders of 19 tracks each, or a total of 15,352 tracks.

The criteria used in selecting the type of storage medium for a given application must be flexible because of the changing price/performance ratios of storage devices. However, a few fundamental criteria have been developed to aid in this decision-making. If a file is to be processed using a direct-access technique or is to be used in an interactive system, disk storage must be used. A file that is to be processed sequentially can be stored on either tape or disk, so a more definitive selection procedure has been developed. The factors used in determining the medium follow:

● Data files smaller than 18 tracks are most cost effective on disk.

● Data files between 18 and 30 tracks are most cost effective on disk when the file is accessed at least once a month.

● Data files larger than 30 tracks are most cost effective on disk when the file is accessed at least once a day.

A data file that does not fall into one of the above categories is stored on tape. In each medium selection decision, the cost used for comparative analysis is determined by the following equation:

$$\text{COST} = (\text{number of accesses} \times \text{charge per access}) + \text{handling \$} + \text{storage \$}$$

The criteria above are rather simplistic for two reasons. First, the cost of making a wrong decision about which medium to use is negligible when compared to the staff time required to develop, execute, and maintain a detailed model to aid in determination. Additionally, management at Procter & Gamble believes that, eventually, computer systems will determine how data will be stored. This determination will be based on established criteria, thus permitting a machine decision to be made.

One example of sequential-access processing is the open-order file application. The open-order master file contains data pertinent to the processing of customer orders. It is used twice each day. On an average day, approximately one-third of the file is changed.

During the processing of this application, the records in the old open-order master file are merged with records indicating orders that have been shipped. The key fields used in this process are sales code—customer number, invoice number, and invoice number group. Once the merge has taken place, a new open-order master file is created by extracting orders that have been shipped. A sub-file containing only the key fields is then created from the new open-order master file to indicate the current open orders. This sub-file is used to update several other master files. If it were not created, it would be necessary to use the complete, new open-order master file for all updating. This would require considerably more CPU time.

The open-order master file is maintained on magnetic tape. The asso-

TABLE 7—1
RELATIVE COSTS OF
STORAGE MEDIA

OPEN-ORDER FILE	MAGNETIC TAPE	MAGNETIC DISK
Number of accesses	2/day	2/day
Charge per access	.01/100 accesses	.10/100 accesses
Handling cost	.70 + .40 tape-drive/minute	0.00*
Storage cost	1.75 reel/month	.10 track/month
Total cost	$3.41/month	$75/month

*No handling cost is incurred for disk storage because Procter & Gamble maintains all disks online.

ciated sub-file is stored on magnetic disk. The size of the open-order master file was the major determinant leading to the selection of tape as the storage medium. This application is processed twice daily, requiring 2:40 CPU time for each run. If stored on magnetic disk, it would require one-half of the disk space available. The much smaller sub-file accessed many times each day and requires significantly less disk space. The computations used in storage media selection for the open-order file are shown in Table 7—1. The cost savings achieved by selecting magnetic tape rather than magnetic disk are readily apparent.

For each order on the open-order master file, there is a corresponding name and address entry on a name and address master file. When an order is shipped or a new order received, the purchaser's name and address must be either deleted from or added to this master file. This update takes place by keying on the sales code-customer number to identify master records that must be updated. This master file is updated once each day and would require over 6000 tracks on a magnetic

disk. For these reasons, the file is maintained on tape.

A subsequent operation in the update application is to compare the current open-order identification file and the name and address master file to create a file of extracted name and address records used in daily processing, such as the preparation of customer billings. This extracted file is stored on tape and is accessed six times each day. When the initial decision was made to store this file on tape, the decision criteria were different from today's. New technological advances have made it more cost effective to maintain this file on disk, and it will probably be converted to this medium. Figure 7—17 depicts the linkage between these files.

The selection of disk or tape is one that is based on constantly changing technology. A cost-effective decision made last year is very likely no longer the correct choice. The decision criteria employed by Procter & Gamble are relatively uncomplicated, yet they facilitate efficient storage-device determination.

DISCUSSION POINTS

1. What are the characteristics of magnetic tape and magnetic disk that cause different charges to be assessed for storage and access costs?

2. Do you agree with the criteria used by Procter & Gamble in the selection of the storage medium to be used for a specific application?

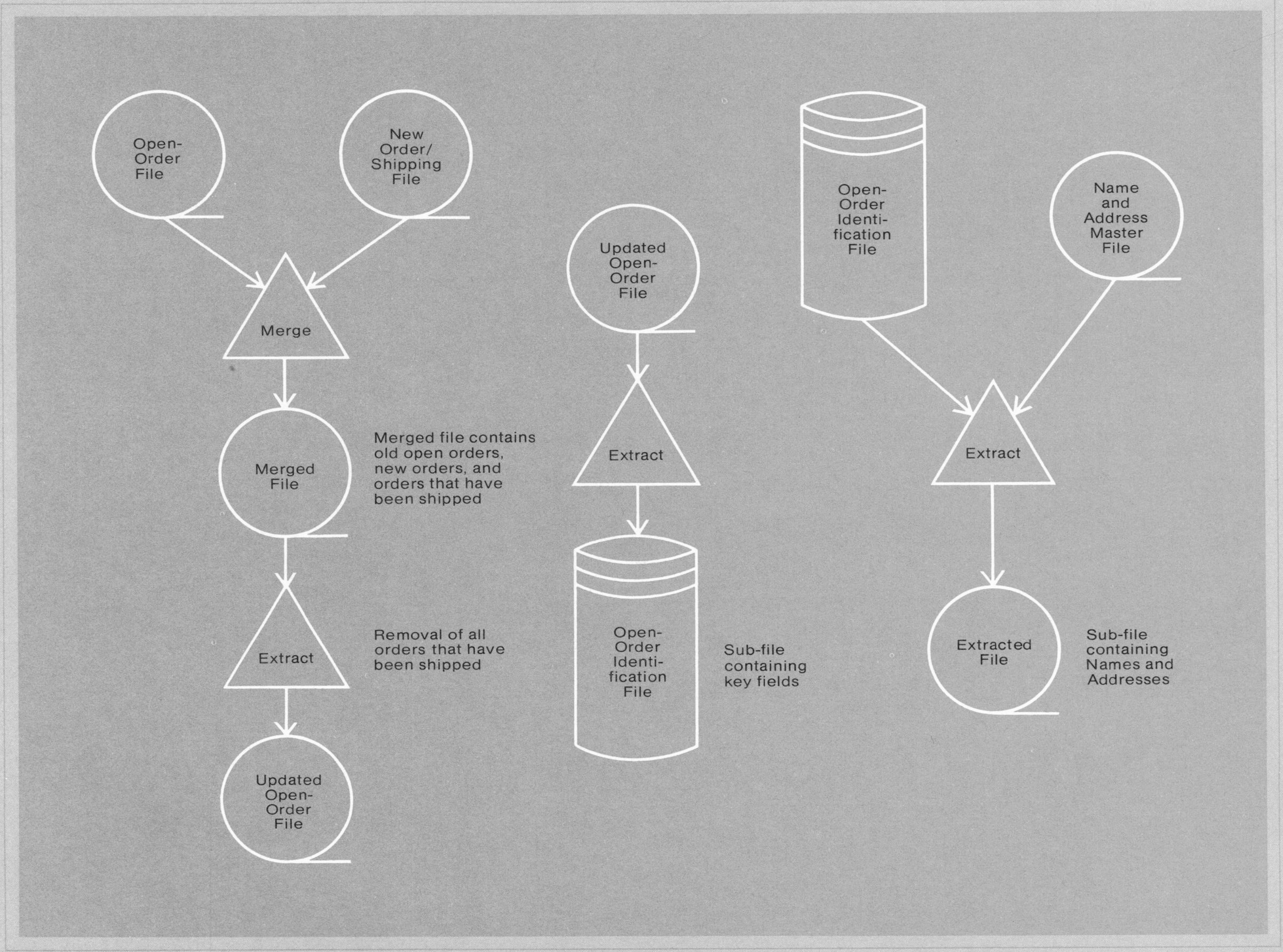

FIGURE 7–17
Relationship between Files

COMPUTER SYSTEMS | 8

OUTLINE

I. Overview of Computer Systems
   A. Large Computer Systems
      1. Multiprocessing
      2. Multiprogramming
      3. Virtual Storage
   B. Medium-Size Computer Systems
      1. Flexibility
      2. Peripheral Devices
      3. Sophisticated Software
   C. Small Computer Systems
      1. Decentralized Computing Capability
      2. Batch-Processing Applications
      3. Program Support
   D. Minicomputer Systems
      1. Limited-Task and General-Purpose Applications
      2. Minicomputer Networks
   E. Microcomputer Systems
      1. Miniaturization Technology
      2. Professional and Non-Computer-Professional Applications

II. Industry Structure
   A. Main-Frame Sector
   B. Minicomputer Sector
   C. Plug-Compatible Peripheral Equipment Sector
   D. Other Sectors
III. Computer Systems—A Management Perspective
   A. Purchase and Rental Price Considerations
   B. Cost and Availability of Maintenance
   C. Vendor Support and Training
   D. Software Costs and Capabilities
   E. Speed, Storage Capacity, and Peripherals
   F. Computer Staff Requirements
   G. Flexibility and Compatibility Considerations

INTRODUCTION

During the past decade there has been a rapid growth in the computer market. New products are constantly being introduced. They perform tasks ranging from monitoring fuel mixtures in automobiles to modeling the economies of entire nations. A microcomputer is used for the former, but a large-scale computer system is needed for the latter. Computer systems today are available in a wide spectrum of sizes and capabilities to handle a variety of problems.

This chapter looks at the various categories into which computer systems can be grouped. The general categories include large, medium-size, small, minicomputer, and microcomputer systems. Although the distinction between medium-size and large computers, or between microcomputers and minicomputers, is not always clear cut, an attempt is made to delineate the characteristics of each category and to identify applications for which particular systems are most appropriate. The chapter concludes with a brief discussion of the factors that must be considered when acquiring a computer system.

LEAVE THE DRIVING TO THE COMPUTER

Reprinted from "U.S. News & World Report."

U.S. News & World Report,
Dec. 26, 1977/Jan. 2, 1978,
p. 86

HILDESHEIM, WEST GERMANY The bane of all motorists—traffic jams—could become a thing of the past if experiments going on here pay off.

Volkswagen and Blaupunkt, the latter an electronics firm, are hard at work on a new computer system intended to automatically route drivers around congested intersections, accidents, and other delays that can make trips miserable.

First developed by Blaupunkt in 1975, this guidance system features a small computer installed in the auto and linked to a network of roadside computers that record traffic patterns in their area. The system works like this:

When a driver starts out on a trip, he or she punches out the destination on a keyboard mounted in the vehicle, using a four-digit code made up of numbers that stand for different locations. The roadside computers in the area to be traveled pick up this signal and relay back to the driver information on the best route. That message, which ap-

pears on a display panel in the car, is delivered in less than a second.

PREDICTING TROUBLE

But backers say that the advantages don't end there. Since the roadside computers know in advance where the cars are going and constantly monitor traffic in the immediate area, they can predict potential trouble spots. That enables the computers to suggest changes in a driver's route to avoid tie-ups during a trip. The motorist also is forewarned about fog, ice, snow, or other hazardous conditions that lie ahead.

Says Peter Braegas, head of Blaupunkt's basic-development department: "The idea is as simple as this: Tell me where you want to go, and I'll tell you the best way to get there."

Designers say the system beats broadcasted traffic reports because it caters to the individual motorist. They point out that in a country with so many foreign visitors, broadcasts can often confuse drivers whose understanding of the language may be limited.

Consumers will be able to have this system in their cars, say Blaupunkt officials, for about the same cost as a car radio. Besides the computer panel, the only other equipment is a small aerial to pick up signals from the roadside units.

AT GREAT EXPENSE

The cost of setting up a national network of roadside computers, of course, would be great. It's estimated that installing the system on major West German highways would cost from 130 million to 175 million dollars—a sum that would multiply in a country the size of the United States. But designers stress that part of the expense would be

offset by fewer road repairs because of better traffic distribution—not to mention the potential for reducing accidents.

The Federal Transport Ministry in Bonn is prepared to subsidize testing of the system next year on a 75-mile stretch of highway in the Bonn area. Also slated for 1978 is a new test track to be built by Volkswagen and Blaupunkt at Ehra. The system is expected to be ready for market in five years.

There already are signs that the public would be delighted with the new technology. A more modest type of guidance system has been tried on highways running between Frankfurt and Darmstadt and between Dernbach and Heumar. Those experiments have used electronic circuitry buried under the highways to measure traffic-flow patterns and relay that information to a central computer.

At the same time, a monitoring official at a central station feeds alternative routes into the computer, which then makes changes that are posted on rotating road signs along the highways. The signs, which look like prisms, are motorized and turn when signaled by the computer. About 90 percent of the drivers take the alternative routes suggested by the signs.

However, this system doesn't take into account a car's destination. Nor does it communicate continuously with indi-

173

vidual cars, as in the more sophisticated system that Blaupunkt and Volkswagen are developing.

INCREASING CONGESTION

Why is a traffic-control system needed? Heinz Funck, senior technician with Blaupunkt, explains: ''Cars and roads are better than they were 20 years ago, but it takes people longer to get where they want to go because of all the congestion. The number of cars is increasing faster than we can build roads.''

Funck adds that it will be much more difficult to build new roads in the future because of the shortage of funds and increasing environmental concerns.

Interest in the new technology is spreading to other countries. Japan already is testing similar control systems, and visitors from around the world have toured the facilities here to pick the brains of technicians.

Minicomputer systems, such as the one described in this article, are being developed to handle a wide variety of applications. This chapter gives an overview of distributed networks like the one described above and of many other computer-system configurations available.

OVERVIEW OF COMPUTER SYSTEMS

Computers have come a long way since the days of the room-sized ENIAC of the 1940s. Technological advances such as *large-scale integrated (LSI) circuitry* have decreased both costs and sizes of computer systems. Computer processing speeds have increased at exponential rates. These advances, along with more sophisticated programming languages and techniques, have contributed to a tenfold increase in the number of computers installed during the last decade.

Until the mid-1960s, most computer systems were of the large-scale variety, commonly occupying an entire room. The costs of these systems prohibited their use by small businesses and government agencies. Equipment configurations normally consisted of a single CPU and several I/O devices, all at a centralized location. All data processing was performed at this centralized location, and reports were distributed (often by mail) to individual users at their offices.

In the last decade, an entirely new concept in computing—the *minicomputer*—has become entrenched in nearly all types of business and industry. These computers cost less than $20,000. They perform many of the functions previously performed only by large computers. Their low cost and small size have contributed to a trend toward increasing decentralization and distribution of computing power. They can be used as stand-alone general-purpose computers, or they can be used to augment a large central computer in almost limitless applications. Since special facilities are not required for minicomputers, they can be located nearly anywhere that people are working.

To meet the diverse needs of businesses and other organizations, broad lines of both large computers and minicomputers have been introduced. Large computers have been scaled down to create medium-size and small versions of the same computers, having similar capabilities. Minicomputer systems can be expanded upward to provide capabilities similar to those of small and even medium-size computers. At the bottom end of the minicomputer spectrum is the *microcomputer*. Microcomputers can perform many of the functions of minicomputers at significantly lower costs. The wide range of computer offerings provides expandability and increased flexibility to computer users.

It is hard to distinguish between the various categories of computer systems. Their sizes, costs, and capabilities frequently overlap. Normally, computer systems are classified by their cost, but this method of classification is arbitrary. We distinguish between five general classes of computers: large, medium, small, minicomputer and microcomputer.

Large Computer Systems

Large computer systems provide the fastest operating speeds and the greatest storage capacities of all categories of computer systems. These computers have operating speeds measured in nanoseconds. They can hold more than one million characters in main storage. In some models, main storage can be expanded to hold over eight million characters.

175

Costs for large computer systems range from $1,000,000 to $12,000,000, depending on the amount and types of peripheral equipment used.

Many alternative equipment configurations are possible with large systems. Large computers can support many magnetic-tape drives, disk drives, printers, card readers, and remote terminals (see Figure 8–1). In a *multiprocessing system,* two or more large CPUs are used to process jobs simultaneously. Processing need not halt entirely if one CPU fails. The CPUs can share resources so that optimum processing efficiency is achieved.

Perhaps the most powerful feature of large computer systems is the sophisticated software they are capable of supporting. Under *multiprogramming,* several programs are stored within one CPU at the same time. The CPU executes instructions of one program until an I/O operation is needed. Rather than remain inactive while the I/O operation takes place, the CPU executes instructions of one of the other programs in primary storage. Several users can access the same central computer and receive almost simultaneous results. Thus, large computers are frequently used to provide time-sharing capabilities.

Large computer systems also frequently offer *virtual storage,* a facility which involves both hardware and software. As mentioned previously, a computer can execute only one instruction at a time. Virtual storage allows only the needed portion of a program to be held in storage; the remainder of the program is stored on a direct-access storage device (usually magnetic disk). Thus, program size is not limited to the available main storage size. These advanced systems concepts can be implemented in smaller systems also, but they are usually standard features in large systems.

Large computer systems offer the ultimate in flexibility of usage. They are often used when large amounts of data must be stored online for immediate updating, or for quick response to inquiries. Because of their massive storage capacity and high operating speeds, large systems are used for high-volume processing in scientific, engineering, and business applications. Their unmatched computational capabilities are especially important in research and development processing.

FIGURE 8–1
Large Computer System

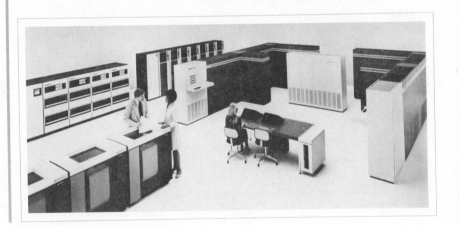

Large central computers can also be connected to a number of smaller computers or minicomputers in a distributed processing network. Jobs that are too large for the smaller computers can be relayed to the large central computer, and the results can be transmitted back to users at the remote sites. Large data files can be stored at the central computer location and shared by all users via the network.

Medium-Size Computer Systems

Medium-size computer systems generally offer the same capabilities as large systems. However, main-storage capacities are somewhat smaller, and processing speeds are not as fast. These computers are very flexible; they can be expanded to meet the needs of users. For example, the main-storage capacity of a medium-size computer is typically greater than 100,000 characters and expandable up to 1,000,000 characters. The purchase prices for these systems range from less than $200,000 to over $1,000,000.

A large number of peripheral devices can be connected to a medium-size CPU (see Figure 8–2). Several disk drives can be used to store large data files online for direct-access processing. Multiple tape drives and card readers can be used for batch processing. Terminals at remote sites can be used for data-entry and information-output.

Medium-size computer systems can support much of the sophisticated software available with large systems. Virtual storage can be used to augment main-storage capacity, thus allowing programs to be run as though main storage were unlimited. Multiprogramming can also be supported by these systems. In multiprogramming environments, both direct-access and batch processing can be performed concurrently. In addition, management inquiries can be entered from remote terminals, and responses can be returned in seconds. A fairly sophisticated management information system (MIS) can be implemented. All major programming languages can be used with medium-size computer systems.

FIGURE 8–2
Medium-Size Computer System

177

These systems can be used for both scientific and business applications. They are used for business applications when the volume of processing does not justify the use of a large computer.

Small Computer Systems

Small computer systems offer an attractive alternative to both manual and unit-record data-processing systems. First-time users of computer equipment often find that a small computer system can assist management in the control of various operations at a lower cost than other methods of data processing. Large users of computer resources often use small computers in situations that require decentralized computing capability.

Small computers generally have main-storage capacities ranging from 8000 to over 100,000 characters, depending on the model. The purchase prices for small computers are typically between $50,000 and $250,000. However, as new technology continues to develop and economies of scale are reached in production, the costs of such systems may decline as much as 25 percent.

Most small computer systems are used for batch-processing applications, although magnetic-disk units can be connected to the CPU to provide direct-access processing capabilities (see Figure 8–3). Besides magnetic-disk units, a limited number of other peripheral devices such as magnetic-tape units, card readers, and printers can be used. These devices allow data to be prepared offline for batch processing at a later time. Offline data preparation helps to insure that the limited main-storage capacity of the small computer is used efficiently.

A typical card-oriented, small computer system is shown in Figure 8–4. Systems such as this are part of a natural transition from electromechanical punched-card equipment to computer systems. The most common form of input is the punched card. Special-purpose punched-card equipment is used for sorting, collating, and punching operations.

FIGURE 8–3
Small Computer System with
Direct-Access Capabilities

FIGURE 8—4
Card-Oriented Small
Computer System

Thus, these small computer systems are perfectly suited for low-volume batch-processing applications. Many users of small computers find that these systems provide faster, more efficient data processing at a lower cost than electromechanical punched-card data-processing systems.

Normally, small computer systems can support fewer programming languages than medium-size and large computer systems. However, new advances in hardware and software have expanded small computer capabilities to include virtual storage and multiprogramming. The manufacturer usually provides various programs to the purchaser of a small computer system since the organization buying the computer is usually too small to engage in its own program development. In many cases, the cost of the computer programs needed to run the system is greater than the cost of the equipment.

Minicomputer Systems

Minicomputers constitute the most rapidly developing segment of the computer market. Designed to fit the needs of small-scale operations, they have many applications in industry and science. A minicomputer has the components of a full-size system—primary storage, arithmetic/logic unit, and control unit. It can be programmed to perform many of the tasks of larger computers. The processors of minicomputer systems have sufficient speed to give high performance; however, they have smaller memories and, consequently, smaller storage capabilities (see Figure 8–5).

Minicomputers generally have main-storage capacities ranging between 4000 characters and 64,000 characters. They are physically small; several models weigh less than 50 pounds. The description "mini," however, generally refers to the low cost of purchasing or renting a system. The purchase price ranges from $2000 to $100,000, depending on the complexity of the system. Especially in recent years, these costs have been declining.

The minicomputer is a very flexible piece of hardware. It requires no special room facilities (such as air conditioning) and can be plugged into

179

FIGURE 8—5
Minicomputer

a standard 115-volt electrical outlet. Virtually all types of I/O devices can be connected to a minicomputer. A typical equipment option consists of a teletypewriter, video-display terminal, disk-storage unit, magnetic-tape drive, card reader, paper-tape read/punch unit, and printer. Data is normally entered via a keyboard. The most popular storage media are cassette tapes and floppy disks. Paper tape is often used for offline program and data storage.

The low cost of a minicomputer system is attractive to small and medium-size businesses. Traditionally, minicomputers were used for specific tasks such as controlling manufacturing processes and machine speeds, automatic testing and inspection, and data communications. Scientific and engineering users generally used minicomputers as super slide rules to achieve fast, accurate answers without incurring the large costs of major computer systems.

Cost reductions, increased processing capabilities, and advances in software have increased the range of possible applications to the point where a minicomputer can now be thought of as a general-purpose, rather than limited-task, machine. Today, minicomputers can support high-level programming languages such as FORTRAN, COBOL, RPG, and BASIC, as well as assembly language. Program packages for billing, order entry, payroll, accounts receivable, sales analysis, and many other applications are available. Indeed, advances in software are essential to full utilization of the hardware capabilities.

Many large firms have instituted networks involving minicomputers to replace or accent larger facilities. A network provides for a distributed type of data processing by interconnecting minis for coordination while still allowing local processing within separate units of a company. As mentioned earlier, minicomputers are often used to facilitate data entry. Data is edited, arranged, and validated before it is forwarded to a larger computer. Minicomputers will be used increasingly as stand-alone systems for many specialized and general-purpose business functions.

Microcomputer Systems

Microcomputers offer the ultimate in miniaturization. Like the mini-computer, the microcomputer has all the attributes of a large computer. Its *microprocessor* is analogous to the CPU of a full-size computer. It can be connected to I/O devices such as paper-tape readers, keyboard terminals, and cassette-tape units.

An entire microcomputer fits on a board less than 60 inches on a side. The microprocessor fits on a single silicon chip the size of a nail head (see Figure 8–6). The microprocessor has about the same computing power as the room-sized CPU of a first-generation computer. Like the CPU of a large system, a microprocessor includes control logic, instruction de-coding, and arithmetic-processing decoding. The microprocessor itself costs less than $10. When the microprocessor is combined with memory and I/O devices, the resulting microcomputer is almost as powerful as a minicomputer and costs less than $2000.

FIGURE 8–6
Microprocessor on a Chip

Microcomputers are being used in a variety of applications. Their major use is in industrial automation, where they are used for manufacturing and process control. More recent innovations include microprocessor-equipped sewing machines, microwave ovens, gas pumps, programmable calculators, chemical analyzers, cash registers, and auto emission controllers. Singer has equipped their Athena 2000 sewing machine with a microprocessor that stores the information necessary to produce any of 24 stitching patterns. The microprocessor controls the movement of the needle and the movement of the fabric feed mechanism to produce the desired stitch. Another recent development is the use of microprocessors in gas stations to reduce the number of attendants needed to run the station. One such device can control 12 separate gas pumps and automatically display the customer's bill on a CRT located in an operator's office. Some minicomputers have several microprocessor chips as components. However, a microcomputer is several times slower than a minicomputer, and probably will not replace the minicomputer for many years. A typical microcomputer is shown in Figure 8–7.

Because of the limited storage capabilities of the microcomputer, it has not been of interest to large firms. But it has attracted a surprising number of non-business users such as students, lawyers, educators, and engineers. Many of these people have acquired microcomputers as a hobby interest; some microcomputers are offered in ready-to-assemble kit form for less than $400. These hobbyists are gradually discovering many important uses for microcomputers, in the home as well as in business.

This new wave of non-computer-professional people owning and using microcomputers has helped to establish the computer in every facet of life. Computer use is no longer restricted to business and business products. As the cost of microcomputers continues to decline, more families and individuals will take advantage of their capabilities. A

FIGURE 8–7
Microcomputer

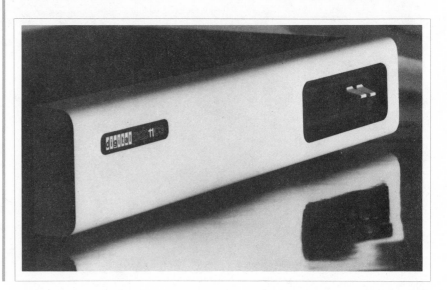

schoolteacher can grade exams or maintain a running total of a student's attendance and performance in class; a homeowner can compute house payments, car payments, utility bills, and other expenses during a given week, month, or year; educational programs can be created to aid students in learning text material. Technological advances, whereby microcomputers are becoming increasingly versatile, powerful, smaller, and less expensive, virtually guarantee the widespread adoption of these devices.

INDUSTRY STRUCTURE

The computer industry comprises a large and growing sector of our country's economic activity. The leading user of computers is still the United States government, but the business world is rapidly closing the gap. Major technological innovations during the past two decades, coupled with the rapidly declining costs of hardware, have caused a "computer explosion." Computers are being used to do tasks ranging from payroll preparation to guiding satellites and spaceships.

At present, there is little indication that the rapid growth in the computer industry has slowed. However, with the maturation of the industry, its structure has become more clearly defined. In this section, we take a closer look at the different sectors of the industry and analyze the nature of their business.

Main-Frame Sector

International Business Machines (IBM) Corporation dominates this sector of the industry. Other main-frame manufacturers include Burroughs, Honeywell, Univac, National Cash Register (NCR), and Control Data Corporation (CDC). Amdahl is a newcomer to the main-frame business.

When we refer to a computer *main frame*, we generally mean the CPU (control unit, ALU, and primary storage) of a full-scale computer. Competition in this market is limited to the few manufacturers listed above. Entry into the market is restricted by the huge capital investment required. Also, extensive economies of scale are involved in the areas of research and development, hardware design, and design of applications and system software. The large and well-established companies can spread these costs over a greater number of units; this gives them a pricing advantage. Also, the practice of renting or leasing hardware acts as a capital barrier to a small company trying to penetrate the main-frame market.

Minicomputer Sector

The minicomputer market has experienced a phenomenal growth rate in the past five years. The industry has been growing at a rate of 35 to 40 percent annually. However, recent analysis indicates that this growth rate is declining, and that the market will stabilize in the near future. The leading manufacturer in this sector is Digital Equipment Corporation (DEC). Other major manufacturers are Hewlett-Packard, Data General, Honeywell, General Automation, and Texas Instruments. Smaller manufacturers are Wang Laboratories, Systems Engineering Laboratories, Inc. (SEL), and Prime Computer, Inc. IBM and Burroughs have also entered this market.

Initially, minicomputers were developed for specific applications such as process control and engineering calculations. However, the present minis are more flexible, provide greater capabilities, and support a full line of peripherals. The growth in minicomputer applications has led to the concept of distributed processing. Minicomputers are now being used in time-sharing applications, numerically controlled machine tools, industrial automation, and word-processing equipment.

Plug-Compatible Peripheral Equipment Sector

The growth in this sector has also been great. The impetus to this growth has been the standardization of computer components, and the increasing competitiveness exhibited by many firms in this part of the market. Until the late 1960s, there were only a few *independent computer peripheral equipment manufacturers* (*ICPEMs*). However, between 1965 and 1970, many firms entered the peripheral equipment market. Among them were Telex, Memorex, California Computer Products, Ampex, and a number of other small firms. They offer *plug-to-plug compatible* (*plug-compatible*, for short) devices. Plug-to-plug compatibility implies interchangeability between the original manufacturer's peripheral device and the independent manufacturer's peripheral. The use of the independent peripheral is transparent to the main frame—that is, the original device.

Several factors accounted for the successful entry of independent manufacturers into the plug-compatible peripheral equipment market.

● The capital barrier to entry was lower because the manufacturer could concentrate on a limited market (e.g., tape drives or disk drives), and not get involved in developing other hardware.

● The potential market was large, and the profit margins were high.

● Peripheral devices were comprising an increasingly large fraction of the total hardware outlay for a computer-based system. (Peripherals currently represent about 70 percent of the total value of the hardware of a system.)

● Technological progress in the peripheral device area had been slow compared to that made in computing capabilities.

By making peripheral devices that were plug-to-plug compatible with IBM equipment, ICPEMs directly threatened IBM's market share. The actions taken by IBM to maintain its leadership position in the industry and prevent the ICPEMs from nibbling away at its share of the market resulted in anti-trust litigation against IBM. Some of the strategies that IBM adopted included redesigning products to prevent competitors from achieving plug-to-plug compatibility, offering new lease terms to maintain its customer base, and providing new products at lower prices.

Other Sectors

The other sectors within the computer industry are: (1) software and consulting services; (2) service bureaus and computer utilities; and (3) microcomputer market.

The software and consulting services sector comprises firms that specialize in developing instructions to control the operations of computers. The two basic types of software are system software and applications software. *System software* consists of programs written to coordinate the operation of all computer circuitry, allowing the computer to run efficiently; *applications software* consists of programs designed to solve specific problems or processing needs (e.g., payroll). Both system software and applications software are often sold as "packages." Each package is a collection of programs that work together to accomplish specific processing objectives.

The software and consulting services sector has grown substantially, despite the fact that many users have their own staffs to design systems and develop new applications software. The market for externally supplied software packages and other computer-related consulting services is expected to grow faster in the future. More and more users are realizing that the cost of purchasing software from outside suppliers is generally less than the cost of developing it in-house. Moreover, the software is debugged and well documented. Some suppliers also provide ongoing maintenance.

Entry into the software segment is easy because there are no capital or software barriers. Most *original equipment manufacturers* (*OEMs*) have unbundled—that is, they have begun to charge separately for maintenance, software support, and so on. Consequently, software firms do not need to be concerned about users being locked into the OEM's software. The performance of this sector was rather poor in the early 1970s due to reduced demand and many new entrants. However, a shakedown has occurred since then, and the firms that remain in this sector are doing much better.

Service bureaus and *computer utilities* supply time-sharing capabilities to clients. In addition to hardware, a service bureau may also provide software services in the form of applications packages. A computer utility differs from a service bureau in that it offers a regional or national communication network, linking many large processors. Great economies of scale can be achieved. Thus, a utility should be able to provide low-cost computing power to a large number of customers. However, the growth of computer utilities has been restricted. Some reasons are:

- The costs of all sizes of hardware have continued to drop. Consequently, a cost-effective system of any size can be established to meet a customer's needs.

- Data-communication costs have been increasing.

- The complexities of a large network can result in high overhead.

- In-house minicomputer systems have been linked together to form distributed networks.

Recently, the microcomputer market has received greater attention. Prior to this period, microprocessors were being used in intelligent terminals, process control, and calculators. But now, a whole new vista has opened, with the potential of providing low-cost computers to individuals. Radio Shack and several other retailers of electronic equipment have entered the home-computer market. Many of the larger computer manufacturers may use their technical knowledge to produce better and cheaper microcomputers for the individual hobbyist, and thus penetrate this expanding market.

COMPUTER SYSTEMS—A MANAGEMENT PERSPECTIVE

Management is faced with alternative methods of meeting data-processing requirements. Some firms choose to own their computer resources and do in-house processing; other firms have an outside service bureau handle their data processing. Other alternatives include time-sharing, manual methods, and combinations of methods. Determining the best type of system for an organization is an exceedingly complex task.

The selection is further complicated by the myriad of equipment configurations available. We have discussed five general categories of computer systems: large, medium, small, minicomputer, and microcomputer systems. Given the peripheral devices discussed in Chapters 4, 6, and 7, a seemingly infinite number of configurations is possible.

Here are some of the major considerations when deciding which type of computer system to purchase (or lease):

- Purchase prices and monthly rental prices of equipment

- Cost and availability of maintenance

- Vendor support and training

- Software costs and capabilities

- Speed of CPU

- Storage capacity and expandability of main storage

- Number and types of peripherals supported by CPU

- Size of computer staff and skill requirements

186

- Flexibility of system

Purchase and Rental Price Considerations

The purchase prices of the CPU and peripheral devices prohibit all but the largest firms from buying and owning a large computer system. Traditionally, large and medium-size computer systems have been rented or leased. From the user's point of view, leasing or renting offers several advantages. First, lease payments are fully tax-deductible. Second, since equipment is leased, it is easier to adapt the system to changing requirements by exchanging CPU models and accessories. A firm need not worry about new technological advances rendering its equipment obsolete, since the firm is not committed as it would be if it owned the system. Also, leasing does not require large, one-time expenditures for computer equipment. Normally, it takes five years of lease payments to reach the purchase price of the equipment. Minicomputers and microcomputers, because of their low cost, are almost always purchased.

Cost and Availability of Maintenance

Maintenance costs and quality of service must not be overlooked when acquiring a computer system. These costs are normally included in the lease price, but they are not considered a part of the purchase price. Therefore, when a system is purchased, maintenance is a separate contractual matter. The costs can be significant (often several thousand dollars a month for large systems). Maintenance services can be performed by either the computer manufacturer or a specialized maintenance firm. The quality of service is vital because a computer breakdown can totally disrupt work flow.

Vendor Support and Training

Vendor support and training are especially important when first installing or radically changing a computer system. The expertise of the vendor can be invaluable during design and implementation. Most vendors offer training classes to educate expected users of the systems they sell or lease. But the quality and amount of training offered differs greatly. The cost for these services may be included in the price of the equipment. If this support is provided without extra charge, it is said to be bundled.

Software Costs and Capabilities

Many large computer systems are justified solely because of the sophisticated software they can support. For large firms, multiprogramming and virtual-storage capabilities may be necessities. These capabilities can be fully exploited only with large and medium-size computers.

Software is a significant expense. In minicomputer systems, the software costs may be more than the hardware costs. Large computer users can frequently purchase many prewritten programs, but similar programs may not be available for small computers and minicomputer

187

systems. Firms owning minicomputer and microcomputer systems must be prepared to develop a large share of their software.

Speed, Storage Capacity, and Peripherals

The speed and storage capacity of the CPU is of keen concern to computer users. The volume and type of processing to be done normally determines the size of computer needed.

Large businesses with a high volume of data processing frequently need the maximum computer capabilities available. Firms that use computers for scientific applications need a very fast computer, but a large storage capacity may not be as essential. Small organizations may find a minicomputer meets all their requirements. Large businesses frequently use small computers in many applications where response time and storage capacity are not critical. For example, a minicomputer costing only $50,000 can do much of the same work as computers costing $2,000,000. Simply stated, a minicomputer that costs one-fortieth as much as a large computer can do much more than one-fortieth of the work.

Computer Staff Requirements

Besides paying for hardware and software, an organization must pay the salaries of its computer staff. The computer staff generally consists of managers, system analysts, programmers, data-entry personnel, computer operators, and computer technicians. Most computer-related jobs require a high degree of skill and training. These specialized services do not come cheaply; the computer staff may account for a significant portion of an organization's monthly payroll expense.

Small and minicomputer systems do not require as much staff support as large systems, but certain skill requirements may be even higher than those for larger systems. For example, firms using minicomputers may need highly skilled programmers to do program-development work because no prewritten programs are available for their minicomputers.

Flexibility and Compatibility Considerations

The *flexibility* of a system is reflected as the degree to which the system can be adapted or tailored to meet changing requirements. Many manufacturers design their systems using a modular approach. This approach permits the addition of components to a system configuration, thereby allowing for growth and adaptation as an organization's needs change. An organization can start with a relatively slow, less expensive system, and then change to a larger CPU or add more peripherals when needed. Systems designed with emphasis on this modular concept are usually fairly flexible.

Software compatibility also affects the flexibility of the system. *Compatibility* refers to the degree to which programs must be modified when a firm changes computers. From the firm's point of view, the number of required program changes should be minimal, since reprogramming is both costly and time-consuming. An organization must plan for future needs as well as present needs. Fortunately, many manufacturers offer systems which can be enlarged with few or no required program changes.

Discussion

While this list of considerations is by no means complete, it demonstrates the complexity involved in choosing a computer system. Other key considerations are the size of the organization and the type of organizational structure used. For example, a large, highly centralized organization may have little choice but to acquire a large computer system. In contrast, small businesses and decentralized organizations often find that all their data-processing needs can be met with minicomputer systems. With the expanded capabilities of minicomputers and small computer systems, and the great potential offered by microcomputer systems, developing sound criteria for evaluating system alternatives is essential.

A summary of the types of computer systems discussed in this chapter is given in Table 8–1. All types of systems have certain advantages and disadvantages; they must be weighed in relation to the information requirements of the organization.

TABLE 8–1
COMPUTER SYSTEMS COMPARED

	LARGE COMPUTER SYSTEMS	MEDIUM-SIZE COMPUTER SYSTEMS	SMALL COMPUTER SYSTEMS	MINICOMPUTER SYSTEMS	MICROCOMPUTER SYSTEMS
Purchase Price ($)	1–12 million	200,000–1,000,000	50,000–250,000	2,000–100,000	1,000–10,000
Main-Storage Capacity	Extremely large	Large	Medium	Medium	Limited
Ability to Support Numerous I/O Devices	Excellent	Excellent	Good	Fair	Poor
Processing Speed	Extremely fast	Fast	Moderately fast	Moderately fast	Relatively slow
Programming Language and Other Software Availability	Many options	Many options	Some options	Limited options	Very limited options
Environmental Requirements	Controlled environment	Controlled environment	Controlled environment	No special site preparation	No special site preparation
Computational Power	Very high	Very high	High	Relatively limited	Limited

SUMMARY

● Computer systems can be grouped into various categories, depending on size, cost, and capabilities. Different configurations can be established to meet the diverse needs of businesses and other organizations.

● Large computer systems are used by organizations that regularly need to process large amounts of data at high speeds. These systems can provide multiprogramming and virtual-storage capabilities. Multiprocessing is also possible if two or more CPUs are connected together. Large computers can support many peripheral devices. They can also be connected to a number of smaller computers to do distributed processing. Large systems are suitable for applications that require quick response times and massive amounts of data stored online for immediate updating.

● Medium-size computer systems have less main-storage capacity than large systems, but they provide similar capabilities. Multiple peripheral devices can be connected to the CPU, and remote terminals can be used for data-entry and information-output. Both direct-access and batch processing are possible if multiprogramming capabilities exist. Such systems support all major programming languages. Medium-size systems are suitable for both scientific and business applications.

● Small computers are generally used for low-volume batch-processing applications. Many are card-oriented. They can support a limited number of I/O devices and fewer programming languages. Offline collection and preparation of input data allows efficient utilization of the limited main-storage capacity of a small computer.

● Minicomputers are small and rugged. Their price and performance vary widely. They can support all types of I/O devices. Cassette tapes and floppy disks are popular auxiliary-storage media. Minicomputers have been used for process control, data communications, and scientific computations. Lower costs and advances in software have greatly increased the flexibility of minicomputers and made them very attractive to small and medium-size computer users. They can be used for an ever-increasing variety of applications. They are being included in distributed networks and being used increasingly as stand-alone systems as well.

● Microcomputers are based on miniature-size microprocessors. They are being used in industrial automation, programmable calculators, cash registers, and home applications. The potential of these low-cost, compact microcomputers appears almost limitless.

● The main-frame sector of the computer industry is dominated by IBM, although several other manufacturers provide a limited degree of competition. Entry into the main-frame market is restricted by large capital investment requirements and economies of scale that can be achieved only by large firms.

● Minicomputers are being manufactured in an increasing percentage as they become increasingly affordable by small businesses. Capital requirements are not as great as in the case of main-frame manufacturers, and the market for minicomputers is much more competitive.

● The plug-compatible peripheral equipment market has experienced considerable growth. Most plug-compatible equipment is designed to operate in conjunction with IBM equipment. This has prompted IBM to redesign products, thus preventing competitors from achieving plug-to-plug compatibility.

● The unbundling of maintenance, software, and support by manufacturers has created opportunities for software and consulting service firms to enter the computer market. Service bureaus and computer utilities are experiencing increased competition from the emerging microcomputer market.

● Selection of the optimum computer configuration for an organization is a complex task. Important factors to be considered when deciding which type of system to acquire include: purchase/rental prices of the hardware, maintenance costs, vendor support, software costs and capabilities, hardware capabilities, staff requirements, and system flexibility.

REVIEW QUESTIONS

1. Discuss the major features of large and medium-size computer systems. Identify typical applications in which such systems can be used to advantage, giving reasons.

2. Are small computer systems appropriate for online direct-access processing? If not, for what types of applications are they suited?

3. How may a large organization with a large centralized computer system benefit by using small computers? Explain.

4. Compare and contrast minicomputer systems with microcomputer systems. What do you perceive to be the future of minicomputers and microcomputers?

5. Suppose you have been hired as the computer system manager for a small car rental agency that has decided to discard its manual data-processing system in favor of electronic methods. What factors must you consider in acquiring a computer system for the agency?

6. What are the major sectors of the computer industry? How competitive are these sectors relative to each other?

SOUTHERN RAILWAY COMPANY

LOOK AHEAD-LOOK SOUTH

The 84-year-old Southern Railway Company is a very profitable, highly innovative organization. It has a long history of leadership in many areas of the railroad industry. It is the eighth-largest railroad in the United States and, unlike many United States railroads, has achieved its success by operating only railroads. Some lines have oil (Union Pacific), timber (Burlington Northern), or coal (Norfolk & Western). Still others, like IC Industries and Santa Fe Industries, have become diversified holding companies.

Southern Railway has had a long and successful evolution of computer application. They currently have a very large installation in Atlanta. The central system hardware consists of four IBM System/370 Model 158s and two IBM System/360 Model 50s. Some examples of applications processed by these computers are: a real-time, car movement system designed to keep track of freight cars and trains on the lines of the railroad, accounting, payroll, marketing and sales analysis, statistical reporting, engineering and car distribution functions, and inquiry systems that provide information for car-distribution and field personnel.

At the opposite end of the spectrum, Southern also uses microcomputers. They act as communication terminals and measure inquiry volume and response time. Southern has installed, and operates, approximately 100 minicomputers at yard sites for local operational support. One of the most interesting applications involves a sophisticated network of minicomputers at the Sheffield, Alabama, automatic railroad classification yard. The system, a $15-million, 2½-year project, uses a distributed approach; the data needed for the Sheffield operation is transmitted from the central computer complex in Atlanta.

The computer activity at the Sheffield rail yard is divided into two distinct systems—a management information system (MIS) and a process control (PC) system. Five minicomputers are

linked together to form these systems—two on PC, one on MIS, and two on backup.

The purpose of a rail yard is to receive inbound trains in the receiving area, reclassify the individual train cars in the classification area, and consolidate the new classifications of cars for forwarding to the proper destination. In the Sheffield automatic classification yard, the switching is done by the PC minicomputers.

The information flow really starts long before a train arrives at Sheffield. Throughout the 13 southeastern states served by Southern, about 400 stations report every movement of every car and train to the central online/real-time system. The central computer complex in Atlanta, consequently, has current data about every car and train on more than 10,500 miles of track. About two hours before a train arrives at Sheffield, the Atlanta computer transmits an "advanced consist" to Sheffield. The consist tells the makeup of the train, specifying the precise sequence, destination, weight, and so on, of each car. This data is stored by the MIS minicomputer and printed to assist yard personnel in planning.

When the train arrives at the Sheffield yard, the yard supervisor decides which receiving track the cars go onto and informs the MIS minicomputer via a CRT. It updates the inventory of the receiving yard. At the end of the receiving tracks is a small hill over which each inbound car is pushed; as it rolls free over the hill, it is switched onto one of the 32 classification tracks. This process is controlled by the PC minicomputers and other instrumentation, including photo-electric cells, weigh-in-motion scales, wheel sensors, speed-reading radars, and wind gauges. There are 600 inputs to the PC minis from the various devices in the yard. As each car starts to roll over the hill, its weight is calculated, length determined, axles counted, and rate of speed change measured. Also determined at this point are the curves the car must negotiate and the distance it must roll to reach its classification track so that it will strike the last car already there at less than four miles per hour (see Figure 8—8).

After making these calculations, a "master retarder" is instructed by the minicomputer to slow the car to the calculated speed and to align the switches that will direct the car to the proper track. The car enters the complex of switches and is directed to its assigned track. At the other end of the classification track, a locomotive pulls the cars, under radio instruction, from that track and moves them to the forwarding yard where they are coupled into trains for a subsequent road haul.

The MIS minicomputer also assists in the classification process. When the cars are ready to go over the small hill, the yard supervisor uses the CRT to enter the receiving track, number of cars, and beginning and ending car numbers. From this, the MIS minicomputer prepares a list of every car, the sequence, and the classification track (depending on its route, destination, contents, etc.) to which it should go. The speed at which the cars should be shoved to the hill is then selected. The PC mini takes over the control of the "switching" locomotive and adjusts speed as the cars approach the hill.

A CRT displays the first 10 cars to go over the hill, and a closed-circuit TV shows the supervisor the actual operation. He or she visually compares the car on the TV with the first car on the CRT list. If they are the same,

193

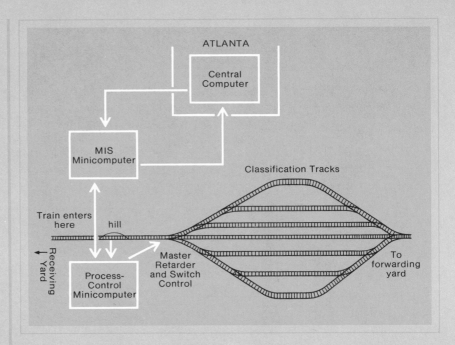

FIGURE 8–8

Computer-Controlled
Railroad Classification Yard

the supervisor does nothing else. As the first car clears the hill, the list on the CRT rolls up one. The process is repeated for each car.

As each car completes its switching, the PC mini sends (to the MIS mini) data regarding which track the car actually went to. If this data is not the same as the data in the original list, the differences are analyzed. Appropriate messages are updated and displayed to the yard supervisor. Occasionally, a car does not go to the proper track. If the first car rolled slowly and the second car rolled fast and caught up with, or came too close to, the first car, the PC mini may have deemed it unwise to throw switches between them. If so, it allowed the second car to go to the wrong track. These moves must receive attention.

Finally, the yard supervisor requests CRT displays of the contents of the tracks. He or she decides which cars, and in what sequence, will make up an outbound train. This decision is keyed in as a work order which, in turn, is relayed by radio to the "pullback" locomotive engineer. As the train leaves the forwarding yard, the supervisor records that the train is leaving the particular track. The MIS mini updates the inventories and sends the consist of the outbound train to the central computer in Atlanta.

Only control instructions—no data— are entered into the system. Full advantage is taken of the already existing, centralized data in the Atlanta computer. The concept of the distributed data base, where the data needed for local operation is transmitted and processed locally, is extremely important for complete reliability. Trains must be classified 24 hours a day, regardless of computer or communication problems. Distributed computers and data bases are essential for high-reliability operations in this application.

194

DISCUSSION POINTS

1. Why is the concept of distributed computers and data bases extremely important for operations that require complete reliability?

2. What types of applications does Southern Railway process on their large computers? For what purpose do they use minicomputers?

section ▌▌▌

PROGRAMMING

9
SYSTEM AND
APPLICATIONS SOFTWARE

10
THE PROGRAMMING PROCESS

11
PROGRAMMING LANGUAGES

12
STRUCTURED-DESIGN CONCEPTS

13
ADVANCED SOFTWARE TOPICS

section III

PROGRAMMING

9
SYSTEM AND
APPLICATIONS SOFTWARE

10
THE PROGRAMMING PROCESS

11
PROGRAMMING LANGUAGES

12
STRUCTURED-DESIGN CONCEPTS

13
ADVANCED SOFTWARE TOPICS

SYSTEM AND APPLICATIONS SOFTWARE | 9

OUTLINE

I. Programs
   A. System Programming
   B. Applications Programming
II. Operating Systems
   A. Operating-System Functions
   B. Types of Operating Systems
      1. Batch (Stacked-Job)
      2. Real-Time
   C. Operating-System Components
      1. Control Programs
         a. Supervisor Program
         b. Job-Control Program
         c. Input/Output
            Management System

2. Processing Programs
   a. Language Translators
   b. Library Programs
   c. Utility Programs
III. Levels of Language
   A. Machine Language
   B. Assembly Language
   C. High-Level Programming
      Languages
IV. Language Translation

INTRODUCTION

The computer is a powerful, general-purpose machine that can solve a variety of problems. Previous chapters have covered the major hardware components of a computer system. They have shown how these components are used to store and process data and generate information. However, the computer cannot be used to solve problems without the use of computer programs. Programming is a critical step in data processing because if programs are not correctly used, the system delivers information that cannot be used.

This chapter examines several different aspects of computer software. Differences between system programming and applications programming are examined. The various functions performed by operating-system software are discussed. The chapter emphasizes the logical progression from machine-language programming to programming in high-level languages more oriented toward problem solving. A section on conversion of high-level languages into code that the computer can execute is also presented.

COMPUTERIZED CAMERAS, KNIVES SCULPT QUICKLY

Roger Field

Science Digest, "Consumer Notebook" section, April, 1977, pp. 77, 78

A company in the radar business, Dynell Electronics Corporation in Melville, N.Y., has combined optical mapping techniques with computer technology to produce instant automatic sculpture. Right now, the system is used mainly to sculpt heads. But, refined further, it could produce scaled reproductions of almost any object, quickly and inexpensively. For example, its originators foresee a day when a dentist might remove a decayed tooth and have a similar system replicate it in high-temperature alloy—without making awkward and often imprecise casts in the patient's mouth.

Recently, I was the first reporter to see the entire Dynell process for automatic sculpture. The company's president, Paul Dimateo, who took me through it from start to finish (using my own head as an example), says the system took five years to develop and cost the firm $3 million. Here's how it works:

First, you're seated in a hydraulic chair, dead center between a battery of eight special cameras. All lenses are aimed at a single point, and your head must be perfectly positioned on that spot. You hold still for two seconds, while the cameras click and special shutters whirr and clack. What's happening—although Dynell is very secretive about certain portions of the process—is that your face is being "mapped" by white light, select points at a time. As film pours through the cameras, they retain all this topographical information in the form of line smears, not real images. Then, the film is developed and a special optical reader goes to work converting the curved patterns to a digital format that can be understood by a minicomputer.

The net result of this preprocessing is a roll of magnetic tape that contains, in essence, the total shape of your head. And here's where the process really gets interesting: Placed on a minicomputer, that tape is analyzed to determine the location of every point on the face, and the computer steers cutting tools that create the sculpture out of a hunk of white wax—a formulation the company calls "paralene" which has a higher melting point than most waxes and is somewhat more permanent because of a polymer additive.

First comes a coarse cut on a machine that contains a computer-driven motor sporting a rotating bit. This bit enters a rectangular plexiglass cage through a small hole and proceeds to bore away large amounts of wax from one-quarter of the sculpture at a time. The wax goes flying in all directions, and every few minutes, a quarter is completed and the piece automatically rotates 90 degrees. In half an hour or so, a crude approximation emerges of the final piece.

Next, the coarse-cut head is placed on a fine-cut machine for finishing. Again, the computer controls the cutting process, but this time it's done with 20 dazzling blades, attacking the head simultaneously from two sides. The head rotates into position, and the blades sweep back and forth, making many passes and worming away more modest amounts of paralene. Forty minutes later, the fine cut is complete and the result is an excellent representation—eyebrows, locks of hair, creases, even moles. Not every sculpture comes out perfectly, though, as the smallest glitch in the computer program or error in interpretation of the film can cause a cutting tool to make a deep gash in a cheek or prune off a nose entirely. Your "head" might need to be redone. But, generally speaking, the results are most impressive. The computer knocked out several versions of my head in wax, and even to me they all looked fine, except for a minor flaw in my scalp in one.

From here, the only hand that ever touches the piece goes to work, touching up tiny details, or possibly giving an added smoothness you may desire for skin surfaces. Then it's coated with urethane to make a mold. Into this mold is poured any one of a number of materials, depending on what you want. You could have his head in bonded aluminum, bonded bronze, a stone-like solid plastic, a clay-looking plastic, or conceivably, the original paralene wax.

Prices range from $150 a half-size head in white paralene to $350 for a large three-quarter-size in bonded bronze. And great variation is possible: A bust could be made small enough to fit a ring or pendant chain. This is done on a third machine that chisels ultrasonically in brass, glass, and many other relatively hard materials. Or, conceivably, if you were willing to take the risk, you could have your likeness in sapphire or rare jade by supplying the raw material.

The company says a sculpture is ready the following week if all goes well. But if push comes to shove, a given piece can be produced overnight. A sculptor tells me a comparable bronze head carved manually would cost several times the Dynell charge, and might not achieve the desired likeness.

Right now, the only location doing "sittings" is a small shop on Madison Avenue in New York City called "The Studio for Solid Photography." Dynell opened it recently and installed its special photographic equipment in a small room behind the gallery. Passersby have no idea what goes on behind that door, not to mention the exotic equipment that carves up paralene out in Melville, on Long Island. But the company hopes to make an exciting business of computer sculpting and get a return on its investment. Meanwhile, it seems to be selling its highly customized product at relatively bargain prices. And your own head carved by computer is obviously quite a conversation piece.

Imagine the complexity of the software that supports the sculpting process! The following material describes programs, operating systems, and levels of language that help to make such sophisticated applications possible.

PROGRAMS

When a problem is to be solved with the aid of a computer, certain procedures must be followed. Despite the apparent complexity and power of the computer, it is merely a tool manipulated by an individual. Step-by-step instructions providing the problem solution are required. As stated earlier, this series of instructions is known as a *program*. The individual who creates the program is the *programmer*. There are two basic types of programs: (1) *applications programs,* which solve user problems (such as payroll); and (2) *system programs,* which coordinate the operation of all computer circuitry.

System Programming

System programs directly affect the operation of the computer. They are designed to facilitate the use of the hardware and to help the computer system run quickly and efficiently. For example, a system program allocates storage for data being entered into the system. We have already seen that computers differ in main-storage capacity, in the methods used to store and code data, and in the number of instructions they can perform. Consequently, system programs are written specifically for a particular type of computer and cannot be used (without modification) on different machines.

System programming is normally provided by the computer manufacturer or a specialized programming firm. Thus, system programs are initially written in a general fashion to meet as many user requirements as possible. However, they can be modified, or tailored, to meet an organization's specific needs.

A system programmer maintains the system programs in good running order and tailors them, when necessary, to meet organizational requirements. Since system programmers serve as a bridge between the computer and applications programmers, they must have the technical background needed to understand the complex internal operations of the computer. Because each organization uses a different set of applications programs, system programs must be modified (tuned) to insure computer efficiency at each organization's installation.

Applications Programming

Applications programs perform specific data-processing or computational tasks to solve the organization's management problems. They are usually developed within the organization, although some can be purchased. The job of the applications programmer is to use the capabilities of the computer to solve a specific problem. Typical examples of applications programs are those used in inventory control and accounting. Applications programmers who work in banks write programs to update checking and savings account balances.

Applications programs can be written without an in-depth knowledge of the computer. The applications programmer concentrates on the particular problem to be solved. Once a problem is clearly defined and understood, the actual writing of a program to solve it is usually relatively simple.

OPERATING SYSTEMS

In early computer systems, a human operator monitored computer operations, determined the priority of programs (the order in which submitted programs were run), and handled input and output operations. With the significant increases in processing speeds of CPUs and the need for efficient use of all computer resources, human operator intervention for control purposes became unrealistic. Time delays and human errors occurred while the operator developed solutions and implemented the necessary procedures.

In the 1960s, *operating systems* were developed to help overcome this problem. An operating system is a collection of programs designed to permit a computer system to manage its own operations. This approach provides a control system which can operate at computer speeds. Instead of a human operator preparing the I/O devices to be used for each program and loading the programs into storage, the operating system assumes responsibility for all jobs to be run.

Operating-System Functions

The functions of an operating system are geared toward attaining maximum efficiency in processing operations. Most operating systems are designed to allow several programs to share the same computer resources. The operating system handles the allocation of these resources to the users requesting them. It automatically resolves conflicts that occur when, for example, two or three programs request the use of the same tape drive or main-storage locations. In addition, the operating system performs an accounting function. It keeps track of all resource usage as needed for charging user fees and for evaluating the efficiency of CPU utilization.

A procedure for scheduling jobs on a priority basis is often used. Although it may seem logical to run programs in the order in which they are submitted, this is not always the most practical approach. For instance, assume five programs are submitted for processing within a short period of time. Suppose one program requires one minute of CPU time and the other four require one hour each. It may be reasonable to process the short program first. A system of priorities can be established, based on considerations such as the required processing time and the need for the expected output. In this way, programs that produce vital reports can be processed before less important ones.

Types of Operating Systems

There are two basic types of operating systems: *batch* (or *stacked-job*) and *real-time.* In a stacked-job processing environment, several user programs (jobs, or job steps) are grouped into a batch and processed one after the other in a continuous stream. For example, in the morning an operator may load all jobs to be processed during the day into a card reader and input them into the system. The stacked-job operating system will direct processing without interruption until all jobs are complete, thus freeing the operator to perform other tasks.

A real-time operating system can respond to spontaneous requests for system resources, such as management inquiries entered from online terminals.

Many operating systems can handle both batch and real-time applications simultaneously. These systems direct processing of a job stream but also respond to interrupts from other devices (such as online terminals) in direct communication with the CPU.

Operating-System Components

An operating system is an integrated collection of subsystems. Each subsystem consists of programs that perform specific duties (see Figure 9–1). Since all operating-system programs work in unison, CPU idle time is avoided and utilization of computer facilities is increased. Two types of programs make up the operating system: *control programs* and *processing programs.*

Control Programs   Control programs oversee system operations and perform tasks such as input/output, scheduling, handling interrupts caused by error conditions, and communication with the computer operator or programmers. The processing programs of the operating system are executed under the supervision of control programs.

The *supervisor program* (also called the *monitor,* or *executive*) is the major component of the operating system. It coordinates the activities of all other parts of the operating system. Usually, operating-system programs are stored on an auxiliary storage device (disk, tape, or drum) known as the *system residence device.* The supervisor calls for these system programs as needed and loads them into main storage. It schedules I/O operations and allocates channels to various I/O devices. It also sends messages to the computer operator indicating the status of particular jobs, error conditions, and so on. Since the supervisor is needed at all times, it remains in primary storage thoughout processing.

FIGURE 9–1
Operating-System Components

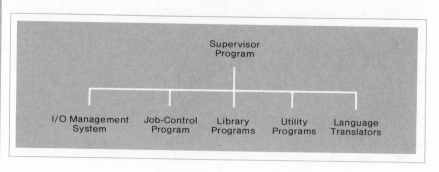

The operating system requires job-control information in order to perform its mission. A *job-control language* (*JCL*) serves as the communication link between the programmer and the operating system. Job-control statements are used to specify the beginning of a program, identify the program to be executed, describe the work to be done, and indicate the I/O devices required. The *job-control program* is a control program that translates the job-control statements written by a programmer into machine-language instructions that can be executed by the computer.

In most computer systems, the data to be processed is stored on high-speed input devices such as magnetic-tape units or disk units. In these systems, job-control statements are entered on cards from an input device other than the data input device. For example, the job-control cards may be entered in a stream from a card reader as shown in Figure 9–2a. Among other things, these cards specify which data files and input devices are required. As each job is processed, the system instructs the operator to load the particular tapes or disk packs needed for the job.

In some systems, programs and data are read into storage from the same input device (see Figure 9–2b). No additional I/O devices are required in this instance, but it is not an efficient method for processing large programs or data files. This method is most often used when programs are being tested, before storing them on the system residence device.

Typically, a number of job steps are required to execute a program. Thus, several job-control statements are needed to indicate which operations are to be performed and the devices needed to perform them.

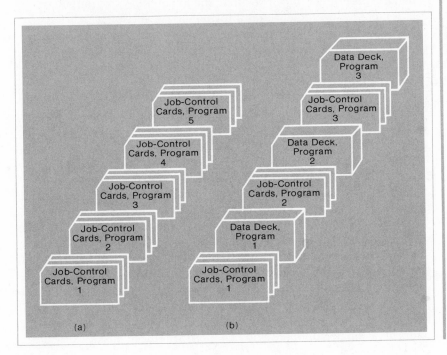

FIGURE 9–2

Continuous Job Streams for Stacked-Job Processing System

However, once the job-control program has interpreted a job-control statement and issued the commands necessary to carry out the step, it is not needed again until that job step has been completed and another is to be done. Therefore, the supervisor calls the job-control program into main storage only when it is needed to interpret a job-control statement.

The control programs of the operating system must be able to control and coordinate the CPU while receiving input from channels, executing instructions of programs in storage, and regulating output. I/O devices must be assigned to specific programs, and data must be moved between them and specific memory locations. The *input/output management system* oversees and coordinates these processes.

Processing Programs   The operating system contains several processing programs that facilitate efficient processing operations. The processing programs are available to the user to simplify program preparation and execution. The major processing programs contained in the operating system are the language translators, library programs, and utility programs.

Applications programs are seldom (if ever) written in machine language, because of the complexity and time that would be required to write them. Instead, most programs are written in a language closely resembling English. A *language-translator program*, as its name implies, translates English-like programs written by programmers into machine-language instructions (1s and 0s).

A number of programming languages are available. Common examples are FORTRAN, COBOL, and PL/1. The programmer must specify (in a job-control statement) the language in which a program is written. When the program is to be executed, the job-control program interprets that job-control statement and informs the supervisor which language translator is needed. The supervisor then calls the appropriate language translator from the system residence device. The language translator converts the program into machine language so it can be executed.

Library programs are user-written or manufacturer-supplied programs and subroutines which are frequently used in other programs. Rather than write these routines every time they are needed, they are written and stored in a *system library* (usually on magnetic disk or tape) and called into main storage when needed. They are then linked together with other programs to perform specific tasks. A *librarian program* manages the storage and use of library programs by maintaining a directory of programs in the system library; it contains appropriate procedures for adding and deleting programs.

Operating systems also include a set of *utility programs* that perform specialized functions such as transferring data from one I/O device to another. For example, a utility program can be used to transfer data from punched cards to magnetic tape or the reverse.

Other programs known as *sort/merge programs* are also utility programs. They are used to sort records into a particular sequence to facilitate updating of files. Once sorted, several files can then be merged to form a single, updated file. To perform these tasks, job-control statements are used to specify the sort and merge programs. These programs or routines are then called into storage when needed.

LEVELS OF LANGUAGE

The programmer uses a sequence of instructions to communicate with the computer and to control program execution. As computers have developed in complexity, so have programming languages. Today there are three levels of language groups, known as machine languages, assembly languages, and high-level languages (see Figure 9–3).

Machine Language

Machine language is as old as the computer itself. It is the code that designates the proper electrical states in the computer. Machine language is expressed as combinations of 0s and 1s. It is the only language the computer can execute directly; therefore, it can be called the language of the computer.

Each type of computer has its own machine language. That language is not transferrable to another type of computer. Each machine-language instruction must specify not only what operation is to be done but also the storage locations of data items. Due to these requirements, machine-language programming is extremely complex, tedious, and time-consuming. Figure 9–4 shows a sequence of machine-language instructions for a UNIVAC System 70/7. It contains operation codes and primary-storage addresses, expressed in the hexadecimal number system.

Assembly Language

Because machine-language programming is difficult, other languages have been developed. An *assembly language* is similar to a machine language but one step removed from it in the direction of human understanding. Programmers who are using assembly languages must be very conscious of the computer and must designate not only operations to be performed but also storage locations. This requirement is similar to that of machine language. However, instead of the 0 and 1

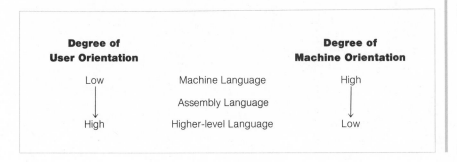

FIGURE 9–3
Language Levels

Degree of User Orientation		Degree of Machine Orientation
Low	Machine Language	High
	Assembly Language	
High	Higher-level Language	Low

```
48 00 23C0
4C 00 23C2
40 00 2310
D2 01 2310 2310
48 00 2310
4E 00 2028
F3 17 3002 2028
9G F0 3003
```

FIGURE 9–4
Machine-Language Instructions Expressed in the Hexadecimal Number System

groupings of machine language, convenient symbols and abbreviations are used in writing programs. For instance, "STO" may stand for STORE, and "TRA" may stand for TRANSFER. Even with these conveniences, programming in assembly language is cumbersome, although not as difficult as machine-language programming (see Figure 9–5).

FIGURE 9–5
Assembly-Language Program

```
PGM1        START    0
            PRINT    NOGEN
            SAVE     (14, 12)
            BALR     2,0
            USING    *,2
            OPEN     (IOIN,(INPUT))
FIRST       GET      IOIN,NUMB
            PACK     WORKA,A
            PACK     WORKB,B
            ZAP      WORKC,WORKA
            AP       WORKC,WORKB
            UNPK     C,WORKC
            OI       C+1,X'F0'
            PUT      PRINT,OUTA
            B        FIRST
ENDOFJOB    CLOSE    IOIN
            CLOSE    PRINT
            RETURN   (14,12)
NUMB        DS       0CL80
A           DS       CL1
B           DS       CL1
            DS       CL78
OUTA        DS       0CL132
            DS       CL1
C           DS       CL2
            DS       CL129
WORKA       DS       PL1
WORKB       DS       PL1
WORKC       DS       PL2
            END      PMG1
```

High-Level Programming Languages

High-level languages are the culmination of sophistication in programming languages. They are procedure- and problem-oriented. They are designed so that most of the programmer's attention can be directed to problem solving rather than to computer operations. Many high-level languages are English-like and allow use of common mathematical terms and symbols. The time and effort needed to write a program are reduced, and programs are easier to correct and modify.

High-level languages are so called because they are farthest removed from the hardware; they least resemble the 0 and 1 combinations of machine language. Whereas one assembly-language instruction is generally equivalent to one machine-language instruction, one high-level-language statement can accomplish the same result as a half-dozen or more machine-language instructions. The principal reason for this is that the addresses for many of the required storage locations do not have to be specified; they are handled automatically.

Figure 9–6 illustrates one statement written in the COBOL high-level language and the machine-language instructions that correspond to it. The machine-language instructions are expressed in the hexadecimal number system.

Machine-language and assembly-language programs are written for a particular computer and cannot generally be executed on other computers. Programs in high-level languages can usually be transferred from one computer to another with little change. Many high-level languages have been developed. FORTRAN, COBOL, and PL/1 were mentioned previously. Other examples are BASIC, APL, and RPG. Each has certain advantages, disadvantages, and applications areas. These languages will be discussed in Chapter 11.

LANGUAGE TRANSLATION

As noted above, machine language is the only language the computer can execute directly. A sequence of machine-language instructions and appropriate data can be entered into the computer and results produced (see Figure 9–7).

FIGURE 9–6

One COBOL Statement and Corresponding Machine-Language Instructions

(a) **COBOL**

```
       STANDARD-ROUTINE.
         MULTIPLY HOURS-WORKED BY WAGE-PER-HOUR GIVING GROSS-PAY.
```

(b) **MACHINE LANGUAGE**

```
*STANDARD-ROUTINE
         000778                    PN=02 EQU  *
MULTIPLY 000778 F2 71 D 1E8 7 010        PACK 1E8(8,13),010(2,7)   TS=01      DNM=1-201
         00077E F2 73 D 1F0 7 012        PACK 1E0(8,13),012(4,7)   TS=09      DNM=1-223
         000784 FC 42 D 1E8 D 1E5        MP   1E8(5,13),1E5(3,13)  TS=04      TS=014
         00078A F3 43 6 000 D 1EC        UNPK 000(5,6),1EC(4,13)   DNM=1-347  TS=05
         000790 96 F0 6 004              OI   004(6),X'F0'         DNM=1-347+4
         000794 58 10 D 21C              L    1,21C(0,13)          VN=02
         000798 07 F1                    BCR  15,1
```

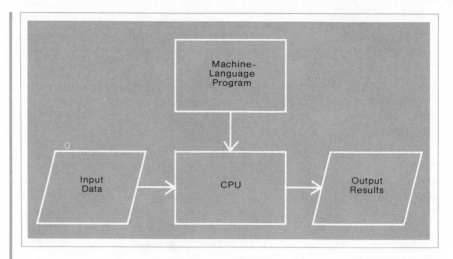

FIGURE 9–7
Machine-Language
Execution

Assembly and high-level languages are much more widely used by programmers, but programs written in these languages cannot be executed directly by the computers. So, an assembly-language or a high-level-language program is converted into machine-executable form by a language-translator program. The sequence of instructions written in either assembly language or high-level language by the programmer is called a *source program*. The language-translator program transforms the source-program statements into a machine-executable program known as an *object program*. The sequence of machine-language instructions (object program) provided by the language translator accomplishes the same operations as a program written originally in machine-language form.

The translator program for an assembly language is called an *assembler program*. A high-level-language translator is called a *compiler program*. Both assemblers and compilers are designed for specific machines and languages. For example, a compiler that translates a source program written in FORTRAN into a machine-language program can only translate FORTRAN (see Figure 9–8). The same is true for all high-level and assembly languages.

During compilation or assembly (the translation process), the object program is generated. The programmer also receives an assembly listing or a source-program listing with indications of any errors the assembler or compiler detected during translation. The errors are usually violations of the rules associated with the particular programming language. For example, if a statement begins in column 6 on a punched card but it should begin in column 8, an error message will be generated. Similarly, an error message will be generated if language keywords such as WRITE and COMPUTE are misspelled. Only after all errors have been corrected can the resultant object program be submitted to the computer to be executed. Therefore, several attempts at successful compilation or assembly may be needed. The complete process of compilation and execution of a COBOL program is shown in Figure 9–9. In this case, the

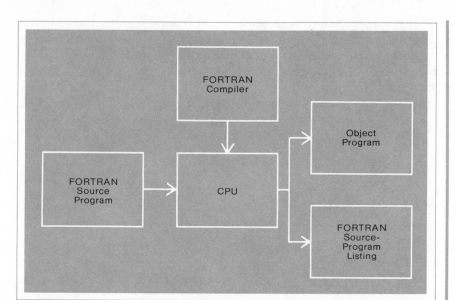

FIGURE 9–8
FORTRAN Program
Translation

FIGURE 9–9
COBOL Program Translation
and Execution

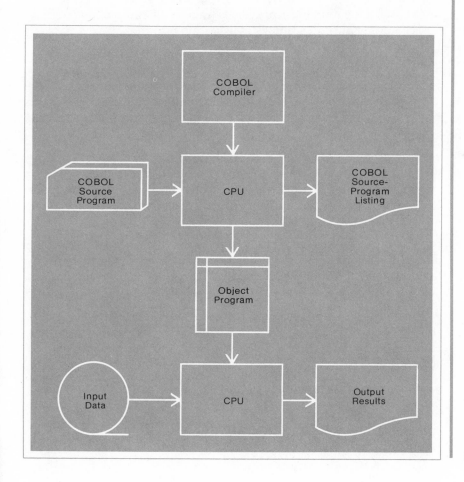

COBOL program has been punched on cards, and the data for the program has been stored on magnetic tape.

Compilers and assemblers are integral parts of operating systems. As mentioned earlier, the programmer indicates on a job-control statement the specific language of the source program. The appropriate translator is loaded into primary storage and produces the object program to be executed by the computer.

SUMMARY

● A program is a series of step-by-step instructions required to solve a problem. Applications programs solve user problems whereas system programs coordinate the operation of all computer circuitry.

● System programs are generally provided by the computer manufacturer or a specialized programming firm. Applications programs are usually developed within the organization, although some can be purchased.

● An operating system is a collection of programs designed to permit a computer system to manage its own operations. It allocates computer resources among multiple users, keeps track of all information required for accounting purposes, and establishes job priorities.

● Batch (stacked-job) operating systems allow uninterrupted processing of a batch of jobs without operator intervention. Real-time operating systems can respond to spontaneous requests for system resources, such as management inquiries entered from online terminals. Operating systems that can handle both batch and real-time applications are available.

● An operating system consists of control programs and processing programs. The supervisor is the major component of the operating system. It controls the other subsystems: job-control program, input/output management system, library programs, utility programs, and language translators.

● A job-control language (JCL) is the communication link between the programmer and the operating system. Job-control statements specify the beginning of a program, identify the program to be executed, and describe the work to be done.

● The input/output management system is part of the operating system control programs. It receives input from channels, regulates output, assigns I/O devices to specific programs, and coordinates all I/O activities.

● Language translators convert English-like programs into machine-language instructions. Library programs consist of programs and subroutines which are frequently used in other programs. They are stored in a system library (usually on magnetic tape or disk) and called into main storage when needed.

● Utility programs perform specialized functions like sorting, merging, and transferring data from one I/O device to another.

● There are three levels of language groups: (1) machine language is expressed as combinations of 0s and 1s and is the only language the computer can execute directly; (2) assembly language provides convenient symbols and abbreviations for writing programs; and (3) high-level languages are English-like, procedure- and problem-oriented, and can usually be transferred from one computer to another with little change.

● A sequence of instructions written in assembly language or high-level language is called a source program. The language translator converts the source program into a machine-language equivalent known as an object program.

● The translator program for an assembly language is called an assembler program. A high-level-language translator is called a compiler program. Compilers and assemblers are integral parts of operating systems.

REVIEW QUESTIONS

1. Distinguish between applications programs and system programs. Give examples of both types of programs and explain why they belong to that particular category.

2. What are the major functions performed by an operating system? Is an operating system that can handle stacked-job processing more complex and sophisticated than one that allows real-time processing? Explain.

3. What are the major components of an operating system? Briefly explain the functions of each component.

4. What is the primary purpose of a job-control language?

5. Who is most likely to use utility programs and why?

6. How do high-level languages differ from machine languages?

7. Distinguish between a source program and an object program. In doing so, explain why language translators are required.

NCR CORPORATION

NCR

The first cash register was invented in 1879 by a Dayton cafe owner, James Ritty, and his brother John. By 1883, the National Manufacturing Company had been formed to manufacture the new device. John H. Patterson, who was using two cash registers in his small store in Coalton, Ohio, found that they proved to be the difference between operating at a loss and making a profit. Patterson bought 25 shares of stock in the National Manufacturing Company. He became its secretary and a member of the Board of Directors. In 1884, he purchased a controlling interest and changed the company's name to the National Cash Register Company.

Patterson's first factory employed 13 people and produced as many as five cash registers a week. By 1900, the company's registers were widely used throughout the United States and overseas. Today, almost 100 years later, the corporation employs 65,000 people and has sales and service facilities in more than 100 countries.

To more accurately reflect the corporation's commitment to providing total electronic data-processing systems to a variety of industries world-wide, the Board of Directors changed the company's name in 1974 from the National Cash Register Company to the NCR Corporation. While NCR is still involved in the design and manufacture of retail systems, its market has expanded to encompass many other types of products.

NCR Corporation today is a multinational organization engaged in developing, producing, marketing, and servicing business equipment and computer systems. Its product line includes electronic data-processing systems, electronic point-of-sale terminals for retail stores and financial institutions, a variety of data-entry and retrieval terminals, individual freestanding business equipment, business forms, supplies, and related accessories.

NCR develops applications software as well as system software to support its equipment. A major new application is NCR MISSION (Manufacturing Information System Support Integrated On-Line). One of the largest applications ever undertaken by the company, MISSION can be used as a single- or multiple-plant system for the complete control of an industrial company's manufacturing operations.

Numerous NCR plants across the nation and abroad are involved in the design and manufacturing of hardware and software for NCR products. The plants are decentralized in nature. Each plant has a separate Management Information System (MIS) Department to support it and produce the systems it needs. In an attempt to incorporate all common manufacturing systems used by the plants, a group called the Manufacturing Control System (MCS) was formed to oversee all the MIS departments. This overall MIS function was staffed with applications programmers from outside the company. They brought new thoughts and ideas to NCR. The group interviewed the NCR plant managers to determine their individual needs. They found these needs to be not only common among NCR management, but also similar to those found in any type of manufacturing plant. The MCS group broke the system into subunits and assigned these subunits to separate plants for development. The design of system files, transaction processing, and I/O interfaces was required.

A Design Review Committee of user personnel from three different plants was established to evaluate the design and documentation produced by the various developing plants and to insure that the systems satisfied user specifications. Upon agreement of the final design, the MIS department within each plant proceeded with applications programming.

The total system design includes 11 applications modules that work together and draw upon common resources. Four of these modules, or subsystems, have been completed: the Bill of Material, Material Management, Inventory Management, and Material Requirements Planning.

The only difference between MISSION and an application designed specifically for customer use is that it was originally designed for use in NCR's manufacturing plants. Therefore, the system had to go through the normal system tests before it was ready for use. The first of these tests is known as BETA test. For MISSION, it was a complete in-house system test of the four completed applications subsystems. This is followed by GAMMA test, which insures the quality of the application. The final procedure is Customer Verification Test (CVT). Normally, the system is installed in a user site for this test. In the case of MISSION, the system was installed in one of NCR's plants.

Because of MISSION's successful debut internally, the four completed subsystems have been made available to NCR customers. Each applications subsystem is made up of 25 to 200 separate programs. For example, the Bill of Materials application contains 100 separate programs, half of which accept input from online terminals.

Development of a system such as MISSION requires many people and a lot of time. MISSION was started in 1974. The first complete year was spent in doing system analysis and building a staff. It will probably be 1980 before all 11 applications modules of the system are ready for the marketplace.

The applications programs must be supported by system software. NCR's software includes several operating systems, each tailored for maximum efficiency in either a batch or an online/real-time environment. The batch operating system handles all input and output operations automatically and contains the routines necessary to intermix data transfers. The operating system can accommodate new hardware designs and peripheral equipment without reprogramming.

The online/real-time operating system functions in either of two ways. In a dedicated, single-purpose online mode, it processes inquiry and updating trans-actions as they occur. In a dual programming mode, it accommodates both a high-priority, online foreground program and a low-priority, batch background program in a single system. When the foreground program has no data to process, control is given to the background program until online processing is again required. This procedure permits the user to take full advantage of CPU time otherwise wasted when an online system is inactive.

NCR also offers five high-level language compilers. They are NEAT/3, COBOL, FORTRAN, NCR RPG, and NCR BASIC. NEAT/3 is NCR's comprehensive, proprietary programming language that can be used for all general business applications. It is a narrative, job-oriented language that permits the user to accomplish many machine functions with a single statement.

Supporting applications software and operating systems is an integral part of the NCR total-systems concept. The company's broad range of software products is one of their greatest strengths in helping make customers' investments in NCR systems more productive.

DISCUSSION POINTS

1. Describe the two modes in which NCR's real-time operating system functions.

2. What are the advantages of purchasing an applications package such as MISSION instead of developing it in-house? What are the disadvantages?

THE PROGRAMMING PROCESS | 10

OUTLINE

I. Program Development
   A. Defining the Problem
   B. Planning a Problem Solution
   C. Writing the Program
   D. Program Debugging
   E. Testing the Program
      1. Dump
      2. Trace
II. Basic Logic Patterns
   A. Simple Sequence
   B. Selection

   C. Loop
   D. Branch or Link
III. Program Flowcharting
   A. Modular and Detailed
      Flowcharting
   B. Developing a Flowchart
IV. Documentation
V. Programming Case Study

INTRODUCTION

Many people solve problems instinctively; they do not have to identify each step in the solution process. Many times, the initial steps in solving a problem are completed before the final steps are even known. Unfortunately, a computer lacks these human capabilities. Solving a problem with the help of a computer requires a great deal of planning. All the steps required to solve the problem must be identified and coded into a logical instruction sequence before the computer can be used to perform the computations and get the correct result.

The stages involved in the development of a program are identified and discussed in this chapter. Program debugging and testing techniques are illustrated. The four traditional, basic patterns of program logic that can be used to solve any problem are explained. Both modular and detailed flowcharts are discussed in detail. The importance of documentation is emphasized. Finally, a sample program is developed to illustrate the complete programming process.

LET'S GO, BIG BEIGE MACHINE!

Jim Kaplan

Sports Illustrated,
Aug. 22, 1977, p. 42

An outfit known as the International Federation for Information Processing held the world chess championships last week, and although there were television lights in the hall, running commentary over a mike, and delays in the action, there wasn't a single complaint by the players. As a matter of fact, the players didn't mind at all. They were computers.

The occasion was the second World Computer Chess Championships at Toronto's Hotel Toronto. Sixteen programs from eight countries fought it out while an overflow crowd cheered, International Master David Levy did play-by-play, and the programmers talked and joked even as their computers broke down. Suddenly, chess was in danger of becoming a social event.

But computer chess is more than a sideshow, and when chess masters get over their knee-jerk objections to playing machines, they will discover that the computers are the best thing to happen to the game since the Fischer boom. The best programs are no match for masters, but someday they may extend the frontiers of chess knowledge. Freed from stereotyped lines of play, computer programs create bizarre and unexpected variations. They play wild and woolly games, alternately veering into winning and losing positions. And in their present, erratic state, they sometimes make more human errors than humans. A computer once took 86 minutes to ponder a move that was in the book.

The history of chess-playing machines dates back to 1770, when Baron Wolfgang von Kempelen unveiled his automatin at the court of Empress Maria Theresa of Austria. The machine consisted of a desk with a chessboard on top, manned by a human-like figure dressed as a Turk. It created an instant sensation. It was not until half a century later, after Napoleon among others had played it, that the Turk was exposed as a fake manipulated by a man inside. The first uninhabited computers that could play an acceptable game of chess came out in the 1950s, but the chess Establishment held them in contempt until 1976, when Northwestern University's CHESS 4.6, the brains of Control Data's beige-colored CYBER 176 computer, beat all-human fields in the Minnesota Open and California B division tournaments.

Now controversy has replaced contempt. Among the spectators in Toronto was Mikhail Botvinnik, 66, the Soviet world champion for 13 years. Botvinnik, who is working on a program of his own, says, ''Man is limited, man gets tired, man's program changes very slowly. Computer not tired, has great memory, is very fast.'' Disagreeing was 92-year-old Edward Lasker, the first master to play against a computer. ''Some thoughts you can't program,'' he said.

Chess is computerized much the same as anything else. All the vital information—material value, board squares, mobility—is given numerical value, with the machine striving for maximum worth. Set to analyze as many as one million variations of a move and plan eight moves ahead, the best computers can outplay their programmers, especially in complicated tactical situations. They are weaker at what programmers call ''heuristics''—the ability to approximate human thinking—and fall down in such areas as position and spatial relationships.

Just how far computers have come, the overflow crowds in Toronto hoped to discover in the expected showdown between CHESS 4.6, the North American champion, and the Soviets' defending world champion KAISSA, which is named after the goddess of chess. Unfortunately, the match short-circuited. The Soviets took the chance of reprogramming their computer a few weeks before the tournament. They failed to discover a bug, and it cost them an opening-day match with an aggressive Duke University program named, inevitably, DUCHESS. Because the tournament was being played under the Swiss system, with winners playing winners and losers playing losers, the big U.S.–U.S.S.R. match didn't come off. CHESS 4.6 sailed by DUCHESS in the third round and met Ma Bell's own BELLE in the finals.

Perhaps it was just as well. BELLE was every bit as lovable as *Star Wars'* R2-D2. Asked by its programmer, Ken Thompson, if it would beat 4.6, BELLE spewed out lengthy answer from the *I Ching.* An excerpt: ''The Prince shoots at a hawk on a high wall. He kills it. Everything serves to further.'' Alas, 4.6's program was further along. Watching it gobble up BELLE, University of Minnesota computer scientist Warren Stenberg remarked, ''The pawn structure looks like a horde of Brazilian army ants.'' In a special exhibition the following night, CHESS 4.6 beat KAISSA, establishing itself as the world's best, and its young programmers, Larry Atking (31) and David Slate (32), as the game's new hotshots.

Even announcer Levy was impressed, and he is just a year away from winning a $2000 bet that he can go a decade without losing to a computer. ''I'd need odds the next time,'' he said. Added Monty Newborn, author of *Computer Chess,* ''Seven years ago the best players came to laugh. This time they came to watch. Seven years from now they'll come to learn.''

The United States Chess Federation, which has been slow to acknowledge computer growth, recently voted to allow computers to take part in human tournaments but has not decided whether computers will be allowed to win prize money. If computers ever dominate human play, they may eventually be restricted to their own tournaments. Will they reduce chess to a mathematical formula? No problem yet. There are as many variations to a chess game as there are grains of sand in the universe.

''The first time I saw a computer it was playing in a Massachusetts tournament,'' says Shelby Lyman, who did television commentary during the Fischer–Spassky series. ''I never saw a more depressed person than the guy who was playing it. Finally, the thing got to the end game and lost. I went around saying, 'Boy, is that thing stupid.' That was 1972. Now I'm impressed.

''If computers became better players than people, I would be delighted. I mean, why not? It wouldn't stop humans from playing. Someday computers could help the top masters. Why should we be afraid of such things?''

The logic of chess lends itself quite readily to imaginative computer programming. Similar operations must be followed in both programming and chess playing, namely, analyzing the problem, planning, and simulating various solutions. This chapter focuses on the program-development process.

219

PROGRAM DEVELOPMENT

If we elect to use a computer to solve a problem, the solution must first be reduced to a series of specific steps, or instructions. These instructions must be extremely detailed; they must also be expressed in a language the computer can understand. The names and locations of files must be specified; the sizes of data fields must be designated; and the logic and calculations to be used must be spelled out. Once the solution is defined and reduced to specific steps, the computer can be used, with all its capabilities, to execute the steps—to process the input and produce the appropriate output.

Regardless of the complexity of the problem to be solved, computer problem-solving includes five steps:

1. Defining the problem

2. Designing a problem solution

3. Writing the program

4. Submitting the program for compilation, and locating and correcting any errors the compiler detects

5. Testing the program with sample data and locating and correcting any remaining errors

Normally, these steps are performed in the sequence shown. Obviously, the problem must be defined and the solution planned before the program can be written. At times, however, the programmer may need to retrace earlier steps to correct oversights or to define the problem in greater detail.

Several people are usually involved in the solution process: managers, system analysts, programmers, and clerical workers. In some cases, one individual has sole responsibility for solving the problem. Nevertheless, all efforts must be carefully coordinated to achieve the desired results.

Defining the Problem

Defining the problem begins with recognizing the need for information. In many cases, the process is initiated by a management request for information. In other cases, an analyst works with the manager to determine the specific information requirements.

The objective of the program must be stated clearly and concisely at the outset. So, the analyst or programmer begins with a definition of the outputs requested. A detailed description of the information needed or the task to be accomplished is established at this time. If a program is to produce printed reports, the layout and the information to be contained in each report must be defined.

Next, the input required to accomplish the objective of the program must be determined. This involves a statement of not only what input is needed, but also where the input will originate. It may be necessary to design a system to collect the necessary data, if that data is not already available.

The manipulations and calculations to be performed must be determined in the problem-definition step. This may involve describing files and records and designing data-collection and input documents. The complexity and time required in the problem-definition step depend on whether the system is being newly designed or being modified. In all cases, however, all findings from this step should be clearly documented for future reference.

Planning a Problem Solution

When the problem definition has been completed, the design of the solution (one or more computer programs) begins. The programmer usually breaks the problem into subunits (segments) and works out a tentative program flow. Breaking the problem into manageable subunits at this point greatly simplifies the program-coding task that must be performed later.

A computer operates in a logical manner. The programmer must structure the problem solution to meet this requirement. Therefore, a logical sequence of tasks must be outlined. The computer instructions may exhibit the same step-by-step logic that a human would use to solve the same problem.

A programmer frequently draws a *flowchart* to visualize the program logic. The flowchart is a diagrammatical representation of the program. (Flowcharting is discussed in greater detail later in this chapter.) Instead of designing a program while writing it, the programmer can sketch out a flowchart and notice flaws or omissions in the problem solution before beginning to actually write the program.

Writing the Program

After the programmer has defined the problem and designed a solution, the program is written in a specific language. Normally, the type of programming language to be used is considered in the solution-planning step, since this decision may affect the solution to the problem as well as the ultimate structure of the program. As we will see in the next chapter, programming languages are usually designed for specific types of applications. For example, FORTRAN is a language designed primarily for scientific applications; COBOL is normally used for business applications.

One key to success in using a computer is to always keep in mind that the computer can do only what it is instructed to do. It cannot correct logical mistakes. If the programmer is using a machine language or an assembly language, careful consideration must be given to the computer hardware. With a high-level language, the programmer can concentrate on problem-solving rather than on computer technology.

221

When the programmer writes (or *codes*) the problem solution in a programming language, special coding forms can be used (see Figure 10–1). These forms are designed to reflect the rules of the particular programming language, such as column restrictions. In addition, the use of coding forms helps to reduce clerical errors in coding and to simplify keypunching.

Program Debugging

After the program has been written, it is submitted to the computer. If a high-level language was used, the compiler that translates the program can detect grammatical errors, such as misspellings and incorrect punctuation. Errors in programs are called *bugs,* and the process of locating, isolating, and eliminating bugs is called *debugging.* The amount of time that must be spent in debugging depends on the quality of the program. A newly completed program rarely executes successfully the first time it is run. In fact, one-third to one-half of a programmer's time is spent in debugging.

To help the programmer debug a program, the compiler can provide a listing of all compiler-detected errors. This error-message listing may give the number of each statement in error. It may also describe the nature of the error (see Figure 10–2). Only after all errors have been corrected can the program be run with test data.

Testing the Program

When a compilation without errors is achieved, it is time for a test run. This run involves executing the program with input data that is either a

FIGURE 10–1

Some Commonly Used
Coding Forms

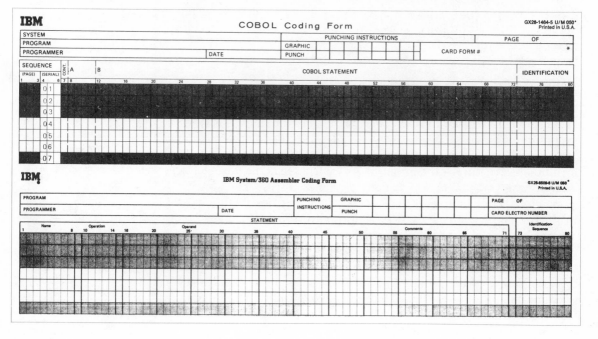

STATEMENT NUMBER	ERROR CODE	ERROR MESSAGES
1972	IKF1080I–W	PERIOD PRECEDED BY SPACE. ASSUME END OF SENTENCE.
1999	IKF1080I–W	PERIOD PRECEDED BY SPACE. ASSUME END OF SENTENCE.
2074	IKF1043I–W	END OF SENTENCE SHOULD PRECEDE 02. ASSUMED PRESENT.
2399	IKF2126I–C	VALUE CLAUSE LITERAL TOO LONG. TRUNCATED TO PICTURE SIZE.
2432	IKF1043I–W	END OF SENTENCE SHOULD PRECEDE 02. ASSUMED PRESENT.
2481	IKF1080I–W	PERIOD PRECEDED BY SPACE. ASSUME END OF SENTENCE.
2484	IKF1080I–W	PERIOD PRECEDED BY SPACE. ASSUME END OF SENTENCE.
2623	IKF1004I–E	INVALID WORD NOTE. SKIPPING TO NEXT RECOGNIZABLE WORD.
2623	IKF1007I–W	MINUS SIGN NOT PRECEDED BY A SPACE. ASSUME SPACE.
2623	IKF1007I–W	**NOT PRECEDED BY A SPACE. ASSUME SPACE.

representative sampling of actual data or a facsimile of it. Often, sample data that can be manipulated easily by the programmer is used so that the computer-determined output can be compared with programmer-determined correct results. The output should be easily recognizable upon inspection. This allows the programmer to see if the computer produces correct output.

A complex program is frequently tested in separate units so that errors can be isolated to specific sections. This aids in narrowing the search for the cause of an error. The programmer must correct all mistakes. Running and rerunning a specific unit may be necessary before the cause of an error can be found. The programmer rewrites the particular part in error and resubmits it for another test. Care is needed so that a correction of one logical error does not give rise to several others. Otherwise, this in turn extends the debugging time.

Each section of the program must be tested (even sections that will be used infrequently). If exception-handling instructions are part of the program, the sample input data should include items that test the program's ability to spot and reject improper data items. The programmer often finds *desk-checking* (desk-debugging) helpful. With this method, the programmer pretends to be the computer. By reading each instruction (and thus simulating how the computer would process a data item), the programmer attempts to catch any flaws in the program logic.

After a programmer has worked to correct the logic of a program for an extended length of time, he or she may tend to overlook errors or assume a clarity that in reality does not exist. For this reason, programmers sometimes trade their partially debugged programs among themselves. As each programmer steps through a "fresh" program, mistakes in logic that were hidden to the original programmer may be uncovered.

There are many cases where program errors are especially difficult to locate. In such cases, two commonly used diagnostic procedures are usually available to the programmer: dump programs and trace programs.

A dump program lists the contents of registers and main-storage locations. In some systems, the resultant printout, or *dump*, lists storage values in hexadecimal notation (see Figure 10–3). Trying to understand

FIGURE 10–2
Compiler-Detected Errors

```
USER STORAGE
                         CORE ADDRESSES SPECIFIED-      000000 TO '000390
J00C00    05C0E020  C0520064  E000C0B7  00064770    C032E020  C0860007  41200006  4130C0B7    *................................*
J00C20    45A0C17E  F235C107  C0B7FA33  C10BC107    47F0C006  4120000A  F393C174  C10B4130    *..A.2.A.....A.A..0.......3.A.A...*
J00C40    C17445A0  C218E020  C10F0064  E020C173    000B07FE  F1E3C8C5  E2C540C1  D9C540E3    *A...B..A......A......1THESE ARE T*
J00C60    C8C540E5  C1D3E4C5  F540D9C5  C1C44040    40404040  40404040  40404040  40404040    *HE VALUES READ                  *
J00C80    40404040  40404040  40404040  40404040    40404040  40404040  40404040  40404040    *                                *
J00CA0    40404040  40404040  40404040  40404040    40404040  40404040  40F0F2F1  F2F0D0F5    *                        02120.5*
J00CC0    F5F5F5F5  F5F5F5F5  F5F5F5F5  F5F5F5F5    F5F5F5F5  F5F5F5F5  F5F5F5F5  F5F5F5F5    *5555555555555555555555555555555555*
 LINES    0000E0-0000E0     SAME AS ABOVE
J00100    F5F5F5F5  F5F5F5F5  F5002120  0DF0F0F0    C0F0E3C8  C540E2E4  D44006C6  40E3C8C5    *555555555....000.0THE SUM OF THE*
J00120    40E5C1D3  E4C5E240  C9E24C040  40404040    40404040  40404040  40404040  40404040    * VALUES IS                      *
J00140    40404040  40404040  40404040  40404040    40404040  40404040  40404040  40404040    *                                *
J00160    40404040  40404040  40404040  40404040    40404040  4040F5F5  F5F5F5F5  F5F5F5F5    *                     5555555555*
J00180    0620954E  30004780  C19A9560  30004770    C1AC1A32  940F3000  47F0C1A0  1A3294CF    *........A.......*A.......*0A.....*
J001A0    30001B32  92F03000  A1220001  07FAE020    C1B40064  07FA40C6  C9D9E2E3  40C3C8C1    *......0...........A... FIRST CHA*
J001C0    D9C1C3E3  C5D940E2  C5D5E740  E3D640E7    C9D540E6  C1E240D5  D6E340C1  40E2C9C7    *RACTER SENT TO XIN WAS NOT A SIG*
J001E0    D5404040  40404040  40404040  40404040    40404040  40404040  40404040  40404040    *N                               *
```

FIGURE 10-3
Storage Dump

such a dump can be a cumbersome procedure; but once dump-reading is learned, it can be a very useful debugging technique. The programmer can determine whether data and instructions have been correctly stored in the proper locations. In this manner, errors can be traced to specific statements or data, and corrections can be made.

A *trace* produced by a trace program is much easier to use than a dump. The trace lists the steps followed during program execution in the order they occurred. The programmer can specify that all or specific portions of a program are to be traced. The trace is used in combination with the desk-checking procedure described above to see if the correct flow of execution has occurred. The values of selected variables can also be displayed in the trace. This can be helpful in determining if the necessary calculations have been performed correctly.

BASIC LOGIC PATTERNS

At times it may seem hard to believe that all of the varying problems that face users can be solved by the repeated use of a limited set of instructions. What is even more remarkable is that four basic patterns of program logic can be used to solve any problem. These four patterns are available in all computer languages; the languages vary only in the phrases that are used to express them.

Currently there is significant debate as to whether all four logic patterns should be employed. Supporters of structured programming maintain that the branch or link logic is not only unnecessary but also counterproductive. Since most programmers today still follow the traditional approach, all four program logic patterns are presented here (see Figure 10-4). However, since structured programming is gaining rapid acceptance, a later chapter is devoted to it.

PROGRAM FLOWCHARTING

When a programmer is attempting to develop the solution to a problem, many difficulties with regard to interrelationships and logic may arise. Flowcharting provides a visual frame of reference for this aspect of a

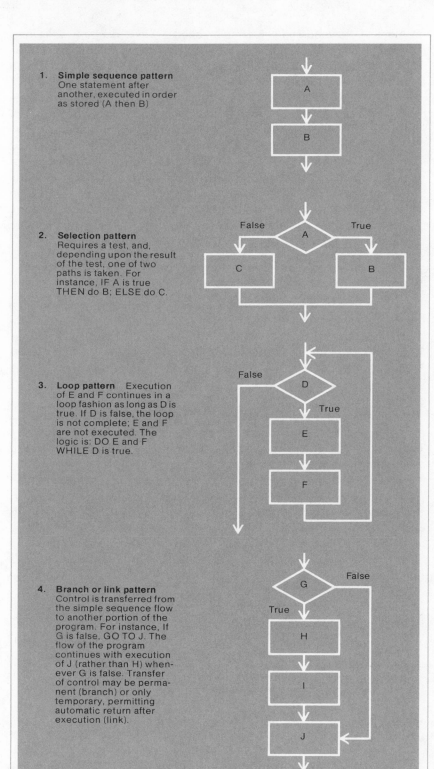

1. **Simple sequence pattern**
   One statement after another, executed in order as stored (A then B)

   A

   B

2. **Selection pattern**
   Requires a test, and, depending upon the result of the test, one of two paths is taken. For instance, IF A is true THEN do B; ELSE do C.

   False   A   True

   C   B

3. **Loop pattern** Execution of E and F continues in a loop fashion as long as D is true. If D is false, the loop is not complete; E and F are not executed. The logic is: DO E and F WHILE D is true.

   False   D   True

   E

   F

4. **Branch or link pattern**
   Control is transferred from the simple sequence flow to another portion of the program. For instance, If G is false, GO TO J. The flow of the program continues with execution of J (rather than H) whenever G is false. Transfer of control may be permanent (branch) or only temporary, permitting automatic return after execution (link).

   G   False

   True

   H

   I

   J

FIGURE 10–4
Four Traditional Program Logic Patterns

225

problem. A flowchart is sometimes called a *block diagram* or a *logic diagram*. It is constructed in a step-by-step fashion, similar to an outline. Each operation of the proposed program can be represented by an appropriate block on the flowchart.

A program flowchart shows the processing details needed to solve a problem. The flowchart serves as both a guide when coding the program and a helpful reference tool when debugging it. The flowchart also serves as invaluable documentation. The program may be modified several times during its life span, and the flowchart is an excellent reference guide for programmers who must make the changes. Thus, the flowchart should be complete, up-to-date, and easy to read. To help achieve these objectives, the American National Standards Institute (ANSI) has adopted a set of flowcharting symbols. These symbols are commonly accepted and used by programmers (see Figure 10–5).

Modular and Detailed Flowcharting

There is no set of rules determining the amount of detail required in a flowchart. As mentioned previously, complex programs can be simplified by breaking them into segments and handling a segment at a time. Therefore, it may be desirable to prepare two levels of flowcharts for a problem. One outlines the general flow and major segments of the program, and the other lists the detailed processing required in the segment.

A flowchart that outlines the general flow and major segments of a program is called a *modular program flowchart,* or *macro flowchart.* The major segments of the program are called *modules.* A *detailed program flowchart,* or *micro flowchart,* is used to depict the processing steps within one module. One set of flowcharts usually comprises one macro flowchart and several micro flowcharts.

An example can be used to illustrate the flowcharting process. This example deals with a problem that is common to all businesses today: accurately and efficiently calculating a payroll. The business, Heim & Sons Roofing Company, has many employees working different hours for different rates; they must be paid at scheduled times. The payroll is to be calculated by a computer program.

The following data is available for five employees of the Heim & Sons Roofing Company during the last one-week period:

EMPLOYEE NAME	HOURS WORKED	WAGE/HOUR
Lynn Mangino	35	8.00
Thomas Ritter	48	4.75
Marie Olson	45	5.50
Lori Dunlevy	40	5.00
William Wilson	50	7.00

FIGURE 10—5
Flowcharting Symbols

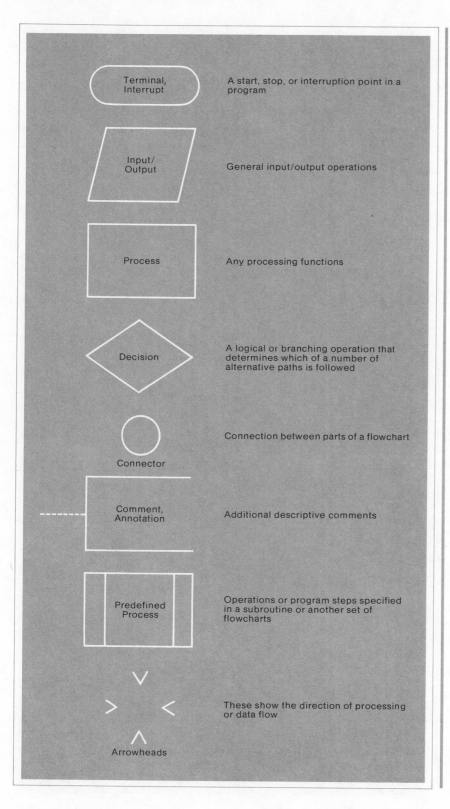

Terminal, Interrupt	A start, stop, or interruption point in a program
Input/ Output	General input/output operations
Process	Any processing functions
Decision	A logical or branching operation that determines which of a number of alternative paths is followed
Connector	Connection between parts of a flowchart
Comment, Annotation	Additional descriptive comments
Predefined Process	Operations or program steps specified in a subroutine or another set of flowcharts
Arrowheads	These show the direction of processing or data flow

227

To calculate an employees's gross pay, the hours worked are multiplied by the wage per hour. If an employee's gross pay is greater than $250, then the tax rate is 20 percent. Otherwise the tax rate is 14 percent. An employee's tax is calculated by multiplying gross pay by tax rate. The tax is then subtracted from gross pay to determine net pay.

Figure 10–6 shows examples of modular and detailed flowcharts for the payroll program. Notice that the modular flowchart contains only the major steps to be performed in the program. The block labeled CALCULATE TAX is one of the modules in the program. It is further expanded using a detailed flowchart to show the individual operations to be performed in that module. In complex programs, each module may be written by a different programmer. The modules may be tested individually, thus simplifying the debugging process. The focus of this

FIGURE 10–6

Modular and Detailed Flowcharts

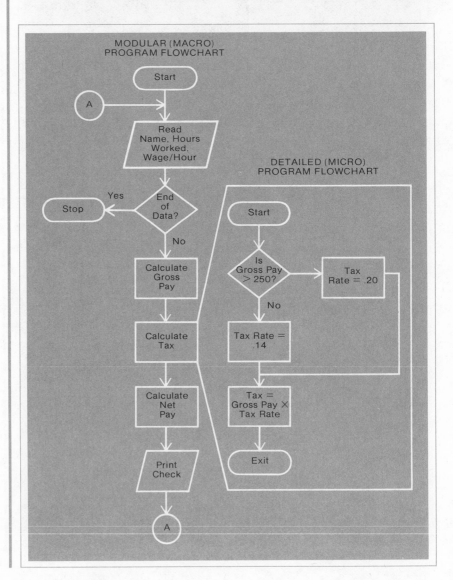

discussion is detailed flowcharting. Other flowcharting techniques will be discussed in Chapters 12 and 14.

Developing a Flowchart

A flowchart can be constructed for any situation that can be broken into separate steps. Assume, again, that the gross pay of an employee is to be calculated and a percentage of the gross pay is to be removed as tax, to yield the net pay. The following steps are required:

1. Input name, hours worked, wage/hour.

2. Calculate gross pay.

3. Calculate tax.

4. Calculate net pay.

5. Output name, net pay.

A diagram of this solution can be sketched with four types of flowcharting symbols (see Figure 10–7). The symbols are: *terminal* (⬭), *input/output* (▱), *process* (▭), and *flowline* (→). Their meanings are given in Figure 10–5, if you need to refer to them.

Notice that the flowchart begins at the top of the page and can be read from top to bottom. All flowchart blocks must contain text that is both understandable and concise. Use of a personal shorthand that is not recognizable by others is not advisable. It makes the diagram confusing.

The pay program outlined in Figure 10–7 will compute the net pay for one employee. One method of expanding the program to calculate net pay for more employees would be to repeat steps 1–5 for each employee. A program flowchart to calculate net pay for two employees appears in Figure 10–8. Imagine the flowchart needed to calculate net pay for 100, or even 1000, employees.

A shorter way to achieve the same results is to create a branch back to the beginning of the duplicated section of the program logic. In this instance, the branch is unconditional; the flow always returns to step 1 when step 5 has been completed. The branch is shown in Figure 10–9 by use of flowlines (flowchart on the left), and by use of *connector symbols* (○ flowchart on the right).

These flowcharts do not include a stop symbol indicating the end of the program. Since the branch is unconditional, the loop does not have an opportunity to terminate. Execution of a program coded with this logic would never end. Since programs that fail to end are not useful, a method of checking for the appropriate time to end should be instituted. We need one more type of symbol on the flowchart—the *decision symbol* (◇).

The decision symbol in Figure 10–10 represents a test for the presence of employee data in the input list. If another employee's statistics have been read, the calculation and output steps are repeated; if not, the

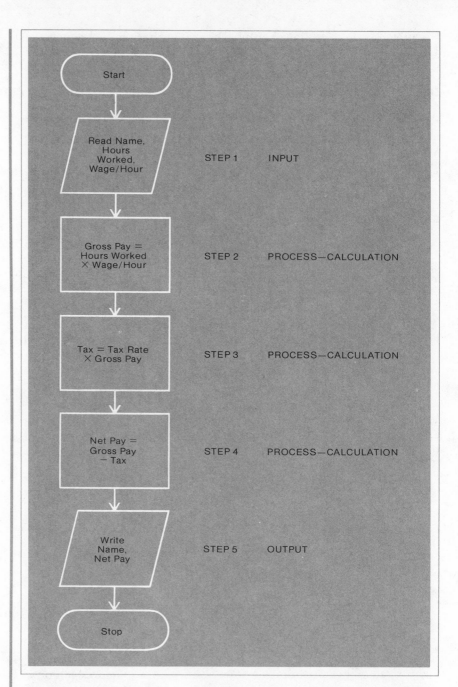

FIGURE 10—7
Pay Program Flowchart I

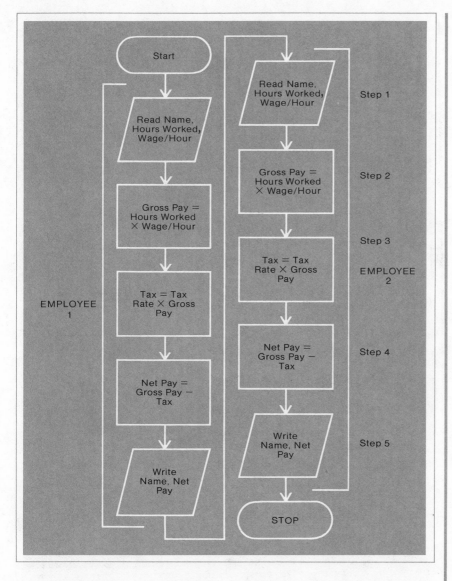

FIGURE 10—8
Pay Program Flowchart II

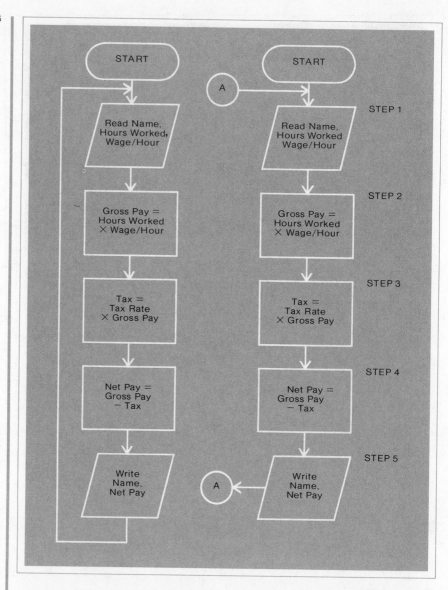

FIGURE 10—9
Pay Program Flowchart III

program terminates. This test is an example of a conditional branch. Branching to a different path is possible, but need not always occur. The particular path that is taken depends on the result of the test, "yes" or "no." (The decision block does not allow for "maybe.")

As a final example of flowcharting techniques, we again expand our net pay diagram. (See Figure 10–11.) Previously, we calculated the gross pay without regard to the specific number of hours worked. Now, if an employee has worked more than 40 hours, that employee is to receive time-and-a-half for all hours over 40. A decision block can be used to compare the hours worked to 40. If the hours worked are less than or equal to 40, the calculation flow shown in our previous examples is

followed.

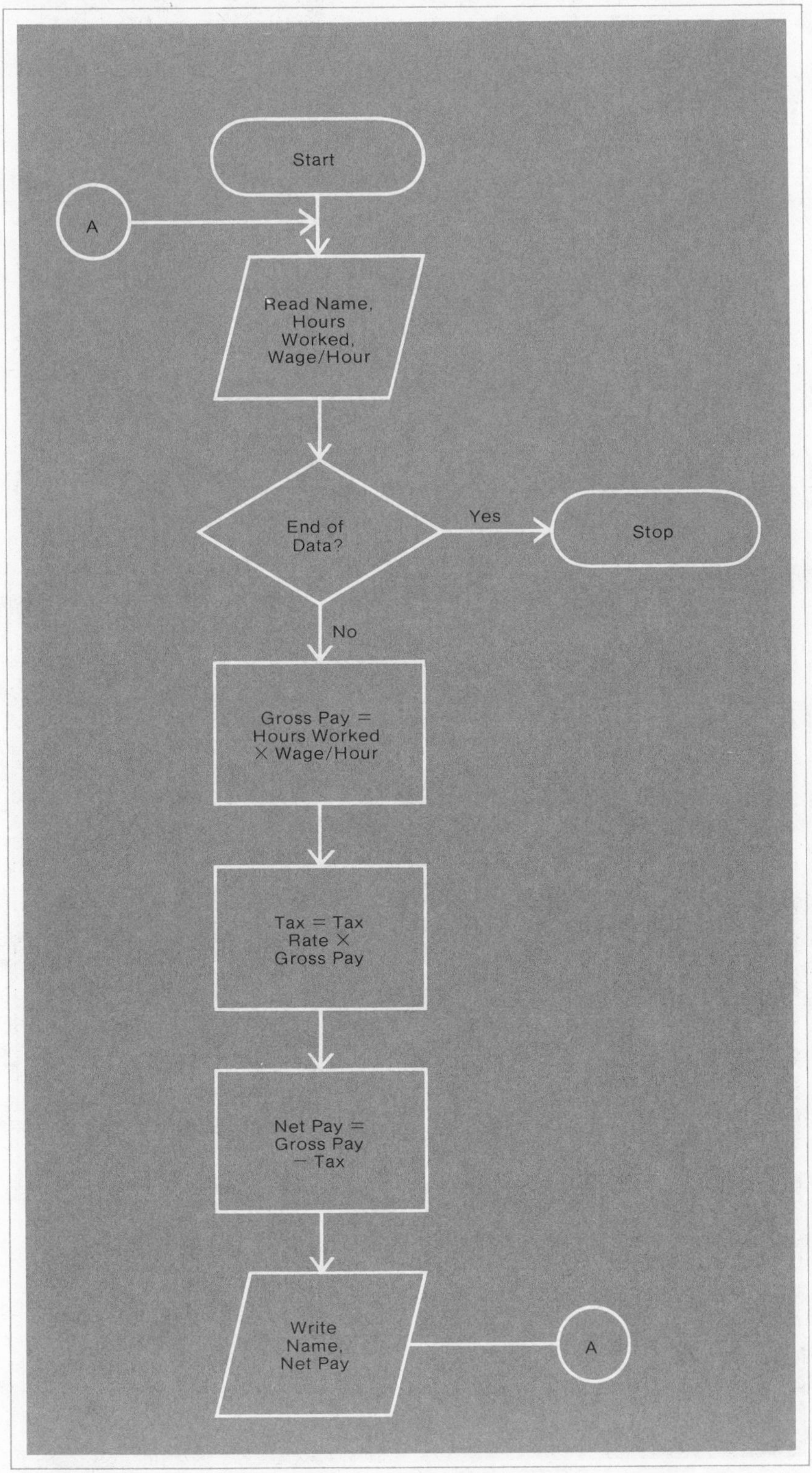

FIGURE 10—10
Pay Program Flowchart IV

FIGURE 10–11
Pay Program Flowchart V

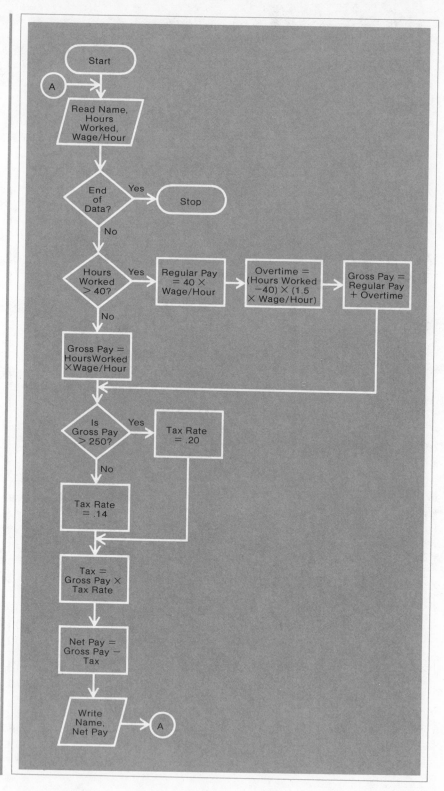

Furthermore, if an employee's gross pay is greater than $250, a tax rate of 20 percent applies. Otherwise, the tax rate is 14 percent. A decision block is used to compare the gross pay with 250. (Recall similar logic in the detailed program flowchart in Figure 10–6.)

DOCUMENTATION

Documentation consists of written descriptions and explanations of programs and other materials associated with an organization's data-processing systems. Documentation of system and program designs is one of the most important (and, unfortunately, one of the most neglected) requirements for success in a data-processing application. The importance of complete documentation has long been known, but many firms are only now beginning to insist that complete documentation is a prerequisite to implementing a new program or changing an existing one.

Proper program documentation serves as a reference guide for programmers and analysts who must modify or update existing programs and system procedures. Without it, a programmer may have to spend days or weeks trying to ascertain what a program does and how it does it. In many cases, programs are designed to operate under a fixed set of conditions and constraints. When organizations change and grow, program modifications are needed to meet the changing needs of the organization. Therefore, documentation helps management to evaluate the effectiveness of data-processing applications and to determine where changes are desirable.

Documentation is essential to those who must perform manual functions required by the system. When staff changes occur, new employees need complete documentation of all clerical procedures within the system. This information helps them to understand their jobs and how to carry them out. Finally, documentation provides instructions to the computer operator about the requirements (tape drives, card readers, etc.) for running particular programs.

The process of documentation is an ongoing process. It begins with the initial request for information. The individual making the request should be identified. So should those who will be charged with the responsibility of designing the system and the required programs. The names of the persons who must approve the request should be provided.

During the problem-definition phase, the problem should be stated clearly in a short narrative statement. The objectives of the program that will be created to solve the problem should be included with the problem statement. Several other descriptions are necessary. They include:

● A complete description of the contents and formats of all data inputs, outputs, and files to be used.

- A statement of the hardware requirements for running the program, such as magnetic-tape drives, disk drives, and card readers. Estimated processing time and storage requirements should also be stated.
- A statement of software requirements, such as utility programs and library programs. This statement may also identify the programming language to be used and list the reasons for choosing it.

Several aids for the programmer are available in this phase. Forms such as those shown in Figure 10–12 are particularly useful. Besides serving as documentation, these forms help in planning specific details of the program.

In the planning phase, the most important documentation produced is the flowchart. If the application is complex, both modular and detailed program flowcharts should be prepared. Descriptive comments may be included for each processing step. Completeness and accuracy are essential. If changes are made to the program, they must be reflected in the flowchart also. In this manner, all program documentation stays up-to-date.

There are two tools the programmer can use to simplify the flowcharting process. One is a flowcharting template (see Figure 10–13). The flowcharting template contains the commonly used program flowcharting symbols as well as several special-purpose symbols used in system flowcharting. (System flowcharting will be discussed in Chapter 14.) The template is normally made of plastic, and the symbols are represented by cut-outs which can be traced.

The second flowcharting tool is a pad of flowcharting worksheets. Typical worksheets contain 50 rectangles in which flowcharting symbols can be drawn (see Figure 10–14). Each rectangle is labeled with a letter and a number. These labels are helpful when connector symbols are needed, since distinct areas of the form can be pointed to within the connector symbols.

All the documentation for a program or system can be combined to form a *user's manual.* This manual contains program documentation designed to aid persons not familiar with a program in using the

FIGURE 10–12
Multiple-Card Layout Form and Print Chart

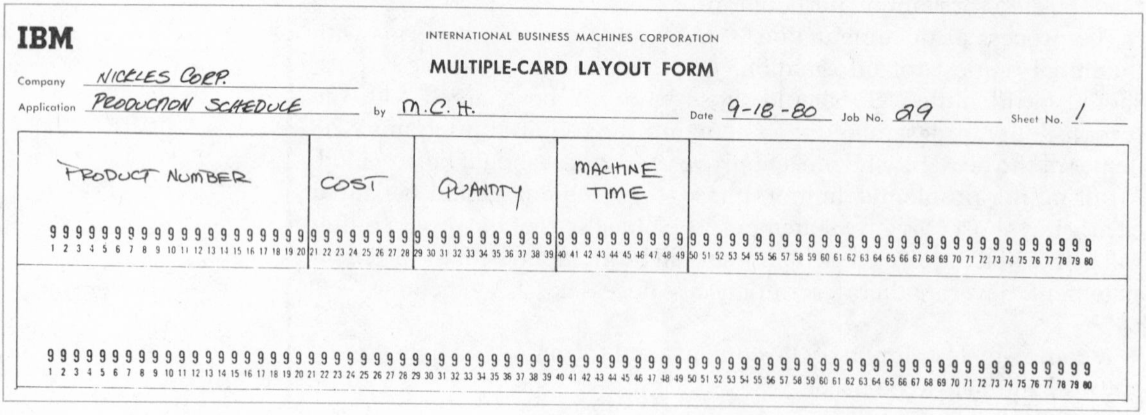
IBM
INTERNATIONAL BUSINESS MACHINES CORPORATION
MULTIPLE-CARD LAYOUT FORM
Company NICKLES CORP.
Application PRODUCTION SCHEDULE by M.C.H. Date 9-18-80 Job No. 29 Sheet No. 1

PRODUCT NUMBER | COST | QUANTITY | MACHINE TIME

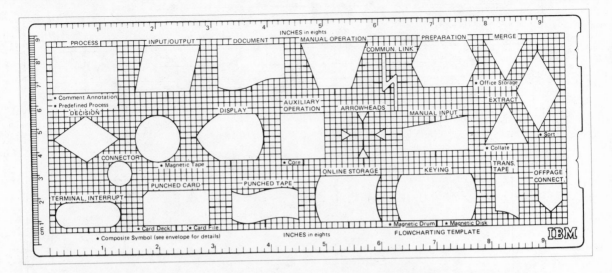

FIGURE 10–13
Flowcharting Template

program. It serves as a reference guide for managers who must evaluate the program and for programmers who must modify it. An *operator's manual*, sometimes known as a *run book*, should also be prepared. It contains the instructions needed to run the program. The computer operator who must run the program is the major user of the operator's manual.

PROGRAMMING CASE STUDY

The objective of this case problem is to calculate the average numerical grade for each student in a class and to determine his or her final letter grade for the course.

Our input will be the student names and the five numerical grades each received during the course. Our output requirements are to print the headings "Name," "Average," and "Final Grade," corresponding to the names of the students, average numerical grades, and final letter grades, which also are to be printed as output.

The final grade for each student is to be based upon the following grade scale:

AVERAGE	FINAL GRADE
90–100	A
80–89	B
70–79	C
60–69	D
0–59	F

Thus, the job requirements have been defined: the input will be student names and their grades; the required computation is the

237

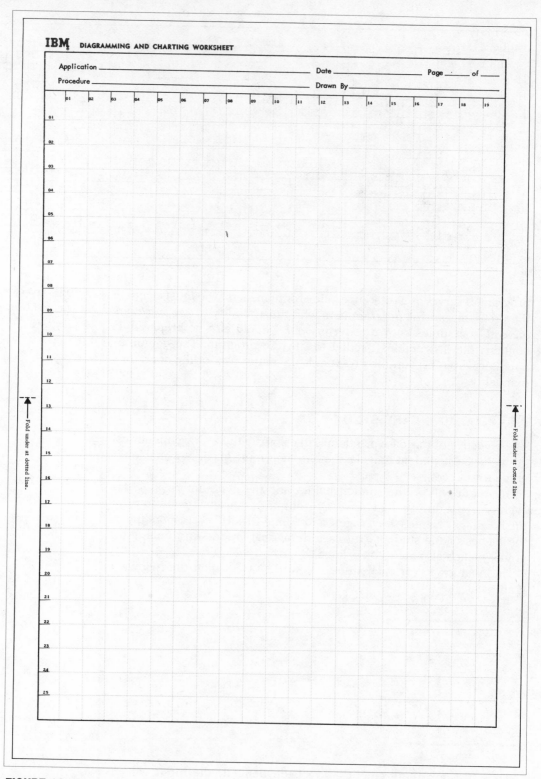

FIGURE 10–14
Flowcharting Worksheet

determination of average and final grades; and the required output is the student names, averages, and final grades listed under appropriate headings. It is important to remember that the problem solution must be defined logically, and that the computer must be given all relevant data and instructions.

The first step in designing a problem solution is to determine a basic instruction flow. Output headings can be printed before the student data is read as input. Since each student has five grades, the student name and five grades must be input, and the grades added together. When the addition has been completed, the average can be calculated. Once the average has been determined, the appropriate final letter grade can be assigned according to the grade scale. After the final letter grade has been established, the name, average, and final grade can be printed. When the data for one student has been processed, the data for the next student can be read and processed, and so on, until no more student statistics are available.

The flow can be placed into steps, as follows:

1. Print headings.

2. Read student's name and five grades.

3. Total the student's grade average.

4. Calculate the student's grade average.

5. Determine the final letter grade based on the grade scale.

6. Print name, average, and final grade.

7. Repeat steps 2–6 for all students.

8. Stop.

A flowchart for the solution of this case problem is given in Figure 10–15. The relationship between the steps above and the blocks on the flowchart is also pointed out.

After the flowchart has been constructed and the logic reviewed, the next task is to express the solution in a programming language. In this case, we use BASIC. The completed source program can then be entered into the computer via the keyboard of a terminal. Then it can be translated into an object program. A listing of the source program and notification of errors (if any) detected by the compiler will be generated. Then it can be executed.

Figure 10–16 shows the source-program listing. Figure 10–17 shows the output produced during the execution of the program.

SUMMARY

● In solving a problem, a programmer follows five steps: (1) defining the problem; (2) designing a problem solution; (3) writing the program; (4) submitting the program for compilation; and (5) testing the program with sample data.

239

FIGURE 10–15
Case-Study Flowchart

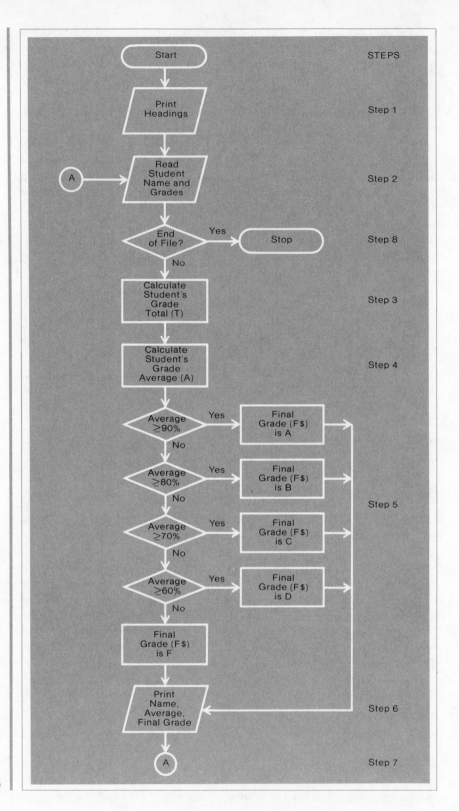

240

```
GRADE       21:54       TUESDAY JULY 25, 1978

100 REM THIS PROGRAM WILL ADD 5 INDIVIDUAL GRADES
110 REM FOR A STUDENT, CALCULATE THE AVERAGE, AND THEN
120 REM DETERMINE THE STUDENT'S FINAL GRADE
130 PRINT 'NAME', 'AVERAGE', 'FINAL GRADE'
140 PRINT
150 READ N$, G1, G2, G3, G4, G5
160 LET T = G1,+G2+G3+G4+G5
170 LET A = T/5
180 IF A >= 90 THEN 240
190 IF A >= 80 THEN 260
200 IF A >= 70 THEN 280
210 IF A >= 60 THEN 300
220 LET F$ = 'F'
230 GO TO 310
240 LET F$ = 'A'
250 GO TO 310
260 LET F$ = 'B'
270 GO TO 310
280 LET F$ = 'C'
290 GO TO 310
300 LET F$ = 'D'
310 PRINT N$, A, F$
320 GO TO 150
330 DATA 'FRED J. SMITH', 70, 65, 24, 100, 98
340 DATA 'JASON R. JACKSON', 97, 96, 59, 78, 60
350 DATA 'JOHN S. LAWSON', 90, 94, 88, 98, 96
360 DATA 'SUSAN EAKINS', 83, 76, 87, 89, 95
370 DATA 'MARY Q. JOHNSON', 66, 79, 83, 75, 70
999 END
```

FIGURE 10—16
BASIC Case Program with
Sample Data

FIGURE 10—17
Case-Study Output

```
RUN GRADE

GRADE       21:54       TUESDAY JULY 25, 1978

NAME                    AVERAGE FINAL GRADE

FRED J. SMITH           71.4    C
JASON R. JACKSON        78      C
JOHN S. LAWSON          93.2    A
SUSAN EAKINS            86      B
MARY Q. JOHNSON         74.6    C

LINE 150:   END OF DATA

TIME 0 SECS
```

● Defining the problem begins with recognizing the need for information, and then preparing a concise statement of what output is needed. The input, and the manipulations to be performed on this input to generate the required output, can then be identified.

● Designing a solution to the problem involves breaking the program into subunits, and outlining the logical sequence of steps required in each subunit. Flowcharts are used to visualize the program logic.

● The next step is to write the program in a specific language. Selection of an appropriate language is important because it may affect the solution to the problem. Special coding forms are available for the various programming languages; they help to reduce clerical errors and simplify keypunching.

● Programs are then debugged and tested. Testing is done using sample data so that the computer-determined output can be compared with predetermined correct results. Dump programs and trace programs provide diagnostics to help debug programs.

● There are four traditional patterns of program logic: simple sequence, selection, loop, and branch (or link). They can be used singly or in combination to solve any problem.

● A flowchart is a block diagram, constructed in a step-by-step fashion to provide a visual frame of reference for a problem's interrelationships and logic. The flowchart symbols most frequently used are: terminal, input/output, process, flowline, and decision.

● Flowcharts are prepared at two levels: general and detailed. The former are referred to as modular (macro) flowcharts; the latter are called detailed (micro) flowcharts.

● Program documentation is essential throughout the programming cycle. It simplifies modification and updating of existing programs and system procedures and is a must for the successful continuation of any program.

REVIEW QUESTIONS

1. Why is a complete problem definition critical to successful program development?

2. Explain some of the tools and techniques used in program debugging and testing.

3. Discuss the four traditional, basic logic patterns that can be used to solve any problem.

4. For what purposes are flowcharts used? Distinguish between modular flowcharts and detailed flowcharts, noting similarities and differences.

5. Why is documentation required? What types of documentation are needed during the various steps of program development?

On May 10, 1876, Colonel Eli Lilly, a Civil War veteran, began operation of a small laboratory in downtown Indianapolis, Indiana. The laboratory was dedicated to the manufacture of quality medications. With total assets of $1400 in fluid extracts and cash, Lilly began producing pills and other medicines. In 1881, the firm, which had since incorporated as Eli Lilly and Company, moved to the location in downtown Indianapolis that today continues to house its principal offices and research headquarters.

Two of the most well-known medical discoveries toward which Lilly provided substantial contributions are insulin and the Salk polio vaccine. At the University of Toronto in 1921, Banting and Best discovered that diabetes could be controlled by injections of an extract of animal pancreas glands. Their discovery led to a cooperative effort between the two scientists and Lilly in the development of insulin; it provided the foundation for modern diabetes management. In the case of the polio vaccine, independent research conducted by Lilly during the 1940s was combined with Dr. Salk's technique for making poliomyelitis vaccine. The capability to mass-produce the vaccine resulted in a 95 percent decrease in the incidence of polio within six years after its introduction.

Besides manufacturing pharmaceutical products, Lilly has diversified into cosmetics, agricultural products, and veterinary medicines, through its subsidiaries. Altogether, Lilly International has 36 affiliates in foreign countries, including 15 manufacturing plants in 13 of these countries and a major research center in England. The company also owns one-half interest in affiliated companies with manufacturing facilities in Spain and England.

With interests in business and research scattered across the globe, Eli Lilly and Company has developed an extensive data-processing operation structured to support every department of the corporation. The Scientific Information Systems Division handles activities related to research and development. The Information Systems Development Division supports the firm's business

application

ELI LILLY AND COMPANY

243

data-processing needs. The Corporate Computer Center consists of two large IBM computers and one Digital Equipment Corporation computer. They receive and process data transmitted to the Center via remote job-entry (RJE) teleprocessing and time-sharing terminals located in user departments of the corporation in United States and overseas locations. The Corporate Computer Center supports more than 100 time-sharing terminals, over 100 teleprocessing devices, and at least 50 RJE stations. In a typical business day, over 7000 programs are executed.

The Information Systems Development Division employs approximately 160 people. Here lies the responsibility for the design, development, and maintenance of business information systems. The division is composed of functional development groups. Each group works with line management and staff groups in the development of applications programs. The programs are designed to reduce operating expenses or provide information for more effective management. Marketing activities, manufacturing departments, financial systems, all phases of engineering, patent and general legal, corporate affairs, and industrial relations are supported by this organization.

When a user department requests a major new application, a *system study* is initiated. The study is characterized by several phases. Figure 10–18 indicates the flow of these phases and their related activities.

The scope of the entire project is first determined to establish initial specifications and to assign a priority of importance to the proposal. A feasibility study is then conducted to insure that the necessary personnel and hardware are available to support the system. If the application appears feasible, an ex-

tensive management review is conducted. The goal of the entire system study is to totally justify the system before programmers begin work on the coding. Emphasis is placed on the determination of feasibility, workability, and requirements of the proposed application. The importance of these steps cannot be overemphasized; they are vital to the success of the application.

Following the system study and the project approval, the detailed design of the new application begins. The definition of the problem and the macro-structured (general) design of the solution have already been prepared during the system study, so the programmers can launch immediately into the detailed design and coding of the problem solution. The first step in this process is the grouping of elements from the system structure chart (a graphic representation of the problem solution) into logical program modules. Since Lilly stresses *structured design* and *modular programming* (which divide a program into logical sections), the second step in the coding phase is the development of individual *program structure charts.* These charts show the programming modules of the problem solution and the relationships between them.

With the program structure charts as guides, the programmers begin to write the program. To facilitate this process, preprinted IBM coding forms are used to format the instructions. Each programmer codes entire modules of the program. The completed coding forms are given to keypunch operators to prepare computer input. The value of the coding forms now becomes evident, since they not only aid the programmers but also greatly speed the keypunching process.

After a module has been keypunched, it is submitted for compilation. Any cleri-

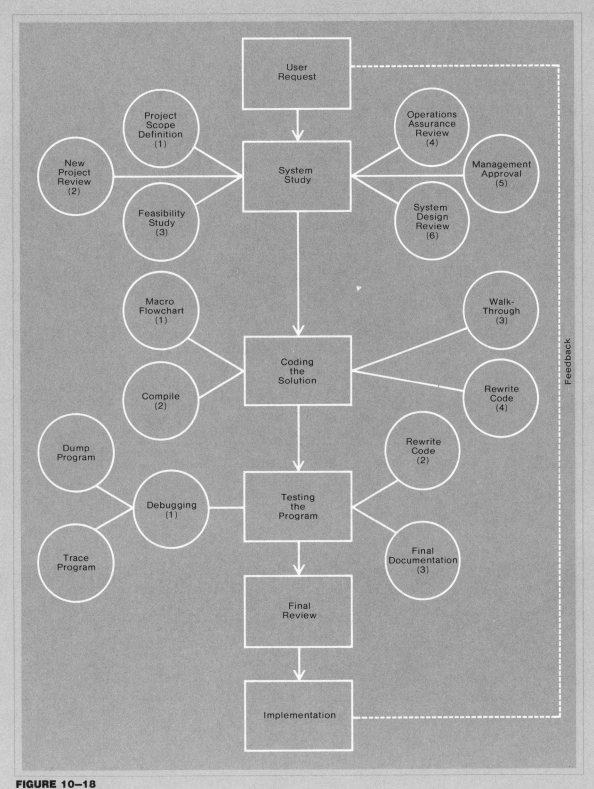

FIGURE 10–18
Application-Development Process at Eli Lilly and Company

cal errors are detected during the compilation process. This step is repeated until an error-free compilation ("clean compile") is achieved. The programmer then conducts a *walk-through,* explaining the purpose of the program to a previously uninvolved third party. This person, usually a fellow programmer, can provide fresh insights into areas where the purpose of the program is unclear (and thus requires additional comments). The person can also desk-check the program and identify logic errors that the programmer has overlooked. At this point, prior to the actual testing, the program is usually recompiled using a compiler program that *optimizes* the machine-language code (builds the most efficient instruction sequences, for repetitive processing purposes). It may also provide diagnostic messages indicating possible logic problems that need to be resolved.

The program is now ready to be executed using real, or "live," test data, representative of what may be processed in real-life situations. If the data is processed correctly, the program is ready for use. However, correct processing seldom occurs on the first run. To identify the causes of errors, the programmer may submit trial runs with abnormal terminations that produce dumps at the end of execution. (Since the dumps are printed in hexadecimal notation, Lilly trains its programmers in hexadecimal-to-decimal conversion.) Occasionally, an error is so subtle that the programmer cannot determine its cause by analyzing a dump. In this case, a trace program can be used to indicate the execution flow through the entire sequence of instructions. The programmer can then determine if the flow has mistakenly entered some section of the program.

After the solution has been completely coded and thoroughly tested, a final review of the application is made by members of the staff who will be involved in its operation. This review includes a check to see that (1) the code conforms to established programming standards; (2) documentation requirements have been satisfied; and (3) the program is ready to be designated as in "production" status. If the total application is found to be acceptable, it is released for implementation.

The application is allowed to operate for two to three months following implementation. After this period of time, the user area and operations staff review the application. They either document their acceptance or suggest revisions.

The complexity of activities involved in the development of a new application, from the system study to the coding and testing, is directly reflected in the cost associated with such an undertaking. Failure to properly perform any of the steps in the process can result in, at best, considerable difficulty and, at worst, a complete failure of the application. For this reason, the stringent standards described above have been adopted by Eli Lilly and Company to minimize these difficulties, if not totally eliminate them.

DISCUSSION POINTS

1. In the application-development at Eli Lilly, who is responsible for each of the steps listed in this chapter?

2. What are the flowcharting implications of Lilly's emphasis on structured design and modular programming?

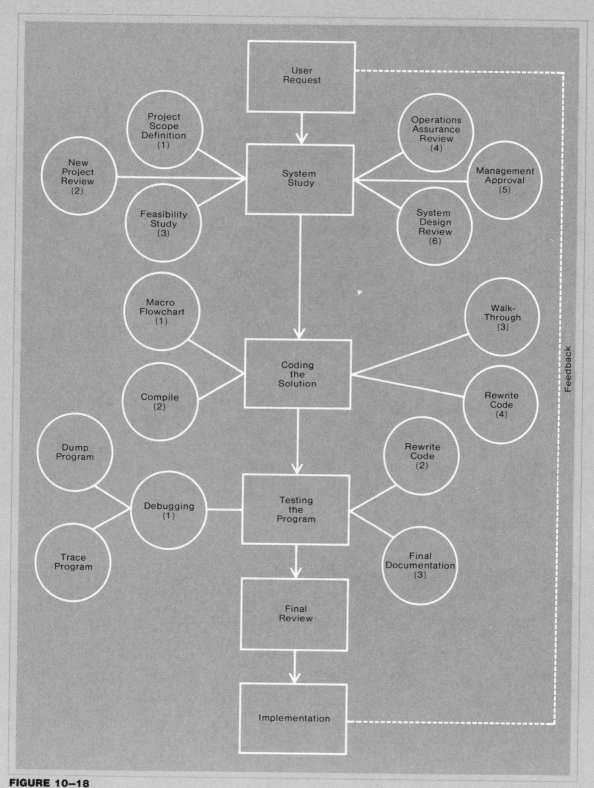

FIGURE 10—18

Application-Development Process at Eli Lilly and Company

cal errors are detected during the compilation process. This step is repeated until an error-free compilation (''clean compile'') is achieved. The programmer then conducts a *walk-through,* explaining the purpose of the program to a previously uninvolved third party. This person, usually a fellow programmer, can provide fresh insights into areas where the purpose of the program is unclear (and thus requires additional comments). The person can also desk-check the program and identify logic errors that the programmer has overlooked. At this point, prior to the actual testing, the program is usually recompiled using a compiler program that *optimizes* the machine-language code (builds the most efficient instruction sequences, for repetitive processing purposes). It may also provide diagnostic messages indicating possible logic problems that need to be resolved.

The program is now ready to be executed using real, or ''live,'' test data, representative of what may be processed in real-life situations. If the data is processed correctly, the program is ready for use. However, correct processing seldom occurs on the first run. To identify the causes of errors, the programmer may submit trial runs with abnormal terminations that produce dumps at the end of execution. (Since the dumps are printed in hexadecimal notation, Lilly trains its programmers in hexadecimal-to-decimal conversion.) Occasionally, an error is so subtle that the programmer cannot determine its cause by analyzing a dump. In this case, a trace program can be used to

indicate the execution flow through the entire sequence of instructions. The programmer can then determine if the flow has mistakenly entered some section of the program.

After the solution has been completely coded and thoroughly tested, a final review of the application is made by members of the staff who will be involved in its operation. This review includes a check to see that (1) the code conforms to established programming standards; (2) documentation requirements have been satisfied; and (3) the program is ready to be designated as in ''production'' status. If the total application is found to be acceptable, it is released for implementation.

The application is allowed to operate for two to three months following implementation. After this period of time, the user area and operations staff review the application. They either document their acceptance or suggest revisions.

The complexity of activities involved in the development of a new application, from the system study to the coding and testing, is directly reflected in the cost associated with such an undertaking. Failure to properly perform any of the steps in the process can result in, at best, considerable difficulty and, at worst, a complete failure of the application. For this reason, the stringent standards described above have been adopted by Eli Lilly and Company to minimize these difficulties, if not totally eliminate them.

DISCUSSION POINTS

1. In the application-development at Eli Lilly, who is responsible for each of the steps listed in this chapter?

2. What are the flowcharting implications of Lilly's emphasis on structured design and modular programming?

PROGRAMMING LANGUAGES | 11

OUTLINE

I. Batch-Oriented Programming
   Languages
   A. Assembly Language
      1. Machine-Oriented
      2. Label, Op Code, Operand
   B. COBOL
      1. General Organization of the
         Program
      2. Coding Rules
      3. Punctuation and Spacing
      4. Reserved Words and
         Programmer-Defined Words
      5. Input/Output
      6. Arithmetic
      7. Control
      8. Characteristics
   C. FORTRAN
      1. General Organization of the
         Program
      2. Coding Rules and
         Punctuation
      3. Data Types and Variable
         Names
      4. Input/Output
      5. Format Specifications

      6. Arithmetic
      7. Control
   D. PL/1
      1. Procedure-Oriented
      2. Free-Form
      3. Modular
   E. RPG
      1. Problem-Oriented
      2. File, Input, Calculation,
         Output Specifications
II. Interactive Programming
    Languages
    A. BASIC
       1. Time-Sharing
       2. Program Statements,
          System Commands, Editing
          Commands
    B. APL
       1. Execution and Definition
          Modes
       2. Special Character Set
III. Programming Languages—A
     Comparison

INTRODUCTION

There has been a tremendous growth in the hardware capabilities of modern computers during the past decade. However, benefits from the hardware technology cannot be realized unless there are complementary developments in software. Various programming languages have been developed to increase the usefulness of computers. The future of information processing appears to depend less on the development of better technologies and more on the effectiveness with which we use existing capabilities. Thus, developments in software and programming techniques can be expected to play a key role in the future success of computer-based systems.

This chapter highlights the major programming languages used today. The unique features and characteristics of each language are discussed, and typical applications are identified. The discussions of COBOL and FORTRAN are more extensive than those of other languages. The payroll program developed in Chapter 10, with which the reader is already familiar, is used as a sample program in discussing the different languages. The chapter ends with a critical comparison of the languages. The factors that should be considered in selecting the most appropriate language for a particular application are pointed out.

MUSECOM II

Don Heckman

High Fidelity Magazine,
August, 1977, p. 106

The growing alliance between music and computer technology is one of the most fascinating and potentially rewarding developments since the invention of electrical recording in the mid-twenties. The ways in which computer elements can make life easier for the musician and the recording technician are only beginning to be explored, and are gaining almost daily, both on the large-scale corporate research and development level and in the semi-pro do-it-yourself area.

One of the most familiar applications is the use of digital electronics to create practical delay systems free of the irritating problems inherent in spring reverbs and tape loops. Digital memory is used for program storage in synthesizers and recording studio mixdown boards. Its ability to recall any element of a mix has been an enormous boon to harried producers and engineers. And digital sequencers are capable of maintaining and recalling any assigned sequences of sounds.

Musecom, Ltd., in Playa del Rey, California, has come up with a further, and quite startling, application of computer technology to music—the Musecom II. Very simply, it is an instrument that instantly notates any musical work fed into it through its keyboard terminal. The four basic components—an electronic piano keyboard, a video monitor, an incremental plotter, and a small computer—are housed in modern wood cabinetry. Features include access to all key signatures, major and minor; a metronome that can be set for any rhythm, both with subdivisions and with accents; eighty time signatures; easy

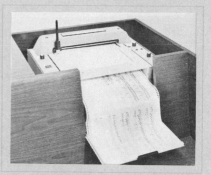

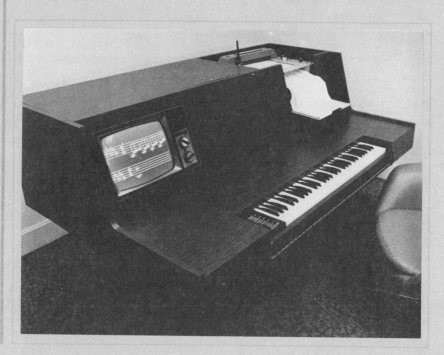

248

transposition from/to any key; instant display of whatever is played, measure by measure, on the video screen; audible replay of recorded material; scoring capability on a single treble staff, a single bass staff, or the grand staff; and printing of the final score through the incremental plotter.

The instrument is not difficult to operate. After the user determines his choice of rhythms, staff, time signatures, key signatures, etc., he plays the keyboard. The printed music appears simultaneously on the video screen. If there are mistakes or changes, the score can be rolled back and any kind of adjustments—rhythms, notes, keys— can be made in the notation. And the composer can listen to his creation at any point during its conception. When the music is complete, a notated score is delivered through a slot on the right side.

The unit was developed by Jim Troxel, a Los Angeles studio musician and percussionist. The key element, he says, was teaching the minicomputer to "converse in standard music notation."

Otherwise, the composer would have to convert musical elements into computer language.

The Musecom's potential for non-reading composers and for schools, recording studios, and music publishing companies is enormous—although it may deprive music copyists of a profession. For the moment, the price (around $18,000 and up) will minimize technological unemployment. Access to it would seem to be limited to the most financially successful musicians and composers. But historically, the cost of electronically sophisticated hardware has gone down with time.

Troxel looks to the future development of an input terminal more powerful than a keyboard. He envisions a system in which any musical sound—sung or played—can be picked up and converted into sheet music. It would be feasible to provide a telephone service wherein the subscriber could phone into a Musecom terminal, sing or play his composition, and receive a neatly printed copy of it in the mail the following day. Troxel sees that development as close as a year and a half away.

The fact that Musecom II can be used by people totally unfamiliar with computers speaks highly of today's software and hardware technology. The typical programming languages that support this achievement are discussed in this chapter.

BATCH-ORIENTED PROGRAMMING LANGUAGES

Batch-oriented programming languages are normally used in solving problems for which immediate responses are not required. A batch program is submitted to the computer as a single unit, containing both instructions and data. Once the instructions and data have been input to the CPU, processing takes place, without any programmer or user intervention.

Most batch programs are developed within an organization to solve specific problems of a recurring nature. For example, payroll processing is usually done in batch mode. Each week or month, the same payroll processing functions must be performed. A batch program (or programs) that indicates the steps necessary to process the payroll can be written once, and then used repeatedly to process different sets of data. Other common batch-processing applications are accounts receivable, inventory control, and billing.

Batch programs are not executed as they are submitted to the computer. Instead, several batch programs are stored temporarily on an auxiliary storage device until the CPU is ready to execute them. Several jobs may be read in at the same time and processed at different times during the day or night, depending on their priority.

There are three categories of batch programming languages: *machine-oriented*, *procedure-oriented*, and *problem-oriented*. An assembly language is an example of a machine-oriented language. The programmer using a machine-oriented language must pay close attention to the machine functions that take place during program execution. A machine-oriented language is very similar to actual machine language.

In contrast to the machine-orientation of assembly languages, high-level languages are either procedure- or problem-oriented. When a procedure-oriented language is used, the programming emphasis is placed on describing the computational and logical procedures required to solve a problem. Common procedure-oriented languages are COBOL, FORTRAN, and PL/1. A problem-oriented language is one in which the problem and solution are described without detailing necessary computational procedures. The most popular problem-oriented language is RPG.

This lack of machine-orientation in high-level batch-oriented programming languages reduces the amount of coding required to solve a problem; thus, the programmer's task is simplified. However, programs written in these languages require more storage and execution time than comparable programs written in assembly languages.

The common batch-oriented programming languages are assembly language, COBOL, FORTRAN, PL/1, and RPG. Some batch-oriented languages, such as PL/1, are also available in special versions developed specifically for online, interactive processing. However, our discussions of these languages in this chapter revolve around their use as batch languages. A discussion of other languages especially suited for interactive processing follows later in this chapter.

Assembly Language

As stated in Chapter 10, assembly languages were developed to alleviate many of the disadvantages of machine-language programming. Programming in a machine language is very tedious and time-consuming. Machine-language instructions must be written as combinations of numerals. They are difficult to remember and to use. Also, when programming in a machine language, the programmer must know the storage locations used for instructions and data.

When programming in an assembly language, the programmer can use symbolic names, or *mnemonics*, to specify machine operations. The mnemonics are English-like abbreviations used instead of binary operation codes. For example, Table 11–1 shows how some common arithmetic operations can be coded in an assembly language and the binary representations of the operations.

Notice that many of the operations listed in Table 11–1 involve the use of registers, which are temporary storage areas for holding data and instructions. The mnemonic codes for assembly-language instructions differ, depending on the type and model of computer. Thus, assembly-language programs can only be written by persons who know the computers that will execute the program.

There are three basic parts in an assembly-language instruction: a *label*, an *op code*, and an *operand* (see Table 11–2). The label is a programmer-supplied name that represents the first storage location used for the instruction. When the programmer wishes to refer to the instruction, he or she can simply specify the label, without regard to its storage location.

The op code is a mnemonic that tells the operation to be performed (refer again to Table 11–1). The operand represents the address of an item to be operated on. There may be one or two operands in an instruction. The remainder of the coding-form line can be used for remarks that explain the operation being performed (remarks are optional). The payroll program developed in Chapter 10 (see Figure 10–11) is coded in assembly language as shown in Figure 11–1.

OPERATION	TYPICAL ASSEMBLY-LANGUAGE MNEMONIC CODE	TYPICAL BINARY OP CODE
Add memory to register	A	01011010
Add register to register	AR	00011010
Compare memory locations	CLC	11010101
Divide register by memory	D	01011101
Load from memory into register	L	01011000
Multiply register by memory	M	01011100
Store register in memory	ST	01010000
Subtract memory from register	S	01011011

TABLE 11–1

EXAMPLES OF ASSEMBLY-LANGUAGE MNEMONIC CODES

TABLE 11–2

THE PARTS OF
ASSEMBLY-LANGUAGE
INSTRUCTIONS

LABEL	OP CODE	OPERANDS A and B	REMARKS
READRT	GET	INCARD,INWORK	READ INTO INWORK
	MVC	LIMOUT,LIM	SET UP PRINT LINE
	PACK	LIMP(3),LIM	PACK LIMIT
LOOP	AP	ANSP,CTR	ADD CTR TO ANSP

STMT	SOURCE STATEMENT		
1		START	
2	PAYROLL	BALR	12,0 } Set Up Registers
3		USING	*,12
4		XPRNT	HEADING,45 } Print Headings
5	READCRD	XREAD	CARD80
6		CLC	EOF,"C'99' } Read Data Card
7		BE	DONE
8		PACK	WKHR!,HOURS
9		PACK	WKRATE,RATE
10		ZAP	GROSS,ZERO } Convert Data to Decimal Form and Initialize Variables
11		ZAP	OVRTME,ZERO
12		ZAP	REG,ZERO
13		CP	WKHRS,FORTY
14		BH	OVERTIME
15		AP	GROSS,WKRATE } Compute Regular Pay
16		MP	GROSS,WKHRS
17		B	TAXRATE
18	OVERTIME	AP	OVRTME,FORTY
19		MP	OVRTME,WKRATE
20		AP	GROSS,WKRATE
21		SP	WKHRS,FORTY } Compute Overtime Pay
22		MP	WKHRS,ONEHLF
23		MP	GROSS,WKHRS
24		MVN	GROSS+5(1),GROSS+6
25		ZAP	GROSS(7),GROSS(6)
26		AP	GROSS,OVRTME
27	TAXRATE	CP	GROSS,=P'25000'
28		BH	UPPERRTE
29		ZAP	RATE,LOW } Determine Tax Rate
30		B	TAXES
31	UPPERRTE	ZAP	RATE,HIGH
32	TAXES	ZAP	TOTAXES,GROSS
33		MP	TOTAXES,RATE
34		AP	TOTAXES,=P'50' } Compute Taxes
35		MVN	TOTAXES+5(1),TOTAXES+6
36		ZAP	TOTAXES(7),TOTAXES(6)
37		SP	GROSS,TOTAXES
38		MVC	PRPAY,MASK } Calculate Net Pay and Edit Print Line
39		ED	PRPAY,GROSS
40		MVC	PRNAME,NAME } Print Output Line
41		XPRNT	LINE,32

```
STMT    SOURCE  STATEMENT
  42              B       READCRD
  43 DONE         XPRNT   HEADING,1
  44              BR      14
  45 *
  46 *
  47 *
  48 CARD         DS      0CL80
  49 NAME         DS      CL16
  50 HOURS        DS      CL2
  51              DS      CL2          }  Input Card File Definitions
  52 RATE         DS      CL4
  53              DS      CL54
  54 EOF          DS      CL2
  55 HEADING      DS      0CL45
  56              DC      CL1'1'
  57              DC      CL4'     '
  58              DC      CL13,EMPLOYEE NAME'
  59              DC      CL10'
  60              DC      CL7'NET PAY'        }  Output Print
  61              DC      CL10'                  File Definitions
  62 LINE         DS      0CL30
  63              DC      CL1' '
  64 PRNAME       DS      CL16
  65 PRPAY        DS      CL15
  66 GROSS        DS      PL7
  67 WKRATE       DS      PL3
  68 OVRTME       DS      PL7
  69 REG          DS      PL7
  70 WKHRS        DS      PL4
  71 FORTY        DC      PL2'40'       }  Variable Definitions
  72 ONEHLF       DC      PL2'150'
  73 LOW          DC      PL2'14'
  74 HIGH         DC      PL2'20'
  75 ZERO         DC      PL4'0000'
  76 TOTAXES      DS      PL7
  77 MASK         DC      X'402020202020202020202021482121'  }  Edit Field
  78              END     PAYROLL
  79                      =C'99'
  80                      =P'50'
  81                      =P'25000'
```

Output:

```
    EMPLOYEE NAME      NET PAY

LYNN MANGINO           224.00
THOMAS RITTER          212.42
MARIE OLSON            209.00
LORI DUNLEVY           172.00
WILLIAM WILSON         308.00
```

There are some advantages to using assembly language. First, it can be used to develop highly efficient programs, in terms of storage and processing time required. The programmer works with very close control of the machine. Second, the assembler program performs certain checking functions and generates error messages (as needed) that are useful in debugging. Third, assembly language is conducive to modular programming techniques. In a modular programming approach, a program is broken into a number of separate modules or programming units. The advantage of these techniques is that the logic of the total program becomes more manageable. Instead of one extensive program, it becomes a group of small, understandable programming segments.

The main disadvantage of assembly language is that it is cumbersome to use. Generally, one assembly-language instruction is translated into one machine-language instruction. This one-for-one relationship between assembly language and machine language leads to long program-preparation times.

Another disadvantage of assembly language is the high level of skill required to use it effectively. The programmer must know the computer to be used. He or she must be able to work with binary and/or hexadecimal numbers and with codes such as EBCDIC. It is true that the problem must be fully defined and a solution carefully planned, but the task of writing the solution in assembly language is often the most difficult phase in the solution process.

Finally, assembly language is machine-dependent; a program written for one computer generally cannot be executed on a different computer. When equipment is changed, substantial reprogramming may be required.

Assembly language is often used when writing operating systems. Because of the functions these programs perform, they are machine-dependent in nature. The potential efficiency of assembly language makes it well suited for operating-system programming.

COBOL

COBOL (Common Business Oriented Language) is the most frequently used business programming language. Before 1960, no language that was well suited to solving business problems existed. Recognizing this inadequacy, the Department of Defense called together representatives of computer users, manufacturers, and government installations to examine the feasibility of establishing a common business programming language. This was the beginning of the CODASYL (Conference of Data Systems Languages) Committee. By 1960, the committee had established the specifications for COBOL. The government furthered its cause by refusing to buy or lease any computer that did not support COBOL.

One of the objectives of the CODASYL group was to establish a language that was machine-independent. When several manufacturers began offering different modifications and extensions of COBOL, a need for standardization became apparent. Consequently, in 1968 the American National Standards Institute (ANSI) established and published guidelines for a standardized COBOL. It became known as ANSI COBOL. In 1974, a revised version of the standards was published in which the language definition was expanded. The CODASYL Committee continues to examine the feasibility of modifying or incorporating new features into COBOL.

Another key objective of the designers of COBOL was to make the language look like English. Their intent was that programs written in COBOL should be understandable to even casual readers. Figure 11–2 shows the payroll application coded in the COBOL language.

General Organization of the Program COBOL programs have a formal, uniform structure. Many statements must appear in the same forms and positions in every COBOL program. The basic unit of a COBOL program is the sentence. Sentences are combined to form paragraphs, and paragraphs are combined into sections. At the broadest level, sections are contained within divisions.

Every COBOL program is divided into four divisions: *IDENTIFICA-TION, ENVIRONMENT, DATA,* and *PROCEDURE.* Therefore, the four statements below must appear in every COBOL program. They must be in the order shown (with other statements between them), and each must occupy a separate line (card).

Statement	Purpose of the Division
IDENTIFICATION DIVISION	Provides documentation of the program— at the minimum, the program name.
ENVIRONMENT DIVISION	States the type of computers used for compiling the COBOL source program and for executing the resultant object program.
DATA DIVISION	Describes the data items and files used by the program.
PROCEDURE DIVISION	Contains the processing steps to be executed.

Not all COBOL divisions have sections, and not all sections have paragraphs. The possible divisions, sections, and paragraphs are shown below.

Division	Sections	Paragraphs
IDENTIFICATION DIVISION	No sections	PROGRAM ID AUTHOR INSTALLATION DATE WRITTEN REMARKS
ENVIRONMENT DIVISION	CONFIGURATION SECTION	SOURCE-COMPUTER OBJECT-COMPUTER

255

Division	Sections	Paragraphs
	INPUT/OUTPUT SECTION	FILE CONTROL
		I/O CONTROL
DATA DIVISION	FILE SECTION	No paragraphs
	WORKING STORAGE SECTION	
PROCEDURE	Sections named by	Paragraphs named by
DIVISION	programmer as needed	programmer as needed

The PROGRAM-ID paragraph (IDENTIFICATION DIVISION) is required. PROGRAM-ID must be followed by a period and a name for the program (see Line 2 in Figure 11–2). The name may contain up to 30 characters. They may be any combination of alphabetic and numeric characters. The only special character permitted is the hyphen. It cannot appear as the first or last character.

FIGURE 11–2

Payroll Program in COBOL

The INPUT-OUTPUT SECTION (ENVIRONMENT DIVISION) is vital

```
00001    IDENTIFICATION DIVISION.
00002    PROGRAM-ID. PAYROLL.
00003    ENVIRONMENT DIVISION.
00004    INPUT-OUTPUT SECTION.
00005    FILE-CONTROL.
00006        SELECT CARD-FILE ASSIGN TO UR-2540R-S-SYSIN.
00007        SELECT PRINT-FILE ASSIGN TO UR-S-SYSPRINT.
00008    DATA DIVISION.
00009    FILE SECTION.
00010    FD   CARD-FILE LABEL RECORDS ARE OMITTED.
00011    01   PAY-CARD.
00012        02 EMPLOYEE-NAME PICTURE A(16).
00013        02 HOURS-WORKED PICTURE 99.
00014        02 WAGE-PER-HOUR PICTURE 99V99.
00015    FD   PRINT-FILE LABEL RECORDS ARE OMITTED.
00016    01   PRINT-LINE.
00017        02 NAME         PICTURE A(16).
00018        02 FILLER       PICTURE X(5).
00019        02 AMOUNT       PICTURE $$$$.99.
00020    WORKING-STORAGE SECTION.
00021    77   GROSS-PAY       PICTURE 999V99.
00022    77   REGULAR-PAY     PICTURE 999V99.
00023    77   OVERTIME-PAY    PICTURE 999V99.
00024    77   NET-PAY         PICTURE 999V99.
00025    77   TAX             PICTURE 999V99.
00026    77   OVERTIME-HOURS  PICTURE 99.
00027    77   OVERTIME-RATE   PICTURE 999V999.
00028    77   BLANK-LINE      PICTURE X(132) VALUE SPACES.
00029    PROCEDURE DIVISION.
00030        DISPLAY 'EMPLOYEE NAME             ', 'NET PAY'.
00031        DISPLAY BLANK-LINE.
00032        OPEN INPUT CARD-FILE, OUTPUT PRINT-FILE.
```

if files are used by the program. In the FILE-CONTROL paragraph, each file must be assigned a name, and the input or output device with which the file will be associated must be specified (see Lines 5–7 in Figure 11–2).

In the DATA DIVISION, all storage locations used during execution of the program must be named and described. Those that are parts of input and output files are declared in the FILE SECTION. A sentence beginning with FD is required for each file used. The FD sentence is followed by a record description for each type of record contained in the file. (See Lines 9–19; one input file and one output file are used in this program. The input file contains a record (PAY-CARD) for each employee. The output file contains PRINT-LINE records.)

All other storage locations are described in the WORKING-STORAGE SECTION (see Lines 20–28).

A descriptive entry in either storage area has certain mandatory parts. For example:

FIGURE 11-2
Continued

```
00033   WORK-LOOP.
00034       READ CARD-FILE AT END GO TO FINISH.
00035       IF HOURS-WORKED IS GREATER THAN 40 THEN GO TO
00036           OVERTIME-ROUTINE.
00037       MULTIPLY HOURS-WORKED BY WAGE-PER-HOUR GIVING GROSS-PAY.
00038       GO TO TAX-COMPUTATION.
00039   OVERTIME-ROUTINE.
00040       MULTIPLY WAGE-PER-HOUR BY 40 GIVING REGULAR-PAY.
00041       SUBTRACT 40 FROM HOURS-WORKED GIVING OVERTIME-HOURS.
00042       MULTIPLY WAGE-PER-HOUR BY 1.5 GIVING OVERTIME-RATE.
00043       MULTIPLY OVERTIME-HOURS BY OVERTIME-RATE GIVING
00044           OVERTIME-PAY.
00045       ADD REGULAR-PAY, OVERTIME-PAY GIVING GROSS-PAY.
00046   TAX-COMPUTATION.
00047       IF GROSS-PAY IS GREATER THAN 250 THEN MULTIPLY GROSS-PAY
00048           BY 0.20 GIVING TAX ELSE MULTIPLY GROSS-PAY BY 0.14
00049           GIVING TAX.
00050       SUBTRACT TAX FROM GROSS-PAY GIVING NET-PAY.
00051       MOVE EMPLOYEE-NAME TO NAME.
00052       MOVE NET-PAY TO AMOUNT.
00053       WRITE PRINT-LINE.
00054       GO TO WORK-LOOP.
00055   FINISH.
00056       CLOSE CARD-FILE, PRINT-FILE.
00057       STOP RUN.
```

Output:

```
        EMPLOYEE NAME      NET PAY

        LYNN MANGINO       $224.00
        THOMAS RITTER      $212.42
        MARIE OLSON        $209.00
        LORI DUNLEVY       $172.00
        WILLIAM WILSON     $308.00
```

Level Number	Name	PICTURE Clause
77	GROSS-PAY	PICTURE 999V99

The possible level numbers are:

01: indicates that the item is a complete record.

02 through 49: indicate that the item is part of a record.

77: indicates that the item is independent, that is, does not form part of a record.

Any item that is not broken into smaller parts is called an elementary item. Each elementary item must have a PICTURE clause. The abbreviation PIC may be used instead of the word PICTURE. The PICTURE clause specifies the number and type of characters to be stored. In our example, the following symbols appear in PICTURE clauses:

Symbol	Meaning
9	Numeric
A	Alphabetic
X	Alphanumeric (numeric, alphabetic, or special)
V	Decimal-point location

Parts that are further divided do not require PICTURE clauses.

Here are some PICTURE clauses from the payroll program and their meanings:

00026 77 OVERTIME-HOURS PICTURE 99—Numeric value, two digits in length; no decimal-point location is designated.

00017 02 NAME PICTURE A(16)—Alphabetic data item, 16 characters in length. A 16-letter word may be stored. This description could be written as 16 consecutive As, but the symbol followed by a count with enclosing parentheses is an easier way to tell the total number of As required.

00028 77 BLANK-LINE PICTURE X(132)—*Alphanumeric* data; any combination of numeric, alphabetic, and special characters, 132 characters in length. In this case, the 132 characters are spaces and will cause a totally blank print line.

00014 02 WAGE-PER-HOUR PICTURE 99V99—Numeric value, with two digits to the left of the decimal point and two digits to the right.

Coding Rules Some rules that apply when coding COBOL programs follow.

1. Six types of entries must begin in columns 8, 9, 10, or 11 (Margin A of the COBOL coding form); they are:

Division names
Section names

Paragraph names
Entries beginning FD
Entries beginning 01
Entries beginning 77

2. All other coding begins in column 12 or a subsequent column (Margin B).

3. No coding intended for the computer can extend beyond column 72. Columns 1–6 and 73–80 are available to the programmer for remarks.

4. Column 7 is used only under special circumstances; a hyphen (-) in this column indicates continuation of the prior line (card).

Punctuation and Spacing The one essential punctuation mark in COBOL is the period. Every sentence must end with a period. So must all division, section, and paragraph names. At least one space must follow a period. (A period followed immediately by another character is treated as an error.)

A sentence may "run on" from line to line, without the continuation indicator, unless a word is broken at the end of a line. Conversely, a line may contain more than one sentence, with the exception of division and section names, which cannot share lines (cards) with other coding.

Reserved Words and Programmer-Defined Words A COBOL reserved word is used for a specified purpose and has a particular meaning to the COBOL compiler. The complete reserved word list consists of over 250 words. Examples are DISPLAY, READ, MULTIPLY, BY, and CLOSE. (See these and others in Figure 11–2.)

Programmer-defined words, or data names, are chosen by the programmer to represent data items referred to in the program. Each data name may consist of up to 30 characters. Letters, numbers, and embedded hyphens are allowed. The use of hyphens can enhance readability and help to prevent inadvertent use of reserved words. Embedded spaces are not permitted within data names. Each data name must be a single word.

For example, in Figure 11–2, HOURS-WORKED, WAGE-PER-HOUR, and GROSS-PAY are some of the data names chosen by the programmer. They represent the values of an employee's hours, wage, and calculated gross pay, respectively.

Input/Output Four COBOL verbs are used to perform data input and output functions: ACCEPT, READ, DISPLAY, and WRITE. The ACCEPT verb is used to obtain data from the system input devices. The general format is:

ACCEPT data-name.

ACCEPT may be followed by one data name. This name is usually a 77-level item or an 01-level item (record name), which may be further subdivided in a record description.

259

READ is used to refer to values treated as complete files. The general format is:

READ file-name AT END statement.

Although READ must be followed by a file name, reading is actually done one record at a time. All fields within the record are transmitted at once and arranged in storage according to the DATA DIVISION record description. To read the next record, a branch back to READ (or another READ) is required. Consider the following sentence (Line 34) in the sample program:

READ CARD-FILE AT END GO TO FINISH.

The computer reads values from one punched card into the three data locations reserved for the record named PAY-CARD of the file. CARD-FILE (EMPLOYEE-NAME, HOURS-WORKED, and WAGE-PER-HOUR). The statement following AT END is executed only after the last record in the file has been read. Control of the program is transfered to the FINISH paragraph (Line 55). Program execution is terminated.

The DISPLAY verb is available for low-volume output. The general format is:

$$\text{DISPLAY} \begin{bmatrix} \text{data-name-1} \\ \text{literal-1} \end{bmatrix}, \begin{bmatrix} \text{data-name-2} \\ \text{literal-2} \end{bmatrix}, \cdots$$

For example, the sentence

DISPLAY 'EMPLOYEE NAME   ', 'NET PAY'.

contains two literals (which must be in quotes); the sentence

DISPLAY BLANK-LINE.

contains a data name.

The WRITE verb is used to output data as part of an organized file. Each record used as part of a file must have been introduced by name in the FILE SECTION. Whereas the READ statement mentions only a file name, the WRITE statement mentions only a record name. The general format is:

WRITE record-name.

Thus, the sentence (Line 53 in sample program)

WRITE PRINT-LINE.

transmits as output the individual fields (NAME, FILLER, AMOUNT) of the record PRINT-LINE.

Arithmetic Arithmetic computations are called for by any of four verbs or five symbols (arithmetic operators):

Verbs   **Symbols**

ADD   +
SUBTRACT   −
MULTIPLY   *
DIVIDE   /
                 ** (exponentiation—no
                    verb equivalent)

The arithmetic sentences in the sample program follow these formats:

$$\text{ADD} \begin{bmatrix} \text{data-name} \\ \text{numeric literal} \end{bmatrix}, \begin{bmatrix} \text{data-name} \\ \text{numeric literal} \end{bmatrix} \text{GIVING data-name.}$$

$$\text{SUBTRACT} \begin{bmatrix} \text{data-name} \\ \text{numeric literal} \end{bmatrix} \text{FROM} \begin{bmatrix} \text{data-name} \\ \text{numeric literal} \end{bmatrix} \text{GIVING data-name.}$$

$$\text{MULTIPLY} \begin{bmatrix} \text{data-name} \\ \text{numeric literal} \end{bmatrix} \text{BY} \begin{bmatrix} \text{data-name} \\ \text{numeric literal} \end{bmatrix} \text{GIVING data-name.}$$

$$\text{DIVIDE} \begin{bmatrix} \text{data-name} \\ \text{numeric literal} \end{bmatrix} \text{INTO} \begin{bmatrix} \text{data-name} \\ \text{numeric literal} \end{bmatrix} \text{GIVING data-name.}$$

In these formats, the numeric literal is any value written as a number. Thus,

MULTIPLY WAGE-PER-HOUR BY 40 GIVING REGULAR-PAY.

multiplies the value stored in the data name WAGE-PER-HOUR by a numeric literal (40) and stores the result of the calculation in the data name REGULAR-PAY.

The COMPUTE verb is another method of specifying arithmetic computations in COBOL. The general format is:

COMPUTE data-name = arithmetic expression.

The following sentences (Lines 40–45 in the sample program)

MULTIPLY WAGE-PER-HOUR BY 40 GIVING REGULAR-PAY.
SUBTRACT 40 FROM HOURS-WORKED GIVING OVERTIME-HOURS.
MULTIPLY WAGE-PER-HOUR BY 1.5 GIVING OVERTIME-RATE.
MULTIPLY OVERTIME-HOURS BY OVERTIME-RATE GIVING OVERTIME-PAY.
ADD REGULAR-PAY, OVERTIME-PAY GIVING GROSS-PAY.

are equivalent to one single sentence:

COMPUTE GROSS-PAY = WAGE-PER-HOUR * 40 + (HOURS-WORKED − 40)
   * (1.5 * WAGE-PER-HOUR).

261

Obviously, the COMPUTE form is more convenient for lengthy computations.

Control An unconditional branch calls for the sequential flow of program control to be altered—that is, for statements to be executed "out of order." In COBOL and other high-level languages, the words GO TO are frequently used for this purpose. The COBOL general format of the unconditional branch is:

$$\text{GO TO} \begin{vmatrix} \text{paragraph-name} \\ \text{section-name} \end{vmatrix}.$$

A conditional statement allows an alternative control flow to be followed, depending on a condition tested during program execution. Most conditional statements in COBOL and other high-level languages begin with the word IF. The statement has the following general format:

$$\text{IF} \begin{bmatrix} \text{data-name-1} \\ \text{literal-1} \\ \text{arithmetic-expression-1} \end{bmatrix} \text{IS (NOT)} \begin{bmatrix} \text{equal to } (=) \\ \text{greater than } (>) \\ \text{less than } (<) \end{bmatrix}$$

$$\begin{bmatrix} \text{data-name-2} \\ \text{literal-2} \\ \text{arithmetic-expression-2} \end{bmatrix} \text{THEN statement-1 (statement-2)} \ldots$$

An example of a condition, or relation test, from the sample program (Lines 35 and 36) is:

IF HOURS WORKED IS GREATER THAN 40 THEN GO TO OVERTIME-ROUTINE.

If the stated condition (HOURS-WORKED IS GREATER THAN 40) is not true, then control passes to the next sentence following the period. The statement following THEN is ignored.

An extended format for COBOL IF sentences is also available. It is:

IF condition THEN statement-1
    ELSE statement-2.

For example:

IF GROSS-PAY IS GREATER THAN 250 THEN TAXRATE = .20
    ELSE TAXRATE = .14.

Characteristics COBOL offers many advantages as a business programming language. Because of its English-like nature, little additional documentation is needed. COBOL programs tend to be self-explanatory. COBOL is a procedure-oriented language; the programmer need not be concerned with detailed machine functions. Program testing and debugging is simplified, because the logic of the program is easy to follow. One primary advantage of COBOL is its standardization. This allows a firm to switch computer equipment with little or no rewriting of existing programs.

The effort to make COBOL as English-like as possible has resulted in some disadvantages. A large and sophisticated compiler program is needed to translate a COBOL source program into machine language.

As a result, COBOL is not available on some small computers. (But there are some COBOL compilers supporting subsets of the language that can be used with minicomputers.) Also, COBOL tends to be a wordy language. It may take many more statements to solve a problem using COBOL rather than a more compact language such as FORTRAN. Finally, COBOL's computational abilities are limited. For this reason, it is seldom used for scientific and mathematical applications.

FORTRAN

FORTRAN (*For*mula *Trans*lator) is the oldest high-level programming language. Its origins trace back to the mid-1950s. At that time, most programs were written in either assembly language or machine language. Efforts were made to develop a programming language that resembled English, but could be translated into machine language by the computer. This effort, backed by IBM, produced FORTRAN—the first commercially available high-level language.

Early FORTRAN compilers contained many errors. They were not always efficient. Moreover, several manufacturers offered various versions of FORTRAN, all of which were usable only with their computers. Although many improvements were made, early FORTRAN suffered from a lack of standardization. In response to this problem, ANSI laid the groundwork for a standardized FORTRAN. In 1966, two standard versions of FORTRAN were recognized. These standardized versions were called ANSI FORTRAN and Basic FORTRAN. They were very similar to two earlier versions, FORTRAN IV and FORTRAN II. In spite of this attempt to standardize FORTRAN, most computer manufacturers have continued to offer their own extensions to the language. Therefore, the compatibility of FORTRAN remains a problem today.

In 1957, when FORTRAN was first released, the computer was primarily used by engineers, scientists, and mathematicians. Consequently, FORTRAN was developed to meet their needs. Its purpose has remained unchanged today. FORTRAN is a procedure-oriented language with extraordinary mathematical capabilities. It is especially applicable where numerous complex arithmetic calculations are necessary. Large algebraic expressions can be expressed in FORTRAN. However, it is not well-suited for programs involving file maintenance, editing of data, or production of documents. Figure 11–3 shows the sample payroll program in FORTRAN.

General Organization of the Program The basic unit of a FORTRAN program is a statement. (It corresponds to a sentence in COBOL.) There is only one statement that must appear in every program: END. In contrast to the four divisions of a COBOL program, a FORTRAN program contains only one overall structure, which incorporates all storage declarations, computations, and input/output definitions. In FORTRAN, most variables (storage areas) need not be declared before use, and record descriptions are contained in FORMAT statements within the program.

263

```
FORTRAN IV G LEVEL 21                    MAIN                    DATE = 78214
0001        WRITE (6,1)
0002      1 FORMAT ('1', 'EMPLOYEE NAME', 5X, 'NET PAY'/' ')
0003      2 READ (5,3) NA,NB,NC,ND,NHOURS, WAGE, IEND
0004      3 FORMAT (4A4, I2, 2X, F4.2, 54X, I2)
0005        IF (IEND. EQ.99) STOP
0006        IF (NHOURS.GT.40) GO TO 10
0007        GROSS = FLOAT(NHOURS)*WAGE
0008        GO TO 15
0009     10 REG = 40.*WAGE
0010        OVERTM=FLOAT(NHOURS-40)*(1.5*WAGE)
0011        GROSS=REG+OVERTM
0012     15 IF (GROSS.GT.250.) GO TO 20
0013        RATE = .14
0014        GO TO 25
0015     20 RATE = .20
0016     25 TAX=RATE*GROSS
0017        PAY = GROSS - TAX
0018        WRITE (6,50) NA,NB,NC,ND,PAY
0019     50  FORMAT (' ', 4A4, 3X, F6.2)
0020        GO TO 2
0021        END
```

Output:

```
    EMPLOYEE NAME        NET PAY

    LYNN MANGINO         224.00
    THOMAS RITTER        212.42
    MARIE OLSON          209.00
    LORI DUNLEVY         172.00
    WILLIAM WILSON       308.00
```

FIGURE 11–3
Payroll Program in
FORTRAN

Four types of statements are used in FORTRAN programs:

● Control statements determine the sequence in which operations are performed. Operations such as choosing between alternatives and branching to another part of the program are governed by control statements.

● Arithmetic statements direct the computer to perform computations.

● Input/output statements instruct the computer to read data from, or write data to, an I/O device.

● Specification statements describe the arrangement of data read from an input device, or information written to an output device.

Coding Rules and Punctuation   The position of a FORTRAN statement and its associated statement number (if there is one) must conform to

264

certain restrictions. The statement itself must be written in columns 7 through 72 of a coding line (card). Columns 73 to 80 are ignored by the FORTRAN compiler during translation. If a FORTRAN statement has an associated statement number, that number must appear in the first five columns of the line.

The period, required at the end of every COBOL sentence, is not used in FORTRAN except as a decimal point. The only other punctuation used in FORTRAN is the comma. It is required in some statements, as noted below.

Data Types and Variable Names   Two kinds of variable names are used in FORTRAN to designate storage locations for integers, real numbers (also called reals), and alphanumeric characters. An integer is a number written without a decimal point (e.g., 17), and a real number is one written with a decimal point (e.g., 6.3). A data item that is to be treated as an integer must be assigned a variable name beginning with one of the letters I, J, K, L, M, or N. If the variable name begins with any other letter, the compiler treats the data item as a real number. The following rules apply when choosing a name:

1. A name can contain no more than six characters.

2. Each character must be either a letter or one of the digits 0 through 9.

3. The first character must be a letter.

An example of an integer variable name from the sample program is NHOURS. Examples of real variable names are WAGE, GROSS, and PAY.

In FORTRAN, only four alphanumeric characters can be represented by one variable name. Thus, to store alphanumeric data consisting of more than four characters, more than one variable name is needed. For example, assume a data card contains an employee's name in the first 16 columns. Four variable names must be used for the storage required:

```
WILLIAM WILSON__
  \  /   \  /   \  /   \  /
  NA     NB     NC     ND
```

Notice that only two characters are stored in the locations set aside for the variable name ND. The remaining space is filled with blanks.

Input/Output   In FORTRAN, input and output functions are specified by the verbs READ and WRITE. The READ statement has the general form:

```
  READ (J,K)    list
K FORMAT (   )
```

J is a number that tells the computer the input device to be used to enter data. K is an integer constant, the statement number of an associated FORMAT statement (see "FORMAT Specifications") below. The list consists of variable names for which values are to be entered. Thus, the statements

```
2 READ (5,3) NA,NB,NC,ND,NHOURS,WAGE,IEND
3 FORMAT (4A4, I2, 2X, F4.2, 54X, I2)
```

indicate that data is to be input and tell which variables are to hold the data. The 5 indicates that the input device is a card reader. The 3 is the statement number of the FORMAT statement. Every READ statement must be accompanied by a FORMAT statement that tells how the input data is arranged.

The WRITE statement has the following general form:

```
  WRITE (M,N)    list
N FORMAT ( )
```

M is a number indicating which output device is to be used. N is an integer constant, the statement number of the associated FORMAT statement. The list contains the variable names whose values are to be output.

Every WRITE statement must be accompanied by a FORMAT statement. It tells how values are to be spaced on the output. In the sample program, the statements

```
  WRITE (6,50) NA,NB,NC,ND,PAY
50 FORMAT (' ', 4A4, 3X, F6.2)
```

indicate that the values stored in the five listed variables are to be printed out on a line printer (designated by the number 6). The FORMAT statement tells how they are to look as output.

Format Specifications In the READ and WRITE statements and their corresponding FORMAT statements, there is a specification for each value that is to be input or output. A specification code indicates the type of the data field, the number of characters in the field, and the number of decimal places (if any) in the field. The common format specification codes are:

aIw (describes integer data fields)

aEw.d (describes real data fields)

aFw.d (describes real data fields)

aAw (describes character data fields)

wH   (indicates literal data)

wX   (indicates that a field is to be skipped on input or filled with blanks on output)

where:

a is an integer constant used to denote the number of times the code is to be used. If omitted, the code is used only once.

w   is an integer constant that specifies the number of characters in the field.

d   is an integer constant that specifies the number of decimal places to the right of the decimal point.

An explanation of the codes contained in the following FORMAT statement and of its use with the READ statement is given below.

```
2 READ (5,3) NA, NB, NC, ND, NHOURS, WAGE, IEND
3 FORMAT (4A4, I2, 2X, F4.2, 54X, I2)
```

4A4   specifies that 4 groups of 4 alphabetic characters will be read from the first 16 columns of a data card and stored in NA, NB, NC, and ND.

I2   specifies that a 2-digit integer will be read from the next two columns of the data card and stored in NHOURS.

2X   specifies that the next two columns of the data card will be skipped (irrespective of whether or not they contain data).

F4.2   specifies that a real number will be read from the next four columns of the data card and stored in WAGE; two of the digits will be stored to the right of an assumed decimal point (if there is no decimal point in the data field).

54X   specifies that the next 54 columns of the data card will be skipped.

I2   specifies that a 2-digit integer will be read from the next two columns of the data card and stored in IEND.

Arithmetic   In FORTRAN, mathematical operations are designated as follows:

Symbol	Meaning
+	Addition
−	Subtraction
*	Multiplication
/	Division
**	Exponentiation

Every FORTRAN arithmetic statement has the following form:

variable = arithmetic-expression

The left-hand side of the statement must be a variable (not a constant or an expression). The arithmetic expression may be a variable, a constant, or any properly formed FORTRAN expression. Thus, the following statements from the sample program are correctly formed statements.

```
REG = 40. * WAGE
GROSS = REG + OVERTM
RATE = .14
```

267

Control In FORTRAN, as in COBOL, the statement that alters the normal sequential order of program execution is the GO TO statement. The general format for this unconditional branch is:

`GO TO statement number`

For example, the following statement in the sample program

`GO TO 2`

transfers control to statement 2, the READ statement. Thus, once an employee's net pay has been calculated and printed, the computer returns to statement 2 and reads another data card.

The FORTRAN conditional statement beginning with the word IF is written in the following manner:

`IF (condition) statement`

When the computer encounters this statement, it examines the condition and determines whether it is true or false. If it is true, the computer executes the statement to the right of the parentheses before executing the next statement in the program. If it is false, the computer immediately executes the next statement in the program.

The conditions with which the sample program is concerned are comparisons. In FORTRAN, there are six comparison operators:

Operator	Meaning
`.EQ.`	Equal to
`.NE.`	Not equal to
`.GT.`	Greater than
`.LT.`	Less than
`.GE.`	Greater than or equal to
`.LE.`	Less than or equal to

The following statement in the sample program:

`15 IF (GROSS.GT.250.) GO TO 20`

says that if the employee's gross pay is greater than $250, control is to pass to statement 20. (The employee's tax rate will be 20 percent.) Otherwise, the statement following the IF statement will be executed. (The employee's tax rate will be 14 percent.)

Although other high-level programming languages such as COBOL and PL/1 are better suited for business data processing, use of FORTRAN for certain types of business applications is increasing. For example, FORTRAN is often used for quantitative analysis involving techniques such as linear programming and regression analysis. As Figure 11–3 shows, FORTRAN does not have much resemblance to English. For this reason, FORTRAN programs must be well documented.

PL/1

PL/1 (*P*rogramming *L*anguage One) was designed as an all-purpose, procedure-oriented language usable for both scientific and business applications. With the increased use of management-science techniques such as linear programming and regression analysis, the business programmer needs a language with greater computational capabilities than COBOL. By the same token, a language with greater file-manipulation ability than FORTRAN is desired by the scientific programmer. PL/1 combines the best features of both COBOL and FORTRAN; thus, it is a more flexible high-level language. PL/1 was introduced during the early 1960s for use with IBM System/360 computers. It is still primarily an IBM-sponsored language, although its use is spreading to other computers.

All of the languages we have discussed so far—assembly language, FORTRAN, and COBOL—impose some rather strict coding rules on the programmer. Column restrictions are prevalent. In contrast, PL/1 is a free-form language with very few coding restrictions.

The basic element in a PL/1 program is the statement. Each PL/1 statement is terminated by a semicolon. The statements are not confined to individual lines or paragraphs, and need not begin in certain columns (see Figure 11–4).

In addition to its free-form characteristic, PL/1 has many other desirable features. PL/1 programs can be constructed in a modular fashion. Separate logical procedures, called *blocks*, can be combined to form a complete program. This simplifies writing of the program and facilitates the use of structured-programming techniques (discussed in the next chapter).

The PL/1 compiler has certain *default* features, thus reducing the number of statements needed in a program. A default is a course of action chosen by the compiler when several alternatives exist, but none has been explicitly stated by the programmer. The default is the alternative determined by the compiler or language designers to be most often required. For example, if the programmer does not specify the types of data to be represented by particular variable names, the compiler assumes that data items beginning with the letters I through N represent integer values.

The PL/1 compiler also contains several *built-in functions* that the programmer can use. Examples are SQRT (for taking square roots) and LOG (for finding logarithms). The availability of these built-in functions greatly simplifies the programmer's task. He or she need only refer to a required function by name to cause the corresponding pretested, correct routine to be executed and the results made available to his or her coding.

PL/1 was designed to be used by both novice and expert programmers. The beginning programmer can quickly learn to write programs using the basic features of the language. As knowledge of the language is developed, the programmer can use the more powerful features of PL/1 to write complex programs.

269

```
PAYROLL: PROCEDURE OPTIONS (MAIN);

STMT LEVEL NEST BLOCK              SOURCE STATEMENT

  1                        PAYROLL: PROCEDURE OPTIONS (MAIN);
  2     1    1             DECLARE NAME        CHARACTER (16);
  3     1    1             DECLARE HOURS      FIXED DECIMAL (2);
  4     1    1             DECLARE WAGE       FIXED DECIMAL (3,2);
  5     1    1             DECLARE GROSS_PAY  FIXED DECIMAL(5,2);
  6     1    1             DECLARE TAXRATE    FIXED DECIMAL (2,2);
  7     1    1             DECLARE TAX        FIXED DECIMAL (4,2);
  8     1    1             DECLARE NET_PAY    FIXED DECIMAL (5,2);
  9     1    1             PUT PAGE LIST ('EMPLOYEE NAME', 'NET PAY');
 10     1    1             PUT SKIP;
 11     1    1             START: GET LIST (NAME, HOURS, WAGE);
 12     1    1             ON ENDFILE GO TO FINISH;
 13     2    2             IF HOURS > 40 THEN
                               GROSS_PAY = 40*WAGE + 1.5*WAGE*(HOURS-40);
 16     1    1               ELSE GROSS_PAY = HOURS*WAGE;
 17     1    1             IF GROSS_PAY > 250 THEN TAXRATE = .20;
 19     1    1               ELSE TAXRATE = .14;
 20     1    1             TAX = TAXRATE*GROSS_PAY
 21     1    1             NET_PAY = GROSS_PAY = TAX;
 22     1    1             PUT SKIP (1) LIST (NAME, NET_PAY);
 23     1    1             GO TO START;
 24     1    1             FINISH: END PAYROLL


PAYROLL       14:50    AUGUST 3RD, 1978
```

Output:

```
EMPLOYEE NAME          NET PAY

LYNN MANGINO           224.00
THOMAS RITTER          212.42
MARIE OLSON            209.00
LORI DUNLEVY           172.00
WILLIAM WILSON         308.00
```

FIGURE 11—4
Payroll Program in PL/1

Various subsets of PL/1 containing only portions of the full language have been developed. These subsets are especially geared toward educational use. Below is a PL/1 program written in PL/C, a subset of PL/1 developed at Cornell University.

Although PL/1 is a very powerful language, it has some inherent disadvantages. First, a large amount of storage is required for the PL/1 compiler. This prohibits its use on small computers. Due to the complexity of the PL/1 compiler, the translation of source programs into machine language takes slightly longer for PL/1 than it does for other high-level languages.

RPG

RPG (*Report Program Generator*) is a problem-oriented language originally designed to produce business reports. Basically, the programmer using RPG describes the type of report desired. Normally, very little logic has to be specified. A generator program is used to build (generate) a program to produce the report. Therefore, little programming skill is required to use RPG.

Since RPG was initially intended to support the logic of punched-card equipment, it is used primarily with small computer systems. Many firms that formerly used electromechanical punched-card processing equipment have upgraded their data-processing operations to small computer systems. These firms usually have relatively simple, straightforward data-processing needs. In such cases, a small computer system supporting RPG can provide significantly improved data-processing operations. Management reports can be produced in a fraction of the time required by electromechanical methods.

RPG is now used for file processing as well as for the preparation of printed output. The programmer does not code the statements required. Instead, he or she completes specification forms such as those shown in Figure 11–5. All files, records, and fields to be manipulated must be defined by entries in specific columns on the specification forms. The operations to be performed and the content and format of output files are described similarly. The entries on the RPG forms are keypunched, combined with job-control cards, and submitted to the computer. The RPG generator program builds an object program from the source program, and the object program is executed by the computer.

RPG is easy to learn, since the basic pattern of execution is fixed; a minimal amount of effort is required of the programmer. Since RPG does not require large amounts of main storage, it is one of the primary languages of small computers and minicomputers. It provides an efficient means for generating reports requiring simple logic and calculations. RPG is commonly used to process files for accounts receivable, accounts payable, general ledgers, and inventory.

The computational capabilities of RPG are limited. Some RPG compilers can generate machine-language instructions for up to 30 different operations. However, compared to COBOL, FORTRAN, or PL/1, its looping, branching, and decision capabilities are restricted. RPG is not a standardized language; therefore, RPG programs may require a significant degree of modification if they are to be executed on a computer other than the one for which they were initially written. This is especially true if a firm changes computer manufacturers. However, if a firm stays with a particular manufacturer's equipment, its RPG programs can generally be run on a similar but more powerful computer with only slight modifications.

INTERACTIVE PROGRAMMING LANGUAGES

Interactive programming languages allow the programmer to communicate directly with the computer. They are designed to allow programs

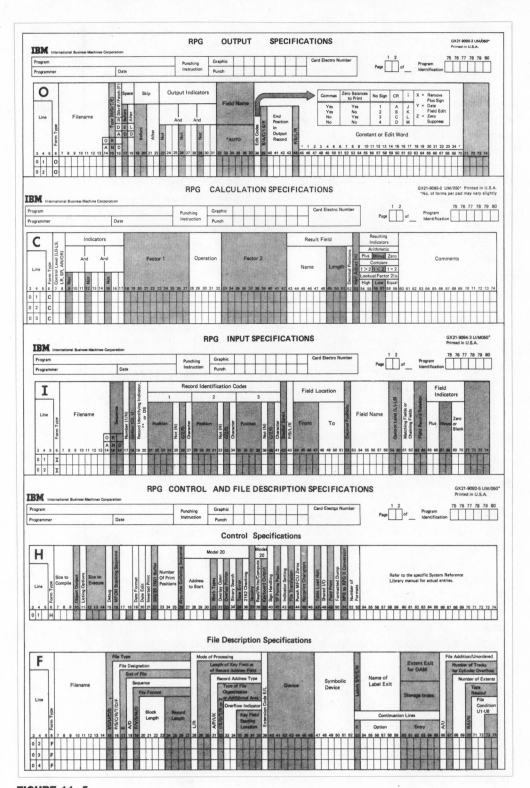

FIGURE 11-5
RPG Program Specification
Forms

and data to be submitted directly to the computer from remote terminals in a conversational fashion. The programs are translated (compiled) and executed, and the results returned to the remote terminal in a matter of seconds. In contrast, programs submitted in a batch environment may spend several hours in a queue before they are executed and the results returned to the user.

Programs written for interactive computing are generally relatively simple. They usually process small amounts of data. Typical interactive programs are one-time requests for information and inquiries into data files. Most systems designed to handle interactive computing permit several programmers to use the system at the same time. With the help of the fast response time, programs can be written and debugged in a short period of time.

The two major interactive programming languages are BASIC and APL. These languages are discussed in this section.

BASIC

BASIC (*B*eginners' *A*ll-Purpose *S*ymbolic *I*nstruction *C*ode) was developed at Dartmouth College for time-sharing use. Because BASIC is easy to learn, it can be used by people with little or no programming experience. Novice programmers can write fairly complex programs in BASIC in only a matter of hours.

The growth in the use of time-sharing systems has been accompanied by an increase in the use of BASIC. Most computer manufacturers offer both large and small computers capable of supporting BASIC. Although BASIC was originally intended to be used by colleges and universities for instructional purposes, many companies have adopted BASIC for their data-processing needs.

A BASIC program consists of a series of sequentially numbered statements. Each statement occupies a separate line. Following the line number is a keyword, such as PRINT or READ, which identifies the type of statement. The line numbers can range from 1 to 99999. The programmer can use the line numbers as labels to refer to specific statements in branching and looping operations. The line numbers must be in ascending sequence, but they do not need to be in increments of 1. Increments of 10, for example, make it easier for the programmer to insert lines between other lines. Figure 11–6 shows the payroll program coded in BASIC.

Three types of entries are typed from the terminal when writing a BASIC program:

Programming-language statements are used to write the BASIC program. BASIC statements such as IF, GO TO, PRINT, and INPUT are similar, if not identical, to statements used in other high-level languages.

System commands are used to communicate with the operating system. For example, the terminal user must type the system command RUN to direct the computer to begin program execution. To terminate program execution, the user types the system command STOP.

273

```
PAYROLL          14:50     AUGUST 3RD, 1978

10    REM THIS PROGRAM CALCULATES A WEEKLY
15    REM PAYROLL FOR FIVE EMPLOYEES
20    PRINT 'EMPLOYEE NAME', 'NET PAY'
30    PRINT
40    READ N$, H, W
50    IF H > 40 THEN 70
60    LET G = H*W
65    GO TO 100
70    LET R = 40*W
80    LET O = (H-40) * (1.5*W)
90    LET G = R+O
100   IF G > 250 THEN 130
110   LET T = .14
120   GO TO 140
130   LET T = .20
140   LET T2 = T*G
150   LET P = G-T2
160   PRINT N$, P
170   GO TO 40
180   DATA 'LYNN MANGINO', 35, 8.00
190   DATA 'THOMAS RITTER', 48, 4.75
200   DATA 'MARIE OLSON', 45, 5.50
210   DATA 'LORI DUNLEVY', 40, 5.00
220   DATA 'WILLIAM WILSON', 50, 7.00
230   END

RUN PAYROLL

PAYROLL

EMPLOYEE NAME     NET PAY

LYNN MANGINO      224.00
THOMAS RITTER     212.42
MARIE OLSON       209.00
LORI DUNLEVY      172.00
WILLIAM WILSON    308.00

LINE   40:   END OF DATA
```

FIGURE 11—6
Payroll Program in BASIC

● Editing commands are used for inserting changes in, or deleting parts of, the source program. For instance, the programmer can delete an incorrectly keyed letter or number by simply pressing the backward-arrow (←) key and then typing the correct character.

As the sample program illustrates, it is possible to write any of a wide variety of simple programs in BASIC with only a few types of statements.

The first two lines (Lines 10 and 15) of the sample program are remarks. A remark is used to provide information for the programmer and/or anyone else reading the program; it provides no information to the computer. To indicate a remark, the REM key word is used. It is followed immediately by the comment.

Lines 20 and 30 are PRINT statements. When the computer executes line 20, the words "EMPLOYEE NAME" and "NET PAY" will be printed. Execution of line 30 will cause a blank line to be printed.

The READ statement (line 40)

```
40 READ N$, H, W
```

causes the data in the DATA statement (lines 180–220) to be read and assigned to the variables whose names are N$, H, and W. That is, the employee's name will be stored in the location N$; the hours worked will be stored in H; and the employee's wage will be stored in W. In BASIC, a numeric variable name may be a single letter or a single letter followed by a digit. Character-string variables are distinguished from numeric variables by the use of a dollar sign ($) as the last character of character-string variable names.

The IF-THEN statement (Line 50)

```
50 IF H > 40 THEN 70
```

specifies that if the value represented by the variable name H (the number of hours the employee worked) is greater than 40, control should be transferred to statement 70. Statement 70 is where the calculation of overtime pay begins. If H is not greater than 40, the computer executes the next statement in sequence (Line 60, in the example).

Line 60 is a LET statement:

```
60 LET G = H * W
```

This LET statement says: "LET the variable G be set equal to the value obtained by evaluating the expression H * W." In other words, the data stored in H is multiplied by the data stored in W, and the result is stored in G. G represents the employee's gross pay.

Statement 160 is a PRINT statement:

```
160 PRINT N$, P
```

It prints the value of the variable N$ and the value of the variable P. The variable N$ holds the employee's name. P holds the final result of the arithmetic calculation of the employee's net pay.

Statement 170 tells the computer to go to statement 40 instead of continuing execution in sequence. Since statement 40 is the READ statement, more data will be read.

Statements 180, 190, 200, 210, and 220 are DATA statements. The BASIC compiler takes all the data appearing in all the DATA statements in the program and forms a list of data. As READ statements are encountered, data items are read consecutively from this list. When all the data has been read, and the READ statement is attempted, the message "LINE 40: END OF DATA" is printed on the terminal.

Every BASIC program must have an END statement which instructs the computer to terminate compilation of the program. It must be the last (highest-numbered) statement in the program. In the sample program, statement 230 marks the end of the program.

The BASIC programming language is a flexible language; it can be used for both scientific and business applications. Many BASIC statements are similar to those used in FORTRAN. BASIC is not suitable for handling large amounts of input and output because of its interactive nature. However, it can be used effectively to access large amounts of data stored on disk or tape at a central location.

At the present time, a BASIC standard exists, but it covers only a small subset of the BASIC language. BASIC programs written for one system may need substantial modification before being used with another system. Many extensions to BASIC have been developed, but only at the expense of increasing the difficulty of learning and using the language. As firms continue to expand online, real-time programming applications, the use of BASIC will continue to increase.

APL

APL was first conceived in 1962 by Kenneth Iverson. He described the APL language in his book, *A Programming Language*. He also worked with IBM to develop the language. It became available to the public through IBM in 1968. Over the years, APL has been expanded and has gained many enthusiastic supporters. Several businesses now use APL as their main programming language.

The full power of APL is best realized when it is used for interactive processing via a terminal. A programmer can use APL in two modes. When APL is used in an *execution mode*, the terminal can be used much like a desk calculator. An instruction is keyed in on one line, and the response is returned immediately on the following line. When APL is used in a *definition mode*, a series of instructions is entered into memory; the entire program is executed on command from the programmer. In a manner similar to BASIC, the APL user enters programming-language statements to develop a source program, system commands to communicate with the operating system, and editing commands to modify the source program. However, APL bears little resemblance to any high-level programming language discussed thus far.

Both character-string data and numeric data can be manipulated using APL. It is especially well suited for handling tables of related numbers known as *arrays*. To simplify the programmer's task, a number of operators (up to 50 or more) are provided for array manipulation, logical comparisons, mathematical functions, branching operations, and so forth. The operators are represented by symbols on a special APL keyboard (see Figure 11–7). Some examples of APL coding are shown in Table 11–3.

APL operators can be combined to perform some very complex operations with a minimum of coding. Its lack of formal restrictions on input and output, and its free-form style make APL a very powerful language. It can be learned quickly by programmers.

There are a few disadvantages of APL. First, it is very difficult to read. Second, as mentioned above, a special keyboard is required to enter APL

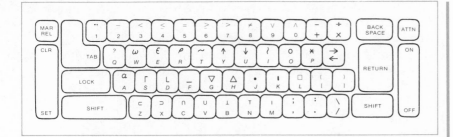

FIGURE 11-7
APL Keyboard

statements. Fortunately, the large offering of new, low-cost terminals capable of handling several type fonts has greatly reduced, if not eliminated, this problem. Another limitation of APL is the large amount of primary storage required by the APL compiler. Usually, only large and medium-size systems are capable of supporting APL. However, if a network of remote terminals is connected to a large central computer, APL can be made available to users at these remote sites. Time-sharing networks such as this have led to increased use of APL.

PROGRAMMING LANGUAGES—A COMPARISON

When implementing an information system, an important decision must be made concerning the type of programming language to use. The decision is almost entirely based on the applications involved. Some questions must be asked:

● What languages is the selected (or available) computer system capable of supporting?

● Will the applications require mostly complex computations, or file processing, or report generation?

● Is a fast response time crucial or will batch processing be satisfactory?

● Are equipment changes planned in the future?

● How frequently will programs need modification?

The size of the computer system is an obvious constraint on language choice. The limited main-storage capacity of small computers usually prohibits the use of languages such as COBOL, FORTRAN, and PL/1,

TABLE 11-3
APL CODING

APL CODING	ENGLISH TRANSLATION
A + B	A plus B
A ← 25	A = 25
A ⌊ B	Finds the smaller of A and B
V1 ← 2 5 11 17	Creates a vector of 4 components and assigns this vector to V1
⌈/V1	Finds the maximum value in the vector V1

277

which require significant amounts of main storage and sophisticated hardware. If the system is punched-card-oriented, RPG is a good choice. The computational capabilities of RPG are limited, but in many cases they can supply sufficient information for the management of small firms. If interactive processing is desired, BASIC should be considered. It can be used on many small computers and minicomputers. Subsets of COBOL and FORTRAN that can be used on small systems have also been developed.

For large systems, the type of processing is the key consideration in choosing a language. Business applications typically involve large amounts of data, but relatively few calculations are performed on the data. Substantial file processing (requiring many I/O operations) is performed. Thus, many business applications are *input/output-bound*. In such cases, COBOL and PL/1 provide the necessary power for efficient operations. When choosing between COBOL and PL/1, management must weigh the importance of standardization versus ease of programming. Although PL/1 has been standardized, it is still primarily an IBM language. In contrast, COBOL is available on all large computers but may require greater programming effort.

Scientific programming applications usually require many complex calculations on relatively small amounts of data. Therefore, they tend to be *process-bound*. The computational capabilities of FORTRAN make it ideal for such applications. Standardization is another attractive feature of FORTRAN. Another alternative is PL/1. As more manufacturers offer PL/1 compilers, it becomes a more attractive, more often available alternative. If interactive computing is desired, both APL and BASIC can be used. Although BASIC is easier to learn and use. APL has some very powerful features not available in BASIC. APL, however, is not available on all large computers and requires a special keyboard.

Because of the diversity of programming languages, many firms choose to use several languages. For example, scientific programs can be written in FORTRAN. File-updating programs can be written in COBOL. Programs for interactive processing can be written in BASIC. It is also possible to write part of a program in one language, and another part in a different language. This involves compiling the different portions of the program in separate steps, and linking together the resultant object programs. These steps can be specified in the job-control statements for the program.

There has been a definite trend away from programming in assembly language. Because of the one-to-one relationship between assembly-language instructions and machine-language instructions, programming in assembly language is very time-consuming. Assembly-language programs may be very efficient, but writing them is very laborious. In contrast, high-level languages shift the programming emphasis away from detailed computer functions, toward procedures for solving problems. High-level-language compilers require significant amounts of main-storage capacity, but the languages are much easier to use than machine-oriented languages.

278 As hardware costs have decreased, many more firms have determined that they can afford computers capable of supporting high-level languages. At the same time, labor costs have increased; program development and maintenance have become significant expense items. Thus, high-level languages have increased in popularity. These languages not only require less programming time, but also are much more machine-independent than assembly languages. When main-storage capacity is a critical constraint, however, assembly languages are the best, if not the only, alternative available. This situation is frequently encountered in minicomputer systems.

As in choosing hardware, there are many considerations in choosing software. A comparison chart reflecting some of the key considerations is shown in Table 11–4.

SUMMARY

● Programming languages can be classified into two categories—batch-oriented and interactive. Batch-oriented languages can be further classified as machine-oriented, procedure-oriented, or problem-oriented.

● Machine-oriented languages, like assembly language, are very similar to machine language. Procedure-oriented languages emphasize the computational and logical procedures for solving a problem. Common procedure-oriented languages are COBOL, FORTRAN, and PL/1. Prob-

TABLE 11–4

PROGRAMMING-LANGUAGE COMPARISON

	ASSEMBLY LANGUAGE	FORTRAN	COBOL	PL/1	RPG	BASIC	APL
Strong Math Capabilities	X	X		X		X	X
Good Character-Manipulation Capabilities	X		X	X		X	X
English-like			X	X			
Available on Many Computers	X	X	X		X	X	
Highly Efficient	X						
Standardized		X	X	X		X	
Requires Large Amts. of Storage			X	X			X
Good Interactive Capability						X	X
Procedure-Oriented		X	X	X			
Problem-Oriented					X		
Machine-Dependent	X				X		

lem-oriented languages describe a problem without detailing the computational steps necessary to solve it. RPG is a popular problem-oriented language.

● Programs in problem- and procedure-oriented languages are simpler to code but require more execution time than comparable programs written in lower-level, machine-oriented languages.

● An assembly-language programmer uses symbolic names for machine operations. Programming is less tedious and time-consuming than it would be if a machine language were used. Assembly-language programs are efficient in terms of storage and processing time required. However, assembly-language programming requires a high level of skill, and the language itself is machine-dependent.

● COBOL is the most popular business programming language. It was designed to be very English-like and self-documenting. Standardization of COBOL has helped to make it machine-independent. The main disadvantage of COBOL is that a large and sophisticated compiler is required to convert a COBOL source program into machine language.

● FORTRAN was the first high-level language to be developed. It is procedure-oriented and well-suited for scientific and mathematical applications.

● PL/1 is an all-purpose, procedure-oriented language suited to both scientific and business applications. It combines features of both COBOL and FORTRAN. The modularity of PL/1 facilitates structured programming. PL/1 compilers require a large amount of storage and are not available on small computers.

● RPG is designed to produce business reports. The output format needs to be specified, but the RPG generator program can build a program to provide the output. Little programming skill is required to use RPG. It is popular with users of small computers and minicomputers. However, RPG has limited computational capabilities and is not totally machine-independent.

● Interactive programming languages are used to communicate directly with the computer in a conversational mode. Response time is almost immediate. Interactive programs are fairly simple. Typical examples are one-time requests for information and inquiries into data files. Two major interactive programming languages are BASIC and APL.

● BASIC is an easy-to-learn language, well-suited for instructional purposes. It is an ideal language for time-sharing systems. It is flexible, and can be used for both scientific and business applications. Because many features of the language are not standardized, it is machine-dependent.

● APL is a very powerful interactive language. It can be used in an execution mode or a definition mode. Both character-string data and numeric data can be manipulated. Because APL has a large number of unique operators, it requires a special keyboard. The APL compiler needs a large amount of primary storage; this restricts its use to medium-size and large computers.

● Factors to consider when selecting an appropriate programming language include: What languages can the computer support? Are computations simple? Is output format important? What response time is required? Are equipment changes planned in the future? How often will programs be modified?

● There is an increasing trend toward the use of high-level, procedure-oriented languages.

REVIEW QUESTIONS

1. Distinguish between machine-oriented languages and procedure-oriented languages, giving examples of each.

2. Name the four divisions of a COBOL program. What is the function of each division?

3. Explain the special features of FORTRAN. For what types of applications is FORTRAN preferred and why?

4. What advantages does PL/1 have over other high-level languages? Why has PL/1 not been accepted widely?

5. Identify some applications for which RPG is appropriate. Explain why you selected these applications.

6. Compare BASIC with APL. What are some of the unique characteristics of APL?

OHIO CITIZENS TRUST COMPANY

The Ohio Citizens Trust Company opened for business on March 28, 1932, with 25 employees and capital funds totaling $350,000. After a 1959 merger with the Spitzer-Rorick Trust and Savings Bank, the bank's total deposits exceeded $100 million. Today, with total deposits exceeding $400 million, Ohio Citizens is a progressive financial institution and a major resource for Toledo community development.

Through the years, the bank has pioneered and popularized many services in the greater Toledo area. Personal loans, drive-up windows, money orders, charge cards, freight payment, payroll systems, and EveryDay interest passbook savings are among the most notable. In 1975, the bank introduced an automatic loan plan called checkLOAN which provides extra funds whenever needed for approved checking customers. The 24-hour money machines, OCEY BANKS, were also introduced during that year.

"OC Transfer," the first bank telephone transfer system offered in the marketplace, was developed in 1977. This system allows a customer to transfer funds between checking, savings, and checkLOAN. It operates 24 hours a day, seven days a week.

Offering financial services to both retail and commercial communities, the bank processes an average of 436,000 transactions per week. Millions of dollars worth of computers and other facilities

are used to record and process nearly 90,000 daily transactions.

The Operations Center of Ohio Citizens, in downtown Toledo, houses the corporate data-processing facilities. Two main-frame computers, an IBM System/360 Model 50 and an IBM System/370 Model 148, provide information support for all departments. ENTREX is the primary key-entry system. Charge-card processing, installment loans, and stock transfers are supported by remote data-entry stations in those departments. ENTREX is a key-to-disk data-entry system where the data is collected, stored, retrieved, and forwarded to the application computer systems for processing. The data is entered on a keyboard with a video display screen and stored directly on a disk; the data on the disk is transferred to tape or transmitted through telecommunications for daily processing.

Other recent innovations aid Ohio Citizens in efficient processing. The online, real-time savings system directly connects tellers' terminals with a computer for savings passbook transactions. The bank has also installed Central Information File, an online, data-base-like application. The basic file contains data, financial and otherwise, about all of the bank's customers and utilizes audio response equipment for inquiry from the branch offices and other departments. Bank personnel can use a touch-tone telephone to learn account information such as available balance. The response is a computer-generated voice message. In conjunction with businesses in the area, Ohio Citizens has an automatic payroll deposit system.

Ohio Citizens is also an active member of the Automated Clearing House (ACH) payment system. With this sys-

tem, customers can have billing payments withdrawn from their accounts directly, without ever seeing their bills, or can arrange for recurring payments such as payroll or Social Security benefits deposited directly into their bank accounts. The customer signs an authorization form with the participating company or organization whereby the bill or payment is transmitted through an originating bank to the Midwest Automated Payment Center at the Federal Reserve Bank in Cleveland. The Center then forwards a transaction to the customer's bank for processing. Member banks receive the transactions on magnetic tape and process them accordingly.

Three programming languages are used in Ohio Citizens' data-processing applications: COBOL, BASIC, and assembly language. In the Controller's Division of the bank, most accounting-oriented financial reports are processed as BASIC applications. The division uses an IBM 5100 microcomputer with a CRT for these applications. The applications are online, real-time programming applications for which data is submitted directly to the computer from remote terminals; the results are returned in a matter of seconds.

The Daily Statement application, for example, prepares a daily balance sheet report and a formatted report of the bank's six checking-account balances. Controller's Division personnel enter (via the CRT keyboard) the new balance of each account received from the Proof Department. The current day's balance, month-to-date and year-to-date figures, and a statistical comparison of the balances with other financial data of the bank are produced. The Commercial Loan Accounts Accrual Report application daily computes the accrued interest on loan accounts.

These applications are conducive to BASIC programming because the procedure is the same every day and involves only inputting data.

Two other programs, although not run daily, are written in BASIC. One is a Return-on-Investment Analysis program, which determines instantaneously the return on investment for the bank. The other is a Budget Modeling application. Because the BASIC program is so quick and simple to change, it provides an excellent environment for manipulating alternative budget models.

In the data-processing department, programs are written in assembly language and COBOL. Originally, all programming was done in assembly language. Because the department's first IBM 360 computer was a Model 30, a small computer with only 32K bytes of main storage, it was necessary to use a compact language. The transition to larger equipment has made the use of the more English-like COBOL possible. Many programs have already been converted to it.

The assembly-language programs written for System/360 machines can be run on System/370 equipment. Because of its speed and efficiency, assembly language will continue to be used for teleprocessing monitors and MICR support. Also, some applications require I/O devices that can only be supported with assembly language provided by the equipment manufacturer. These programs and the operating systems will continue to be programmed in assembly languages.

All batch applications in the department will eventually be written in COBOL. The Installment Loan and Payroll applications are two original assembly-language applications that have already been rewritten in COBOL.

The above three languages were selected by Ohio Citizens in order to match the requirements of the applications with the strengths of the languages. The online, real-time programs are written in BASIC so that results can be obtained quickly. Operating systems and programs that require assembly-language I/O support will continue to be written in assembly languages. COBOL has been selected as the application language of the future because of its standardization, programming ease, and readability.

DISCUSSION POINTS

1. Ohio Citizens is converting their assembly-language programs to COBOL. Discuss the advantages and disadvantages of such a conversion.

2. Why is BASIC an ideal language for applications such as budget modeling?

STRUCTURED-DESIGN CONCEPTS | 12

OUTLINE

I. Structured-Design Methodology
  A. Top-Down Design
    1. Modular Approach
    2. Structure Charts
  B. Documentation and Design
    Tools
    1. HIPO
    2. Pseudocode
II. Structured Programming
  A. Standardized Method of
    Program Problem-Solving

B. Control Patterns
    1. Simple Sequence, Selection,
    Loop
    2. "GO-TO-less" Programming
III. Management of System Projects
  A. Chief Programmer Team
    1. Chief Programmer / Analyst
    2. Backup Programmer
    3. Librarian
  B. Structured Review and
    Evaluation
    1. Informal Design Review
    2. Formal Design Review

INTRODUCTION

With recent advances in computer technology, hardware costs have continued to decrease while capabilities have expanded. Unfortunately, the same cannot be said of program and system development costs. Modern business environments have become more complex and dynamic in nature. Systems designed to supply information to management must be continually re-designed or modified in response to the changing needs of management. As more time is spent in system design and maintenance, the costs for such services continue to rise dramatically in relation to hardware costs.

These problems have caused a greater emphasis to be placed on simplicity and well-thought-out logic in system and program design. Several tools for simplifying the tasks of programmers and system analysts have recently attracted considerable attention. A sound methodology for program and system development is a necessity. The concept of top-down design and the tools for its implementation are discussed in the following section. These techniques apply to both system and program development. A later section is devoted specifically to structured programming. Also included is a section on the management of system projects.

"VIEWDATA" MAKES TV INTO COMPUTER

Fernand Auberjonois
(the *Blade's* European
correspondent)

The Toledo Blade,
March 5, 1978, p. 1

LONDON There'll be no place like home when the British post office starts operating its "Viewdata" service which turns the ordinary television set into a computer, encyclopedia, travel booking agent, two-way Telex machine, and memory bank.

This will happen, postal officials say, in about 12 months. And they regard the development as the greatest invention since television. By 1984, the year that George Orwell picked at random a long time ago to mark the birth of the new era when people shall be "programmed," nearly half the sets in Britain may be "adapted" to provide a variety of services to the living room.

At a press conference in London last Tuesday, the head of the post office telecommunications division, Peter Benton, said the government is committing nearly $400 million to the Viewdata project for the next seven years, nearly $100 million of which will be spent to launch the scheme next year.

Viewdata is operated jointly by the post office, the television networks, and subscribers who provide information stored by the General Post Office.

QUESTIONS FOR MEMORY BANK

The viewer will use his adapted set to ask questions from the memory bank. The answers will come out in print and graphs, in black and white or color. By June 1, when the market trials are due to begin, the post office will have accumulated a small fund of knowledge: 110,000 pages of information sent in by the 100 organizations now under contract to act as "providers." By June, 1979, the bank will have 800,000 pages stored.

The receiver looks very much like the ordinary living room set, but it is connected to the Viewdata service over telephone lines. In Britain the telephone service is government-operated.

Connection with the Viewdata computer will be established by pressing a button. For precise questions and answers the subscriber will use a code in figures on a remote control unit which looks like a pocket calculator. The post office will charge per page for the answers provided.

The receiver becomes a sender by the addition of an alphabetic keyboard. Messages will be sent out to the computer or to other subscribers. Eventually the home receiver will be made "intelligent" with a computer of its own, no bigger than a postage stamp.

TO DISPLAY SMALL ADS

Television networks will be linked with the system to display small ads. This causes publishers some concern. But the receiver is still, at this moment, a costly gadget: One must pay $1400 for the adapted color set. In Britain, the average price of a color receiver is about $640.

Post office technicians predict that eventually the price of the adapted set will be $100 to $200 more than the regular color set. Black and white Viewdata sets will be available in June for about $700. They can also be rented.

There is a great deal of competition right now between manufacturers of Viewdata sets. The system itself could be a substantial earner of foreign currency. It has been bought by the West German post office. Holland and Australia are negotiating. France is developing its own system.

Two questions have been raised by the computerization of the home TV set. One is: "Who needs it?" The other,

286

perhaps more to the point: ''Who will be feeding what into the Viewdata bank?''

1,500 SUBSCRIBERS AT START
When the Viewdata tests begin in June and for a period of about two years, there will be 1,500 subscribers, mostly medium-size firms, colleges, and societies. Later, individual viewers will join in.

As to the possible misuse of data by providers intent on distributing propaganda, this is something several newspapers have been concerned with. So has the government. And so have critics who believe the government must be watched. There is bound to be a demand for controls.

The potential problems associated with the design of such an ambitious project as Viewdata necessitate very careful planning and development. Structured design and other techniques used in the management of complex system projects, as discussed in this chapter, must be employed.

STRUCTURED-DESIGN METHODOLOGY

Top-Down Design

Chapter 10 mentioned that a problem can be simplified by breaking it into segments, or subunits. This is known as a *modular approach* to problem-solving. A problem solution is defined in terms of functions to be performed. Each step, or module, in the solution process consists of one or more logically related functions. Thus, a problem solution may consist of several independent modules which, together, perform the required tasks.

The use of modules greatly facilitates the solution planning process. But the modules must be meaningfully organized. *Top-down design* is a method of defining a solution in terms of major functions to be performed, and further breaking down these major functions into subfunctions. To accomplish this, problems are dealt with at varying levels of complexity.

At the highest level is the main control logic. It is most critical to the success of the solution. Each module at this level contains only a broad description of a particular step in the solution process. It is further broken down into several lower-level modules. They contain more detail as to the specific steps to be performed. Depending on the complexity of the problem, several levels of modules may be required. The lowest-level modules contain the greatest level of detail.

When the top-down approach is used, the modules of the problem solution are related to each other in a hierarchical, or tree-like, manner. As an aid, the modules and their relationships can be depicted graphically using a *structure chart*. As an example, a structure chart for an inventory-processing application is shown in Figure 12–1.

At the highest level in the hierarchy is the main *control module*. It is represented by the block labeled "Inventory Processing." This module is further broken down into lower-level modules. The inventory-processing application involves three basic functions: reading a master inventory record and a sales transaction card; computing the reorder quantity; and writing an updated master file and purchase orders. The "Reorder Quantity" module can be further divided into "Compute Current Inventory" and "Compute Order Requirements" modules. Finally, computing the current inventory involves two modules: "Determine Beginning Inventory" and "Determine Units Sold." Notice how the level of detail increases at lower-level modules.

The flow of control in the structure chart is from top to bottom, demonstrating the top-down design of the solution. In other words, each module has control of the modules directly below it, but it is controlled by the module directly above it. The higher-level modules are both processing modules and control modules; they control other modules below them in the hierarchy. At the lowest level, only processing modules are involved.

The complete structure chart for the inventory processing application is shown in Figure 12–2.

When top-down design is used, certain rules must be followed. First, an attempt should be made to make each module independent of all

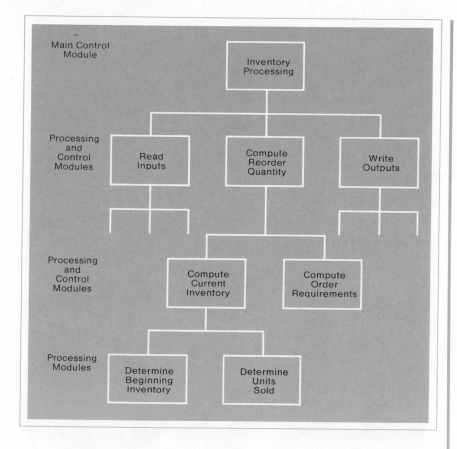

FIGURE 12—1
Portion of Structure Chart
for Inventory Processing

other modules. In other words, each module should be executed only when control is passed to it from the module directly above it. Similarly, once a module has been executed, control should be passed back to the module directly above. The return process continues until the main control module is reached.

Another rule of the modular approach is that each module should be relatively small. The purpose of this rule is to facilitate the translation of modules into program statements. Many advocates of the modular approach suggest that each module should consist of no more than 50 or 60 lines of code. When module size is limited in this manner, the coding for each module can fit on a single page of computer printout. This simplifies testing and debugging procedures.

Yet another rule is that each module should have only one entrance point and one exit point. This also makes the basic flow easy to follow.

When top-down design is used, the complete solution is not established until the lowest-level modules have been designed. However, this does not prevent higher-level modules from being coded and tested at earlier stages in the development cycle. To do this, *dummy modules* are created and used in place of the lower-level modules for testing purposes. Significant errors in higher-level modules can be isolated by observing whether control is correctly transferred between the higher-level modules and the dummy modules. As the lower-level modules are

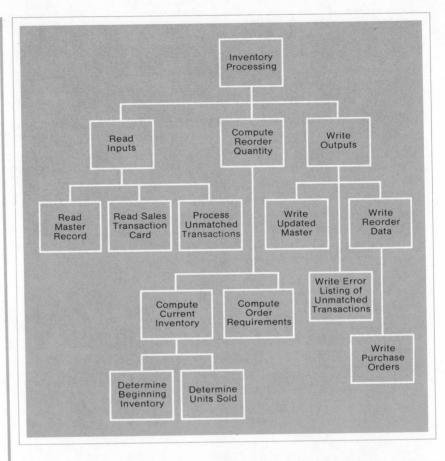

FIGURE 12–2
Structure Chart for Inventory
Processing with Four Levels
of Processing Modules

designed and coded, they can replace the dummy modules and be similarly tested. In this manner, by the time the lowest-level modules have been coded, all other modules have already been tested and debugged.

When top-down design is used, structure charts provide an excellent means of documentation. However, structure charts show only functions, their relationships, and the flow of control; they do not show the processing flow, the order of execution, or how control will be transferred to and from each module. Therefore, structure charts must be supplemented with system charts, program flowcharts, record layouts, and so on. We discussed program flowcharts and layout forms in Chapter 10. System charts will be discussed in Chapter 14. Two helpful documentation aids—HIPO and pseudocode—are discussed in the following section.

Documentation and Design Tools

HIPO   The term *HIPO* is an acronym for *H*ierarchy plus *I*nput-*P*rocess-*O*utput. HIPO diagrams are visual aids commonly used as supplements to structure charts. Whereas structure charts emphasize only structure and function, HIPO diagrams show the inputs and outputs of program modules.

A typical HIPO package consists of three types of diagrams. They describe a program, or system of programs, from the general level to the detail level. At the most general level is the *visual table of contents*. The visual table of contents is almost identical to a structure chart, but it includes some additional information. Each block in the visual table of contents is given an identification number that is used as a reference in other HIPO diagrams. Figure 12–3 shows a visual table of contents for the inventory-processing application mentioned earlier in this chapter.

Each module in the visual table of contents can be described in greater detail using an *overview diagram*. The overview diagram includes the inputs, processing, and outputs of a module. The reference number assigned to the overview diagram shows where the module fits into the overall structure of the system as depicted in the visual table of contents. If the module passes control to a lower-level module in the hierarchy for some specific processing operation, that operation is also given a reference number. An overview diagram for the "Read Inputs" module (2.0) is shown in Figure 12–4.

Finally, the specific functions performed and/or data items used in each module are described in a *detail diagram*. The amount of detail used in these diagrams depends on the complexity of the problem involved. Enough detail should be included to enable a programmer to understand the functions and write the code to perform these functions.

HIPO diagrams are an excellent means of documenting systems and programs. The varying levels of detail incorporated in the HIPO diagrams allow them to be used by managers, analysts, and programmers to meet needs ranging from program maintenance to overhaul of entire systems.

Pseudocode Flowcharts are the most commonly used method of expressing program logic, but a technique known as *pseudocode* is becoming increasingly popular. Pseudocode is an English-like description of the processing steps in a program. At times, flowcharts become lengthy and difficult to read, especially those for complex programs. In some cases, it is difficult to express the logic of processing steps within the commonly used flowcharting symbols. When pseudocode is used, the program solution follows an easy-to-read, top-down sequence.

Certain key words such as IF, THEN, and ELSE are used in pseudocode. However, there is no rigid set of rules to be followed. Thus, pseudocode is a simple technique to learn and use. Figure 12–5 contrasts pseudocode and program flowcharting. As the example indicates, pseudocode is understandable, even to those unfamiliar with the program logic. The actual program can be coded easily, directly from the pseudocode.

STRUCTURED PROGRAMMING

Emphasis on the art of programming and the flexibility that high-level languages provide has encouraged poor programming techniques. For example, many programs contain numerous branches that continually

291

FIGURE 12–3
Visual Table of Contents for Inventory-Processing Example

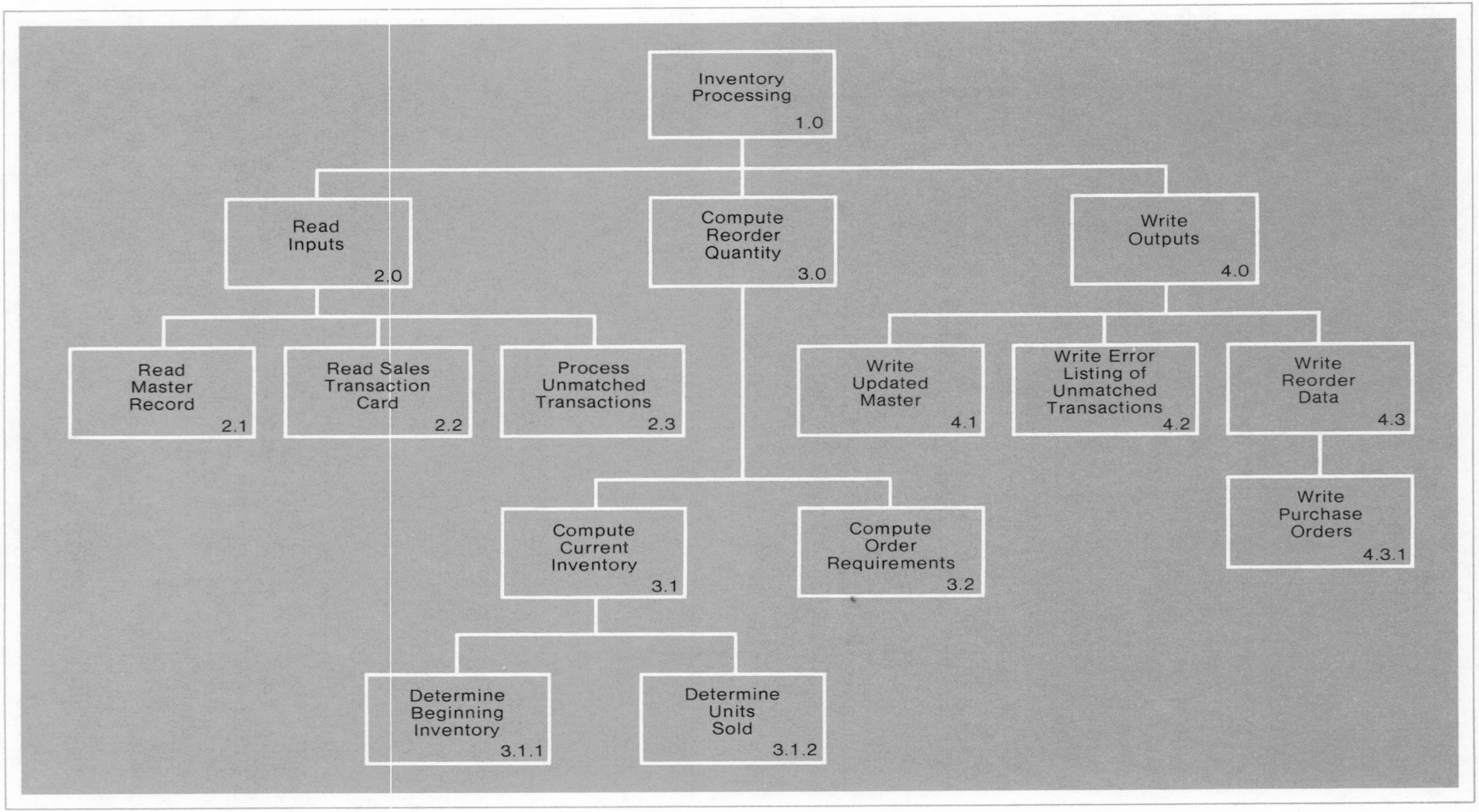

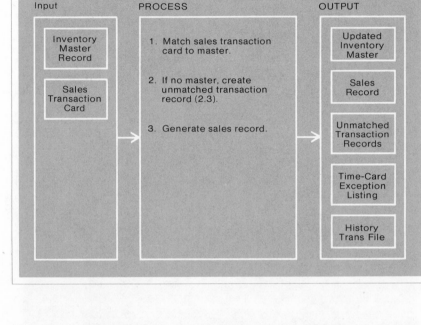

Author: M. Andrews   System/Program: Inventory Processing Date: 6/1/80
Diagram ID: 20   Name: Inventory   Page: 1 of 1

Input   PROCESS   OUTPUT

Inventory Master Record

Sales Transaction Card

1. Match sales transaction card to master.

2. If no master, create unmatched transaction record (2.3).

3. Generate sales record.

Updated Inventory Master

Sales Record

Unmatched Transaction Records

Time-Card Exception Listing

History Trans File

FIGURE 12–4
HIPO Overview Diagram for "Read Inputs" Module

alter the sequential flow of processing. These programs may work successfully, but the often-confusing logic can be understood only by the original programmer. This increases the costs and difficulties associated with program maintenance. Furthermore, without a standardized method of attacking a problem, a programmer may spend far more time than necessary in determining an appropriate solution and developing the program. To counter these tendencies, a concept known as *structured programming* has been widely publicized.

There are three objectives of structured programming:

1. To reduce testing time
2. To increase programmer productivity
3. To increase clarity by reducing complexity

Structured programming encourages well-thought-out program logic. The top-down modular approach discussed earlier in this chapter is used during development of the program design. The structured program itself is written using only three basic control patterns: simple sequence, selection, and loop (see Figures 12–6 and 12–7). When these three patterns and the modular approach are used, programs can be read from top to bottom and are easier to understand. An attempt is made to keep programs as simple and straightforward as possible. Too often, programmers consider the programs they write as their own creations,

293

FIGURE 12–5

Example of Pseudocode

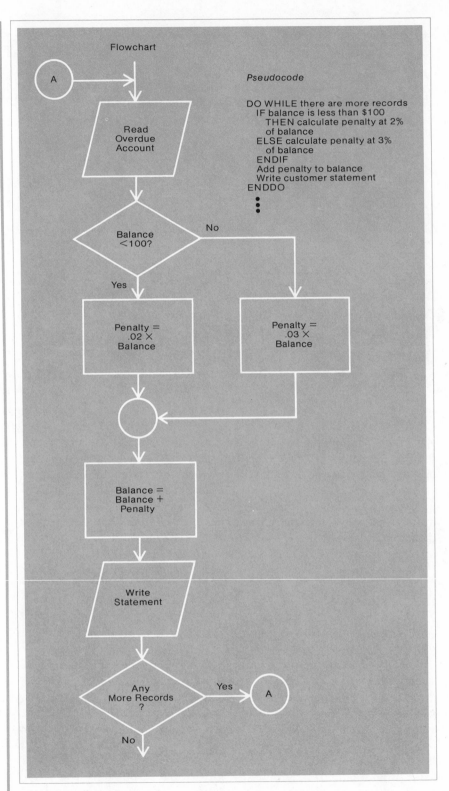

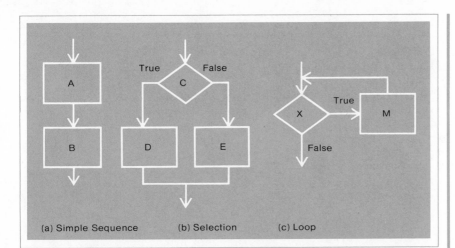

(a) Simple Sequence   (b) Selection   (c) Loop

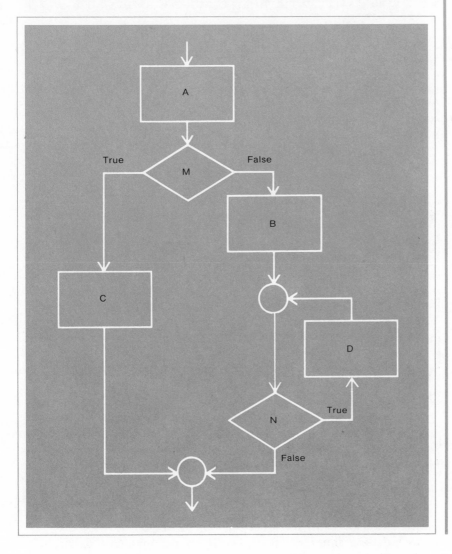

FIGURE 12—6
Basic Structured-
Programming Control
Patterns

FIGURE 12—7
Sample Flowchart of
Structured Programming

```
00032
00033     WORK-LOOP.
00034        READ CARD-FILE AT END GO TO FINISH.
00035        IF HOURS-WORKED IS GREATER THAN 40 THEN GO TO
00036           OVERTIME-ROUTINE.
00037        MULTIPLY HOURS-WORKED BY WAGE-PER-HOUR GIVING GROSS-PAY.
00038        GO TO TAX-COMPUTATION.
00039     OVERTIME-ROUTINE.
00040        MULTIPLY WAGE-PER-HOUR BY 40 GIVING REGULAR-PAY.
00041        SUBTRACT 40 FROM HOURS-WORKED GIVING OVERTIME-HOURS.
00042        MULTIPLY WAGE-PER-HOUR BY 1.5 GIVING OVERTIME-RATE.
00043        MULTIPLY OVERTIME-HOURS BY OVERTIME-RATE GIVING
00044           OVERTIME-PAY.
00045        ADD REGULAR-PAY, OVERTIME-PAY, GIVING GROSS-PAY.
00046     TAX-COMPUTATION.
00047        IF GROSS-PAY IS GREATER THAN 250 THEN MULTIPLY GROSS-PAY
00048           BY 0.20 GIVING TAX ELSE MULTIPLY GROSS-PAY BY 0.14
00049           GIVING TAX.
00050        SUBTRACT TAX FROM GROSS-PAY GIVING NET-PAY.
00051        MOVE EMPLOYEE-NAME TO NAME.
00052        MOVE NET-PAY TO AMOUNT.
00053        WRITE PRINT-LINE.
00054        GO TO WORK-LOOP.
00055     FINISH.
00056        CLOSE CARD-FILE, PRINT-FILE.
00057        STOP RUN.
```

(a) Unstructured Portion of COBOL Program

FIGURE 12–8

Unstructured vs.
Structured COBOL
Code

without regard to others who may have to modify them. Structured programming discourages the use of "tricky" logic that is confusing to everyone (sometimes, even to the original programmer).

A basic guideline of structured programming is that each module should have only one entry point and one exit point. This allows the flow of control to be followed easily by the programmer. When the modular approach is used, the one-entry/one-exit guideline is easy to incorporate into the program. A program having only one entrance and one exit is called a *proper program*.

It must be emphasized that the branch pattern, characterized by the GO TO statement, is not advocated in structured programming. In fact, structured programming is sometimes called "GO-TO-less programming." A GO TO statement causes an unconditional branch from one part of the program to another. Excessive use of GO TO statements results in continual changes in the execution flow of the program. Often the flow is transferred to totally different logical sections of the program. Programs containing many GO TO statements are difficult to modify because they are obscure and complicated. In contrast, structured-programming logic flows from the beginning to the end of a program, without backtracking to earlier sections (see Figure 12–7).

296 Some programming languages are more conducive to structured

```
00033    WORK-LOOP.
00034      READ CARD-FILE AT END CLOSE CARD-FILE, PRINT-FILE, STOP RUN.
00035      IF HOURS-WORKED IS GREATER THAN 40
00036        THEN PERFORM OVERTIME-ROUTINE
00037        ELSE PERFORM STANDARD-ROUTINE.
00038      PERFORM TAX-PAY-COMPUTATION.
00039      PERFORM PRINTING.
00040      GO TO WORK-LOOP.
00041    STANDARD-ROUTINE.
00042      MULTIPLY HOURS-WORKED BY WAGE-PER-HOUR GIVING GROSS-PAY.
00043    OVERTIME-ROUTINE.
00044      MULTIPLY WAGE-PER-HOUR BY 40 GIVING REGULAR-PAY.
00045      SUBTRACT 40 FROM HOURS-WORKED GIVING OVERTIME-HOURS.
00046      MULTIPLY WAGE-PER-HOUR BY 1.5 GIVING OVERTIME-RATE.
00047      MULTIPLY OVERTIME-HOURS BY OVERTIME-RATE GIVING
00048        OVERTIME-PAY.
00049      ADD REGULAR-PAY, OVERTIME-PAY GIVING GROSS-PAY.
00050    TAX-PAY-COMPUTATION.
00051      IF GROSS-PAY IS GREATER THAN 250 THEN MULTIPLY GROSS-PAY
00052        BY 0.20 GIVING TAX ELSE MULTIPLY GROSS-PAY BY 0.14
00053        GIVING TAX.
00054      SUBTRACT TAX FROM GROSS-PAY GIVING NET-PAY.
00055    PRINTING.
00056      MOVE EMPLOYEE-NAME TO NAME.
00057      MOVE NET-PAY TO AMOUNT.
00058      WRITE PRINT-LINE.
```

(b) *Structured Portion of COBOL Program*

FIGURE 12–8
Continued

programming than others. Especially well-suited for structured programming are PL/1, COBOL, and ALGOL (another language developed by a coordinated effort of user groups and computer manufacturers, and in widespread use in Europe). Languages such as FORTRAN and BASIC lack some features that many people consider essential for structured programming. For example, it is sometimes difficult to avoid the use of GO TO statements in these languages. However, careful planning and well-placed GO TO statements can result in well-structured programs, regardless of the language used. Figure 12–8 compares a portion of an unstructured COBOL payroll program with a structured version.

Management's difficulties in implementing structured programming may originate from a resistance to change. However, the use of structured programming not only significantly improves programming practices, but also represents potential cost savings.

MANAGEMENT OF SYSTEM PROJECTS

Throughout this chapter, we have presented various tools—top-down design, modular design, HIPO diagrams, and structured programming—all of which are intended to aid in designing an efficient, easy-to-maintain system in a minimum amount of time. However, even the most organized and well structured system may have errors and omissions that can render the system useless. Thus, continuous review of the system during the development cycle is essential. While errors and oversights will almost certainly surface after a system becomes operative (sometimes even months or years later), these problems can be minimized through careful planning, coordinating, and review of the system effort.

Chief Programmer Team

As an important first step in coordinating a system effort, a *chief programmer team (CPT)* is sometimes formed. The CPT concept involves organizing a small number of programmers under the supervision of a chief programmer. The goals of the CPT approach are to produce a software product that is easy to maintain and modify, to improve programmer productivity, and to increase system reliability. Organizations have applied the CPT concept to implement systems well ahead of schedule and with a minimal number of errors in programming.

The chief programmer is responsible for overall coordination and development of the programming project. A lead analyst works with the chief programmer in large system projects. In such cases, the lead analyst may supervise the general system design effort, while the chief programmer concentrates on the technical development (JCL, program coding, etc.) of the project.

Usually, a backup programmer is assigned as an assistant to the chief programmer. The backup programmer is a highly qualified specialist who may help in system design, testing, and evaluation of alternative designs. The chief programmer and backup programmer normally code the most critical parts of the overall system, but work together with one or more other programmers to integrate all parts into a complete system. The chief programmer is responsible for the success of the project.

Under this approach, both structured programming and top-down design are used. Separate modules of the system are programmed and tested by different programmers. In recognition of the fact that communication among programmers and analysts is essential, the CPT concept incorporates the use of a *librarian* to help maintain complete, up-to-date documentation of the project. The librarian relieves the team programmers of many clerical tasks they would otherwise have to perform. The duties of the librarian include:

- Preparation of computer input from coding forms completed by programmers

- Submission and pickup of inputs and outputs of computer runs

- Maintaining up-to-date source-program listings in archives available to all programmers

- Updating test data and implementing changes in programs and job-control statements as required

- Maintaining up-to-date documentation

Communication among team members is enhanced with this approach because all program descriptions, coding, and test results are current and visible to everyone involved in the effort. In addition, this approach enables the chief programmer to maintain control of costs and of human and computer resources, and to insure adherence to standards.

The organizational structure of a chief programmer team is shown in Figure 12–9. As mentioned previously, the structure of the chief programmer team varies, depending on the complexity of the system project.

Structured Review and Evaluation

Obviously, an important goal of a system effort is to produce an error-free system in the shortest possible time. This requires a careful review of the system effort before it is implemented. Early detection of errors and oversights can prevent costly modifications later.

One approach used in the early phases of system development is an *informal design review*. The system design documentation is reviewed by selected management, analysts, and programmers. This is usually done prior to the actual coding of program modules. After a brief review period, each person responds with suggestions for additions, deletions, and modifications to the system design.

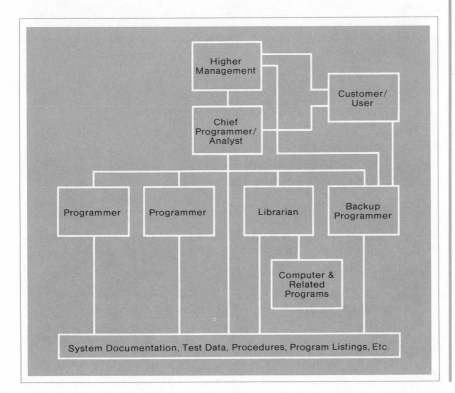

FIGURE 12–9

Chief Programmer Team Organization

A *formal design review* is sometimes used after the detailed parts of the system have been sufficiently documented. The documentation at this point may consist of program flowcharts, pseudocode, and/or narrrative descriptions. Sometimes called a *structured walk-through*, the formal design review involves distributing the documentation to a review team of two to four members. This team studies the documentation and then meets with the program designers to discuss the overall completeness, accuracy, and quality of the design. The reviewers and program designers often trace through the programs using desk-checking as discussed in Chapter 10. Both valid and invalid data are used to ascertain the program's exception-handling and standard procedures.

After programs have been coded and executed on the computer, their outputs can be compared with hand-calculated results for verification. Any discrepancies can be noticed and problems corrected. Using this approach, few, if any, errors will remain undetected when the system finally becomes operative.

SUMMARY

● Top-down program design and structured programming are techniques that have been developed to reduce program development and maintenance costs.

● In the top-down approach, a program is broken down into functional modules. The highest-level module is the main control module. It is further broken down into lower-level modules. Structure charts are used to graphically depict the program modules and their relationships. The flow of control in the structure chart is from top to bottom.

● When using top-down design, the programmer codes the higher-level modules first and tests them. Lower-level modules are then coded and tested. This facilitates debugging because errors can be isolated to particular modules.

● Two methods of documentation used with top-down design are HIPO diagrams and pseudocode. HIPO diagrams show the input, output, and processing steps of each module. HIPO documentation consists of three types of diagrams—a visual table of contents, overview diagrams, and detail diagrams.

● Program logic can be expressed in pseudocode, which is an English-like description of the processing steps in a program. In pseudocode, the program solution follows a top-down sequence. The technique is easy to learn and use.

● Structured programming is a "GO-TO-less" programming concept. It uses only three basic control patterns—simple sequence, selection, and loop. Some languages like PL/1, COBOL, and ALGOL are well-suited to structured programming.

● The chief programmer team (CPT) concept involves organizing a small number of programmers under the supervision of a chief programmer. Usually, the chief programmer is assisted by a highly qualified backup programmer. These two people code the most critical parts of the overall system. A librarian maintains complete, up-to-date documentation of the project. The organization of the CPT varies according to the complexity of the project.

● Systems must be reviewed before implementation. In an informal design review, the system design documentation is reviewed prior to actual coding to determine any changes that may be desirable. After a detailed system design is complete, a formal design review is held to check its completeness, accuracy, and quality. Desk-checking and test data are used to check all programs.

REVIEW QUESTIONS

1. Explain top-down design. Why is this technique being used for system and program design?

2. What is the role of HIPO and pseudocode in structured-design methodology? Do you think that these tools offer any significant advantages over traditional methods of documentation? Explain.

3. Structured programming avoids the use of GO TO statements. Does this reduce the flexibility of the programmer and make coding more difficult?

4. What benefits can be realized by using structured programming? Give reasons to support your answer.

5. Explain the chief programmer team concept. What is the role of the librarian in this approach to system design?

In the late 1880s, a young man named George M. Verity, manager of a small roofing company, was looking for a reliable source of quality steel sheets for his company. Since these sheets were not easy to find, Verity decided to become his own supplier and organized a new company, ambitiously named the American Rolling Mill Company. It was the first company to bring together all the steps necessary to make steel, roll it flat into sheets, and galvanize, corrugate, and fabricate the sheets into a finished product. Today, Armco Inc. is a highly-diversified, 77-year-old company headquartered in Ohio. Employing 52,000 people, Armco is the nation's fifth largest tonnage producer of steel, traditionally ranking third in the industry in assets, sales, and profits.

At the plant in Butler, Pennsylvania, about 3700 Armco men and women make the electrical steels for power generation and distribution. These steels are used in electrical equipment such as transformers, motors, and other devices that generate, distribute, and use electric power. This plant is now the world's largest producer of electrical steels. It also makes large quantities of stainless steel sheets and strips.

Throughout the data-processing structure at Armco, large computers, minis, and microcomputers are being used. More specifically, these systems include IBM, Four-Phase, Westinghouse, and Process Computing Systems hardware. The regional CPUs are located at Armco corporate headquarters in Middletown, Ohio. They consist of two IBM System/370 Model 168s with disk and tape units. All general office and Butler regional applications are processed on this equipment. Butler jobs are handled by an IBM remote job-entry

(RJE) terminal, and keypunch data is transmitted using a Four-Phase key-to-disk system with 10 display-entry stations.

The data-processing center at Butler houses two IBM System/7 minicomputers which are tied to the regional equipment at Middletown. With this communication capability, the Butler plant can transfer any data they process to the equipment at headquarters. The minicomputers and attached disks handle the Butler Information Management System test and production systems, time-sharing option, and local applications development. Figure 12–10 illustrates the hardware configuration.

The data-processing department at Butler presently has 41 employees. Computerized data-processing is used in the areas of payroll, cost accounting, production inventory control, metallurgical testing of customer shipments, forecasting production requirements, and management information reports. Other applications include an automated shipping system that tracks shipping inventory and prints out necessary

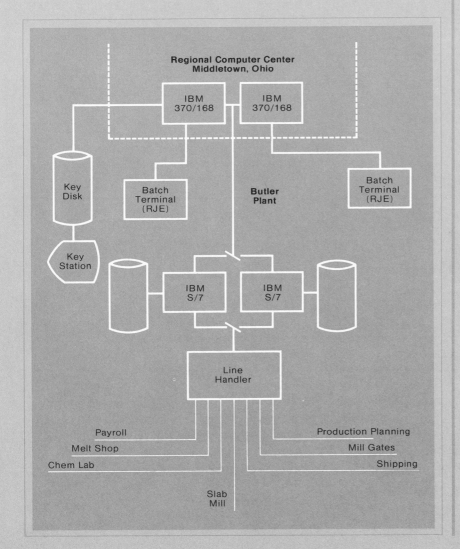

FIGURE 12–10
Regional Computer Center

303

shipping documents, a personnel data system that keeps complete employment records of all employees, a badge reader and time-keeping system, and a maintenance job-order control system.

The data-processing department uses a structured approach in planning, coding, and testing programs. The typical flow constructs are established, and coding rules for statements, comments, segmentation, indentation, and so on, are applied. The EDP personnel chose the structured features they felt most applicable to their philosophy and discarded others. For instance, they do not use a librarian or detailed HIPO diagrams. In the HIPO vein, however, they have implemented the use of structure charts. PL/1 is used in coding because of its structured qualities.

Computer programs are developed through a process known as a "unit development" procedure. When a user problem is presented to a programming team, it is reviewed and broken into segments. Each team member is assigned one or more of the resulting segments for planning and development. He or she creates a unit development plan (UDP) to estimate the effort needed to develop that particular program or group of programs. The UDP clarifies early, and in writing, the specific functions that a program is to perform. It is a valuable tool in the detection of errors while the program is still in the design stage. It also provides a means of scheduling checkpoints with the program user, thus promoting user involvement with project development.

The UDP is initiated by a very general, brief, written assignment statement from the project leader to a team member. The assignment statement includes a definition of the task, recommendations for interfacing with other tasks, and a target completion date. It also includes procedural recommendations such as edits, timing, and important tests (see Figure 12–11).

When the team member receives the assignment statement, he or she sets up a schedule of subtargets and prepares the unit development plan. Three standard items must be included in the UDP:

● Data definition list and flow plan: The definition list is an itemizing of all input and output. The flow plan specifies the flows needed, the approach to be used on them (structured, top-down, etc.), and an estimate of the time needed to complete the flows.

● Coding and clean compile estimates: These are estimates of the time needed to code the program, keypunch the code, and clean-compile the program (eliminate all compiler-detected errors).

● Test and documentation plans: The test plan defines the edit needs and the test conditions that will be used to validate the program. It may also include an estimate of the number of compilations and test runs anticipated. The documentation plan includes a list of the documentation and training considerations.

Throughout development of the UDP, the team meets once a week to discuss the project progress. After the UDP has been completed by the team member, it is reviewed by the project leader and a user representative. At this time, the team member and project leader review the target dates that each has estimated. A final target date is assigned. The project leader and user representative can then either approve the UDP or meet with the team member to resolve any differences.

The approved UDPs are then assembled, and the whole project plan is

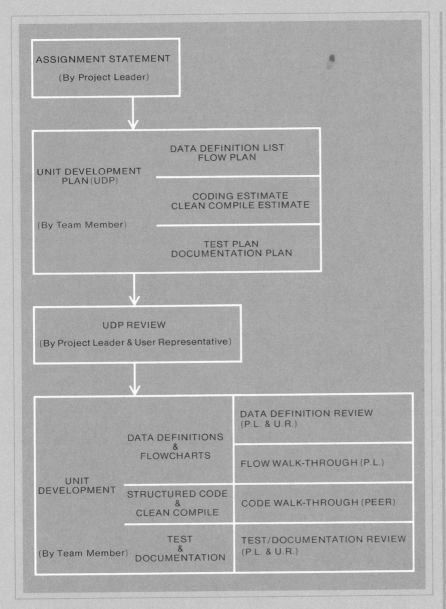

reviewed for approval. Upon approval, the team members begin the unit development effort.

Figure 12–11 illustrates the relationship of the UDP to the actual unit development. The development begins with data definitions and flowcharts. Typical flow constructs have been established as standards:

● Every structure has one entrance and one exit.

● Every connector has two arrows going in and one arrow coming out.

● Every structure should have the potential of being compressed into one box.

● Each modular structure must be independent of other modular structures.

305

These initial steps are concluded with a data definition review by the project leader and user representative and a flow walk-through by the project leader.

The next step for the programmer is the actual program coding. Some structured-programming conventions that have been established for PL/1 programming follow:

● Every procedure must be a proper program, with one entry and one exit.

● No GO TO or RETURN statements are allowed.

● There must be only one statement per line and only one data characteristic (attribute) per line.

The code is then keypunched, compiled, and reviewed with another team member.

Finally, the program is validated with data which tests the conditions and edit needs of the program, and then documented. Both the test and the documentation are reviewed by the project leader and user representative.

Armco is committed to the structured approach because of the many benefits derived from it. The major benefit is found in the area of planning and organization of projects. The modular approach and the weekly team reviews have led to a tremendous reduction in errors. For example, one of the projects included 50 programs and, after implementation, was found to have only two errors. Furthermore, the logic flow discussions between team members aid greatly in any follow-up and documentation.

DISCUSSION POINTS

1. What specific benefits has Armco found in the structured approach? What are some other advantages to this approach?

2. In what stages of the programming process does Armco use the structured approach? Do you think this is typical of many businesses or unique to Armco?

ADVANCED SOFTWARE TOPICS | 13

OUTLINE

I. Multiprogramming
  A. Increasing CPU Active Time
    1. MFT (Multiprogramming with a Fixed Number of Tasks)
    2. MVT (Multiprogramming with a Variable Number of Tasks)
  B. Problems
    1. Memory Management
    2. Scheduling
II. Virtual Storage
  A. Limitations of Multiprogramming
  B. Virtual Storage vs. Real Storage
  C. Segmentation
  D. Paging
III. Multiprocessing
  A. Multiprocessing Configurations
    1. Small Front-End Processor and Large Main-Frame
    2. Multiple Large CPUs
IV. Software Packages
  A. System Packages
  B. Applications Packages
  C. Choosing Packages

INTRODUCTION

An electronic data-processing system that provides timely and relevant information is essential to the successful operation of a large, complex organization. Present computer systems can execute instructions in nanoseconds, provide large storage capacities, and transfer data at extremely high speeds. Tremendous improvements have also been made in peripheral equipment such as card readers, printers, CRTs, and other I/O and communication devices. This hardware evolution has been accompanied by significant software developments.

This chapter discusses some of the more advanced software developments that have occurred in the past ten years. The concepts of multiprogramming and multiprocessing are introduced. The use of virtual storage to avoid real-storage limitations is discussed in detail. Finally, there is an explanation of different types of software packages and the factors that go into the selection of a package.

PORTABLE UNITS LOWER JET FUEL USE

Computerworld,
October 17, 1977, p. 47

ONTARIO, CALIF. Multimillion-dollar corporate jet and turboprop aircraft are being helped to reduce costly fuel consumption by computerized flight scheduling and planning that utilize portable data terminals

A computer-based flight planning service used by corporate pilots, as well as airlines and the U.S. Navy, is Jetplan from Lockheed Aircraft Service Co. Jetplan provides, via Computer Devices, Inc. (CDI), portable Miniterm units and an IBM time-sharing CPU, the information required by pilots so maximum travel with the lowest fuel consumption is possible.

Corporate pilots have access to worldwide weather reporting, route analyses, and complete performance data for more than 50 jets and turboprop aircraft.

"Corporate jets are considered important business tools, and fuel savings mean real dollars saved, as well as reduction of energy consumption. This is a real, attainable goal sought by most major corporations," according to Lou Reinkens, manager of aviation services for Lockheed.

That's where Jetplan comes in. Instead of two or more hours of calculations, the corporate pilot plugs his portable Miniterm terminal into a wall outlet and inserts a telephone into the built-in acoustic coupler. He dials the computer and types in his aircraft, desired route, and payload. Within seconds, the pilot gets back a complete flight plan.

Although the Jetplan service is available to users via Telex and TWX, more than 100 subscribers use CDI Miniterm 1203s available directly from Lockheed.

"Pilots use Miniterms directly from airports—even using pay phones—or in their hotel rooms. Because they can talk to the CPU and get complete flight plans in only seconds, they can wait until just before boarding time to optimize their fuel loads with the terminals," Reinkens said.

Jetplan is a good example of the many uses of time-sharing. What makes all this possible are the multiprogramming capabilities of the CPU. These and other advanced software techniques are discussed in this chapter.

MULTIPROGRAMMING

One major advantage of computer processing over manual data processing is the speed that is possible, given the internal (i.e., CPU) processing capabilities of a computer system. Even though the CPU is designed to handle a large volume of data-processing activities, it frequently remains idle because I/O devices do not have the same capabilities.

When the CPU is very active, the system as a whole is more efficient. Although the CPU is fast, it can operate on only one instruction at a time. Furthermore, the CPU cannot operate on data until the data is in primary storage. This means that the CPU often must wait until I/O operations have been completed. Since I/O operations are much slower than CPU processing, a significant amount of time may be wasted while the CPU is in a wait state (see Figure 13–1). (Recall our discussions of input/output-bound situations in Chapters 6 and 11.)

Multiprogramming is a technique that helps increase CPU active time. It allows for effective allocation of computer resources and also aids in offsetting slow I/O speeds. Under multiprogramming, several programs are resident in the primary storage unit at the same time. Although the CPU can execute only one instruction at a time, it can execute instructions from one program, then another, then another, and back to the first again. Instructions from one program are executed until an interrupt for either input or output is generated. The I/O operation is handled by a channel, thus freeing the CPU to rotate processing. That is, the CPU shifts its attention to another program in memory until that program requires input or output. This rotation occurs so quickly that the execution of the programs in storage appears to be simultaneous. Instead of using the term *simultaneous*, we say, more precisely, that the CPU executes the different programs in a *concurrent* fashion, which means "over the same period of time."

The programs that are in main storage during multiprogramming must be képt separate. This is accomplished through the use of *partitions*. Each partition is an area reserved in memory for one program. There are two approaches to multiprogramming. One approach is known as *m*ultiprogramming with a *f*ixed number of *t*asks (MFT). Each task is simply a unit of work such as one program or one module of a program. Under MFT, the number of partitions is fixed; hence, only a fixed number of programs can be in memory at any one time (see Figure 13–2). However, all partitions need not be the same size. For example, several partitions may be large enough to hold 110K

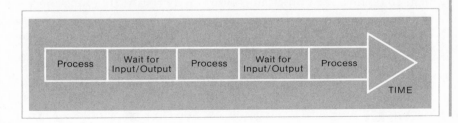

FIGURE 13–1
Processing in
Input/Output-Bound
Situation

309

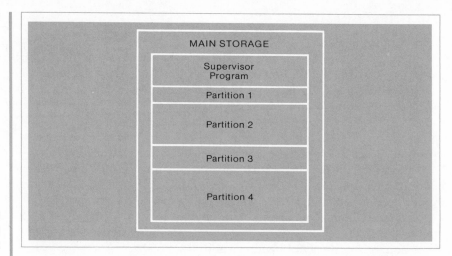

FIGURE 13–2
Multiprogramming
Partitions

characters (remember, $K = 1024$). Others may be large enough to hold 190K, 256K, and so on. The computer's operating system can allocate, to a program, the partition that most closely approximates the storage required by that program; but a program can never exceed the size of the partition allocated to it.

Under *multiprogramming with a variable number of tasks* (MVT), the size of a partition is not fixed; it may change, depending on the storage requirements of the programs to be executed. The control program in an MVT environment can vary not only the sizes of partitions but also the number of them and their locations in memory. Thus, several small programs or a few large programs may be in main storage at the same time. The term *region*, rather than *partition*, is often applied when talking about MVT systems, since each area in memory is not a constant, fixed size as is the case with MFT.

Although multiprogramming increases the system's flexibility and efficiency, it also creates some problems. First, there must be a way of keeping the programs separate. This is known as *memory management*, or *memory protection*. For example, one program must be prevented from reading data into storage locations reserved for another program. The same situation exists with I/O devices—two programs cannot access the same tape or disk drive. These problems are handled by operating-system control programs.

A second problem that arises with multiprogramming is the need to schedule programs, thereby determining which one will receive service first. To do this, each program is assigned a priority. In a time-sharing system the programs being used for online processing must be capable of responding immediately to users at remote locations. Thus, these programs are assigned the highest priority. The highest-priority programs are loaded into *foreground partitions* and are called *foreground programs*. Similarly, programs of lowest priority are loaded into *background partitions* and are called *background programs* (see Figure 13–3). Background programs are typically executed in a batch mode. When a

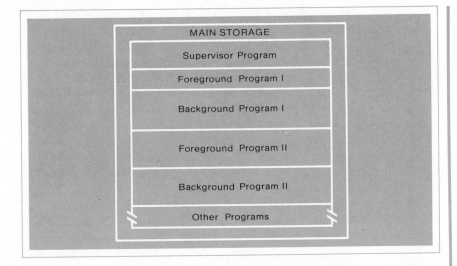

MAIN STORAGE

Supervisor Program

Foreground Program I

Background Program I

Foreground Program II

Background Program II

Other Programs

FIGURE 13–3
Foreground and
Background
Programs in a
Multiprogramming
Environment

foreground program is interrupted for input or output, control is transferred to another foreground program of equal or lower priority or to a background program.

For large systems with several foreground and background programs, scheduling is not a simple task. In rare cases, two programs of the same priority may request CPU resources at the same time. The method of deciding which program gets control first may be arbitrary. For example, the program that has been in main storage the longer may receive control first. Fortunately, the operating system is capable of handling such problems as they occur.

VIRTUAL STORAGE

Multiprogramming increases system efficiency because the CPU can concurrently execute programs instead of waiting while I/O operations occur. A limitation of multiprogramming, however, is that each partition must be large enough to hold an entire program; the program remains in memory until its execution is completed.

Another limitation of this approach is that all the instructions of a program are kept in primary storage throughout its execution, whether they are needed or not. Yet, a large program may contain many sequences of instructions that are executed infrequently. For example, the program may consist of several modules, but most of the processing may be done by only one or two modules. While this processing occurs, the other modules (representing the bulk of the program) are not needed. Hence, the space they occupy is not used efficiently. As processing requirements increase, the physical limitations of memory become a critical constraint, and the productive use of memory becomes increasingly important.

For many years, the limited amount of main storage has been a barrier

311

to applications. Programmers have spent much time trying to find ways to trim the sizes of programs so that they can be fit into available main storage. In some cases, attempts have been made to segment programs (break them into separate modules) so that they can be executed in separate job steps. Doing this manually is both tedious and time-consuming. While hardware costs have decreased and storage capacities have increased, this storage problem still exists in high-volume processing systems where large programs are required.

To alleviate these problems, an extension of multiprogramming called *virtual storage* has been developed. The basic concept is that only a portion of a program (that portion which is needed immediately) has to be in primary storage at any given time; the rest of the program and data can be kept in much larger auxiliary storage. Since only part of a program is in primary storage at one time, the size limitation of the memory is minimized. This gives the illusion that primary storage is unlimited. Also, virtual storage makes it possible for more programs to be executed within a given time period since portions of several programs can be resident in primary storage simultaneously.

To implement virtual storage (or *virtual memory* as it is sometimes called), a direct-access storage device such as a magnetic-disk unit is used to augment primary storage. The term *real storage* is usually given to primary storage within the CPU, while *virtual storage* refers to the direct-access storage (see Figure 13–4). Both real and virtual storage locations are given addresses by the operating system. If data or instructions needed are not in the real (main) storage area, the portion of the program containing them is transferred from virtual storage into real storage. Another portion currently in real storage may be written back to virtual storage. This process is known as *swapping*. If the portion of the program in real storage has not been modified during execution, the portion from virtual storage may be simply laid over it because copies of all parts of the program are kept in virtual storage.

FIGURE 13–4

Schematic of Virtual Storage

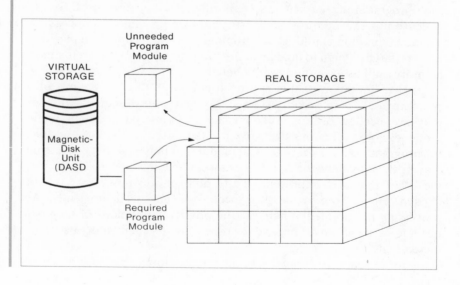

312

There are two main methods of implementing virtual-storage systems, both of which use a combination of hardware and software to accomplish the task. The first method is called *segmentation*. Each program is broken into variable-size blocks called *segments*. The segments are logical parts of the program. For example, one segment may contain data used by the program; another segment may contain a subroutine of the program; and so on. Storage space is allocated by the operating system software, based on the sizes of these logical segments.

When segmentation is used, a two-part address must be kept for each instruction within a segment. One part of the address identifies which segment of the program the instruction belongs to; the second part identifies the relative location of the instruction within that segment. Since the locations of all segments must be readily available at all times, their addresses are kept in real (main) storage in a segment table (see Figure 13–5). These functions are handled by the virtual-storage operating system.

A second method of implementing virtual storage is called *paging*. Primary storage is divided into fixed-size physical areas called *page frames*. All page frames for all programs are the same size, and this size depends on the characteristics of the particular computer. In contrast to segmentation, paging does not consider the logical portions of programs.

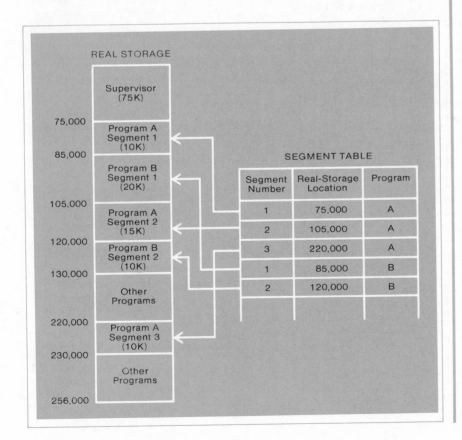

FIGURE 13—5
Segmentation

Instead, the programs are broken into equal-size blocks called *pages*. One page can fit in one page frame of primary storage (see Figure 13–6).

As with segmentation, paging requires that two-part addresses be kept in real storage for each program instruction. The usage of page frames is recorded in a page-frame table which resides in real storage. In addition, a page table is maintained to monitor pages which are currently in real storage, and their locations.

In both paging and segmentation, the operating system handles the swapping of pages or segments whenever a portion of the program that is not in real storage is referenced during processing.

Virtual storage offers tremendous flexibility to programmers and system analysts who are designing new applications. Time can be devoted to solving the problem at hand, rather than to fitting programs into storage. Moreover, the use of main storage is optimized since only needed portions of programs are in main storage at any time.

One of the major limitations of virtual storage is the requirement for extensive online auxiliary storage. Also, the virtual-storage operating system is highly sophisticated and requires significant amounts of storage. If virtual storage is not implemented wisely, much time can be wasted in locating and exchanging program pages or segments.

MULTIPROCESSING

Multiprocessing involves the use of two or more central processing units linked together for coordinated operation. Stored-program instructions are executed simultaneously, but by different CPUs. The CPUs may

FIGURE 13–6

Paging

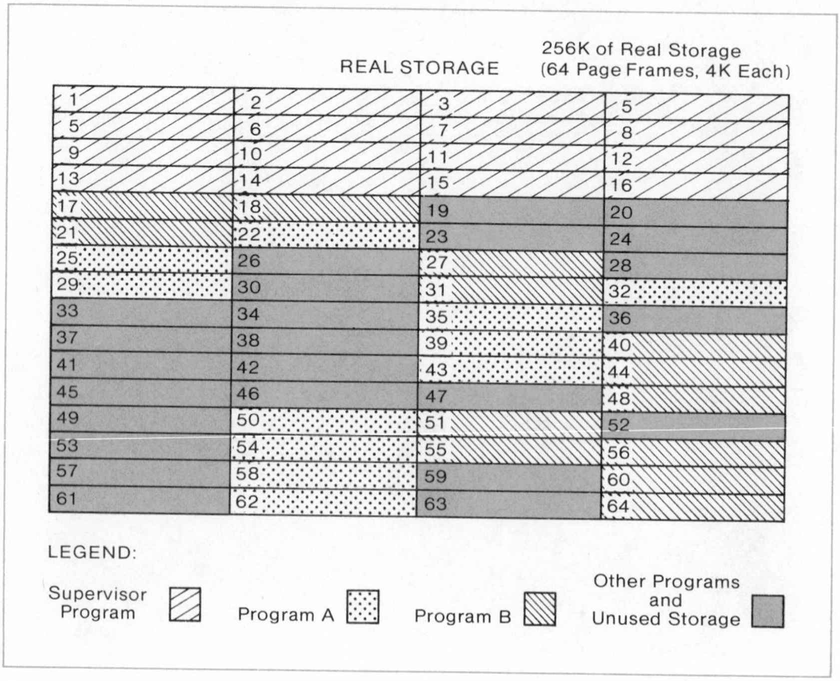

execute different instructions from the same program, or they may execute totally different programs. (In contrast, under multiprogramming, the computer appears to be processing different jobs simultaneously, but this is not really the case. The stored-program instructions are executed concurrently.)

Multiprocessing systems are designed to achieve a particular objective. One common objective is to relieve a large CPU of tasks such as scheduling, editing data, and file maintenance so that it can continue high-priority or complex processing without interruption. To do this, a small CPU (often a minicomputer) is linked to the large CPU. All work coming into the system from remote terminals or other peripheral devices is first channeled through the small CPU. It coordinates the activities of the large one. Generally, the small CPU handles all I/O interrupts and so on, while the large CPU handles the "number crunching" (large mathematical calculations). A schematic of this type of multiprocessing system is shown in Figure 13–7.

The small CPU in Figure 13–7 is commonly referred to as a *front-end processor*. It is an interface between the large CPU and peripheral devices such as online terminals.

A small CPU may also be used as an interface between a large CPU and a large data base stored on direct-access storage devices. In this case, the small CPU is solely responsible for maintaining the data base. It is often termed a *back-end processor*. Accessing data and updating specific data fields are typical functions that a small CPU performs in this type of multiprocessing system.

Many large multiprocessing systems have two or more large CPUs. These large CPUs are no different from those used in single-CPU (stand-alone) configurations. Each CPU may have its own separate memory, or a single memory may be shared by all of them. The activities

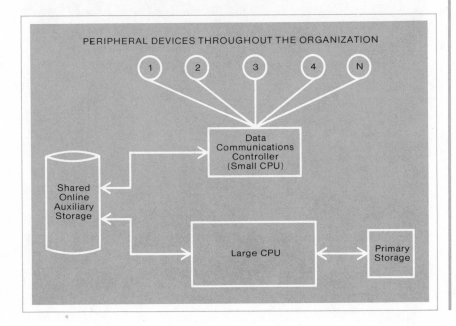

FIGURE 13–7

Multiprocessing System with Small Front-End Processor and Large Main-Frame of each CPU can be controlled in whole or in part by a common supervisor program. This type of system is used by organizations with extremely large and complex data-processing needs. Each large CPU may be dedicated to a specific task such as I/O processing or arithmetic processing. One CPU can be set up to handle online processing while another handles only batch processing. Alternately, two CPUs may be used together on the same task to provide rapid responses in the most demanding data-processing applications. Many multiprocessing systems are designed so that one or more of the CPUs can provide backup if another one of the CPUs malfunctions. A multiple-large-CPU configuration is depicted in Figure 13–8. This system also uses a small CPU to control communications with peripheral devices and perform "house-keeping" chores (input editing, validation, and the like).

Coordinating the efforts of several CPUs requires highly sophisticated software and careful planning. The scheduling of workloads for the CPUs involves making the most efficient use of computer resources. The implementation of such a system is a time-consuming endeavor. It may require the services of outside consultants as well as those provided by the equipment manufacturers. The payoff from this effort is a system with capabilities extending far beyond those of a single-CPU system.

FIGURE 13–8
Multiple-Large-CPU
Multiprocessing System
Configuration

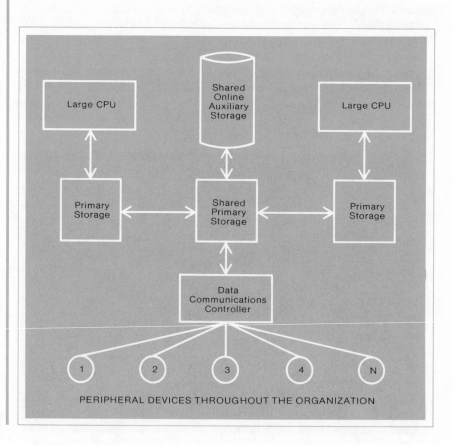

316

SOFTWARE PACKAGES

Many organizations employ programmers to develop programs for their internal operations. This approach, called *in-house development*, allows for programming creativity while satisfying customer/user requirements. However, it requires significant expenditures for staff. In addition, many organizations may write programs to accomplish the same basic objectives, thus duplicating effort.

Because of these disadvantages, interest groups have been created for the purpose of sharing software among organizations operating in similar environments. Firms specializing in software development have been formed to meet the growing demand for prewritten programs. Software and consulting activities are requiring an ever-increasing share of data-processing expenditures, thereby reducing the proportion spent on hardware. Most computer manufacturers supply some or all of these services (often, at a separate cost), but there is a large and growing market for externally supplied computer services.

A *software package* is a set of standardized computer programs, procedures, and related documentation designed to solve problems of a specific application. Proprietary software packages are developed and owned by an organization, but sold or leased to many users. There are packages available to handle almost any computer function. Their costs range from less than $50 to more than $100,000. When a package that fits a user's requirements exists (or can be adapted easily), its cost is almost certainly less than that of in-house development. Furthermore, such packages are usually debugged and documented, and ongoing maintenance and support are usually guaranteed.

System Packages

System packages are sets of programs that make it possible to operate computers more conveniently and efficiently. Traditionally, system packages were *bundled;* that is, they were provided to the customer/user by the equipment manufacturer at no additional cost. When many major computer manufacturers moved to unbundle system software, interest in the commercial aspect of program development began to accelerate. Programs similar to those which had been supplied "free" by the manufacturers were made available, but at significant additional costs. Users of computer equipment were given an incentive to shop around to find suitable software at costs to their liking.

System packages exist in many forms. Examples include operating systems, data-base management systems, report generators, job-accounting systems, compilers, input/output control routines, and diagnostic routines. Since these packages are normally machine-dependent, they are most often supplied by the equipment manufacturers; however, an increasing number are being made available by independent software suppliers. System packages comprise about 25 percent of all currently available software packages, but they account for more than 50 percent of total revenues.

317

Applications Packages

Applications packages are sets of programs for performing specific, well defined, data-processing or computational tasks. Applications packages have long been available for engineering and scientific applications. The Statistical Package for the Social Sciences (SPSS) and the Generalized Package for System Simulation (GPSS) are examples. These packages include routines for performing matrix inversion, regression analysis, probability functions, and so on. Many statistical packages are designed to be used easily, even by inexperienced users, but they are normally available only for large systems.

Packages for business applications are available for almost any kind of computer. They are available for payroll, accounts receivable, accounts payable, general ledger, inventory control, production scheduling, and many other common business data-processing functions. Such packages are written in a general way, and then tailored to the requirements of individual firms. About 75 percent of all packages are applications packages. Although they are available from equipment manufacturers, the fastest-growing market is for those supplied by independent software firms.

Choosing Packages

A major decision made by computer users is whether to buy a prewritten software package or to develop the software in-house. In-house development often suffers from serious delays, underestimated resource and time requirements, poor documentation, and high development costs. In contrast, purchased packages are normally available at a fixed cost (known in advance). They can be installed and made to operate within a relatively short time period. In addition, good documentation can be made a prerequisite for purchased software. Thus, there are many factors favoring the purchase of prewritten packages.

Unfortunately, implementing prewritten packages is seldom a simple endeavor. Due to their generalized nature, prewritten packages may be difficult to tailor to meet a firm's unique requirements. The costs of modification, installation, conversion, and testing software packages can be significant. Also, the costs for training and maintenance must not be overlooked. The overriding concern is, of course, whether the package can meet the requirements of the user. The more modification needed, the greater implementation costs become.

Many proprietary packages have been extremely successful, and have many satisfied users. Others have been dismal failures. For this reason, firms considering buying or leasing a proprietary package often elect to contact current users of the package. This practice has much merit. Inferior packages will be recognized as such, and will soon fade from the market.

The use of proprietary software packages is expected to increase over the next several years as more firms discover the potential benefits. As more systems are implemented using proprietary software, in-house developers will concentrate more on unique projects that offer new challenges.

SUMMARY

● The CPU may be idle for a significant amount of time because of the speed disparity between the CPU and I/O devices. Multiprogramming is used to increase the efficiency of CPU utilization.

● With multiprogramming, several programs are resident in the primary storage unit at the same time. Instructions from one program are executed until an interrupt for either input or output is generated. Then the CPU shifts attention to another program in memory until that program requires input or output.

● The programs in main storage are kept separate using partitions. In multiprogramming with a fixed number of tasks (MFT), the number of partitions is fixed; in multiprogramming with a variable number of tasks (MVT), the size and number of partitions can be varied according to needs.

● Multiprogramming requires memory protection and a method of assigning priorities to programs. High-priority programs are loaded into foreground partitions, and low-priority programs are loaded into background partitions.

● A complete program may not fit into a partition. Also, certain segments of a program may be executed infrequently. The problems arising from these constraints are alleviated by use of virtual storage.

● Virtual storage involves loading only the part of a program needed, in primary storage. The remainder of the program is kept in secondary storage. This gives the illusion that primary storage is unlimited.

● Segmentation is a method of implementing virtual storage whereby each program is broken into variable-size segments. Each segment is a logical subunit of the complete program. Paging uses equal-size blocks called pages, without considering logical parts of the program.

● Multiprocessing involves the use of two or more CPUs linked together for coordinated operation. Separate programs can be processed simultaneously by different CPUs.

● Small computers can be linked to main frames as either front-end processors or back-end processors. The former interfaces between the CPU and I/O devices; the latter acts as an interface between the large CPU and a data base stored on a DASD.

● Large CPUs are linked together to handle extremely large and complex data-processing needs. Each CPU may be assigned to a specific task, or it may be used with other CPUs on the same task to provide rapid response.

● A software package is a set of standardized computer programs, procedures, and related documentation for a particular application. Software packages are becoming popular because of their relatively low cost and the fact that they are usually tested, debugged, and documented.

● System packages are designed to increase the efficiency and convenience of computer operations. Historically bundled with equipment, they now must be purchased separately.

● Applications packages are used to solve specific problems. They are available for a variety of scientific and business applications.

● Implementing packages can be difficult because they must be modified to meet the user's specific needs. Costs of installation, conversion, and testing can be high. Current users of a package should be contacted to get a report on its performance before buying or leasing it.

REVIEW QUESTIONS

1. Distinguish between multiprogramming and multiprocessing. What are some of the problems that must be solved in a multiprogramming environment?

2. What advantages does MVT offer over MFT? Does a payroll processing program belong in a foreground partition or a background partition? Explain.

3. Why were virtual-storage systems developed? Compare and contrast the two techniques used to implement virtual-storage capabilities—segmentation and paging.

4. A corporation is implementing a large, data base management system that can respond to inquiries from online terminals. What kind of a multiprocessing configuration would be suitable for this application?

5. Why are software packages becoming more popular? What are some of the disadvantages of buying a package instead of developing the program or set of programs in-house?

In 1883, 25-year-old Bernard H. (Barney) Kroger and his friend B. A. Branagan opened a small store in Cincinnati, Ohio, with $722 in capital. It was named "The Great Western Tea Company" and sold coffees, teas, sausages, staples, and chinaware. At the end of the first year, with assets amounting to $2620, Kroger bought out the store and ran it by himself.

Today, 94 years after Barney Kroger opened his first store, the Kroger Company is the sixth largest retailing company in the United States as ranked by total sales. Kroger Food Stores is the country's third largest supermarket chain; it has 1188 stores in 21 states. The superstore is Kroger's basic store today. With sizes ranging from 25,000 to 45,000 square feet, these stores offer specialty and personal-service departments such as delicatessens, bakeries, wine shops, and greeting-card departments.

Kroger also manufactures and processes food for sale by these supermarkets, a tradition which began before the turn of the century. The company operates eight regional bakeries and five dairies in addition to a sausage plant, a cheese plant, egg production facilities, egg grading and packing plants, a peanut butter plant, a candy plant, and a general processing plant.

The Kroger Company headquarters are at Cincinnati, Ohio. The data-processing facilities, which centrally serve and support the corporate activities, are also there. The present operation is

application

THE KROGER COMPANY

concentrated in two main-frame computers at headquarters. Most of the transaction activity is transmitted to them by private leased lines connecting 15 other marketing-area locations. Thirteen of these marketing-area locations consist of an area headquarters, an area warehouse, and 50 to 100 supermarkets. Each marketing-area location also has a data-processing staff. This configuration is illustrated in Figure 13—9.

The MIS Department at the Cincinnati headquarters services most departments in the company to some degree. These include merchandising and buying, warehousing, transportation, store operations, finance and accounting, manufacturing, personnel, and market research. Current applications in these departments include order-entry and billing, inventory control, payroll, accounts payable, and accounting.

The department presently has a staff of about 125 employees. Ninety of these employees are involved in system analysis and programming. The remaining

35 are concerned with operations, communications, and data entry.

Additionally, five Kroger supermarkets (one in Indianapolis, three in Cincinnati, and one in Columbus) have complete electronic-scanning operations. These stores communicate directly with their area headquarters, which in turn communicate with corporate headquarters. Plans have been made to install complete scanning operations in 15 to 20 additional stores.

The biggest processing demand on the system is the order-entry inventory-control system. In fact, this application was Kroger's primary justification for automation. Ordering inventory is the highest-priority process in the retail grocery business. The business depends on correct and timely ordering. In support of 1200 stores, the Cincinnati headquarters may process as many as 50,000 orders per week.

So that orders can be processed at any time of the day (to afford maximum benefits to each store), the head-

FIGURE 13—9
Kroger Company
Headquarters

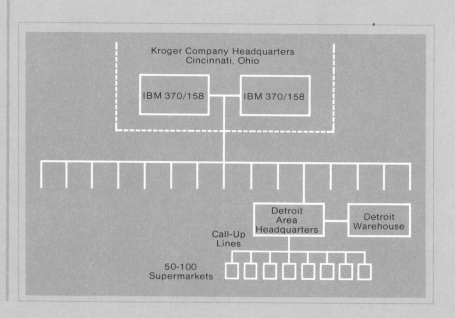

quarters data-processing department operates full-time, 24 hours a day, 7 days a week. Because of the need to process orders at any time, some part of the computer must be dedicated to order-entry at all times. The response time, capacity, and volume requirements of the order-entry and inventory-control processes led to the need for multiprogramming and multiprocessing capabilities.

The multiprocessing system consists of two IBM System/370 Model 158 CPUs that communicate with each other and execute programs simultaneously. With the multiprocessing capability, both CPUs are used together on the order-entry processing to provide the stores with rapid service. If one CPU is busy when an order is input for processing, the other CPU takes over. The system can process 80 percent of the order-entry input within 15 minutes of the time the input is entered. Furthermore, the multiprocessing environment allows uninterrupted order processing if one of the CPUs breaks down.

The system is also capable of multiprogramming—the concurrent processing of two or more programs. If the order-entry and inventory-control processes were the only applications that needed to be executed, there would probably be no need for multiprogramming. However, numerous other programs must be run; without multiprogramming capabilities, applications would be backlogged.

The operating system that controls Kroger's System/370 computers is OS/MVS (Operating System/Multiple Virtual Storage). The control program of OS/MVS incorporates multiprogramming. It initiates, or routes, each task to a main-storage partition. In the Kroger control program, there are 16 task ini-

tiators. For example, there is an initiator for batch-processing jobs that routes those particular tasks to a designated partition, and three initiators for test jobs, or program development, which route those tasks to other partitions.

A snapshot of the system at any moment may show the following tasks being performed concurrently:

- Eight to ten programmers may be working on the development of programs or program modifications.

- The sausage plant may be working on the optimization of product blends and yields.

- The centralized cash control department may be processing accounts payable.

- The personnel department may be generating exception reports, searching personnel files for promotion candidates, or reviewing salaries.

- The inventory control department may be processing store orders.

- The time-sharing option (TSO) system software has 100 potential users, of which 12 to 21 users may be logged onto the system at any one time. These users include Kroger Management Information System personnel as well as outside users from Kroger bakeries, dairies, and chicken hatcheries.

These multiprogramming/multiprocessing capabilities reduce the time a user must wait for available CPU time and alleviate the physical limitations of I/O operations. In multiprogramming, everything is shared. For example, if a user indicates a need for tape space, any available tape space is used.

If Kroger's operations were not processed in a multiprogramming environment, they would be burdened with the

323

need for redundant computer power as well as for redundant I/O equipment. To accomplish the work they do now without multiprogramming capabilities, the hardware requirements would be astronomical.

DISCUSSION POINTS

1. Discuss the reasons for Kroger's move to a multiprocessing, multiprogramming environment. What advantages have these capabilities provided?

2. How are Kroger's CPUs used in order-entry processing?

section **IV**

SYSTEMS

14
SYSTEM ANALYSIS AND DESIGN

15
PROCESS DESIGN

16
MANAGEMENT INFORMATION
SYSTEMS

SYSTEM ANALYSIS AND DESIGN | 14

OUTLINE

I. System Analysis
   A. Data Gathering
      1. Interviews
      2. System Charts
      3. Questionnaires
   B. Data Analysis
      1. Grid Charts
      2. System Flowcharts
      3. Decision Logic Tables
II. System Design
   A. Review of Goals and Objectives
   B. Development of System Model
   C. Evaluation of Organizational Constraints
   D. Defining I/O Requirements
   E. Developing Alternative Designs
   F. Cost/Benefit Analysis of Alternatives
   G. System Recommendation
III. System Implementation
   A. Personnel Training
   B. Testing the System
   C. System Conversion
      1. Parallel Conversion
      2. Pilot Conversion
      3. Phased Conversion
      4. Crash Conversion
   D. System Auditing
   E. System Maintenance and Follow-up

INTRODUCTION

In computer-based information systems, the hardware and software technologies discussed earlier are applied as tools to the collection, storage, and retrieval of information helpful to management (e.g., sales analysis, investment analysis) or otherwise required for routine business procedures (e.g., payroll, income tax). A knowledge of these technologies is necessary to effectively use them in management information systems.

This chapter focuses on the development of computer-based information systems. The development process involves making a *system study* to identify and develop needed informational improvements within an organization. There are three distinct phases in any system study: (1) system analysis, (2) system design, and (3) system implementation. *System analysis* is an evaluation of the current procedures and operations of an organization to enhance understanding and determine critical problem areas. The *system-design* phase is a logical extension of the analysis to determine alternative solutions to solve the problems uncovered earlier and, eventually, to ascertain the best solution. The last step of the system study is *system implementation,* which includes follow-up to insure error-free operation and user acceptance of the system.

Jeffrey Beeler
CW Staff

Computerworld,
October 10, 1977, p. 16

DALLAS — Braniff International and the U.S. Postal Service have applied at least some of the elements of an electronic mail network to an experimental ticket-processing system that has been undergoing tests here since Aug. 12.

The ticket-by-mail system, which Braniff officials claim is the first of its kind in the airlines business, is built around the company's existing flight reservations computer, an IBM 2314 disk drive unit, and a teleprinter at the Dallas Post Office.

When a customer reserves a flight at Braniff's Love Field office and asks to receive his ticket by mail, a clerk enters the necessary reservations data through an online terminal into the airline's 1M-byte IBM System/360 Model 65 main-frame, which sends the information to the post office.

There, a Di/An Controls, Inc., 8100 teleprinter generates the customer's ticket, which a postal employee stuffs into an open-windowed envelope for delivery in the next day's mail.

The main advantage of such a system is speedier ticket delivery, according to Lou Garcia, a Braniff vice president. Within five minutes of the time a customer makes a reservation at the Braniff office here, the system can process a ticket and have it ready for mailing.

The usual lead time for customers who request their tickets by mail is several days, primarily because manual ticket delivery is a complicated procedure involving many clerical steps and several reservations officials, Garcia explained.

Although he said the system has performed "very nicely" during its first two weeks of tests, Garcia declined to speculate on the viability of the ticket-by-mail concept. Braniff officials supervising the tests will delay their evaluations and recommendations until all the results become available in mid-November, Garcia explained.

Even if the system does go into regular service, however, it will print tickets for only about 70 customers a day, "a relatively small percentage" of Braniff's total daily volume here, Garcia admitted.

Airline reservations information systems are extremely complex. They are also largely responsible for the success of modern passenger air travel. An undertaking such as the addition of this ticket-by-mail system requires careful system analysis, design, and implementation. This chapter describes how these tasks are carried out.

SYSTEM ANALYSIS

Every organization has methods of transferring information from one person to another. Examples are by memo, by a letter in a file cabinet, or on a computer printout. An *information system* is an integrated network of personnel, equipment, and procedures designed to satisfy the information requirements of management. Some information systems are computerized; others are manual.

There are several reasons why management may want to review its present information system. Among these are:

● The present system is not functioning properly.

● A new aspect has been added, such as a new product or procedure. For example, the government has imposed a new regulation.

● A new development in computer technology that the organization can benefit from has occurred. For example, the introduction of point-of-sale terminals can have a great impact on a retail business.

● The organization wants to update the entire information system. This desire may be due to an increase in the size or sales volume of the organization, or a competitive incentive to operate in the most efficient and effective manner.

Even when there are compelling reasons to review the present system, it does not follow automatically that a new system should be developed. This decision should be based on need. Even if an organization has the personnel, technology, and other resources required to develop a new application system, it should not do so unless it needs that system and will benefit from the implementation. The goal of system analysis is to determine whether or not this need exists.

The first step in system analysis is to formulate a statement of system objectives. This is essential to the identification of information requirements. Subsequent to the statement of objectives, the system analyst should have a general understanding of what needs to be done. This should be communicated to management in the form of a proposal. The salient points of the proposal should include:

● A clear and concise statement of the problem, or reason for the system analysis

● A statement delineating the scope of the system analysis, and its objectives

● An identification of the information that must be collected, and the potential sources for this information

● A preliminary schedule for conducting the analysis

The purpose of the proposal is to insure that management is aware of the resources that will be required during the system analysis. It also helps the system user to be sure the system analyst has identified the problem correctly and understands what the system analysis should accomplish.

Once the proposal has been accepted, the analyst can proceed with the analysis. This involves two steps: data gathering and data analysis.

Data Gathering

This step is the collection of raw data, or facts, that are relevant to the system project. The potential sources for this data include the present system, other areas within the organization, and external sources. In rare instances, a completely new system is to be developed. Usually, this is not the case. Therefore, the analyst often begins by analyzing the existing system. The advantage of this approach is that the analyst can evaluate the current operations to determine if minor changes are needed or if a new system is required. This study should also indicate what resources (management, clerical, and equipment) are available, and how they can be used in the changed or new system. However, studying current operations is expensive. It can also lead to the inclusion of unnecessary constraints in a new design.

Other internal data sources include the forms used by the organization, files, organization charts, and employees. In addition to these sources, the analyst may need to go to external sources—other organizations that have developed similar systems, textbooks, trade journals, and even the customers of the organization. All of these sources may provide valuable insights into what the system does and what it is supposed to do.

Some tools and techniques used for data collection are described below.

Interviews Preliminary interviews provide data about current operations and procedures, and the user's perception of what the system should do. Follow-up interviews and discussion sessions provide checkpoints to verify the accuracy and completeness of the procedures and documentation within the system.

System Charts Given the source documents that provide the system input, the processing steps needed are flowcharted using *system charts.* The devices and files used are identified; the resulting output is indicated; and the departments that use the output are pointed out.

Questionnaires These forms are used to collect more details about system operations. By keying questions to specific steps in a system chart, specific facts can be obtained: the volume of input and output, the frequency of processing, the time required for various processing steps, and the personnel and equipment used.

Data Analysis

After data has been collected and documented, the next phase involves organizing and integrating it to put everything into proper perspective. The facts can then be analyzed, and alternate solutions explored. Whereas the focus during data collection is on *what* is being done, the focus during data analysis is on *why* certain operations and procedures are being used. The analyst looks for ways to improve these operations if advisable.

The various techniques and tools used to analyze data are explained below.

Grid Charts   The tabular or grid format of *grid charts* is employed to summarize the relationships that exist between the components of a system. Figure 14–1 is a grid chart indicating which departments use which documents of an order-writing, billing, and inventory-control system.

A special type of grid chart is an I/O chart. It shows the relationships that exist between system inputs and outputs. The input documents are listed in the rows on the left. The output reports are identified in the columns on the right (see Figure 14–2). If a particular source document is used in the preparation of an output report, an X is placed at the intersection of the appropriate row and column. These charts help the analyst to identify subsystems—parts of the system that may be relatively independent of each other.

System Flowcharts   As we saw in Chapter 10, program flowcharts are concerned with operations on data. They do not indicate the form of

FIGURE 14–1
A Grid Chart

Document \ Department	Order Writing	Shipping	Billing	Inventory	Marketing	Accounts Receivable
Sales Order	X				X	
Shipping Order	X	X	X	X		
Invoice			X		X	X
Credit Authorization					X	X
Monthly Report					X	X

| | of | sheets | | | | | **DATA ANALYSIS SHEET** | | | | **AREA:** *TITLE VII* | |

			INPUT				ELEMENTS OF DATA				OUTPUT							

Data Analysis Sheet — INPUT / ELEMENTS OF DATA / OUTPUT

INPUT columns: Form 1, Form 3A, Form 3B, Form 4, Referral

OUTPUT columns: Form 2, Form 5, Form 6, Form 7, Form 8, Form 9

DOC. NAME INPUT/OUTPUT DATA	Form 1	Form 3A	Form 3B	Form 4	Referral		DATA CODE	DESCRIPTION	NR CHAR	A/N	DEC	Form 2	Form 5	Form 6	Form 7	Form 8	Form 9
	X							DATE/INITIAL PARTICIPATION									
	X	X	X	X				NAME				X	X				
	X			X				SOCIAL SECURITY NUMBER									
	X			X	X			ADDRESS				X	X				
	X							DATE OF BIRTH									
	X		X					RACE									
	X		X	X				SEX									
	X				X			PHONE NUMBER									
	X		X					MEANS OF TRANSPORTATION				X					
	X		X					DOCTOR									
	X		X					DOCTOR'S PHONE NUMBER									
	X							EMERGENCY CONTACT									
	X							EMERGENCY PHONE NUMBER									
	X							PHYSICAL HANDICAP									
								WEEKLY CALENDER TRANSPORTATION				X	X				

CLASS OF DATA — CODE

FIXED ELEMENTS
IDENTIFYING — I
QUANTITATIVE — Q

VARIABLE ELEMENTS
REPORTED — R
GENERATED — G
CONSTANTS — C

CODE
GEN FLOW REF
VOL
FREQ

FIGURE 14—2 I/O Chart

input (e.g., terminal keyboard, cards, or tape) or the form of output (e.g., display, document, disk, or tape). For any of these forms, a *general input/output symbol* ( ) is used.

In contrast, *system flowcharts* concentrate on what processing is done rather than how. They emphasize the flow of data through the entire data-processing system, without describing details of internal computer operations. A system flowchart represents the interrelationships among various system elements.

The general input/output symbol used in program flowcharting is not specific enough for system flowcharting. A variety of specialized input/output symbols are needed to identify the wide variety of media used in input/output activities. The symbols are miniature outlines of the actual media (see Figure 14–3).

In a like manner, specialized process symbols are used instead of the *general process symbol* ( ) to represent specific processing operations on a system flowchart. For example, a trapezoid is used to indicate a manual process such as keypunching (see Figure 14–4).

The difference in emphasis in the two forms of flowcharting is due to the different purposes served. A program flowchart aids the programmer in writing a source program. It specifies the details of operations so that the programmer can code the steps precisely. In contrast, a system flowchart is designed to represent the general information flow. System flowcharts often represent many operations within one process symbol.

FIGURE 14–3
System Flowcharting—
Specialized Input/Output
Symbols

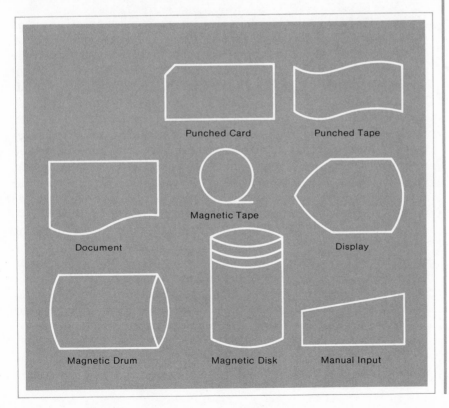

Punched Card Punched Tape

Magnetic Tape

Document Display

Magnetic Drum Magnetic Disk Manual Input

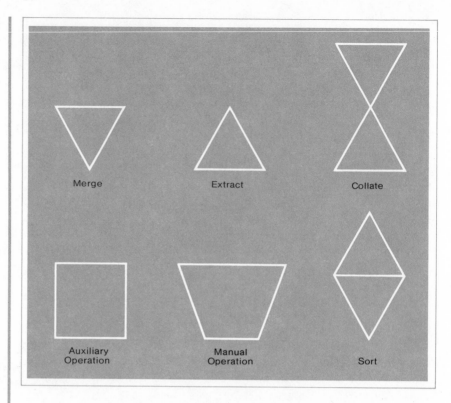

FIGURE 14—4
System Flowcharting—
Specialized Process
Symbols

Figure 14–5 shows the updating of an inventory master file. The *online storage symbol* (⬭) indicates that the file is kept on an online external storage medium such as disk or tape. The file is used to keep track of the raw materials and finished products of the organization. How current this information is depends on how often the master file is updated. If the master file is updated as soon as a product is shipped or a raw material supply depleted, then the information it provides is up-to-date. Usually, however, the updating is done on a periodic basis. All changes that occur during a specific time period are batched and then processed together to update the inventory master file. Reports from the shipping, receiving, and production departments are collected. The data from this set of documents is transferred onto cards. These cards and the inventory master file then serve as input for the updating process.

The flowchart in Figure 14–5 outlines the steps in the updating process. In addition to updating the inventory master file, the system generates three reports. These reports give management information about inventory, order shipments, and production. Notice that in the system flowchart, one process symbol encompasses the entire updating process. A program flowchart must be created to detail the specific operations to be performed within the updating process.

Decision Logic Tables   A *decision logic table* (DLT) is a tabular representation of the actions to be taken under different sets of conditions.

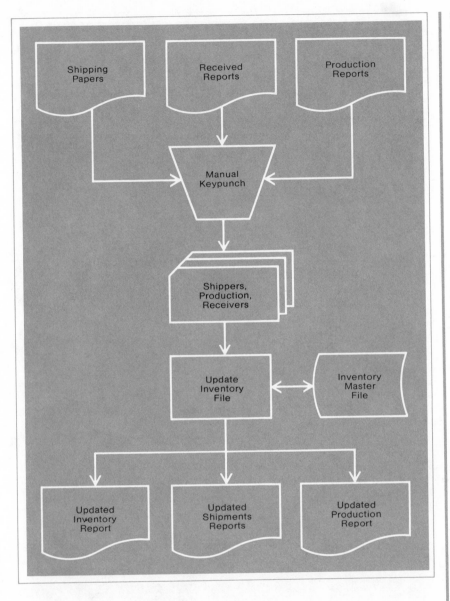

FIGURE 14–5
Sample System Flowchart

Thus, the decision table expresses the logic for arriving at a particular decision under a given set of circumstances. The structure within a decision table is based on the proposition "if this condition is met then do this."

The basic elements of a decision logic table are shown in Figure 14–6. The upper half lists conditions to be met, and the lower half shows actions to be taken. That is, the *condition stub* describes the different conditions; the *action stub* describes the possible actions. *Condition entries* are made in the top right section. *Action entries* are made in the bottom right section.

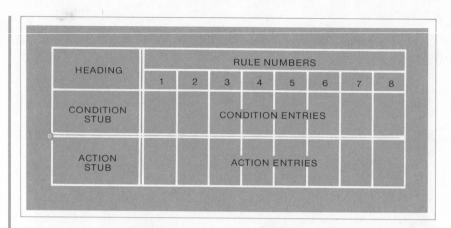

FIGURE 14–6
Decision Logic Table

A decision table is not needed for conditions that can be communicated and understood easily. However, in the case of multiple conditions, a decision table serves as a valuable tool in analyzing the decision logic involved. Figure 14–7 shows a decision table for selecting applicants for an assembly-line job.

The rules for selecting applicants are based on the age, education, and experience of the candidates. The applicants must be at least 18 years of age to be considered for the position. They must have at least a high school education or a year's experience to be interviewed for further evaluation. They are hired directly if they meet both requirements.

In Figure 14–7, the Y's mean yes, the N's mean no, and the X's indicate which actions are to be taken. The decision table is read as follows:

Rule 1: If the applicant's age is less than 18 years, then reject him or her.

FIGURE 14–7
Decision Logic Table
for Selecting Applicants

SELECTING APPLICANTS		RULES				
		1	2	3	4	5
CONDITIONS	AGE < 18 YEARS?	Y	N	N	N	N
	HIGH SCHOOL EDUCATION?		N	N	Y	Y
	EXPERIENCE > 1 YEAR?		N	Y	N	Y
ACTIONS	REJECT	X	X			
	INTERVIEW			X	X	
	HIRE					X

Rule 2: If the applicant is at least 18 years old, but has no high school education and experience less than 1 year, then reject him or her.

Rule 3: If the applicant is at least 18 years old, has no high school education, but has experience of more than 1 year, then call him or her for an interview. Once a candidate has been selected for an interview, another decision table may be needed to evaluate the interview.

Rule 4: If the applicant is at least 18 years old, has a high school education, but has less than 1 year of experience, then call him or her for an interview. Again, another decision table might be used at this point to evaluate the interview.

Rule 5: If the applicant is at least 18 years old, has a high school education, and has work experience of more than 1 year, then hire him or her.

A more detailed decision logic table is shown in Figure 14–8. The first step in constructing such a table is to determine the conditions that need to be considered. In this case the conditions that must be evaluated are: (1) Is the credit rating of the customer AAA?; (2) Is the quantity ordered above or equal to the minimum quantity for a discount?; and (3) Is there enough stock on hand to fill the order? These conditions are listed in the condition-stub section of the decision table.

The next step is to determine the possible actions that may take place. These are: (1) bill at a discount price, or (2) bill at a regular price; and (3) ship the total quantity ordered, or (4) ship a partial order and back-order the rest. These possibilities go in the action stub.

Once the conditions and possible courses of action have been identified, the decision table is completed by relating the conditions to

FIGURE 14–8
DLT for Order Processing

ORDER PROCESSING	Rules							
	1	2	3	4	5	6	7	8
Credit Rating of AAA	Y	Y	Y	Y	N	N	N	N
Quantity Order >= Minimum Discount Quantity	Y	N	N	Y	Y	N	Y	N
Quantity Ordered >= Stock on Hand	N	Y	N	Y	N	Y	Y	N
Bill at Discount Price	X			X				
Bill at Regular Price		X	X		X	X	X	X
Ship Total Quantity Ordered		X		X		X	X	
Ship Partial and Back-Order Remaining Amount	X		X		X			X

corresponding action entries. The decision table can then be used to make the appropriate decision. Thus, Rule 4 of the DLT could be interpreted as follows: "If the customer has a credit rating of AAA and the quantity ordered is equal to or above the minimum discount quantity and there is enough stock on hand, then the customer is to be billed at the discount price and the total order is to be shipped."

Because decision tables present logic in a summarized form and are easy to understand, they are used to record facts collected during the investigation of the old system. They can also be used to summarize aspects of the new system. In the latter case, they guide programmers in writing programs for the new system.

After the data has been collected and analyzed, the next task of the system analyst is to communicate the findings to management. The *system analysis report* should include the following items:

- A restatement of the scope and objectives of the system analysis
- An explanation of the present system, the procedures used, and any problems identified
- A statement of all constraints on the present system and any assumptions made by the analyst during this phase
- A preliminary report of alternatives that seem feasible at this point in time
- An estimate of the resources and capital required to either modify the present system or design a new system. This estimate should include costs for a feasibility study to determine whether or not to continue the system study.

Only if management approves this report can the system analyst proceed to detailed system design.

SYSTEM DESIGN

System design is concerned with the formulation of specifications for the proposed new system, to achieve the objectives identified during the system-analysis phase. The specifications include the I/O requirements, files, procedural details, and hardware needs of the proposed system.

The emphasis during system analysis is on what is being done and why; in system design the emphasis shifts to how things should be done to meet the newly verified system requirements. Translating the information requirements identified during system analysis into a feasible and detailed design plan requires originality and creativity. The analyst develops alternate designs, determines the cost effectiveness of the alternatives, and then makes recommendations.

A problem encountered by the analyst when considering design alternatives is that of conflicting objectives within the organization. For example, the shipping department may want additional trucks to improve delivery service, but the finance department may be unwilling to make the additional capital investment. The overall goals of the organization must be the determining factor when resolving these functional area problems.

The design process is the second phase in the system life cycle (see Figure 14-9). It consists of the following steps:

1. Reviewing the verified system goals and objectives

2. Developing a conceptual model of the system

3. Evaluating the organizational constraints

4. Defining output and input requirements

5. Developing alternative design proposals to meet the requirements

6. Preparing a *cost/benefit analysis* for each alternative

7. Recommending the most appropriate alternative, and offering a plan for implementation of that alternative

Each of these steps is discussed in more detail below.

Review of Goals and Objectives

The objectives of the new or revised system are identified during system analysis, and stated in the system analysis report. Before the analyst can proceed with system design, these objectives must be reviewed. The system goals and objectives identified at this point are not identical to

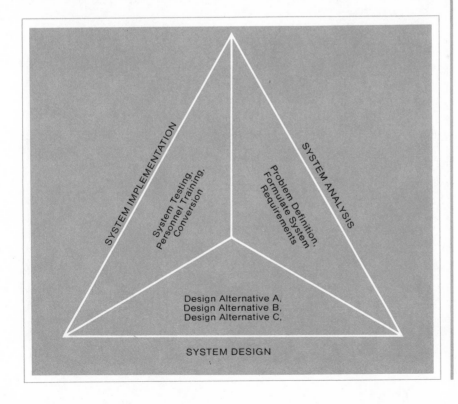

FIGURE 14—9
System Life Cycle

user information requirements. Rather, they are defined so that all user needs can be met within them. For example, the finance department may want a report of customers who have been delinquent in payments. This requirement can be met within the goals of the accounts-receivable system, stated as: (1) to maintain an accurate and timely record of the amounts owed by customers; (2) to provide control procedures that insure that any abnormal developments are detected and reported on an exception basis; and (3) to provide relevant information regarding accounts receivable, on a timely basis, to different levels of management to help achieve overall company goals.

Development of System Model

In this second step of the design phase, the analyst attempts to represent symbolically what is visualized as the system's major components. This enables the analyst to verify his or her understanding of the system and of its purported goals. Figure 14–10 is a conceptual model (system flowchart, in this case) of an accounts-receivable (A/R) system.

Evaluation of Organizational Constraints

No organization has unlimited resources. Consequently, the system analyst has to recognize the constraints imposed by the limited availability of resources. One of the important tasks of the analyst is to use the resources available in an optimum manner to achieve the system objectives. Typically, the constraints involve a limited budget, specific

FIGURE 14–10
Model of an
Accounts-Receivable
System

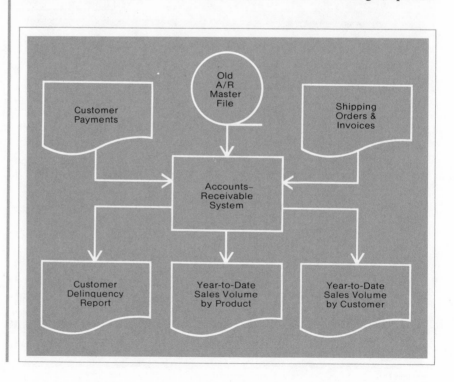

time requirements within which the system must be operative, and staff and hardware availability.

The analyst can usually design an ideal system to meet all requirements. However, the cost of such a system may be prohibitive. This is one of the reasons why an analyst should provide alternative designs with different costs and capabilities. Management can then decide which alternative best suits the organization's needs and budget.

It is important that the system be designed and implemented within a realistic time span. Furthermore, the analyst has to work under the assumption that the new or revised system should not require additional resources in the form of staff and hardware, unless a major system overhaul is being done. Thus, before proceeding to the detailed system design, the analyst must critically assess and evaluate the constraints imposed by organizational requirements, and how they will impact the system development.

Defining I/O Requirements

To be able to decide the kinds of inputs that are going to be needed, the analyst must look at the desired outputs. By working backward, the inputs required to generate the outputs can be determined.

During this step, the analyst should get the user involved. The questions to be answered include: (1) What information needs to be generated? and (2) What are the desired formats for the reports that will provide this information? The user should comment on whether the right kinds of information are being produced and whether the report formats are appropriate.

It is important that the analyst assign priorities to the different outputs from the system. Obviously, the outputs that are most important to the achievement of the system objectives should be given highest priority.

Developing Alternative Designs

Once the outputs and inputs have been correctly identified, the next step is to decide how the input data should be manipulated to convert it into useful and meaningful information. Since data can be processed in a variety of ways to achieve the same results, the analyst is concerned here with developing alternative designs to meet the system requirements.

The system analyst must also examine the hardware needed to support the proposed designs. If the existing equipment will not adequately serve the needs of the new system, additional hardware must be selected.

Important factors to be considered in each alternative design include: the structure and form of reports, the program specifications needed to guide programmers in code preparation, the data bases or files required, the clerical procedures that will be used, and the process-control measures that will be instituted. Providing adequate system controls is essential in any system proposal. Input data must be verified for accuracy; various checks are required to prevent errors during processing; and, finally, output controls are needed to insure the correctness of the information produced.

The processing requirements will differ for different alternatives. For example, one alternative may involve batch processing and sequential file organization; another may provide for random-access processing using direct-access storage devices and online terminals. The data collection, data processing and file updating, data storage and retrieval, processing controls, and information reporting will differ, depending on the particular alternative selected for implementation.

Cost/Benefit Analysis of Alternatives

The next phase in system design involves evaluating each alternative to assess its benefits and the costs that will be incurred to realize the benefits. The decision as to which alternative is preferable will be based primarily on economic considerations. Therefore, both benefits and costs must be quantified so that they can be compared. This may be especially difficult to do for benefits that seem *intangible*. For example, how does one estimate the benefit derived from better customer service resulting from a new or improved information system?

By analyzing customer sales, one may find that a company is losing 10 percent of its gross sales due to the unavailability of products needed to fill orders. A new system could increase the customer service level from its present 80 percent to 90 percent. This could, in turn, reduce lost sales to only 5 percent. On the basis of this analysis, one could compute the revenue increase due to better customer service.

If a particular benefit cannot be quantified and measured, then it is reasonably safe to assume that it will never be realized.

The costs attributable to an alternative will include direct costs like the initial investment required for materials and equipment; set-up costs related to data collection, data processing, and information distribution; and the cost of converting from the old system to the new one. In addition, there are always indirect, or overhead, costs that cannot be easily identified with the proposed system. Examples include management salaries, insurance, taxes, and rent.

In analyzing alternatives, the analyst must use quantitative methods such as sampling and modeling as well as qualitative factors such as judgment, common sense, and experience. Selection of an alternative will be based upon the cost/benefit ratios derived.

System Recommendation

The final step in system design is recommending to top management the best alternative and offering a plan for its implementation. The selection of an alternative usually presents no problem, since a cost/benefit analysis has already been done for each design. The analyst recommends the alternative that offers the maximum benefits as compared to the costs involved.

When presenting a recommendation, the analyst should also present a plan for system implementation. This plan should indicate the resources required in terms of personnel and equipment. A time schedule for the implementation should be proposed. The installation plan should identify activities, like system testing, personnel training, and system auditing, which must be done before system implementation is complete.

The presentation of alternative designs, in conjunction with a recommendation and a project plan for system implementation, officially terminates the design phase.

SYSTEM IMPLEMENTATION

The final phase in the development and operation of new or revised systems is *system implementation*. This involves the following activities:

1. Personnel training

2. Testing the system

3. System conversion

4. System auditing

5. System maintenance and follow-up

The goal of system implementation is to insure that the system is completely debugged and operational, and is accepted by the users.

Personnel Training

There are two groups of people who interface with a system. The first group includes the people who develop, operate, and maintain the system. To the second group belong those who use the information generated by the system to support their decision-making. Both groups must know what they can expect from the system and what responsibilities they have to insure its smooth and trouble-free operation. One of the primary responsibilities of the system analyst is to see that education and training are provided to these people.

The user group includes general management, staff personnel, line managers, and other operating personnel. It may also include the organization's customers and various suppliers with whom the company does business. These users must be told what the system can do for them and what inputs it will need from them.

The personnel who will be operating the system must be trained regarding such aspects as preparation of input data, using appropriate media for input, loading and unloading of auxiliary storage devices, and handling of problems that occur during data processing.

The necessary education and training can be provided in large-group seminars, or in smaller, tutorial training sessions. The latter approach is more personal. It can be fairly costly, but it is appropriate for complex tasks. Another approach, used almost universally, is on-the-job training. As the name implies, an employee learns while actually working at his or her job. To start with, the employee is given simple tasks and told how to do them. As soon as those are learned, the employee progresses to more difficult tasks, and so on, until all have been mastered.

Personnel training and education are expensive, but they are essential to successful system implementation.

Testing the System

Before a system becomes operational it must be tested and debugged. Testing occurs at various levels. The lowest level is program testing. Programs are divided into distinct logical modules. Each module is tested to insure that all input is accounted for, the proper files are updated, and the correct reports are printed. Only after each module has been debugged should the modules be linked together and the complete program tested.

Once all program testing is complete, system testing can proceed; this level of testing involves checking all the applications programs that support the system. All clerical procedures used in data collection, data processing, and data storage and retrieval are included in system testing.

Two test methods discussed in Chapter 10 are often used in system testing: (1) desk-checking and (2) processing test data. The former involves mentally tracing the sequence of operations performed on a particular transaction to determine the correctness of the processing logic. This approach is least costly, but it is not always reliable. In the second method, the analyst can take "live" data that has already been processed, and submit it to the new system. If the results match previously determined correct output, the system is functioning as expected.

System Conversion

The switch from an old system to a new one is referred to as conversion. The conversion involves not only the changes in the mode of processing data, but also the changes in equipment and in clerical procedures.

Different approaches can be used to accomplish the conversion process. The most important ones are explained below.

● **Parallel conversion.** In this approach, the new system is operated side-by-side with the old one for some period of time. An advantage of this approach is that it offers data security, since no data is lost if the new system crashes. Also, it gives the user an opportunity to compare and reconcile the outputs from both systems. However, this method is rather costly.

● **Pilot conversion.** This approach involves initially converting only a small piece of the business to the new system. For example, the total new system may be implemented on just one production line of the company. This minimizes the risk to the organization as a whole, in case unforeseen problems occur. It also enables the organization to identify any problems and correct them before implementing the system in other areas. A disadvantage of this method is that the total conversion process usually takes a long time.

● **Phased conversion.** In this method, the old system is gradually replaced by the new one over a period of time. The difference between this method and pilot conversion is that in phased conversion the new system is segmented; only one segment is implemented throughout the organization before proceeding to the next segment. This allows the organization to adapt to the change because it takes place gradually over an extended period of time. One drawback to the approach is that an interface must be developed between the new system and the old one during the conversion process.

● **Crash conversion.** This method is sometimes referred to as *direct conversion.* The conversion takes place all at once. Since the old system is discontinued immediately upon implementation of the new one, the organization has nothing to fall back on if problems arise. The approach can be used advantageously if the old system is not operational, or if the new system is totally different from the old one in structure and design. Because of the high risk involved, this approach requires extreme care in planning and extensive testing of all system components.

System Auditing

After the conversion process is complete, the system must be audited. This involves the analysis of system accomplishments in terms of initial objectives. The evaluation should address the following questions:

1. Does the system perform as planned and deliver the anticipated benefits? How do the operating results compare with the initial objectives? If the benefits are below expectation, what can be done to improve the cost/benefit tradeoff?

2. Was the system completed on schedule and with the resources estimated?

3. Is all output from the system used?

4. Have old system procedures been eliminated and new ones implemented?

5. What controls have been established for input, processing, and output of data? Are these controls adequate?

6. Have users been educated about the new system? Is the system accepted by users? Do they have confidence in the reports generated?

7. Is the processing turnaround time satisfactory or are delays frequent?

347

All persons involved in the system implementation should be aware that a thorough audit of the system will be performed. The anticipated audit acts as a strong incentive; it helps to insure that a good system is designed and delivered on schedule.

System Maintenance and Follow-up

All too often, management believes that after a system has been installed and is operational, nothing more has to be done. This belief is a fallacy. Improvements must be made continually in all systems. The purposes of system maintenance are to detect and correct errors, to meet new information needs of management, and to respond to changes in the environment.

One of the important tasks of the analyst during system follow-up is to insure that all system controls are working correctly. All procedures and programs related to the old system should have been eliminated. Many of the problems that the system analyst deals with during system maintenance and follow-up are problems that were identified during the system audit.

A well planned approach to system maintenance and follow-up is essential to the continued effectiveness of an information system.

SUMMARY

● An information system is an integrated network of equipment, procedures, and personnel designed to satisfy the information requirements of management. Information systems may be either manual or computerized.

● Every system study consists of three distinct phases: analysis, design, and implementation. System analysis is an evaluation to enhance understanding and determine problem areas. System design is the formulation of alternative solutions to solve problems uncovered in the analysis phase. System implementation involves making the design operational and insuring error-free operations and user acceptance.

● During system analysis, the analyst gathers data relevant to the system project to help in understanding the advantages and limitations of the present system, and to help in designing the new system. Data gathering is facilitated by interviews, questionnaires, and the preparation of system charts.

● Data collection focuses on what is being done in the present system, while data analysis focuses on why certain procedures and operations are being used. Tools frequently used in data analysis are grid charts, system flowcharts, and decision logic tables.

● System design is concerned with the formulation of specifications for the proposed new system, to achieve the objectives identified during the system-analysis phase. The specifications include the I/O requirements, files, hardware needs, and procedural details of the proposed system.

● System design encompasses several steps: reviewing the system goals and objectives; developing a conceptual model of the system; evaluating organizational constraints; defining I/O requirements; developing alternative designs; preparing a cost/benefit analysis for each alternative; and recommending the best alternative and a plan for its implementation.

● System implementation is the final phase in system development. It involves personnel training, system testing and conversion, system auditing, and system maintenance and follow-up.

● Converting to a new system can be done in several ways. In parallel conversion, both the old and the new systems operate together for a period of time. In pilot conversion, the new system is first implemented in only a part of the organization to determine its adequacies and inadequacies; the latter are corrected before full-scale implementation. In phased conversion, the old system is gradually replaced with the new system by implementing only portions of the system at a time. In crash conversion, the total new system is implemented at once.

● Once a new system is operational, it must be audited to ascertain that the initial objectives of the system are being met, and to find any problems occurring in the new system. System maintenance is the continued surveillance of system operations to determine what modifications are needed to meet the changing needs of management and to respond to changes in the environment.

REVIEW QUESTIONS

1. What is system analysis and what are some reasons why a firm may engage in system analysis work? For what reasons may a firm decide not to analyze its present systems?

2. What techniques are frequently used by the system analyst to collect data about current systems and to evaluate management needs? Would you expect internal or external data sources to be most helpful to the system analyst in designing new systems? Explain.

3. Distinguish between system flowcharts and program flowcharts. What purposes does each serve?

4. What steps are involved in the design phase of the system life cycle? Why does an analyst develop alternative designs before making recommendations? How are alternative designs evaluated?

5. What are some of the methods used in training personnel in new system procedures? Which groups of individuals must undergo training?

6. Why is a system audit an essential part of system implementation? What is the difference between a system audit and system maintenance?

MARATHON OIL COMPANY

Marathon Oil Company is a fully integrated oil company. Its general offices are in Findlay, Ohio. Exploration, production, transportation, and marketing of crude oil and natural gas, as well as refining, transporting, and marketing of petroleum products, are its primary activities. The pursuit of these activities has led to significant international operations extending to five continents and involving about 13,000 employees. With sales in excess of $4 billion, Marathon is ranked among the 50 largest industrial corporations in the United States.

Two distinct computer centers are maintained by the Marathon Oil Company. One is the Computer Sciences Department at the Research Center in Littleton, Colorado. The primary function of this department is support of petroleum engineering, geophysical, and research work conducted at the Research Center. The computer system itself comprises twin Burroughs 6800 main-frames and the necessary peripheral tape and disk drives. Several online pieces of equipment directly associated with research activities are also used.

The other computer facility is located at the corporate headquarters in Findlay. It is devoted primarily to business-related computing. The computer system consists of an IBM System/370 Model 168 and a variety of peripheral devices, including printers, tape drives, disk drives, CRTs, and a telecommunication network. Additional hardware includes optical-scanning equipment, key-to-disk minicomputers, and microfiche processing equipment.

The Computer Services Organization at Findlay encompasses four functional areas: Systems Development, Operations Research, Facilities Planning, and Computer Operations. The applications developed and operated at Marathon range from a simple payroll procedure to the computer control of refining operations. It is not unusual to find one project development group updating an existing billing system while another group is developing a highly sophisticated engineering application. Thousands of programs have been developed to handle user requests. An average of 1500 jobs (5200 programs) are processed each day.

The Systems Development Division within the Computer Services Organization employs approximately 130 individuals who are concerned with the maintenance of current systems and the development of new systems arising from user requests. Marathon uses PRIDE, a standard methodology for system development marketed by M. Bryce & Associates. In all, seven phases of system analysis and design are outlined in the PRIDE methodology.

Phase I of this approach is essentially a feasibility study, during which the following-steps occur:

1. Project Scope. The overall nature of the project is defined in this step. Emphasis is placed on what this study intends to accomplish.

2. Information Requirements. Data is collected during extensive interviews with individuals who will interface with the new system and become its primary users.

3. Recommendations and Concepts. A general flowchart of the proposed system is developed during this step. The flow of key documents through the system is depicted on it. A narrative is included to explain the flow.

4. Economics. This step emphasizes the projected costs of developing the proposed system and the annual costs associated with the operation of it. Any savings generated by the system are included, as well as a payout schedule.

5. Project Plan. This is the final step in Phase I. A calendar schedule outlining the time required to complete the proposed system is set up.

Several alternatives are usually generated during Phase I. These alternatives are then presented to management who selects what it believes is the most feasible alternative. The chosen alternative is then carried forward into Phase II.

During Phase II, all major functions of the system are identified. The total system is divided into logical subsystems. Each subsystem is thoroughly documented through the use of flowcharts. Included within the flowcharts are subsystem identification, the inputs and outputs associated with the subsystem, and the files to be accessed, referenced, and/or updated by the subsystem. Any output report generated by the subsystem is also formatted at this time. A narrative covering the subsystem is included to clarify any points not represented by the flowcharts. The entire package is then presented to management for final approval. Once the design has been approved by management (at the end of Phase II), no other formal presentation of the entire system is made, although the final details of each subsystem are reviewed.

Phase III entails subsystem design and focuses directly on the project plan for each subsystem. Administrative procedures and computer procedures are thoroughly documented in a subsystem design manual. Flowcharts and narratives are again used as documentation tools. During this phase it is not unusual to discover overlooked outputs such as control totals that should be provided by the system. These are incorporated, and the final formats for all output reports are developed.

In Phase IV, a separation of activities between analysts and programmers occurs. The analysts begin work on the administrative procedure design, which is denoted as Phase 4–1. The key activity is the development of a user manual. The system design manual generated during Phase II generally becomes the first chapter of this manual. The remaining chapters are devoted to the component subsystems. Necessary input documents are designed and added to each subsystem definition. The previously designed output documents are usually carried forward. The procedures or methods to be used in inputting data are defined.

While the analysts are developing the user manual, programmers are busy with program design, which is Phase 4–2. Extensive use of HIPO techniques occurs during this phase, which eventually leads into Phase V. During Phase V, the actual programs are produced. This phase tends to be overlapped with Phase VI. Each program module is tested during this phase.

The activities of the analysts and programmers are carefully coordinated so that the user manual and the programs are completed at approximately the same time. The entire system is now ready to begin the final phase outlined in the PRIDE methodology—a complete systems test. Phase VII involves extensive volume tests and comprehensive training of the system users.

An example of a system developed internally is the Medical Claims System designed to speed the processing of medical claims submitted by Marathon employees. Prior to the development of this system, each claim was processed manually. First, a medical claims processor thoroughly checked the claim's validity. After all the medical bills associated with the claim had been received, the processor filled out a worksheet to complete the claim. The processor was then able to prepare a check payable to the employee in accordance with the policy.

The new system greatly simplifies and speeds this processing. Once the entire claim has been collected, it is entered into the system via a CRT. This is the last time a human needs to interface with the claim. The system handles all subsequent processing, including generation of the check.

The bar chart in Figure 14–11 indicates the time involved in each phase of the development of this system.

More than 4600 person-hours were required. This means that if one person

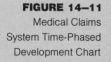

FIGURE 14–11
Medical Claims System Time-Phased Development Chart

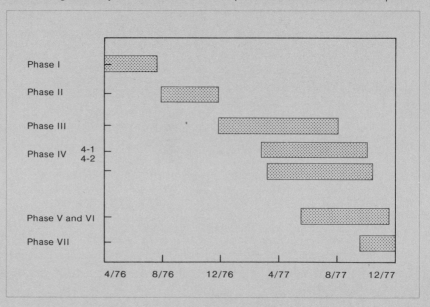

were to devote 40 hours a week to the development of such a system, it would require over two years. Such an occurrence would be extremely unusual, since several analysts and programmers are usually working on more than one project at the same time.

During 1977, the Systems Development Division was actively involved in the development of many new systems and in maintaining systems already in operation. Despite continual efforts to satisfy user demand, a sizable backlog of requests remains virtually untouched. As users continue to become more comfortable with computer interaction, the demands on this division will undoubtedly continue to grow.

DISCUSSION POINTS

1. What type of conversion process would you recommend for the Medical Claims System? What advantages and disadvantages are associated with this approach?

2. Is the structured approach outlined in the PRIDE methodology an effective technique for conducting system analysis, design, and implementation? Should such a detailed procedure always be followed?

PROCESS DESIGN | 15

OUTLINE

I. Batch/Sequential Processing
  A. Characteristics
    1. Data Base
    2. Master File
    3. Transaction File
    4. Media
  B. Example of Batch Processing
  C. Interrogating Sequential Files
  D. Assessment of
    Batch/Sequential Processing
II. Inline/Direct-Access Processing
  A. Direct-Access Addressing
    1. Directory Method
    2. Randomizing

  B. Examples of
    Inline/Direct-Access
    Processing
  C. Interrogating Direct-Access
    Files
  D. Assessment of
    Inline/Direct-Access
    Processing
III. Indexed-Sequential File
  Organization

INTRODUCTION

Updating is a common business practice—keeping bank account balances current, maintaining inventory levels in certain ranges, and making employee records up-to-date. A typical business or other organization stores a wide variety of data ranging from employee records to inventory levels to customer purchase histories. While some types of data require constant updating (e.g., inventory levels), other types require only periodic updating (e.g., payroll). Depending on the nature of the data, its usage, and the processing it requires, there are a variety of ways it can be organized and stored to guarantee that the correct information can be made available to the right person at the appropriate time.

This chapter presents the methods most commonly used to update data stored in computer files. The concepts of batch and inline processing are discussed together with the methods used to organize and locate individual records by each processing method. Examples of applications of these methods are provided to further enhance understanding of how they are used. In addition, their advantages and disadvantages are pointed out.

CHECKING OUT TOMORROW

Time, February 20, 1978, p. 49

Americans spend more than $153 billion a year on food and other purchases in supermarkets and grocery stores, and have an abiding suspicion that they are getting gypped at the check-out counter. Their mistrust should be considerably allayed, and the waiting lines shortened, by the ever-growing number of computers that are taking over the tally.

At a computer-equipped check-out line, all the clerk has to do is pass each item over a Cyclopean eye linked to a cash register and a scale. In a twinkling, the eye "reads" the striped UPC (Universal Product Code) symbol, by which the computer system identifies the product, brand name, and other pertinent information about the item. (The store manager can program into the computer price changes for specials or daily fluctuations.) Then the computer prints out both the name of the item (say, one 4-oz. can of sliced French beans) and the price on the receipt list.

The miracle-chip brain of the check-out computer is amazingly versatile. If, for example, a customer buys two cans of tomato soup priced at two for 49¢, the computer will charge 25¢ for the first can that crosses the eye. Then, no matter how many different items have been handled in between, when the second can passes across the eye, the computer—remembering the first—will charge only 24¢ for it.

If an item is not code-marked, or if the clerk mistakenly positions it so that the marking is on the upper surface (and thus invisible to the scanning eye), the computer signals that it has not charged for that merchandise; it will then be added manually to the bill by the check-out clerk. In handling produce that must be weighed, the computer reads the code on the plastic bag containing, say, a half-dozen Delicious apples, but delays ringing up the charge until the bag has been placed on the computer-connected check-out scale. Then, programmed with the price per pound, it calculates and prints out the cost; this largely eliminates the time-consuming process of clerkly computation.

Unbeknown to the shopper, the check-out computer also logs each outgoing item against inventory in the store or a centralized warehouse, warning the manager when he must reorder and thus greatly reducing the frequency of the "Sorry, we're sold out" dirge. Obviously, the consumer benefits from computerized marketing. So does the store. Since supermarkets operate on a profit margin of about 2% or less, the savings can be crucial.

Though the purchase price for a sophisticated eight-lane check-out system can be more than $110,000, some 200 systems are already operating in supermarkets around the nation. Some chains are, well, waiting in line for them. In time, chips in check-out counters will be as much a supermarket staple as the crunchy kind that comes in bags and tins.

Imagine the sophistication required to access data on one can of Campbell's tomato soup (differentiating it not only from the store brand of tomato soup, but also from hundreds of other grocery items) and update the inventory at the same time. This chapter describes how both steps are possible through inline/direct-access processing.

BATCH/SEQUENTIAL PROCESSING

Data can be manipulated in many ways. As shown in Chapter 1, an individual employee record may contain data concerning home address, social security number, wage per hour, withholding tax, and gross income. So that this data can be used in different ways without restructuring, it is organized in an integrated manner.

We introduced several terms in discussing employee records: a field, which is a data item; a record, which is a collection of data items that relate to a single unit; and a file, or data set, which is a grouping of related records (see Figure 15–1).

To design an *integrated file*, or *data base*, it is necessary to discover all the information needs that must be satisfied and then tailor the file to meet those needs. A possible data base of the ABC Company has already been shown (see Figure 15–1). A distributor may keep all data about its goods—reorder point, selling price, current inventory level, etc.—listed together under the item numbers of the goods. This is also a possible data base.

If the set of records in a file is very small, then it may not be difficult to randomly search the file for a particular record. But given a high volume of records, this method is impractical. A special structuring technique is needed to organize the records. Employee records can be arranged according to social security number (look again at Figure 15–1). An inventory file can be arranged according to part number. In any case, the identifier, or *key* (social security number, part number), used to locate the particular record must be unique. No duplicate keys can exist in the file.

An organization's method of processing all or a certain portion of its data should be determined by specific job requirements. For example: Is an up-to-the-minute account balance needed at all times, or is a weekly

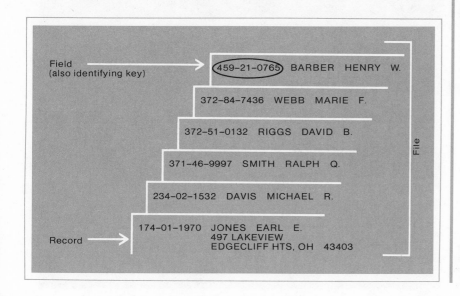

FIGURE 15–1
Employee Data—
ABC Company

357

or monthly balance report adequate? If periodic reports are satisfactory, then batch processing can probably be used (see Figure 15–2). Each data item is only as current as the particular batch in which it is grouped. For periodic reports such as payroll information, this method of processing is acceptable.

The basic file, say, of employee records or inventory records, being updated is called a *master file*. The records containing changes to be made to the master file are called a *transaction file*. The master file is organized with respect to the identifier chosen as a key, and the transactions are ordered according to the same key.

Both the master file and the transaction file serve as input to the computer system. The computer compares one or more keys on the master file with the first key on the transaction file. When a match occurs, the proper record in the master file has been found. The updating of the master file can then take place.

FIGURE 15–2
Batch Processing

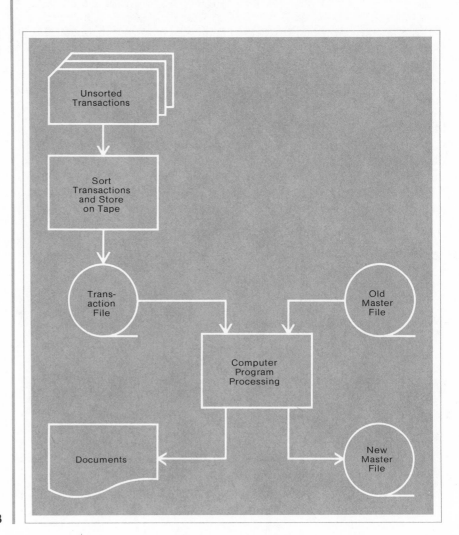

Two media commonly used for sequential processing are punched cards and magnetic tape. There is no method of immediately going to an individual record on the master file. The entire master file must be read each time it is updated. The preliminary sorting that the transaction file undergoes insures that the master file is read only once during a run. Processing time for updating, using a sequential processing method, is the amount of time needed to read the entire master file, process the transaction records, and rewrite the entire master file. Each time the master file is updated, a new master file reflecting not only the changes but also the accounts that remain the same is formed. For security reasons, the old master file and the transaction records are maintained for reconstruction of the new (current) master file if necessary.

Example of Batch Processing

The billing operation is well suited to batch processing because customer bills need to be prepared only at scheduled intervals. It uses standard procedures and deals with a large number of records.

The processing of customer records results in the preparation of bills for customers and an update of the amount owed by each customer. Magnetic tape is an appropriate medium for this application because all customer records have to be processed in a sequential order.

The procedure for preparing the billing statements involves the following steps:

Step 1: The transaction cards indicating which items have been shipped to the customer are keypunched and verified. One card is used for each item shipped (see Figure 15–3a).

Step 2: The data on the cards is transferred to magnetic tape. The card-to-tape program also edits the input data. Editing checks include tests to make sure that contents of fields are within reasonable limits, numeric fields have numeric data, alphanumeric fields have alphanumeric data, and so forth. The card-to-tape run provides a report of invalid transactions so that they can be corrected (see Figure 15–3b).

Step 3: In this step, the transaction records are sorted according to customer number. This is done because the customer master file is arranged in customer number order (see Figure 15–3c).

Step 4: The sorted transactions are used to update the customer master file. The process involves reading the transaction records and master records into main storage. There may be more than one transaction record for a master record. The master record is updated to reflect the final amount owed by the customer. If a master record has no matching transactions, it is left unchanged. Usually, during an update, a report is also printed for management. For example, during the billing update, a listing of customers who have exceeded their credit limits may be printed (see Figure 15–3d).

Step 5: In the last step, the customer bills are prepared using the data generated from the previous step (see Figure 15–3e).

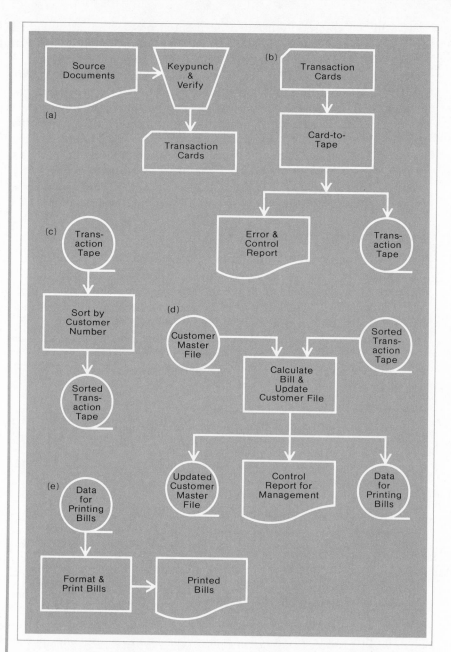

FIGURE 15–3
Billing Operations

Interrogating Sequential Files

How inquiries into a *sequential file* on magnetic tape are handled depends on the type of inquiry. Let us consider the following inquiries into ABC's employee file.

1. List the records of employees with social security numbers 234–02–1532 and 372–84–7436.

2. List all customers from the area with zip code 43403.

The employee file is sequenced according to social security number. In the first case, only the key will be checked. The file will be searched from the beginning. As soon as the required social security numbers are located, the records will be listed and the search stopped. If the numbers are in the last two records on the file, then the entire file will be searched.

For the second inquiry, the entire file will have to be searched. The zip-code field of each record will be checked to see if it matches 43403. This illustrates one problem with sequential files. If an inquiry is based on a field other than the key of the master file, then much time is wasted in the search process. In this case, a second customer file ordered by zip code could be created. This would result in maintenance of multiple files and duplication of data.

Assessment of Batch/Sequential Processing

Some advantages of batch processing and sequential file design follow:

● It is suitable for many types of applications—payroll, billing, preparation of customer statements, and so forth. In all these cases, it is not necessary to update records as transactions occur. Payrolls and customer statements are prepared only at scheduled intervals. The delays resulting from accumulating data into batches have no adverse impact.

● The method is economical when the number of records processed is high. Thus, in a billing application, at least half of the customer records may be updated during a run. Due to the large volume of transactions, the processing cost per record is low. Economies of scale are achieved.

● The design of sequential files is simple.

● Magnetic tape, a low-cost medium, can be used to maximum advantage.

● Input and output rates are higher than those achieved with direct input of transactions from keyboard terminals.

The disadvantages of this mode of processing include:

● The entire file must be processed, even if very few records need to be updated.

● Transactions must be sorted in a particular sequence. This takes time and can be expensive.

● The master file is only as up-to-date as the last processing run. In many instances (such as a customer inquiry as to how much is owed), the delay in the processing of the master file results in old and, thus, incorrect information being given in response to an interrogation of the file.

● The sequential nature of the file organization is a serious handicap when inquiries reference a field other than the one used as a key in the master file.

INLINE/DIRECT-ACCESS PROCESSING

In contrast to a batch-processing system, an inline system does not require grouping or sorting of transaction records prior to processing. Data is submitted to the computer in the order it occurs. Direct-access storage devices (DASDs) make this type of processing possible. A particular record on a master file can be accessed directly and updated without having to read all preceding records on the file. An up-to-the-minute report is always available.

For example, assume Ralph Smith's address had to be changed in the employee master file (Figure 15–1). With inline/direct-access processing, the computer can locate that record without sequentially processing the records that precede it. Various techniques are used to accomplish direct-access processing.

Direct-Access Addressing

A major consideration with inline processing is finding the record to be updated. To be able to locate the record, a device-dependent address must be known. The address is usually a number between 5 and 7 digits in length that is related to the physical characteristics of the direct-access storage device. The address can be obtained from a directory or by performing a transformation process on the record key (also called *randomizing*).

In the first method, the directory contains the reference numbers and corresponding addresses of storage locations of records. Thus, during processing the computer searches the directory to locate the addresses of particular records.

Assume the ABC Company's employee master file is on a direct-access storage device. Employee Ralph Smith's record could be located using this approach. The directory (or table) would consist of two columns: the first containing the key of the record (social security number); and the second containing the address of that record. The computer would quickly scan the first column until it found Ralph Smith's social security number. It would pick up the corresponding address of the record from the second column.

With the second method of addressing, an arithmetic manipulation is performed on the record key to obtain an address. No new identification key is required, and there is no need to create a directory. However, this method may produce *synonyms*—two or more records whose keys transform to the same address. This problem is resolved by carrying in the record located at the calculated address a *pointer* field that points to the next record having the same calculated address. During processing, the program derives the address from the key and goes to that location. If the record at that location does not have the right key, the computer looks at the pointer field to continue its search for the record.

Examples of Inline/Direct-Access Processing

Many applications are not suited for batch processing. One example is an airline reservation system. To assign seats on flights, up-to-date information must be available. Coordination of sales effort is necessary so that a passenger in Cleveland and one in Detroit do not purchase the same seat on the same flight to New York. If data for an airline were processed once a week, plane flights would be oversold many times. With an inline system, a ticket agent can submit a flight number and the quantity of seats required and obtain the necessary information quickly. This can only be achieved because the data about all flights does not need to be read; only the flight in question is checked. The computer system has an up-to-date report on all flights at all times.

Another example of direct-access processing is a savings account system at a bank. The bank can maintain a current status of all savings accounts by updating each account as soon as a deposit or withdrawal is made. Customer records are stored on a DASD, and terminals are installed at all branch offices and hooked directly to the computer. The terminals are used for both input and output (see Figure 15–4).

When a bank customer makes a deposit or withdrawal, the amount of the transaction, the type of transaction (deposit or withdrawal), and the customer account number are communicated to the central computer through the typewriter-like terminal at the branch office. The computer immediately locates the record corresponding to that account number on the DASD and updates the account. It sends a message giving the current balance back to the terminal. The message is then printed on the customer's savings book. It is important to note that it is possible to directly locate the desired record on the DASD and that only one record is updated. Sequential processing is unsuitable for this kind of application.

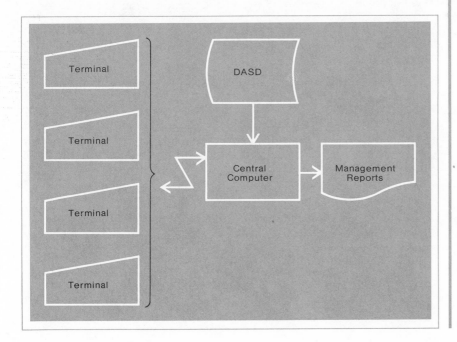

FIGURE 15–4
Inline Processing

Interrogating Direct-Access Files

To see how direct-access files handle inquiries, let us again look at the two inquiries discussed in connection with sequential files:

1. List the records of employees with social security numbers 234–02–1532 and 372–84–7436.

2. List all customers from the area with zip code 43403.

Given the first inquiry, the records of the two employees can be located directly because the addresses can be derived by one of the two methods described earlier.

The approach used for the second inquiry will depend on the organization of the file. If much processing is done based on a geographic breakdown of employees, a directory relating zip codes and record addresses can be created (see Figure 15–5). This may be the case if ABC is a large diversified corporation with people working at sites all over the country. However, if ABC is a small company at just one location, a directory to locate employee records by zip code may serve no purpose. In that situation, it would not speed up processing.

Assessment of Inline/Direct-Access Processing

The advantages of inline/direct-access processing follow:

● Transaction data can be used directly for updating records via online terminals without first being sorted.

● The master file is not read completely each time updating occurs. Only the master records to be updated are read during a run. This saves time and money.

● It takes only a fraction of a second to access any record on a direct-access file.

● Direct-access files provide more flexibility in handling inquiries.

● Several files can be updated concurrently using direct-access processing. For example, when a credit sale is made, the inventory file can be updated; the customer file can be changed to reflect the current accounts-receivable figure; and the sales file can be updated to show which employee made the sale. Several runs would be required to accomplish the same goals using sequential processing.

FIGURE 15–5
Directory for Zip Codes

ZIP CODE	ADDRESS
43403	12043
43403	12140
44151	12046
44153	12143
44200	12146
44201	12045

● Random-access processing is suited to applications involving files which have low *activity* and high *volatility*. Activity refers to the proportion of records processed during an updating run, and volatility refers to the frequency of changes in a file during a certain time period.

Some disadvantages of direct-access processing are:

● During processing, the original record is destroyed and replaced by the updated record. If the updating was correct or incorrect, the original record has been lost. (This is in contrast to batch processing where a complete new master file is created from the old master.) Consequently, to provide backup, an organization may make a magnetic-tape copy of the master file once a week, and keep the current weekly transactions so that master-file records can be reconstructed if necessary.

● Since many users have access to records stored on direct-access devices in inline systems, the chances of accidental destruction of data are greater. Special programs are required for careful editing of input data and for performing other checks to insure that data is not lost. Also, there exists the possibility of confidential information falling into unauthorized hands; additional security procedures are necessary to reduce this risk.

● Implementation of direct-access systems is more difficult because of the greater complexity and the high level of programming (software) support that such systems need.

● Direct-access file organization leads to some unused file locations because of the randomizing technique employed. It also requires keeping track of these unused locations for use as overflow areas for synonyms and later additions.

INDEXED-SEQUENTIAL FILE ORGANIZATION

Sequential processing is suitable for applications where the proportion of records processed in an updating run (file activity) is high. However, sequential files provide slow response times and cannot adequately handle file inquiries. On the other hand, direct-access processing is inappropriate for applications like payroll which require that almost every record be processed during a run. Therefore, when a single file must be used for both batch processing and inline processing, neither direct-access nor sequential file organization will accomplish both tasks efficiently. The same inventory file that is used in a weekly batch run for re-ordering parts by the purchasing department may be used daily on an inquiry basis by sales personnel to check on stock availability. To some extent, the limitations of both types of file design can be minimized by using a compromise approach to file organization—*indexed-sequential.*
    In this structure, the records are stored sequentially on a direct-access storage device. In addition, an *index* to selected record keys and their

365

corresponding addresses is established. The file can be accessed directly by matching a record key against the index table to get an approximate address of the record that has that key. The computer can then go to that location and check records in a sequential manner until it locates the desired record.

This approach is similar to the way one locates a house in an unfamilar city. The address specifies the street and house number, for example, 213 S. Clay Street. The first step is to get to S. Clay Street. Then we check the number of the closest house. Let's say it is 219. Then, we proceed down the street to check if the next house is 221 or 217. If it is 217, we proceed in the same direcion until 213 is located. This is quicker than randomly checking all house numbers on S. Clay Street because we know that the numbers are in sequence. The odd-numbered houses are on one side of the street, and the even-numbered houses are on the other side.

In contrast, the direct-access method can be compared to finding a particular landmark on a city map by means of coordinates. Knowing these, we can immediately zero-in on the exact location of the landmark.

Thus, an indexed-sequential file provides direct access because a particular record can be accessed without processing all the records before it. However, since all the records are ordered according to a key, such a file can also be processed sequentially. But the processing time for direct-access processing of an indexed-sequential file will be longer than if the file were organized for direct addressing. Similarly, an indexed-sequential organization requires a great deal of additional overhead in the form of indexes as compared to a sequential organization.

SUMMARY

● Storing data for subsequent processing requires that the data be organized in a logical fashion. A field is an individual data item; a record is a collection of data items relating to a single unit; and a file is a grouping of related records. An integrated file is called a data base.

● Batch/sequential processing involves storing records in a sequence based on a unique identifier called a key. These records form a master file. All changes to be made to the master file are collected and processed in a batch to update the file. These changes form a transaction file; they must be ordered in the same sequence as the master file. After processing, there is a new master file, an old master file, and a transaction file.

● Batch processing is normally used when files are large and need to be updated only periodically, such as for payroll or billing. However, sequential file organization is not well suited to responding to inquiries since the file must be read from the beginning to locate a desired record.

● In an inline system, transaction records are processed as they occur, without prior sorting or grouping. This method requires the use of high-speed, direct-access storage devices (DASDs).

● In a direct-access file, records may be located by any of several techniques. In direct-access addressing, an address assigned to each record indicates the location of the record on a particular storage device. A directory which contains the reference numbers of these records and their storage locations is often kept. Alternatively, an arithmetic manipulation may be performed on the record key to obtain the record address.

● Inline/direct-access processing is most often used when changes are frequent, but only a small proportion of master records must be updated at any single time.

● Indexed-sequential file organization is suitable where the proportion of records to be processed in an updating run is high. Records are stored in sequence on a direct-access storage device. An index to selected record keys and their corresponding addresses is established. When records in indexed-sequential files are accessed, the index table gives the approximate address of the record, and the records near that location are read sequentially until the correct one is found. Both indexed-sequential and direct-access file organizations are well-suited to responding to inquiries into data files.

REVIEW QUESTIONS

1. Why does batch processing require a sequential file organization? How are sequential files updated?

2. Under what circumstances is batch processing applicable? What are the limitations of this approach?

3. What are two commonly used methods for addressing direct-access files? Explain briefly the differences between these methods.

4. Direct-access processing is best suited to what types of applications?

5. Contrast indexed-sequential file organization with sequential and direct-access file organizations. What advantages does indexed-sequential organization have over the other two approaches?

Dana's origins date to 1904. Clarence Spicer, a mechanical engineering student at Cornell University, adopted the idea of replacing the sprockets and chains being used to transmit the power from the engine to the rear axle in automobiles with a universal joint and driveshaft. The Spicer Manufacturing Company was founded in Plainfield, New Jersey, to manufacture and market these universal joints. Several automobile makers were changing from the chain drive to a universal-joint drive at this time. Production was hard pressed to meet sales. An order for 96 sets of universal joints and driveshafts was received in 1905 from the Wayne Automobile Company. Nearly 16 weeks of around-the-clock production were required to fill the order. Today, Dana produces and ships 2.5 million joint sets in a similar 16-week period.

The company has continued to expand and prosper. Its major products today are axle parts, transmissions, universal joints, clutches, industrial products, engine parts, and frame and chassis parts. International sales have grown from

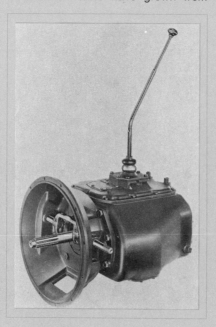

about $1 million in 1950 to over $390 million in 1977. Total sales have increased from $153 million to almost $1.8 billion during the same period.

The Spicer Transmission Division of Dana has an extensive data-processing center. It supports the Spicer Transmission Division and another plant in Tipton, Indiana. It also maintains some financial information and centralized accounts-receivable for the corporate headquarters. Seventeen management personnel and eight operators are involved in the preparation of data for subsequent processing by the computer at this facility. The CPU is an IBM System/370 Model 148 capable of storing one million characters. Seventeen remote terminals are used in the centralized accounts-receivable system. Seventeen additional terminals at the Spicer plant complex are used for online sales, new product development, and personnel record-keeping applications.

The variety of needs of users at the Spicer Transmission Division requires both inline/direct-access and batch/sequential modes of processing. Most applications programs used in these processes are written in COBOL. The entire COBOL program library contains some 2000 programs. Although recent emphasis has been placed on the development of online applications, batch processing remains a vital aspect of the overall data-processing activities.

One system that operates in a batch mode is the material requirements planning (MRP) system. This system is extremely important to the production and purchasing departments of the division, because production planning schedules are heavily dependent upon a sufficient supply of the parts required in the assembly of a given product, such as a transmission. A shortage is extremely expensive because the entire assembly line must either be halted until the needed parts arrive, or be converted to another assembly process. Carrying a large supply of parts in inventory is also expensive, so the purchasing department must strive to have no more inventory than is needed to meet demand.

Any transactions affecting inventory have an impact on the MRP system. During a typical day, many such transactions occur—deliveries of goods, shipments of goods, withdrawals of goods from inventory, and so on. As these transactions occur, they are recorded on a diskette. This diskette becomes a transaction file. It is processed nightly against the master files contained in the MRP system. These master files can be used to produce planning reports, inventory shortage and overage reports, and material buying reports.

Approximately 150 reports are available through the MRP system. They can be generated at regular intervals or on user demand. Consider, as an example, an inventory shortage report. This report can include item number, description, quantity on hand, quantity on order, expected future requirements, requirements during past periods, shortage quantities, the division placing the orders, and even the specific buyer who is responsible for the item. Reports of such a comprehensive nature, provided in a timely manner, are invaluable to management.

Another batch-processing application is the payroll system. The office staff and production workers are paid on a weekly basis. The salaried management personnel are paid on a semimonthly basis. An additional complication arises because the office staff are paid at hourly rates. The input for these employees is encoded on punched cards as depicted in Figure 15–6.

This data is sequentially processed against a master file, using the employee number as a key. The master file used to process payroll is also used to maintain all personnel information. The data pertinent to payroll includes employee pay rates and year-to-date tax figures. Together, the punched-card file and the master file contain all the data necessary for the calculation of the employee's pay and the computer generation of a paycheck. The entire payroll can be processed in five to six hours.

The two batch systems above adequately serve certain user needs. However, many users also need to access data immediately to effectively perform their jobs. The engineering department is an example of such a user group.

The Spicer Transmission Division has produced approximately 5000 different types of transmissions over the years. The specifications for these transmissions are maintained in a transmission file. When a customer submits specifications for a new product, such as a heavy truck transmission, the engineer-

DANA CORPORATION

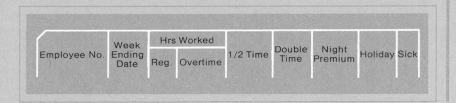

FIGURE 15–6
Format of Employee Input

369

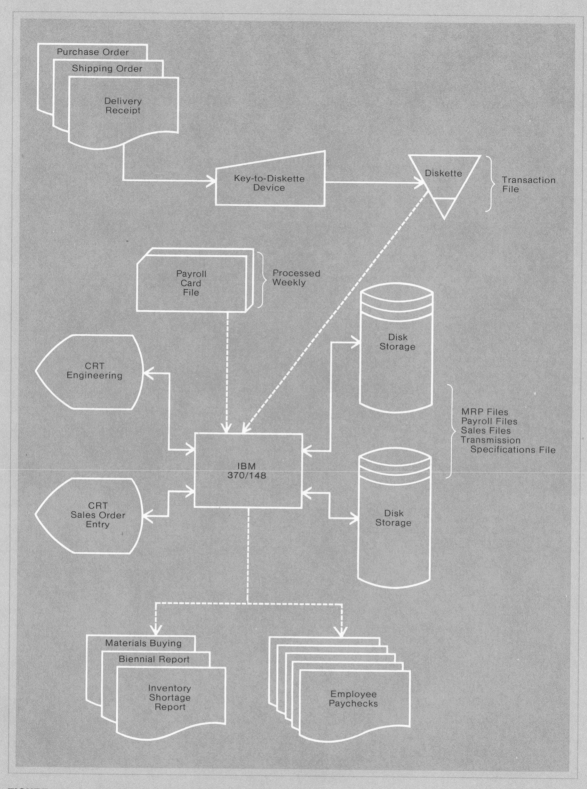

FIGURE 15—7

Data-Processing Environment at Dana Corporation

ing department must determine how that product will be produced. When the order is received, an engineer keys into the keyboard of a CRT any number of major component specifications for the ordered transmission. The computer searches the transmission file and indicates transmissions that have been produced previously that contain the largest number of identical parts. By determining the similarity of the new product to these previously produced transmissions, the engineer can determine the development or retooling necessary to produce the new product and provide the purchaser with accurate time and cost estimates.

A vitally important inline/direct-access system used extensively by the Spicer Transmission Division is the sales order-entry system. This system makes use of a complex data base containing data about customers, pricing, and part-number interchange. When a customer order is received, a sales entry clerk uses a CRT to obtain customer data such as the shipping address, terms, and party to be charged. The order information and part number are then entered. Since the customer's part number is often different from the number used by Dana to represent a part, the data base converts the cus-tomer part number to its respective Dana classification. The order is then submitted for processing. A computer-generated shop order is produced and entered into the manufacturing system. A customer acknowledgment form is also created for mailing to the buyer. The customer's order is also entered into a customer open-order file. It is through this file that a sales representative can inquire into the status of a customer's order at any time. This capability is used hundreds of times a day in response to customer inquiries. A schematic of the processing environment at Dana is presented in Figure 15–7.

As can be seen from the four applications presented above, a wide variety of circumstances dictate whether an application will be processed in inline/direct-access or batch/sequential mode. In general, applications that only need to be processed periodically, such as payroll, can be performed in batch mode. Systems requiring immediate updates must be processed inline/direct-access. Since it is usually more expensive to maintain an inline/direct-access application, management must be careful in the selection of a processing method for each new application.

DISCUSSION POINTS

1. What criteria are used by Dana to determine if an application will be processed batch/sequential or inline/direct-access?

2. Would an indexed-sequential file organization be appropriate for the sales order-entry application?

371

MANAGEMENT INFORMATION SYSTEMS | 16

OUTLINE

I. Information Requirements of
Managers
II. Effectiveness of MIS
III. Decision-Oriented Reporting
of MIS
  A. Information Reports
    1. Scheduled Listings
    2. Exception Reports
    3. Predictive Reports
    4. Demand Reports
  B. Management and MIS
IV. Design Alternatives
  A. Decentralized
  B. Distributed
  C. Hierarchical
  D. Centralized
V. Data Base Concepts
  A. Data Organization
    1. Physical vs. Logical

    2. Simple
    3. Inverted
  B. Data Base Management
    System (DBMS)
  C. Data Base Administrator
VI. Managing Information Systems
  A. Organization of Data
    Processing
  B. Top Management and User
    Involvement
  C. Managing System
    Development
  D. Managing Computer
    Operations
VII. Security
  A. Major Hazards
  B. Security Measures

INTRODUCTION

For many years, computers have been used to perform routine and repetitive operations formerly done manually. Although labor time is saved when functions such as payroll preparation and order writing are done by computer, these types of applications are not especially helpful to management in planning for the future or in controlling daily activities. To achieve its full potential, the computer must be integrated with people and procedures to provide information useful in decision-making. Simply having a computer does not insure an effective information system.

This chapter emphasizes the decision-oriented reporting of the management information system. Types of information needed by different levels of management are discussed. Several approaches to designing an information system to meet these information needs are presented. Data base concepts and data organization techniques are presented also, since these are vital to the design of an effective MIS. The management of the information system is discussed, with emphasis on organizational structure, management and user involvement in the MIS, and management of system development projects and computer operations.

The final section emphasizes security considerations involved in the operation of an information system. Security threats from natural disasters and human malice are discussed. Some preventive measures are suggested.

MIS FOR PRO BASKETBALL

Donald R. Moscato

Journal of Systems Management, November, 1976. pp. 24–25

Professional basketball fans are continually engaging in open debate regarding the strengths and weaknesses of particular athletes and their respective teams. However, the basic available facts about player performance show a scarcity of information on points scored, field goals and free throws attempted, field goals and free throws made, minutes played, assists, and rebounds.

Any information system design should consider the types of decisions which must be made by its users (coaches, players, scouts, owners, media, and league officials) and the particular information requirements needed to support them. Information requirements must be built upon basketball's basic transactions or activity units. For example, a field goal, a free throw, a steal, a rebound, a turnover, and a foul are some of the more obvious elemental activities. Each of these activities is of little value unless we add additional modifiers which characterize time, place, and form utility.

For example, the fact that a basket was made by a player is recorded in the score book under the existing arrangement. However, the score needs to be qualified as to how important it was in affecting the tempo of the game, was the game already won or lost, from where on the court was the shot made? From the "user's" viewpoint these are more important than the final score.

The coach gets paid for producing a winning team. He needs to know how does each player contribute to the team's standing. At present there are only crude statistics for this decision-making.

Other than "drawing power" there are few measures to evaluate a player's performance. Points scored, assists, rebounds, etc., are aggregate measures and do not capture the value of an athlete in a definitive manner. Contract negotiations can become more enhanced with the availability of more analytical information. Both owners and players will be able to cite particular attributes of player performance to strengthen their positions.

Scouts can analyze the data and provide supportive information to coaches on particular strategies against given players and teams. A new dimension to the notion of team balance can be developed by a given organization. The media will be able to explain hidden relationships and proposed strategies to their listeners and readers. League officials would serve as a clearinghouse of the data base of information. They could provide a service to all teams, the media, and other additional parties.

BUILDING THE DATA BASE

The heart of an effective data base system for pro basketball is in the coding structure employed to collect the data. The constraints are to capture the most data, quickly and at a reasonable cost. Basketball is a fast, dynamic game; however, it is not played continuously. Transactions occur at points in time during a given game by specific individuals, at specific places on a well-defined court. From a data-gathering point of view, basketball is a structured closed system that requires a coding system to capture the data and process it into useful information for decision-making.

The first step of the system design process is to develop a data element dictionary describing the game of basketball. For example, a field goal made can be recorded as just that or as a field goal made from a particular zone at a point in time in a particular quarter. With transaction data collected at the detailed level it allows analysis by the sub-items in the code, i.e., shots by zone, by tempo of the game, by quarter. Ultimately, it would be possible to build a trace-driven simulator of any given game if one wanted to collect the necessary data. While this is interesting it is not economically feasible.

One must differentiate between the data-collection process and the data-input process. In the data-collection process, special coding forms will have to be developed to facilitate the new scoring method. Each quarter will have a separate form to record the time-stamped transactions. Color coding the transactions could improve the efficiency of the data collection. The data would be recorded with the use of multiple spotters located in different locations of the arena. The accuracy of the data could be cross-checked with video monitors and traditional scoring procedures. The critical element is the ability to time-stamp the transaction.

Immediately after the game, the coded score sheets would be teleprocessed to the central data-processing facility. Since the data was captured at the elemental level the burden of summari-

zation and computation is placed upon the CPU. Within a short time the information would be available to the users.

OTHER DESIGN FEATURES

The real value of an MIS is in its potential as a decision support system. The availability of the data in a disaggregated form allows the user to experiment with the construction of new and more realistic measures of player and team effectiveness. Indices could be developed for various requirements. For example, one might rate players on their defensive prowess by considering the components of 'defense' and then constructing an appropriate index based on data in the data base.

The user could use his measurements of what is important to the decision at hand. Eventually, the most acceptable measures will be accepted as standards.

SUMMARY

To date, most applications of the computer in sports have been of a clerical nature. It is my belief that we can utilize the computer in sports in the same sense that it has been utilized in business—as an aid to the decision-making process.

As we can see from this article, computerized MISs are becoming essential in areas other than business. How these systems support decision-making and are used in various management settings is the emphasis in this chapter.

375

INFORMATION REQUIREMENTS OF MANAGERS

Typical data-processing applications involve manipulating data and producing reports. When an organization acquires a computer, the increased data-processing capability frequently results in the production of an overabundance of statistics—many of which are confusing and unnecessary. Computers are a definite asset in producing output such as payroll reports and bank statements. This use of computer power is a faster way of producing the same kinds of reports formerly prepared manually. A new concept has been introduced that extends computer use beyond routine reporting and into the area of management decision-making. This approach is known as a *management information system* (*MIS*). An MIS is a formal information network using computer capabilities to provide management information necessary for decision-making. The goal of an MIS is to get the correct information to the appropriate manager at the right time.

In considering a management information system, an organization must insure that it has the following characteristics:

● **Reports that are decision-oriented:** This can be achieved by providing information that is accurate, timely, complete, concise, and relevant. If the information does not have these characteristics, then the reports are not useful for decision-making.

● **Room for expansion and future growth:** The survival and growth of any organization depends on how well it adapts to the changing environment. Therefore, the MIS must be flexible enough to handle the changing needs of an organization. It should also have the capability to handle any increase in user requirements.

● **Results that the user needs:** As noted above, the primary objective of an MIS is to provide management information necessary for decision-making. An MIS cannot be successful if it does not meet the requirements of the user.

In designing management information systems, it is important to distinguish between the needs of different levels of management. Three levels of decision-making are generally recognized in an organization. They are depicted in Figure 16–1.

● **Strategic planning and creative decision-making:** This level pertains to activities which are future-oriented. They have a great deal of uncertainty associated with them. Examples include establishing goals and determining strategies to achieve the goals. Different strategies may involve decisions regarding introduction of new product lines, determination of new markets, acquisition of physical facilities, setting financial policies, generating capital, and so forth.

● **Tactical decision-making:** The emphasis here is on activities required to implement the strategies that have been determined at the top level. Thus, most middle-management decision-making is tactical in nature.

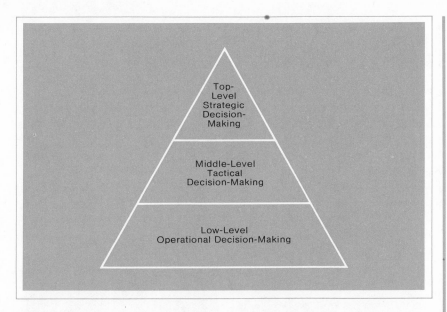

FIGURE 16–1
Levels of Decision-Making

Some of the different types of activities included in this level are
planning working capital, production scheduling, formulating budgets,
short-term forecasting, and personnel administration. Much of the
decision-making at this level pertains to control and short-run planning.

● **Operational decision-making:** This is the lowest level in the hierarchy. It includes the operating decisions made by first-line supervisors
and foremen to insure that specific jobs are done. The many activities
which pertain to this level include maintaining inventory records,
preparing sales invoices, determining raw material requirements, shipping orders, and assigning jobs to workers. Most of these operations can
be programmed because the decisions are deterministic. They follow
specific rules and patterns established at higher levels of management.
The major function of management at this operational level is controlling company results—keeping them in line with planned expectations
and taking corrective actions if necessary.

Since the information needs at the three levels of decision-making are
likely to differ, data has to be structured differently for each level. For
routine operating decisions like payroll preparation and replenishment
of inventory, separate employee files and inventory files are needed. As
we move up the pyramid to the middle level and top level, the data
should be organized to provide interrogative access and to be able to
handle routine types of information reports.

The operational level feeds summary information to the middle level,
and this in turn provides top-level management with further summary
reports (see Figure 16–2).

In addition to the horizontal breakdown of an organization into three
management levels, there exists a vertical functional breakdown. This

377

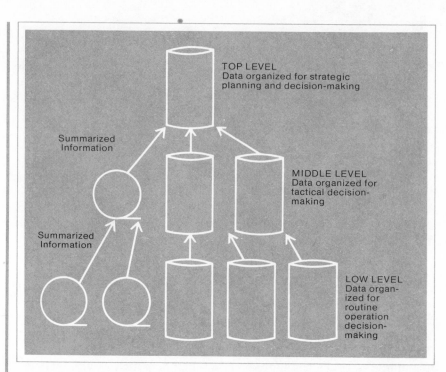

TOP LEVEL
Data organized for strategic
planning and decision-making

Summarized
Information

MIDDLE LEVEL
Data organized for
tactical decision-
making

Summarized
Information

LOW LEVEL
Data organ-
ized for
routine
operation
decision-
making

FIGURE 16–2
Information Needs Differ
with Levels of
Decision-Making

generates separate streams of information flow (see Figure 16–3). For example, the operational level of the marketing department might produce detailed sales reports for each product, but feed only a summary of these reports to the middle level of marketing management. This summary, which might show sales figures for each division of the company, is again summarized to show sales figures for the whole company and is then fed to the top-level marketing management.

FIGURE 16–3
Functional
Information Flow

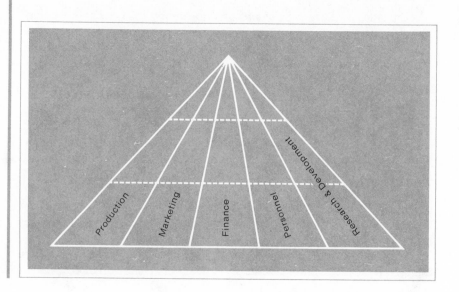

Production

Marketing

Finance

Personnel

Research & Development

EFFECTIVENESS OF MIS

To be effective, a management information system must be designed to meet the information requirements of all three levels of management. A major difficulty arises when such a system is designed, because of the differing nature of the decision-making process at each level. The information system must be tailored to provide appropriate information to each level.

Decisions made at the technical level are generally routine and well-defined. The needs of first-level supervisors can be met by normal administrative data-processing activities such as preparation of financial statements and routine record-keeping. Although this level of decision-making is fairly basic, it provides the data-processing foundation for the entire organization. If the information system proves faulty at this level, the organization faces an immediate crisis.

Tactical decision-making is characterized by an intermediate time horizon, a high use of internal information, and significant dependence on rapid processing and retrieval of data. The major focus of decisions deals with the determination of the most efficient use of organizational resources. Many of these middle-level decisions are ill-structured. An effective MIS can be an invaluable aid by providing relevant, concise, and timely information to support the manager in decision-making.

The main problems in MIS design arise when considering the information requirements of top-level management. It is extremely difficult, if not impossible, to clearly delineate top-level information needs because most problems are nonrepetitive, have a great impact on the organization, and involve a great deal of uncertainty. Most information systems at present serve the needs of the two lower levels, but are not adequately designed to cope with the variety of problems encountered by top management. However, well-designed management information systems can provide information which will help reduce the complexity and uncertainty of situations encountered at this level. Table 16–1 provides a summary of differences among the three levels of decision-making.

CHARACTERISTICS	LEVELS OF DECISION-MAKING		
	Technical	Tactical	Strategic
Time Horizon	Daily	Weekly/Monthly	Yearly
Degree of Structure	High	Moderate	Low
Use of External Information	Low	Moderate	Very high
Use of Internal Information	Very high	High	Moderate/Low
Degree of Judgment	Low	Moderate	Very high
Information Online	Very high	High	Moderate
Level of Complexity	Low	Moderate	Very high
Information in Real-Time	High	High	High

TABLE 16–1
CHARACTERISTIC DIFFERENCES IN LEVELS OF DECISION-MAKING

DECISION-ORIENTED REPORTING OF MIS

Typically, a management information system generates the following kinds of reports:

● **Scheduled listings:** These are produced at regular intervals and provide routine information to a wide variety of users. Since such listings attempt to provide information to many users, they tend to supply an overabundance of data, most of which may not be relevant. Such listings constitute the majority of output of current computer-based information systems.

● **Exception reports:** These are action-oriented management reports. Performance is monitored, and any deviation from expected results triggers the generation of an exception report. Such reports can also be produced during routine batch-processing. Exception reports are useful because they ignore all normal events and focus management's attention on the few abnormal situations which require special handling. This saves time and effort.

● **Predictive reports:** These are used for anticipatory decision-making (planning). Future results are projected on the basis of decision models. The levels of complexity of the models may range from very simple to highly complex. The usefulness of a model depends on how well it can predict future events. Management can manipulate the variables included in a model to get responses to "what if" kinds of queries. Thus, such models are suited to tactical and strategic decision-making.

● **Demand reports:** These are produced only on request. Since they are not required on a continuing basis in the total life of the MIS, they are often requested and displayed through online terminals. However, the MIS must have an extensive and appropriately structured data base if it is to provide responses to random queries. No data base can contain everything, but the data base of a well-designed MIS should include data that may be needed to respond to user inquiries. Demand reporting can be expensive, but it provides quick responses to unanticipated inquiries and permits decision-makers to obtain relevant and specific information on a timely basis.

Although an MIS can assist management, it cannot guarantee decision-making success. One problem that frequently arises is determining what information is needed by management. To many, decision-making is an individual art. Experience, intuition, and chance affect the decision-making process. In designing a system, the analyst relies on the user when determining information requirements. Frequently, a manager requests everything the computer can provide. The result is an overload of information. Instead of assisting the manager, information overload creates another problem: how to distinguish what is relevant from what is irrelevant.

After an MIS has been installed, management does not always feel as though the change is beneficial to decision-making. Often, the people who must use the system were not involved in the analysis and design of it. Managers frequently expect totally automatic decision-making after implementation of an MIS; they fail to recognize that only routine decisions can be programmed. Examples of routine decisions are ordering materials when inventory stock goes below a certain point and scheduling production. Decisions that are dependent upon more than quantitative data require human involvement, because the computer system has no intuitive capability. By making information available, the MIS helps to reduce uncertainty surrounding the decision-making process.

The future of an MIS depends largely upon the attitudes of management. In a very real sense, the success of the system is dependent upon user involvement. As routine decisions are taken over by the computer, managers may become resistant to future changes, either because their responsibility for decision-making is reduced, or because they fear the computer may make their positions obsolete. An MIS is most apt to be successful when it is implemented in an organization that is presently operating on a sound basis, rather than in an organization seeking a miracle.

DESIGN ALTERNATIVES

When considering alternative design structures, the analyst faces a virtually unlimited range of possibilities. This section covers four basic design structures: *decentralized, distributed, hierarchical,* and *centralized* (see Figure 16–4). These structures should be viewed as designated checkpoints along a continuous range of design alternatives rather than as separate, mutually exclusive options. For example, a system design may incorporate attributes from both the distributed system and the decentralized system. It is not limited to just one type. Computer systems do not exist in a vacuum; they must be designed to meet the needs of the organizations they serve.

In a decentralized design approach, the authority and responsibility for computer support is placed in relatively autonomous organizational operating units. These units usually parallel the management decision-making structure. Normally, there is no central control point; the authority for computer operations goes directly to the managers in charge of the operating units. Since there is no central control, each unit

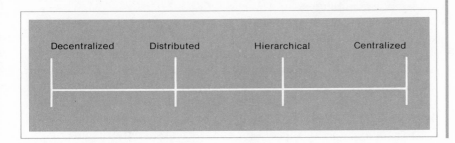

FIGURE 16–4
Design Structures

is free to acquire hardware, develop software, and make personnel decisions independently. Communication between units is limited or nonexistent, thereby ruling out the possibility of common or shared applications. Responsiveness to user needs is normally high because close working relationships are reinforced by the proximity of the system to its users. This decentralized design approach can only be used where an existing organizational structure supports decentralized management. It cannot provide support for the management information system concept. An example of the decentralized design approach is shown in Figure 16–5a.

The distributed design approach identifies the existence of independent operating units but recognizes the benefits of central coordination and control. The organization is broken into the smallest activity centers requiring computer power to support them. These centers may be based on organizational structure, geographical location, functional operations, or a combination of these factors. Hardware (and often people) are placed within these activity centers to support their tasks. Total organization-wide control is often evidenced by standardized classes of hardware, common data bases, and coordinated system development. The distributed computer sites may or may not share data elements, workload, and resources, depending on whether or not they are in communication with each other. An example of the distributed design approach is given in Figure 16–5b.

The hierarchical design is applied in an organizational-chart approach. There are multiple levels within the organization with varying degrees of responsibility and decision-making authority. In addition to this, the organization may have functional subdivisions like production, finance, and marketing, or it may have regional subdivisions based upon geographical considerations. The flow of information is between the different levels of management. Requests for information come down the different levels, and summarized information flows up these levels. There is limited communication between the subdivisions.

In hierarchical design, each management level is given the computer power necessary to support its task objectives. At the lowest level of the pyramid, limited support is usually needed because the work at that level is considered technical in nature. Middle-level support is more extensive, because managerial decisions at that level require more complicated analysis (hence, more information processing). Finally, top-level executives seek little detailed information. They deal with general issues, requiring information that can be obtained only with greater processing and storage capabilities.

In a hierarchical system, there is also a segregation of data bases along regional or functional lines. The data bases within each level may or may not be standardized. Communication between levels is essential, but the line of responsibility for computer systems is normally traced through several levels rather than handled within all levels of the organization. The tendency, then, is for the largest group of people and machines—those at the top level—to assume responsibility for coordination and control. An example of this design approach is shown in Figure 16–5c.

382 The most traditional design approach involves the centralization of

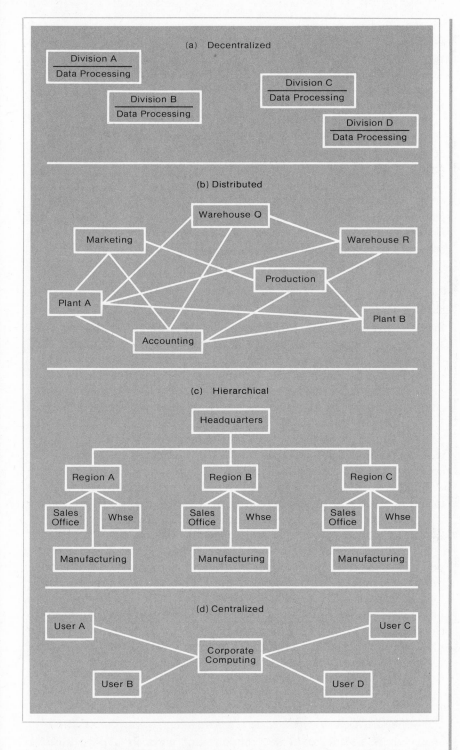

FIGURE 16–5
Sample Design Structures

computer power within an organization. A separate department is set up to provide data-processing facilities for the entire organization. The personnel of the electronic data-processing (EDP) department, like other staff personnel, support the operating units of the organization in meeting their task objectives. All program development, as well as all equipment acquisition, is controlled by the EDP group. Standard regulations and procedures are employed with respect to an organization-wide system. The capability for distant units to use the centralized equipment is provided through remote access via a communication network. A common data base exists, permitting authorized users to access information (see Figure 16–5d).

The advantages of the centralized approach are that it permits economies of scale, reduces redundancy and duplication of data, and results in better utilization of data-processing capability. However, a centralized design is not always best suited to all divisions of an organization. Response to division needs is generally slow because priorities are assigned based on overall organizational needs. Also, many managers prefer to control their own data-processing needs; they are reluctant to relinquish authority to a central EDP staff group.

DATA BASE CONCEPTS

Prior to the integrated MIS approach, departments had their own separate data files and collected their own input. The accounting data structure was set up to suit financial accounts; the marketing structure was designed to facilitate sales reports; and the production data was oriented toward inventory levels and scheduling. These files frequently contained duplicate data about customers, employees, and products.

In contrast, the installation of an MIS requires the use of some form of general data storage. The organization's data must be stored in such a way that it can be accessed by multiple users for varied applications. The cornerstone of an MIS is its data base.

A *data base* is a grouping of data elements structured to fit the information needs of all functions of an organization. The data is independent of its use. It is not structured specifically for one application task; instead, it is usable in all operations within the organization.

In addition to reducing data redundancy and increasing data independence, the data base concept provides flexibility. When a change needs to be made to data in the data base, it needs to be made only once (at least in most cases, since there is only one copy of the data). There is no need for multiple changes as are required when separate files are stored. The integration of data permits the results of updating to be available to the entire organization. Furthermore, the system can respond to information requests that previously would have bridged several departments' individual data files.

Data Organization

Data can be arranged in several different ways in a data base. A distinction must be made between the physical arrangement of data, which refers to how the data is stored on a data-recording medium, and the logical structure of the data, which refers to how the data is viewed by an applications program. A logical file may extend across more than one physical file. Conversely, a physical file may contain one or more logical files. A file is physically associated with a direct-access storage device such as a disk storage unit or with a sequential medium such as magnetic tape or punched cards.

Magnetic tape is very useful for storing large masses of data; however, the sequential nature of tape severely restricts the variety of approaches to data organization that can be employed. To permit direct access to and retrieval of data items, a DASD must be used. The capabilities provided by a DASD are needed to handle the variety of logical relationships that exist among data elements. Routines can be established to retrieve any combination of data elements from any number of different storage devices, in any manner or order desired, as specified by user requirements. Increased sophistication of operating software has relieved the applications programmer of the burden of physically arranging the data in files. Logical data structures are an attempt to model the real-world relationships that exist among data items. These data structures must be defined by the programmer.

There are two basic types of logical structures: simple and inverted. A *simple structure* (or *list*) is just a sequential arrangement of data records. All the records have the same logical significance, and they are viewed as independent entities. Figure 16–6 illustrates such a structure. If the records are ordered (i.e., arranged in a specific sequence), then the list is referred to as a *linear structure*.

A list can be subdivided into groups to provide valuable information. Each group has one "owner" record and any number of "member" records. Such a list, a customer-order file, is illustrated in Figure 16–7. The owner record of each group contains the customer number, name, and address. Each member record consists of the item number, item description, quantity ordered, and total price.

A typical file, with a simple structure, is shown in Figure 16–8. Each record of the file has five characteristic fields called *attributes*—name, title, education, department, and sex. Such a file structure is appropriate for generating reports, but it is cumbersome for handling inquiries. To overcome its limitations, an *inverted structure* can be introduced.

The inverted structure is more suited to responding to inquiries. This structure is built by preparing sublists for each attribute and cross-referencing each value in the original file to other values by means of its address. Figure 16–9 shows the result of inverting the file shown in Figure 16–8. The major advantage of the inverted structure is that a variety of inquiries can be handled quickly and efficiently. However, a major disadvantage is that all values must be linked and indexed to permit fast retrieval.

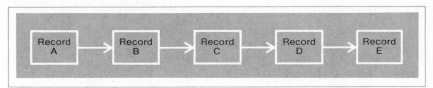

FIGURE 16—6

Example of a
Simple Structure

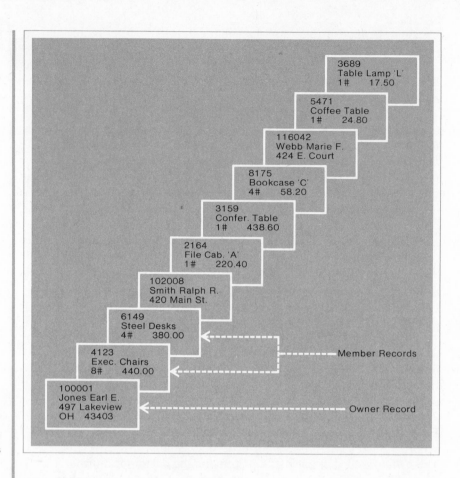

FIGURE 16—7
Customer-Order File with
Owner and Member Records

ADDRESS	NAME	TITLE	EDUCATION	DEPARTMENT	SEX
018021	Borgelt	Asst. Prof.	Ph.D.	Marketing	Male
018024	Henkes	Professor	D.Sc.	Management	Male
018046	Pickens	Instructor	M.S.	Accounting	Male
018020	Deluse	Asst. Prof.	Ph.D.	Marketing	Female
018016	Kozak	Assoc. Prof.	Ph.D.	Accounting	Male
018412	Gadus	Assoc. Prof.	Ph.D.	Accounting	Male
018318	Cross	Asst. Prof.	M.B.A.	Management	Female

FIGURE 16—8
File with
Simple Structure

Some typical inquiries and responses obtained from the inverted file follow.

Question: How many female assistant professors do we have and what are their names?

Response: Total of 2: Deluse, Cross

Question: List the names of all employees who have a Ph.D.

386 Response: Borgelt, Deluse, Kozak, Gadus

NAME		TITLE		EDUCATION		DEPARTMENT		SEX	
Value	Address	Value	Address	Value	Address	Value	Address	Value	Address
Borgelt	018021	Instructor	018046	M.S.	018046	Marketing	018021	Male	018021
Henkes	018024	Asst. Prof.	018021	M.B.A.	018318		018020		018024
Pickens	018046		018020	Ph. D.	018021	Management	018024		018046
Deluse	018020		018318		018020		018318		018016
Kozak	018016	Assoc. Prof.	018016		018016	Accounting	018046		018412
Gadus	018412		018412		018412		018016	Female	018020
Cross	018318	Professor	018024	D. Sc.	018024		018412		018318

Question: List the management department staff and their titles.

Response: Henkes, Professor; Cross, Assistant Professor

Question: How many instructors do we have and what are their education backgrounds?

Response: One, M.S.

Question: List the names of the staff members who have an M.B.A. and teach in the accounting department.

Response: None

FIGURE 16–9
Inverted Structure

In addition to the two file structures that we have discussed, there are other more complex structures. Examples are the hierarchical (tree) structure and the network structure. These structures are suitable for applications that require multiple linkages among data items. A detailed explanation of these structures is beyond the scope of this text.

Data Base Management System (DBMS)

A *data base management system* (*DBMS*) facilitates the use of a data base. It is a set of programs that provides: (1) a method of arranging data to limit duplication; (2) an ability to make changes to the data easily; and (3) a capability to handle direct inquiries that require access to the data. In effect, the DBMS serves as the major interface between the data base and three principal users—the programmer, the operating system, and the manager (or other information user). By installing an available DBMS, an organization greatly reduces its need to develop detailed data-handling capabilities.

One of the major purposes of a DBMS is to effect physical data independence. Physical independence permits the physical layout of data files to be altered without necessitating changes in applications programs. This insulation between a program and the data with which the program interacts is extremely desirable. The programmer does not have to pay attention to the physical nature of the file. He or she can simply refer to the specific data that the program needs.

387

Most existing data base management systems provide the following facilities:

● Integration of the data into logical structures that model the real-world relationships among data items

● Provision for storing the volume of data required to meet the needs of multiple users

● Provision for concurrent retrieval and updating of data

● Method of arranging data to eliminate duplication and thereby to avoid the inconsistencies that arise from duplication

● Provision for privacy controls to prevent unauthorized access to data

● Controls to prevent unintended interaction or interference among programs that run concurrently

● Capability for data base interface from within applications programs coded in available programming languages (and yet, not be restricted to just one of them)

Some of the limitations of the data base approach are:

● An error in one data record may be propagated throughout the data base.

● Design and implementation of a data base system requires highly skilled, well trained people.

● Elimination of duplication and redundancy makes it more difficult to reconstruct records if data is lost due to a programming error or system malfunction.

● Major attention must be given to the security of the system, since all the data resources of the organization can be accessed once the data base has been accessed.

Data Base Administrator

The development of data base systems has created the need for a person to manage the data base—a *data base administrator*. This person is responsible for the creation, maintenance, and updating of the data base.

The data base administrator's technical functions include:

● Establishing a data dictionary as a means of standardizing data definitions and insuring the uniqueness of each data item

● Advising system analysts and users about file design

● Designing security controls to guard against unauthorized access to the data base

In addition to these technical responsibilities, the data base administrator has planning, organizing, and control responsibilities. The administrator plans changes and alterations in the data base; organizes the data items into appropriate structures for easy access; and monitors the data base to detect response, usage, and security problems.

The data base administrator must have both managerial and technical expertise to handle these and other data base responsibilities. Sometimes, a data base administration staff is established as a support group to carry out these functions.

MANAGING INFORMATION SYSTEMS

Organization of Data Processing

Traditionally, data-processing activities have been performed within the functional departments of organizations. However, because of increased record-keeping requirements, the ever-present need for current information, and the necessity to adapt to a complex, changing environment, many organizations have been forced to consolidate their data-processing operations. The computer has been used increasingly as a tool to manage the paper explosion that threatens to engulf many organizations.

The rapid growth of computer-based data processing has affected the location of the EDP department in an organization's structure. In most organizations, data processing originated in the accounting area, since most record-keeping was done there. However, management then recognized that information is a scarce and valuable resource of the entire organization. There is increasing emphasis on the data-processing activity and on its elevation in the organizational structure.

Look at the organizational chart for a typical manufacturing firm in Figure 16–10. It indicates two general locations for the EDP department.

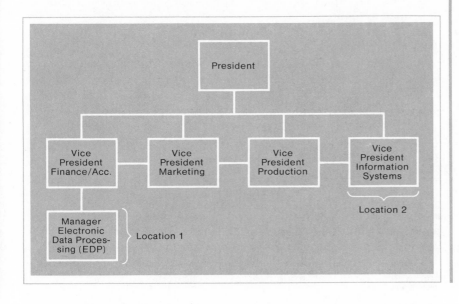

FIGURE 16–10
Possible Locations for
EDP Department in
Organizational Structure

Location 1 is the traditional one: the EDP manager reports to the vice president of finance and accounting. This location is satisfactory only if the other functional areas do not need or desire to use computer capabilities. Unless the processing requirements of the finance department are extensive, the computer is not used to its full potential under such an arrangement.

Thus, this location has the following drawbacks:

● Bias toward financial applications in setting job priorities. Since the data-processing manager reports to the financial vice president, he or she will obviously give high priority to financial applications.

● Being at a lower level in the organizational hierarchy prevents the data-processing personnel from advising different functional divisions on suitable applications, and inhibits overall integration of the data-processing function.

Location 2 overcomes these limitations. Elevating the data-processing activity to the same status as the traditional line functions (production, marketing, finance) reflects the corporate-wide scope of information. Instead of referring to the activity as the EDP department, the organization often refers to it as the Management Information System (MIS) Department, to stress the increased importance of this function. The Vice President of Information Systems provides valuable input concerning which new applications are appropriate for the organization. The independent status of the MIS Department also helps to insure that each functional area gets impartial service and that their particular information requirements are integrated to meet organizational goals.

The internal organizational structure of the MIS Department itself can take various forms. Perhaps the most common breakdown is by data-processing function: system analysis and design, programming, and computer operations. This type of organizational structure is illustrated in Figure 16–11.

An alternative type of structure emphasizes project assignments. Analysts and programmers are combined in teams to work on specific projects. Such a team also includes personnel from user departments who assist throughout the life cycle of the project. As projects are completed, teams are restructured and team members are assigned to new projects. Such an approach is illustrated in Figure 16–12.

Top Management and User Involvement

Time and again it has been demonstrated that a management information system cannot succeed without top-management support and extensive user involvement. Unless top management is convinced that an MIS can bring tangible benefits to the organization, it may fail to provide adequate support to this area in terms of capital and human resources. The result will be a poor system which in turn fails to provide adequate support of management decision-making. Even with top

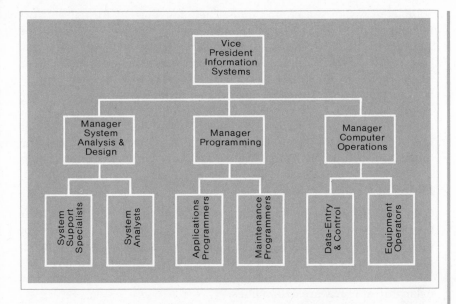

FIGURE 16—11
Functional Organization
of MIS Department

management's support, success is not assured. The intended users of information must be convinced that the system will be a benefit. This can be achieved only if the users are involved in the development of the new system. They should help to decide what the system will do, and thus share direct responsibility for the benefits/losses that may accrue from it.

Managing System Development

System analysis, design, and implementation were discussed in detail in Chapter 14. It is the responsibility of the MIS (data-processing) manager to monitor the total system development cycle to insure that projects are

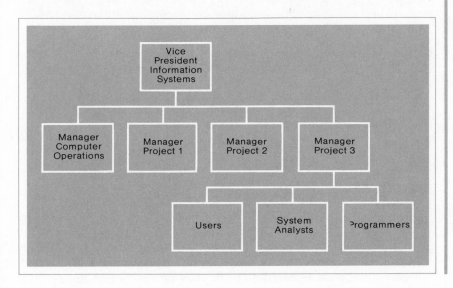

FIGURE 16—12
Project Organization of
MIS Department

completed within reasonable time schedules. Various formal network techniques like *PERT* (*P*rogram *E*valuation and *R*eview *T*echnique) and *CPM* (*C*ritical *P*ath *M*ethod) are available for project planning and control. To use such techniques, the project must be broken into distinct activities; the sequence in which the activities are to be performed must be determined; and a time estimate must be established for each activity. Then, a scheduling chart can be designed. The responsible manager can monitor the progress of the project by comparing estimated completion times for different stages of the project with actual times. If delays occur, the reasons behind them must be identified and corrective actions taken.

Managing Computer Operations

Most modern computer systems cost millions of dollars. There is an increasing concern that the CPU and peripheral devices of a system be used efficiently. Management can collect data and analyze it to determine the degree of utilization of the hardware. Higher efficiency and increased *throughput* can be obtained by proper job scheduling and balancing of hardware capabilities.

In addition to effective hardware utilization, the data-processing manager must strive for a high degree of maintainability and reliability. Preventive maintenance schemes must be developed for both the hardware and the software. Better systems can be achieved through the following practices:

- Establishing standard procedures to control actions that initiate and implement change

- Using a modular approach for both hardware and software so that systems can be expanded; a complete switch to new equipment and new programs should not be required

- Strict adherence to documentation standards. Software maintenance is impossible if an organization does not have extensive documentation to clarify how specific programs do the processing within various applications

- Implementing standard control and audit procedures to ascertain that the administrative policies and procedures established by management are followed

- Planning for all contingencies so that data-processing interruptions do not become catastrophic

SECURITY

A computer system can be a great advantage to an organization that uses its capabilities to improve information flow. However, it can also lead to great problems in the area of data *security*. Data in storage is susceptible to fraud, embezzlement, fire, flood, unintentional mistakes, and employee malice. As a result, data protection has become a key issue at most, if not all, computer installations.

Data security can be penetrated by a visitor who casually picks up a stack of punched cards and keeps them as souvenirs, by an operator who hits a button and mistakenly erases a tape, by an employee who manipulates data for his or her own benefit, by an outsider who breaches security and accesses confidential information, or by a natural disaster that destroys part or all of the computer installation.

Major Hazards

The major hazards to which most computer systems are exposed are fire, natural disasters, environmental problems, theft, fraud, and sabotage.

- *Fire:* This is one of the more apparent problems because most computer installations use combustible materials—punched cards, paper, and so on. Additionally, if a fire gets started, water cannot be used to extinguish it because the water may damage magnetic storage media and hardware. Carbon-dioxide systems are also hazardous because of danger to employees who may be trapped in the computer room. Halon is a nonpoisonous chemical gas that can be used in fire extinguishers, but systems that use halon are more costly than carbon-dioxide or water systems.

- *Natural disasters:* Many computer centers have been damaged or completely destroyed by floods, cyclones, hurricanes, and earthquakes. Floods pose a serious threat to the computer hardware and wiring. However, water in the absence of heat will not destroy magnetic tapes unless the tapes are allowed to retain moisture over an extended period of time. Protection against natural disasters should be considered when the location for the computer center is chosen. For example, if a proposed area is prone to floods, the center should be located at a higher and safer spot.

- *Environmental problems:* Usually, computers are installed in buildings that were not originally planned to accommodate them. Thus, water and steam pipes may run through a computer room. Bursting of these pipes can result in extensive damage. Pipes on floors above the computer room are also potentially hazardous. All ceiling holes should be completely sealed. Other environmental problems include power failures, brownouts (temporary surges or drops in power), external radiation, and destruction of data on magnetic media due to magnetic fields created by electric motors in the vicinity of the computer room.

- *Theft:* Computer installations are particularly vulnerable to theft. Yet, security procedures are lax at most computer centers. A clever person may steal thousands of dollars worth of equipment. For example, hardware valued at nearly $20,000 was stolen recently from the University of Connecticut's Institute of Materials Science. More serious, however, is the theft of data and software. Magnetic tapes and disks can be copied easily and quickly, without leaving any trace. Several state policemen in Boston, Massachusetts, were investigated for allegedly selling criminal history files to private investigators, who in turn sold them to credit-reporting agencies.

393

Outsiders can also be involved in computer crimes. Remote terminals can be used to communicate with the computer from external locations. Telecommunication lines provide opportunities for wire-tapping and establishing unauthorized communication links. Systems involving telephone lines can be breached easily, particularly if knowledge of an appropriate telephone number is all that is needed to gain access to the system.

● *Fraud:* United States businesses lose millions of dollars every year because of fraud and embezzlement. Computers are playing an increasingly prominent role in such criminal activities. The prime reason for this is that detection of irregularities can be extremely difficult in computer-based systems. Input data can be easily manipulated, especially by people who work for the business organization. A teller at New York's Union Dime Savings Bank netted about $1.5 million over a period of three years. When a customer made a deposit, the teller pocketed all the money and used a computer terminal to update the customer's account by transferring money from one of many other accounts that had been inactive for years.

Other methods used by embezzlers include writing improper computer programs, altering files, and tapping communication channels to illegally intercept or transmit data. In one scheme, a programmer at a bank coded a routine to transfer the fractional pennies from interest payments on savings accounts to his account. Since thousands of customers were serviced, this added up to a substantial amount of money. Another widely cited example of fraud involved the Equity Funding Life Insurance Company of Los Angeles. In this particular case, officers of the company created thousands of fictitious insurance policies and then sold the bogus policies to other insurance companies. The computer was used to create the phony policies and keep track of the vast amount of data associated with them.

● *Sabotage:* This represents the greatest risk to any computer installation. It is extremely difficult and expensive to provide adequate security against deliberate sabotage. Radical students, disgruntled employees, and people outside of organizations have discovered that great damage can be done by sabotaging computer centers with little risk of apprehension. For example, magnets can be used to scramble code on tapes; bombs can be planted; and communication lines can be cut.

Security Measures

There is no simple solution to the security problem. To combat potential dangers, organizations have instituted various security measures. Some of these restrict access to computerized records. Others are used to reconstruct destroyed data. Some examples are given below:

● Authorized users are given special codes and numbers. Remote-terminal users have their own unique codes, and batch-processing users have specific job cards.

394 ● The scope of computer access is proportionate to a user's security clearance and job responsibility. Specific portions of the data base can only be accessed by those whose job requirements necessitate such access.

● Installations are guarded by internal security. For example, access to the data-processing department may be restricted to personnel with special badges and keys.

● Backup copies of data are stored outside the organization location, and recovery procedures are established.

These security measures are not complete. They may not prevent internal sabotage, fraud, or embezzlement. An organization member with a special access code may steal classified information. In fact, computer crimes have been called the "white-collar crimes of the future." Banks and insurance companies are especially susceptible. Many organizations have had such problems. Often, they do not wish to report the incidents because of the bad publicity and the difficulty in solving the crimes.

SUMMARY

● A management information system is a formal information network using computer capabilities to provide management information necessary for decision-making. The goal of an MIS is to get the correct information to the appropriate manager at the right time. The MIS should produce reports that are decision-oriented, have room for expansion and future growth, and produce results that the user needs.

● Three levels of decision-making can be distinguished in an organization: (1) strategic planning and creative decision-making is handled by top management; (2) tactical decisions are made by middle management; and (3) operational decisions are made by lower-level management. Data must be organized and defined differently at each level. Difficulties in structuring data increase as one moves toward higher-level decision-making.

● An MIS typically generates four kinds of reports: (1) scheduled listings produced at regular intervals; (2) exception reports, generated when deviations from expected results occur; (3) predictive reports used for projecting future outcomes; and (4) demand reports, which answer random requests for information.

● There are virtually an unlimited number of ways an MIS can be designed. Common approaches are the decentralized, distributed, hierarchical, and centralized structures. In the decentralized approach, authority and responsibility for computer support are placed in relatively autonomous organizational units. In the distributed approach, computer support is placed in key activity centers, and information may be shared among them. In the hierarchical approach, each management level is given the computer power needed to support its task objectives. The centralized approach generally uses a single computer department to provide data processing for the entire organization.

395

● A data base is a grouping of data elements structured to fit the information needs of all functions of an organization. The data base concept reduces data redundancy and provides increased flexibility.

● A simple structure is a logical structure of data in which all records are arranged sequentially and viewed as independent entities. An inverted structure incorporates lists of attributes and addresses of items having these attributes for easy cross-referencing of data. An inverted structure requires much online storage, but it is ideal for responding to inquiries.

● A data base management system (DBMS) is a set of programs that provides: (1) a method of arranging data to limit duplication; (2) an ability to make changes to the data easily; and (3) a capability to handle direct inquiries.

● The internal structure of an organization must insure that the MIS provides impartial service to each functional area and that their particular information requirements are integrated to meet organizational goals. Top-management support and user involvement in MIS design and evaluation are essential to the success of the MIS project.

● Management of the system department involves monitoring the total system development cycle to insure that projects are completed within reasonable time schedules. Management of computer operations involves striving for effective utilization of hardware and a high degree of maintainability and reliability.

● Security is a key consideration in computer installations. Data in computer files is susceptible to: natural hazards such as fire, floods, and earthquakes; crimes involving fraud, embezzlement, theft, and sabotage; and unintentional employee mistakes.

REVIEW QUESTIONS

1. Top management is involved in strategic planning and creative decision-making. Why is it especially difficult to supply needed information to this level of management? What are some differences in the information needs of top, middle, and lower-level management?

2. Which types of reports are most helpful in planning for the future? Which types of reports are generated most easily by the MIS?

3. Contrast the distributed and centralized MIS design alternatives. Which of these alternatives is likely to be more responsive to user needs?

4. What is a data base? How can a data base be structured to respond to a variety of inquiries? Should the data base be designed to answer all possible inquiries? Explain.

5. Why is top-management and user involvement in the design of an MIS essential?

6. "White-collar crimes" are a major problem of computer security. What steps can be taken to remedy this problem? How effective have current remedies been?

Since 1903, Ford Motor Company has grown from a tiny operation in a converted Detroit wagon factory to a multinational enterprise with more than 300,000 stockholders. Today, Ford serves tens of millions of customers throughout the United States and overseas. It is the world's fourth largest industrial enterprise in terms of sales, with revenues totaling $38 billion and assets exceeding $19 billion. It is also the second largest auto company in the world.

Ford Motor Company entered the age of computers in 1955. Today there are data-processing centers in every Ford division and support equipment in every plant, both in the United States and abroad. The number of computers used for business applications exceeds 200. The computers vary in size and capacity and are supplied by a number of manufacturers, including IBM, Hewlett-Packard, Honeywell, Burroughs, and Univac.

In the industrial control area, the number of computers exceeds 500. Most of them are minicomputers supplied by Digital Equipment Corporation, General Automation, and Control Data. Corporate-wide, there are over 2000 system analysts, programmers, and operations researchers and almost 3000 operating personnel. The number of systems exceeds 2500. There are over 50,000 associated programs and modifications.

The Ford Communications and Data Processing Center in Dearborn, Michigan, is one of the largest data-processing centers in private industry. Ten large-scale computers are available to provide data-processing services to the company's Dearborn-area facilities. The center is also the headquarters for Ford's world-wide communication activities. A network of teletypes connected to Ford's communications processor transmits thousands of messages per day throughout the world.

Successful applications of computers in all phases of the company's activities range from product development to management control. With the aid of the computer, Ford analyzes market data to monitor customer reaction to present products and to suggest possible product improvements to meet the changing needs of its customers. In the area of product design and development, body-design engineers use a computer-directed scanner to translate the dimensions of clay models into digital coordinates. For capacity and product

planning, a computer forecasting model projects total car and truck demand several years into the future. For production planning, a computer makes monthly forecasts of orders by body styles, options, and option combinations.

The development of computer systems has helped Ford management to improve operations related to the crucial area of customer service. By developing dealer-oriented applications close to the retail level, management can more efficiently control and monitor sales and inventory. Computer/communication systems have improved parts service to dealers and to independent service facilities. Efficient parts service in an operation as extensive as Ford is vital to good customer service. There are over 226,000 different parts needed to service all Ford vehicle products sold in the U.S. More than 7000 Ford and Lincoln-Mercury dealers and 1000 independent distributors cannot be expected to stock all 226,000 parts.

Therefore, a system has been developed to allow dealers to order and receive parts in the most timely manner and at the same time to allow corporate management to control inventory.

Figure 16–13 shows the flow of a parts order originated by any of the approximately 35 million customers owning Ford-built vehicles in operation. Each dealer stocks from 8,000 to 12,000 parts and must depend on the Ford parts distribution system to replenish this inventory as well as to ship parts not normally stocked.

Dealers are serviced by 21 Ford Parts Distribution Centers (PDCs) across the nation, based on a hierarchical stocking pattern with the fastest-moving parts stocked at the greatest number of locations. Twelve of these PDCs individually stock from 14,000 to 15,000 of the fastest-moving parts. Eight other PDCs individually stock from 30,000 to 40,000 different parts; this stock is made up of the fastest-moving inventory as well as

FIGURE 16–13
Ford's Volume of
Customers, Dealers, and
Parts Distribution Centers

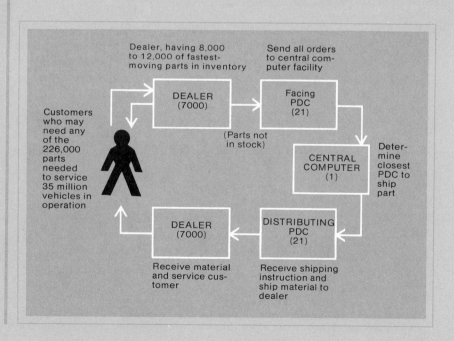

inventory that moves at an intermediate speed. The final PDC is the National Parts Distribution Center. It carries the 160,000 to 180,000 different parts which make up the slowest-moving inventory. Each dealer places a parts order with the nearest (facing) PDC but the parts may be shipped from any one of the 21 PDCs.

A system has been developed by the Ford Parts and Service Division to get parts to dealers quickly. Distributed-processing capabilities allow an individual dealer to order any part from his or her facing distribution center. The system was designed in-house and has been in use for over five years.

Each dealer can communicate part orders to the facing PDC by telephone, mail, or a specialized input terminal. All the PDCs have small computers through which dealer orders are transmitted by leased lines to the Ford Parts and Service central computer facility at Dearborn. The system is centered around a data base at the central facility which determines the location from which each ordered part will be sent.

An individual dealer is faced with three ordering alternatives: (1) weekly stock order with which the stock supply normally ordered is replenished and for which a 5 percent incentive discount is received; (2) a unit-down order which ships ordered parts every other day and for which no discount is received; and (3) a critical order for which parts are shipped within 24 hours and for which a

10 percent surcharge must be paid (see Table 16–2). Each order condition requires a different search pattern contained within the data base.

As an example, for a unit-down order condition, the data base contains a logical order pattern for each of the dealers. For each dealer ordering any specific part, the pattern centers around the most economical warehouse/transportation combination for supplying the part. If the part is not available at the closest location that normally stocks the part, a computer search is made at the next three closest stocking locations. If the part is still not available, it is placed on a back-order at the closest location that normally stocks the part. ·

If, for example, a Toledo Ford dealer needs an exhaust manifold for a 1966 Mustang, that dealer notifies the facing PDC in Cleveland (see Figure 16–4). From the Cleveland PDC computer, the order is transmitted to the Ford Parts and Service central computer facility at Dearborn; the central computer searches the data base and finds the PDC closest to the Toledo dealer that has the part. If the Cleveland PDC normally stocks these exhaust manifolds, it is the first logical stocking location for the Toledo dealer. If the part is found there, it is shipped, and the master part file is updated to show the shipment of one exhaust manifold from the Cleveland PDC. However, if the Cleveland PDC is temporarily out of the part, the master part file in Detroit is

ORDER CONDITION	INCENTIVE	PART LOCATION SEARCH
Weekly stock order	5% discount	First normal stocking PDC
Unit-down order	No discount	Up to four closest stocking PDCs
Critical order	10% surcharge	Up to 21 PDCs

TABLE 16–2
ORDERING ALTERNATIVES

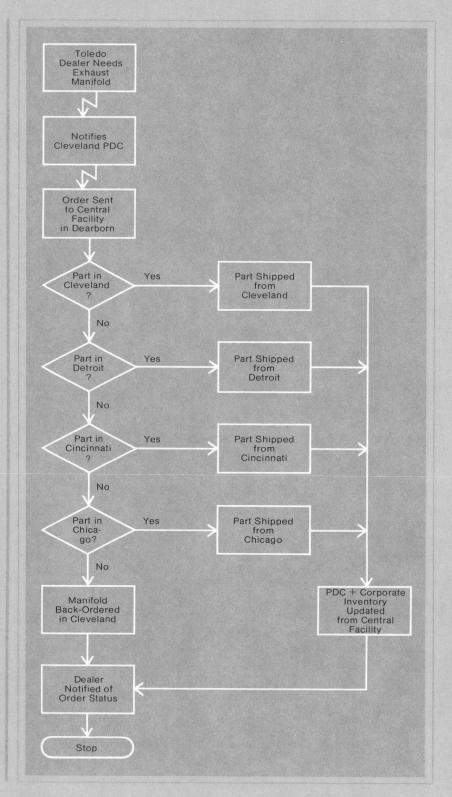

searched for the exhaust manifold. Again, if the part is located, it is shipped, and the master file is updated. If it is still not located, the part file in Cincinnati is searched. If the part is located, the normal procedure occurs. If not, the procedure is repeated once again for Chicago. If the exhaust manifold is not found during the computer search of the fourth location, it is put on a back-order at the Cleveland facing PDC. The entire search process is done in a fraction of a second.

When the part has been located, the Cleveland facing PDC sends the dealer a hard-copy listing of the part that has been ordered and the location from which it will be shipped. The central facility at this time processes the order and updates the inventory for the PDC from which the part is being sent as well as quantitatively controlling corporate inventory.

The system was designed for real-time operation to help dealers get parts which they normally do not carry in stock, on a timely basis. This system is also used for normal stock reorder. By maintaining an inventory record of each part stored at each center, it also provides timely inventory information to management. An up-to-the-minute report can be generated to show exactly what parts and how many of them are in stock at any distribution center.

DISCUSSION POINTS

1. How is the parts-ordering system used as a management tool for corporate decision-making?

2. What benefits do the individual Ford dealers derive from this system?

section **V**

ISSUES OF INDIVIDUAL CONCERN

17
CAREER OPPORTUNITIES

18
COMPUTERS AND SOCIETY

CAREER OPPORTUNITIES | 17

OUTLINE

I. People and Their Roles
  A. Information System Manager
  B. System Analyst
  C. Programming Personnel
    1. Applications
    2. Maintenance
    3. System
  D. Data-Processing Operations Personnel
    1. Librarian
    2. Computer Operator
    3. Data-Entry Operator
  E. Data Base Administrator
II. University Programs
  A. Undergraduate Programs
    1. Organizational Concentration
    2. Technical Concentration

  B. Graduate Programs
III. Professional Associations
  A. American Federation of Information Processing Societies (AFIPS)
  B. Association for Computing Machinery (ACM)
  C. Data Processing Management Association (DPMA)
  D. Association for Systems Management (ASM)
  E. Institute for Certification of Computer Professionals (ICCP)

INTRODUCTION

Future career opportunities in the rapidly growing computer industry seem to be practically limitless. An increasing number of skilled people will be needed to support the tremendous growth in data-processing activities. The computer field is not only expanding rapidly, but also constantly changing. Colleges and professional associations are continually trying to help students and practitioners stay abreast of new developments in the area of data processing.

This chapter takes a close look at computer-related occupations. The responsibilities and required personal characteristics and training for various data-processing positions are discussed. Also, university programs for training individuals for careers in data processing are described. Finally, some of the professional associations that promote the continued education of computer practitioners are identified.

BURGEONING COMPUTER SOFTWARE INDUSTRY FORESEES FIVEFOLD INCREASE IN JOBS BY 1985

N. R. Kleinfield
Staff Reporter

The Wall Street Journal,
May 12, 1977, p. 40

AGS Computers, Inc., has an open offer to its employees that will land them $1000 if they refer a programmer to the company. The Union, N.J., company doesn't have to hire the person for the employee to get his loot. It just wants to know about him.

"Of course, we've had people refer their wives and all that," says Lawrence Schoenberg, the company's president. "We've had some good people referred. But, the sad truth of the matter is, it hasn't really worked. We're still short. Now, we're thinking about upping the ante. We need bodies."

Unemployment may be awesome in many industries these days. But at companies like AGS Computers, which sells computer software, jobs are going begging. A need for qualified computer experts is besetting the data-processing industry, and the worst hit by the labor shortage appears to be the rapidly growing software industry.

Software, by and large, consists of the programs, or sets of instructions, used to tell a computer what to do and how to do it. The industry essentially was born in June 1969 when International Business Machines Corp. began to sell software and hardware (the actual computers) separately, rather than strictly as a unit. This allowed the formation of companies that could furnish competing software packages.

ASTONISHING GROWTH

Around 800 independent software suppliers have come into being in the U.S., employing roughly 42,000 computer specialists. There is no telling how many available jobs there are—estimates hover around 15,000—but demand is increasing at an astonishing rate. By 1985, it's expected there will be 232,000 computer specialists in the field.

Demand for computer specialists is booming among all companies that use the electronic devices. Computer makers also develop software and frequently sell systems complete with programs, and users sometimes set up departments to develop their own software. According to the U.S. Labor Department, employment of computer specialists by all these sources is expected to swell to 476,000 people by 1985 (the department's most recent tabulation, using 1974 figures, had 308,000 people in the field).

As this happens, software companies are figuring on siphoning away a good many specialists currently working in data-processing departments of companies, and on attracting new people entering the field. Hence, while the software companies now employ less than 15% of all computer specialists, by 1985 they expect to employ around half of them.

The people will be needed because software purchases are mushrooming. According to Software Association statistics, U.S. software purchases soared to $840 million last year from $655 million in 1975 and $500 million in 1974. (Of the total cost of a computer system to a user, software accounts for about 75%.) Frost & Sullivan, an international market research firm, estimates that software expenditures will climb to a remarkable $3.5 billion in 1984. The Software Association says this projection is "very conservative."

BUTCHER AND BAKER

Demand for software reflects burgeoning use of the computer. John Imlay, president of the Software Association, says, "The cost of computer power has come down so far that the butcher, the baker, and the candlestick maker can afford computers. Minicomputers, for instance, are available to virtually anyone. The creative uses of this new level of computers are endless—video games, and everything. And so this new technology has opened up varied thousands of jobs."

Frost & Sullivan reckons that the cost of computer power today is a tenth of what it was only three years ago. As some indication of how widespread use has become, it's estimated that from 20,000 to 100,000 individuals now own computers. Minicomputer growth means more software-related jobs. Monmouth County, N.J., recently advertised for a county police computer officer. The county is willing to pay $18,500 a year to someone not only familiar with police functions, but also with five years of computer experience.

Says Mr. Imlay: "With the lower cost of hardware, the small company can afford a machine, so the concept of, say, a bookkeeper becomes that of a computer operator. What was the bookkeeper with a quill 10 years ago has become a full-fledged computer programmer. More and more people who weren't previously exposed to computers are now expected to know how to use them."

"WE'LL PAY YOU"
It is around 7 to 10 times cheaper for a company to purchase software from a professional supplier than to try to develop it in-house, software people say, and so more and more orders are flowing to software suppliers. They are desperate for people to handle them.

AGS Computers' Mr. Schoenberg says, "The major thing holding this company back from further growth is the manpower shortage. We're constantly 20 to 30 people short in a company of 150 people. We put an ad in *The New York Times* classified section, which, if you'll notice, is about a third full of data-

processing ads. The ad basically said to come in and be your own employment agency. It said that if you came in and we hire you, we'll pay you the fee you would have paid an agency to get a job. The ad attracted virtually no notice."

John Imlay, who is also president of Atlanta-based Management Science America, Inc., has watched his company's ranks explode from 70 people in 1970 to over 300 now. Last year, he hired 120 people. He expects to hire 160 more this year, if he can find them.

Charles Fox, President of Fox & Associates, an Atlanta recruitment firm that specializes in the data-processing field, reports that the average job opening took three to five days to fill in 1972. These days, it requires 12 to 16 days. Mr. Fox says he wouldn't be shocked if the figure jumped to 16 to 20 days by year's end. "Beyond that, I wouldn't even want to predict," he adds. "The long-term opportunities in the software industry are exceptional. A top-level woman and the very specialized programmer are the hardest of all to find."

IBM ABOVE THE BATTLE
Training seems to be at the root of the problem. Training breadth and quality are insufficient to meet market needs. General programmers of two years experience remain most in demand, though most companies don't want to do training. They may lack time or money for it, and once they do train someone, there is no guarantee that the employee won't scoot over to another firm.

IBM, which does a lot of training of computer specialists, says it isn't having any particular trouble tracking down programmers for its "limited openings." Besides IBM's considerable reputation, industry people feel that the company's

407

willingness and ability to train have kept IBM above the labor shortage problem.

Lloyd Baldwin, vice-president of administration of Pansophic Systems, Inc., an Oakbrook, Ill., software supplier, suspects that part of the trouble is that the industry hasn't communicated its requirements to computer schools effectively. Furthermore, he says, technological changes are occurring in the industry at a much more rapid pace than curriculum changes in computer schools. Thus many school graduates aren't overly marketable. But at good schools such as Chubb Institute for Computer Technology, in Short Hills, N.J., graduates are much sought-after.

"We had a rule of thumb awhile ago," says Peter Enander, Chubb's director, "that if 50% of our students had jobs as programmers by graduation, we were on target. In the next four to six weeks, we figured the rest would have jobs. By graduation last November, it turned out all but two students had jobs out of 22 graduating."

Chubb's enrollment is growing apace. It favors students with two years of college or work experience, and enrolls numerous converts from other fields. "We get the English major who couldn't get a job, or the person who goes out and teaches a couple of years and burns himself out," Mr. Enander says.

"We had a person who worked four years as an auto mechanic. He graduated and is working as a programmer and the company loves him. We had a furniture stripper who's been hired as a programmer. We get all kinds."

TRAINING THE KEY

Ultimately, the software industry is hopeful that more Chubbs will sprout, as well as more computer courses in colleges. It recognizes that part of the answer to its labor shortage will have to be increased training by companies themselves. "No question about it," one industry man says. "We need these people. We can't find them. We've got to turn them out ourselves."

For those who qualify, the rewards can be great. Starting salaries average about $10,000 a year, but the figure can rise to $30,000 or so within five years.

Whether enough applicants will be turned out remains problematical. Milton Wood, president of Wood Computer Associates, a Chicago-based recruitment firm, says "Right now, an individual competent in software can pick who he wants to work for, what part of the country he wants to work in, and, to a large extent, how much he wants to make. There's going to be more training, but I don't see the demand being overshadowed by the supply for at least 10 years. It's downright incredible."

The computer has been responsible for the elimination of jobs and displacement of personnel in some industries; but, as we can see from this article, it has also opened new fields of employment for thousands. This chapter outlines some of the careers available in the computer industry.

PEOPLE AND THEIR ROLES

A typical computer installation in a business organization is expected to perform at least three basic functions: system analysis and design, programming, and computer operation. Personnel with the education and experience required to work in these areas are needed. In addition, an information system manager is needed to coordinate the activities, set goals for the data-processing department, and establish policies and procedures to control and evaluate both personnel and projects in progress.

Information System Manager

The *information system manager* is responsible for planning, organizing, staffing, and controlling all data-processing activity. Historically, "data-processing managers" have been programmers or system analysts who have worked their way up to management positions with little formal management training. But the increasing emphasis on "information systems" and "information management" has resulted in a change. Professional managers with demonstrable leadership qualities and good communication abilities are being hired to manage the information system department.

The *management information system (MIS) manager* is responsible for planning and tying together the entire information resources of the firm. The manager must organize the physical and human resources of the department to achieve company goals. He or she must devise effective control mechanisms to monitor progress. This means that the MIS manager must possess the following knowledge and skills:

- A thorough understanding of the organization, its goals, and its business activities

- Leadership qualities to motivate and control a group of highly skilled people

- Knowledge of data-processing methods, and familiarity with available hardware and software

A man or woman seeking a career in information system management should have a college degree. For managing business data-processing centers, a degree in business administration with a concentration in the area of management information systems is desirable. Obviously, practical experience is required before a person can handle high-level management responsibilities.

System Analyst

The *system analyst* is the key person in the analysis, design, and implementation of the formal information system. The analyst has the following responsibilities:

409

● Assisting the user in determining information needs

● Gathering facts about the existing system and analyzing them to determine the effectiveness of current processing methods and procedures

● Designing new systems, recommending system changes, and being involved in implementing these changes

The analyst's role is critical to the success of any management information system. He or she acts as an interface between the users of the MIS and the technical personnel such as the programmers, machine operators, and data base administrators. This role becomes more important as the cost of designing, implementing, and maintaining information systems rises.

To be effective, the system analyst should possess the following characteristics:

● A general knowledge of the firm, its goals and objectives, and the products and services that it provides

● Familiarity with the organizational structure of the company, and the management rationale for selecting that structure

● Comprehensive knowledge of data-processing methods and of current hardware, and familiarity with available programming languages

● The ability to plan and organize one's own work, and to cooperate and work effectively with both technical and nontechnical personnel

● A high level of creativity, including the ability to communicate clearly and persuasively

System analysts should be college graduates with backgrounds in management, computer science, data processing, and mathematics. Many universities offer majors in management information systems; their curricula are designed to train people to be system analysts.

System analysis is a growing field. According to the United States Department of Labor, system analysts can look forward to brighter employment prospects through the mid-1980s than workers in almost any other occupation. However, there may be some occupational changes. Job opportunities in data-processing service firms may stabilize because more users will be installing their own systems. Offsetting this will be the small users' rising needs for analysts to design systems for small computers.

Programming Personnel

Generally there are three levels of programmers in most organizations: *applications programmers, maintenance programmers,* and *system programmers.* Persons in any of the three categories should possess the following basic skills:

● Good command of the programming language or languages in which programs will be written

● A knowledge of general programming methodology and of the relationship between programs and computer hardware

● Analytical reasoning ability and attention to detail

● Creativity and discipline to develop new problem-solving methods

Applications programming constitutes the bulk of all programming tasks. It involves taking a broad system design prepared by the analyst and converting it into instructions for the computer. In addition to the basic skills outlined earlier, an applications programmer should have some idea of the objectives of the organization, and a basic understanding of accounting and management science if he or she is involved in business data processing.

Program maintenance is a very important but neglected activity. Many large programs are never completely debugged, and there is a continuing need for improvement of major programs. To be effective, a maintenance programmer needs considerable experience, and a high level of analytical and logical ability. Complete and consistent documentation is an invaluable aid in program maintenance.

System programmers are responsible for maintaining system software. They are expected to develop utility programs, maintain compilers and assemblers, and be involved in decisions concerning hardware/software additions or deletions. To be able to perform these duties effectively, a system programmer should have: (1) a comprehensive background in the theory of computer-language structure and syntax, and (2) extensive and detailed knowledge of the hardware being used and the software that controls it.

Educational requirements for programmers vary. For example, a system programmer should have a formal educational background in computer science or professional training in that area. In general, however, a college degree, though desirable, is not a prerequisite for a programming job. There are many technical colleges that emphasize programming, and many individuals and private organizations teach programming in two- to three-month courses.

The demand for applications programmers has been great during the past five years. Although growth is expected in the future, it will be slower and some changes are anticipated. With the development of simpler, interactive high-level languages, users will be able to communicate with the computer very easily. Consequently, the emphasis will shift from efficient coding to problem-solving.

Data-Processing Operations Personnel

The *librarian* is responsible for the control and maintenance of the files and programs stored on cards, magnetic tapes, and magnetic disks which are kept in the computer library for subsequent processing or

411

historical record-keeping. The librarian's other tasks include transferring backup files to an alternate storage site, purging old files, and supervising the periodic cleaning of magnetic tapes and disks.

The librarian's job is important because he or she controls access to stored master files and programs. Computer operators and programmers do not have access to the tapes or disks without the approval of the librarian. This prevents unauthorized changes or processing runs.

The educational background required for this particular job is not extensive. A high school diploma is adequate. In addition, the individual must have some knowledge of basic data-processing concepts, and should possess clerical record-keeping skills.

A *computer operator's* duties include setting up the equipment for particular jobs, and mounting and removing tapes or disks as needed. This person should be able to identify any operational problems and take appropriate corrective action. Most modern computers have sophisticated operating systems which direct the operator through messages generated during processing. However, the operator is responsible for reviewing errors made during operation, determining their causes, and maintaining operating records.

Most people in this job receive their training as apprentice operators. Few have college degrees. Formal training is available through technical schools and some junior colleges. To be effective, training must include on-the-job experience.

A *data-entry operator's* job involves transcribing data into a form suitable for computer processing. He or she uses a keypunch or key-entry device to transfer data from source documents to punched cards, magnetic tape, or magnetic disk. In online systems, data is entered directly from operating sites.

Usually, all forms of data-entry require manual dexterity and alertness on the part of the operator. No extensive formal education is required (a high school diploma is sufficient); however, all personnel in this category should be trained carefully, to minimize the incidence of errors.

Data Base Administrator

With the increasing trend toward data base management, a new role has been created in the data-processing area—that of the *data base administrator* (*DBA*). The primary responsibilities of this individual include:

● Developing a dictionary of standard data definitions so that all records are consistent

● Developing and designing the data base

● Maintaining the accuracy, completeness, and timeliness of the data base

● Designing the data base security system to guard against unauthorized access and use of files

● Facilitating communication between analysts and users of the data base

● Advising analysts, programmers, and system users as to the best ways to use the data base

To handle these responsibilities, the data base administrator must have a high level of technical expertise. In addition, he or she must have the ability to communicate effectively with diverse groups of people. Looking at the functions that a data base administrator performs, we can conclude that the job requires a college education with concentration in the areas of data processing and management. Since this is a newly created position, most individuals working at this job were selected because of their practical experience in developing data base systems. However, many colleges now offer courses in data base management, and one can expect organizations to recruit individuals with appropriate backgrounds.

A block diagram showing career paths available to people in the computer-operations area and system and programming area is given in Figure 17–1.

UNIVERSITY PROGRAMS

Considerable attention has been paid recently to the development of educational programs for the training of qualified people in the area of information systems. Because the field has evolved so quickly, most educational institutions have not been able to react fast enough to

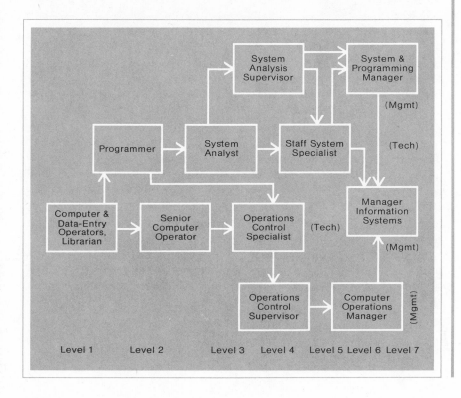

FIGURE 17–1
EDP Career Paths

develop programs that provide the background and basic skills required of computer professionals. In the past, a college degree may not have been necessary to pursue a career in information systems; but informal surveys have shown that a college degree is an implicit requirement for entry-level positions in the areas of programming and system analysis and design in most firms using modern computer equipment.

Recognizing the disparity between the educational needs of information system personnel and the availability of adequate undergraduate and graduate programs to satisfy these needs, the Curriculum Committee on Computer Education for Management was formed by the Association of Computing Machinery (ACM). One of the main tasks of the committee was to formulate recommendations for curricula in the area of information systems. The basic recommendations of this committee for undergraduate programs for information system specialists were presented in terms of two concentration options:[1]

● *Organizational concentration:* This option is designed to prepare a person to be an effective computer user. The undergraduate student, therefore, combines information-system course work with the academic area of emphasis in a field of application such as business or government.

● *Technological concentration:* This option is designed to prepare a person for an entry-level job in a data-processing department. The typical graduate starts as a programmer and, through practical experience and advanced education, moves into the area of system analysis and design.

The committee suggested a set of 11 undergraduate courses. Seven of these are needed to get the organizational concentration; eight are required for the technological concentration. Four courses are common to both areas of concentration. The complete set of 11 courses, and the breakdowns for organizational and technological concentrations, are shown in Figure 17–2.

For a graduate professional program in information system development at the master's level, the committee formulated a set of 13 courses. These courses are grouped into four categories as shown in Figure 17–3.[2]

The relationships of the courses and course groupings are illustrated in Figure 17–4. The arrows indicate the precedence relationships between the courses. The labels outside the boxes indicate the general areas of knowledge and abilities to which the proximate courses are relevant.

Academic programs at the doctoral level reflect the particular interests of the faculty and thus vary considerably from one university to another. Therefore, the ACM Curriculum Committee on Computer Education for Management has not made any recommendations for such programs.

---

[1]*Communications of the ACM* Vol. 16, No. 12 (December 1973).
[2]*Communications of the ACM* Vol. 15, No. 5 (May 1972).

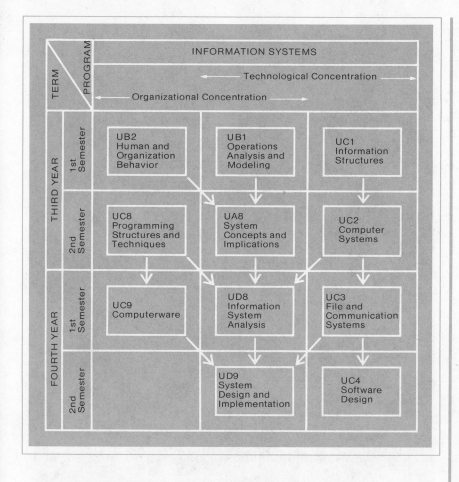

FIGURE 17–2
Undergraduate Courses

FIGURE 17–3
Courses Suggested for
Graduate Program

Course Group A: Analysis of Organizational Systems
  A1. Introduction to Systems Concepts
  A2. Organizational Functions
  A3. Information Systems for Operations and Management
  A4. Social Implications of Information Systems

Course Group B: Background for Systems Development
  B1. Operations Analysis and Modeling
  B2. Human and Organizational Behavior

Course Group C: Computer and Information Technology
  C1. Information Structures
  C2. Computer Systems
  C3. File and Communication Systems
  C4. Software Design

Course Group D: Development of Information Systems
  D1. Information Analysis
  D2. System Design
  D3. Systems Development Projects

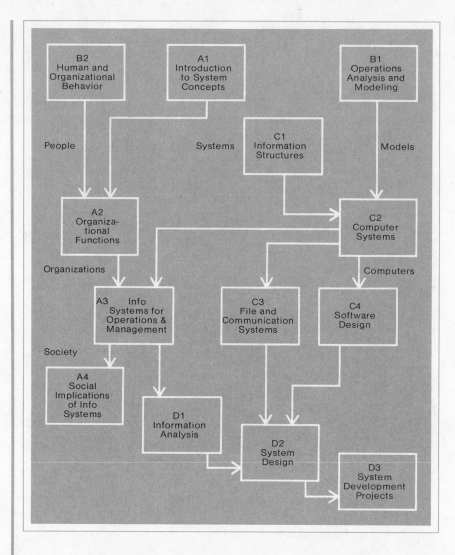

FIGURE 17–4
Course Relationships

Although the ACM committee has developed fairly comprehensive curricula for both undergraduate and graduate programs in information systems, not many universities have adopted these suggestions in their entirety. Two general trends have emerged.

1. The Computer Science Department (which is usually part of the College of Arts and Sciences) is offering a technical concentration in information systems by providing mostly hardware- and software-oriented courses. These are supplemented with courses in traditional business areas like general management and accounting.

2. The College of Business is offering a concentration in information-systems/data-processing through the accounting department or an autonomous information system department. This approach provides the student with a fairly comprehensive background in business-related areas and with moderate technical expertise in areas such as programming, system analysis, and system design.

The objective of both approaches above is to prepare individuals for entry-level positions in the field of information systems. The former may be more suited for occupations stressing scientific applications of computers; the latter is deemed more appropriate for data-processing jobs in business organizations.

PROFESSIONAL ASSOCIATIONS

These professional societies have been formed to increase communication among professional people in computer fields, to continue the professional education of members, and to distribute current knowledge through publication of professional journals.

American Federation of Information Processing Societies (AFIPS)

The American Federation of Information Processing Societies is a national federation of professional societies established to represent member societies on an international basis for the advancement and dissemination of knowledge of the information processing societies. AFIPS was organized in 1961. There are two categories of AFIPS participation: (1) member societies that have a principal interest in computers and information processing, and (2) affiliated societies that, although not primarily concerned with computers and information processing, have a major interest in this area. Some of the prominent constituent societies of AFIPS are the Association for Computing Machinery (ACM), the Data Processing Management Association (DPMA), the Institute of Electrical and Electronic Engineers, Inc. (IEEE), and the American Society for Information Sciences (ASIS). Affiliated societies of the AFIPS include the American Institute of Certified Public Accounting (AICPA) and the American Statistical Association (ASA).

Association for Computing Machinery (ACM)

The ACM is the largest scientific, educational, and technical society of the computing community. Founded in 1947, this association is dedicated to the development of information processing as a discipline, and to the responsible use of computers in increasingly complex and diverse applications. The objectives of the association are:

● To advance the science and art of information processing, including the study, design, development, construction, and application of modern machinery, computing techniques, and programming software

● To promote the free exchange of ideas in the field of information processing in a professional manner, among both specialists and the public

417

● To develop and maintain the integrity and competence of individuals engaged in the field of information processing

The ACM has established Special Interest Groups (known as SIG's) within the society to address the wide range of interests in the computing field. For example, SIGSMALL was established for those members of the ACM interested in small computers, and SIGPLAN was formed to address interests in programming languages.

Data Processing Management Association (DPMA)

Founded in Chicago as the National Machine Accountants Association, the DPMA was chartered in Illinois in December 1951. At that time the first electronic computer had yet to come into commercial use. The name "machine accountants" was chosen to identify persons associated with the operation and supervision of punched-card equipment. The society took its present name in 1962.

DPMA is one of the largest world-wide organizations serving the information-processing and management community. It comprises all levels of management personnel. Through its educational and publication activities, DPMA seeks to encourage high standards in the field of data processing and to promote a professional attitude among its members. Its specific purposes are:

● To promote and develop education and scientific inquiry in the field of data processing and data-processing management

● To inculcate among members a better understanding of the nature and functions of data processing

● To study and develop improvements in equipment related to data processing

● To supply members with current information in the field of data-processing management, and to cooperate with them and with educational institutions in the advancement of the science of data processing

● To encourage and promote a professional attitude among members in their approach to, and understanding and application of, the principles underlying the science of data processing

Association for Systems Management (ASM)

The Association for Systems Management was founded in 1947. It is headquartered in Cleveland, Ohio. The ASM is an international organization and is engaged in keeping its members abreast of the rapid growth and change occurring in the field of system management and information processing. It provides for the professional growth and development of its members and the system profession through:

● Extended programs in local and regional areas in the fields of education and research

● Its annual conference and committee functions in research, education, and public relations

● The promotion of high standards of work performance by members of the ASM and members of the system profession

● Publication of the *Journal of Systems Management*, technical reports, and other works on system subjects of current interest to system practitioners

The ASM has five technical departments: Data Communications, Data Processing, Management Information Systems, Organization Planning, and Written Communications. An ASM member can belong to one or more of the technical departments, depending upon his or her particular interests.

Institute for Certification of Computer Professionals (ICCP)

The ICCP is a nonprofit organization, established in 1973, for the purpose of testing and certifying knowledge and skills of computing personnel. A primary objective of the ICCP is to pool the resources of constituent societies so that the full attention of the information-processing industry can be focused on the vital tasks of development and recognition of qualified personnel.

The establishment of the ICCP was an outgrowth of studies made by committees of the DPMA and the ACM, during which the concept of a "computer foundation" to foster testing and certification programs was formulated. In 1974 the ICCP acquired the testing and certification programs of DPMA, including the *Certificate in Data Processing* (*CDP*) examination, which DPMA had begun in 1962. All candidates for the CDP examination must have at least five years of work experience in a computer-based information-system environment. The examination consists of five sections: data-processing equipment, computer programming and software, principles of management, quantitative methods, and system analysis and design. Any qualified person is eligible to take the examination. All five sections must be completed successfully to receive the certificate.

The ICCP is involved in the improvement of existing programs and the establishment of new examinations for various specialties. A framework for a broad spectrum of tests and the relationship of these tests to job functions and curricula is under development.

SUMMARY

● An information system manager is responsible for planning, organizing, staffing, and controlling data-processing activities. This individual must have good leadership qualities, a thorough knowledge of the organization, a knowledge of computer-processing methods, and good communication abilities.

419

● A system analyst assists in the analysis, design, and implementation of formal information systems. This individual must assist the user in determining information needs, analyze existing systems to determine their effectiveness, and design new systems or recommend system changes. The system analyst is the interface between the users of an MIS and the technical personnel such as programmers and computer operators.

● Programming personnel include applications programmers, maintenance programmers, and system programmers. All three types of programmers must have a thorough knowledge of the programming languages they use, a knowledge of programming methodology, analytical reasoning ability, and creativity for developing new problem-solving methods.

● Data-processing operations personnel perform the tasks necessary for actual computer operations. A librarian is responsible for the control and maintenance of files and programs which are kept in the computer library for subsequent processing or historical record-keeping. The computer operator sets up equipment for program runs, and corrects operational problems that occur during processing. A data-entry operator is responsible for transcribing data into a form suitable for computer processing.

● A data base administrator oversees the development and maintenance of a complete, accurate, and secure data base to serve the organization. Since this individual has the most knowledge of the firm's data base, he or she must advise analysts, programmers, and system users as to the best ways to use the data base.

● In response to the growing need for well-trained data-processing personnel, many universities and colleges are developing more complete graduate and undergraduate programs for students in computer science and information systems. The Curriculum Committee on Computer Education and Management has recommended two separate concentration options for undergraduate curricula: an organizational concentration to prepare individuals to be effective computer users; and a technical concentration to prepare individuals for entry-level positions in a data-processing department.

● Many universities are designing their programs using one of the two approaches. In the first approach, the Computer Science Department offers technical courses supplemented with traditional business and management courses. In the second approach, the College of Business offers a concentration in information systems with greater emphasis in business-related areas, and moderate emphasis in technical areas. Both approaches are designed to train students for entry-level positions in a data-processing department.

● There are many professional organizations in the field of computers and information systems. These associations encourage increased communication and diffusion of knowledge among computer practitioners through publications, seminars, and other educational programs.

REVIEW QUESTIONS

1. Contrast the job responsibilities of the system analyst and the applications programmer. Which position requires the greater educational background? Explain.

2. The data base administrator occupies a newly created position in the data-processing department. What has created the need for this position?

3. Various college curricula for students planning careers in data processing were discussed in this chapter. Do you agree with the programs now being offered? What changes do you recommend?

4. If you choose a career in data processing, will you join any of the professional associations discussed in this chapter? If yes, which ones? If no, why?

CIVIL SERVICE COMMISSION

In addition to the opportunities available in private industry, the federal government, through the Civil Service Commission, offers a virtually unlimited range of career opportunities in computer-related fields. Applications presently in operation include the analysis of air traffic patterns, the structure of chemical compounds, foreign policy determination, and missile design. In nearly every instance in which the government touches the lives of United States citizens, a computer is providing support. Consider the difficulty of issuing retirement checks or income tax refunds, tabulating election results, or monitoring driver's license applications without the assistance of computers.

The federal government obviously needs people to support these various activities. These individuals are broadly classified in four major groups: computer system administrators, computer specialists, computer operators, and computer aides and technicians. Table 17–1 indicates the total numbers of

people employed in these classifications, the corresponding average salaries, and the federal agencies that hire the most significant numbers. The Department of Defense employs nearly 60 percent of these individuals, but there are also a substantial number of jobs in civilian agencies.

The computer specialist classification includes programmers, system analysts, equipment analysts, and computer specialists. More people are employed under this classification than under the other three classifications combined. A programmer plans and develops the machine logic and program steps necessary to perform the data manipulations involved in applications programs as specified by the system analyst. The analyst must possess the ability to logically relate the activities involved in the flow of data through the system, as well as extensive knowledge of hardware capabilities. Equipment analysts must be technically oriented since they are often responsible for

TABLE 17–1
EDP EMPLOYMENT BY
FEDERAL
AGENCIES

| JOB TITLE | AVERAGE SALARY | DEPARTMENT | | | | | |
		Defense	Treasury	HEW	Agriculture	Other	TOTAL
Computer System Administrator	$28,037	755	158	200	46	464	1,623
Computer Specialist	$21,882	14,891	1,457	2,065	925	6,041	25,379
Computer Operator	$12,965	7,082	1,008	940	201	2,132	11,363
Computer Aides and Technicians	$15,144	3,961	424	409	306	1,349	6,449

evaluating equipment prior to purchase decisions. A computer specialist is an individual with outstanding abilities in more than one of the areas described above. He or she usually is involved in a broad range of activities.

Computer system operators and peripheral-equipment operators are grouped under the computer operator category. The system operator is concerned with the operation of the computer control console and the devices with which it is connected. A peripheral-equipment operator works with card readers and card punches, printers, optical scanners, and other related equipment.

Aides and technicians do support work associated with computer operations. Typical tasks performed by a technician include the translation of program routines and detailed logic steps designed by others into machine-readable instructions and code, developing charts showing the flow of documents and data in specified areas, and revising programs.

Of unique benefit to federal data-processing employees are the educational development programs available through the Civil Service Commission's Bureau of Training. The Bureau of Training is divided into many functional areas, one of which includes training and education programs in automatic data processing (ADP).

The Civil Service Commission segments the entire country into ten regions which serve as a basis for distributed operations. The Bureau of Training has established regional ADP Management Training Institutes in these regions. The courses offered by these institutes fall into three broad categories—user education, computer specialist training, and upward mobility training.

User education programs are designed for people whose jobs are affected by the computer in some way, but who are not directly involved in the operation of the computer. The courses offered include Management Introduction to ADP, Executive Seminar in ADP, and Introduction to ADP Systems Analysis. The purpose of these courses is not to help an individual develop extensive technical competence, but rather to familiarize him or her with the capabilities of an ADP system.

The upward mobility training curriculum is designed to provide ADP technical training for government personnel in lower-level jobs who want to upgrade their skills. These people are usually working in dead-end jobs and have no previous training in data processing. Beginning courses in this sequence include Introduction to Computer Operation, Introduction to Computer Programming, and Basic Card-Punch Operating Training.

The most technically involved courses are offered in the area of computer specialist training. As mentioned earlier, computer specialists are employees who are involved in programming, system analysis, and equipment analysis. These courses are designed to provide further training to those integrally involved in the everyday operation of a computer facility. As new and better technologies evolve, these specialists must keep abreast of the latest advancements.

Largest of the ADP Management Training Institutes is the Automatic Data Processing Management Training Center (ADPMTC) in Washington, D.C. Participants in the ADPMTC courses have direct access to a third generation, medium-scale, batch processing computer which provides opportunities for "hands-on" experience. In 1976, this center conducted 220 course sessions for more than 4800 government employees. Indications are that this number will continue to grow.

The ADPMTC offers training in each of the three categories described above. The courses offered at this center are more in-depth and more comprehensive than those offered at the regional centers. Figure 17–5 indicates the variety of educational opportunities available to computer specialists. From basic courses such as COBOL, FORTRAN, and BASIC programming, the trainee can progress to advanced programming techniques, system analysis, and eventually , complex telecommunication and data base concepts.

Fundamentals of ANS COBOL is an example of a programming course offered, which is structured to help participants develop a working knowledge of the COBOL programming language. The two-week workshop covers such topics as computer fundamentals, the program-development process, a description of the four divisions in a COBOL program, and the actual writing and testing of programs. The knowledge gained from this course serves as the foundation for COBOL Programming Techniques, a course dealing with file storage, input/output control, sorting, and file-processing methods as executed in the COBOL programming language.

The individual who is already proficient in programming can select from among various advanced courses, such as Structured Design. This course is designed to help participants understand design techniques which support structured programming, team organization, top-down approach, and HIPO. These techniques become more important as the government obtains the massive buildups of online storage required for data bases. The course in Data Base Management Systems ties the structured-design fundamentals together with complex data base concepts and functions. Topics covered include data base software, evaluation, and various DBMS packages currently available.

The goal of all the programs offered by the ADP Management Training Center is to develop competent personnel to staff federal agencies. By training those already familiar with agency operations, a higher level of efficiency can be readily achieved. The federal govern-

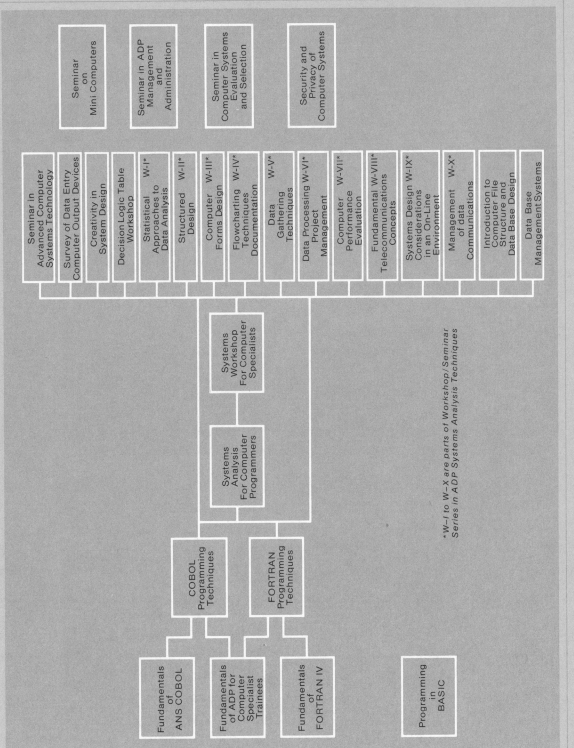

FIGURE 17-5
Computer Specialist Training

ment strives not only to provide jobs for many people in data processing and related fields, but also to enable them to upgrade their job skills. This opportunity makes government employment extremely attractive.

DISCUSSION POINTS

1. Generally, what courses would be beneficial in an undergraduate curriculum to adequately prepare a graduate for a computer-related job with the Civil Service Commission? How do these courses compare with those offered by ADPMTC for computer specialists?

2. As an entry-level programmer, what courses might you select at the ADP Management Training Center to enhance your professional development?

COMPUTERS AND SOCIETY | 18

OUTLINE

I. The Privacy Issue
  A. Data Banks
  B. Fair Credit Reporting Act of 1970
  C. Privacy Act of 1974
II. Automation
  A. Job Displacement
  B. Robotics
III. Artificial Intelligence
  A. Heuristics
  B. Speech Interpretation
  C. Print and Script Reading
  D. Natural-Language Processing

IV. Personal Computing
  A. Use in Small Business and Professions
  B. Use in the Home
  C. Computer Stores
V. Societal Impact
  A. Education
  B. Health Care
  C. Law Enforcement
  D. Entertainment/Sports
VI. Perspective

INTRODUCTION

After learning how computers operate and how they are used in management information systems, we are perhaps somewhat willing to acknowledge that they can have an enormous impact on society. The computer has improved our standard of living. It has changed life styles and job requirements. It has also created major problems in the areas of security and privacy. The degree of impact that computers have in the future will be significantly influenced by our ability and foresight in recognizing and finding suitable solutions to these computer-related problems.

This chapter examines some of the problems of privacy and some of the remedies currently being applied to them. Special attention is also given to the impact of increased automation. Some of the highlights of artificial-intelligence research are included in an attempt to answer the question of whether computers can think, listen, or read. And the growing trend toward personal computing is discussed. Finally, the influence that computers have had on society is depicted through an exploration of some interesting and significant applications.

THE FILE FAMINE: A CASE OF COMPUTER CONSUMPTION

Art Buchwald

Washington Post, April 10, 1975

Several years ago I predicted that there were so many computers in operation in the United States that there would soon be a data famine in the country. I said that, unless new methods were developed to produce data, computer people would soon be fighting each other and possibly resorting to violence to get enough information to satisfy the appetites of their machines.

Unfortunately, I predicted this data war would start in 1984. Little did I realize it had already begun.

Everyone holds the FBI, the IRS, the CIA, local law enforcement agencies, as well as credit companies, responsible for invading the privacy of American citizens. But these organizations are not to blame. The responsibility rests with the computers they have bought or leased that have to be fed constantly to justify their existence.

Let us take the FBI, for example. They purchased their computers to keep track of criminals and subversives in the United States. In no time the computers had absorbed the name and description of every racketeer, car thief, bomb thrower, and cattle rustler in the country.

Every scrap of information had been thrown in, but the computers kept demanding more. Frantic FBI officials sent out Telex messages to their field offices. "Urgent—send us everything you have in your files. Computers are desperate for new data. No matter how inconsequential or nonverifiable we will take it. Director insists each field office responsible for one ton of raw data per week. If you fail to meet quota you will be sent to Billings, Mont."

The FBI field offices tried to obey. All waste paper was sent to Washington.

Agents broke into local police station offices to steal their files; foreign embassies were rifled; union records were filched. But still many of the G-men could not make their quotas. So they started sending in information on citizens who had nothing to do with crime or subversion. Some field agents sent in entire telephone books from their areas; others made reports on members of the American Legion, the Elks, the Shriners, and the Daughters of the American Revolution. A few agents were so hardpressed they mailed in raw files on their own wives and children.

But the FBI computers kept chewing up the information at a faster rate than anyone in the Bureau could produce it. There was talk of putting the computers on a six-hour day and only operating them four days a week. But when the computers heard about this (an agent had fed the suggestion into a computer to find out if it was feasible), red lights started to flash all over the computer center, and a readout indicated that if their work-time was cut every FBI machine would self-destruct in protest.

It was then decided the only way to assure a sufficient supply of data was to keep files on everybody, from college students to people on Social Security. Experts figured that if the FBI could get enough data on them they could keep the computers busy until 1976. That is the only reason the FBI has your name on their list right now.

The CIA faced the same crisis as the FBI did, but it had a problem because by law the CIA is not supposed to keep files on American citizens.

After 25 years the CIA had tons of information on every country in the world; and although it occasionally was able to come up with fresh data, it was not enough to satisfy the voracious appetites of their machines, which incidentally were much larger than those of the FBI. Several years ago the CIA had no choice but to start feeding information on Americans. When Congress found out about this, the CIA had to suspend this operation, which left them in a pickle. Their computers were becoming restless and surly and their printouts indicated there could be an in-house revolt.

So last month the CIA chiefs realized they had no choice. In order to get enough data for their computers for the next three years they decided to do a psychological profile on every man, woman, and child in the People's Republic of China.

Although Buchwald's "file famine" is hilarious, its purpose is to direct attention to a very real problem—privacy. The computer's ability to integrate and amass a great deal of data about individuals should be a concern to all of us. In this final chapter we discuss this issue as well as automation, artificial intelligence, and other areas of the computer's impact on society.

THE PRIVACY ISSUE

A major effect that computers have had on society is to bring to light the issue of invasion of individual *privacy*. During the past decade there has been an increasing trend toward large, centralized *data banks*. These data banks hold a vast array of intimate and personal data in a form such that it is easily accessible to various individuals and agencies. The ease with which any computer installation can be infiltrated poses a serious threat: personal data may get into the hands of the wrong people. The computer may be used as a tool to create an Orwellian society where the lives of individuals are controlled and manipulated by a "Big Brother" regime.

One of the major problems associated with computerized data banks is the inability of the individual to control what personal data is stored and disseminated by such systems. Furthermore, very little, if anything, can be done to correct any false data entered mistakenly or intentionally.

Let us consider some of the data that is being collected by various government and private agencies. Figure 18–1 shows a small cross-section of the individual files presently maintained by various organizations. An extensive personal dossier could be created by integrating all these files. This constitutes a threat to individual *information privacy*.

FIGURE 18–1

Examples of the Many Files
Maintained by Federal, State,
and Private Agencies

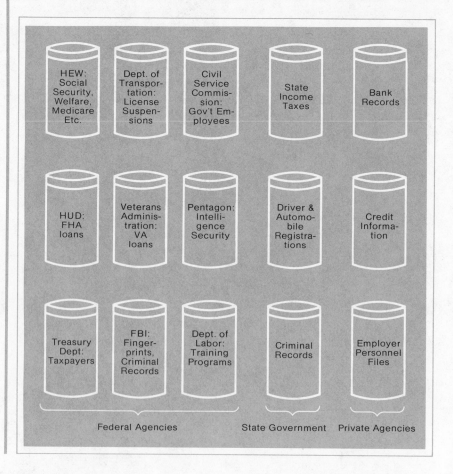

HEW: Social Security, Welfare, Medicare Etc.

Dept. of Transportation: License Suspensions

Civil Service Commission: Gov't Employees

State Income Taxes

Bank Records

HUD: FHA loans

Veterans Administration: VA loans

Pentagon: Intelligence Security

Driver & Automobile Registrations

Credit Information

Treasury Dept: Taxpayers

FBI: Fingerprints, Criminal Records

Dept. of Labor: Training Programs

Criminal Records

Employer Personnel Files

Federal Agencies   State Government   Private Agencies

430

Many of the federal data banks use social security number as a key to access individual records. This is a concern to many people because the use of a common key provides an easy way to correlate and match different pieces of data scattered in various files. In 1966 a recommendation was made by the Task Force on the Storage of and Access to Government Statistics to establish a National Data Center which would consolidate all data compiled by about 20 different federal agencies. The proposal was not implemented (after considerable discussion) because the potential for misuse of the data and for the invasion of individual privacy was just too great.

Centralized data banks are not the only threat to individual information privacy. The increasing trend toward *electronic funds transfer* (*EFT*) has serious implications in the area of individual privacy. More and more financial transactions are being handled electronically. In an EFT system the accounts of the two parties involved in a transaction are adjusted by electronic communication between computers. There is no exchange of money in the form of cash or check. A direct consequence of this processing is that most of the financial transactions of an individual are recorded in a data bank according to some key. Obviously, one can find out a great deal about an individual's life style and habits if one has access to all the financial transactions in which that person has been involved.

Thus, it is easy to see that computer technology has greatly amplified our capability to invade individual privacy. But it is the responsibility of society to protect individual privacy. Some steps to enact appropriate legislation have already been taken, and others are being considered. The first such step was the Fair Credit Reporting Act of 1970. This legislation provided to individuals (1) the right to access credit data about themselves, and (2) an opportunity to challenge and correct any erroneous data. Individuals can also gain access to data about themselves in files collected by federal agencies, according to the 1970 Freedom of Information Act.

The Privacy Act of 1974 was signed on January 1, 1975. It aims at implementing the Code of Fair Information Practices developed by the Department of Health, Education, and Welfare in 1973. The basic provisions of the code are:

● There must be no secret data banks that collect personal information.

● An individual must be able to determine what information about himself/herself is being recorded and how it will be used.

● There must be a provision for an individual to correct or amend information about himself/herself.

● Information collected for one purpose should not be used or made available for any other purpose without the consent of the individual.

● Any organization creating, maintaining, using, or disseminating personal information must insure the reliability of the data and must take precautions to prevent its misuse.

The Privacy Act of 1974 is a step in the right direction, but it applies only to federal agencies. There is still much that needs to be done in the private sector. Resistance to privacy legislation regulating business is to be expected because of the costs involved. These costs include:

● Establishing procedures to tell individuals what data about them is being collected and disseminated

● Provisions to insure that computer installations have adequate physical and system security features to prevent unauthorized access

● Additional checks to verify the accuracy and validity of the data being collected and disseminated

● Replying to individual inquiries and making changes when data is found to be incorrect

Ultimately, these costs must be paid by us, as consumers. Thus, a question arises: "How much privacy do we want, and how much are we willing to pay for it?" Our answer to this question will reflect the extent to which we value individual privacy, and will determine what safeguards we are willing to support to protect it.

AUTOMATION

As indicated early in this text, the term *automation* refers to machine-directed processes. Ever since the Industrial Revolution, automation has been of great concern to people. As technology has advanced, more and more processes have been automated, leading to greater efficiency and lower costs. But if we look at the other side of this advancement, we see machines replacing people. And with the advent of computers, the fear that automation will lead to unemployment and depersonalization has taken on even greater significance. Whether these fears are justified is yet to be seen.

If we look at the past three decades, the evidence does not indicate that increased automation leads to increased unemployment. To be sure, there has been displacement of workers; but each new technology has created enough new employment opportunities to more than compensate for the jobs that have been eliminated. For example, the invention of the automatic weaving machine eliminated many jobs in the garment industry; this effect was offset by the creation of a whole new industry involved in the manufacture and marketing of the new equipment.

Nevertheless, many people argue, the impact of computers is going to be much more significant, because computer technology provides for much more versatile and complex automation. Computers, instead of humans, can be used to control automatic machines and entire assembly lines. Grocery stores can be automated—that is, a person can call in an order, and a computer can record it, access the required items, and even arrange for the delivery of them. Other computers can control entire processes in oil refineries. They start with crude oil and process it into tar, heating oil, diesel oil, gasoline, and so forth.

Several studies have been conducted to determine the effects of computer automation on jobs. The results have not been conclusive. The United States Labor Department made a study of 20 companies just beginning to use computers. It found that, of a total of 3000 employees, about 16 percent retired or left within one year of a computer installation. Obviously, we can expect a certain amount of job displacement, because the computer can take over many routine, clerical types of jobs. However, the extent to which such displacement occurs also depends to a great extent on other factors. Among them are:

● The goals that are sought from the use of the computer. Is the objective to be able to handle an increasing workload with the same personnel, or is it to reduce costs by eliminating jobs?

● The growth rate of the organization. If the organization is expanding, it is much easier to absorb workers whose existing jobs are being eliminated; many new jobs must be created to cope with the increasing business.

● The planning that has gone into the acquisition and use of the computer. With careful preparation, an organization can anticipate the personnel changes that a computer system will bring about. It can make plans either to reassign the affected people or to help them to find new jobs with other organizations. First-time use of a computer-based system will definitely create new jobs in the areas of computer operations, data-entry, programming, and system analysis and design. Usually, however, the skills and education required for these jobs differ from those required for the eliminated jobs. In spite of this, some of the displaced employees can be trained to handle such jobs as operating computer equipment (loading and unloading tapes, etc.), keypunching, or using some other mode of data entry.

The use of computer-controlled machines is also causing some job displacement in production-oriented environments. Industrial robots, as these machines are sometimes called, are a far cry from the endearing C-3PO pictured in *Star Wars*. Usually such a machine is just a mobile arm ending in some sort of vice-like grip. It is attached to a box that houses the control unit. The arm can perform tasks ranging from picking up objects from one point and placing them at another, to handling spray guns and welding torches. Robots not only operate machine tools, but also are capable of interacting with and controlling the machines they operate. For example, a punching machine can signal a mechanical arm that it has punched a component. The arm then automatically removes the part and communicates back to the machine to punch another component.

Robots have been designed to simulate the motion of the human shoulder and elbow; they move horizontally, vertically, or at some other angle. In addition, the hand (or vice-like grip) can rotate and twist just

433

like the human wrist. If the robots are mounted on tracks or wheels, they are also capable of limited locomotion. At present, most of these robots are being used to perform very simple, repetitive tasks. They are found most often in industrial environments which are potentially dangerous for humans. For example, robots can be used in high-radiation environments (like nuclear reactors) to handle parts that are too hot or too cold, or to operate machines such as stamping mills and electric saws that can seriously maim a careless operator.

In the future, robots will be used increasingly to perform more complex and sophisticated tasks. A prototype for the robot of the future has been developed at Stanford Research Institute by Nils Nilsson, Charles Rosen, and others. This machine is capable of exploring and familiarizing itself with a limited environment. It can then react appropriately to a set of instructions like, "Proceed from your present location at (6,9) to location (15,1), picking up the object at (12,4) on your way."

The progress in the field of *robotics*, although impressive, is not yet striking enough to indicate that machines will soon replace humans. We need only take note of the extremely controlled and artificial environments, and the very simple tasks that such machines are now performing, to conclude that there is much progress yet to be made before computerized robots will entirely replace the working and lower-middle classes. Equally remote is the age of leisure and abundance pictured by many, where computers perform all the tasks necessary to keep humans well-fed and clothed, and where people devote themselves to the arts or other esoteric pursuits.

Some concluding remarks can be made about employment and the automation issue:

● Automation may cause job displacement and some temporary unemployment in the short run.

● Although automation may reduce the direct labor required to do a given amount of work, it tends to generate employment opportunities in other areas.

● Our economic growth could not proceed at such a rapid rate without automation and computers. Thus, computers are indirectly responsible for creating jobs because they facilitate economic growth.

● It is possible that a long-run impact of automation will be an increase in the leisure time available to people. If so, this impact will spur the growth of leisure-time industries and provide new jobs.

● The impact of job displacement due to automation can be reduced by providing job training and education. A flexible and mobile work force can find alternative employment without much trouble.

ARTIFICIAL INTELLIGENCE

So far in our discussion of the computer as a problem-solving tool, the problems used as illustrations have been well-structured. Each one could be solved with a carefully defined procedure. For example, to solve our payroll problem, we developed a structure that did not need to be changed each time the payroll was calculated. However, many problems that we face are solved by processes quite different from the conscious, deliberate methods that are used to solve problems in mathematics or logic. We do not always think rigidly, according to a set of strictly defined rules. Many problem solutions involve not only logic, but also intuition, creativity, and intelligence. Examples of such problems include: (1) deciphering someone's scribbled messages, (2) playing a game that requires strategy or deception, and (3) distinguishing literally intended meanings from sarcasm. Such problems are not difficult for humans to solve; they are natural tasks that we do every day. But the question of whether or not techniques can be developed to enable computers to solve problems that seem to require imagination or intelligence is one that continues to challenge researchers.

Research efforts are currently aimed at preparing programs that can do tasks that have never been done automatically and that usually have been assumed to require human intelligence. This field of research is called *artificial intelligence*. It is largely devoted to developing computers that can solve abstract problems. However, there are also some practical applications.

Research efforts in artificial intelligence have been directed mainly toward such fields as heuristics, speech understanding, print and script reading, and natural-language processing.

The word *heuristic* means "helping to learn or discover." Heuristic processes are methods of problem-solving in which the precise means of achieving a solution are not spelled out—strategies are discovered during the course of solving the problem. Generally, heuristics are used to solve problems that are too complex or time-consuming to yield to conventional mathematical analysis. For example, when putting together a jigsaw puzzle, we may always try to put together the border pieces first. This heuristic may help in one type of puzzle but not in another. Nevertheless, it provides a foundation for starting to solve the problem.

One successful example of techniques being developed to program heuristic processes into computers involves determining the structure of an organic compound from certain measurements. Any set of atoms can arrange themselves in hundreds of thousands of ways, and each arrangement makes up a different molecule. Therefore, to determine the structure of a molecule, all possible configurations must be considered. The computer produces a list of all possible structures and then is given data about the mass of a molecule. It can then determine whether a structure being considered would produce characteristics similar to those described by the data.

Artificial-intelligence researchers are also attempting to program computers to understand speech. This is a very difficult task because of variations in intonation and pitch, pauses, errors, hesitations, incomplete words, and different pronunciations of words. Consequently, most research in this area has been restricted to programming machines to perform specified tasks in response to spoken commands, using a very limited vocabulary and simple sentence structure. One such system, for

435

example, accepts spoken commands to move chess pieces. There are only 31 words and a small number of action statements like "move" and "check" in the computer's vocabulary. The computer can test whether or not a statement makes sense, because it has a record of where all the pieces are on the board and knows the legal moves.

Researchers are now trying to program computers to read handwritten script or print. This capability can be very useful for such applications as sorting mail. In fact, the USSR and Japan use readers that can process 20,000 pieces of mail an hour with 93 percent accuracy. The system requires that the address code be written in preprinted boxes on the envelope.

Considerable research effort has also been devoted to developing techniques so that computers can process natural languages: for example, to summarize text, or to translate text from one language to another. This is very difficult because many of the statements we speak, hear, and read are highly ambiguous and assume a thorough understanding of words, grammar, and the world we live in. However, approximate translations of technical text (which is more straightforward than general writing) from Russian to English are now possible.

Although attempts to model human characteristics with computers have met with limited success, the capabilities of computers are increasing at a fantastic rate. Computers can now be programmed to learn by experience, follow an argument, ask pertinent questions, and write pleasing poetry and music. As research in artificial intelligence continues to yield new programming techniques, and combines them with the sophisticated hardware of robots, the future may be in sight for the bright, personable R2-D2 character.

PERSONAL COMPUTING

A trend gaining widespread popularity is the utilization of microcomputers for personal computing, a concept which for years was discussed only as a science fiction novelty. Today there are more than 200,000 general-purpose microcomputers in American homes and small businesses and their number is increasing by over 40 percent per year.

The personal-computing concept involves applying the processing capabilities of a microcomputer to the processing needs of the individual. The movement toward personal computing evolved from the hobby-oriented activity of engineers, programmers, electronic buffs, and other technically competent and inquisitive individuals. These computer hobbyists built their computers from scratch or purchased ready-to-assemble computer kits. Within a few hours, the hobbyist could put together a real computer, complete with a keyboard for data-entry and TV-like display tube. The idea caught on quickly; there is now an enthusiastic and growing population of computer hobbyists.

At the sight of a true consumer market, manufacturers began to offer user-oriented microcomputer systems. These small systems were pre-assembled and equipped with programs to do simple jobs, such as balancing a checkbook or playing a game of backgammon. As more user-oriented microcomputers emerged, the growth of personal computing began.

The applications possible on a personal computer are practically unlimited. Among the most practical and profitable uses of personal computers are those in small businesses and professions. Businesses have found they can use them for doing such things as controlling inventories, estimating costs, maintaining tax records, and evaluating bids and contracts. School teachers can devise exams and compute grades. A doctor can keep patients' records. A college football coach can figure out the most potent combinations of players and strategies.

The most promising market for the microcomputer is in the home. It may soon become as common in the home as color television is now. Thus far, home computers have typically been used for amusement. The list of games programmed for home computers includes bridge, chess, Battleship, backgammon, and Monopoly. However, there are many ways in which a personal computer can be used for practical tasks.

The small computer is a natural as an aid in financial matters. It can help do income taxes and balance checkbooks. It can also maintain the family budget and tell the best time to get a new car.

The homemaker can make extensive use of a microcomputer. The computer can be used to maintain a Christmas-card list, file recipes, work out a dinner menu with what food is in the refrigerator, or start the roast with a phone call from the office. It is a unique, low-cost baby-sitter; thousands of computer games are available. Also, when minute wires are placed underneath a baby's crib mattress, the computer can signal the baby's movements in the crib or even detect irregularity in the baby's breathing, and sound an alarm.

When sensors, motors, and switches are added to the microcomputer, it can be used to run a wide range of gadgets around the home. For example, it can keep various rooms of the house at desired temperatures, thus conserving energy. It can enhance security by locking doors and controlling burglar alarms. The microcomputer can water the lawn according to ground moisture, signal water seeping into the basement, and open and shut drapes. Thus, the applications of a personal computer are as far-ranging as the individuals who imagine them.

A computer for the home can be purchased for about the same price as a good stereo system; those available range in price from $275 to $5000. The personal computing market started in 1975 when MITS introduced the Altair 8800, a computer kit for under $500. The Altair 8800 series has been the pacesetter in microcomputer development. Their complete computing capabilities at a low cost make them ideal for home computing.

The Radio Shack chain has developed the TSR-80 microcomputer system for a little less than $600. This system is adaptable to both small business applications and home computing. The computer can be programmed using the BASIC programming language, which makes the system readily usable by almost anyone. Radio Shack has also developed a software library designed to provide the user with useful programs such as payroll, finance, home-recipe, and backgammon/blackjack games.

Although the production of microcomputers has been dominated by a host of small firms, large manufacturers such as RCA, Texas Instruments, and Heath have now moved into the field.

Personal-computing equipment has been, until recently, mainly a mail-order business. Products have been shipped directly from manufacturers. With the emergence of the home-computer concept, however, a new retailing phenomenon has evolved—the computer store. These stores are structured to appeal almost exclusively to the small business person or personal user. Today there are more than 1000 home computer dealers in this country. The best stores offer a variety of products and services manufactured by several firms. Demonstration systems are on display so the customer can experiment with the system in much the same manner as a test drive can be taken before purchasing a car. Additionally, microcomputer experts are available to answer questions and provide technical guidance to the computer novice.

The home computer may be the answer to many of the problems in our society, ranging from energy regulation to food consumption. The time has come for the machine that has changed our lives to become a part of our lives.

SOCIETAL IMPACT

The computer is evident in all segments of society. It influences not only our means of conducting business, but also the way we live. The use of computers is widespread, and a complete survey of computer applications is beyond the scope of any single book. But a cross-section of some of the most important and most striking uses depicts the significant roles that computers play in our lives. To this end, applications in the areas of education, health care, law enforcement, and entertainment/sports are described here.

The potential impact of computer applications in education is significant. Computers are used for student instruction, as well as for administrative data processing. When used for instruction, computers can provide richer, more meaningful experiences in learning, more individualized instruction, and better learning through practice. Computer applications in administrative processes help schools to operate more efficiently.

Because computers are now simple enough for students to operate, and hardware is inexpensive enough for schools to purchase, they are rapidly changing the methodology of education. The student who uses the computer in a math curriculum, for example, learns an effective approach to the solution of any problem. The computer demands that a problem be divided into steps; in writing programs, the student gains a better understanding of problem-solving in general.

Computer simulations are a base for vivid demonstrations in the physical sciences. For example, the computer can simulate the descent of a lunar module. Its single retro-rocket can be controlled by the student; that is, he or she can attempt to bring the module in for a soft landing. In the biology class, the computer can compress time, allowing many interesting facts about evolution to be presented. A computer can chart a 30-million-year evolution in minutes. Through simulation, the student can appreciate the effects of pollution, for example, the flow of waste into a river. In a physics class, the computer can simulate the use of expensive equipment, such as lasers, and illustrate such concepts as special relativity and projectile motion. The key to the success of these simulations is the fact that the student controls what happens; the computer only tells the student the consequences of his or her decisions. Thus, the student gains a better understanding of what happens in the real world.

The computer controls the learning situation in what is known as computer-assisted instruction (CAI). In fact, the computer may either supplement or replace the teacher. CAI can be drill work, exercises, remedial or enrichment material, tests, or simply a dialogue between the computer and the student.

Computers assist in administrative tasks such as student scheduling, counseling, and grade reporting. Using them to score tests is now a fairly routine application, especially in schools with large classes.

The computer's popularity is also growing within the medical community. Computer systems are being applied in biomedical research and in areas of direct patient care and treatment. Diagnostic systems assist physicians in identifying many disorders and diseases; automated laboratory systems can perform dozens of tests in less time than it takes to do one test using a former method.

Many hospitals use computers to monitor the vital signs of patients in intensive care. Equipment designed to check breathing, pulse rate, and other critical life signs is plugged into the computer. The computer samples the readings of each patient on a regular basis, perhaps several times a second. It compares each patient's actual readings with critical limits and sounds an alarm if any monitored life sign deviates significantly from normal.

Similar monitoring equipment and techniques are also used during surgery. The computer integrates data for both the surgeon and the anesthesiologist. Thus, the strategy behind a surgical procedure can be changed during the operation. Anesthesiologists can determine the appropriate amount of anesthesia by monitoring vital life signs such as blood pressure, blood oxygen saturation, body temperature, pulse and respiration rate, and brain, heart, and muscle responses.

Computers play an integral part in the administrative functions of hospitals, including accounting, billing, and inventory control. Drugs are controlled to prevent theft and misuse. Most hospitals also automate employee payroll, bed allocation, X-ray, surgery, and other facility scheduling.

The field of law enforcement benefits greatly from the use of computers. Computers have helped to reduce the possibility of mistaken identity, prevent the release from custody of criminals wanted in other districts, improve the probability of apprehension, reduce court delays, and make sentencing fairer.

439

Nationwide, the use of computers in law enforcement varies, depending on the availability of money, the degree of local interest, crime rates and patterns, and the sophistication of the local police department. The National Crime Information Center (NCIC) is a complex computerized electronic data-exchange network developed by the FBI to complement computerized systems in local and state enforcement agencies. All states, many major metropolitan areas, and some federal law enforcement agencies have access to the NCIC through the interfacing of local police department computers or remote terminals. The online information system contains over six million records of wanted persons and stolen articles—vehicles, license plates, firearms, securities, boats, and so on.

The NCIC handles nearly 260,000 transactions daily. Over 700 of them result in the identification of wanted fugitives or items of stolen property. This system provides better protection to the public. Prosecution has often resulted from data disseminated by the FBI to other agencies. Examples are:

● Indictment of 16 persons in New York City for conspiring to dispose of $18.2 million in stolen and counterfeit securities in the United States and Europe

● Arrest of three people in Orlando, Florida, for possession of heroin worth $200,000

● Confiscation of $5 million worth of hashish by Drug Enforcement Agency (DEA) agents in Las Vegas in what was described as the largest seizure of hashish ever made in the United States

In the world of professional sports, computer-controlled scoreboards add to the excitement of games. No longer does the scoreboard merely keep track of the score. Word messages such as the batting order, the names of various groups in attendance, and sports trivia questions can be entered into the system via a terminal keyboard. The system can recompute a player's batting average prior to each time at bat. It can then display the latest possible statistic. Animated cartoons celebrating home runs or intercepted passes are stored on auxiliary storage devices from where they can be retrieved and displayed quickly. The computer-controlled scoreboard fills slow spots in the game with interesting action, adds to the excitement of high spots, keeps the fans informed, and, in general, makes the game more exciting.

The computation of odds in horse racing and player analysis for the professional football draft are other interesting applications. Computers are used to analyze opponent's past trends, analyze strategies, and time events.

PERSPECTIVE

Computer technology has had a more significant impact on society than any other factor since the Industrial Revolution. The extent of this impact has led many to classify the present era as the *Information*

Revolution. In an extremely short time, computers have moved out of the laboratory and into an indispensable position in modern life. This rapid progress has generated many problems as well as spectacular results.

Some people born and educated before widespread implementation of computers refuse to recognize their existence. Psychological barriers are raised, and no attempt is made to understand the logical base of computer operations. Technological obsolescence often requires job restructuring or retraining; this tends to increase resistance to computer applications. Computer professionals must commit themselves to continuing education if they want to remain current in this dynamic field. These problems are people-oriented rather than dependent upon scientific advancements. As such, they are more difficult to solve.

The world as we know it today would be impossible if all the advances attributed to computers were removed. For example, airlines could not continue to function without computerized airline reservation systems; space travel would be impossible without simulation and control programs; and our economic system would grind to a halt without the tremendous speed of the computer upon which the banking industry relies so heavily for processing cash flow.

One point must be understood: Not all computer applications are beneficial or even effective. The computer is only a tool used by analysts and programmers to assist in solving problems. If a solution is inappropriate or incorrect, then the computer system has the same deficiencies. Computer power is a fact of technological achievement; harnessing this power is a function of the individuals who control computer use. The principal limitation on computer application is the imagination and ingenuity of the human counterpart.

SUMMARY

● The possibility of someone gaining access to large amounts of data about individuals has raised the issue of invasion of privacy. Compounding the problem are the possibilities that the data may be incorrect and that many individuals may not even know that the data bank exists.

● Some steps taken to resolve the problems surrounding the privacy issue are: (1) the Fair Credit Reporting Act of 1970, which provides to individuals the right to access credit data about themselves and to challenge any erroneous data; and (2) the Privacy Act of 1974, which outlines steps giving people more control over data about themselves collected by federal agencies. The cost of protecting individual privacy will ultimately be passed on to the individuals being protected.

● Automation refers to machine-directed processes. Automation through the use of computers has eliminated some jobs, created new jobs, and modified others. The amount of job displacement as a result of the computer depends on the goals sought from its use, the growth rate of the organization, and the amount of planning that went into the acquisition of the computer.

441

● Computer-controlled machines, including robots, are being used for simple, repetitive taks and for tasks deemed too dangerous for humans, often in industrial environments. These machines are far from displacing the working class.

● Artificial intelligence is a field of research attempting to develop and improve techniques for programming computers to solve problems that seem to require imagination, intuition, or intelligence. Some of the research efforts have been directed to such areas as heuristics, speech understanding, print and script reading, and natural-language processing.

● Personal computing is a trend gaining widespread popularity, both in small businesses and in the home. Applications of microcomputers in the home range from entertainment to more practical tasks such as monitoring energy and security devices.

● Computer systems are an important part of our society. Applications in fields such as education, health care, law enforcement, and entertainment have significantly influenced the way we live.

REVIEW QUESTIONS

1. Name five organizations or institutions where data about you is stored. How much could a stranger tell you about yourself if he or she consolidated all the data into a single, integrated file?

2. Robots and other computer gadgets are used extensively in science-fiction movies and television shows. Do you think these kinds of machines will actually be developed? Why or why not?

3. Do you see any possible impact of progress in artificial intelligence on employment or unemployment? Explain.

4. What computer capabilities make computer-assisted instruction possible?

Leisure time is an integral part of society today. People everywhere find time for amusement and recreation. Among the most unique entertainment experiences of the past two decades are "theme parks," a concept created by Walt Disney in his imaginative reworking of the old-time amusement parks. These parks enchant visitors by surrounding them with a whole new world, shutting out reality and allowing them to ". . . leave today and enter the world of yesterday, tomorrow, and fantasy."

There are now nearly 50 major theme parks across the nation. But the grandfather of these parks, and still the leader of the industry, is Disneyland. Opened at Anaheim, California, in 1955, Disneyland is visited by more people each year than all professional football and basketball games of the year combined. It draws more than twice the combined annual attendance at Yosemite, Yellowstone, and the Great Smokies national parks.

From Anaheim, the Disney imagination spread across the United States to Lake Buena Vista, Florida, where Walt Disney World opened in 1971. An investment of more than 700 million dollars, Walt Disney World is the number-one destination resort in the world. Disneyland and Disney World's annual revenues of $411,238,000 (1977 Annual Report) account for about 40 percent of the theme park industry total.

Computers play an integral part in the operation of the Disney theme parks. They are directly used for entertainment-facility control as well as for monitoring and controlling the park's operating conditions. One use of the computer for entertainment-facility control is the animation of lifelike figures for the numerous show attractions. A distributed system involving seven computers controls the WEDway Peoplemover transportation system at Walt Disney World. The RCA Space Mountain double roller coaster is also computer-controlled. The roller coasters run next to each other on two almost identical courses, inside a huge six-story concrete planetarium. For safety, the cars on each roller coaster must stay at least 18 seconds apart. This safety feature is controlled by a computer. If a car begins to gain on the one ahead of it, the car (i.e., the tailgater) is

application

WALT DISNEY PRODUCTIONS

© Walt Disney Productions

© Walt Disney Productions

slowed down. Computers also release the blast-off roar in the final tunnel of the ride and control the 40 projectors in Space Mountain that create the Milky Way, meteors, and stars.

In the major hotels, or theme resorts, in the California parks, data-entry terminals are used for guest reservations, registrations, and checkouts. For example, as guests prepare to leave, they check out at any of the terminals in the hotel lobby where the clerk punches their room numbers into the terminal keyboards. The terminals print itemized statements for payment at the cashier's window.

At Walt Disney World, a computerized monitoring and control system checks the operating conditions of everything from fire alarms to golf-course sprinklers. If an equipment malfunction or an alarm condition such as a fire occurs, the system will identify the problem by flashing coded messages on visual-display terminals located at two fire stations and two security locations, and on the maintenance console in the main service area.

"Audio-Animatronics," a patented Disney invention, is one of Disney's most important and popular contributions to the entertainment world. The system is known as the Digital Animation Control (DAC) System or the Disney Audio-Animatronic Control System. In this system, voices, music, and sound effects are electronically combined and synchronized with lifelike movements of three-dimensional objects ranging from birds and flowers to humans. Eight major attractions at Walt Disney World use Audio-Animatronics—the Mickey Mouse Revue, the 37 presidents in Liberty Square's Hall of Presidents, Country Bear Jamboree, Haunted Man-

sion, Enchanted Tiki Birds, Mission to Mars, Pirates of the Caribbean, Jungle River Ride, and Carousel of Progress.

A very simplified configuration of the DAC System is shown in Figure 18-2. As the figure shows, the system is divided into two areas: a central area and a show area. The equipment in the central area is used only to support the animator's task; the equipment in the show area is used both to move the Audio-Animatronics (A.A.) figures and to allow the animator to communicate with the figures via the computer.

To compose a show, an animator sits at the programming console of the DAC System and activates the desired function. The system uses a general-purpose computer with a 32,000-word memory. The console itself is a desk-sized housing which contains several dozen switches and indicator lights. Within the console are several small electronic packages. The most important of these is the analog-to-digital converter (ADC). By manipulating switches on the console, the animator sends data to the computer. It is processed to make the figures move. As the animator moves the figures, their actual positions are represented by electrical signals or voltages (analog data). These signals are converted by the ADC to numerical (digital) data which is easily recognized by the computer. The data goes so fast from the console to the computer and back out to the figure that the animator appears to have direct and instantaneous control.

The action is actually generated in a "frame-by-frame" sense, as in film animation. The computer saves data for each "frame's worth" of figure movements in a show's data base. Once the animator decides that the show, or ses-

444

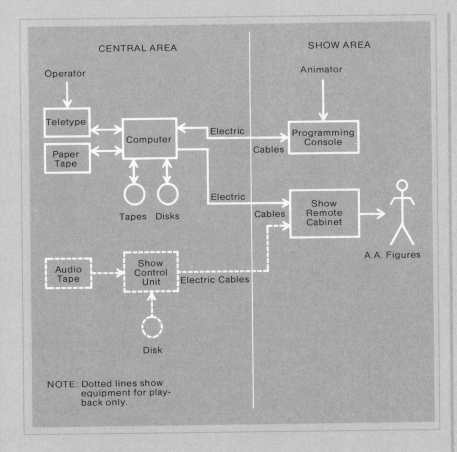

CENTRAL AREA

Operator

Teletype

Paper Tape

Computer

Tapes   Disks

Audio Tape

Show Control Unit

Disk

SHOW AREA

Animator

Programming Console

Electric Cables

Electric Cables

Show Remote Cabinet

A.A. Figures

Electric Cables

NOTE: Dotted lines show equipment for play-back only.

FIGURE 18—2
Simplified DACS Configuration for Animation Only

sion of a show, is ready, all the data for that show or session is saved on magnetic tape.

When the show has finally been edited and fully satisfies the animators and art directors, it is prepared for repetitive automatic playback. The results of the animation process are transferred from the magnetic tape onto a magnetic disk. The show control unit, in the central area, is a machine which plays the show over and over. It is not a computer but only a glorified record-player. The "record" is the show control disk. Essentially, the character movements are activated from electronic signals on the magnetic disks. Digital instructions are sent by wire to a control mechanism in the base of the animated figures. The mechanism converts the digital instructions into linear motions. Slight movements, such as the fluttering of an eyelash, result when the control triggers a magnetic device. The movement of a leg or head, or Lincoln standing up to deliver a speech, is done by a hydraulic double-action piston. Devices used in conjunction with the show control unit allow a show to be played in perfect synchronism with a sound track.

In a typical 30-minute show, there can be up to 1000 analog functions—character movements, stage effects, and sound effects. Characters in the foreground of a show are the most sophisticated; they have the most elaborate

445

circuits and functions. Mickey Mouse in the Mickey Mouse Revue, for example, has 38 functions. He even keeps time with the music.

Thus, computers are indispensable in theme parks. They aid not only the operation of the parks but also the generation, animation, and monitoring of animated shows and park rides, an essential part of park entertainment.

DISCUSSION POINTS

1. A computerized automatic monitoring and control system is used at Walt Disney World to monitor the operating conditions of fire alarms and golf-course sprinklers. What could a similar system be used for in the park's hotels?

2. In what way is the action generation of the Audio-Animatronic figures similar to film animation?

APPENDIX

BASIC PROGRAMMING

This appendix introduces the BASIC programming language. It is not intended to be an exhaustive treatment of BASIC, but rather a presentation of common programming concepts and how the BASIC user applies them.

There are eight sections in the appendix. In Section I, the student is introduced to the components of the BASIC language: BASIC statements, the BASIC character set, variables, character strings, constants, and computational operations. This section also discusses the relationship of BASIC to time-sharing. The student is taught to use a computer terminal and is shown applicable system commands on three computer systems. Editing commands and error messages are also presented.

Section II shows complete BASIC programs. These programs introduce the concepts of assigning values to variables with the READ, DATA, LET, and INPUT statements. Simple processing concepts are explained with the LET statement. Outputting data is discussed with the PRINT statement. REM and END statements are also included. These fundamentals of programming are illustrated with representative examples. After completing the first two sections, the student will be able to write and run a variety of simple BASIC programs.

Sections III and IV expand the student's repertoire of common programming techniques to include branching and looping. Introduced here are additional BASIC statements that can be used to perform these operations: GO TO, ON/GO TO, IF/THEN, and FOR/NEXT. The new techniques and statements are explained with many examples.

Section V presents extended input/output features: the RESTORE, TAB, and PRINT USING statements. Section VI introduces one- and two-dimensional arrays, the DIM statement, and MAT statements. Section VII explains some common mathematical functions that are part of the BASIC language. The subroutine capabilities available to BASIC users are described. Section VIII discusses file processing.

Six of the eight sections conclude with comprehensive programming problems. The problems allow the student to recognize the applicability of the material presented in each section. Newly acquired programming skills are incorporated with those learned in previous sections.

Although a version of BASIC has been standardized, the instructions available are limited. Since it has not been widely implemented, this appendix will not be restricted to a discussion of this version. However, many of the instructions available through the standardized compiler are presented.

A problem associated with this lack of a widely accepted, standardized BASIC compiler is the implementation-dependent nature of many of the instructions. The instructions presented in this appendix include those available through most systems. The author has noted those instances where the instructions are implementation-dependent. Most of the examples have been executed on an IBM system.

The challenge of learning a new computer language can be fun and interesting. The BASIC programming techniques presented here can be applied to use the computer as a powerful problem-solving tool.

BASIC Programming

A BASIC program is a sequence of statements that tells the computer how to solve a problem. There are three types of facilities used in writing a BASIC program:

● Programming-language statements are used in the BASIC program itself. BASIC statements such as IF, GO TO, PRINT, and INPUT are similar, if not identical, to statements in other high-level programming languages.

● System commands are used by the programmer to communicate with the operating system. For example, the programmer may key in the system command RUN to direct the computer to begin program execution. To terminate program execution, the programmer may key in the system command BREAK.

● Editing commands are used to insert changes or to delete parts of a source program. For instance, the programmer can delete an incorrectly keyed letter or number by simply keying in a backward arrow (←) and then keying in the correct character.

All three types of facilities are examined in subsequent sections of this appendix.

The BASIC Character Set

There are three types of characters used in BASIC:

1. Alphabetic characters: ABCDEFGHIJKLMNOPQRSTUVWXYZ

2. Numeric characters: 0123456789

3. Special characters: .," + * − / = ( ) < > $ and the blank, or space

Variables, Character Strings, and Constants

Any data that is to be used in a program must be stored in the computer, either prior to or during execution. The computer has a great number of storage locations, each of which can hold a piece of data. These storage locations can be given names by the programmer. For convenience, the names are used to refer to the data stored in the locations. These programmer-supplied names are called *variable names*. They are "variable" because the value stored in a location can vary as the program is executed. However, each variable name can represent only one value at a time.

A *numeric variable name* represents a number that is either supplied to the computer by the programmer or a user, or internally calculated by the computer during execution of the program. In BASIC, a numeric variable name may be either a single alphabetic letter or a single alphabetic letter followed by one numeric digit. The following examples show valid and invalid numeric variable names:

VALID NUMERIC VARIABLE	INVALID NUMERIC VARIABLE	
A	A*	—Invalid character (*)
X	3S	—Does not start with a letter
I	XYZ	—Too many characters
A2	NAME	—Too many characters
X4	7	—Does not start with a letter

It is possible to process alphabetic or alphanumeric, as well as numeric, data. Alphanumeric data is a sequence of letters, digits, and/or special characters that is stored under a variable name. Such a sequence is commonly referred to as a *character string*. For example, "115 OAK HILLS MANOR" is a string of 19 characters: 3 digits, 3 blanks, and 13 letters.

Character strings are always enclosed in quotation marks. The maximum number of characters allowed in a character string varies from system to system. The following examples show character strings:

```
"ELLEN"
"352-9144"
"THE ANSWER IS"
"75"
```

A *string variable name* can assume the value of a character string. The characters are either supplied by the programmer or a user, or assigned to the string variable name during execution of the program. String variable names are distinguished from numeric variable names by the use of the dollar sign ($) following a single alphabetic letter. The following examples show valid and invalid string variable names:

VALID	INVALID	
N$	A6$	—Contains a digit
H$	6$	—No alphabetic character
D$	$	—No alphabetic character

Constants are values that actually appear in numeric form in a BASIC statement. A constant may appear with or without a decimal point or sign (+ or −). If a constant does not have a sign, it is assumed to be positive. The only characters allowed in a BASIC constant are digits, a decimal point, and a plus or minus sign (no commas). Below are examples of valid and invalid BASIC constants:

VALID	INVALID	
12	5,280	—Contains a comma
−13.3	16X	—Contains an alphabetic character
3.14159	A3	—Contains an alphabetic character
+0.0268	Y	—No digit

Computational Operations

The computer must be directed to perform any computations required to solve a problem. There are specific symbols that must be used and rules that must be followed to express computations in BASIC. The *arithmetic operation symbols* that may be used are shown below.

BASIC ARITHMETIC OPERATION SYMBOL	OPERATION	ARITHMETIC EXAMPLE	BASIC ARITHMETIC EXPRESSION
+	Addition	$A + B$	A + B
−	Subtraction	$A - B$	A − B
*	Multiplication	$A \times B$	A * B
/	Division	$A \div B$	A/B
** or ↑	Exponentiation	A^B	A**B or A↑B

An *arithmetic expression* can be a constant or a variable or any combination of constants and/or variables linked by the above BASIC operation symbols. Thus, some examples of valid expressions are:

```
(A1/B) * C
N**3
(X + 1.4) * Y
```

When more than one arithmetic operation is to be performed within an arithmetic expression, there is a *hierarchy*, or *priority, of operations* which the computer follows. When parentheses are present in an expression, the operation within the parentheses is performed first. If parentheses are nested, the operation in the innermost set of parentheses is performed first. Thus, in the expression

```
(3 * (Y**2) + 5)/10
```

the first operation to be performed is to raise Y to the second power.

Within the parentheses, as well as outside the parentheses, operations are performed according to the following rules of priority:

PRIORITY	OPERATION	SYMBOL
First	Exponentiation	** or ↑
Second	Multiplication or Division	* or /
Third	Addition or Subtraction	+ or −

Operations with high priority are performed before operations with lower priority. Thus, exponentiation operations are performed first. If more than one exponentiation operation appears in an expression, they are performed in order from right to left:

`4**2**3 = 4**(2**3)`   2 is first raised to the third power, and this result (8) is then used as the power of 4.

Multiplication and division operations have second priority. They are performed by the computer after all exponentiation operations have been performed. If more than one multiplication or division operation appears in a statement, they are evaluated from left to right:

`9/3*2 = (9/3)*2`   9 is first divided by 3, and the result of the division (3) is multiplied by 2.

Addition and subtraction operations are performed last. As with multiplication and division operations, evaluation occurs from left to right when more than one addition or subtraction operation is present:

`3-2+5 = (3-2)+5`   2 is first subtracted from 3, and the result (1) is added to 5.

The following arithmetic expression is evaluated as shown here:

```
A**2  +  B/(2 * A)
 ↑    ↑    ↑    ↑
 2    4    3    1
```

1. The parentheses indicate that 2 * A is to be performed first.

2. Since exponentiation has the highest priority, A^2 is computed.

3. Division has the next priority, so B is divided by the already computed product of 2 * A.

4. Finally, because addition has the lowest priority in this expression, A^2 is added to the result of B/(2 * A).

Time-Sharing

The concepts of time-sharing were presented in depth in Chapter 5. We saw that a time-sharing system allows two or more users to share a computer facility. They use typewriter-like terminals instead of punched cards to enter programs and data into the system. Once entered, programs can be edited online for error correction. The system also enables

453

users to store programs between uses. The most unique feature of a time-sharing system is the user's ability to "interact" with a running program in a conversational manner. This direct interaction with the computer makes it a very powerful problem-solving tool.

The BASIC programming language does not require a time-sharing system; however, the most effective applications of its capabilities are generally implemented in a time-sharing environment. The user controls the time-sharing system by typing various system and editing commands. Every system includes many such commands, but their forms vary between systems. In fact, the effect of apparently identical commands may differ between systems. The user should consult the computer manufacturer's reference manuals for complete details on system commands and BASIC statements as implemented on a particular system. This section discusses the fundamental system and editing commands necessary to effectively use the BASIC programming language with the Digital Equipment Corporation (DEC), IBM, and Hewlett-Packard (H-P) systems. The commands are summarized in Table A-1.

The user must initially connect the terminal to the computer. Some terminals are already online; the user only needs to turn on such a terminal and press the RETURN key once to begin. Other terminals depend on dial-up facilities. The user must first call the computer via a telephone used for data transmission. Knowledge of an appropriate telephone number is required to access the computer. When the computer "answers," a high-pitched tone is transmitted over the telephone line. This signals that the computer is ready to receive data from the user. The telephone is then placed firmly into an acoustic coupler (see Chapter 5), which links the terminal to the computer through the telephone line. As with a terminal that is always online, the user must press the RETURN key once. This signals the computer to begin the sign-on procedure.

The sign-on procedure varies with the particular system in use. On the DEC system, the user first enters

↑C

The computer prints a period. The user now enters

LOGIN

and presses the RETURN key. The procedure from this point on is similar for all three systems.

Each system requests the user to enter his/her number, password, or both, as shown below. Each user has a unique number or password which protects his/her data files and programs from other users.

```
ON AT 16:46  FRIDAY AUGUST 25, 1978  LINE 48          IBM
USER NUMBER,PASSWORD--

HELLO-                                                H-P

#                                                     DEC
```

The user enters the number or password, and presses the RETURN key. All user-entered lines must be terminated by pressing the RETURN key; this signals to the computer that the input is complete. This procedure is shown below with the user-entered data shaded.

```
ON AT 16:46  FRIDAY AUGUST 25,1978   LINE 48          IBM
USER NUMBER,PASSWORD--IBA013,START

HELLO-1013, START                                     H-P

#17,12                                                DEC
```

The IBM system immediately types over the user number and password to protect it from inadvertent disclosure.

```
ON AT 16:46  FRIDAY AUGUST 25, 1978   LINE 48
USER NUMBER,PASSWORD--░░░░░░░░░░░░░░░░
```

The DEC and H-P systems prepare a mask composed of several characters, and wait for the user to type the password on top of the mask. The mask is simply a group of characters, typed one on top of another so that what is typed is unreadable:

```
░░░░░░░
```

After receiving a valid user number and password, the computer responds with the message

```
READY
```

The user then specifies the language in which programming will be done. This step is shown below.

```
ENTER BASIC        IBM

RBASIC             DEC

BASIC              H-P
```

On a DEC system, the computer responds

```
NEW OR OLD--
```

to find out if the user is going to enter a new program or use one saved earlier. In this case, the user responds by typing

```
NEW
```

The computer types

```
NEW FILE NAME--
```

The user must give the program a name, such as

```
FIRST1
```

Once again, the computer responds with the message

```
READY
```

In the IBM and Hewlett-Packard systems, the computer responds with READY immediately after the name of the language to be used has been entered. The user can then enter, line by line, the BASIC program.

As the BASIC program is entered, at the end of each line, the RETURN key is pressed. If the user wants to see a listing of the program as it exists in the computer up to a point, he/she can type the system command

LIST

The computer lists the program, in line-number sequence.

After the program has been completely entered, it is ready to be translated into machine language and executed. To request this, the user types the system command

RUN

If there are no errors in the use of the BASIC language (i.e., *syntax errors*), the program will be executed. If there are errors, the BASIC compiler that translates the program will indicate which lines are in error (see below). The errors must be corrected before the program can be executed.

```
NNUM            11:56   AUGUST 18,1978
10 LET A = 123456
20 LET B = 6789012345
30 LET C = .0004568
40 LET D = 33.600
50 PRINT A+4, B*C, D-A, C/D
60 PRINT A, B, C( D
70 END


RUN

NNUM            11:57   AUGUST 18,1978
```

⟶   LINE   60:   SYNTAX ERROR IN EXPRESSION

TIME 0 SECS.

60 PRINT A, B, C, D

1. To correct a line, type the line number and the correct statement. If two lines have the same number, the more recently typed one takes precedence.

2. To delete a line, type the command DELETE and the line number, for example: DELETE 20. Line deletion can also be accomplished by typing the line number and then pressing the RETURN key.

3. To insert a line, pick a number between the numbers of the lines where insertion is to occur; use this number for the line number of the statement to be inserted.

4.   If an error is made while typing a line, use a backward arrow (←) for each character, up to and including the incorrect character; then type correct ones.

When all errors have been corrected, the user again types the system command

```
RUN
```

If a program is running, and for some reason the user wishes to stop it, he/she can either type the command STOP or press the BREAK key on the terminal. This causes data transmission to terminate.

If the user wants to make changes in the program, once it has been executed, it is not necessary to retype the whole program. The lines are changed, as discussed above. When the program is ready to be executed again, RUN is typed once more. The LIST, RUN, and editing commands discussed are identical on all three systems.

Many times the user wants to store a program and data permanently so that the entire program does not have to be re-entered the next time he/she wants to use it. This is accomplished on all three systems by using a SAVE command containing the program name. The DEC system requires that a program be given a name at the time it is first entered. The Hewlett-Packard and IBM systems do not. But a program must be assigned a name by which it can be stored and accessed. The NAME command is used to do this as shown below.

```
NAME FIRST1          IBM

NAME-FIRST1          H-P
```

The program can now be saved on secondary storage. The SAVE command is used as follows:

```
SAVE FIRST1          IBM

SAVE                 H-P & DEC
```

To recall a stored program from secondary storage, the following command is used:

```
LOAD FIRST1          IBM

GET-FIRST1           H-P
```

On a DEC system, the user enters OLD when the computer asks

```
NEW OR OLD--
```

The computer then responds

```
OLD FILE NAME--
```

The user enters the name of the stored program, in this case FIRST1. The computer responds with the message READY on all three systems.

When the user is finished and wants to leave the terminal, a log-off command must be entered. On a DEC system, the user enters

↑C

	DEC	H-P	IBM
Sign-On Procedures			
User enters	↑C		
Computer responds	.		
User enters	LOGIN		
Computer responds	#	HELLO-	ON AT 16:46 AUGUST 30TH,1978 USER NUMBER,PASSWORD--
User enters	17,12	1013,START	IBA013,START
Computer responds	0000000	READY	READY
User enters	IBA013		
Computer responds	READY		
Language Selection			
User enters	RBASIC	BASIC	ENTER BASIC
Computer responds	NEW OR OLD--	READY	READY
User enters	NEW		
Computer responds	NEW FILE NAME--		
User enters	FIRST1		
Computer responds	READY		
System Commands			
To print out a program	LIST	LIST	LIST
To execute a program	RUN	RUN	RUN
To name a program	Specified during language selection	NAME-	NAME
To store a program	SAVE	SAVE	SAVE
To recall a program	Enter OLD during language selection	GET-	LOAD
Sign-Off Procedure			
User enters	↑C	BYE	OFF
Computer responds	.		
User enters	KJOB		
Computer responds	CONFIRM		
User enters	K		

TABLE A—1
TIME-SHARING
COMMANDS

The computer returns a period. The user should now enter

KJOB

The computer responds with the message

CONFIRM

The user enters

K

The computer prints two lines indicating the amount of processing time used.

The log-off procedure is less complicated on the IBM and H-P systems. The IBM termination command is

```
OFF
```

The computer responds

```
OFF AT 16:41
PROC. TIME...    0 SEC.
TERM. TIME...    2 MIN.
```

On the H-P system, the termination command is

```
BYE
```

The computer prints the same information as shown for the IBM system.

A BASIC program is made up of statements. Each statement consists of a line number followed by an English word that indicates the type of statement. A simple BASIC program is shown in Figure A–1. This program performs the task of converting 9 inches to its equivalent in centimeters. The output of an actual computer run of the program shows that the metric equivalent of 9 inches is 3.5433 centimeters.

This example contains some fundamental BASIC statements. The statement in line 10 is a REM (remark) statement. It is used to document the program. Line 20 is a READ statement. This statement causes a data value used by the program (it appears in the DATA statement in line 50) to be read and assigned to the variable whose name is I. In line 30, the actual conversion from inches to centimeters is carried out by means of the LET statement. The number of centimeters is computed by multiplying the number of inches (found in the variable I) by .3937. The result of the conversion is then assigned to the variable C.

Line 40 is a PRINT statement. It instructs the computer to print two numbers: the value of variable I, which is the number of inches; and the value of variable C, which is the number of centimeters.

Line 50 is a DATA statement. As noted above, it supplies data to the READ statement. If, for example, we decide to find the centimeter equivalent of 15 inches, we need only change the DATA statement and return the program. The END statement in line 99 indicates to the BASIC compiler that the end of the program has been reached.

Although this program is extremely simple, it embodies most of the elements common to programs. The READ and DATA statements serve to input data; the data is processed using the LET statement; and output is produced by the PRINT statement. This section more closely examines these fundamental BASIC statements.

Line Numbers

Each statement in a BASIC program begins with a line number. The line numbers can be used as labels, to refer to specific statements in

SECTION II
Fundamental
BASIC Statements

459

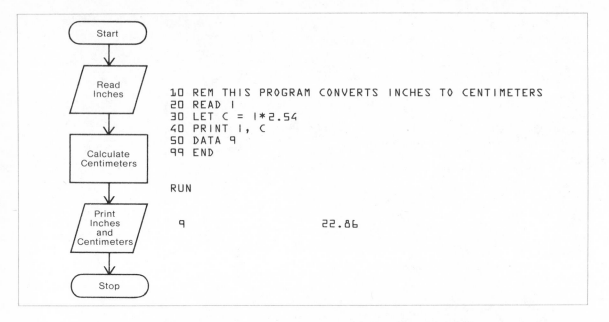

```
10 REM THIS PROGRAM CONVERTS INCHES TO CENTIMETERS
20 READ I
30 LET C = I*2.54
40 PRINT I, C
50 DATA 9
99 END


RUN

9                        22.86
```

the program. Line numbers can be integer values only, ranging from 0 to 99999, and each statement must have a different line number. Program statements are executed in the sequence in which they are numbered, from low to high. The statements need not be entered in numerical order, but they must be numbered in the order in which they are to be executed.

Line numbers do not have to be specified in increments of 1. Using increments of 10, for example, makes it easier to insert new statements between existing statements. If it were necessary to insert a new statement in the sample program (Figure A–1) between statements 10 and 20, the new statement could be numbered 15 without disturbing the order of the existing statements or causing the prógrammer to have to renumber all subsequent statements.

Existing Statements

```
10 REM THIS PROGRAM CONVERTS INCHES TO CENTIMETERS
20 READ I
```

New Statement

```
15 PRINT "THIS IS OUR FIRST BASIC PROGRAM"
```

The REM Statement

The general format of the REM (remark) statement is:

line# REM comment

The comment, or remark, is supplied by the programmer to document the program. The remark provides information for the programmer or anyone else reading the program; it provides no information to the computer. Thus, remarks are comments only; they are not instructions to be executed by the computer.

460

If the length of a remark exceeds 75 spaces (the maximum number of spaces on the output line on teletype terminals), a second REM statement must be entered to continue the remark. Figure A–2 illustrates the use of the REM statement.

The DATA and READ Statements

In order for the computer to solve a problem, it must be provided not only with instructions telling it what to do, but also with data to use when carrying out the instructions. One way to input data to the computer is with DATA and READ statements.

The general format of the DATA statement is:

line# DATA constant list

The constant list consists of numeric or character-string constants, which are to be used as input to the program. Items in the constant list must be separated by commas. The DATA statement can be placed anywhere in the program before the END statement. More than one DATA statement can be used if desired.

The BASIC compiler takes all the data items in all the DATA statements and forms one combined data list. The data items are loaded consecutively into the list before the computer executes the program. At any given time, there is one value at the top of the list. After it is used, the next one comes to the top of the list.

The program in Figure A–3 calculates a simple payroll for two employees. Figure A–4 illustrates how the data items from the DATA statements are loaded consecutively into the data list.

We are now in a position to understand statements 10, 20, and 50 in the program:

```
10 READ X, N$
20 READ H, W
50 READ X, N$, H, W
```

These statements are READ statements. They cause the data to be read from the program and assigned to variables. The general format of the READ statement is:

line# READ variable list

When the READ statements are executed, the values in the data list are assigned consecutively to the variables in the READ statements. Each READ statement causes as many values to be taken from the data list as there are variables in the READ variable list. Figure A–5 illustrates this process of assigning values from the data list to variables.

```
10 REM THE COMMENTS WRITTEN IN REMARK STATEMENTS
20 REM HELP EXPLAIN THE PURPOSE OF SPECIFIC PROGRAM
30 REM STATEMENTS OR THE PURPOSE OF THE OVERALL
40 REM PROGRAM.  REM STATEMENTS CAN BE PLACED
50 REM ANYWHERE THROUGHOUT THE PROGRAM.   THEY DO
60 REM NOT INTERFERE WITH THE EXECUTION OF THE PROGRAM.
```

FIGURE A–2
Use of
REM Statement

461

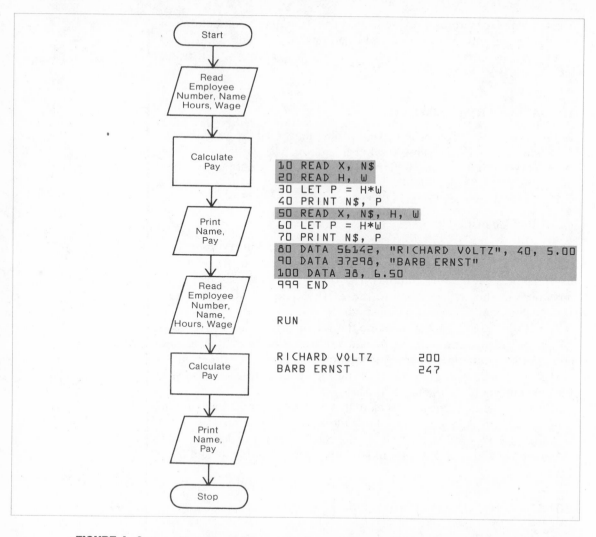

```
10 READ X, N$
20 READ H, W
30 LET P = H*W
40 PRINT N$, P
50 READ X, N$, H, W
60 LET P = H*W
70 PRINT N$, P
80 DATA 56142, "RICHARD VOLTZ", 40, 5.00
90 DATA 37298, "BARB ERNST"
100 DATA 38, 6.50
999 END


RUN


RICHARD VOLTZ        200
BARB ERNST           247
```

Statement 10 says to the computer: "Take the value from the top of the data list, put it in the storage location named X, and throw away any value already in X. Then take the next value from the data list and assign it to variable N\$, throwing away any value already there." After statement 10 has been executed, the number 56142 is in storage location X and the character string RICHARD VOLTZ is in storage location N\$. The number 40 is at the top of the data list.

DATA Statements

```
80 DATA 56142, "RICHARD VOLTZ", 40, 5.00
90 DATA 37298, "BARB ERNST"
100 DATA 38, 6.50
```

Data List

```
56142
RICHARD VOLTZ
40
5.00
37298
BARB ERNST
38
6.50
```

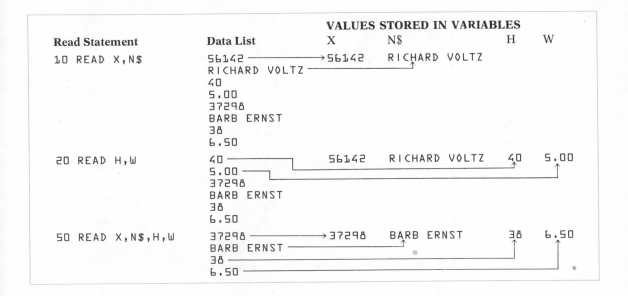

		VALUES STORED IN VARIABLES			
Read Statement	Data List	X	N$	H	W
10 READ X,N$	56142 ⟶	56142	RICHARD VOLTZ		
	RICHARD VOLTZ ⟶				
	40				
	5.00				
	37298				
	BARB ERNST				
	38				
	6.50				
20 READ H,W	40 ⟶	56142	RICHARD VOLTZ	40	5.00
	5.00 ⟶				
	37298				
	BARB ERNST				
	38				
	6.50				
50 READ X,N$,H,W	37298 ⟶	37298	BARB ERNST	38	6.50
	BARB ERNST ⟶				
	38 ⟶				
	6.50 ⟶				

The same process occurs when the computer encounters statement 20. The data from the top of the list (40) is placed in storage location H. The number 5.00 is assigned to W.

When statement 50 is executed, the number at the top of the data list (37298) is assigned to the variable X. The number 56142 that was assigned to X by statement 10 is overlaid by the new value. In the same manner, the character string BARB ERNST is assigned to the variable N$; the number 38 is assigned to the variable H; and the number 6.50 is assigned to W. When these values are assigned, the values previously stored in the variables are also overlaid.

This process illustrates the basic concept of non-destructive read, destructive write, discussed in Chapter 1 of the text. Once the data items are assigned to storage locations, they remain there until new data items are recorded over them. Thus, all four variables represent more than one value during execution, but never more than one at a time.

If a READ statement is attempted after the data list in a program has been exhausted, a message is produced, indicating that the end of the data list has been reached. The message indicates the line number of the READ statement. For example, if line 60 was such a READ statement, the computer would print

LINE 60:   END OF DATA

The LET Statement

Another method of assigning values to variables is by means of a LET statement. With the LET statement, previously determined values can be assigned to numeric or string variables. Or, arithmetic computations can be evaluated and the result assigned to a variable. Most arithmetic

FIGURE A–5

Assigning Values from Data List to Variables

463

computations are specified in LET statements. The general format of the LET statement is:

line# LET variable = expression

The expression can be any constant or variable (character-string or numeric), or a combination of constants, variables, and arithmetic operators.

When a LET statement is encountered, the computer:

1. Evaluates the expression on the right-hand side of the equal sign, and

2. Inserts that value in the storage location (variable) indicated on the left-hand side of the equal sign, overlaying any value currently in that location.

Some examples of LET statements follow:

```
10 LET A = 3
15 LET X = Y + Z
20 LET D = (10 + B + 15)/(M + 4)
25 LET B = C
30 LET N$ = "TODAY'S DATE"
```

Notice that the expression on the right-hand side of the equal sign may

FIGURE A–6

Use of
LET Statements

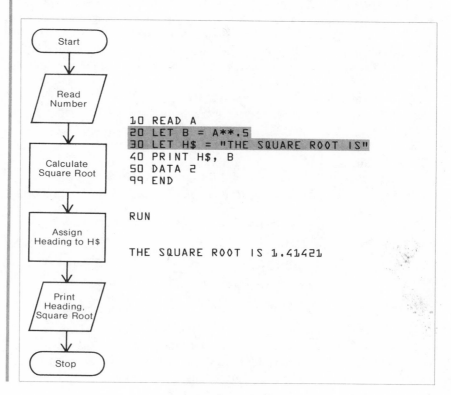

```
10 READ A
20 LET B = A**.5
30 LET H$ = "THE SQUARE ROOT IS"
40 PRINT H$, B
50 DATA 2
99 END


RUN


THE SQUARE ROOT IS 1.41421
```

be quite simple, such as the 3 in line 10, or a complex computation, such as $(10 + B + 15)/(M + 4)$.

Figure A–6 shows a BASIC program that calculates the square root of the number 2.

Statement 20 of this program is a LET statement:

```
20 LET B = A**.5
```

The computer interprets this statement as follows: "LET the variable B be equal to the value obtained by evaluating the expression A**.5." In other words, the square root of the number stored in A (2) is found (A is taken to the .5 power), and the result (1.41421) is stored in the storage location named B. The value of the variable A (which is 2) remains unchanged.

Sometimes a programmer wants to assign the same value to several different variables. This can be done in different ways. Suppose the value of the expression 8.5 * C must be stored in the variables X, Y, and Z. One way to do this is to write several LET statements:

```
10 LET X = 8.5 * C
20 LET Y = X
30 LET Z = X
```

Another way is to use just one LET statement:

```
10 LET Y = Z = X = 8.5 * C
```

or

```
10 LET X,Y,Z = 8.5 * C
```

The last two statements are examples of multiple assignment statements. They are alternative methods of assigning one value to several variables.

The LET statement can also be used to assign a character-string value to a string variable name. For example, the statement in line 30 stores the character string "THE SQUARE ROOT IS" in the variable H$.

```
30 LET H$ = "THE SQUARE ROOT IS"
```

The following examples show valid and invalid LET statements:

Valid LET Statements	Invalid LET Statements	
`10 LET B = 10`	`10 LET 10 = B`	—Variable, not constant, must be on left-hand side of equal sign.
`20 LET X = (A+B)/C`	`20 LET (A+B)/C = X`	—Expression cannot be on left-hand side of equal sign.
`30 LET D$ = "EMPLOYEE NAME"`	`30 LET N2 = "EMPLOYEE NAME"`	—N2 is not a valid string variable name.

The LET statement can also be used to perform two other programming tasks: accumulation and initialization. The process of accumulating involves adding a constant or variable repeatedly to a special variable in order to keep a running total. Initialization involves giving a numeric or string variable an initial value at the beginning of a program; this is very important when the program is going to keep a running total. These two processes are discussed in detail in Section III.

The PRINT Statement

The PRINT statement produces printed output. It has the general form:

$$\text{line\# PRINT} \begin{cases} \text{variable} \\ \text{literal} \\ \text{arithmetic-expression} \\ \text{combination-of-above} \end{cases}$$

The BASIC programs discussed above showed the use of PRINT statements. So does Figure A–7. This program calculates the average and total rainfall for the month of May. The input data values are the average weekly rainfall amounts, in inches, for the four weeks in May.

Printing Variables   The statements

```
20 PRINT H$
80 PRINT R1, R2, R3, R4
```

tell the computer to "PRINT the data in storage locations H$, R1, R2, R3, and R4." The value in H$ is MAY RAINFALL. The values in R1, R2, R3, and R4 are the average weekly rainfalls that were read as data. Therefore, statements 20 and 80 cause the output in the shaded areas below to be printed:

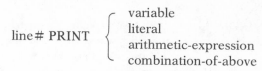

```
MAY RAINFALL

WEEK 1          WEEK 2          WEEK 3          WEEK 4
   2               2.5             1.5               1
THE TOTAL RAINFALL IN MAY WAS 7 INCHES
THE AVERAGE RAINFALL IN MAY WAS 1.75 INCHES
```

Printing has no effect on the contents of storage locations. Rather, it allows the user to see what the contents are. Normally, each time the computer encounters a PRINT statement, it begins printing output on a new line. There are exceptions, discussed later.

Printing Literals   A *literal* is an expression, label, heading, or term consisting of alphabetic, numeric, or special characters, or a combination of any of these three. A character-string literal must be enclosed in quotation marks. It can be printed. For example, the statement

```
70 PRINT "WEEK 1", "WEEK 2", "WEEK 3", "WEEK 4"
```

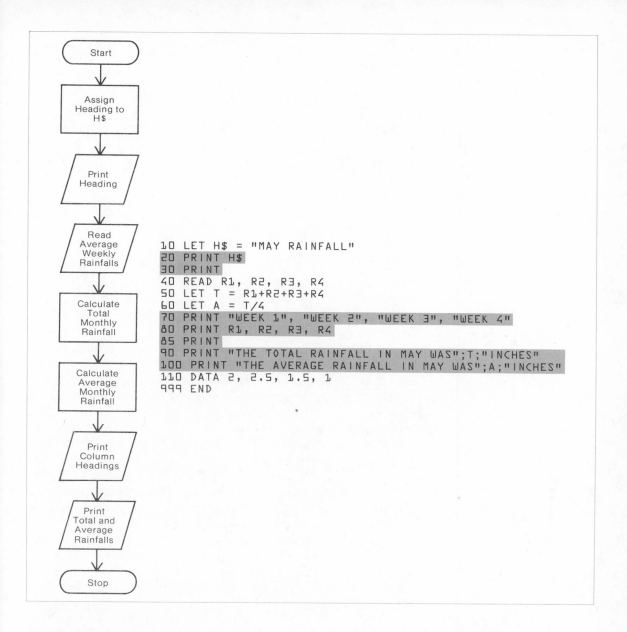

```
10 LET H$ = "MAY RAINFALL"
20 PRINT H$
30 PRINT
40 READ R1, R2, R3, R4
50 LET T = R1+R2+R3+R4
60 LET A = T/4
70 PRINT "WEEK 1", "WEEK 2", "WEEK 3", "WEEK 4"
80 PRINT R1, R2, R3, R4
85 PRINT
90 PRINT "THE TOTAL RAINFALL IN MAY WAS";T;"INCHES"
100 PRINT "THE AVERAGE RAINFALL IN MAY WAS";A;"INCHES"
110 DATA 2, 2.5, 1.5, 1
999 END
```

Flowchart (left column, top to bottom):
Start → Assign Heading to H$ → Print Heading → Read Average Weekly Rainfalls → Calculate Total Monthly Rainfall → Calculate Average Monthly Rainfall → Print Column Headings → Print Total and Average Rainfalls → Stop

contains four literals. The literals are to appear as column headings on the program output. When statement 70 is executed, they are printed out exactly as written except that the quotation marks do not appear.

```
MAY RAINFALL

WEEK 1          WEEK 2          WEEK 3          WEEK 4
2               2.5             1.5             1
THE TOTAL RAINFALL IN MAY WAS 7 INCHES
THE AVERAGE RAINFALL IN MAY WAS 1.75 INCHES
```

Numeric literals do not have to be enclosed in quotation marks to be printed. Thus, the statement

```
10 PRINT 167
```

causes the numeric literal 167 to be printed.

Skipping Lines   Output produced with BASIC is single-spaced. If the programmer wants the computer to skip a line, he/she uses a PRINT statement with nothing following the word PRINT. Thus, when the computer executes statements 30 and 85 in the RAINFALL program, blank lines appear on the output.

```
30 PRINT
85 PRINT
```

```
        MAY RAINFALL

⟶
        WEEK 1         WEEK 2          WEEK 3           WEEK 4
          2             2.5             1.5               1

⟶
        THE TOTAL RAINFALL IN MAY WAS 7 INCHES
        THE AVERAGE RAINFALL IN MAY WAS 1.75 INCHES
```

Printing the Values of Expressions   The computer can print not only literals and the values of variables, but also the values of arithmetic expressions. First, the expression is evaluated. Then the result (i.e., the value of the expression) is printed. Usually, the value is rounded to six significant digits (i.e., the leftmost digit that is not zero and the five digits to its right). If the value is extremely large or extremely small, the computer may print it in exponential, or scientific, notation. The character E is used to represent the decimal base 10. (This form is also called floating-point—the number is represented by a fraction and an exponent which indicates the usual position of the decimal point.) For example, a value such as .004568 is printed in exponential form as 4.568E-3. None of this affects the values of the numbers in the storage locations; they remain in their original state.

The program in Figure A–8 deals with expressions in both decimal and exponential forms.

FIGURE A–8
Expressions Printed
in Both Decimal
and Exponential Notations

```
10 LET A = 123456
20 LET B = 6789012345
30 LET C = .0004568
40 LET D = 33.6E3
50 PRINT A+4, B*C, D-A, C/D
60 PRINT A,B,
70 PRINT C,D
80 END


RUN


123460       3101221       -89856       1.35952E-08
123456       6.78901E+09    4.56800E-04   33600
```

When the PRINT statement in line 50 is executed, the four expressions are evaluated and their values printed. Notice that the extremely large and small numbers printed by statements 60 and 70 are printed in exponential notation.

Print Zones and Punctuation On some terminals, each output line consists of 75 print positions. The line is divided into five zones, each fifteen characters wide. It can be thought of as typewriter output produced with tab stops every fifteen spaces. The beginning columns of the five print zones are shown below:

Print zone	First column
1	1
2	16
3	31
4	46
5	61

When more than one item is to be printed on a line, two punctuation marks can be used to control the spacing of the output: the comma and the semicolon.

The comma is used to separate items that are to be printed according to the five print zones. Thus, in the RAINFALL program, the commas in the statements

```
70 PRINT "WEEK 1", "WEEK 2", "WEEK 3", "WEEK 4"
80 PRINT R1, R2, R3, R4
```

cause the output to be spaced according to the print zones. Statement 70 says: "Print the literal WEEK 1 in the first zone (starting in column 1); then print the literal WEEK 2 in the second zone (starting in column 16); and so on." Statement 80 says: "Print the value of R1 in the first zone; then print the value of R2 in the second zone; R3 in the third zone; and R4 in the fourth zone."

Col. 1   **Col. 16**   **Col. 31**   **Col. 46**

```
WEEK 1        WEEK 2        WEEK 3        WEEK 4
 2             2.5           1.5           1
```

```
THE TOTAL RAINFALL IN MAY WAS 7 INCHES
THE AVERAGE RAINFALL IN MAY WAS 1.75 INCHES
```

If there are more than five items to be printed, as in

```
10 PRINT P, H, M, E, X, Y
```

the computer runs out of zones. The value of Y is printed in the first zone of the next line.

In spacing output across the page, a print zone can be skipped by a technique that involves enclosing a space (the character blank) in quotation marks. The entire zone appears empty, or blank. Thus,

```
10 PRINT "TOTAL SCORE", " ", "AVERAGE SCORE"
```

causes the literal TOTAL SCORE to be printed in the first zone beginning in column 1; the second zone to be blank; and the literal AVERAGE SCORE to be printed in the third zone beginning in column 31.

As mentioned earlier, output generated by a PRINT statement normally begins in the first zone of a new line. However, if the previously executed PRINT statement ends with a comma, the output of a PRINT statement starts in the next available zone. Thus, in Figure A–8, the statements

```
60 PRINT A,B,
70 PRINT C,D
```

produce the following output:

```
123456   6.78901E+09   4.56800E-04   33600
```

To avoid the inflexibility of the fixed print zones which result when using commas, semicolons can be used in PRINT statements. Using the semicolon instead of the comma causes output to be packed more closely on a line. When a semicolon is used between positive numeric data items, two blanks, or spaces, appear between the printed output values (one space for the semicolon and one for the assumed positive sign). When the semicolon controls printing of a negative number, only one blank precedes the minus sign. Notice the difference in output spacing when semicolons are used instead of commas:

Statements: 10 PRINT 1,2,-3
               99 END

Output: 1   2   -3

Statements: 10 PRINT 1;2;-3
               99 END

Output: 1 2 -3

If a semicolon is used to separate a number or numeric variable from a preceding literal, a single space appears between the printed output values if the number is positive:

```
90 PRINT "THE TOTAL RAINFALL IN MAY WAS"; T;"INCHES"
100 PRINT "THE AVERAGE RAINFALL IN MAY WAS"; A; "INCHES"


MAY RAINFALL

WEEK 1            WEEK 2            WEEK 3            WEEK 4
  2                2.5              1.5                1
THE TOTAL RAINFALL IN MAY WAS 7 INCHES
THE AVERAGE RAINFALL IN MAY WAS 1.75 INCHES
```

No space appears if the number is negative. In like manner, when a semicolon separates two literals, no spacing is provided.

If the semicolon is the last character of the PRINT statement, the output medium (generally, a paper document) is not advanced when the printing by the statement is completed. So, the output generated by the next PRINT statement execution continues on the same line.

The END Statement

Every BASIC program must conclude with an END statement. The END statement indicates the end of the program. It must be assigned the highest line number in the program. The general format of the END statement is:

line# END

Thus, in the RAINFALL program,

999 END

is a complete END statement. The use of an all-9s line number for the END statement is a common programming practice. This convention serves as a reminder to the programmer to include the END statement and helps to insure that it is positioned properly.

The INPUT Statement

BASIC can be used in interactive mode—that is, BASIC programs can be written in such a way that user participation is required to achieve desired results. The user/programmer does not have to specify or supply all the problem data in DATA statements. He/she can enter data as it is needed during execution of the program. In essence, the user carries on a conversation with the computer while the program is being executed.

The statement that allows user interaction with the computer is the INPUT statement. The INPUT statement is like a READ statement in that it is a way to assign values to variables—but the data is typed in by the user as it is needed, rather than supplied in a DATA statement in the program. The INPUT statement causes the computer to stop execution and await data; the user can then respond by keying in the data. This method of entering data allows the input data values to be supplied at program execution time.

The general format of the INPUT statement is:

line# INPUT variable-list

INPUT statements are placed in a program wherever data is needed. When the computer reaches an INPUT statement during program execution, it stops executing the program, prints a question mark (?), and waits for the user to supply the necessary data. When the data has been entered, execution proceeds from where it stopped.

Since the INPUT statement signals the need for data with only a question mark, it is good programming practice to precede each INPUT statement with a PRINT statement. That statement should print a line (message) explaining to the user what data is to be entered. This practice is particularly important in a BASIC program that contains numerous INPUT statements; otherwise, when the user sees only a question mark requesting data, he/she may not know what data values are to be entered and in what order.

Figure A–9 shows a metric conversion program similar to the one at

471

the beginning of this section (see Figure A–1). It uses an INPUT statement rather than READ/DATA statements to supply data values.

The computer prints the literal INCHES before asking for input. The semicolon ending statement 10 insures that no space is left after the literal; thus, the question mark produced by INPUT immediately follows the word INCHES, as shown in the output of the run.

The number following the first question mark in Figure A–9 was typed by the user. That number was assigned to the variable I. Statements 30 through 50 convert the number to centimeters, print the result (the value of C), and skip one line. Then the computer returns to line 10 and asks for another input. When the user wants execution to stop, he/she can press the BREAK key.

Comprehensive Programming Problem

A local pet store, The Pet Shed, is having its annual clearance sale this month. It offers the following pets, at the indicated sale prices:

Pet	Sale Price
Fish	.53
Kittens	2.98
Puppies	5.69
Birds	3.95

FIGURE A–9

Use of INPUT Statement

```
10 PRINT "INCHES";
20 INPUT I
30 LET C = I*2.54
40 PRINT "CENTIMETERS:";C
50 PRINT
60 GO TO 10
99 END


RUN


INCHES?9
CENTIMETERS: 22.86

INCHES?15
CENTIMETERS: 38.1

INCHES?42
CENTIMETERS: 106.68

INCHES?34
CENTIMETERS: 86.36

INCHES?36
CENTIMETERS: 91.44

INCHES?10
CENTIMETERS: 25.4

INCHES?

STOP.
```

During the first two weeks of the sale, The Pet Shed sold 117 fish, 39 kittens, 25 puppies, and 63 birds. Management wants to know the gross sales for each item, as well as the total gross sales, for the two-week period. You are to write a BASIC program to calculate these figures.

Because the report of this sale will become part of The Pet Shed's monthly financial report, the output should be in a form that is understandable to stockholders as well as to management. Thus, the following output format is required:

```
              THE PET SHED
              ANNUAL CLEARANCE SALE

FISH SALES     KITTEN SALES    PUPPY SALES    BIRD SALES

$ XX.XX        $ XXX.XX        $ XXX.XX       $ XXX.XX

TOTAL GROSS SALES WERE    $ XXX.XX
```

It is also required, for documentation purposes, that the program contain remarks and that a flowchart of the program be developed.

Problem Solution

Figure A–10 shows a solution to this programming problem, in both flowchart and BASIC-language forms.

The BASIC statements presented in Section II allow the user/programmer to write relatively uncomplicated programs. Many programs solve problems that require more sophisticated logic. This section introduces additional programming concepts and corresponding BASIC statements.

Figure A–11 shows a program that calculates a salesperson's commission based on the following table:

Sales	Commission Rate
$000–$499	0%
$500–$999	1%
$1000–$1499	3%
$1500–$1999	7%

For example, if a salesperson sells $1200 worth of merchandise, his/her commission equals .03 $\times$ $1200, or $36.

Several BASIC statements are introduced in this sales program. Statements 160 and 170 allow control to be transferred to a statement that does not immediately follow the statement being executed.

Statement 160 is an IF/THEN statement. It permits a *conditional transfer* of control.

```
160 IF N$ = "NO MORE" THEN 290
```

The computer first checks the character-string value stored in the variable N$. If this value is NO MORE, the end of the input data has been reached, so control transfers to the END statement. If the value is not

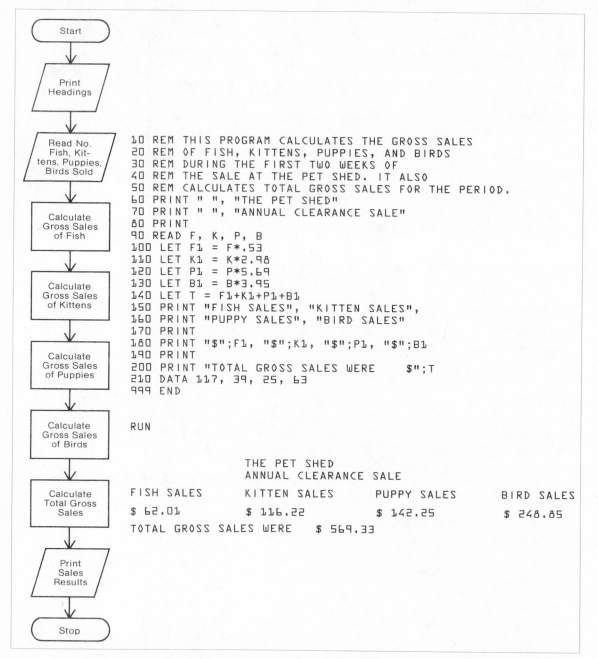

```
10 REM THIS PROGRAM CALCULATES THE GROSS SALES
20 REM OF FISH, KITTENS, PUPPIES, AND BIRDS
30 REM DURING THE FIRST TWO WEEKS OF
40 REM THE SALE AT THE PET SHED. IT ALSO
50 REM CALCULATES TOTAL GROSS SALES FOR THE PERIOD.
60 PRINT " ", "THE PET SHED"
70 PRINT " ", "ANNUAL CLEARANCE SALE"
80 PRINT
90 READ F, K, P, B
100 LET F1 = F*.53
110 LET K1 = K*2.98
120 LET P1 = P*5.69
130 LET B1 = B*3.95
140 LET T = F1+K1+P1+B1
150 PRINT "FISH SALES", "KITTEN SALES",
160 PRINT "PUPPY SALES", "BIRD SALES"
170 PRINT
180 PRINT "$";F1, "$";K1, "$";P1, "$";B1
190 PRINT
200 PRINT "TOTAL GROSS SALES WERE    $";T
210 DATA 117, 39, 25, 63
999 END


RUN


                    THE PET SHED
                    ANNUAL CLEARANCE SALE
FISH SALES          KITTEN SALES        PUPPY SALES        BIRD SALES
$ 62.01             $ 116.22            $ 142.25           $ 248.85
TOTAL GROSS SALES WERE    $ 569.33
```

FIGURE A–10
BASIC Sales Program

NO MORE, the flow of execution continues sequentially to the next statement (statement 170).

Statement 170 is called an ON/GO TO, or computed GO TO, statement. It also permits a conditional transfer of control.

```
170 ON S/500 GO TO 200,220,240
```

When the value of sales (S) divided by 500 equals 1, control branches to statement 200; the LET statement calculates the commission for an

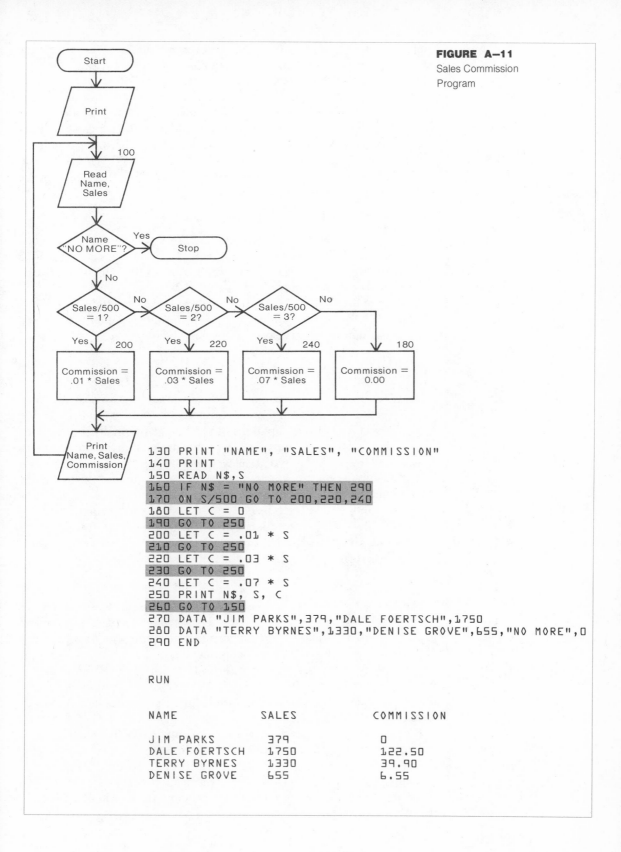

```
130 PRINT "NAME", "SALES", "COMMISSION"
140 PRINT
150 READ N$,S
160 IF N$ = "NO MORE" THEN 290
170 ON S/500 GO TO 200,220,240
180 LET C = 0
190 GO TO 250
200 LET C = .01 * S
210 GO TO 250
220 LET C = .03 * S
230 GO TO 250
240 LET C = .07 * S
250 PRINT N$, S, C
260 GO TO 150
270 DATA "JIM PARKS",379,"DALE FOERTSCH",1750
280 DATA "TERRY BYRNES",1330,"DENISE GROVE",655,"NO MORE",0
290 END


RUN


NAME            SALES               COMMISSION

JIM PARKS       379                 0
DALE FOERTSCH   1750                122.50
TERRY BYRNES    1330                39.90
DENISE GROVE    655                 6.55
```

employee selling less than $999 worth of merchandise. Similarly, if the expression S/500 equals 2, control branches to statement 220; when the expression equals 3, control branches to statement 240.

Conditional transfers, as just discussed, are very important in the execution of most programs. The sales program also contains *unconditional transfers,* caused by GO TO statements. When a GO TO statement is encountered, the flow of execution proceeds to the statement whose number immediately follows the words GO TO. The GO TO in line 260, for example, transfers control to statement 150, which is the READ statement for inputting data.

```
260 GO TO 150
```

The use of the GO TO statement in line 260 allows a required sequence of statements to be executed repetitively, until all sales commissions have been processed. This repetitive processing of the same sequence of statements is called *looping.*

The unconditional and conditional transfer statements, GO TO, IF/THEN, and ON/GO TO, appear in all but the most elementary BASIC programs. Their use is developed more fully below.

The Unconditional Transfer GO TO Statement

All BASIC programs consist of series of statements, which are normally executed in sequential order. Sometimes, however, it is desirable to perform statements in a pattern other than sequentially. In the sales commission program (Figure A–11), for example, imagine the difficulty that would be encountered if all statements had to be written, and rewritten, in the order in which they were to be executed. And, to further appreciate this point, imagine there were 100 salespersons. Many of the statements would have to be written 100 times. Fortunately, there are alternatives. One is to change the flow of execution to re-execute statements. The programmer can use the GO TO statement to do this. The general format of the GO TO statement is:

line# GO TO transfer-line#

The GO TO statement is called an unconditional transfer statement because the flow of execution is altered *every time* the GO TO statement is performed. This allows the programmer to bypass or to repeatedly execute statements in the program as needed.

Consider the program in Figure A–12. It multiplies two numbers and prints the results. The inefficiency in the use of statements is readily apparent. Each time the read/multiply/print processes are required, statements are re-specified.

The same results are accomplished using a GO TO statement in Figure A–13. The statement GO TO 10 in line 40 directs the computer back to statement 10. A loop pattern is formed. In this example, the message "LINE 10: END OF DATA" was printed when an attempt was made to read data after the data list was exhausted. The execution of the program was terminated.

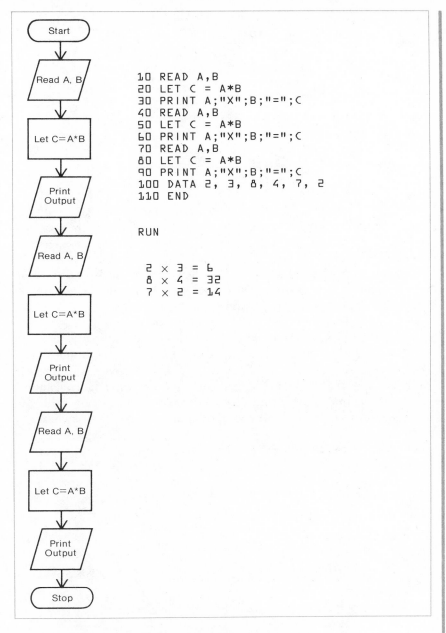

```
10 READ A,B
20 LET C = A*B
30 PRINT A;"X";B;"=";C
40 READ A,B
50 LET C = A*B
60 PRINT A;"X";B;"=";C
70 READ A,B
80 LET C = A*B
90 PRINT A;"X";B;"=";C
100 DATA 2, 3, 8, 4, 7, 2
110 END


RUN


2 X 3 = 6
8 X 4 = 32
7 X 2 = 14
```

FIGURE A–12
Straight-Line
(Sequential-Only) Program

The Conditional Transfer IF/THEN Statement

Often, within a program, it is necessary to transfer the flow of control only when a specified condition or relationship is true. The IF/THEN statement is used to accomplish a transfer of this nature. Unlike the GO TO statement, which always causes a transfer of control, the IF/THEN statement is a conditional transfer statement; it causes a transfer *only* when a specified condition is true. If the condition is false, execution flows to the next statement in sequence. The general format of the IF/THEN statement is:

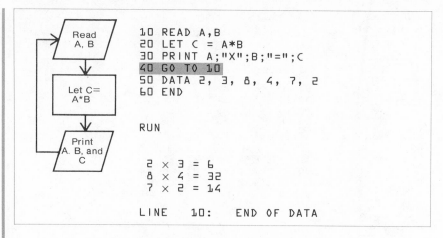

Use of GO TO
Statement

line # IF test-condition THEN line #

The condition or relationship that is tested may involve either numeric or character-string data. The *relational symbols* that may be used in stating test conditions are shown below.

As the numeric examples suggest, numeric relationships have a variety of applications. The applicability of character-string comparisons may not be as obvious. One application was used in the sales commission program (Figure A–11). Recall that an IF/THEN statement was used to check for the end of the data list. Detecting the end of the data available for processing and transferring control to the END statement avoided the printout of an END OF DATA message such as we saw in Figure A–13.

Some examples of valid IF/THEN statements are given below.

(a)
```
10 IF X > 6 THEN 99
20 LET A = 5
        .
        .
99 END
```
If X is greater than 6, transfer to statement 99; otherwise execute the next statement (20).

(b)
```
10 IF K <> N THEN 50
20 PRINT N$, K
        .
        .
50 LET K = K + 1
```
If K is not equal to N, transfer to statement 50; otherwise execute the next statement (20).

BASIC RELATIONAL SYMBOL	MEANING	BASIC NUMERIC EXAMPLE	BASIC CHARACTER-STRING EXAMPLE
<	Less than	$A < B$	$N\$ < $ "JONES"
<=	Less than or equal to	$C1 <= 10$	"SMITH" $<=$ "JONES"
>	Greater than	$X + Y > C$	$P\$ > $ "825-3846"
>=	Greater than or equal to	$B3 + 5 >= M$	"BLACK" $>=$ T$
<>	Not equal to	$A <> B$	"BURTON" $<>$ "NELSON"
=	Equal to	$D + E = F$	$N\$ = $ "LAST DATA"

The program in Figure A–14 uses both numeric and character-string comparisons to search a firm's employee records to find an employee suitable for promotion. The firm is looking for a manager for its data-processing department. The individual must be a system analyst with at least 10 years experience.

The program reads in the name, occupation, and years of experience of each candidate. A character-string comparison is made to determine if the employee is a system analyst:

```
110 IF O$ <> "SYSTEM ANALYST" THEN 160
```

This test condition is stated in such a way that if the test condition is true, the computer branches directly to statement 160; the second test condition (line 120) does not have to be checked.

The other job qualification requirement is 10 or more years of experience. A numeric comparison is used to determine if the employee satisfies this requirement:

```
120 IF Y < 10 THEN 160
```

As above, if the test condition is true, the computer branches directly to statement 160.

The program output indicates that only one of the candidates, Robert Johnson, should be considered for promotion to the data-processing manager position.

FIGURE A–14

Use of Numeric and Character-String Comparisons

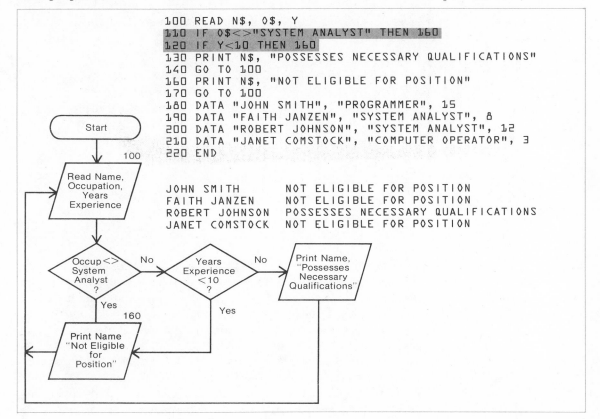

```
100 READ N$, O$, Y
110 IF O$<>"SYSTEM ANALYST" THEN 160
120 IF Y<10 THEN 160
130 PRINT N$, "POSSESSES NECESSARY QUALIFICATIONS"
140 GO TO 100
160 PRINT N$, "NOT ELIGIBLE FOR POSITION"
170 GO TO 100
180 DATA "JOHN SMITH", "PROGRAMMER", 15
190 DATA "FAITH JANZEN", "SYSTEM ANALYST", 8
200 DATA "ROBERT JOHNSON", "SYSTEM ANALYST", 12
210 DATA "JANET COMSTOCK", "COMPUTER OPERATOR", 3
220 END
```

```
JOHN SMITH        NOT ELIGIBLE FOR POSITION
FAITH JANZEN      NOT ELIGIBLE FOR POSITION
ROBERT JOHNSON    POSSESSES NECESSARY QUALIFICATIONS
JANET COMSTOCK    NOT ELIGIBLE FOR POSITION
```

The Computed GO TO Statement

The computed GO TO statement instructs the computer to evaluate one expression and, based on its value, branch to one of several points in a program. The computed GO TO essentially operates as multiple IF/THEN statements; any one of several transfers may occur, based on the value of the expression. Since a transfer occurs only under specific circumstances, the computed GO TO statement is a conditional transfer statement. The general format of this statement is:

line# ON expression GO TO transfer-line-#1, 2, . . . , #n

The expression is always evaluated to an integer, and the line numbers following GO TO must identify statements in the program. The general execution of the ON/GO TO statement proceeds as follows:

1. If the value of the expression is 1, control is transferred to the first statement indicated.

2. If the value of the expression is 2, control is transferred to the second statement indicated.
$$\vdots \qquad\qquad \vdots \qquad\qquad \vdots$$
n. If the value of the expression is n, control is transferred to the nth statement indicated.

Several examples are presented below to illustrate the operation of this statement.

(a) `10 ON X GO TO 50,80,100`   If X = 1, control goes to line 50.
If X = 2, control goes to line 80.
If X = 3, control goes to line 100.

(b) `30 ON N/50 GO TO 90,110`   If N/50 = 1, control goes to line 90.
If N/50 = 2, control goes to line 110.

If the expression in a computed GO TO statement does not evaluate to an integer, the value is truncated (any digits to the right of the decimal point are ignored). Typically, if the expression evaluates to an integer greater than the number of statement numbers following GO TO, or to an integer less than 1, the entire computed GO TO statement is bypassed; control passes to the next sequential statement. (Some systems type an error message such as "ON -5 LN #15" if the test condition value is less than 1 or exceeds the number of statement numbers in the GO TO list. Each user/programmer should consult the reference manual for the specific system in use.) Examples of both instances are shown on the next page.

Statement	Value of Variable	Action
`40 ON N/3 GO TO 60,80`	N = 7	$7 \div 3 = 2.33$. The expression is evaluated as the integer 2, and control passes to statement 80.
`60 ON X GO TO 100,140,170` `70 LET X = Y`	X = 4	The value of X exceeds the number of statement numbers in the GO TO list. Control passes to statement 70.

The program segment in Figure A–15 may help to clarify the use of the ON/GO TO statement. In this example, the ON/GO TO statement is used to group individuals into appropriate age categories. The conditional transfer to an appropriate LET statement allows the number of individuals in each age group to be totalled.

Statement 130 is an ON/GO TO statement:

`130 ON A/10 GO TO 150,170,190`

When this statement is executed, the individual's age is divided by 10. If the integer result is 1, control transfers to statement 150. If the result is 2, control transfers to statement 170. If the result is 3, control transfers to 190. The first two input values for age (see Figure A–15) are processed as shown below.

Age	Action
25	$25 \div 10 = 2.5$ Evaluated as the integer 2; control passes to statement 170.
16	$16 \div 10 = 1.6$ Evaluated as the integer 1; control passes to statement 150.

The variables A1, A2, and A3 are used to maintain running totals for the age groups. They are called *accumulators*. When using an accumulator, it is important to assign a beginning value to the variable used as the accumulator; doing so insures that no other value is stored there. This process is called *initialization*. It is accomplished by statement 100, a LET statement:

`100 LET A1,A2,A3 = 0`

This statement causes zero to be assigned to each of the variables.

Statements 150, 170, and 190 illustrate the accumulation process. For example, the purpose of statement 150 is to keep a running total of the number of individuals in the age group of 10 to 19 years.

`150 LET A1 = A1 + 1`

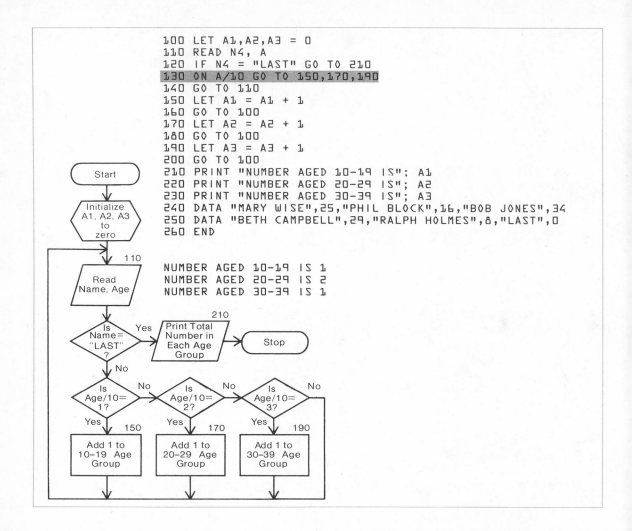

```
100 LET A1,A2,A3 = 0
110 READ N4, A
120 IF N4 = "LAST" GO TO 210
130 ON A/10 GO TO 150,170,190
140 GO TO 110
150 LET A1 = A1 + 1
160 GO TO 100
170 LET A2 = A2 + 1
180 GO TO 100
190 LET A3 = A3 + 1
200 GO TO 100
210 PRINT "NUMBER AGED 10-19 IS"; A1
220 PRINT "NUMBER AGED 20-29 IS"; A2
230 PRINT "NUMBER AGED 30-39 IS"; A3
240 DATA "MARY WISE",25,"PHIL BLOCK",16,"BOB JONES",34
250 DATA "BETH CAMPBELL",29,"RALPH HOLMES",8,"LAST",0
260 END
```

```
NUMBER AGED 10-19 IS 1
NUMBER AGED 20-29 IS 2
NUMBER AGED 30-39 IS 1
```

FIGURE A–15

Use of Computed
GO TO Statement

Each time this LET statement is executed (when control has been transferred from statement 130), 1 is added to the current value of A1. Thus, this statement counts the number of individuals aged 10 to 19. If A1 had not been initialized to zero, there may have been a value other than zero in that location. The final count, or total, would have differed accordingly.

(The ON/GO TO statement is not a standard feature of all BASIC systems. The user's reference manual should be consulted before attempting to use this statement.)

The STOP Statement

The STOP statement is, in essence, an unconditional transfer statement that diverts the flow of execution directly to the END statement whenever it is encountered. The general format of the STOP statement is:

482 line# STOP

The STOP statement at the left below performs the same task as the GO TO 99 statement at the right. That is, the following program segments are equivalent.

```
30 STOP     30 GO TO 99
   .            .
   .            .
   .            .
99 END      99 END
```

The STOP statement differs from the END statement in that STOP may appear as often as necessary in a program. For example, Figure A–16 presents a simple program using three STOP statements. The flow of execution is determined by the values of A and B. For example:

Values of A	B	Flow of Execution
3	4	10, 20, 30, 80, 90, 110
8	8	10, 20, 30, 40, 50, 110

Looping Procedures

The programming flexibility provided by the loop pattern takes advantage of a powerful capability of the computer. Rather than repetitively write a particular sequence of statements (once for each data item, or set of data items, to be processed), we set up a loop pattern to reuse a stored sequence of statements for each data item or set of data items.

A major consideration when constructing a loop is the error message that results from an attempt to read data from a data list after all data in the list has been read. To avoid this error message, it is necessary to control execution of the loop by indicating to the computer when the end of the data list has been reached. BASIC has two techniques for loop control: trailer values and counters.

A loop controlled by a *trailer value* contains an IF/THEN statement that checks for the last item in the data list. This last item is supplied after the last data item, but it is not actually part of the data to be processed. Either numeric or alphanumeric data can be used as a trailer value. The programmer should always select a trailer value that

```
10 READ A,B
20 IF A>B THEN 60
30 IF A<B THEN 80
40 PRINT A;"EQUALS";B
50 STOP
60 PRINT A;"IS GREATER THAN";B
70 STOP
80 PRINT A;"IS LESS THAN";B
90 STOP
100 DATA 7,5
110 END

7 IS GREATER THAN 5
```

FIGURE A–16
Use of STOP
Statement

483

will never appear as a data value. Otherwise an undesired halt in processing may occur.

Figure A–17 shows a program containing a loop pattern controlled by a trailer value. The program reads a baseball player's name, times at bat, and hits, and then calculates his/her batting average. The condition checked in statement 40 is N\$ = "END OF DATA". If this condition is true, the flow of processing drops out of the loop to the END statement. If the condition is false, the THEN 999 portion of the IF/THEN statement is not executed. The flow of processing continues in sequential order to statement 50.

A second method of controlling a loop requires the programmer to create a *counter* that counts the number of times a loop has been executed. The counter is simply a numeric variable that is incremented by one each time the loop is processed. The steps involved in setting up a counter are:

1. Initialize the counter to give it a beginning value.

2. Modify the counter each time the loop is executed.

3. Test the counter to determine if the loop has been executed the desired number of times.

FIGURE A–17
Baseball Program—Loop
with Trailer Value

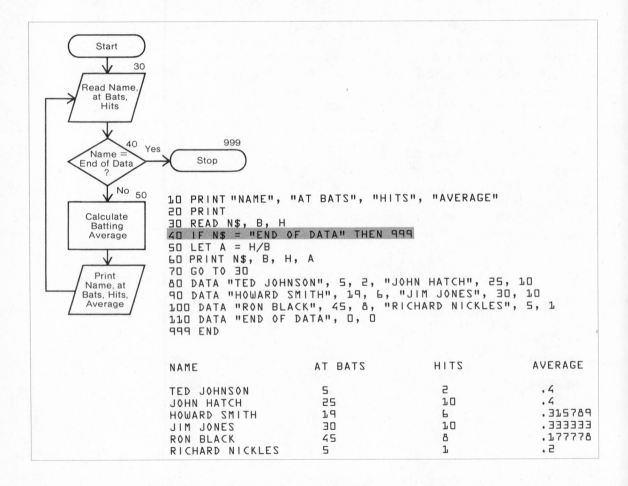

```
10 PRINT "NAME", "AT BATS", "HITS", "AVERAGE"
20 PRINT
30 READ N$, B, H
40 IF N$ = "END OF DATA" THEN 999
50 LET A = H/B
60 PRINT N$, B, H, A
70 GO TO 30
80 DATA "TED JOHNSON", 5, 2, "JOHN HATCH", 25, 10
90 DATA "HOWARD SMITH", 19, 6, "JIM JONES", 30, 10
100 DATA "RON BLACK", 45, 8, "RICHARD NICKLES", 5, 1
110 DATA "END OF DATA", 0, 0
999 END
```

NAME	AT BATS	HITS	AVERAGE
TED JOHNSON	5	2	.4
JOHN HATCH	25	10	.4
HOWARD SMITH	19	6	.315789
JIM JONES	30	10	.333333
RON BLACK	45	8	.177778
RICHARD NICKLES	5	1	.2

For example:

```
20 LET X = 0
30 READ A ←
40 LET T = A**2
50 PRINT A, T
60 LET X = X + 1                          Loop
70 IF X < 5 THEN 30 ─
80 PRINT X
90 DATA 14, 15, 16, 17, 18
 •
 •
 •
```

In the example above, the loop is executed five times since the initial value of the counter X is 0. The IF/THEN statement is used to check the value of the counter. When X equals 5 (after the fifth time through the loop), the test condition is false; the sequence of execution flows to the next sequential statement.

The baseball program in Figure A–17 can be modified to use a counter as shown in Figure A–18. Note, however, that a counter is effective only

FIGURE A–18

Baseball Program—Loop with Counter

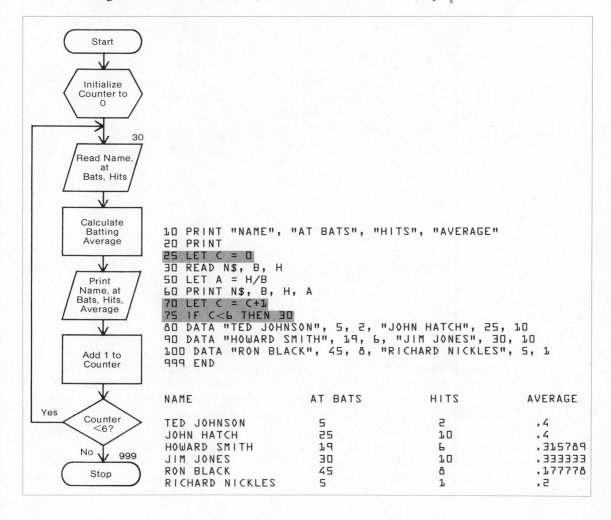

```
10 PRINT "NAME", "AT BATS", "HITS", "AVERAGE"
20 PRINT
25 LET C = 0
30 READ N$, B, H
50 LET A = H/B
60 PRINT N$, B, H, A
70 LET C = C+1
75 IF C<6 THEN 30
80 DATA "TED JOHNSON", 5, 2, "JOHN HATCH", 25, 10
90 DATA "HOWARD SMITH", 19, 6, "JIM JONES", 30, 10
100 DATA "RON BLACK", 45, 8, "RICHARD NICKLES", 5, 1
999 END
```

NAME	AT BATS	HITS	AVERAGE
TED JOHNSON	5	2	.4
JOHN HATCH	25	10	.4
HOWARD SMITH	19	6	.315789
JIM JONES	30	10	.333333
RON BLACK	45	8	.177778
RICHARD NICKLES	5	1	.2

when the programmer knows exactly how many times the loop should be executed. When uncertainty exists, it is best to use a trailer value.

Comprehensive Programming Problem

Management Consultant Services, Inc. (MCS) is a service firm employing 10 people. The controller for MCS is faced with the problem of calculating the total dollar values of federal withholding taxes deducted from the employees' salaries during the past year. Rather than calculate these figures manually, the controller has decided to use the firm's computer facility, and has asked a programming consultant to develop a program to calculate the figures. Since a report must be submitted to the president of MCS, the controller has requested that the output be formatted so that it can be read easily.

The controller has a list of the employees and their salaries, and a tax table to follow in the computation of withholding tax. Both of these are shown below.

Employee	Gross Income
Mary Bruno	$38,000
Ronald Grove	$22,000
Paul Anthony	$29,000
Angela Posillico	$8,500
Steven Clare	$12,750
Lissa Sarniak	$23,450
Mark Green	$15,400
Daniel Horton	$19,200
Kathleen Dufore	$32,011
Debra Russo	$29,325

Yearly Gross Income	Tax Rate
0– 9,999	.08
10,000–19,999	.11
20,000–29,999	.16
30,000–39,999	.23

Problem Solution

Figure A–19 shows a solution to this programming problem.

In Section III, two methods of controlling loops were discussed: counters and trailer values. This section presents two BASIC statements used primarily for loop control: FOR and NEXT.

In the counter procedure for loop control, the counter variable is set to some initial value. Then the processing statements in the loop are executed once. Then the variable is incremented (stepped) by an amount (up or down) and tested against a loop terminal value. If the loop has not been executed the required number of times, the statements in the loop are executed again. Eventually, the variable exceeds the designated

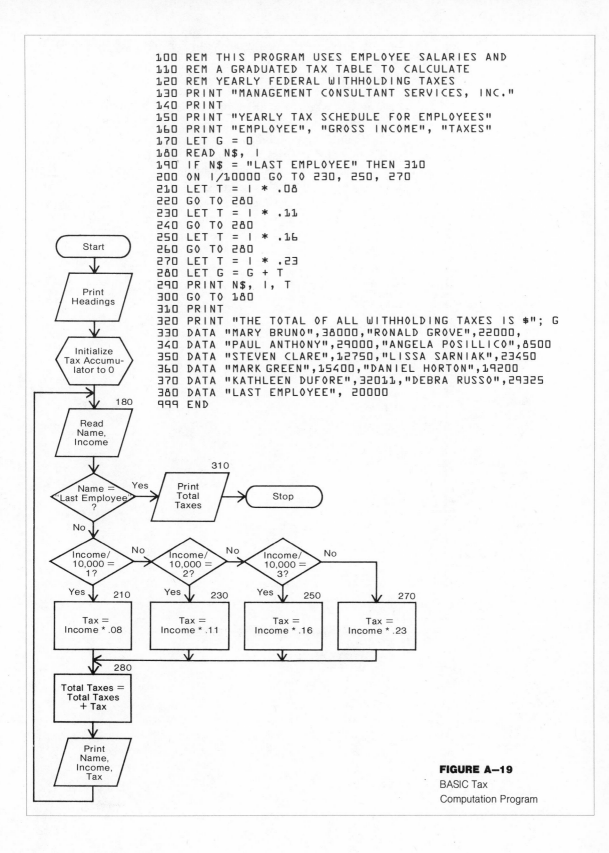

```
100 REM THIS PROGRAM USES EMPLOYEE SALARIES AND
110 REM A GRADUATED TAX TABLE TO CALCULATE
120 REM YEARLY FEDERAL WITHHOLDING TAXES
130 PRINT "MANAGEMENT CONSULTANT SERVICES, INC."
140 PRINT
150 PRINT "YEARLY TAX SCHEDULE FOR EMPLOYEES"
160 PRINT "EMPLOYEE", "GROSS INCOME", "TAXES"
170 LET G = 0
180 READ N$, I
190 IF N$ = "LAST EMPLOYEE" THEN 310
200 ON I/10000 GO TO 230, 250, 270
210 LET T = I * .08
220 GO TO 280
230 LET T = I * .11
240 GO TO 280
250 LET T = I * .16
260 GO TO 280
270 LET T = I * .23
280 LET G = G + T
290 PRINT N$, I, T
300 GO TO 180
310 PRINT
320 PRINT "THE TOTAL OF ALL WITHHOLDING TAXES IS $"; G
330 DATA "MARY BRUNO",38000,"RONALD GROVE",22000,
340 DATA "PAUL ANTHONY",29000,"ANGELA POSILLICO",8500
350 DATA "STEVEN CLARE",12750,"LISSA SARNIAK",23450
360 DATA "MARK GREEN",15400,"DANIEL HORTON",19200
370 DATA "KATHLEEN DUFORE",32011,"DEBRA RUSSO",29325
380 DATA "LAST EMPLOYEE", 20000
999 END
```

FIGURE A—19

BASIC Tax
Computation Program

terminal value. At that point, the computer proceeds to the remainder of the program.

For example, assume we are to write a program to compute and print the square and cube of each of the integers from 1 to 5. From Section III, we know at least one possible approach (see Figure A–20).

Because the requirement for looping arises repeatedly in programming, BASIC language designers have provided the statements FOR and NEXT to help programmers express loops more concisely. The program in Figure A–21 does the same thing as the program in Figure A–20 (this can be verified by examining the output).

Not only are there fewer statements (two have replaced four), but also the loop control information is contained in one statement (line 10). Notice the following flowchart symbol, which is used in Figure A–21:

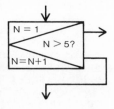

FIGURE A–20
Counter-Controlled Loop

```
10 LET N = 1
20 IF N > 5 THEN 60
30 PRINT N, N**2, N**3
40 LET N = N+1
50 GO TO 20
60 END


RUN

1                    1                    1
2                    4                    8
3                    9                    27
4                    16                   64
5                    25                   125
```

FIGURE A–21
Use of FOR
and NEXT Statements

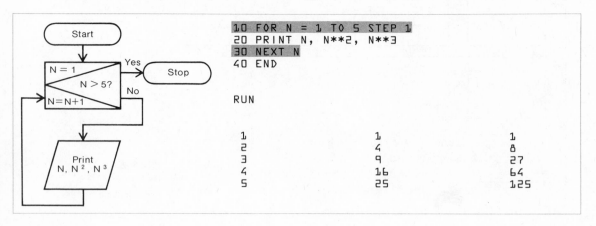

```
10 FOR N = 1 TO 5 STEP 1
20 PRINT N, N**2, N**3
30 NEXT N
40 END


RUN

1                    1                    1
2                    4                    8
3                    9                    27
4                    16                   64
5                    25                   125
```

This symbol is a non-ANSI flowchart symbol, which is very convenient for representing a loop process. The initial, terminal, and step value for the loop control variable are shown in one symbol.

The statements within a loop written in this manner are the FOR statement, its associated NEXT statement, and the statements between these two. The variable whose value is to be changed whenever the loop is executed (in this case N) is indicated in both the FOR and NEXT statements:

```
10 FOR N = 1 TO 5 STEP 1
   .
   .
   .
30 NEXT N
```

The number following the word STEP tells the computer how much the value of the loop control variable is to change each time the loop is executed. The initial, terminal, and step values are indicated in that order in the FOR statement. The general format of the FOR statement is:

line# FOR variable = initial-value TO terminal-value STEP step-value

The STEP clause may be omitted; the step value is then assumed to be 1. Thus, the following statements are equivalent:

```
20 FOR X = 1 TO 25
20 FOR X = 1 TO 25 STEP 1
```

The computer does the following things when it encounters a FOR statement:

1. It sets the loop control variable to the indicated initial value.

2. It tests to see if the value of the variable is already past the indicated terminal value.

3. If the value of the variable is not past the terminal value, the statements in the loop are executed.

4. If the value of the variable is already past the terminal value, control is transferred to the statement following the associated NEXT statement.

When the NEXT statement is encountered at the end of a loop execution, the computer does the following things:

1. It adds the step value to the value of the loop control variable.

2. It goes back to the FOR statement.

This processing continues until the value of the loop control variable is past the terminal value (see step 4 above).

Now assume we are to write a program to generate and print all the odd integers between 1 and 10. We can use FOR and NEXT statements as shown below.

489

```
10 FOR J = 1 TO 10 STEP 2
20 PRINT J
30 NEXT J
40 END

RUN

    1
    3
    5
    7
    9
```

A line-by-line analysis of the execution of the program follows.

Line Number	Result
10	J is 1, not > terminal value 10
20	PRINT J
30	Increase J by 2 to 3; go back to line 10
10	J is 3, still OK
20	PRINT J
30	Increase J to 5; go back to line 10
10	J is 5, still OK
20	PRINT J
30	Increase J to 7; go back to line 10
10	J is 7, still OK
20	PRINT J
30	Increase J to 9; go back to line 10
10	J is 9, still OK
20	PRINT J
30	Increase J to 11; go back to line 10
10	J is 11, too big; go down to line 40
40	End of program

Note that when the value of the loop control variable J exceeds the terminal value 10, control is passed to the statement immediately following the NEXT statement (the END statement in line 40).

To generate and print the sequence of numbers 100, 90, 80, 70, . . . , 20, 10, we can use the following code:

```
10 FOR I = 100 TO 10 STEP -10
20   PRINT I
30 NEXT I
40 END

RUN

  100
   90
   80
   70
   60
   50
   40
   30
   20
   10
```

Notice that the step value in this example is negative. The loop is terminated when the value of the loop control variable I "exceeds" the specified terminal value 10. In this case, though, the value of I "exceeds" in a downward sense—the loop is terminated when I is smaller than the terminal value.

The step size used in a FOR statement should never be zero. This value would cause the computer to loop an endless number of times. Such an error condition is known as an infinite loop.

Transfer can be made from one statement to another within a loop. The program in Figure A–22 reads 5 pairs of numbers and prints the sum of any pair whose value is less than 100. Control stays in the loop but bypasses statement 50 if the sum is greater than or equal to 100.

Note, however, that transfer from a statement within a loop to the FOR statement of the loop is illegal. Such a transfer would cause the loop control variable to be reset (rather than simply a continuation of the loop process). Therefore, an infinite loop would be formed.

Loops can be nested. That is, all of one loop can be part of the body of one or more other loops. An example of a nested loop is shown below.

```
┌FOR I = 1 TO 10
│ ┌FOR J = 1 TO 10
│ │   .
│ │   .
│ │   .
│ └NEXT J
└NEXT I
```

FIGURE A–22

Transfer of
Control within a Loop

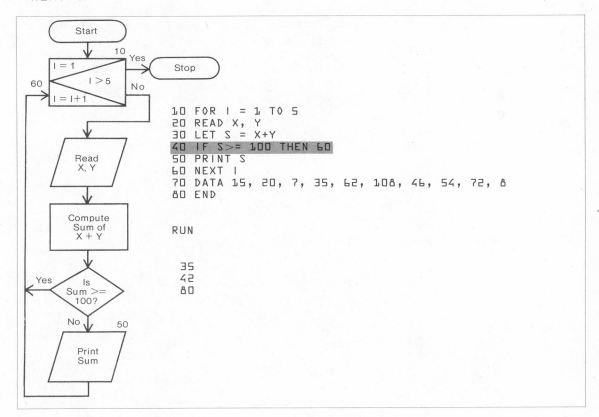

```
10 FOR I = 1 TO 5
20 READ X, Y
30 LET S = X+Y
40 IF S >= 100 THEN 60
50 PRINT S
60 NEXT I
70 DATA 15, 20, 7, 35, 62, 108, 46, 54, 72, 8
80 END


RUN


35
42
80
```

In this case, each time the outer loop is executed once, the inner loop is executed 10 times.

The following example illustrates the mechanics of the nested loop. The outer loop will be executed 2 times since N varies from 1 to 2. The inner loop will be executed 3 times each time the outer loop is executed once. Thus, the inner loop will be executed a total of 2 × 3, or 6, times.

```
       ┌─ 10  FOR  N = 1 TO 2
          20   ┌FOR K = 1 TO 3
Outer ─┤  30    PRINT N, K          ── Inner
Loop      40    NEXT K                 Loop
       └─ 50  NEXT N
```

The output of the above program segment is produced as follows:

(a) First time through outer loop; N = 1

1	1	First time through inner loop; K = 1.
1	2	Second time through inner loop; K = 2.
1	3	Third time through inner loop; K = 3.

(b) Second time through outer loop; N = 2

2	1	Inner loop; K = 1.
2	2	Inner loop; K = 2.
2	3	Inner loop; K = 3.

An application of nested loops is shown in Figure A–23. The program prints three multiplication tables.

The inner loop controls the horizontal length of each row. It prints

1 × B = ☐   2 × B = ☐   3 × B = ☐

for each value of B. The outer loop controls the number of rows printed (that is, how many values of B there are).

Comprehensive Programming Problem

Sam Bricker, the owner of Sam's Tavern and Carryout, has tabulated the following sales figures for the cases of beer sold last week:

Day	Sales
1	16
2	12
3	10
4	30
5	25
6	28
7	14

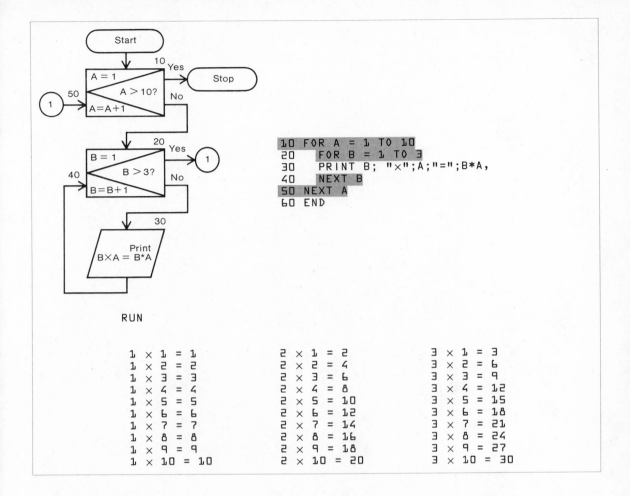

```
10 FOR A = 1 TO 10
20    FOR B = 1 TO 3
30      PRINT B; "×";A;"=";B*A,
40    NEXT B
50 NEXT A
60 END
```

RUN

```
1 × 1  = 1        2 × 1  = 2        3 × 1  = 3
1 × 2  = 2        2 × 2  = 4        3 × 2  = 6
1 × 3  = 3        2 × 3  = 6        3 × 3  = 9
1 × 4  = 4        2 × 4  = 8        3 × 4  = 12
1 × 5  = 5        2 × 5  = 10       3 × 5  = 15
1 × 6  = 6        2 × 6  = 12       3 × 6  = 18
1 × 7  = 7        2 × 7  = 14       3 × 7  = 21
1 × 8  = 8        2 × 8  = 16       3 × 8  = 24
1 × 9  = 9        2 × 9  = 18       3 × 9  = 27
1 × 10 = 10       2 × 10 = 20       3 × 10 = 30
```

Sam wants to be able to visualize graphically the sales trend for the week. He has asked you to write a program that will produce a bar graph showing the sales trend. Each bar can be produced by printing a number of asterisks (*) equal to the number of cases of beer sold during a particular day. The output should look like this:

FIGURE A–23
Use of Nested Loop

```
DAY     SALES

1       16      ****************
2       12      ************
3       10      **********
4       30      ******************************
5       25      *************************
6       28      ****************************
7       14      **************
```

Problem Solution

Figure A–24 shows a solution to this programming problem.

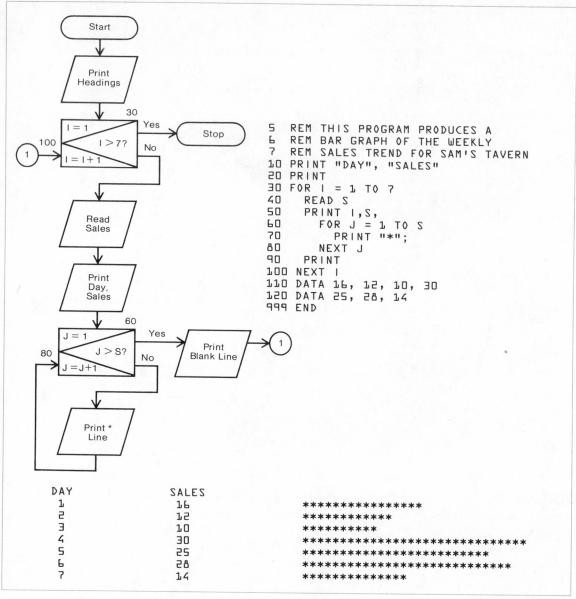

```
5    REM THIS PROGRAM PRODUCES A
6    REM BAR GRAPH OF THE WEEKLY
7    REM SALES TREND FOR SAM'S TAVERN
10   PRINT "DAY", "SALES"
20   PRINT
30   FOR I = 1 TO 7
40      READ S
50      PRINT I,S,
60        FOR J = 1 TO S
70          PRINT "*";
80        NEXT J
90      PRINT
100  NEXT I
110  DATA 16, 12, 10, 30
120  DATA 25, 28, 14
999  END
```

DAY	SALES	
1	16	****************
2	12	************
3	10	**********
4	30	******************************
5	25	*************************
6	28	****************************
7	14	**************

FIGURE A–24   BASIC Sales Trend Bar Graph Program

The RESTORE Statement

Items from a data list are usually processed only once by a READ statement. But in some instances, data must be re-read within a program—for example, to perform several types of calculations on the same numbers, or to reuse character strings. This re-reading can be provided for by the RESTORE statement.

The general format of the RESTORE statement is:

line# RESTORE

When this statement is executed, it causes the next encountered READ statement to start reading data at the *beginning* of the data list, regardless of how many data items from the list have already been read. The use of RESTORE is illustrated in Figure A–25.

Data List

    15
    25
    35

When statement 10 is executed, 15 is stored in A, 25 in B, and 35 in C. The RESTORE statement in line 20 says to the computer: "Restore the data list to its original state." So, when statement 30 is executed, 15 is stored in D and 25 is stored in E. This step does not alter the values already assigned to A, B, and C—they remain the same. The RESTORE in line 40 causes the computer to go to the beginning of the data list again. When the READ statement in line 50 is executed, 15 is stored in X. The variables A, B, C, D, E, and X have the following values when statement 55 is encountered:

$$A = 15$$
$$B = 25$$
$$C = 35$$
$$D = 15$$
$$E = 25$$
$$X = 15$$

```
10 READ A, B, C
20 RESTORE
30 READ D, E
40 RESTORE
50 READ X
55 PRINT A;B;C;D;E;X
60 DATA 15, 25, 35
99 END


RUN


15    25    35    15    25    15
```

FIGURE A–25
Re-reading Items in a Data List

```
5 REM THIS PROGRAM TOTALS THE
6 REM NUMBER OF MIDTERM GRADES,
7 REM DETERMINES 10 PERCENT OF
8 REM THE TOTAL AND PRINTS THOSE
9 REM SCORES THAT ARE A'S.
10 LET T = 0
20 LET N = 0
30 READ G
40 IF G = 00 THEN 70
50 LET T = T+1
60 GO TO 30
70 LET P = .1*T
80 RESTORE
90 READ G
100 PRINT G
110 LET N = N+1
120 IF N = P THEN 150
130 GO TO 90
140 DATA 98,92,84,79,75,72,67,41,40,25,00
150 END


RUN

98
```

FIGURE A–26

Use of RESTORE
Statement

As another application of the RESTORE statement, consider the following problem situation:

An instructor is allowed to give A's to 10 percent of a class on midterm exams. The midterm grades for the class have already been recorded in descending order in a DATA statement. A program must be written to (1) find the total number of grades (this implies reading the data list once), (2) determine 10 percent of that number, and then (3) re-read the list of grades so that it can print the top 10 percent.

A program to solve this problem is shown in Figure A–26.

The TAB Function

The major limitations in outputting data can be somewhat alleviated by the use of commas and semicolons in PRINT statements. However, the programmer is still restricted to printing data in predefined zones that may not be appropriate.

The TAB function allows output to be printed in any of the columns that make up an output line. Using this function, the programmer can structure the program output in a meaningful format.

The general format of the TAB function is:

TAB (expression)

If the TAB function appears in a PRINT statement, it must immediately precede the variable or literal to which it applies. The expression in parentheses determines the column in which printing is to begin. For example, the statement

```
60 PRINT TAB(15); A$; TAB(25); B
```

causes: (1) the printer to be spaced to column 15; (2) the character string represented by the variable A$ to be printed beginning in column 15; (3) the printer to be spaced to column 25; and (4) the numeric data represented by the variable B to be printed.

In most PRINT statements, if the TAB function is used, the semicolon should be used rather than the comma. If a comma had been used following the variable A$ above, for example, the printer would have spaced to column 30 (the third print zone) before detecting the TAB (25) request. Once a column has been passed, the printer is not backspaced to the column specified in the TAB function. Instead, the printing begins at the specified column in the next print line. For this reason, it is generally best to use semicolons rather than commas in PRINT statements that contain references to the TAB function.

The PRINT statements below demonstrate the usefulness of the TAB function.

```
90 PRINT TAB(31); "EMPLOYEE LIST"
95 PRINT
100 PRINT TAB(23); "NAME"; TAB(48); "TELEPHONE NUMBER"
```

```
1          16           31           46           61           75
```
```
                       EMPLOYEE LIST
                  NAME                    TELEPHONE NUMBER
```

The report and column headings in this example are centered on the output page. An easy formula for determining the column in which printing should begin when centering output on a 75-position line follows:

(75 − Number of characters in heading) ÷ 2 =
Column number of first character

In the example above, the heading EMPLOYEE LIST contains 13 characters. By substituting the value 13 into the formula, $(75 - 13) \div 2 = 31$, we can determine that the heading should begin in column 31. (The availability of the TAB function is implementation-dependent. The reference manual for the system in use should be consulted.)

The PRINT USING Statement

Another convenient method for controlling output is the PRINT USING statement. With this statement, the programmer can avoid print-zone restrictions. He/she can "dress up" the output using certain features of the statement. Each PRINT USING statement has an associated image statement that describes the format (image, or layout) of the data items to be printed.

The general format of the PRINT USING statement is:

line # PRINT USING image-statement-line #, expression-list

497

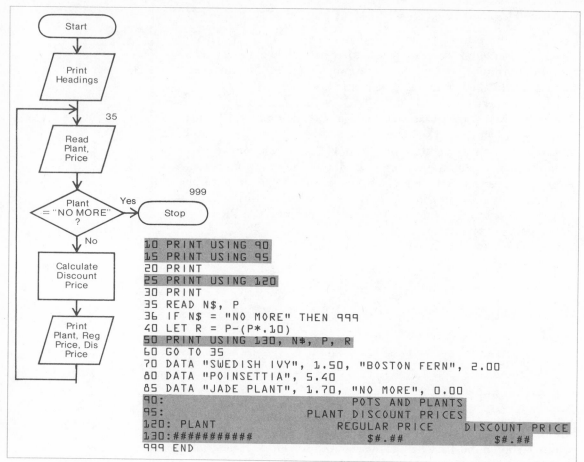

```
10 PRINT USING 90
15 PRINT USING 95
20 PRINT
25 PRINT USING 120
30 PRINT
35 READ N$, P
36 IF N$ = "NO MORE" THEN 999
40 LET R = P-(P*.10)
50 PRINT USING 130, N$, P, R
60 GO TO 35
70 DATA "SWEDISH IVY", 1.50, "BOSTON FERN", 2.00
80 DATA "POINSETTIA", 5.40
85 DATA "JADE PLANT", 1.70, "NO MORE", 0.00
90:                       POTS AND PLANTS
95:                    PLANT DISCOUNT PRICES
120: PLANT              REGULAR PRICE        DISCOUNT PRICE
130:##########          $#.##                 $#.##
999 END
```

FIGURE A–27

Use of PRINT
USING Statement

The line number of the image statement is the number of the **BASIC** statement that tells the computer how to print the data items in the expression list of the **PRINT USING** statement. The expression list consists of a sequence of variables or expressions separated by commas; it is similar to the expression list in any **PRINT** statement.

The general format of the image statement is:

line#: sequence-of-format-control-characters

In some systems, the letters FMT are used instead of the colon. Special format control characters are used in the image statement to describe the output image and to control spacing and strategic positioning of data on the output line.

To understand **PRINT USING**, assume a program is to be written for the Pots and Plants Company to calculate price figures for its August "10% Off Every Plant" sale. The program is to produce the following report:

```
                 POTS AND PLANTS
               PLANT DISCOUNT PRICES

  PLANT              REGULAR PRICE        DISCOUNT PRICE

SWEDISH IVY            $1.50                $1.35
BOSTON FERN            $2.00                $1.80
POINSETTIA            $5.40                $4.86
JADE PLANT            $1.70                $1.53
```

The first three lines of the report consist solely of literal data (headings). These headings are produced by statements 10 through 30 and the corresponding image statements:

```
10 PRINT USING 90
15 PRINT USING 95
20 PRINT
25 PRINT USING 120
30 PRINT
```

```
90:                   POTS AND PLANTS
95:                 PLANT DISCOUNT PRICES
120: PLANT            REGULAR PRICE        DISCOUNT PRICE
```

These image statements specify only headings. The images (heading lines) consist only of literal data, and there are no format control characters. The headings are output exactly as shown in the image statements.

The following format control characters are used in the program to control the other output images:

Format Control Character	Controls Image for
#	alphanumeric and numeric data.
$	dollar sign.

The format control character # is used as a placeholder for alphanumeric and numeric data. Line 50 causes the values of the variable N$ **499** (the names of the plants), and the values of the variables P and R (the regular and discount prices of the plants), to be printed where the # symbols are in the image statement in line 130. (In some systems, instead of the #, an L is used for alphanumeric data, and a 9 is used for numeric data.) The plant name is printed in the first 11 columns. The regular price is printed in the second field of #'s, with two digits to the right of the decimal point since there is a decimal point before the last two #'s. The discount price (with the 10 percent discount applied) is printed in the third field of #'s, again with two digits to the right of the decimal point.

When a leading $ is required at the beginning of a field, the format control character $ is placed at the beginning of the image field (# characters). The computer prints the dollar sign at whatever print position the $ is typed.

The programs so far have used *simple variables* such as A, N$, and D2 to represent single values. Values can be assigned to storage locations with READ, INPUT, and LET statements. Once they are assigned, they can be referenced in any expression. However, if a *group* of values is to be stored in this fashion, each value must have a different variable name. It is desirable, when dealing with a group of values, to have a single name for the entire group.

To achieve this, programmers make extensive use of *arrays*. Arrays may be either *one-dimensional*, sometimes called *lists*, or *two-dimensional*, often called *tables*.

One-Dimensional Arrays

A one-dimensional array is a list of storage locations in memory in which data elements can be stored. The entire array is given one name. Individual elements are indicated by telling their positions in the array. The general concept is simple. For example, assume a store sells 500 different items. To read and store the prices of these 500 items, we could use the statement

```
10 READ A, B, C, . . . , Z, A1, . . . , A9, . . . , Z9
```

for the first 286 prices. However, there would be no variable names available for the remaining prices.

A much better approach is to use a single letter to represent the type of information (P for price) and then refer to the price of the first item as P(1), the price of the second as P(2), and so on. For example, the 500 prices can be read and stored in locations reserved for P by the following statements:

```
10 FOR I = 1 TO 500
20   READ P(I)
30 NEXT I
```

Thus, one variable name (P) represents a complete storage area; each individual price has a position in the storage area.

Any letter can be used as the name of an array. The particular element in the array is indicated within parentheses immediately following the name of the array. Only a single letter can be used for the name of an array. Using N8 as an array name, for example, is illegal. A letter selected as the name of an array should not be used for anything else.

Two lists of numbers, array A and array J, are shown below. The reference A(5) refers to the fifth element in array A, which is 32; similarly, J(3) refers to the third element in array J, which is 102.

Array A	Array J
10	8
15	46
16	102
27	
32	

A particular element in an array can also be referenced using a legal expression inside the parentheses. For example:

```
A ( K )
J ( N )
X ( B+C )
```

When an array element is indicated by an expression, the computer:

1. evaluates the expression inside the parentheses,

2. rounds the result to the nearest integer, and

3. uses the indicated element in the array.

For example, if the computer encounters A(K), it looks at the current value of K, which indicates the position of the desired element in array A. Assume that

```
I = 2
N = 3
K = 5
```

Then:

A(I) refers to A(2)—the second element in array A—15.

J(N) refers to J(3)—the third element in array J—102.

A(K) refers to A(5)—the fifth element in array A—32.

A(I+N) refers to A(5)—the fifth element in array A—32.

The FOR and NEXT statements can be an efficient method of reading data into an array. The following program reads and stores a list of 10 numbers in an array named J.

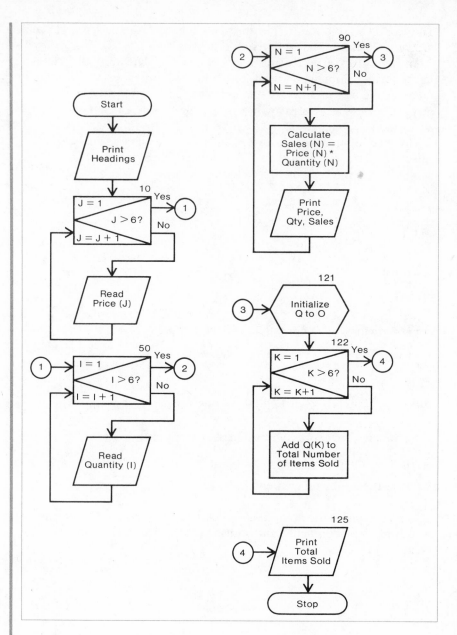

FIGURE A–28
Use of Arrays

```
5    PRINT "PRICE",  "QUANTITY SOLD",  "SALES"
6    PRINT
10 FOR J = 1 TO 6
20    READ P(J)
30 NEXT J
40 DATA .75, 2.98, 10.39, 4.99, .59, 62.88
50 FOR I = 1 TO 6
60    READ Q(I)
70 NEXT I
80 DATA 11, 95, 6, 17, 89, 5
90 FOR N = 1 TO 6
100   LET T(N) = Q(N)*P(N)
110   PRINT P(N), Q(N), T(N)
120 NEXT N
121 LET Q1 = 0
122 FOR K = 1 TO 6
123    LET Q1 = Q1+Q(K)
124 NEXT K
125 PRINT
126 PRINT "THE TOTAL QUANTITY SOLD WAS";Q1;"ITEMS"
130 END


RUN


PRICE          QUANTITY SOLD        SALES
 .75           11                   8.25
 2.98          95                   283.1
 10.39         6                    62.34
 4.99          17                   84.83
 .59           89                   52.51
 62.88         5                    314.4

THE TOTAL QUANTITY SOLD WAS 223 ITEMS
```

FIGURE A—28
Use of Arrays
(continued)

```
10 FOR I = 1 TO 10
20    READ J(I)
30 NEXT I
40 DATA 10, 20, 30, 40, 50, 60, 70, 80
50 DATA 90, 100
100 END
```

The first time through this program loop, the control variable I equals 1. When statement 20 is executed, the computer reads a number from the data list and stores it in J(1)—the first storage location in array J. The second time through the loop, I equals 2. The next number is read into J(2)—the second location in the array. The loop processing continues until all 10 numbers have been read and stored.

Now, assume we are to print the first eight numbers in array J in a single column. The following statements do just that.

```
70 FOR N = 1 TO 8
80    PRINT J(N)
90 NEXT N
100 END
```

```
RUN
```

```
10
20
30
40
50
60
70
80
```

References to specific elements of arrays are often called *subscripted variables*. The quantity inside the parentheses is the *subscript*. In contrast, simple variables are *unsubscripted variables;* they are quite different. An unsubscripted variable, say P3, is used to refer to a single storage location named P3 (not an array). The subscripted variable P(3) represents the third item in an array P.

Arrays are used in the program in Figure A–28. Two one-dimensional arrays, or lists, are read as input: a price list, stored in the array P, contains a list of the prices of six items; and a quantity list, stored in the array Q, contains a list of the quantities sold of the items. In the main part of the program, a third array, T, is generated. It is a list of the gross sales of the items.

The program begins with a segment that establishes the price array P. In lines 10 through 30, the variable J is set equal to 1, and a number is read from the data list and assigned to P(1). As the looping continues, P(2) is given a value, then P(3), and so on. When the looping is finished, the array P contains the prices of the items. That is, P(1) is .75; P(2) is 2.98; and so on.

```
10 FOR J = 1 TO 6
20   READ P(J)
30 NEXT J
40 DATA .75, 2.98, 10.39, 4.99, .59, 62.88
```

```
P(1)
P(2)
P(3)
P(4)
P(5)
P(6)
```

The next segment of the program fills the array Q with values in the same manner. The values read into Q are the quantities of the six items sold. So, after execution of the loop in lines 50 through 70 has been completed, the array Q contains the following values:

```
Q(1) = 11
Q(2) = 95
Q(3) = 6
Q(4) = 17
Q(5) = 89
Q(6) = 5
```

Once the arrays have been stored in the computer, it is possible to manipulate the array elements to obtain desired information. For example, the main part of the program calculates the gross sales for each of the six items and stores the results in the array T. These computations are accomplished by multiplying the elements in the price array P by the corresponding elements in the quantity array Q. All these arrays are then printed.

```
90 FOR N = 1 TO 6
100  LET T(N) = Q(N)*P(N)
110  PRINT P(N), Q(N), T(N)
120 NEXT N
```

The first time this loop is processed, the value of N is 1. Thus, in line 100, the value in Q(1), 11, is multiplied by the value in P(1), .75; the result, 8.25, is stored as the first element in the array T, T(1). Execution of statement 110 causes all three values to be printed. Statement 120 increases the value of N to 2 and returns to statement 90. The process is repeated to compute the remaining 5 elements in array T. When execution of the loop has been completed, the array T contains the following values:

```
T(1) = 8.25
T(2) = 283.10
T(3) = 62.34
T(4) = 84.83
T(5) = 52.51
T(6) = 314.40
```

We are also to determine the total number of items sold. We know that the array Q contains the quantity sold for each item. All we need to do is add all the elements in Q. This is accomplished by the following program segment:

```
121 LET Q1 = 0
122 FOR K = 1 TO 6
123    LET Q1 = Q1+Q(K)
124 NEXT K
125 PRINT
126 PRINT "THE TOTAL QUANTITY SOLD WAS";Q1;"ITEMS
```

We intend to accumulate the total in the variable Q1. Therefore, Q1 must first be initialized to zero. As the FOR/NEXT loop is executed repetitively, the individual elements of Q are added to the total. When K equals 1, the value of Q(1), 11, is added to Q1; then K is incremented to 2, and the value of Q(2), 95, is added to Q1; and so on.

If we wanted the total quantity sold of only the first two items, we could simply alter the number of times the FOR/NEXT loop was processed:

```
121 LET Q1 = 0
122 FOR K = 1 TO 2
123    LET Q1 = Q1 + Q(K)
124 NEXT K
```

The DIM Statement

When a programmer uses an array, the BASIC compiler does not know automatically how many elements the array will contain during execution. Unless told otherwise, it makes provisions for a limited number. Usually, the compiler is designed to assume that such an array will have no more than 10 elements. Consequently, it reserves space for 10 elements in the array. The programmer cannot write a statement that refers to an array element for which space has not been reserved.

If an array is to contain more than 10 elements, the programmer can specify the number of elements in a DIM statement. (DIM is short for dimension.)

The general format of the DIM statement is:

line# DIM variable1(limit1), variable2(limit2), . . .

The variables are the names of arrays. Each limit is an integer constant that represents the number of storage locations required for a particular array.

Assume space is needed to store 25 elements in an array named X. The statement

```
DIM X(25)
```

reserves storage locations for 25 elements. There is no problem if fewer than 25 values are actually read into the array, but it is not possible for X to contain more than 25 values. Array subscripts can vary from 1 to the limit declared in the DIM statement, but no subscript can exceed that limit.

Any number of arrays can be declared in a DIM statement. For example,

```
DIM A(30), B(20), J(100)
```

declares A, B, and J as arrays. Array A may contain up to 30 elements; B up to 20 elements; and J up to 100 elements.

DIM statements must appear in a program before the first executable statement. A good programming practice is to place them at the very beginning of the program.

Two-Dimensional Arrays

An array does not have to be a single list of data. It can also be in the form of a table, which is simply several lists grouped together. For example, assume that Andy's Hamburger Chain operates nine restaurants—three in each of three different cities. Andy has received the following table of data concerning the number of hamburgers that each of the nine stores sold today.

City	Main	RESTAURANT Branch	Drive-Thru
Toledo	100	50	35
Detroit	95	60	50
Columbus	110	80	100

The rows in the table refer to the cities and the columns refer to the stores. Thus, the number of hamburgers sold in Andy's main restaurant in Columbus can be found in the third row, first column.

This arrangement of data, a table consisting of rows and columns, is called a *two-dimensional array*. In this case we have a two-dimensional array of data that is comprised of three rows and three columns, for a total of nine elements (3 × 3).

Two-dimensional arrays are named by single letters, just like one-dimensional arrays. If a given letter is used for a two-dimensional array, it cannot be used for a one-dimensional array in the same program (and vice versa). An individual element in a table is indicated by a pair of subscripts in parentheses; the row number first and the column number second. The row and column numbers must be separated by a comma.

If we name the above array H, then the numbers of hamburgers sold at the individual stores can be indicated by H(r,c), where r stands for the row in which a number is found and c stands for the column in which it is found:

```
H(1,1)   H(1,2)   H(1,3)
H(2,1)   H(2,2)   H(2,3)
H(3,1)   H(3,2)   H(3,3)
```

507

Thus, H(2,3) represents the number of hamburgers sold at the Drive-Thru in Detroit, found in row 2, column 3. H(1,1) indicates the number of hamburgers sold at the main store in Toledo.

As with one-dimensional arrays, individual elements in two-dimensional arrays may be indicated using any legal expressions:

```
X(3,5)
X(1,5)
X(1,J)
X(2,1+J)
```

The 4 × 8 array X contains the following 32 elements:

```
 10    15    20    25    30    35    40    45
 50    55    60    65    70    75    80    85
 90    95   100   105   110   115   120   125
130   135   140   145   150   155   160   165
```

Assume that

```
I = 4
J = 2
```

Then:

> X(J,I) refers to X(2,4)—the element in the second row and fourth column of array X, which is 65.
>
> X(4,I) refers to X(4,4)—the element in the fourth row and fourth column of array X, which is 145.
>
> X(3,J+4) refers to X(3,6)—the element in the third row and sixth column of array X, which is 115.
>
> X(I,5) refers to X(4,5)—the element in the fourth row and fifth column of array X, which is 150.

As with one-dimensional arrays, the space needed to store a two-dimensional array must be explicitly stated if the array size may exceed a certain limit. Unless told otherwise, most BASIC compilers reserve enough space for an array with up to 10 rows and up to 10 columns. Therefore, if an array may exceed either the row limit, or the column limit, or both limits, the programmer must specify its size in a DIM statement. Thus,

```
10 DIM X(15,15)
```

reserves space for an array X having 15 rows and 15 columns. Similarly,

```
15 DIM A(20,5)
```

reserves space for an array A which has 20 rows and 5 columns.

Reading data into, and printing data from, two-dimensional arrays can be accomplished with nested FOR/NEXT statements. Thus, in Figure A–29, we read Andy's hamburgers sales data into a two-dimensional array, or table, H. The reading of the table follows a row-by-row se-

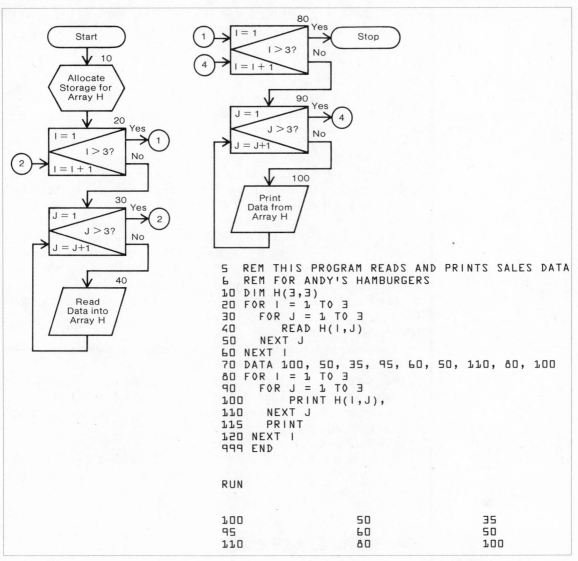

```
5    REM THIS PROGRAM READS AND PRINTS SALES DATA
6    REM FOR ANDY'S HAMBURGERS
10   DIM H(3,3)
20   FOR I = 1 TO 3
30      FOR J = 1 TO 3
40         READ H(I,J)
50      NEXT J
60   NEXT I
70   DATA 100, 50, 35, 95, 60, 50, 110, 80, 100
80   FOR I = 1 TO 3
90      FOR J = 1 TO 3
100        PRINT H(I,J),
110     NEXT J
115     PRINT
120  NEXT I
999  END


RUN


100              50              35
95               60              50
110              80              100
```

FIGURE A—29

Reading and Printing
a Two-Dimensional Array

509

quence, going from left to right across each column. The loops in lines 20 through 60 perform this reading process:

```
20 FOR I = 1 TO 3
30    FOR J = 1 TO 3
40       READ H(I,J)
50    NEXT J
60 NEXT I
70 DATA 100, 50, 35, 95, 60, 50, 110, 80, 100
```

When the program is executed, each data value is represented by the variable H followed by a unique pair of subscripts telling its row, I, and column, J, location. As the data values are read, they fill the table, row by row (i.e., after row 1 has been filled, row 2 is filled, and then row 3). The outer FOR/NEXT loop controls the rows (using the variable I); the inner loop controls the columns (using the variable J). Thus, every time the outer loop is executed once, the inner loop is executed three times. While I is equal to 1, J is equal to 1, 2, and 3. The first three numbers from the data list are read into H(1,1), H(1,2) and H(1,3). Then I is incremented to 2. The inner loop is again executed three times, reading the next three numbers from the data list into the second row, H(2,1), H(2,2), and H(2,3). I is finally incremented to 3, and the third row of the table is filled.

To print all of table H, a PRINT statement in a nested loop can be used. This is also illustrated in Figure A–29.

After data has been read and stored as an array, it is possible to manipulate the array elements. For example, it may be desirable to find out how many hamburgers were sold in Detroit, or how many hamburgers were sold at Drive-Thrus.

Since the data for each city is contained in a row of the array, we want to total the elements in one row of the array (the second row) to find out how many hamburgers were sold in Detroit. This can be done with the following statements:

```
130 LET T= 0
140 FOR J = 1 TO 3
150    LET T = T+H(2,J)
160 NEXT J
170 PRINT
180 PRINT T;"HAMBURGERS WERE SOLD IN DETROIT"
```

Notice that H(2,J) restricts the computations to the elements in row 2, while the column, J, varies from 1 to 3.

To find the number of hamburgers sold at Drive-Thrus, we want to total the elements in the third column of the array:

```
190 LET D = 0
200 FOR I = 1 TO 3
210    LET D = D+H(I,3)
220 NEXT I
240 PRINT D; "HAMBURGERS WERE SOLD AT DRIVE THRUS
```

In these statements, H(I,3) restricts the computations to the elements in the third column, while the row, I, varies from 1 to 3.

Now, suppose we need to know how many Andy's hamburgers were sold altogether. This means we must add all of the elements in the array:

```
250 LET A = 0
260 FOR I = 1 TO 3
270   FOR J = 1 TO 3
280   LET A=A+H(I,J)
290   NEXT J
300 NEXT I
310 PRINT A;"HAMBURGERS WERE SOLD ALTOGETHER"
999 END
```

Figure A–30 shows the complete program for Andy's Hamburger Chain and the resulting output.

Matrices

A matrix can be either a list or a table of data—essentially, the term *matrix* is just another name for a one- or two-dimensional array. The BASIC language has a set of matrix statements that offer convenient, easy ways to carry out array operations. One matrix statement can serve as an alternative method of carrying out an array operation that otherwise requires many statements to perform.

Matrix statements begin with the word MAT. To read data into a matrix, we use the MAT READ statement. The general format of the MAT READ statement is:

line# MAT READ matrix-name(s)

Assume there exists a matrix X:

```
62   99   43
75   28   17
```

The MAT READ and DATA statements needed to read this data are:

```
10 MAT READ X
20 DATA 62,99,43,75,28,17
```

This MAT READ statement is equivalent to a READ within nested FOR/NEXT statements, as shown below.

Array Input with MAT Statement

```
10 DIM X(2,3)
20 MAT READ X
30 DATA 62,99,43,75,28,17
40 END
```

Array Input with Nested FOR/NEXT Statements

```
10 DIM X(2,3)
20 FOR I = 1 TO 2
30   FOR J = 1 TO 3
40   READ X(I,J)
50   NEXT J
60 NEXT I
70 DATA 62,99,43,75,28,17
80 END
```

Similarly, a MAT PRINT statement can be used to print out a matrix. The MAT PRINT statement has the following general format:

line# MAT PRINT matrix-name(s)

511

```
5  REM ANDY'S HAMBURGER CHAIN SALES INFORMATION
10 DIM H(3,3)
20 FOR I = 1 TO 3
30    FOR J = 1 TO 3
40       READ H(I,J)
50    NEXT J
60 NEXT I
70 DATA 100, 50, 35, 95, 60, 50, 110, 80, 100
80 FOR I = 1 TO 3
90    FOR J = 1 TO 3
100      PRINT H(I,J),
110   NEXT J
115   PRINT
120 NEXT I
130 LET T = 0
140 FOR J = 1 TO 3
150   LET T = T+H(2,J)
160 NEXT J
170 PRINT
180 PRINT T;"HAMBURGERS WERE SOLD IN DETROIT"
190 LET D = 0
200 FOR I = 1 TO 3
210   LET D = D+H(I,3)
220 NEXT I
240 PRINT D;"HAMBURGERS WERE SOLD AT DRIVE THRUS"
250 LET A = 0
260 FOR I = 1 TO 3
270   FOR J = 1 TO 3
280   LET A = A+H(I,J)
290   NEXT J
300 NEXT I
310 PRINT A;"HAMBURGERS WERE SOLD ALTOGETHER"
999 END


RUN


100              50              35
95               60              50
110              80              100

205   HAMBURGERS WERE SOLD IN DETROIT
185   HAMBURGERS WERE SOLD AT DRIVE THRUS
680   HAMBURGERS WERE SOLD ALTOGETHER
```

FIGURE A—30

Using a
Two-Dimensional Array

Thus, the statement

```
10 MAT PRINT X
```

is equivalent to the following statements:

```
10 FOR I = 1 TO 2
20    FOR J = 1 TO 3
30       PRINT X(I,J),
40    NEXT J
50    PRINT
60 NEXT I
```

Matrices are read into memory and printed out from memory in row order. The program in Figure A–31 contains MAT statements that read in and print out the 3 × 4 matrix B.

In addition to input/output operations, MAT statements can be used to perform other operations on matrices. The elementary matrix operations that can be handled are summarized on the next page.

BASIC also provides matrix functions that programmers can use to initialize matrices and to determine the transpose (the rows of one matrix become the columns of another) and the identity of a given matrix. These functions are summarized below, where X initially is equal to $\begin{vmatrix} 1 & 2 \\ 4 & 5 \end{vmatrix}$.

OPERATION	BASIC STATEMENT	OPERATION
Initialization	MAT X = ZERO	$X = \begin{vmatrix} 0 & 0 \\ 0 & 0 \end{vmatrix}$
	MAT X = CON	$X = \begin{vmatrix} 1 & 1 \\ 1 & 1 \end{vmatrix}$
Identity	MAT X = IDN	$X = \begin{vmatrix} 1 & 0 \\ 0 & 1 \end{vmatrix}$
Transpose	MAT Z = TRN(X)	$Z = \begin{vmatrix} 1 & -4 \\ 2 & 5 \end{vmatrix}$

```
10 DIM B(3,4)
20 MAT READ B
30 MAT PRINT B
40 DATA 32, 30, 28, 25, 12, 14
50 DATA 16, 17, 18, 20, 22, 24
99 END


RUN


32              30              28              25
12              14              16              17
18              20              22              24
```

FIGURE A–31
Use of MAT
Statements

513

OPERATION	BASIC STATEMENT	OPERATION
Dimension	DIM X(2,2), Y(2,2), Z(2,2)	Establish matrix size
Input/Output	MAT READ X,Y MAT PRINT X,Y	$X = \begin{vmatrix} 1 & 2 \\ -4 & 5 \end{vmatrix} \quad Y = \begin{vmatrix} 5 & 6 \\ 8 & 9 \end{vmatrix}$
Replacement	MAT Z = X	$Z = \begin{vmatrix} 1 & 2 \\ -4 & 5 \end{vmatrix}$
Addition	MAT Z = X + Y	$Z = \begin{vmatrix} 1 & 2 \\ -4 & 5 \end{vmatrix} + \begin{vmatrix} 5 & 6 \\ 8 & 9 \end{vmatrix} = \begin{vmatrix} 6 & 8 \\ 4 & 14 \end{vmatrix}$
Subtraction	MAT Z = X - Y	$Z = \begin{vmatrix} 1 & 2 \\ -4 & 5 \end{vmatrix} - \begin{vmatrix} 5 & 6 \\ 8 & 9 \end{vmatrix} = \begin{vmatrix} -4 & -4 \\ -12 & -4 \end{vmatrix}$
Scalar Multiplication	MAT Z = 3(X)	$Z = 3 \times \begin{vmatrix} 1 & 2 \\ -4 & 5 \end{vmatrix} = \begin{vmatrix} 3 & 6 \\ -12 & 15 \end{vmatrix}$
Multiplication	MAT Z = X * Y	$Z = \begin{vmatrix} 1 & 2 \\ -4 & 5 \end{vmatrix} \times \begin{vmatrix} 5 & 6 \\ 8 & 9 \end{vmatrix} = \begin{vmatrix} 21 & 24 \\ 20 & 21 \end{vmatrix}$

Comprehensive Programming Problem

The Volume Sales Company sells encyclopedias, dictionaries, Bibles, and almanacs door-to-door in the Phoenix, Arizona, area. The company employs seven salespersons. All of them work five days a week. A typical week of sales activity for these salespersons is shown below.

Name	Monday	Tuesday	Wednesday	Thursday	Friday
Sue Herald	89.50	10.82	65.95	86.18	115.85
Sam Spade	45.10	55.95	32.10	95.42	96.50
John Williams	120.35	26.81	96.18	15.85	75.10
Carol Jenner	15.95	200.95	45.20	65.62	80.39
Betty Rubble	65.45	12.50	125.26	95.90	68.75

The sales manager of Volume Sales has asked you to write a program to generate a weekly sales report. The report should show the total sales for each day, and total weekly sales for each salesperson. The report format is specified on the next page.

```
             VOLUME SALES COMPANY
             WEEKLY SALES REPORT
MONDAY        TUESDAY        WEDNESDAY        THURSDAY          FRIDAY
$    .        $    .         $    .           $    .           $    .

             SALESPERSON WEEKLY TOTALS
     SALESPERSON                        WEEKLY SALES
     SUE HERALD                         $      .
     SAM SPADE                          $      .
     JOHN WILLIAMS                      $      .
     CAROL JENNER                       $      .
     BETTY RUBBLE                       $      .
```

Problem Solution

Figure A–32 shows a solution to this programming problem.

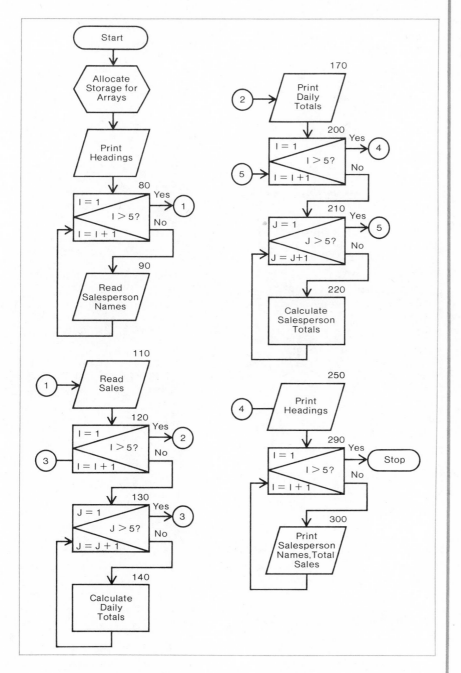

```
10  REM THIS PROGRAM CALCULATES WEEKLY SALES
15  REM FIGURES FOR THE VOLUME SALES COMPANY
20  DIM N$(5)
30  DIM S(5,5)
35  REM PRINT HEADINGS
40  PRINT USING 320
50  PRINT USING 330
60  PRINT
70  PRINT USING 340
75  PRINT
76  REM READ EMPLOYEE NAMES
80  FOR I = 1 TO 5
90     READ N$(I)
100 NEXT I
105 REM READ SALES FIGURES
110 MAT READ S
115 REM CALCULATE SALES FOR EACH DAY
120 FOR I = 1 TO 5
130    FOR J = 1 TO 5
140    LET T(I) = T(I)+S(J,I)
150    NEXT J
160 NEXT I
165 REM PRINT DAILY TOTALS
170 PRINT USING 350,T(1),T(2),T(3),T(4),T(5)
180 REM CALCULATE EMPLOYEE TOTALS
200 FOR I = 1 TO 5
210    FOR J = 1 TO 5
220    LET E(I) = E(I)+S(I,J)
230    NEXT J
240 NEXT I
250 PRINT
255 REM PRINT HEADINGS
260 PRINT USING 360
270 PRINT USING 370
280 PRINT
285 REM PRINT EMPLOYEE SALES TOTALS
290 FOR I = 1 TO 5
300 PRINT USING 380, N$(I), E(I)
310 NEXT I
```

FIGURE A–32

Weekly Sales Report
Program (continued)

```
320:                        VOLUME SALES COMPANY
330:                        WEEKLY SALES REPORT
340:   MONDAY          TUESDAY          WEDNESDAY         THURSDAY          FRIDAY
350:   $###.##         $###.##          $###.##           $###.##           $###.##
360:                        SALESPERSON WEEKLY TOTALS
370:        SALESPERSON                              WEEKLY SALES
380:        #############                              $###.##
400 DATA "SUE HERALD", "SAM SPADE", "JOHN WILLIAMS"
410 DATA "CAROL JENNER", "BETTY RUBBLE"
420 DATA 89.50, 10.82, 65.95, 86.18, 115.85, 45.10
430 DATA 55.95, 32.10, 95.42, 96.50, 120.35, 26.81
440 DATA 96.18, 15.85, 75.10, 15.95, 200.95, 45.20
450 DATA 65.62, 80.39, 65.45, 12.50, 125.26, 95.90, 68.75
999 END
```

```
                       VOLUME SALES COMPANY
                       WEEKLY SALES REPORT
MONDAY          TUESDAY          WEDNESDAY        THURSDAY          FRIDAY

$336.35        $307.03              $364.69        $358.97           $436.59

                   SALESPERSON WEEKLY TOTALS
        SALESPERSON                              WEEKLY SALES
        SUE HERALD                                $368.30
        SAM SPADE                                 $325.07
        JOHN WILLIAMS                             $334.29
        CAROL JENNER                              $408.11
        BETTY RUBBLE                              $367.86
```

FIGURE A—32

Weekly Sales Report Program (continued)

Predefined Functions

The BASIC programming language includes a number of mathematical operations that can be performed by the computer. These mathematical operations are called *predefined*, or *library*, *functions*.

The general format of a reference to a predefined function is:

function-name(argument)

The set of predefined functions available in most BASIC implementations is listed in Table A–2.

In each of these function references, the variable X is used as an *argument*. In BASIC, the argument of a function may be a constant, a variable, a mathematical expression, or another function. The first seven functions listed in Table A–2 are mathematically oriented. Their use extends beyond the scope of this text. The last five functions listed in Table A–2 are discussed here.

The *INT* (*integer*) *function* is used to compute the greatest integer that is less than or equal to the value specified as the argument (X). If the argument value contains digits to the right of a decimal point, the digits are truncated. The INT function does not round a number to the nearest integer. Some examples of arguments, and of corresponding results produced by the INT function, are given below.

X	INT(X)
8	8
5.34	5
16.9	16
−2.5	−3
−6.3	−7
0.7	0

TABLE A–2

BASIC PREDEFINED FUNCTIONS

FUNCTION	PURPOSE
SIN(X)	Trigonometric sine function
COS(X)	Trigonometric cosine function
TAN(X)	Trigonometric tangent function
COT(X)	Trigonometric cotangent function
ATN(X)	Trigonometric arctangent function
LOG(X)	Natural logarithm function
EXP(X)	E raised to the X power
INT(X)	The greatest integer less than X
SGN(X)	The sign of X
ABS(X)	The absolute value of X
SQR(X)	The square root of X
RND(X)	A random number between 0 and 1

Do not be confused by argument values that are negative numbers. When −2.5 is entered as the argument (fourth example above), the INT function returns −3 because −3 is the greatest integer that is less than or equal to −2.5. Similarly, given −6.3, INT returns −7.

One useful application of the INT function is in rounding numbers. Though this function doesn't round, it can be used in an expression that rounds to the nearest integer, tenth, hundredth, or any degree of accuracy that is necessary. The program below rounds an input (original) number to the nearest integer and to the nearest tenth.

```
100 PRINT "ORIGINAL NUMBER", "NEAREST INTEGER", "NEAREST TENTH"
110 READ A
120 LET A1 = INT(A+.5)
130 LET A2 = INT((A+.05) * 10)/10
140 PRINT A, A1, A2
150 DATA 3.54
999 END
```

```
ORIGINAL NUMBER          NEAREST INTEGER          NEAREST TENTH
3.54                     4                        3.5
```

Since the INT function returns the greatest integer less than or equal to the argument, it is necessary to use an expression adding .5 when rounding to the nearest integer and another adding .05 when rounding to the nearest tenth. The examples below demonstrate why this is necessary.

		Original Number	Expression
(a)	Nearest integer	3.68	LET A1 = INT(A + .5)
			A1 = INT(3.68 + .5)
			A1 = INT(4.18)
			A1 = 4
(b)	Nearest tenth	3.68	LET A2 = INT((A + .05) * 10)/10
			A2 = INT((3.68 + .05) * 10)/10
			A2 = INT((3.73) * 10)/10
			A2 = INT(37.3)/10
			A2 = 37/10
			A2 = 3.7

The *SGN (sign) function* yields one of three possible values, depending on the value of the argument. If $X > 0$, $SGN(X) = +1$; if $X = 0$, $SGN(X) = 0$; if $X < 0$, $SGN(X) = -1$.

X	SGN(X)
8.34	+1
0	0
−3.5	−1
.5	1

The argument passed to the SGN function can be a single numeric value or a mathematical expression. Both are demonstrated in the program below.

519

```
10 READ A
20 PRINT SGN(A)
30 PRINT SGN(A/4*(-1))
40 DATA -1
50 END

RUN

-1
 1
```

The *ABS (absolute value) function* returns the absolute value of the argument. The absolute value is always positive, even if the argument is a negative number. The table below presents examples of the results of application of the ABS function.

X	ABS(X)
−2	2
0	0
3.54	3.54
−2.68	2.68

The *SQR (square root) function* determines the square root of the argument. In most BASIC implementations, the argument must be a positive real number. Other BASIC systems ignore the sign of the argument passed to the SQR function.

X	SQR(X)
4	2
16	4
11.56	3.4

The *RND (randomize) function* is used to generate a random number between 0 and 1. A programmer can use this function to generate random data for a program. The term *random* means that any value between 0 and 1 is equally likely to occur when the function is used. Most systems require that the RND function be passed an argument, but some systems ignore the argument, even when specified. Representative output of the RND function is shown below.

```
10 FOR I = 1 TO 5
20 PRINT RND(I)
30 NEXT I
40 END

3.18146E-03
6.35529E-03
9.52911E-03
1.27029E-02
1.58768E-02
```

The RND function can be used to generate numbers greater than 1 by using it and other mathematical operations in a LET statement. The statement

```
LET R = RND(1) * (R1 - R2) + R2
```

computes a real number between R1, the lower limit in a programmer-selected range, and R2, the upper limit in the range. To compute an integer random number within a specified range, the statement

```
LET N = INT(RND(1) * (R1 - R2) + R2)
```

can be used. Sample output produced by these two statements is shown below.

```
10 READ R1,R2
20 LET R = RND(1) * (R1-R2) + R2
30 LET N = INT(RND(1) * (R1-R2) + R2)
40 PRINT "R1", "R2", "R", "N"
50 PRINT R1, R2, R, N
60 DATA 10,20
70 END


RUN


R1              R2              R               N
  10              20              19.9682           19
```

User-Defined Functions

The *DEF (definition) statement* can be used by the programmer to define a function not included in BASIC whenever necessary in a program. The function is defined just once. Then the programmer can use the function (with any of numerous arguments) as often as necessary. Since the DEF statement is nonexecutable, it can be placed anywhere before the first statement that refers to the function it defines.

The general format of the DEF statement is:

line# DEF name(argument) = expression

The name of the function is programmer-supplied. It must begin with the letters FN, which must be followed by any one of the 26 alphabetic characters. There can be only one argument. The expression can contain any mathematical operations that the programmer desires. However, a function definition cannot exceed one line of code.

Sample program segments using DEF statements are presented below.

Statements	Expression	Result

```10 DEF FNR(X) = (X+5)/2```
```20 LET B = 5```
```30 PRINT FNR(B)```
	$\dfrac{X+5}{2}$	5

```10 DEF FNR(A) = ABS(X)```
```20 LET C = -2.68```
```30 PRINT FNR(C)```
	X	2.68

521

Subroutines

Many times, it is necessary to execute an identical sequence of statements at different points in a program. Writing the sequence of statements at each of these points is both wasteful and tedious. To avoid this duplication of effort, a *subroutine* can be used. The subroutine is a sequence of statements not within the main line of the program. When the subroutine is to be performed, a transfer of control to the subroutine occurs. After the subroutine has been executed, control returns to the statement following the statement that transferred control to the subroutine. Two statements are required to define a subroutine: GOSUB and RETURN.

The GOSUB Statement   The GOSUB statement is used to transfer the flow of control from the main line of a program to a subroutine. The general format of the GOSUB statement is

line # GOSUB line #

where the line number following GOSUB identifies the first statement of the subroutine.

The program in Figure A–33 illustrates the use of a subroutine. The program calculates individual and team averages for a bowling team. The data for the program consists of the team members' names and their individual scores.

Statement 190 is a GOSUB statement:

```
190 GOSUB 800
```

Transfer is made to statement 800, which is the first statement of the subroutine.

```
800 REM THIS SUBROUTINE SORTS INDIVIDUAL SCORES INTO
805 REM DESCENDING ORDER
810 FOR J = 1 TO 5
820 LET N = 0
830 FOR I = 1 TO 5
840 IF S(J,I)>=S(J,I+1) THEN 890
850 LET H=S(J,I)
860 LET S(J,I)=S(J,I+1)
870 LET S(J,I+1)=H
880 LET N=1
890 NEXT I
900 IF N=1 THEN 820
905 NEXT J
910 RETURN
```

Thus, once an individual's name and scores have been read and stored in an array, control of the program is transferred to the subroutine where the individual's scores are sorted into descending order. Following execution of the subroutine, control returns to the main line of the program and individual and team averages are calculated and printed.

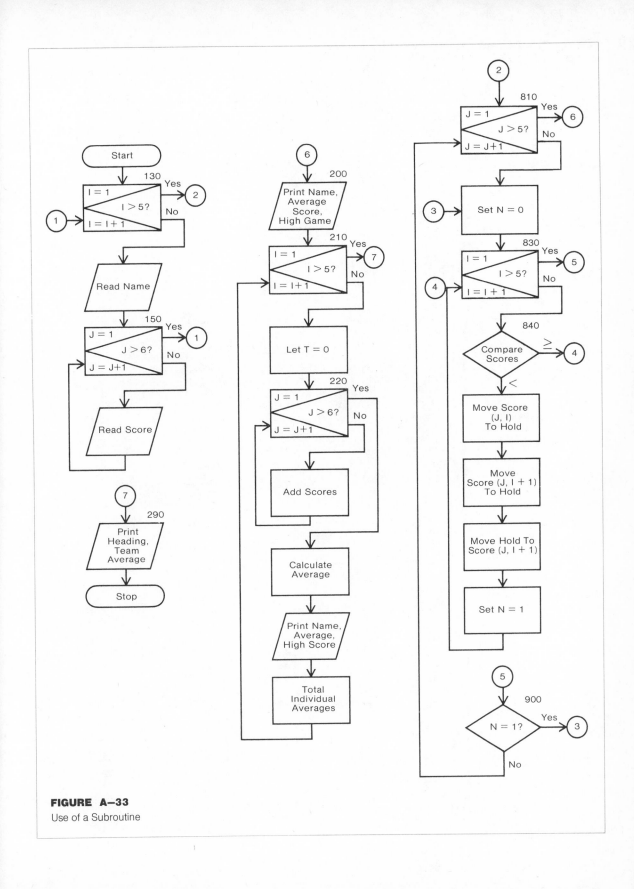

FIGURE A–33
Use of a Subroutine

```
100 REM THIS PROGRAM CALCULATES THE AVERAGE SCORE
110 REM AND THE HIGH GAME FOR EACH MEMBER
120 REM OF A BOWLING TEAM
130 FOR I=1 TO 5
140    READ N$(I)
150    FOR J=1 TO 6
160    READ S(I,J)
170    NEXT J
180 NEXT I
190 GOSUB 800
200 PRINT "NAME","AVERAGE SCORE","HIGH GAME"
205 PRINT
210 FOR I=1 TO 5
215 LET T=0
220    FOR J=1 TO 6
230    LET T=T+S(I,J)
240    NEXT J
250    LET A=T/6
260    PRINT N$(I),A,S(I,1)
270    LET A1=A1+A
280 NEXT I
285 PRINT
290 PRINT "THE TEAM AVERAGE IS";A1/5
300 STOP
310 DATA "LINDA SMITH",200,186,177,205,199,195
320 DATA "BILL DAILY",235,201,215,245,216,226
330 DATA "SUE HERALD",206,210,219,220,207,215
340 DATA "JANE LONG",186,193,181,195,198,188
350 DATA "BOB HOWARD",220,225,216,242,208,213
800 REM THIS SUBROUTINE SORTS INDIVIDUAL SCORES INTO
805 REM DESCENDING ORDER
810 FOR J=1 TO 5
820 LET N=0
830 FOR I=1 TO 5
840 IF S(J,I)>=S(J,I+1) THEN 890
850 LET H=S (J,I)
860 LET S(J,I)=S(J,I+1)
870 LET S(J,I+1)=H
880 LET N=1
890 NEXT I
900 IF N=1 THEN 820
905 NEXT J
910 RETURN
999 END
```

```
NAME                 AVERAGE SCORE        HIGH GAME

LINDA SMITH          193.667              205
BILL DAILY           223                  245
SUE HERALD           212.833              220
JANE LONG            190.167              198
BOB HOWARD           220.667              242

THE TEAM AVERAGE IS 208.067
```

The RETURN Statement To transfer control from a subroutine back to the main line of a program, the RETURN statement is used. Execution of the RETURN statement occurs after processing within the subroutine has been completed. The general format of the RETURN statement is:

line# RETURN

No line number is needed following RETURN because the BASIC compiler creates code that, when executed, returns control to the statement immediately following the most recently executed GOSUB statement. Thus, in Figure A–33,

910 RETURN

returns control to statement 200. The result of the calculation is then printed.

Comprehensive Programming Problem

The biology instructor at North Junior High School teaches an advanced biology seminar. This year, five students were enrolled. Three tests were given during the year. The students' scores on the tests are shown below.

Student	Test 1	Test 2	Test 3
Mike Ames	99	94	97
Julie Smith	82	87	92
Karen Jones	78	85	81
Mark Hayes	88	90	86
Jane Long	78	75	81

The instructor has given this data to a student who is to write a program to calculate the class average on each of the three tests, as well as an average for each student.

Problem Solution

A solution to this problem is given in Figure A–34.

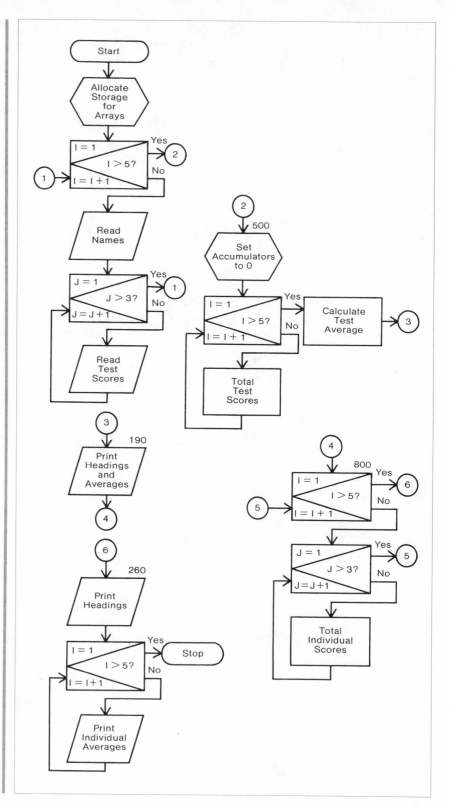

```
60 REM THIS PROGRAM CALCULATES THE CLASS
70 REM AVERAGE ON EACH OF THREE TESTS AND
80 REM AN AVERAGE FOR EACH STUDENT
90 DIM T(5)
100 DIM N$(5)
110 DIM S(5,3)
120 FOR I=1 TO 5
130    READ N$(I)
140    FOR J=1 TO 3
150    READ S(I,J)
160    NEXT J
170 NEXT I
180 GOSUB 500
190 PRINT " ","BIOLOGY CLASS"
200 PRINT " ","AVERAGE CLASS SCORES"
210 PRINT
220 PRINT "TEST 1","TEST 2","TEST 3"
230 PRINT
240 PRINT A1,A2,A3
250 GOSUB 800
260 PRINT
270 PRINT " ","STUDENT AVERAGES"
280 PRINT "NAME"," ","GRADE AVERAGE"
290 PRINT
300 FOR I=1 TO 5
310 PRINT N$(I)," ",INT(T(I)/3+.5)
320 NEXT I
325 STOP
330 DATA "MIKE AMES",99,94,97,"JULIE SMITH",82,87,92
340 DATA "KAREN JONES",78,85,81,"MARK HAYES",88,90,86
350 DATA "JANE LONG",78,75,81
490 REM SUBROUTINE TO CALCULATE TOTAL TEST AVERAGES
500 LET S1,S2,S3=0
510 FOR I=1 TO 5
520 LET S1=S1+S(I,1)
530 LET S2=S2+S(I,2)
540 LET S3=S3+S(I,3)
550 NEXT I
560 LET A1=INT(S1/5+.5)
570 LET A2=INT(S2/5+.5)
580 LET A3=INT(S3/5+.5)
590 RETURN
790 REM SUBROUTINE TO TOTAL INDIVIDUAL TEST SCORES
800 FOR I=1 TO 5
810    FOR J=1 TO 3
820    LET T(I)=T(I)+S(I,J)
830 NEXT J
840 NEXT I
850 RETURN
999 END
```

```
                    BIOLOGY CLASS
                    AVERAGE CLASS SCORES

TEST 1              TEST 2              TEST 3

 85                  86                  87

                    STUDENT AVERAGES
NAME                                GRADE AVERAGE

MIKE AMES                               97
JULIE SMITH                             87
KAREN JONES                             81
MARK HAYES                              88
JANE LONG                               78
```

The BASIC programs for the applications presented so far have contained DATA statements that supplied required data. However, many applications programs must process significant amounts of data each time they are run. To avoid entering the data each time via DATA statements, the data can be stored permanently on a secondary storage medium, such as magnetic tape or magnetic disk. The data stored in this manner is called a *file*, and manipulation of the data is referred to as *file processing*.

In BASIC, file-processing statements are not standardized. Each BASIC user should consult the BASIC language reference manual for the system available to him/her when utilizing file-processing techniques. In this section, we approach file-processing conceptually, so that the user can recognize the techniques required for file processing, regardless of the system used. The examples shown have been run on an IBM system. The statements needed to accomplish the same tasks on DEC and Hewlett-Packard systems are also discussed. An example of a file-processing application is discussed below.

The Andrews Athletic Store maintains an inventory of 10 items. Every two weeks, the store personnel take inventory and reorder any items that are out of stock or in short supply. Mr. Andrews has established an *inventory master file* that contains the item number, item description, quantity on hand, and minimum stock requirement for each item. The contents of this file are shown in Figure A–35.

During each two-week period, Mr. Andrews keeps a record of the quantity of each item sold. The record for the current period is shown in Figure A–36. This record of transactions for the two-week period can be called a *transaction file*.

Before placing an order, Mr. Andrews must determine the quantity on hand for each of the 10 items in inventory. This is done through processing referred to specifically as *file updating*. During the master

ITEM NO.	DESCRIPTION	QTY ON HAND	MINIMUM STOCK REQUIREMENT
305	Basketball	4	10
426	Tennis racquet	2	5
584	Football	8	12
627	Gym shoes	19	30
365	Sweat socks	15	25
891	Baseball	5	10
212	Ball glove	6	14
450	Tennis balls	5	10
360	Golf clubs	3	5
735	Bowling ball	3	8

file update, the transaction file (in this case the two-week inventory transactions record) is matched against the inventory master file. The quantity sold of an item is deducted from the existing quantity on hand of the item to determine the new (i.e., current) quantity on hand. The current quantity on hand is then compared with the minimum stock requirement for the item to determine whether or not stock should be ordered, and if so, how much.

This processing is repeated for each item actioned during the two-week period. The computer can then be used to create a purchase order to be sent to a sporting goods supplier.

The relationship between the files used in this application is presented in Figure A–37.

Before the processing we have just described can occur, the inventory master file itself must have been created. The program in Figure A–38 was used to create this file. The name INVEN has been assigned to the file. The program in Figure A–39 reads and prints the contents of this file.

When writing data to and reading data from a file, a number of input/output statements must be used. In Figure A–38, the OPEN and PUT statements can be seen. The program PRINV in Figure A–39 shows use of the OPEN and GET statements.

The OPEN statement is used to make a file available for reference by a program. The GET statement retrieves data from a file. The PUT statement is used to write data to the file.

After the inventory master file has been created and is available for use, the program in Figure A–40 can be used to update the file as we have described. The CLOSE statement is used twice in this program. First, it indicates to the system that the file is no longer needed for input. Second, it indicates that updating has been completed. By closing the file, the programmer makes certain that no data is inadvertently changed.

Figure A–41 is a representative example of the computer-to-user (and vice versa) interactions that occur during the execution of this program.

After the master file update program has been executed, the quantity on hand fields of the inventory master file reflect the current inventory. Figure A–42 shows the contents of the inventory master file following the update run of Figure A–41.

All that remains to be done at this point is the preparation of a purchase order specifying the quantity of each item to be ordered. Figure A–43 shows the program to create the purchase order and the result of its execution. The PURCH program also performs file processing; the contents of the INVEN file have to be read and manipulated to determine the quantities to be ordered. Note that the INVEN file is again opened (line 130) and closed (line 170).

This example demonstrates the usefulness of file processing. The store manager, Mr. Andrews, is able to maintain an accurate accounting of goods in inventory and to generate a bi-weekly purchase order with a minimum of manual effort. As the size of the file increases, the appli-

529

Item Number	Quantity Sold
305	3
426	2
584	5
627	10
365	8
891	1
212	4
450	3
360	1
735	3

FIGURE A–36
Inventory Transactions
Record

FIGURE A–37
Inventory File Processing

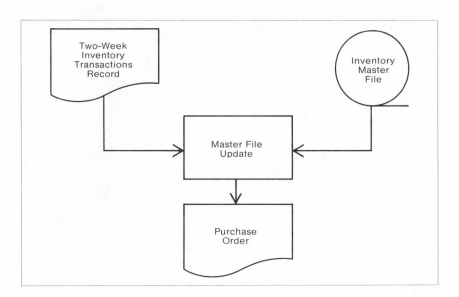

```
100 OPEN 1,"INVEN",OUTPUT
110 FOR I = 1 TO 10
120 READ I,N$,Q,R
130 PUT 1: I,N$,Q,R
135 IF I=735 THEN 200
140 NEXT I
150 DATA 305,"BASKETBALL",4,10,426,"TENNIS RACQUET",2,5
160 DATA 584,"FOOTBALL",8,12,627,"GYM SHOES",19,30
170 DATA 365,"SWEAT SOCKS",15,25,891,"BASEBALL",5,10
180 DATA 212,"BALL GLOVE",6,14,450,"TENNIS BALLS",5,10
190 DATA 360,"GOLF CLUBS",3,5,735,"BOWLING BALL",3,8
200 END
```

FIGURE A—38
Program to Create
Inventory Master File

```
PRINV
100 OPEN 1,"INVEN",INPUT
101 PRINT "ITEM NUMBER","DESCRIPTION","QUANTITY","REQUIREMENT"
105 FOR J= 1 TO 10
110 GET "INVEN",I,N$,Q,R
130 PRINT I,N$,Q,R
135 IF I=735 THEN 150
140 NEXT J
150 END
```

ITEM NUMBER	DESCRIPTION	QUANTITY	REQUIREMENT
305	BASKETBALL	4	10
426	TENNIS RACQUET	2	5
584	FOOTBALL	8	12
627	GYM SHOES	19	30
365	SWEAT SOCKS	15	25
891	BASEBALL	5	10
212	BALL GLOVE	6	14
450	TENNIS BALLS	5	10
360	GOLF CLUBS	3	5
735	BOWLING BALL	3	8

FIGURE A—39
Program to Print
Inventory Master File

531

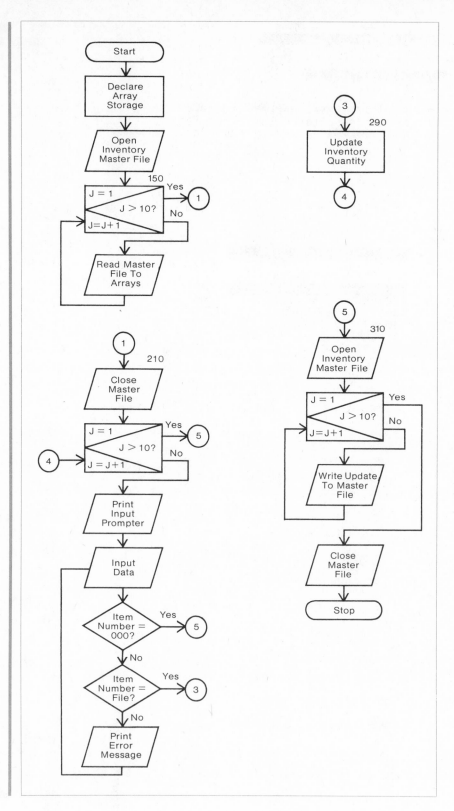

532

```
UPDATE        21:51    SUNDAY AUGUST 27,1978

100 REM THIS PROGRAM UPDATES THE
110 REM INVENTORY MASTER FILE
120 DIM D$(10)
130 DIM F(10,3)
140 OPEN 1,"INVEN",INPUT
150 FOR J = 1 TO 10
160 GET 1: F(J,1)
170 GET 1: D$(J)
180 GET 1: F(J,2),F(J,3)
200 NEXT J
210 CLOSE 1
220 FOR J= 1 TO 10
230 PRINT "ENTER ITEM NUMBER, QUANTITY SOLD"
240 INPUT I1,Q1
250 IF I1=000 THEN 310
260 IF I1=F(J,1) THEN 290
270 PRINT "ITEM NUMBER ERROR, TRY AGAIN"
280 GO TO 240
290 LET F(J,2)=F(J,2)-Q1
300 NEXT J
310 OPEN 1,"INVEN",OUTPUT
320 FOR J = 1 TO 10
325 PUT 1: F(J,1),D$(J),F(J,2),F(J,3)
330 NEXT J
340 CLOSE 1
999 END
```

```
UPDATE        11:16    MONDAY AUGUST 28,1978

ENTER ITEM NUMBER, QUANTITY SOLD
?305,3
ENTER ITEM NUMBER, QUANTITY SOLD
?426,2
ENTER ITEM NUMBER, QUANTITY SOLD
?584,5
ENTER ITEM NUMBER, QUANTITY SOLD
?627,10
ENTER ITEM NUMBER, QUANTITY SOLD
?365,8
ENTER ITEM NUMBER, QUANTITY SOLD
?891,1
ENTER ITEM NUMBER, QUANTITY SOLD
?233,4
ITEM NUMBER ERROR, TRY AGAIN
?212,4
ENTER ITEM NUMBER, QUANTITY SOLD
?450,3
ENTER ITEM NUMBER, QUANTITY SOLD
?360,1
ENTER ITEM NUMBER, QUANTITY SOLD
?735,3
```

```
PRINV        11:18    MONDAY AUGUST 28,1978

ITEM NUMBER      DESCRIPTION         QUANTITY      REQUIREMENT
    305          BASKETBALL              1             10
    426          TENNIS RACQUET          0             5
    584          FOOTBALL                3             12
    627          GYM SHOES               9             30
    365          SWEAT SOCKS             7             25
    891          BASEBALL                4             10
    212          BALL GLOVE              2             14
    450          TENNIS BALLS            2             10
    360          GOLF CLUBS              2             5
    735          BOWLING BALLS           0             8
```

```
PURCH

100 REM THIS PROGRAM CREATES A PURCHASE ORDER
110 DIM D$(10)
120 DIM F(10,3)
125 REM STATEMENTS 130 THROUGH 170 READ THE CONTENTS
126 REM OF THE INVENTORY FILE INTO ARRAYS
130 OPEN 1,"INVEN",INPUT
140 FOR J=1 TO 10
150 GET 1: F(J,1),D$(J),F(J,2),F(J,3)
160 NEXT J
170 CLOSE 1
180 PRINT " ","ANDREWS ATHLETIC GOODS"
190 PRINT " ","BI-WEEKLY PURCHASE ORDER"
200 PRINT
210 PRINT "***************************************************************"
220 PRINT
230 PRINT "ITEM DESCRIPTION"," ","QUANTITY ORDERED"
240 PRINT
245 REM CALCULATE ORDER QUANTITY
250 FOR J= 1 TO 10
260 LET O = F(J,3)-F(J,2)
270 PRINT D$(J)," ",O
280 NEXT J
290 PRINT
300 PRINT "***************************************************************"
310 END



                 ANDREWS ATHLETIC GOODS
                 BI-WEEKLY PURCHASE ORDER
**************************************************************
ITEM DESCRIPTION            QUANTITY ORDERED

BASKETBALL                  9
TENNIS RACQUET              5
FOOTBALL                    9
GYM SHOES                   21
SWEAT SOCKS                 18
BASEBALL                    6
BALL GLOVE                  12
TENNIS BALLS                8
GOLF CLUBS                  3
BOWLING BALL                8
**************************************************************
```

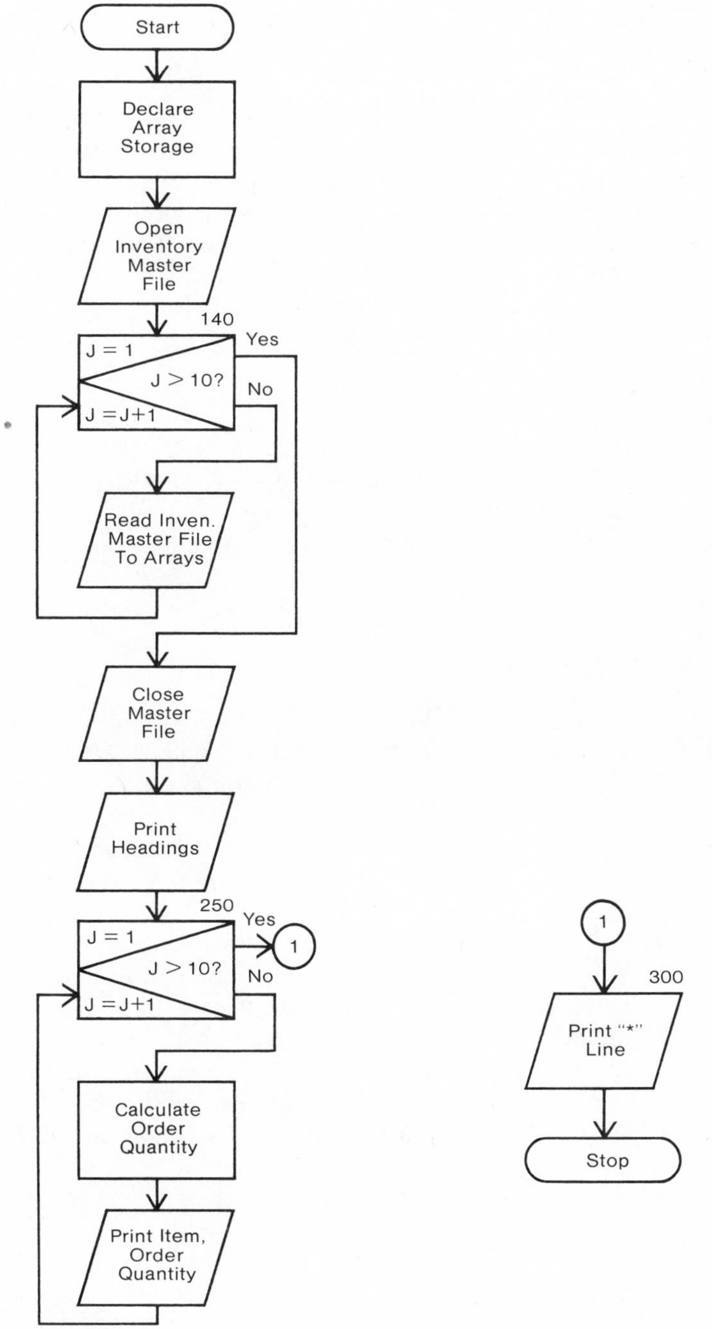

FIGURE A–43
Purchase Order Program and Output (continued)

cability of file-processing techniques becomes increasingly important. The file-processing statements used in the example are explained more fully below.

File Organization

Most BASIC systems require that data files be organized sequentially. Some systems also support sequential processing of indexed sequential files (see Chapter 15 of the text). The files discussed here are sequentially organized files requiring sequential processing. Recall that each record in the inventory master file discussed above consists of an item number, item description, quantity on hand, and minimum stock requirement (see Figure A–35). When stored on magnetic tape, the inventory master file appears as sketched in Figure A–44.

File Creation

The first step in file processing is naming the file. This step attaches a name to the file by which it can be referenced and allocates storage space for the file. The system commands used to name a file are shown below.

FILE file-name   IBM

FILE file-name   H-P

On a DEC system, file creation and storage allocation are performed the first time a file is referenced. Since the FILE command is a command rather than a BASIC statement, no line number is needed.

Once storage space has been allocated for a file, data can be written to and read from the file. The file can contain both numeric and character string data.

The use of the FILE command can be seen in Figure A–45. The computer responds with the message READY, indicating that the file NAME can now be used to store data. First, the file must be opened. Opening a file is similar to opening a door to a house—until the door is open, no one can get in. On an IBM system, the file must be designated as either an INPUT file or an OUTPUT file. An INPUT file is a file from which data will be read during program execution; an OUTPUT

FIGURE A–44
Sequential Inventory
Master File

| 305 BASKETBALL 4 10 | 426 TENNIS RACKET 2 5 | 735 BOWLINGBALL 3 8 |

```
FILE NAME
READY

100 OPEN 1,"NAME",OUTPUT
110 FOR I=1 TO 5
120 READ N$,P$
130 IF N$="LAST" THEN 190
140 PUT 1: N$,P$
150 NEXT I
160 DATA "RICHARD NICKLES","522-7806","JANE CALLOWAY","796-8212"
170 DATA "ROBIN GREEN","521-2906","TOM WATSON","825-3846"
180 DATA "SUE HERALD","663-7684","LAST","000-0000"
190 CLOSE 1
999 END
```

file is a file onto which data will be written. An INPUT file cannot be referenced as an OUTPUT file, and vice versa.

The IBM BASIC statement to open a file has the general format:

OPEN file-number, "file-name", file-type

The file number is a number chosen by the programmer to be used as a reference for the file name that follows. The file name is the name that has been established for the file. The file type is either INPUT or OUTPUT. An OPEN statement for the file NAME appears in line 100 of Figure A–45.

The H-P command for opening a file is implied through a read or write statement (discussed later).

The DEC BASIC statement for opening a file has the general format:

OPEN file-number, channel-number AS "file-name"

The file number is supplied by the programmer and can be used in subsequent statements to refer to the file. The channel number indicates the communication link between the terminal and a storage device. The file name is the programmer-supplied name of the file. Because there is no FILE command on a DEC system, the naming of the file and the allocation of storage space occur when this statement is executed; it is the first reference to the file.

Now that the file NAME has been created and opened, data can be stored in it. This is done in lines 110 through 150 in Figure A–45. The data is first read as input into the variables N$ and P$. Once there, it can be written as output to the file. Character-string and numeric variables must be used for intermediate storage in this manner when working with data files. (An error message results if an attempt is made to read character-string data into a numeric variable.)

The statement used to write data to a file are very similar in the systems. Their formats are shown below.

537

PUT "file-number", variable-list	IBM
PRINT file-number, channel-number, variable-list	DEC
PRINT "file-name", variable-list	H-P

After the data has been written to the file NAME, the file must be closed to insure that another program does not inadvertently access its contents. The general formats of the CLOSE statements on IBM and DEC system are shown below.

| CLOSE file-number | IBM |
| CLOSE file-number | DEC |

The close of a file on an H-P system occurs automatically after a PRINT statement has been executed.

Yet another input/output statement is used to read data as input from a data file. Before the statement can be executed, however, the file must be opened for input (on IBM and DEC systems, using the OPEN statements as discussed above).

The general formats of the statements used to read input from a data file are shown below.

GET file-number: variable-list	IBM
INPUT file-number, channel-number, variable-list	DEC
GET file-name or READ file-number; read item list	H-P

Again, the variable names used in these statements must represent numeric or character-string data, depending on the type of data read from the file.

File Manipulation

In general, BASIC data files are organized sequentially and must be processed accordingly. When files are used only for data input or data output, the programmer's task is relatively simple. Difficulties arise, however, when a file must be referenced, data read and transformed in some manner, and the manipulated data written back to the file. Such processing was illustrated in the inventory application at the beginning of this section: the quantity on hand fields of records in the master inventory file were updated. Since the file is sequential, data cannot be read in, manipulated, and then written to the same file location without back-

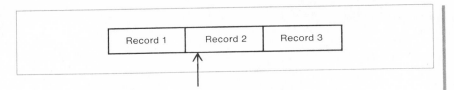

Record 1	Record 2	Record 3

spacing to the beginning of the record that was read (and this is not a reasonable approach—it would take far too long).

Look at the sample data file in Figure A—46. After record 1 has been read, the read/write head of the tape drive (or disk drive) is positioned at the beginning of record 2 (as shown by the arrow). If the manipulated data from record 1 were written back onto the tape, record 2 would be destroyed. To prevent this, file processing in which data fields must be transformed and then written back to the file is accomplished by reading the entire contents of the file into an array or arrays, performing the required data manipulation, and then writing the transformed data back into the original file. We saw this type of processing in Figure A—40. That is, the inventory master file update was accomplished in this manner.

The BASIC file-processing statements introduced in this section are listed in Table A—3. The function of each is identified.

● To open a file:

OPEN file-number, ''file-name'', file-type	I BM
OPEN file-number, channel-number AS ''file-name''	DEC
Implied in GET or READ Statement	H–P

● To write data to a file:

PUT file-number: variable-list	I BM
PRINT file-number, channel-number, variable-list	DEC
PRINT ''file-name'', variable-list	H–P

● To read data from a file:

GET file-number: variable-list	I BM
INPUT file-number, channel-number, variable-list	DEC
GET file-name	
or	H–P
READ file-number	

● To close a file:

CLOSE file-number	I BM
CLOSE file-number	DEC
Implied in PRINT statement	H–P

539

Comprehensive Programming Problem

The News Subscription Service (NSS) is a midwestern business firm that provides mail-order subscription service to a five-state area. The area includes Ohio, Kentucky, Pennsylvania, Indiana, and West Virginia. The NSS maintains a subscriber master file which contains the following data for each subscriber: name, street address, city, state, and zip code.

The NSS is considering circulating a new monthly magazine called "Cincinnati High School Athletics." It wants to determine reader interest in such a publication. To sample its reader interest, the NSS has decided to send a questionnaire to all subscribers living in Cincinnati. The Ohio-area contents of the subscriber master file are shown below.

Name	Street Address	City & State	Zip Code
Richard Nickles	222 Fremont Dr.	Akron,OH	47231
Scott Patrick	212 Willow Way	Cincinnati, OH	45231
Jane Long	615 Oakmont Dr.	Columbus, OH	47621
Sue Herald	197 Bulldog La.	Findlay, OH	48443
Karen Jacobs	487 Sparrow Rd.	Huron, OH	44422
Michael Caine	819 Norcrest Ct.	Cincinnati, OH	45231
Terry Smith	415 Watermill Dr.	Dayton, OH	48451
Cindy Horton	945 Summit St.	Athens, OH	47521
Dave Ball	719 Prince Rd.	Cincinnati, OH	45231
Ellen Lowe	314 Adams Rd.	Akron, OH	47248

Since the reader questionnaires are to be mailed, the NSS has decided to use the subscriber master file to computer-generate mailing labels. First, a program must be written to read the data from the subscriber master file into storage and write it onto a file that can be processed by the computer. Then a program to locate Cincinnati subscribers in the file is required. The required output consists of the name and address of each Cincinnati subscriber, printed as it should appear on an envelope.

Problem Solution

Figures A–47 and A–48 show a solution to this programming problem.

```
100 OPEN 1, "SUB",OUTPUT
110 FOR I=1 TO 10
120 READ N$,A$,C$,S$,Z
130 PUT 1: N$,A$,C$,S$,Z
140 NEXT I
150 CLOSE 1
160 DATA "RICHARD NICKLES", "222 FREMONT DR.", "AKRON", "OH", 47231
170 DATA "SCOTT PATRICK", "212 WILLOW WAY", "CINCINNATI", "OH", 45231
180 DATA "JANE LONG", "615 OAKMONT DR.", "COLUMBUS", "OH", 47621
190 DATA "SUE HERALD", "197 BULLDOG LA.", "FINDLAY", "OH", 48443
200 DATA "KAREN JACOBS", "487 SPARROW RD.", "HURON", "OH", 44422
210 DATA "MICHAEL CAINE", "819 NORCREST CT.", "CINCINNATI", "OH", 45231
220 DATA "TERRY SMITH", "415 WATERMILL DR.", "DAYTON", "OH", 48451
230 DATA "CINDY HORTON", "945 SUMMIT ST.", "ATHENS", "OH", 47521
240 DATA "DAVE BALL", "719 PRINCE RD.", "CINCINNATI", "OH", 45231
250 DATA "ELLEN LOWE", "314 ADAMS RD.", "AKRON", "OH", 47248
999 END
```

FIGURE A—47

Program to Load
Master Subscriber File

FIGURE A—48

Mailing List Generation
Flowchart, Program, and
Output

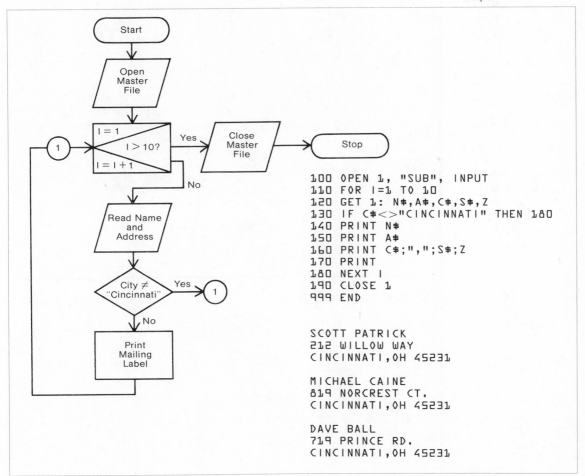

```
100 OPEN 1, "SUB", INPUT
110 FOR I=1 TO 10
120 GET 1: N$,A$,C$,S$,Z
130 IF C$<>"CINCINNATI" THEN 180
140 PRINT N$
150 PRINT A$
160 PRINT C$;",";S$;Z
170 PRINT
180 NEXT I
190 CLOSE 1
999 END


SCOTT PATRICK
212 WILLOW WAY
CINCINNATI,OH 45231

MICHAEL CAINE
819 NORCREST CT.
CINCINNATI,OH 45231

DAVE BALL
719 PRINCE RD.
CINCINNATI,OH 45231
```

STATEMENT	PURPOSE
FUNDAMENTAL	
REM	Provides comments about program
DATA	Supplies data list to program
READ	Reads data from data list
LET	Computes and assigns values
PRINT	Writes variables or literals as output
INPUT	Reads data from user terminal
END	Terminates program
TRANSFER	
GO TO	Unconditional transfer of control
IF/THEN	Conditional transfer of control
ON/GO TO	Conditional transfer of control
STOP	Transfer of control to END statement
FOR/NEXT	Loop control
EXTENDED INPUT/OUTPUT	
TAB	Allows printing in any specified column
PRINT USING	Allows formatted printing
RESTORE	Allows data in a data list to be re-read
ARRAYS	
DIM	Allocates storage space for an array
MAT	Reads and prints data from and to arrays; performs other matrix operations
FUNCTIONS AND SUBROUTINES	
DEF	Allows user to define a function
ABS	Computes absolute value of an expression
SGN	Returns sign $(+1, 0, -1)$ of an expression
INT	Truncates expression to greatest integer less than or equal to the expression
RND	Generates random number
SQR	Computes square root of a number
GOSUB	Transfers flow of control to a subroutine
RETURN	Returns control from subroutine to statement after GOSUB
FILE PROCESSING	
OPEN	Opens a data file
PUT	Writes data to a file
GET	Reads data from a file
CLOSE	Closes a data file

GLOSSARY / INDEX

Access mechanism   The physical device that positions the read/write head of a direct-access storage device over a particular track. **157**

Accounting machine   Forerunner of the computer; could mechanically read data from punched cards, perform calculations, rearrange data, and print results in varied formats. **24**

Accumulator   A register that accumulates results of computations. **50**

Action entry   One of four sections of a decision logic table; specifies what actions should be taken. **337**

Action stub   One of four sections of a decision logic table; describes possible actions applicable to the problem to be solved. **337**

Activity   An indication of the proportion of records processed in a master file. **365**

Address   A part of an instruction that specifies the location of an operand; (2) a unique identifier used to refer to a location. **49**

Address register   A register that holds the address of a location containing a data item called for by an instruction. **50**

Alphanumeric   A character set that contains letters, digits, and special characters such as punctuation marks. **258**

American Standard Code for Information Interchange (ASCII)   A 7-bit standard code used for information interchange among data-processing systems, communication systems, and associated equipment. **53**

Amplitude (of a wave)   The strength of a wave length. **98**

Analog computer   A computer that measures continuous electrical or physical magnitudes rather than operating on digits; contrast with digital computer. **46**

Analog transmission   Transmission of data over communication channels in a continuous wave form. **98**

Analytical engine   A machine conceived by Charles Babbage, capable of addition, subtraction, multiplication, division, and storage of intermediate results in a memory unit; too advanced for its time, the analytical engine was forgotten for nearly 100 years. **22**

APL   A Programming Language; a terminal-oriented, symbolic programming language especially suitable for interactive problem-solving. **276**

Applications program   A sequence of instructions written to solve a specific problem facing organizational management. **202**

Applications programmer   An individual who writes programs to solve specific problems facing organizational management. **410**

Applications software   Programs designed to solve specific problems or processing needs such as a payroll program. **185**

Arithmetic/logic unit (ALU)   The section of the CPU that handles arithmetic computations and logical operations. **47**

Array   An ordered set of data items; also called a table or matrix. **276**

Artificial intelligence   A field of inquiry developing techniques whereby computers can be used to solve problems that appear to require imagination, intuition, or intelligence. **435**

Assembler program   The translator program for an assembly language; produces a machine-language program. **210**

Assembly language   A symbolic programming language that uses convenient abbreviations rather than groupings of 0s and 1s; intermediate-level language in terms of user orientation. **251**

Attribute   A field containing information; a descriptive property associated with a name to describe a characteristic of items that the name may represent. **385**

543

Audio input/output   Data entered into a computer system and responses received through human-voice audio transmissions; widely used, but is presently impractical due to variations in speech patterns and dialects. **133**

Automatic data processing (ADP)   The collection, manipulation, and dissemination of data by electromechanical machines to attain specified objectives. **8**

Automation   Machine-directed processes. **432**

Auxiliary storage   Also known as external storage or secondary storage; supplements primary storage but operates at slower speeds. **29, 57, 149**

Back-end processor   A small CPU serving as an interface between a large CPU and a large data base stored on direct-access storage device. **315**

Background partition   In a multiprogramming system, a partition holding a lower-priority program that is executed only when high-priority programs are not using the system. **310**

Background program   In a multiprogramming system, a program that can be executed whenever the facilities of the system are not needed by a high-priority program. **310**

Backup   Alternate procedures, equipment, or systems used in case of destruction or failure of the original. **59**

Bandwidth   The range, or width, of the frequencies available for transmission on a given channel. **100**

Bar-code reader   A device used to read a barcode by means of reflected light, such as a scanner that reads the Universal Product Code on supermarket products. **127**

BASIC   *B*eginners' *A*ll-Purpose *S*ymbolic *I*nstruction *C*ode; a programming language commonly used for interactive problem solving by users who may not be professional programmers. **273**

Batch/Sequential processing   A method of processing data in which data items are collected and forwarded to the computer in a group; normally uses punched cards or magnetic tape for generating periodic output, e.g., payroll. **30**

Binary coded decimal (BCD)   A computer code that uses unique combinations of zone bits and numeric bits to represent specific characters; examples are 4-bit BCD and 6-bit BCD. **52**

Binary digit   A bit. **52**

Binary number system   The numeric system used in computer operations that uses the digits 0 and 1 and has a base of 2. **51**

Binary representation   Uses a two-state, or binary, system to represent data; as in setting and re-setting the states of a magnetic core. **51**

Binary system   A form of data representation in which two possible states exist. **51**

Bit   A binary digit; the smallest unit of information that can be represented in binary notation. **52**

Block   In block-structured programming languages, a section of program coding treated as a unit. **269**

Block diagram   *See* Flowchart. **226**

Blocked records   The grouping of records on magnetic tape or magnetic disk to reduce the number of inter-record gaps and more fully utilize the storage medium. **154**

Branch pattern   Logic in which control is transferred from the simple sequence flow to another portion of the program. **225**

Bubble memory   A recently developed memory device in which data is represented by magnetized spots (magnetic domains) that rest on a thin film of semiconductor material. **59**

Buffer   Storage used to compensate for a difference in rate of flow of data, or time of occurrence of events, when transmitting data from one device to another. **138**

Built-in function   A common or often-used procedure that is permanently stored in the computer; examples include square root, absolute value, and logarithms. **269**

Bundling   Opposite of unbundling; the practice whereby the cost of a computer system may include not only the CPU but also an operating system, peripheral devices, maintenance agreements, etc.; has largely been dropped as a result of litigation. **317**

Business data processing   The application of the computer and related techniques to solving problems encountered in business, *e.g.*, payroll, inventory, personnel files, etc. **13**

544

Byte   Some number of bits; a unit of storage. **53**

Calculate   To manipulate data in an arithmetic and/or logical manner. **9**

Card punch   *See* Keypunch. **74**

Card reader   A device that translates the holes in punched cards into electrical pulses for input into another device (usually a computer). **76**

Cathode-ray tube (CRT)   A visual-display device that receives electrical impulses and translates them into a picture on a television-like screen. **132**

Centralized   A design alternative whereby computer power is established within one group; includes a common central data base that permits authorized users to gain access to information. **381**

Central processing unit (CPU)   Also known as the "main frame," or heart of the computer; composed of three sections—primary storage unit, arithmetic/logic unit (ALU), and control unit. **47**

Certificate in Data Processing (CDP)   A certificate awarded by the ICCP to qualified candidates who have successfully passed an examination consisting of five sections—data-processing equipment, computer programming and software, principles of management, quantitative methods, and system analysis and design. **419**

Chain printer   An output device that has the character set engraved in type and assembled in a chain that revolves horizontally past all print positions; prints when a print hammer (one for each column on the paper) presses the paper against an inked ribbon that presses against the characters on the print chain. **84**

Channel   A limited-capacity computer that takes over the tasks of input and output in order to free the CPU to handle internal processing operations. **139**

Channel (of paper tape)   One of eight rows used to encode data on paper tape. **151**

Charge-coupled device (CCD)   A silicon storage device where access is 100 times faster than with magnetic bubbles but slower than with semiconductor memory. **162**

Chief programmer team   A method of organization used in the management of system projects where a chief programmer supervises the programming and testing of system modules; programmer productivity and system reliability are increased. **298**

Classify   To categorize data according to certain characteristics so that it is meaningful to the user. **9**

COBOL   *CO*mmon *B*usiness-*O*riented *L*anguage; a high-level programming language generally used for accounting and business data processing. **254**

CODASYL   *C*onference on *Da*ta *S*ystems *L*anguages; a committee formed by the Department of Defense to examine the feasibility of establishing a common business programming language. **254**

Code   To express a problem solution in a programming language; a set of rules for data conversion and representation. **222**

Collator   A piece of punched-card equipment capable of sequence-checking, merging, matching, selecting, and match-merging a deck of punched cards. **79**

Communication channel   A medium for carrying data from one location to another. **99**

Compatibility   The degree to which programs can be run on a different computer system without modification. **33, 189**

Compiler program   The translator program for a high-level language such as FORTRAN or COBOL; translates source-program statements into machine-executable code. **210**

Computer   A general-purpose machine with applications limited only by the creativity of the humans who use it; its power is derived from its speed, accuracy, and memory. **6, 46**

Computer operator   Data-processing operations personnel whose duties include setting up the processor and related equipment, starting the program run, checking to insure proper operation, and unloading equipment at the end of a run. **412**

Computer output microfilm (COM)   Miniature photographic images of output. Computer output is placed on magnetic tape which serves as the input to a microfilm processor. **137**

Computer utility   A regional or national communication network linking many large processors, providing low-cost computing power to a large number of users through increased economies of scale. **185**

Concentrator   A device that systematically allocates communication channels among several terminals. **101**

Concurrent   Over the same period of time; in multiprogramming, processing of operations rotates between different programs, giving the illusion of simultaneous processing. **309**

545

Condition entry   One of four sections of a decision logic table; answers all questions in the condition stub. **337**

Condition stub   One of four sections of a decision logic table; describes all factors (options) to be considered in determining a course of action. **337**

Continuous form   A data-entry form, such as cash register tape, utilized by OCR devices. **130**

Control program   A routine, usually part of an operating system, that aids in controlling the operations and management of a computer system. **204**

Control unit (I/O)   An electronic device, intermediate between a computer and an I/O device, that performs functions such as buffering and code conversion. **138**

Control unit (of CPU)   The section of the CPU that directs the sequence of operations by electrical signals and governs the actions of the various units which make up the computer. **47**

Core storage   A form of high-speed storage using magnetic cores (iron-alloy doughnut-shaped rings). **57**

Cost/benefit analysis   A quantitative form of evaluation in which benefits are assessed and costs associated with achieving the benefits are determined. **341**

CPM   Critical Path Method; *see* PERT. **392**

Crash conversion   A method of system implementation in which the old system is abandoned and the new one implemented at once; also known as direct conversion. **347**

Cut form   A data-entry form such as phone or utility bill, utilized by OCR devices. **130**

Cylinder   All tracks on a magnetic disk that are accessible by the read/write heads with one movement, or positioning, of the access mechanism. **157**

Data   A fact; the raw material of information. **8**

Data bank   A comprehensive collection of libraries of data. **430**

Data base   The cornerstone of a management information system; basic data is commonly defined and consistently organized to fit the information needs of a wide variety of users in an organization. **10, 357, 384**

Data base administrator   The individual responsible for the orderly development of a data base project. **388, 412**

Data base management system (DBMS)   A set of programs that serves as an interface between the data base and three principal users—the programmer, the operating system, and the manager (or other information user); provides a method of arranging data to limit duplication, an ability to make changes easily, and a capability to handle direct inquiries. **387**

Data buffering   Reading data into a separate storage unit normally contained in the control unit of the input/output subsystem. **138**

Data communication   The electronic transmission of data from one site to another, usually over communication channels such as telephone/telegraph lines or microwaves. **98**

DATA DIVISION   The part of a COBOL program that describes the data items and files used by the program. **255**

Data-entry operator   Data-processing operations personnel whose job includes transcribing data into a form suitable for computer processing, e.g., by keypunching. **412**

Data processing   A systematic set of techniques for collecting, manipulating, and disseminating data to achieve specified objectives. **8**

Data recorder   The 96-column punched-card equivalent of a card punch, which stores the characters to be punched for verification and correction until instructed to punch. **76**

Data set   A grouping of related records; also called a file. **98**

Debugging   The process of detecting, locating, isolating, and eliminating errors, or bugs, in a program. **222**

Decentralized   A design alternative whereby computer support is placed in separate organizational units; communication among units is limited or nonexistent. **381**

Decimal number system   A number system based on powers of 10. **51**

Decision logic table (DLT)   A standardized table that organizes relevant facts in a clear and concise manner to aid in the decision-making process. **336**

Default   A course of action chosen by the compiler when several alternatives exist but none has been stated explicitly by the programmer. **269**

Demand report   A report produced only on request and often displayed through online terminals. **380**

Demodulation   The process of retrieving data from a modulated carrier wave. **98**

Density   The number of characters that can be stored on one inch of tape. The storage capacity of the tape depends in part on its density. **152**

Desk-checking   A method used in both system and program debugging in which the sequence of operations is mentally traced to verify the correctness of the processing logic. **223**

Detail diagram   Used in HIPO to describe the specific functions performed and/or data items used in a module. **291**

Detailed program flowchart   Same as micro flowchart; a diagram that depicts the processing steps within one module of a program. **226**

Difference engine   A machine developed by Charles Babbage in 1822; used to compute mathematical tables with results up to five significant digits in length. **22**

Digital computer   The type of computer commonly used in business applications; operates on distinct data (e.g., digits) by performing arithmetic and logic processes on specific data units. **46**

Digital transmission   The transmission of data as distinct "on"/"off" pulses. **98**

Direct-access processing   *See* Inline/Direct-access processing. **29, 103**

Direct-access storage device (DASD)   A storage device on which data can be stored, and from which it can be retrieved in any order, at random, e.g., a disk storage unit; also called random-access storage device. **103, 150**

Direct conversion   *See* Crash conversion. **347**

Disk drive   The mechanical device used to rotate a disk pack during data transmission; common speeds range between 40 and 1000 revolutions per second. **157**

Diskette   *See* Flexible disk. **159**

Disk pack   A stack of magnetic disks. **156**

Distributed   A design alternative whereby each activity center has its own computer power, although total organization-wide control exists. **381**

Distributed system   On equipment configuration characterized by geographically dispersed computers linked together in a communication network; user-oriented but under total organization-wide control. **110**

Documentation   (1) The process of describing, in detail, every phase of the programming cycle and specific facts about the program being produced; (2) the hard-copy results of this process. **235**

Drum printer   An output device consisting of a metal cylinder that contains rows of characters engraved across its surface; one line of print produced with each rotation of the drum. **85**

Dummy module   A temporary program module of coding that is inserted at a lower level to facilitate testing of the higher-level modules; used in top-down design to enable higher-level program modules to be coded prior to completion of lower-level modules. **289**

Dump   Hard-copy printout of the contents of computer memory; valuable in debugging programs. **55**

EDSAC   *E*lectronic *D*elay-*S*torage *A*utomatic *C*omputer; the first "stored-program computer." **27**

Electronic data processing (EDP)   Data processing performed largely by electronic equipment such as computers, rather than by manual or mechanical methods. **8**

Electronic funds transfer (EFT)   A cashless method of paying for services or goods; the accounts of the two parties involved in the transaction are adjusted by electronic communication between computers. **431**

Electrostatic printer   A nonimpact printer in which electromagnetic impulses and heat are used to affix characters to paper. **85**

Electrothermal printer   A nonimpact printer that uses a special type of paper which is heat sensitive and forms characters on the paper using heat. **85**

ENIAC   *E*lectronical *N*umerical *I*ntegrator *a*nd *C*alculator; the first "electronic digital computer." **27**

547

ENVIRONMENT DIVISION   The part of a COBOL program that tells the hardware to be used. **255**

Even parity   A method of coding in which an even number of 1 bits represents each character; enhances detection of errors. **55**

Exception report   A report that monitors performance and indicates deviations from expected results. **380**

Extended Binary Coded Decimal Interchange Code (EBCDIC)   An 8-bit code for character representation. **53**

External storage   Also known as secondary or auxiliary storage; storage not directly controlled by the CPU; supplements main storage. **29, 57**

Field   A meaningful item of data, such as a social security number. **10**

File   a grouping of related records; sometimes referred to as a data set. **10**

First-generation computer   Used vacuum tubes; developed in the 1950s; much faster than earlier mechanical devices, but very slow in comparison to today's computers. **28**

Flexibility   The degree to which a computer system can be adapted or tailored to the changing requirements of the user. **188**

Flexible disk   See Floppy disk. **159**

Floppy disk   Also called a diskette or flexible disk; a low-cost, random-access form of data storage made of plastic and having a storage capacity equivalent to that of 3000 punched cards. **159**

Flowchart   Of two kinds: the program flowchart which is a graphic representation of the types and sequences of operations in a program, and the system flowchart which shows the flow of data through an entire system. **221**

Foreground partition   Also called foreground area; in a multiprogramming system, a partition containing a high-priority applications program. **310**

Foreground program   In a multiprogramming system, a program that has a high priority. **310**

Formal design review   An evaluation of the documentation of a system by a group of managers, analysts, and programmers to determine completeness, accuracy, and quality of design; also called structured walk-through. **300**

FORTRAN   *FOR*mula *TRAN*slator; a programming language used primarily in performing mathematical or scientific operations. **263**

Frequency (of a wave)   The number of times a wave form is repeated during a specified time interval. **98**

Front-end processor   A small CPU serving as an interface between a large CPU and peripheral devices. **103, 315**

Full-duplex channel   A type of communication channel capable of the most versatile mode of data transmission; can transmit data in both directions simultaneously. **100**

Gangpunching   Punching source data from the first card in a deck onto the remaining cards of the deck by using a reproducer. **79**

Garbage in–garbage out (GIGO)   A phrase used to exemplify the fact that the meaningfulness of data-processing results relies on the accuracy and/or relevancy of the data fed to the processor. **7**

Graphic-display device   A visual-display device that projects output in the form of graphs and line drawings and accepts input from a keyboard and/or a light pen. **132**

Grid chart   A table or grid used in system analysis to graphically summarize the relationships that exist between the components of a system. **333**

Half-duplex channel   A type of communication channel through which communication can occur in only one direction at a time, but that direction can change. **100**

Hard-copy   Printed output. **82**

Hardware   The electrical circuitry and physical devices that make up a computer system. **19**

Heuristics   Rules of operation that may or may not work every time; they have to be tested to see if they have value; used to solve complex problems and in situations that do not yield to conventional mathematics. **435**

Hexadecimal number system   A base 16 number system commonly used when printing the contents of main memory to aid programmers in detecting errors. **55**
Hexadecimal representation   A notation in which a group of four binary digits is represented by one digit of the hexadecimal (base 16) number system. **55**
Hierarchical   A design alternative in which each level within an organization is provided with necessary computer power; responsibility for control and coordination goes to the top level. **112, 381**
High-level languages   English-like coding schemes which are procedure-, problem-, and user-oriented. **30, 209**
HIPO   Hierarchy plus *I*nput-*P*rocess-*O*utput; a documentation technique used to describe the inputs, processing, and outputs of program modules. **290**
Hollerith code   A method of data representation named for the man who invented it; represents numbers, letters, and special characters by the placement of holes in 80-column punched cards. **71**

IDENTIFICATION DIVISION   The part of a COBOL program that provides documentation of the program. **255**
Impact printer   A printer that forms characters by physically striking a ribbon against paper. **82**
Index   An ordered reference list of the contents of a file, or the keys for identification or location of the contents. **365**
Indexed-sequential   A file organization technique in which records are placed on a file in sequence and a multiple-level index is maintained, thus allowing both sequential and direct-access processing. **365**
Informal design review   An evaluation of system-design documentation by selected management, analysts, and programmers prior to the actual coding of program modules to determine necessary additions, deletions, and modifications to the system design. **299**
Information   Data that has been organized and processed so that it is meaningful. **8**
Information privacy   An individual's rights regarding the collection, processing, storage, dissemination, and use of data about his or her personal attributes and activites; *see also* Privacy. **430**
Information Revolution   The name given to the present era due to the impact of computer technology on society. **441**
Information system   An integrated network of personnel, equipment, and procedures designed to satisfy the information requirements of management. **331**
Information system manager   The manager responsible for planning, organizing, staffing, and controlling all data-processing activity. **409**
Inhibit wire   A wire through a magnetic core that keeps the contents of the core from being destroyed when read. **57**
In-house development   An organization's use of its own personnel to develop programs for its internal operations. **108, 317**
Initiator   A routine within the control program of the operating system that routes tasks to the appropriate main storage partition for processing. **323**
Ink-jet printer   A nonimpact printer that uses a stream of charged ink to form dot-matrix characters. **87**
Inline/Direct-access processing   Same as random-access processing; a method of processing in which data is submitted to the computer as it occurs; individual records can be located and updated without reading all preceding records on a file. **362**
Input   Data that is submitted to the computer for processing. **7**
Input/output-bound   A situation in which the CPU is slowed down because of I/O operations, which are extremely slow in comparison to CPU internal processing operations. **138, 278**
Input/output management system   A subsystem of the operating system that controls and coordinates the CPU while receiving input from channels, executing instructions of programs in storage, and regulating output. **206**
Instruction   A statement that specifies an operation to be performed and the associated values or locations. **11, 202**
Instruction register   A register where each instruction is decoded by the control unit. **50**

549

Instruction set   The fundamental logical and arithmetic procedures that the computer can perform such as addition, subtraction, and comparison. **6**

Intangible   Something that cannot be defined or quantified easily; sometimes used in system studies to describe benefits to which indisputable dollar values cannot be attached. **344**

Integrated circuit   A small chip less than ⅛ inch square containing hundreds of electronic components permitting much faster processing than with transistors and at a greatly reduced price. **31**

Integrated file   Another name for a data base. **357**

Intelligent terminal   A terminal with an internal processor that can be programmed to perform specified functions, such as data editing, data conversion, and control of other terminals. **134**

Interactive computing   Conversation (interaction) between a user and a central computer via an online terminal. **107**

Interblock gap (IBG)   A space on magnetic tape that facilitates processing; records are grouped and separated by interblock gaps. **154**

Internal storage   Another name for the primary storage unit of the CPU. **29, 47**

Interpreter   A device that prints, on a punched card, the data already punched into that card. **79**

Interrecord gap (IRG)   A space that separates records stored on magnetic tape; allows the tape drive to regain speed during processing. **152**

Interrupt   A control signal from a sensor-band input or output unit that requests the extention of the control unit of the CPU from the current operation. **65**

Inverted structure   A file structure that permits fast, spontaneous searching for previously unspecified information; independent lists are maintained in record keys which are accessible according to the values of specified fields. **385**

Job-control language (JCL)   A language that serves as the communication link between the programmer and the operating system. **205**

Job-control program   A control program that translates the job-control statements written by a programmer into machine-language instructions that can be executed by the computer. **205**

K   A symbol used to denote 1024 (2^{10}) storage units when referring to a computer's primary storage capacity. **54**

Key   A unique identifier for a record; used to sort records for processing or to locate a particular record within a file. **357**

Keypunch   A keyboard device that punches holes in a card to represent data. **74**

Key-to-disk   Hardware designed to transfer data entered via a keyboard to magnetic disk or diskette. **122**

Key-to-tape   Hardware designed to transfer data entered via a keyboard to magnetic tape. **122**

Label   A name written beside an instruction that acts as a key or identifier for it. **251**

Language-translator programs   Software that translates the English-like programs written by programmers into machine-executable code. **206**

Large-scale integrated (LSI) circuits   Circuits containing thousands of transistors densely packed in a single silicon chip. **32, 175**

Laser printer   A type of nonimpact printer that combines laser beams and electrophotographic technology to form images on paper. **87**

Laser storage system   A secondary storage device using laser technology to encode data onto a metallic surface; usually used for mass storage. **163**

Librarian   Data-processing personnel responsible for the control and maintenance of files, programs, and catalogs of same for subsequent processing or historical record-keeping. **298, 411**

Librarian program   Software that manages the storage and use of library programs by maintaining a directory of programs in the system library and appropriate procedures for additions and deletions. **206**

550 *Library programs*   User-written or manufacturer-supplied programs and subroutines that are frequently used in other programs; they are written and stored on secondary media and called into main storage when needed. **206**

Light pen   A pen-shaped object with a photoelectric cell at its end; used to draw lines on a visual-display screen. **132**

Linear structure   Records arranged in sequence; *see* Simple structure. **385**

Link pattern   Logic in which control is transferred temporarily from the simple sequence flow to another portion of the program. **225**

List   *See* Simple structure. **385**

Logic diagram   *See* Flowchart. **226**

Loop pattern   A series of instructions that is executed repeatedly as long as specified conditions remain constant. **225**

Machine language   The only set of instructions that a computer can execute directly; a code that designates the proper electrical states in the computer as combinations of 0s and 1s. **28**

Macro flowchart   *See* Modular program flowchart. **226**

Magnetic core   An iron-alloy doughnut-shaped ring about the size of a pin head of which memory is commonly composed; an individual core can store one binary digit (its state is determined by the direction of an electrical current). **29**

Magnetic disk   A storage medium consisting of a metal platter coated on both sides with a magnetic recording material upon which data is stored in the form of magnetized spots; suitable for direct-access processing. **29, 156**

Magnetic domain   A magnetized spot representing data in bubble memory. **59**

Magnetic drum   A cylinder with a magnetic outer surface on which data can be stored by magnetizing specific portions of the surface. **28**

Magnetic-ink character reader (MICR)   A device that reads characters composed of magnetized particles; often used to sort checks for subsequent processing. **122**

Magnetic tape   A storage medium consisting of a narrow strip upon which spots of iron-oxide are magnetized to represent data; a sequential storage medium. **29, 151**

Main frame   The CPU of a full-scale computer. **47, 183**

Main storage   *See* Primary storage unit. **29, 47, 149**

Maintenance programmer   An individual who continually monitors, debugs, and documents applications programs. **410**

Management information system (MIS)   A formal network that extends computer use beyond routine reporting and into the area of management decision-making; its goal is to get the correct information to the appropriate manager at the right time. **376**

Management information system manager   The manager responsible for planning and organizing the entire information resources of a business firm. **409**

Mark I   The first automatic calculator. **25**

Mass storage devices   A class of secondary storage devices capable of storing large volumes of data; offers cost advantages over disk storage, but is much slower (retrieval time is measured in seconds). **161**

Master file   A file that contains relatively permanent data; updated by records in a transaction file. **358**

Matching   Comparing master records with transaction records to see if certain fields are identical, and extracting the unmatched cards. **79**

Match-merging   The process of merging only cards which are matched; unmatched cards from both the master file and the transaction file are separated. **79**

Memory   *See* Storage. **8, 47**

Memory management   In a multiprogramming environment, the process of keeping the programs in main memory separate. **310**

Merging   An operation where two or more similarly sequenced files are combined into one file. **79**

Microcomputer   A very small computer; often a special-purpose or single-function computer on a single chip. **175**

Micro flowchart   *See* detailed program flowchart. **226**

Microprocessor   The CPU of a microcomputer. **181**

Microprogram   A sequence of instructions wired in read-only-memory; used to tailor a system to meet the user's processing requirements. **61**

Microprogramming The process of building a sequence of instructions into read-only memory to carry out functions that would otherwise be directed by stored program instructions at a much slower speed. **61**

Microsecond One millionth of a second; a term used to specify the speed of electronic devices. **6**

Millisecond One thousandth ($\frac{1}{1000}$) of a second; a term used in specifying the speed of electronic devices. **6**

Minicomputer A computer with the components of a full-sized system but having a smaller memory. **32, 175**

Mnemonic A symbolic name (memory aid); used in symbolic languages (e.g., assembly language) and high-level programming languages. **29, 251**

Modem (data set) A device that modulates and demodulates signals transmitted over communication facilities. **98**

Modular program flowchart Also called macro flowchart; a diagram that represents the general flow and major processing steps (modules) of a program. **226**

Modular programming A programming approach that emphasizes the organization and coding of logical program units, usually on the basis of function. **244, 288**

Modulation A technique used in modems (data sets) to make business-machine signals compatible with communication facilities. **98**

Module A part of a whole; a program segment; a subsystem. **226**

Multiplexer A device that permits more than one terminal to transmit data over the same communication channel. **101**

Multiplexor channel A limited-capacity computer that can handle more than one I/O device at a time; normally controls slow-speed devices such as card readers, printers, or terminals. **139**

Multiprocessing system A multiple CPU configuration in which jobs are processed simultaneously. **176, 314**

Multiprogramming A technique whereby several programs are placed in primary storage at the same time, giving the illusion that they are being executed simultaneously; results in increased CPU active time. **176, 309**

Nanosecond One billionth of a second; a term used to specify the speed of electronic devices. **6**

Next-sequential-instruction feature The ability of a computer to execute program steps in the order in which they are stored in memory unless branching takes place. **12**

Non-destructive read, destructive write The feature of computer memory that permits data to be read and retained in its original state allowing it to be referenced repeatedly during processing. **11**

Nonimpact printer A hard-copy output device that forms images through electrostatic or other nonimpact means. **83**

Numeric bits The four rightmost bit positions of 6-bit BCD used to encode numeric data. **53**

Object program A sequence of machine-executable instructions derived from source-program statements by a language translator program. **210**

Odd parity A method of coding in which an odd number of 1 bits is used to represent each character; facilitates error checking. **55**

Original equipment manufacturer (OEM) A major firm producing computer hardware, such as IBM, DEC, Hewlett-Packard, and NCR. **185**

Offline Pertaining to equipment or devices not under control of the central processing unit. **94**

Online In direct communication with the computer. **30**

"On-us" field The section of a check that contains the customer's checking account number. **122**

Op code Operation code; the part of an instruction that tells what operation is to be performed. **48, 251**

Operand A part of an instruction that tells where to find the data or equipment to be operated on. **49, 251**

Operating system   A collection of programs designed to permit a computer system to manage itself and to avoid idle CPU time while increasing utilization of computer facilities. **32, 203**

Operator's manual   Also called run book; program documentation designed to aid the computer operator in running the program. **237**

Optical-character recognition (OCR)   A capability of devices with electronic scanners that read numbers, letters, and other characters, and convert the optical images into appropriate electrical signals. **129**

Optical-mark recognition (OMR)   A capability of devices with electronic scanners that read marks or symbols and convert the optical images into appropriate electronic signals. **127**

Optimize   A term usually used in reference to machine-language code that has been carefully compiled to yield the most efficient sequence of instructions possible. **246**

Organizational concentration   A course of study recommended by the Association of Computing Machinery for undergraduate programs for information system specialists; prepares students to be effective computer users by combining system coursework with an academic area of emphasis in a field of application such as business or government. **414**

Output   Information that comes from the computer as a result of processing. **7**

Overview diagram   Used in HIPO to describe, in greater detail, a module shown in the visual table of contents. **291**

Page frame   In a virtual-storage environment, one of the fixed-size physical areas into which primary storage is divided. **313**

Pages   In a virtual-storage environment, portions of programs which are kept in secondary storage and loaded into real storage only when needed during processing. **314**

Paging   A method of implementing virtual storage; data and programs are broken into fixed-size blocks, or pages, and loaded into real storage when needed during processing. **313**

Paper tape   A relatively slow, continuous input medium on which data is recorded as vertical combinations of circular holes in horizontal rows called channels; applicable for sequential processing. **150**

Parallel conversion   A system implementation approach in which the new system is operated side-by-side with the old one until all differences are reconciled. **346**

Parity bit   A means of detecting erroneous transmission of data; internal self-checking to determine if the number of 1 bits in a bit pattern is either odd or even; also called check bit. **54**

Partition   In multiprogramming, the primary storage area reserved for one program; may be fixed or variable in size; *see also* Region. **309**

Peripherals   Also referred to as peripheral devices; I/O devices, secondary storage devices, and other auxiliary computer equipment. **103**

PERT   *P*rogram *E*valuation and *R*eview *T*echnique; network model used to plan, schedule, and control complex projects; identifies all activities to be performed, their sequence, the time necessary to complete each activity, and the time required to complete the total project. **392**

Phase (of a wave)   The duration in time of an electrical signal during data transmission. **98**

Phased conversion   A method of system implementation in which the old system is gradually replaced by the new one; the new system is segmented and gradually applied. **347**

Picosecond   One trillionth of a second; a term used to specify the speed of electronic devices. **6**

Pilot conversion   The implementation of a new system into the organization on a piecemeal basis; also known as modular conversion. **346**

PL/1   *P*rogramming *L*anguage One; a general-purpose programming language used for both business and scientific functions. **269**

Plotter   An output device that converts data emitted from the CPU into graphic form; produces hard-copy output. **135**

553

Plug-compatible   Also known as plug-to-plug compatible; implies interchangeability between a manufacturer's original peripheral device and the peripheral of another ("independent") firm. **184**

Pointer   A link; used in randomizing. **362**

Point-of-sale (POS) terminal   A terminal that serves the same purpose as a cash register, but is also capable of relaying sales and inventory data to a central computer for immediate updating of records. **130**

Predictive report   Used for planning; allows an organization to project future results. **380**

Primary storage unit   Also known as internal storage, memory, or main storage; the section of the CPU that holds instructions, data, and intermediate and final results during processing. **47**

Printer   A device used to produce permanent (hard-copy) computer output; impact printers are designed to work mechanically; nonimpact printers use electronic technology. **82**

Printer keyboard   An impact printer designed to print one character at a time. Very similar to an office typewriter except that a program controls the printing. **83**

Print-wheel printer   A device consisting of 120 print wheels, each containing 48 characters. The print wheels rotate until an entire line is in the appropriate print position, then a hammer presses the paper against the print wheel. **84**

Privacy   An individual's right to be left alone; one's private life or personal affairs; *see also* Information privacy. **430**

PROCEDURE DIVISION   The part of a COBOL program that contains the processing steps to be executed. **255**

Process-bound   A condition that occurs when a program monopolizes the processing facilities of the computer making it impossible for other programs to be executed. **278**

Processing program   A routine, usually part of the operating system, that is used to simplify program preparation and execution. **204**

Program   A series of step-by-step instructions that provides a problem solution and tells the computer exactly what to do; of two types—applications and system. **11, 202**

Program flowcharting   Concerned with operations on data within the computer; provides a symbolic representation of each step and thus aids the programmer in writing a source program; also called block diagramming. **224**

Programmable communications processor   A device that relieves the CPU of the task of monitoring data transmissions. **101**

Programmable read-only memory (PROM)   Read-only memory that is programmed by the manufacturer, but can be reprogrammed by the user for special functions to meet the unique needs of the user. **61**

Programmer   The person who writes step-by-step instructions for the computer to execute. **202**

Proper program   A program using the structured approach and top-down design and having only one entrance and one exit. **296**

Pseudocode   An informal design language used to represent the control structures of structured programming. **291**

Pulse form   A pulse of current used to store data in computers. **98**

Punched card   A commonly used, sequential-storage medium in which data is represented by the presence or absence of strategically placed holes. **71**

Punched-card system   The use of punched cards and electromechanical machines to process data. **71**

Random-access processing   *See* Inline/Direct-access processing. **29**

Randomize   to compute relative record numbers from actual keys through any of a number of mathematical techniques. **362**

Read-only memory (ROM)   The part of computer hardware containing items that cannot be deleted or changed by stored-program instructions because they are wired into the computer. **59**

Read/write head   An electromagnet used as a component of a tape or disk drive; in reading, it detects magnetized areas and translates them into electrical pulses; in writing, it magnetizes appropriate areas, thereby erasing data stored previously. **152**

554   *Real storage*   *See* Primary storage unit; contrast with virtual storage. **312**

Real-time   Refers to the capability of a system or device to receive data, process it, and provide output fast enough to control an activity being performed; real-time systems are generally online systems but not all online systems operate in real time. **104, 203**

Record   A collection of data items, or fields, that relate to a single unit. **10**

Region   In multiprogramming with a variable number of tasks, a term often used to mean the internal storage space allocated; a variable-size partition. **310**

Register   An internal computer component used for temporary storage of an instruction or data; capable of accepting, holding, and transferring that instruction or data very rapidly. **49**

Remote-access computing   Communication with a data-processing facility from one or more stations that are distant from that facility. **103**

Remote job-entry (RJE)   Entering jobs into the regular batch-processing stream from a remote facility. **103**

Remote terminal   *See* Terminal. **130**

Reproducer   A piece of punched-card equipment used to transfer data from one card to another; equipment capable of reproducing and gangpunching. **79**

Reproducing   The process of transferring data from one punched card to another. **79**

Response time   The time between completion of data input and start of output. **104**

Ring configuration   A type of distributed system in which a number of computers are connected by a single transmission line in a ring arrangement. **112**

Robotics   The study of robots, their design, manufacture, and use. **434**

RPG   Report Program Generator; a coding scheme used to write programs that provide report-writing functions. **271**

Run book   *See* Operator's manual. **237**

Scheduled listings   The majority of output from an MIS; received at regular time intervals. **380**

Scientific data processing   The application of computer techniques to solving complex scientific problems involving a mathmetical or "number-crunching" orientation. **66, 438**

Secondary storage   *See* Auxiliary storage. **57, 149**

Second-generation computer   Transistors; smaller, faster, and had larger storage capacity than first-generation computers. **29**

Security   Precautions taken by management or built into an EDP system to guard against crimes such as unlawful access to information, fraud and embezzlement, and natural disasters such as fires or floods; security is also set up to protect against unintentional mistakes made by employees working in the EDP system. **106, 392**

Segment   A variable-size block, or portion, of a program used in a virtual storage system. **313**

Segmentation   A method of implementing virtual storage; involves dividing a program into variable-size blocks called segments, depending upon the program logic. **313**

Selecting   Extracting particular cards from a file without disturbing the organization of the other cards. **79**

Selection pattern   Program logic that includes a test; depending on the results of the test, one of two paths is taken. **225**

Selector channel   A limited-capacity computer that can accept input from only one device at a time; used with a high-speed I/O device such as a magnetic-tape or magnetic-disk unit. **139**

Semiconductor memory   Circuity on silicon chips which are smaller than magnetic cores and allow for faster processing; more expensive than core memory and requires a constant source of power. **58**

Sense wire   A wire through a magnetic core that determines whether the core contains a 0 bit or a 1 bit. **57**

Sequence-checking   A function performed by a collator to determine if cards have been sorted in the correct order, or sequence. **79**

Sequential-access storage   Auxiliary storage from which records must be read, one after another, in a fixed sequence, until the needed data is located, e.g., magnetic tape. **150**

Sequential file   Data (records) stored in a specific order, one right after the other. **360**

Service bureau   An organization that supplies computer capabilities to clients utilizing timesharing. **185**

Silicon chip Solid-logic circuitry used in the primary storage of third-generation computers. **58**

Simple-sequence pattern Program logic where one statement after another is executed in order, as stored. **225**

Simple structure Also called a list; a sequential arrangement of data records. **385**

Simplex channel A type of communication channel that provides for unidirectional, or one-way, transmission of data. **100**

Simultaneous At the same time; in multiprocessing, two or more instructions can be executed at exactly the same time necessitating the use of two or more CPUs. **309, 314**

Soft-copy Data displayed on a CRT screen; not a permanent record; contrast with hard-copy. **132**

Software Computer programs; contrast with hardware. **19**

Software package A set of standardized computer programs, procedures, and related documentation designed to solve problems of a specific application; often acquired from an external supplier. **317**

Sort To arrange data elements into a predetermined sequence to facilitate processing. **9**

Sorter A piece of punched-card equipment capable of ordering or grouping punched cards into a predetermined sequence. **79**

Sort/merge programs A part of the operating-system utility programs; used to sort records to facilitate updating and subsequent combining of files to form a single, updated file. **206**

Source-data automation The use of special equipment to collect data at its source. **126**

Source program A sequence of instructions written in either assembly language or high-level language. **210**

Spider configuration A type of distributed system in which a central computer is used to monitor the activities of several network computers. **111**

Stacked-job processing *See* Batch/Sequential processing. **203**

Storage The part of a computer that provides the ability to recall information; memory. **8, 57**

Storage register A register that holds information being sent to or taken from the primary storage unit. **50**

Store To retain processed data for future reference. **9**

Stored program Instructions stored in the computer's memory in electronic form; can be executed repeatedly during processing. **11**

Structure chart A graphic representation of top-down programming, displaying modules of the problem solution and relationships between modules; of two types—system and process. **244, 288**

Structured design A top-down modular approach to programming; *see* top-down design. **244, 288**

Structured programming A top-down modular approach to programming that emphasizes dividing a program into logical sections in order to reduce testing time, increase programmer productivity, and bring clarity to programming. **293**

Summarize To reduce large amounts of data to a more concise and usable form. **9**

Supervisor program Also called a monitor or an executive; the major component of the operating system; coordinates the activities of all other parts of the operating system. **204**

Swapping In a virtual-storage environment, the process of transferring a program section from virtual storage to real storage, and vice versa. **312**

Symbolic language Also called assembly language; uses mnemonic symbols to represent instructions; must be translated to machine language before it can be executed by the computer. **29**

Synonym A record for which the computed, or randomized, address is identical to that of another record. **362**

System analysis A detailed, step-by-step investigation of an organization for the purpose of determining what must be done and the best way to do it. **329**

System analysis report A report given to top management after the system analysis phase has been completed to report the findings of the system study; includes a statement of objectives, constraints, and possible alternatives. **340**

System analyst The communication link or interface between users and technical persons (such as computer programmers and operators); responsible for system analysis, design, and implementation of computer-based information systems. **409**

System charts Graphic representations of source documents, processing steps, files, output, and user departments. **332**

System design Alternative solutions to problems uncovered in the system analysis phase are designed, the cost effectiveness of the alternatives is determined, and final recommendations are made. **329**

System flowcharting The process of using symbols to represent the general information flow; focuses on inputs and outputs rather than on internal computer operations. **335**

System implementation The final phase in the development of a new or revised system; the goal of implementation is to insure that the system is completely debugged and operational, and is accepted by the users. **329, 345**

System library A collection of data sets in which various parts of an operating system are stored. **206**

System program A sequence of instructions written to coordinate the operation of all computer circuitry and to help the computer run fast and efficiently. **202**

System programmer A person who serves as the bridge between the computer and the applications programmer; must understand the complex internal operations of the computer. **410**

System residence device An auxiliary storage device (disk, tape, or drum) on which operating-system programs are stored and from which they are loaded into main storage. **204**

System software A collection of programs written to coordinate the operation of all computer circuitry allowing the computer to run efficiently. **185**

System study A development process to identify and develop needed informational improvements within an organization. **329**

Tape cassette A sequential-access storage medium (similar to cassettes used in audio recording) used in small computer systems for high-density digital recording. **154**

Tape drive A device that moves tape past a read/write head. **152**

Tape pooler A device used to rewrite data on the original tape onto another tape in a highly condensed form; used in key-to-tape systems. **124**

Technological concentration A course of study recommended by the ACM for undergraduates to prepare for entry-level jobs in an information-processing department. **414**

Teleprocessing The combined use of communication facilities, such as the telephone system, and data-processing equipment. **98**

Terminal A device through which data can exit from or be entered into a computer. **98**

Third-and-a-half generation computer Characterized by large-scale integrated (LSI) circuitry, increased speeds, greater reliability, and storage capacities approaching billions of characters. **32**

Third-generation computer Characterized by the use of integrated circuits, reduced size, lower costs, and increased speed and reliability. **31**

Throughput The rate at which work can be handled by an EDP system. **392**

Time-sharing An arrangement in which two or more users can access the same central computer resources and receive what seem to be simultaneous results. **32, 107**

Time-slicing A technique used in a time-sharing system that restricts each user to a small portion of processing time. **108**

Top-down design A method of defining a solution in terms of major functions to be performed, and further breaking down the major functions into subfunctions; the further the breakdown, the greater the detail. **288**

Touch-tone device A terminal used together with ordinary telephone lines to transmit data. **133**

Trace Hard-copy list of the steps followed during program execution in the order they occurred. **224**

Track A horizontal row stretching the length of a magnetic tape on which data can be recorded; one of a series of concentric circles on the surface of a disk; one of a series of circular bands on a drum. **152, 156**

Transaction file   A file that contains new records or modifications to existing records; used to update a master file. **358**

Transistor   A type of circuitry characteristic of second-generation computers; smaller, faster, and more reliable than vacuum tubes, but inferior to third-generation, large-scale integration. **29**

Transit field   The section of a check, preprinted with magnetic ink, that includes the bank number. **122**

Unbundling   The practice of establishing a separate price for each segment of a computer system. **185**

Unit record   One set of information; the amount of data on one punched card. **71**

Universal Product Code (UPC)   A code consisting of 10 pairs of vertical bars that represent the manufacturer's identity and the identity code of the item; commonly used on most grocery items. **129**

UNIVAC I   The first commercial electronic computer; became available in 1951. **27**

User's manual   Program documentation designed to aid persons not familiar with a program in using the program. **236**

Utility programs   A subsystem of the operating system which is capable of performing specialized, repeatedly used functions such as sorting, merging, and transferring data from one I/O device to another. **206**

Vacuum tube   An electron tube in which air has been evacuated; used in first-generation computers. **28**

Verifier   A machine similar to a keypunch used to check the results of keypunching. **75**

Verifying Punch   A device used to validate the data encoded on a punch card. **75**

Virtual storage   Also called virtual memory; an extension of multiprogramming in which portions of programs not being used are kept in secondary storage until needed, giving the impression that primary storage is unlimited; contrast with real storage. **176, 312**

Visual-display terminal   A terminal capable of receiving output on a cathode-ray tube (CRT) and, with special provisions, of transmitting data through a keyboard. **132**

Visual table of contents   Similar to a structure chart; each block is given an identification number that is used as a reference in other HIPO diagrams. **291**

Volatility   An indication of the frequency of changes in a master file. **365**

Walk-through   A step in the programming process in which a programmer who is unfamiliar with a module of code is introduced to its purpose; the new programmer is able to identify logic errors and other difficulties that the initial programmer may have overlooked. **246, 300**

Wand reader   A device used in reading source data represented in optical bar-code form. **129**

Wave form   The form of electrical signals used in transmission over communication channels; each wave is characterized by three elements—amplitude, frequency, and phase. **98**

Wire-matrix printer   A type of impact printer that creates characters through the use of dot-matrix patterns. **84**

Xerographic printer   A type of nonimpact printer that uses printing methods similar to those used in common xerographic copying machines. **87**

Zone bits   Used in different combinations with numeric bits to represent numbers, letters, and special characters. **53**

Zone punch   In the Hollerith code, used in combination with a number punch to represent a letter or special character in Hollerith code. **71**